Pocket
Crossword
Dictionary

GW00645165

General Editor
John Bailie

First published in Great Britain in 1988
Revised and updated in 2001 by
Hamlyn, a division of Octopus Publishing Group Ltd
2–4 Heron Quays, London E14 4JP

ISBN 0 600 61378 X
EAN 9780600613787

A CIP catalogue record for this book is available from the
British Library

Printed and bound in Italy by Amadeus S.r.l., Rome

10 9 8 7 6 5 4 3 2 1

CONTENTS

AGRICULTURE

3

awn
bin
cob
cod
cow
cub
dam
dig
ear
ewe
fen
gid
hay
hoe
hog
hop
ket
kid
kip
lea
ley
moo
mow
pig
pip
ram
rut
rye
sow
ted
teg
tup

4

acre
bale
barn
beam
beef
beet
bent
bere
bigg
bran
bull
byre
calf
cart
clay
corn
cote
crop
culm
curb
dock
dung
farm
fell
foal
gait
herd
hind
holt
hops
hull
husk

kine
lamb
lime
loam
mare
marl
meal
milk
neat
neep
oast
oats
odal
pale
peat
pest
pone
quey
rabi
rake
rape
root
roup
runt
rust
ryot
sand
scab
sear
seed
shaw
silo
silt
skep

slob
sock
soil
soya
span
stot
teff
till
toft
tope
tore
udal
vale
vega
weed
wold
yean
zebu

5

aphid
araba
auger
avena
baler
beans
biddy
borax
bothy
braxy
brize
calve
carse
cavie

chaff	mulch	animal	gimmer
churn	mummy	arable	gluten
clamp	ovine	barley	grains
clone	plant	beeves	grange
couch	ranch	binder	harrow
croft	rumen	botfly	heifer
crone	sheep	bulgur	hogget
crops	shoat	butter	hogsty
dairy	shuck	cattle	hopper
ditch	spelt	cereal	huller
drill	spuds	cloche	hurdle
drove	staig	clover	incult
durum	stall	colter	inning
ergot	stead	corral	inspan
farcy	stich	cotter	intine
flail	stipa	cowman	jument
fruit	stook	cratch	linhay
fungi	straw	cutter	litter
gebur	swill	digger	llanos
glume	swine	disbud	manger
grain	tilth	dobbin	manure
grass	tithe	drover	meadow
graze	tuber	eatage	mealie
guano	veldt	écurie	merino
haugh	vimen	fallow	milium
haulm	vives	farina	millet
hedge	vomer	farmer	milsey
hilum	wagon	farrow	mowing
hoove	wheat	fescue	nilgai
horse	withe	fleece	nubbin
humus	withy	fodder	pampas
kulak	worms	forage	piglet
lande	yield	furrow	pigsty
llano		garget	plough
maize	**6**	garron	podsol
mower	angora	gaucho	polder

porker	avenage	harvest	panicum
potato	bailiff	haycart	pannage
punner	binding	haycock	pasture
pyrene	boscage	hayrick	peonage
raggee	budding	hedging	piggery
rancho	bullock	hencoop	pinetum
realty	buttery	herding	pinfold
reaper	cabbage	hogcote	piscina
roller	calving	hop pole	polders
runrig	combine	hunkers	poultry
scythe	compost	implant	prairie
sheave	copland	infield	praties
sickle	cornage	innings	predial
silage	coulter	kidling	provine
socage	cowherd	lamb-ale	pruning
sowans	cowshed	lambing	pulping
sowing	demesne	laniary	radicle
spruit	digging	lealand	raking
stable	dipping	leasowe	rancher
steppe	docking	lucerne	reaping
stover	drought	maizeña	rearing
tanist	droving	malting	retting
tedder	eanling	marlite	rhizome
travis	erosion	milk can	rokeage
trough	farming	milking	rundale
turnip	fee tail	misyoke	rustler
turves	fertile	morling	savanna
warble	foaling	multure	sickled
weevil	folding	murrain	slanket
	foot rot	nest box	spancel
7	forcing	novalia	spinner
	fox trap	nursery	stacker
acidity	gadsman	orchard	station
aerator	granary	organic	stooker
alfalfa	granger	pabular	stubble
amidine	grazing	paddock	subsoil
anthrax			

swinery
tantony
tax cart
threave
thwaite
tillage
tilling
topsoil
tractor
trammel
trekker
trotter
udaller
vaquero
vitular
wagoner
windrow
yardman

8

acid soil
agronomy
bone meal
branding
breeding
cash crop
clipping
cropping
ditching
drainage
elevator
ensilage
farmyard
fat stock
forestry
fowl pest

gleaning
grafting
hayfield
haymaker
haystack
haywagon
hopfield
kohlrabi
landgirl
longhorn
loosebox
milkcart
Paraquat
pedigree
pigswill
plougher
root crop
rotation
rotavate
ruminant
ryotwari
sainfoin
shearing
sheepdip
vineyard
watering
wireworm
yearling

9

agrestial
allotment
black rust
butterfat
cold frame
cornfield

dairyfarm
dairymaid
disc drill
fertility
free-range
fungicide
gathering
grassland
harrowing
harvester
haymaking
herbicide
hop-picker
horserake
husbandry
implement
incubator
livestock
pasturage
pesticide
phosphate
pig trough
ploughing
rice field
Rotavator
screening
separator
shorthorn
sugar beet
sugar cane
swineherd
thrashing
threshing
trenching
warble fly
winnowing

10

agronomics
agronomist
battery hen
cattle cake
cultivator
fertilizer
harvesting
husbandman
irrigation
mouldboard
plantation
selfbinder
swine fever
transplant
weedkiller
wheatfield

11

agriculture
agrobiology
brucellosis
cake crusher
chaff cutter
chicken farm
cultivation
fertilizing
hydroponics
germination
insecticide
pastureland
poultry farm
reclamation
stock-taking
swath turner
viticulture

weed control

12 AND OVER

agribusiness (12)
agricultural (12)
arable farming (13)
arboriculture (13)
dairy farming (12)
factory farming (14)
feeding-stock (12)
fermentation (12)
horticulture (12)
hydroponics (11)
insemination (12)
market garden (12)
mixed farming (12)
share-cropping (13)
silviculture (12)
smallholding (12)
turnip cutter (12)

ART
Artists, architects, sculptors, cartoonists, etc.

3 AND 4

Adam, Robert
Apt, Ulrich
Arp, Hans
Bell, Vanessa
Bill, Max
Bles, Herri met de
Bol, Ferdinand
Bone, Muirhead
Both, Jan
Boyd, Arthur
Bril, Paul
Bush, Jack
Cano, Alonso
Capp, Al
Caro, Anthony
Cole, Rex Vicat
Cuyp, Jacob
Dadd, Richard
Dali, Salvador

Dick, William
Dine, Jim
Dix, Otto
Doré, Gustave
Dou, Gerrit
Dufy, Raoul
Dyce, William
Dyck, Anthony van
Egg, Augustus
Emin, Tracy
Etty, William
Eyck, Jan van
Feti, Domenico
Ford, Edward
Fry, Roger
Fyt, Jan
Gabo, Naum
Gill, Eric
Goes, Hugo van
  der
Gogh, Vincent van

Gore, Spencer
Goya, Francisco de
Gris, Juan
Gros, Antoine-Jean
Guys, Constantin
Hals, Frans
Heda, Willem
Hemy, Charles
Holl, Elias
Home, Henry
Hone, Nathaniel
Hood, Raymond
Hunt, William
Holman
Ives, James
John, Augustus
Jorn, Asger
Judd, Donald
Kahn, Louis
Kalf, Willem
Kane, John

Katz, Alex
Kent, William
Klee, Paul
Lam, Wilfredo
Lamb, Henry
Lear, Edward
Lely, Peter
Lin, Kim
Loos, Adolph
Low, David
Maes, Nicolaes
Marc, Franz
May, Phil
Miró, Joan
Mola, Pier Francesco
Mor, Anthonis
Nash, Paul
Neer, Aart
Opie, John
Pei, I. M.
Peto, John
Post, Frans
Prem, Heimrad
Rego, Paula
Reid, Robert
Reni, Guido
Rops, Félicien
Rosa, Salvator
Rude, François
Shaw, John Byam
Soto, Jesús Rafael
Tura, Cosmè
Uhde, Fritz von
s, Maerten de
d, James
J. Alden

West, Benjamin
Wit, Jacob de
Witz, Konrad
Wols
Wood, Grant
Wren, Christopher
Zorn, Anders

5

Aalto, Alvar
Abbey, Edwin Austin
Allan, David
Andre, Carl
Antal, Frederick
Appel, Karel
Bacon, Francis
Baily, Edward Hodges
Banks, Thomas
Barry, James
Barye, Antoine-Louis
Beale, Mary
Beuys, Joseph
Blake, William
Bosch, Hieronymus
Bouts, Dirk
Brown, Ford Madox
Burra, Edward
Campi (Family)
Caron, Antoine
Carrà, Carlo
Corot, Jean
Cossa, Francesco del
Costa, Lorenzo
Cotes, Francis
Crane, Walter
Credi, Lorenzo di

Crome, John
Daddi, Bernardo
Dalou, Aimé-Joles
Danby, Francis
Dance, Nathaniel
David, Jacques-Louis
Davis, Stuart
Degas, Edgar
Denis, Maurice
Devis, Arthur
Dossi, Dosso
Dürer, Albrecht
Duvet, Jean
Ensor, James
Ernst, Max
Flynt, Henry
Freud, Lucian
Frink, Elisabeth
Frith, William
Gaddi (Family)
Gaudí, Antoni
Gibbs, James
Gorky, Arshile
Goyen, Jan van
Grant, Duncan
Grosz, George
Hayez, Francesco
Henri, Robert
Heron, Patrick
Hirst, Damien
Homer, Winslow
Hooch, Pieter de
Horta, Victor
Itten, Johannes
Johns, Jasper
Jones, Inigo

Kahlo, Frida
Keene, Charles
Kelly, Ellsworth
Kitaj, Ron B.
Klein, Yves
Klimt, Gustav
Kline, Franz
Koons, Jeff
Kupka, František
Leech, John
Léger, Fernand
Le Vau, Louis
Lewis, Wyndham
Lhote, André
Lippi, Fra Filippo
Lotto, Lorenzo
Louis, Morris
Lowry, L. S.
Macke, August
Manet, Edouard
Marin, John
Maris (Family)
Matta
Mauve, Antoine
Mengs, Anton
Metsu, Gabriel
Monet, Claude
Moore, Henry
Moses, Grandma
Mucha, Alphonse
Munch, Edvard
Myron
Nervi, Pier Luigi
Nolan, Sidney
Nolde, Emil
Ofili, Chris

Orley, Bernard
Orpen, William
Oudry, Jean-Baptiste
Pater, Walter
Peale, Charles
Pencz, Georg
Pilon, Germain
Piper, John
Polke, Sigmar
Pozzo, Andrea
Prout, Samuel
Puget, Pierre
Pugin (Family)
Redon, Odilon
Repin, Ilya
Ricci (Family)
Riley, Bridget
Rodin, Auguste
Rosso, Giovanni
Runge, Philipp Otto
Scott, Samuel
Serra, Richard
Shahn, Ben
Smith, David
Soane, John
Speer, Albert
Staël, Nicolas de
Steen, Jan
Steer, Philip
Stone, Nicholas
Stoss, Jeit
Sully, Thomas
Tacca, Pietro
Takis
Tobey, Mark
Tonks, Henry

Velde, Henri van de
Vicky
Vouet, Simon
Vries, Hans Vredeman de
Watts, George
Witte, Emanuel de
Wyatt, Matthew
Wyeth, Andrew
Yeats, Jack B.

6

Abbate, Niccolò dell'
Abbott, Lemuel
Albers, Josef
Allori, Cristofani
Archer, Thomas
Audran (Family)
Ayrton, Michael
Batoni, Pompeo
Benson, Ambrosius
Benton, Thomas
Berman, Eugene
Bewick, Thomas
Braque, Georges
Bratby, John
Breuer, Marcel
Buffet, Bernard
Butler, Elizabeth
Calder, Alexander
Callot, Jacques
Campin, Robert
Canova, Antonio
Casson, Hugh
Catlin, George
Cibber, Caius
Clerck, Hendrik de

Clouet (Family)
Cooper, Samuel
Copley, John
Cosway, Richard
Cotman, John
Cousin (Family)
Coypel (Family)
Cozens, Alexander
Demuth, Charles
Derain, André
De Wint, Peter
Dobell, William
Dobson, Frank
Dongen, Kees van
Duccio
Dughet, Caspard
Eakins, Thomas
Flavin, Dan
Floris (Family)
Foster, Myles
Fraser, James
Fuller, Isaac
Fuseli, Henry
Geddes, Andrew
Gelder, Aert de
Gérard, François
Gibson, John
Gilman, Harold
Gilpin, Sawrey
Ginner, Charles
Giotto
Girtin, Thomas
Gleyre, Charles
Goujon, Jean
Greuze, Jean
Guardi, Francesco

Guston, Philip
Hassam, Childe
Haydon, Benjamin
Hayman, Francis
Hayter, S. W.
Heckel, Erich
Heyden, Jan van der
Hilton, Roger
Hodler, Ferdinand
Hölzel, Adolf
Hopper, Edward
Houdon, Jean-Antoine
Hudson, Thomas
Hughes, Robert
Huysum, Jan van
Ingres, Jean
Inness, George
Isabey, Eugène
Jagger, Charles
Janson, H. W.
Kaprow, Allan
Kettle, Tilly
Keyser, Hendrick de
Kiefer, Anselm
Knight, Laura
Laroon, Marcellus
Lasdun, Denys
La Tour, Georges de
Lavery, John
Lebrun, Charles
Legros, Alphonse
Le Nain (Family)
Lescot, Pierre
Longhi, Pietro
Lurçat, Jean
Mabuse, Jan Gossaert

McEvoy, Ambrose
Man Ray
Mander, Karel van
Marini, Marino
Martin, John
Masson, Antoine
Massys, Quentin
Matsys, Quentin
Menzel, Adolph
Mesdag, Hendrik
Metsys, Quentin
Millet, Jean-François
Momper, Joos de
Moreau, Gustave
Morley, Malcolm
Moroni, Giovanni
Morris, William
Mytens, Daniel
Nauman, Bruce
Newman, Barnett
Noland, Kenneth
Oliver, Isaac
Orozco, José
Ostade, Adriaen van
Pacher, Michael
Palmer, Samuel
Panini, Giovanni
Parléř, Petr
Paxton, Joseph
Piombo, Sebastiano del
Pisano, Andrea
Porter, Fairfield
Potter, Paulos
Rainer, Arnulf
Ramsay, Allan
Renoir, Pierre

Ribera, José
Rigaud, Hyacinthe
Rivera, Diego
Rivers, Larry
Robbia, Luca della
Robert, Hubert
Romney, George
Rothko, Mark
Rubens, Peter Paul
Rublev, Andrey
Ruskin, John
Sacchi, Andrea
Sandby, Paul
Savery, William
Scarfe, Gerald
Scorel, Jan van
Searle, Ronald
Seurat, Georges
Signac, Paul
Sisley, Alfred
Sluter, Claus
Sodoma, Il
Spence, Basil
Stella, Frank
Straub, Johann Baptist
Stuart, Gilbert
Stubbs, George
Tamayo, Rufino
Tanguy, Yves
Tàpies, Antoni
Tatlin, Vladimir
Tissot, James
Titian
Troost, Cornelis
Turner, J. M. W.
Varley, John

Vasari, Giorgio
Vernet (Family)
Villon, Jacques
Voysey, Charles
Walker, Frederick
Wallis, Alfred
Warhol, Andy
Weenix, Jan Baptist
Weyden, Rogier van der
Wilkie, David
Wilson, Richard
Wilton, Joseph
Wright, Joseph
Zeuxis

7

Alberti, Leon Battista
Allston, Washington
Apelles
Audubon, John James
Balthus
Barlach, Ernst
Barocci, Federico
Bassano (Family)
Bateman, H. M.
Bazille, Jean
Beechey, William
Behrens, Peter
Bellini (Family)
Bellows, George
Berchem, Nicolaes
Bermejo, Bartolomé
Bernini (Family)
Böcklin, Arnold
Boldini, Giovanni
Bomberg, David

Bonheur, Rosa
Bonnard, Pierre
Bordone, Paris
Boucher, François
Boydell, John
Brouwer, Adriaen
Calvert, Edward
Cassatt, Mary
Cellini, Benvenuto
Cézanne, Paul
Chagall, Marc
Chardin, Jean
Chirico, Giorgio de
Christo
Cimabue
Clausen, George
Clodion
Collins, William
Corinth, Lovis
Cornell, Joseph
Cortona, Pietro da
Courbet, Gustave
Coustou (Family)
Cranach, Lucas
Da Vinci, Leonardo
Dalziel (Family)
Dalwood, Hubert
Daumier, Honoré
De Hooch, Pieter
Delorme, Philibert
Delvaux, Paul
De Maria, Walter
Downman, John
Duchamp, Marcel
Edwards, Edward
El Greco

Epstein, Jacob
Flaxman, John
Fontana, Lucio
Fouquet, Jean
Francia
Francis, Sam
Gauguin, Paul
Gertler, Mark
Gibbons, Grinling
Gigante, Giacinto
Gilbert, Alfred
Gillray, James
Gleizes, Albert
Gozzoli, Benozzo
Gropius, Walter
Guarini, Guarino
Harding, Chester
Harnett, William
Hartley, Marsden
Hartung, Hans
Herrera, Francisco
Herring (Family)
Hobbema, Meindert
Hockney, David
Hodgkin, Howard
Hofmann, Hans
Hogarth, William
Hokusai, Katsushika
Holbein, Hans
Hoppner, John
Ictinus
Indiana, Robert
Israëls, Jozef
Jackson, A. Y.
Johnson, Eastman
Klinger, Max

Kneller, Godfrey
Koninck, Philips
Kooning, William De
Lambert, George
Lancret, Nicolas
Lemoyne (Family)
L'Enfant, Pierre
Le Nôtre, André
Lievens, Jan
Limburg (Family)
Lindner, Richard
Linnell, John
Lutyens, Edwin
Maclise, Daniel
Maderno, Stefano
Maillol, Aristide
Mansart, François
Manzoni, Alessandro
Maratta,Carlo
Maratti, Carlo
Marinus
Martini, Simone
Mathieu, George
Matisse, Henri
Mazzoni, Sebastiano
Memlinc, Hans
Michaux, Henri
Millais, John Everett
Morandi, Giorgio
Morisot, Berthe
Morland, George
Morrice, James
Mumford, Lewis
Murillo, Bartolomé
Nasmyth, Peter
Nattier, Jean-Marc

Neumann, Balthasar
O'Keeffe, Georgia
Orcagna, Andrea
Ordóñez, Bartolomé
Palumbo, Peter
Pasmore, Victor
Peruzzi, Baldassare
Pevsner, Antoine
Phidias
Philpot, Glyn
Picabia, Francis
Picasso, Pablo
Pigalle, Jean
Pollock, Jackson
Poussin, Nicolas
Poynter, Edward
Prud'hon, Pierre
Quercia (Family)
Rackham, Arthur
Raeburn, Henry
Raphael
Redouté, Pierre
Reverón, Armando
Ribalta, Francisco
Richter, Adrian
Roberts, David
Rouault, Georges
Russell, Morgan
Sargent, John Singer
Schiele, Egon
Seghers, Gerard
Shannon, Charles
Sheeler, Charles
Shepard, E. H.
Sherman, Cindy
Sickert, Walter

Slevogt, Max
Snyders, Frans
Solomon, Simeon
Soutine, Chaïm
Spencer, Stanley
Stevens, Alfred
Teniers, David
Tenniel, John
Thomson, Tom
Tibaldi, Peliegrino
Tiepolo, Giovanni
Twombly, Cy
Uccello, Paolo
Ugolino
Utrillo, Maurice
Valadon, Suzanne
Van Dyck, Anthony
Van Eyck, Jan
Van Gogh, Vincent
Vermeer, Jan
Vischer (Family)
Vlieger, Simon de
Watteau, Jean-Antoine
Westall, Richard
Woolner, Thomas
Wynants, Jan
Zadkine, Ossip
Zoffany, John
Zuccaro, Taddeo

8

Aaltonen, Wäinö
Ammanati, Bartolommeo
Angelico, Fra
Armitage, Kenneth
Avercamp, Hendrik

Baselitz, Georg
Beckmann, Max
Beerbohm, Max
Bellotto, Bernardo
Boccioni, Umberto
Bramante, Donato
Brancusi, Constantin
Brangwyn, Frank
Bronzino, Il
Brueghel, Jan
Callcott, Augustus
Carpeaux, Jean-Baptiste
Carracci (Family)
Carriera, Rosalba
Castagno, Andrea del
Chadwick, Lynn
Chantrey, Francis
Chillida, Eduardo
Christus, Petrus
Cipriani, Giovanni
Coysevox, Antoine
Daubigny (Family)
Drysdale, Russell
Dubuffet, Jean
Eastlake, Charles
Evergood, Philip
Falconet, Etienne-Maurice
Fielding, Copley
Filarete, Antonio
Flandrin, Hippolyte
Frampton, George
Francken (Family)
Garofalo
Ghiberti, Lorenzo
Giordano, Luca
Girardon, François

Goltzius, Hendrik
González, Julio
Gossaert, Jan
Gottlieb, Adolph
Gravelot, Hubert-François
Guercino, Il
Hamilton, Richard
Hepworth, Barbara
Herkomer, Hubert von
Highmore, Joseph
Hilliard, Nicholas
Hodgkins, Frances
Ibbetson, Julius Caesar
Jacobsen, Georg
Janssens, Abraham
Jordaens, Jacob
Jouvenet, Jean-Baptiste
Kaulbach, Wilhelm de
Keirincx, Alexander
Kienholz, Edward
Kirchner, Ernst
Kollwitz, Käthe
Lairesse, Gerard de
Landseer, Edwin
Lawrence, Thomas
Leighton, Frederic
Leonardo
Lipchitz, Jacques
Lombardo (Family)
Lubetkin, Berthold
Lysippus
Magritte, René
Malevich, Kasimir
Manfredi, Bartolommeo
Mantegna, Andrea
Marshall, Benjamin

Masaccio
Meegeren, Han van
Molenaer, Jan
Mondrian, Piet
Monteiro, José Luis
Mostaert, Jan
Mulready, William
Munkácsy, Mihály
Munnings, Alfred
Nevelson, Louise
Nevinson, Christopher
Niemeyer, Oscar
Overbeck, Johann
Palladio, Andrea
Paolozzi, Eduardo
Patenier, Joachim
Perugino
Piranesi, Giovanni
Pissarro, Camille
Pontormo, Jacopo
Redgrave, Richard
Regnault, Henri
Reynolds, Joshua
Richmond, George
Ricketts, Charles
Robinson, Henry
Rossetti, Dante Gabriel
Rousseau, Henri
Ruisdael, Jacob
Rysbrack, John
Saarinen, Eero
Salviati, Francesco
Sassetta
Schalken, Gottfried
Schinkel, Karl
Severini, Gino

Sluyters, Jan
Solimena, Francesco
Soufflot, Jacques
Stothard, Thomas
Sullivan, Louis
Terborch (Family)
Tinguely, Jean
Topolski, Feliks
Tournier, Nicolas
Trumbull, John
Vanbrugh, John
Van Goyen, Jan
Van Steen, Jan
Vasarely, Victor
Veronese, Paolo
Vigeland, Gustav
Vlaminck, Maurice
Vuillard, Edouard
Wheatley, Francis
Whistler, James
Williams, Frederick
Wölfflin, Heinrich
Wolgemut, Michael
Woollett, William
Zurbarán, Francisco de

9

Altdorfer, Albrecht
Antonello
Bakhuyzen, Ludolf
Bartholdi, Frédéric
Beardsley, Aubrey
Biederman, Charles
Bierstadt, Albert
Bonington, Richard
Borromini, Francesco

Botticini, Francesco
Bourdelle, Antoine
Bourgeois, Louise
Burgkmair, Hans
Caldecott, Randolph
Canaletto
Carpaccio, Vittore
Cavallini, Pietro
Cockerell, Charles
Collinson, James
Constable, John
Cornelius, Peter von
Correggio
De Kooning, Willem
Delacroix, Eugène
Delaroche, Paul
Donatello
Duquesnoy, François
Elsheimer, Adam
Fabritius, Carel
Farington, Joseph
Feininger, Lyonel
Feuerbach, Anselm
Flannagan, John B.
Fragonard, Jean
Friedrich, Caspar David
Géricault, Théodore
Giorgione
Gonçalves, Nuno
Greenaway, Kate
Grünewald, Mathias
Haussmann, Georges
Hawksmoor, Nicholas
Honthorst, Gerard
Jawlensky, Alexei von
Kandinsky, Wassily

Kauffmann, Angelica
Kokoschka, Oscar
Lancaster, Osbert
Lanfranco, Giovanni
Laurencin, Marie
Lissitzky, El
Margarito
Martorell, Bernardo
Mestrovic, Ivan
Nicholson, Ben
Nollekens, Joseph
Northcote, James
Oldenburg, Claes
Oppenheim, Meret
Pechstein, Max
Piazzetta, Giovanni
Pisanello, Antonio
Pordenone, Giovanni
Ravilious, Eric
Reinhardt, Ad
Rembrandt
Remington, Frederick
Rodchenko, Alexander
Roubiliac, Louis
Sansovino, Il
Schlemmer, Oskar
Siqueiros, David
Stanfield, Clarkson
Steenwyck (Family)
Thornhill, James
Vallotton, Félix
Velázquez, Diego
Vitruvius
Whiteread, Rachel
Wouwerman, Philips

10

Alma-Tadema, Lawrence
Archipenko, Alexander
Arcimboldo, Giuseppe
Baumeister, Willi
Berruguete, Alônso
Botticelli, Sandro
Bouguereau, William
Bourdichon, Jehan
Breenbergh, Bartolomeus
Burlington, Earl of
Burne-Jones, Edward
Caracciolo, Giovanni
Caravaggio
Champaigne,Philippe de
Chassériau, Theodore
Coldstream, William
Giacometti, Alberto
Goncharova, Natalia
Heartfield, John
Heemskerck, Maerten van
Holman Hunt, William
Jan van Eyck
Kennington, Eric
La Fresnaye, Roger de
Liebermann, Max
Lorenzetti (Family)
Mackintosh, Charles Rennie
Marochetti, Carlo
Meissonier, Jean
Modigliani, Amedeo
Moholy-Nagy, László
Motherwell, Robert
Ochtervelt, Jacob
Orchardson, William
Pollaiuolo, Antonia

Polycletus
Prampolini, Eurico
Praxiteles,
Richardson, Jonathan
Rowlandson, Thomas
Schongauer, Martin
Schwitters, Kurt
Signorelli, Luca
Squarcione, Francesco
Sutherland, Graham
Tintoretto, Jacopo
Torrigiano, Pietro
Van der Goes, Hugo
Van der Meer, Jan
Van de Velde, Henry
Verrocchio, Andrea del
Waterhouse, Alfred
Ysenbrandt, Adriaen

11

Abercrombie, Patrick
Apollodorus
Bartolommeo, Fra
Butterfield, William
Callicrates
Castiglione, Giuseppe
Chodowiecki, Daniel
Della Robbia, Luca
Domenichino, Domenico
Fra Angelico
Gentileschi, Orazio
Ghirlandaio, Domenico
Giambologna
Gislebertus
Hondecoeter, Melchior D'
Hoogstraten, Samuel van

Le Corbusier
Lloyd Wright, Frank
Margaritone
Maulbertsch, Franz Anton
Nam June Pike
Poelenburgh, Cornelis Van
Polycleitus
Polykleitos
Primaticcio, Francesco
Saint Phalle, Niki de
Terbrugghen, Hendrick
Thorvaldsen, Bertel
Van Ruisdael, Jacob
Vigée-Lebrun, Elisabeth

12 AND OVER

Andrea del Sarto (14)
Baldovinetti, Alesso (12)
Baldung Grien, Hans (12)
Brunelleschi, Filippo (12)
Claude Gellée (12)
Claude Lorraine (14)
de Loutherbourg, Philippe (14)
Fantin-Latour, Henri (12)
Fischer von Erlach (16)
Ford Madox Brown (14)
Gainsborough, Thomas (12)
Gaudier-Brzeska, Henri (14)
Geertgen tot Sint Jans (19)
Gilbert and George (16)
Girodet de Roucy, Anne-Louis (14)
Giulio Romano (12)
Grandma Moses (12)
Guido da Siena (12)

Heath Robinson (13)
Joos van Cleve (12)
Leonardo da Vinci (15)
Lichtenstein, Roy (12)
Lucas van Leyden (14)
Master of Flémalle (16)
Master of Moulins (15)
Michelangelo (12)
Mies van der Rohe, Ludwig (14)
Palma Vecchio (12)
Parmigianino, Il (12)
Piero della Francesca (19)
Piero di Cosimo (13)
Puvis de Chavannes (16)
Rauschenberg, Robert (12)
Rembrandt van Ryn (15)
Sassoferrato (12)
Schmidt-Rotluff, Karl (14)
Simone Martini (13)
Toulouse-Lautrec, Henri de (15)
Van der Weyden, Rogier (12)
Van Ochtervelt, Jacob (13)
Vitruvius Pollio (15)
Winterhalter, Franz Xaver (12)

Terms, movements, schools, etc.

2 AND 3

air
art
bur
del.
exc.
fec.
hue
inc.
inv.
key
mat
oil
op.
pen
pop
sit

4

airy
arts
base
body
burn
burr
bust
cast
chic
Dada
daub
draw
etch
flat
form

gild
halo
icon
kore
limn
line
lipo
mass
Merz
nude
oils
pinx.
pose
size
swag
tone
wash

5

batik
bloom
blush
board
brush
cameo
carve
chalk
couch
delin.
donor
draft
easel
ember
Fauve

fecit
frame
genre
gesso
glair
glaze
glory
gloss
glyph
grave
hatch
inert
ivory
japan
lay-in
lumia
magot
model
mount
mural
Nabis
naive
Op Art
paint
panel
Pietà
prime
print
putto
rebus
resin
salon
scene
sculp

secco
sepia
shade
Stijl
study
stump
tondo
torso
trace
vertu
virtu

6

action
artist
ashcan
bistre
cachet
canvas
colour
crayon
Cubism
depict
design
dipper
doctor
ectype
emblem
emboss
enamel
engild
flambé
fresco
fylfot

gisant
Gothic
ground
incavo
kitcat
kitsch
kouros
limner
mastic
medium
megilp
mobile
mosaic
niello
nimbus
object
offset
ormolu
ox-gall
pastel
patina
pencil
pinxit
plaque
Pop Art
primer
Purism
reflex
relief
rhythm
rococo
school
sculpt
shadow
shippo
sitter

sketch
statue
stucco
studio
uncial
veduta
verism

7

abbozzo
academy
acrylic
ad vivum
amorino
archaic
Art Brut
Art Deco
atelier
aureole
bachiru
baroque
Bauhaus
biscuit
bitumen
bodegón
bottega
camaïeu
cartoon
carving
cassone
classic
collage
contour
Dadaism
daubing
De Stijl

diagram
diorama
diptych
draught
drawing
écorché
etching
excudit
faience
Fauvism
felt tip
fine art
gilding
glazing
gouache
graphic
hot tone
impaint
impasto
Junk Art
lacquer
linocut
lost wax
lunette
modello
montage
mordant
Orphism
outline
painter
palette
picture
pigment
plaster
plastic
pochade

priming
profile
realism
relievo
remodel
replica
reredos
retable
scumble
sfumato
shading
sketchy
stabile
stencil
stipple
support
surface
T-square
tableau
tempera
texture
touch up
tracery
tracing
vanitas
varnish
vehicle
woodcut

8

abstract
academic
acid bath
acrolith
airbrush
anaglyph

aquatint
armature
arriccio
Art Autre
artistic
Barbizon
Blue Four
bozzetto
caryatid
charcoal
concours
cool tone
diaglyph
drypoint
emulsion
engraver
figurine
fixative
freehand
frottage
Futurism
gargoyle
graffiti
graphics
grouping
half-tone
handling
hatching
idealism
intaglio
intarsia
intonaco
luminism
majolica
makimono
mandorla

maquette
Mogul Art
monotype
mounting
naive art
negative
oil paint
ornament
painting
panorama
pastiche
penumbra
plein air
pointing
portrait
pouncing
predella
Rayonism
repoussé
rocaille
Romantic
seascape
seicento
statuary
symmetry
tachisme
tapestry
tectonic
tesserae
throwing
trecento
triglyph
triptych
vignette
warm tone

9

aesthetic
aggregate
alla prima
anti-cerne
appliqué
aquarelle
aquatinta
arabesque
asymmetry
ball-point
bas-relief
Blaue Vier
block book
bric-à-brac
cartouche
cartridge
cloisonné
colourist
crow quill
damascene
damaskeen
dichroism
Die Brücke
distemper
emblemata
embossing
encarnado
encaustic
engraving
facsimile
geometric
gradation
grisaille
grotesque
happening

highlight
hot colour
indelible
Indian ink
intimisme
japanning
landscape
lay figure
life class
lithotint
low relief
mahlstick
Mannerism
marquetry
maulstick
mezzotint
miniature
Minoan Art
modelling
multiples
Nazarenes
Neo-Gothic
oil colour
old master
oleograph
painterly
pen and ink
phototype
plaquette
polyptych
primitive
ready-made
recession
red-figure
sculpture
scumbling

Serial Art
serigraph
sgraffito
sketch pad
statuette
still-life
stippling
strapwork
stretcher
Symbolist
tailpiece
tattooing
tenebrism
Totentanz
undercoat
Vorticism
woodblock
xylograph

10

accidental
achromatic
altarpiece
altogether
anaglyphic
anaglyptic
applied art
Archaic Art
Arte Povera
Art Nouveau
assemblage
atmosphere
automatism
avant-garde
background
biomorphic

body colour
caricature
cartellino
cartoonist
cerography
cire perdue
Classicism
cool colour
cornucopia
craquelure
crosshatch
dead colour
Doelenstuck
drying oils
embossment
embroidery
fitch brush
flat colour
Florentine
foreground
full-length
glass print
graphic art
hair pencil
half-length
India paper
Jugendstil
Kinetic Art
linseed oil
lithograph
marouflage
metal point
mezzotinto
Minimalism
monochrome
Naturalism

night piece
organic art
paintbrush
pantograph
pen and wash
pencilling
pentimento
photograph
pietra dura
plasticity
quadratura
Raphaelism
Raphaelite
repoussoir
Romanesque
section d'or
serigraphy
silhouette
silk screen
Surrealism
Synthetism
terracotta
turpentine
warm colour
water glass
xylography

11

Abstract Art
academician
alto rilievo
aquatinting
Art Informel
battle piece
Biedermeier
black-figure

Blaue Reiter
calligraphy
canvas board
chiaroscuro
chinoiserie
chromograph
cinquecento
Claude glass
colour print
composition
Concrete Art
connoisseur
conté crayon
Cosmati work
Divisionism
draughtsman
Eclecticism
electrotype
engravement
foreshorten
found object
French chalk
ground plane
Hague School
heliochrome
heliochromy
Hellenistic
iconography
Illusionism
imprimatura
life drawing
lithography
marqueterie
masterpiece
neo-Romantic
objet trouvé

oil painting
papier collé
pavement art
perspective
photography
picturesque
Pointillism
porte-crayon
portraiture
poster paint
Primitivism
Renaissance
restoration
Romanticism
scenography
Suprematism
watercolour
wood carving

12

acrylic paint
alkyd colours
anamorphosis
Ashcan School
bird's eye view
bondieuserie
Byzantine Art
camera lucida
cloisonnisme
eidophusikon
illustration
Newlyn School
palette knife
photomontage
Precisionism
quattrocento

scraper board
self-portrait
stained glass
stereochromy
Superrealism
tessellation
tracing linen
tracing paper

13

black and white
camera obscura
complementary
Conceptual Art
crosshatching
daguerreotype
decorative art
degenerate art
etching needle
Expressionism
fête champêtre
figurative art
Flemish School
Glasgow School
glass painting
golden section
Impressionism
line engraving
neoclassicism
neoplasticism
Norwich School
Pre-Raphaelite
primary colour
relief etching
Social Realism
tactile values

underpainting
wood engraving

14 AND OVER

Abstract Expressionism (21)
action painting (14)
cabinet painting (15)
Camden Town Group (15)
chromatography (14)
Constructivism (14)
conversation piece (17)
draughtsmanship (15)
Euston Road School (16)
Florentine School (16)
foreshortening (14)
history painting (15)

International Gothic (19)
Kitchen Sink School (17)
neo-Impressionism (16)
neo-Romanticism (14)
Neue Sachlichkeit (16)
pavement artist (14)
performance art (14)
picture gallery (14)
plaster of Paris (14)
portrait painter (15)
Post-Impressionism (17)
representational (16)
silk-screen printing (18)
Socialist Realism (16)
steel engraving (14)
vanishing point (14)

ASTRONOMY

(a.)=asteroid; (c.)=constellation; (c.p.)=constellation (popular name); (g.)=group of stars; (p.)=planet; (s.)=noted star; (sa.)=large satellite

2–4

Amor (a.)
Apus (c.)
Ara (c.)
Argo (c.)
belt
Bull (c.p.)
coma
Crab (c.p.)
Crow (c.p.)
Crux (c.)

Cup (c.p.)
Dove (c.p.)
Eros (a.)
Fly (c.p.)
Fox (c.p.)
Goat (c.p.)
Grus (c.)
halo
Hare (c.p.)
Hebe (a.)
Io (sa.)
Juno (a.)

Keel (c.p.)
Leo (c.)
limb
Lion (c.p.)
Lynx (c.) (c.p.)
Lyra (c.)
Lyre (c.p..).
Mars (p.)
Mira (s.)
Moon
Net (c.p.)
node

nova
orb
Pavo (c.)
pole
Ram (c.p.)
Rhea (sa.)
Sol
star
Sun
Swan (c.p.)
Vega (s.)
Vela (c.)
Wolf (c.p.)

5

Algol (s.)
Altar (c.p.)
apsis
Aries (c.)
Arrow (c.p.)
Ceres (a.)
Cetus (c.)
Clock (c.p.)
comet
Crane (c.p.)
Deneb (s.)
Digit
Dione (sa.)
Draco (c.)
dwarf
Eagle (c.p.)
Earth (p.)
epact
epoch
error
flare

giant
Hamal (s.)
Hyads (g.)
Hydra (c.)
Indus (c.)
Janus (sa.)
Lepus (c.)
Level (c.p.)
Libra (c.)
lunar
Lupus (c.)
Mensa (c.)
Metis (sa.)
Mimas (sa.)
Musca (c.)
nadir
Norma (c.)
orbit
Orion (c.)
phase
Pluto (p.)
polar
Pyxis (c.)
Regel (s.)
Rigel (s.)
River (c.p.)
Sails (c.p.)
Saros
Shield (c.p.)
solar
space
Spica (s.)
stars
Stern (c.p.)
Table (c.p.)
Titan (sa.)

Twins (c.p.)
umbra
Venus (p.)
Vesta (a.)
Virgo (c.)
Whale (c.p.)

6

albedo
Altair (s.)
Antlia (c.)
apogee
Apollo
Aquila (c.)
Archer (c.p.)
astral
Auriga (c.)
aurora
binary
Bolide
Boötes (c.)
Caelum (c.)
Cancer (c.)
Carina (c.)
Castor (s.)
Charon (sa.)
Chiron (a.)
Chisel (c.p.)
colure
corona
Corvus (c.)
cosmic
cosmos
crater
Crater (c.)
Cybele (a.)

Cygnus (c.)
Davida (a.)
Deimos (sa.)
Dipper (c.p.)
Dorado (c.)
Dragon (c.p.)
Europa (sa.)
Fishes (c.p.)
Fornax (c.)
galaxy
Gemini (c.)
gnomon
Hermes (a.)
Hunter (c.p.)
Hyades (g.)
Hydrus (c.)
Hygeia (a.)
Icarus (a.)
Indian (c.p.)
Leonid
Lizard (c.p.)
lunary
meteor
nebula
Nereid (sa.)
Oberon (sa.)
Octans (c.)
Octant (c.p.)
Pallas (a.)
parsec
Persei (g.)
Phobos (sa.)
Phoebe (sa.)
Pictor (c.)
Pisces (c.)
planet

Pleiad (g.)
Plough (g.)
Pollux (s.)
pulsar
Puppis (c.)
quasar
Saturn (p.)
Scales (c.p.)
Scutum (c.)
Sirius (s.)
sphere
Square (c.p.)
sundog
syzygy
Taurus (c.)
Tethys (sa.)
Toucan (c.p.)
Triton (sa.)
Tucana (c.)
Uranus (p.)
vector
vertex
Viking
Virgin (c.p.)
Volans (c.)
zenith
zodiac

7

Airpump (c.p.)
Alphard (s.)
anomaly
Antares (s.)
apogean
appulse
apsides

Astraea (a.)
auroral
azimuth
big bang
Canopus (s.)
Capella (s.)
Centaur (c.p.)
Cepheid
Cepheus (c.) (c.p.)
cluster
Columba (c.)
cometic
Dog Star (s.)
Dolphin (c.p.)
eclipse
equator
equinox
Eunomia (a.)
faculae
Furnace (c.p.)
gibbous
Giraffe (c.p.)
Hidalgo (a.)
Iapetus (sa.)
Jupiter (p.)
Lacerta (c.)
Mariner
Mercury (p.)
Miranda (sa.)
mock Sun
nebulae
nebular
Neptune (p.)
new moon
Peacock (c.p.)
Pegasus (c.)

perigee
Perseus (c.)
Phoenix (c.) (c.p.)
Polaris (s.)
Procyon (s.)
Proxima (s.)
radiant
Regulus (s.)
Sagitta (c.)
Scorpio (c.)
Sea goat (c.p.)
Serpens (c.)
Serpent (c.p.)
Sextans (c.)
Sextant (c.p.)
sextile
spectra
Sputnik
stellar
sunspot
Thania (sa.)
transit
Trojans (a.)
Umbriel (sa.)
Unicorn (c.p.)

8

Achernar (s.)
aerolite
aerolith
Aipherat (s.)
Almagest
altitude
Amalthea (sa.)
aphelion
Aquarius (c.)

Arcturus (s.)
asterism
asteroid
Callisto (sa.)
Canicula
Circinus (c.)
cometary
Cynosure (c.)
Denebola (s.)
ecliptic
epicycle
Equuleus (c.)
Eridanus (c.)
evection
Explorer
fireball
flocculi
free fall
full moon
galactic
Ganymede (sa.)
Great Dog (c.p.)
half moon
Hercules (c.) (c.p.)
Herdsman (c.p.)
Hesperus
Hyperion (sa.)
isostasy
latitude
Leo Minor (c.)
Loadstar (s.)
Lodestar (s.)
lunation
meridian
meteoric
Milky Way

mock moon
night sky
nutation
occulted
parallax
parhelia
penumbra
perigean
Pleiades (g.)
Pointers
Pole Star (s.)
quadrant
red dwarf
red giant
red shift
Scorpion (c.p.)
Scorpius (c.)
Sculptor (c.)
Ship Argo (c.p.)
sidereal
solstice
spectrum
spheroid
starless
stellary
sublunar
sunspots
Triangle (c.p.)
universe
Vanguard
variable
zodiacal

9

aerolitic
Aldebaran (s.)

Andromeda (c.)
  (c.p.)
anthelion
ascendant
ascension
astrolabe
astrology
astronomy
azimuthal
black hole
canicular
celestial
Centaurus (c.)
Chameleon (c.p.)
coelostat
Compasses (c.p.)
cosmogony
cosmology
Delphinus (c.)
elevation
Enceladus (sa.)
ephemeris
epicyclic
firmament
fixed star
Fomalhaut (s.)
giant star
Great Bear (c.p.)
heliostat
hour angle
libration
light year
Little Dog (c.p.)
longitude
lunisolar
magnitude

meteorite
meteoroid
Minuteman
Monoceros (c.)
North Star
novilunar
Nubeculae
Ophiuchus (c.)
parhelion
planetary
planetoid
Ploughman (c.p.)
Ptolemaic
radio star
reflector
refractor
Reticulum (c.)
satellite
solar wind
stargazer
starlight
sublunary
supernova
Swordfish (c.p.)
synodical
telescope
Telescope (c.p.)
uranology
Ursa Major (c.)
Ursa Minor (c.)
Via Lactea
Vulpecula (c.)

10

aberration
almucantar

altazimuth
apparition
asteroidal
astrologer
astrometer
astronomer
astronomic
Atlantides (g.)
atmosphere
Betelgeuse (s.)
brightness
Canis Major (c.)
Canis Minor (c.)
Cassiopeia (c.)
  (c.p.)
Chamaeleon (a.)
Charioteer (c.p.)
collimator
cometarium
Compass Box
  (c.p.)
Copernican
cosmic dust
cosmic rays
Crab nebula
depression
double star
earthshine
elongation
Euphrosyne (a.)
extrasolar
Flying Fish (c.p.)
green flash
Greyhounds (c.p.)
Horologium (c.)
hour circle

ionosphere
Lesser Bear (c.p.)
Little Bear (c.p.)
Little Lion (c.p.)
lunar cycle
lunar month
lunar probe
mesosphere
Microscope (c.p.)
opposition
Orion's Belt
outer space
paraselene
perihelion
precession
prominence
quadrature
refraction
retrograde
Sea Serpent (c.p.)
selenology
siderolite
solar cycle
solar flare
stargazing
supergiant
terminator
trajectory
Triangulum (c.)
tropopause
uranoscopy
Water Snake (c.p.)
white dwarf

11

astrography

astronomize
Baily's Beads
blazing star
Capricornus (c.)
conjunction
coronagraph
cosmography
declination
Evening Star (p.)
falling star
Gegenschein
giant planet
Hunting Dogs
  (c.p.)
last quarter
Little Horse (c.p.)
major planet
metemptosis
meteorolite
minor planet
Morning Star (p.)
neutron star
observatory
occultation
Orion's Sword
photosphere
planetarium
planisphere
radio source
Sagittarius (c.)
solar system
Southern Fly (c.p.)
spectrology
Telescopium (c.)
terrestrial
uranography

Water Bearer (c.p.)
Winged Horse
  (c.p.)

12

astronautics
astronomical
astrophysics
Charles's Wain (g.)
chromosphere
crescent moon
Doppler shift
eccentricity
first quarter
Halley's comet
heliocentric
interstellar
lunar eclipse
Metonic Cycle
Microscopium (c.)
Saturn's rings
selenography
shooting star
sidereal time
solar eclipse
Southern Fish
  (c.p.)
spectroscope
spiral galaxy
stratosphere
uranographic
Van Allen Belt
variable star

13

Alpha Centauri (s.)

Berenice's Hair (c.p.)
Canes Venatici (c.)
Coma Berenices (c.)
constellation
Crux Australis (c.)
Doppler effect
draconic month
extragalactic
intergalactic
meteorography
Northern Crown (c.p.)
Painter's Easel (c.p.)
River Eridanus (c.p.)
scintillation
Serpent Bearer (c.p.)
sidereal clock
Southern Cross (c.p.)
Southern Crown (c.p.)
Wolf–Rayet star
zodiacal light

14

annular eclipse
Aurora Borealis
Bird of Paradise (c.p.)
Camelopardalis (c.)
Corona Borealis (c.)
interplanetary
Musca Australis (c.)
northern lights
partial eclipse
radio astronomy
radio telescope
right ascension
Sculptor's Tools (c.p.)
summer solstice

transit of Venus
vertical circle
winter solstice
zenith distance

15 AND 16

Alphonsine tables (16)
armillary sphere (15)
astronomical unit (16)
Aurora Australis (15)
celestial sphere (15)
Corona Australis (c.) (15)
Fraunhofer lines (15)
Hubble's constant (15)
Magellanic Clouds (16)
meteoric showers (15)
Piscis Austrinus (c.) (15)
Proxima Centauri (15)
Rudolphine tables (16)
Sculptor's Chisel (c.) (15)
Southern Triangle (c.p.) (16)

BUILDING AND ARCHITECTURE

2 AND 3	berm	gaol	plan
	boss	gate	post
bar	byre	grot	quad
bay	café	haha	quay
cot	cage	hail	rail
den	cell	herm	ramp
hip	club	home	raze
hut	coin	jail	reed
inn	cote	jamb	rink
kip	cove	keep	roof
loo	cowl	khan	room
mew	crib	kiln	ruin
pa	cusp	kirk	sash
pub	cyma	lath	seat
pug	dado	lift	shed
rib	dais	lock	shop
spa	digs	loft	sill
sty	dike	mart	silo
tie	dome	maze	sink
w.c.	door	mews	site
won	drip	mill	slab
	drum	mint	slat
4	eave	moat	slum
	exit	mole	span
adit	face	nave	stay
apse	fane	nook	step
arch	farm	oast	stoa
area	flag	ogee	stud
balk	flat	oven	tent
bank	flue	pale	term
barn	foil	pane	tige
base	fort	pave	tile
bead	foss	pier	toft
beam	fret	pile	tomb
bema			

tope
town
trap
vane
wall
weir
well
wing
xyst
yard

5

abbey
adobe
agora
aisle
alley
ambry
ancon
annex
arena
arris
atlas
attic
aulic
berth
block
booth
bothy
bower
brace
brick
broch
build
cabin

cella
cheek
choir
cleat
close
coign
compo
conch
congé
court
crypt
dairy
depot
domed
Doric
drain
drive
eaves
entry
erect
facet
facia
fence
flats
floor
flush
flute
folly
forum
fosse
foyer
gable
glass
glaze
glyph
grate

griff
groin
grout
gully
gutta
harem
hatch
helix
hinge
hoist
hotel
house
hovel
hydro
igloo
ingle
Ionic
jetty
joint
joist
jutty
kiosk
kraal
latch
ledge
level
lobby
lodge
manor
manse
mitre
motel
newel
niche
ogive
order

oriel
ovolo
paned
panel
patio
plank
plaza
porch
pound
putty
pylon
quirk
quoin
rails
ranch
range
revet
ridge
riser
Roman
salon
scape
serai
sewer
shack
shaft
shelf
shell
slate
slatt
slums
socle
solar
spire
splay
stack

stage	alcove	collar	fluted
stair	annexe	column	fresco
stake	arbour	coping	friary
stall	arcade	corbel	frieze
stand	ashlar	cordon	gablet
stele	ashler	corona	garage
steps	asylum	course	garret
stile	atrium	coving	gazebo
stoep	aviary	cranny	ghetto
stone	awning	crèche	girder
store	bagnio	crenel	glazed
stove	bakery	cupola	godown
stria	barrow	dagoba	Gothic
strut	batten	débris	gradin
study	bedsit	dentil	grange
stupa	belfry	design	griffe
suite	billet	donjon	grille
talon	bistro	dormer	grotto
tepee	bourse	dosser	ground
thorp	bricks	drains	groyne
tiled	bridge	dry rot	gutter
torii	camera	dug-out	hangar
torus	canopy	duplex	header
tower	casino	durbar	hearth
tread	castle	ecurie	hostel
truss	cellar	Empire	impost
Tudor	cement	enwall	insula
vault	châlet	estate	inwall
villa	chapel	exedra	Ionian
wharf	church	façade	kennel
works	cimbia	facing	ladder
	cinema	fascia	lancet
6	circus	fillet	larder
	closet	finial	lean-to
abacus	coffer	flèche	lierne
access	coigne	florid	lintel
adytum			

			7
listel	piazza	studio	academy
lock-up	picket	suburb	acroter
locker	pigsty	subway	air duct
log-hut	pillar	taenia	alcázar
loggia	plinth	tarsia	almonry
lounge	podium	tavern	ancones
louver	portal	temple	annulet
louvre	prefab	thatch	arcaded
lyceum	priory	tholos	archlet
mantel	prison	thorpe	archway
marble	purlin	tiling	armoury
market	putlog	timber	arsenal
metope	quarry	toilet	asphalt
mihrab	rabbet	tolsey	astylar
mitred	rafter	torsel	atelier
module	rancho	trench	balcony
morgue	recess	trough	baroque
mortar	refuge	tunnel	barrack
mosaic	reglet	turret	bastion
mosque	relief	Tuscan	Bauhaus
mud hut	rococo	unroof	beading
museum	rubble	untile	bedroom
mutule	rustic	vallum	boudoir
niched	saloon	veneer	boxroom
Norman	school	vestry	bracket
office	scotia	vihara	brewery
outlet	scroll	volute	builder
pagoda	shanty	wattle	built-in
palace	smithy	wicket	bulwark
paling	soffit	wigwam	butlery
pantry	spence	window	buttery
parget	square	zareba	cabaret
parvis	stable	zenana	cabinet
paving	stairs	zoning	calotte
perron	storey		canteen
pharos	stucco		

capitol	edifice	lagging	pantile
carving	embassy	landing	parapet
cassino	entasis	lantern	parlour
cavetto	eustyle	lathing	parquet
ceiling	factory	lattice	passage
chamber	fencing	laundry	pendant
chancel	festoon	lazaret	pension
chantry	fitment	library	pergola
chapter	fixture	lodging	piggery
château	fluting	low-rise	pillbox
chevron	foundry	lunette	plaster
chimney	gadroon	mansard	portico
cistern	galilee	mansion	postern
citadel	gallery	marquee	pugging
cob wall	gateway	masonry	pyramid
college	godroon	minaret	quarrel
conduit	gradine	minster	railing
contour	granary	moellon	rampart
convent	grating	Moorish	rebuild
cornice	Grecian	Mudéjar	rectory
cortile	groined	mudsill	reeding
cottage	grounds	mullion	rejoint
crocket	hallway	munnion	repairs
cubicle	hay loft	narthex	reredos
culvert	hip roof	necking	respond
curtain	hospice	new town	rockery
De Stijl	housing	nogging	roofing
deanery	hydrant	nunnery	rooftop
demesne	impasto	nursery	rosette
dinette	Islamic	obelisk	rostrum
domical	jib door	offices	rotunda
doorway	kennels	oratory	sanctum
dovecot	keyhole	ossuary	sawmill
dry wall	kitchen	outwork	sea-wall
dungeon	knocker	paddock	section
echinus	kremlin	palazzo	shebeen

shelter
shelves
shingle
shore up
shoring
shutter
slating
stadium
staging
station
steeple
storied
surgery
systyle
tambour
tannery
taproom
tayalot
tegular
telamon
terrace
theatre
thermae
tie-beam
tracery
tracing
transom
trefoil
trellis
tumulus
unpaved
untiled
upright
varnish
vaulted
veranda

viaduct
village
voluted

8

abat-jour
abattoir
abat-voix
abutment
acanthus
air-drain
airtight
anteroom
apophyge
approach
aquarium
aqueduct
arboured
astragal
atheneum
back door
backroom
badhouse
baguette
ballroom
baluster
banderol
banister
bannerol
barbican
basement
basilica
bathroom
bed-sitter
brattice
building

bulkhead
bungalow
buttress
caliduct
canephor
capstone
caryatid
casement
catacomb
causeway
cenotaph
centring
cesspool
chapiter
chaptrel
cincture
cloister
clubroom
cockloft
coliseum
colossal
comptoir
concrete
contract
corn loft
corridor
cow house
crescent
cromlech
cross-tie
crow step
cupboard
curb roof
cymatium
dancette
darkroom

decorate
detached
doghouse
dogtooth
domicile
door jamb
door nail
doorpost
doorsill
doorstep
dovecote
dovetail
dowel pin
drainage
dwelling
Egyptian
elevator
emporium
entrance
entresol
epistyle
erection
espalier
excavate
fanlight
fireclay
fireside
flagging
flashing
flat roof
flooring
fortress
freehold
fretwork
frontage
fusarole

gable end	mortuary	sacristy	terraced
gargoyle	moulding	sail-loft	tesserae
gatepost	newsroom	sale room	toll-gate
geodesic	ogee arch	scaffold	top floor
grillage	open-plan	scullery	town hall
grouting	openwork	seminary	transept
hacienda	orangery	seraglio	trap door
handrail	outhouse	showroom	traverse
hen house	overhang	shutters	triglyph
high-rise	palisade	side door	tympanum
hoarding	panelled	skewback	underpin
hospital	pantheon	skirting	upstairs
hostelry	parclose	skylight	vaulting
hothouse	parterre	slop-shop	verandah
housetop	pavement	smeltery	vicarage
ice house	pavilion	snack bar	vignette
intrados	pedestal	snuggery	voussoir
jalousie	pediment	soil pipe	wainscot
keystone	pilaster	solarium	wardroom
kingpost	pinnacle	spandrel	waxworks
lathwork	plashing	spanroof	well hole
lavatory	platform	stabling	well room
legation	playroom	stairway	windmill
lichgate	plumbing	stockade	windowed
lodgings	pointing	storeyed	woodwork
log cabin	pothouse	stuccoed	woodworm
loghouse	property	subtopia	workroom
lychgate	propylon	suburbia	workshop
madhouse	quarters	sudatory	ziggurat
magazine	refinery	sun-porch	
martello	registry	sun-proof	**9**
medieval	rocaille	taphouse	
memorial	rockwork	tectonic	acropolis
monolith	rood loft	tenement	acroteria
monument	roof tree	terminal	aerodrome
Moresque	ropewalk	terminus	alignment
			almshouse

anthemion	chop house	escalator	hypethral
apartment	clapboard	esplanade	hypocaust
arabesque	classical	estaminet	hypostyle
architect	claustral	excavator	infirmary
archivolt	cloakroom	extension	inglenook
archstone	clubhouse	farmhouse	inner city
art school	coalhouse	file-drain	ironworks
ashlaring	cofferdam	firebrick	kerbstone
athenaeum	colonnade	fireplace	labyrinth
bakehouse	colosseum	flagstone	landscape
banderole	composite	flashings	latticing
bas-relief	construct	floor plan	lazaretto
bay window	consulate	flophouse	leasehold
beadhouse	converted	floriated	letterbox
bell gable	copestone	foliation	lift-shaft
bell tower	courtyard	forecourt	linenfold
belvedere	cross-beam	framework	Mannerist
blueprint	crown post	front door	mausoleum
boathouse	cubby hole	front room	medallion
bolection	cubiculum	gable roof	mezzanine
bow window	Cyclopean	gatehouse	mock Tudor
box girder	cyma recta	glory hole	modernist
brick kiln	decastyle	gravel pit	modillion
brickwork	distemper	green belt	monastery
brutalist	door frame	groundsel	Mozarabic
bunkhouse	door panel	guardroom	music hall
butt joint	dormitory	guestroom	music room
Byzantine	dosshouse	guildhall	neo-Gothic
cafeteria	dowelling	guilloche	Nissen hut
calcimine	drainpipe	gymnasium	octastyle
campanile	dripstone	headpiece	orphanage
cartouche	dust stove	headstone	oubliette
cathedral	earthwork	hermitage	outer door
ceilinged	elevation	homestead	outer gate
cellarage	embrasure	hood mould	outskirts
centering	episenium	houseboat	paintwork

Palladian
panelling
pargeting
parquetry
parsonage
parthenon
partition
party wall
pay office
penthouse
peristyle
pillarbox
playhouse
pleasance
pontlevis
poorhouse
pressroom
prize ring
promenade
quicklime
rail-fence
rainproof
reception
refectory
rendering
reservoir
residence
residency
revetment
ridgepole
ring-fence
roadhouse
roughcast
rusticate
sallyport
scagliola

scantling
scrimshaw
sectional
sepulchre
shopfront
slate roof
spare room
staircase
stanchion
stateroom
stillroom
stinktrap
stockroom
stonewall
stonework
storeroom
stretcher
structure
stylobate
sun-lounge
swing door
synagogue
tablature
tenements
threshold
tollbooth
tollhouse
tower-room
townhouse
treillage
triforium
turf-house
turnstile
undermine
underprop
vestibule

wallpaper
wall-plate
warehouse
wastepipe
watertank
whitewash
window box
windproof
windtight
wine vault
workhouse

10

antechapel
arc-boutant
arched roof
architrave
art gallery
auditorium
backstairs
ballflower
balustered
balustrade
bargeboard
bedchamber
bell-turret
brick earth
brick-built
brownfield
cantilever
catafalque
chimney cap
chimneypot
cinquefoil
clerestory
clock tower

coachhouse
coal cellar
coffee shop
common room
conversion
corbie step
Corinthian
court house
covered way
crenulated
cross-aisle
crown glass
crownpiece
damp-course
decoration
decorative
depository
dining hall
dining room
dispensary
distillery
doll's house
dome-shaped
Doric order
double-hung
double lock
dowel joint
drawbridge
drying room
Dutch tiles
earth house
earthworks
egg and dart
embankment
engine-room
excavation

facia panel
fan tracery
fire escape
first floor
fives court
flamboyant
flint glass
flock paper
footbridge
foundation
functional
garden city
garden wall
glasshouse
glebe house
grandstand
granny flat
Greek cross
greenfield
greenhouse
ground plan
groundsill
groundwork
guardhouse
habitation
hammer beam
hipped roof
hippodrome
hunting box
hypaethral
intramural
Ionic order
jerry-built
label mould
laboratory
lady chapel

lancet arch
Latin cross
lazar-house
lighthouse
living room
lumber-room
luxury flat
maisonette
manor house
manteltree
market town
mitre joint
necropolis
Norman arch
opera house
overmantel
panopticon
passageway
pebble dash
persiennes
pied-à-terre
plastering
plate glass
polychromy
Portakabin
portcullis
post office
power-house
proportion
propylaeum
proscenium
pycnostyle
quadrangle
quatrefoil
ranch house
real estate

repointing
repository
restaurant
retrochoir
ribbed arch
road bridge
robing-room
rock-temple
Romanesque
roof garden
rose garden
rose window
roundhouse
round tower
rubblework
rumpus room
sanatorium
sanitarium
settlement
sink estate
skew bridge
skyscraper
slaked lime
smokestack
split level
state house
storehouse
street door
stronghold
structural
sun parlour
terracotta
tetrastyle
tiring-room
tower block
trust house

Tudor style
tumbledown
undercroft
university
unoccupied
untenanted
varnishing
ventilator
vernacular
vestry room
watch-house
watch-tower
water-tower
way-station
wicket gate
window sash
windscreen
wine-cellar

11

antechamber
barge couple
barge course
barrel vault
caravansary
Carolingian
castellated
cementation
chain-bridge
cinquecento
coffee house
columbarium
compartment
concert hall
coping stone
corbel steps

cornerstone
counterfort
country seat
crazy paving
crenellated
curtail step
cyma reversa
distempered
door knocker
dovetailing
drawing room
dress circle
eating house
entablature
fan vaulting
fingerplate
florid style
foundations
gambrel roof
Graeco-Roman
ground floor
hearthstone
ichnography
kitchenette
lattice work
laundry room
lecture room
linen closet
load-bearing
louver-board
louvre-board
machicoulis
mansard roof
mantelpiece
mantelshelf
manufactory

market-cross
masonry arch
morning room
observatory
oeil-de-boeuf
office block
oriel window
outbuilding
paving stone
picket fence
picture rail
plasterwork
postern gate
public house
reading room
reconstruct
Renaissance
residential
restoration
Roman cement
roofing felt
sarcophagus
scaffolding
service lift
shooting box
sitting room
smoking room
stately home
stringboard
sub-contract
summerhouse
tessellated
tiled hearth
trelliswork
trussed beam
Turkish bath

Tuscan order
undercoated
unfurnished
uninhabited
urban sprawl
utility room
ventilation
wainscoting
waiting room
war memorial
water closet
water supply
weathercock
whitewashed
window frame
window glass
window ledge
wrought iron

12

amphitheatre
architecture
assembly hall
assembly room
auction rooms
billiard room
building line
building site
caravanserai
chapel of rest
chapter house
chimneypiece
chimney shaft
chimney stack
conservatory
construction

country house
covered court
dividing wall
dormer window
double-glazed
draught-proof
dressing-room
Early English
egg and anchor
egg and tongue
entrance hall
fluted column
folding doors
French window
frontispiece
garden suburb
geodesic dome
guest chamber
half-timbered
hôtel de ville
hunting lodge
inner sanctum
Ionian column
kitchen range
labour-saving
lake dwelling
lancet window
lightning-rod
lock-up garage
lodging house
louvre window
machicolated
main entrance
mansion house
meeting house
mission house

neoclassical
pantechnicon
parquet floor
penitentiary
plasterboard
power station
prefabricate
privy chamber
Purbeck stone
purpose-built
quattrocento
retiring room
rooming house
semi-detached
spiral stairs
stained glass
string course
substruction
substructure
subterranean
swinging post
thatched roof
town planning
tracing cloth
tracing linen
tracing paper
transitional
underpinning
unmodernized
unornamental
unornamented
untenantable
unventilated
urban renewal
wainscotting
weatherboard

weatherproof
winter garden

13

accommodation
amphiprostyle
ancient lights
architectonic
architectural
assembly rooms
back staircase
boarding house
breakfast room
building block
butler's pantry
chimney corner
compass window
contabulation
council estate
coursing joint
dormitory town
double glazing
Dutch clinkers
dwelling house
dwelling place
emergency exit
encaustic tile
entrance lobby
establishment
ferro-concrete
fire-resistant
fitted kitchen
floodlighting
furnished flat
Grecian temple
housing estate

lattice window
machicolation
martello tower
master builder
Norman doorway
owner-occupied
palais de danse
Perpendicular
picture window
Portland stone
postmodernism
prefabricated
public library
Purbeck marble
revolving door
satellite town
shooting lodge
skirting board
soundproofing
specification
subcontractor
trading estate
triumphal arch
uninhabitable
vaulting shaft
Venetian blind
vinyl emulsion
wattle and daub

14

airing cupboard
apartment house
architectonics
banqueting hall
bedsitting room
Catherine-wheel

central heating
consulting room
country cottage
drying cupboard
filling station
flying buttress
funeral parlour
lath and plaster
listed building
mezzanine floor
office building
picture gallery
Portland cement

powder magazine
reconstruction
slaughterhouse
superstructure
threshing floor
Venetian window

15

air conditioning
clustered column
community centre
damp-proof course
discharging arch

dormitory suburb
feather-boarding
foundation stone
hydraulic cement
pleasure gardens
reception centre
refreshment room
spiral staircase
state apartments
unfurnished flat
Vitruvian scroll
weatherboarding
withdrawing room

BUSINESS, TRADE AND COMMERCE

2 AND 3	4		
	IOU		debt	gild

2 AND 3

A1
AVC
bid
BOT
buy
CA
COD
cut
due
dun
EC
ECU
fee
FOB
GDP
GNP
HP

IOU
ISA
job
lot
Ltd
MBA
net
owe
par
pay
PEP
RD
rig
SET
sum
tax
tip
VAT

4

agio
back
bail
bank
bear
bill
bond
boom
bull
call
cash
cess
chip
coin
cost
deal
dear

debt
deed
dole
dues
dump
duty
earn
easy
EFTA
even
fees
FIFO
fine
firm
fisc
free
fund
gain
GATT

gild
gilt
giro
glut
gold
good
hire
idle
kite
lend
levy
lien
loan
long
loss
mart
mint
nett
note

owed	at par	folio	score	assets
paid	audit	funds	scrip	assign
PAYE	award	gilts	share	at cost
peag	baron	gnome	shark	avails
perk	batch	goods	short	backer
poll	bears	gross	sight	bailee
pool	bid up	hedge	slash	bailor
post	block	House	slump	banker
puff	board	index	snake	barter
punt	bonds	issue	spend	bazaar
ramp	bonus	labor	stake	bearer
rate	brand	lease	stock	borrow
rent	bribe	limit	tally	bought
ring	bulls	MIRAS	talon	bounce
risk	buyer	money	taxes	bounty
ruin	buy in	notes	teind	bourse
safe	buy up	offer	TESSA	branch
sale	by-law	order	tight	broker
scot	cargo	owing	tithe	bubble
sell	cheap	panic	token	budget
sink	check	paper	trade	burden
sold	chips	payee	trend	bursar
spot	clear	payer	truck	buying
stag	clerk	pound	trust	buy out
swap	costs	price	usury	by-laws
tare	cover	proxy	value	cartel
term	crash	quota	wages	cash in
turn	cycle	quote	worth	change
vend	debit	rally	yield	charge
wage	dough	rates		cheque
	draft	remit	**6**	client
5	entry	repay		corner
	Ernie	rhino	accept	coupon
agent	ex cap	rider	accrue	credit
angel	ex div	scalp	advice	crisis
assay	float	scoop	agency	cum div
asset			amount	

dealer	ledger	profit	staple
deal in	lender	public	stocks
debtor	liable	punter	strike
defray	Lloyd's	purvey	supply
demand	lock-up	quorum	surety
dicker	margin	racket	surtax
docket	market	rating	syndic
drawee	mark-up	realty	tariff
drawer	mature	rebate	taxman
equity	merger	recoup	teller
estate	minute	redeem	tender
excise	moneys	refund	ticket
expend	nem con	remedy	tithes
export	notice	rental	trader
factor	octroi	rentes	tycoon
figure	office	report	unload
fiscal	on call	resale	unpaid
freeze	oncost	resign	usance
gazump	one off	retail	usurer
godown	on tick	retire	valuta
go slow	option	return	vendor
growth	outbid	salary	vendue
hammer	outlay	sample	volume
hawker	outlet	save up	wampum
holder	output	saving	wealth
honour	packet	sell in	wind up
import	parity	sell up	worker
in cash	pay-day	set off	
income	paying	settle	**7**
in debt	pay-off	shares	
indent	payola	shorts	account
insure	pay out	silver	actuary
in-tray	picket	simony	advance
jobber	pledge	specie	allonge
job lot	plunge	spiral	annuity
labour	policy	spread	arrears
			at sight

auction	douceur	insured	per cent
auditor	draw out	interim	poll tax
average	due bill	in trust	portage
backing	dumping	invoice	pre-empt
bad debt	duopoly	jobbers	premium
balance	economy	jobbing	prepaid
banking	embargo	kaffirs	pricing
bargain	endorse	killing	product
bidding	engross	launder	profits
bonanza	entrust	lay days	promote
bullion	ex-bonus	leasing	pro rata
bursary	expense	lending	pyramid
buy back	exploit	limited	realize
cambist	exports	lockout	realtor
capital	factory	lottery	receipt
cashier	failure	lump sum	refusal
ceiling	fall due	manager	reissue
certify	feedback	mint par	release
charter	finance	minutes	renewal
coinage	flutter	name day	reserve
company	for sale	nest egg	returns
consols	forward	net gain	revenue
convert	freebie	no funds	rigging
corn pit	freight	on offer	royalty
crossed	funding	on order	salable
customs	futures	on trust	salvage
cut-rate	gearing	out-tray	selling
damages	go under	package	sell-out
day book	haulage	partner	service
dealing	hedging	payable	sold out
declare	holding	pay cash	solvent
default	imports	payment	spinoff
deficit	imprest	pay rise	squeeze
deflate	indorse	payroll	stipend
deposit	inflate	pay slip	storage
dockage	in funds	pension	striker

subsidy	auditing	day shift	hardware
surplus	back bond	dealings	hoarding
swindle	bailment	defrayed	hot money
takings	bank bill	delivery	huckster
taxable	bankbook	director	importer
tax free	bank giro	disburse	in arrear
tonnage	bank loan	discount	increase
trade in	banknote	dividend	indebted
trading	bank rate	drawings	industry
traffic	bankroll	dry goods	interest
tranche	bankrupt	earnings	in the red
trustee	barratry	embezzle	investor
utility	basic pay	employee	kitemark
vending	below par	employer	lame duck
venture	berthage	emporium	manifest
war bond	blue chip	endorsee	manpower
war loan	book debt	endorser	mark down
warrant	borrower	entrepot	markings
way bill	bottomry	equities	maturing
welfare	business	estimate	maturity
workday	buying in	evaluate	merchant
wound up	carriage	exchange	monetary
write up	cashbook	ex-gratia	monopoly
	cash down	expenses	mortgage
8	cash sale	exporter	net price
	clearing	ex-rights	net worth
above par	commerce	finances	novation
acceptor	consumer	fine gold	on credit
accounts	contango	flat rate	on demand
act of God	contract	gold pool	on strike
after tax	creditor	goodwill	operator
agiotage	credit to	gratuity	ordinary
amortize	cum bonus	hallmark	overhead
ante-date	currency	hammered	overtime
appraise	customer	hard cash	par value
assignee	cut-price	hard sell	passbook
assigner			

pawn shop	solvency	arbitrage	easy terms
pay talks	spending	arrearage	economics
pin money	spot cash	assurance	economies
post paid	sterling	averaging	economize
poundage	straddle	bank stock	emolument
price cut	supertax	blank bill	endowment
price war	swindler	book value	exchequer
proceeds	takeover	bordereau	exciseman
producer	taxation	borrowing	excise tax
property	tax dodge	brand name	executive
purchase	taxpayer	brokerage	export tax
quit rent	trade gap	by-product	extortion
rack rent	transfer	call money	face value
rag trade	Treasury	call price	fair price
receipts	turnover	carry over	fair trade
receiver	underbid	certified	fiat money
recovery	undercut	chartered	fiduciary
reinvest	unquoted	charterer	financial
rent free	wage rate	clearance	financier
reserves	warranty	commodity	fine paper
retailer	watchdog	cost price	firm offer
retainer	wharfage	cum rights	firm price
salaried	windfall	death duty	first call
saleable	write off	debenture	first cost
saleroom		debit note	flotation
salesman	**9**	deck cargo	franchise
scarcity		deduction	free trade
schedule	actuarial	defaulter	fully paid
security	ad valorem	deflation	garnishee
shipment	aggregate	demurrage	gilt-edged
shipyard	allotment	depletion	going rate
showcase	allowance	depositor	guarantee
showroom	annuitant	directors	guarantor
sideline	ante-dated	direct tax	hard money
sinecure	anti-trust	dishonour	hush money
soft sell	appraisal	easy money	import tax
	appraiser		

in arrears
incentive
income tax
indemnity
indenture
inflation
insolvent
insurance
inventory
knock down
late shift
leasehold
liability
liquidate
liquidity
list price
long-dated
loss-maker
luxury tax
mail order
marketing
means test
middleman
mortgagee
mortgagor
near money
negotiate
net income
night safe
on account
on the tail
order book
outgoings
outworker
overdraft
overdrawn

overheads
packaging
pari passu
paymaster
pecuniary
petty cash
piecework
piggy bank
portfolio
preferred
price list
price ring
price rise
prime cost
principal
profiteer
promotion
purchaser
put option
quittance
quotation
ratepayer
ready cash
recession
redundant
reflation
reimburse
repayable
repayment
resources
restraint
reversion
royalties
sell short
shift work
shop floor

short bill
shortfall
short time
sight bill
slush fund
sold short
sole agent
speculate
spot price
stamp duty
statement
stock list
stockpile
strike pay
subscribe
subsidize
surcharge
sweat shop
syndicate
tax return
ticket day
trade fair
trademark
trade name
tradesman
traveller
treasurer
undersell
unit trust
unskilled
utilities
valuation
vendition
viability
wage claim
warehouse

wealth tax
wholesale
winding up
workforce
work sheet
work study
World Bank

10

acceptance
accountant
account day
accounting
accumulate
active bond
added value
adjustment
advice note
appreciate
assessment
assignment
attachment
auctioneer
automation
average out
bank credit
bank return
bankruptcy
bearer bond
bear market
bill broker
bill of sale
block grant
bondholder
bonus issue
bonus share

bookkeeper
bottom line
bucket shop
bulk buying
bull market
calculator
call option
capitalism
capitalist
capitalize
capitation
chain store
chargeable
chequebook
closed shop
closing bid
collateral
colporteur
commercial
commission
compensate
consortium
contraband
conversion
cost centre
credit bank
credit card
credit note
credit slip
cumulative
defalcator
defrayment
del credere
department
depository
depreciate

depression
direct cost
dirty money
drawn bonds
elasticity
encumbered
end product
engrossing
ergonomics
estate duty
Eurodollar
Euromarket
evaluation
excise duty
ex dividend
first offer
fiscal year
fixed costs
fixed price
fixed trust
floor price
forced sale
forwarding
free market
funded debt
green pound
gross value
ground rent
growth area
honorarium
import duty
income bond
industrial
insolvency
instalment
in the black

investment
issue price
job hunting
joint stock
lighterage
liquidator
living wage
long period
loss leader
management
marked down
marketable
mass market
meal ticket
mercantile
monetarism
monetarist
money order
monopolist
monopolize
moratorium
negotiable
never never
night shift
nonpayment
no par value
note of hand
obligation
open cheque
open credit
opening bid
open market
open policy
option rate
overcharge
paper money

pawnbroker
peppercorn
percentage
plough back
pre-emption
preference
prepayment
price index
price level
production
profitable
profits tax
prospector
prospectus
prosperity
prosperous
provide for
purchasing
pure profit
pyramiding
quarter day
ready money
real estate
real income
recompense
redeemable
redemption
redundancy
remittance
remunerate
repurchase
rock bottom
sales force
scrip issue
second-hand
securities

selling day
selling out
serial bond
settlement
share index
short bonds
short-dated
smart money
sole agency
speculator
statistics
stockpiles
stock split
subscriber
tape prices
tax evasion
ticker tape
tight money
trade cycle
trade price
trade union
ultra vires
underwrite
unemployed
upset price
wage freeze
wage policy
Wall Street
wholesaler
working day
work to rule
written off

11

accountancy
account book

acquittance
advance note
advertising
arbitration
asking price
at face value
auction ring
auction sale
average bond
bank account
bank balance
bank holiday
bank manager
bank of issue
bear squeeze
beneficiary
betting shop
big business
billionaire
bill of entry
bimetallism
black market
blank cheque
bonded goods
bond washing
bonus scheme
book-keeping
budget price
businessman
capital gain
cash account
central bank
certificate
circulation
closing down
commitments

commodities
common stock
competition
competitive
comptometer
consignment
consumerism
consumption
co-operative
corporation
cost-benefit
counterfeit
cover charge
cum dividend
customs duty
danger money
days of grace
defence bond
demand curve
demand draft
demutualize
deposit rate
deposit slip
devaluation
direct debit
discounting
dishonoured
distributor
dividend tax
double entry
down payment
economic law
economic man
endorsement
estate agent
expenditure

fixed assets
fixed charge
fixed income
floor trader
fluctuation
foreclosure
free on board
freight note
Gresham's Law
gross income
high finance
hypermarket
hypothecate
income stock
indemnified
indirect tax
industrials
job analysis
joint return
legal tender
life savings
liquidation
loan capital
manufacture
market overt
market place
market price
mass-produce
merchandise
middle price
millionaire
minimum wage
money-lender
negotiation
net interest
net receipts

open account
option price
outstanding
overpayment
overtrading
package deal
partnership
pay on demand
physiocrats
pocket money
point of sale
postal order
poverty line
poverty trap
premium bond
price fixing
price freeze
property tax
purchase tax
Queer Street
raw material
realization
reinsurance
reserve bank
retiring age
revaluation
rights issue
risk capital
safe deposit
sales ledger
sales person
savings bank
seigniorage
self-service
sell forward
shareholder

single entry
sinking fund
small trader
sold forward
speculation
stagflation
stake holder
stockbroker
stockjobber
stock market
stockpiling
stocktaking
subsistence
supermarket
syndicalism
take-home pay
takeover bid
time deposit
time sharing
tracker fund
trading post
transaction
travel agent
undercharge
undervalued
underwriter
with profits

12

above the line
account payee
ad valorem tax
amalgamation
amortization
appreciation
assembly line

balance sheet
banker's draft
banker's order
bargain price
below the line
bill of lading
board meeting
Board of Trade
bond creditor
bonded stores
bottomry bond
branch office
bridging loan
buyer's market
callable bond
capital gains
capital goods
capital stock
carpetbagger
carry-over day
carrying over
cash and carry
cash register
caveat emptor
charter party
clearing bank
closing price
common market
compensation
contract note
cost of living
credit rating
current price
current ratio
customs union
Defence Bonds

denomination
depreciation
differential
direct labour
disbursement
discount rate
disinflation
distribution
Dutch auction
early closing
earned income
econometrics
economy drive
embezzlement
entrepreneur
exchange rate
export credit
first refusal
fiscal policy
fixed capital
floating debt
frozen assets
gate receipts
general store
going concern
gold standard
haberdashery
hard currency
hire purchase
indirect cost
interest rate
invoice clerk
irredeemable
joint account
keep accounts
labour market

laissez-faire
life interest
liquid assets
manufacturer
marginal cost
mass-produced
maturity date
mercantilism
merchant bank
mixed economy
monetization
money changer
national bank
national debt
nearest offer
nominal price
nominal value
official list
opening price
overcapacity
pay as you earn
pay in advance
paying-in slip
policy holder
present worth
price ceiling
price control
price current
price rigging
productivity
profiteering
profit margin
profit motive
profit taking
public sector
rate of growth

raw materials
redeployment
remuneration
remunerative
reserve price
retaining fee
rig the market
rising prices
running costs
sale or return
sales gimmick
sales manager
salesmanship
severance pay
share capital
shareholding
sliding scale
social credit
soft currency
specie points
state lottery
statistician
sterling area
stock in trade
stockjobbery
stockjobbing
street market
surplus value
tax avoidance
tax collector
tax exemption
terms of trade
trade balance
trade barrier
trading stamp
transfer deed

travel agency
treasury bill
treasury bond
treasury note
trial balance
trustee stock
underwriting
unemployment
valued policy
welfare state
works council

13

acceptilation
allotment note
appropriation
articled clerk
asset stripper
average clause
backwardation
bank overdraft
bank statement
blank transfer
budget surplus
bullion market
business cycle
cash dispenser
cash in advance
clearance sale
clearing house
consumer goods
contract curve
cost-effective
credit account
credit control
credit squeeze

crossed cheque
current assets
discount house
discount store
dividend yield
dollar premium
Dow–Jones index
effective rate
excess profits
exchequer bill
financial year
fire insurance
free-trade area
fringe benefit
futures market
gross receipts
guarantee fund
impulse buying
incomes policy
interim report
issued capital
life assurance
life insurance
livery company
Lombard Street
long-dated bill
making-up price
multinational
multiple store
non-cumulative
not negotiable
options market
ordinary share
outside broker
overhead price
paid-up capital

par of exchange
participating
payment in kind
penalty clause
precipice bond
premium income
private sector
profitability
profit and loss
profit sharing
protectionism
public company
purchase price
quota sampling
rateable value
sales forecast
seller's market
service charge
settlement day
share transfer
small business
specification
standing order
Stock Exchange
subcontractor
switch selling
taxable income
tax-deductible
trade discount
trading estate
value added tax
vendor's shares
wasting assets
wheeler-dealer
works councils

14

accident policy
account current
advance freight
apprenticeship
balance of trade
bearer security
bill of exchange
blocked account
break-even point
bureau de change
capital account
capital gearing
capitalization
command
 economy
consumer credit
convertibility
corporation tax
cost accountant
cost accounting
current account
current balance
debenture stock
decimalization
deferred rebate
deferred shares
deposit account
discount market
economic growth
featherbedding
fiduciary issue
finance company
floating charge
founders' shares
fringe benefits

full employment
garnishee order
general average
general manager
half-commission
holder for value
holding company
hyperinflation
imprest account
inertia selling
infrastructure
inscribed stock
insider dealing
insider trading
invisible trade
joint stock bank
letter of credit
limited company
liquidity ratio
Lloyd's Register
loan conversion
macro-economics
managing agents
market research
merchant banker
micro-economics
monthly account
monthly payment
mortgage broker
national income
new issue market
nominal capital
option dealings
ordinary shares
overproduction
oversubscribed

over the counter
preferred stock
private economy
production line
progress chaser
promissory note
pyramid selling
quality control
random sampling
rate of exchange
rate of interest
receiving order
revenue account
shopping centre
short-term gains
simple interest
social security
superannuation
surrender value
trading account
uberrimae fidei
unearned income
venture capital
working capital

15 AND 16

average adjuster
bargain basement
bonded warehouse
building society
business manager
business studies
capital employed
capital gains tax
closing-down sale
commission agent

company director
consignment note
consumer durable
cottage industry
deferred annuity
demutualization
department store
dividend warrant
early retirement
endowment policy
ex-gratia payment
exchange control
family allowance
foreign exchange
golden handshake
insurance broker
insurance policy

interim dividend
investment trust
labour-intensive
lightning strike
liquidity ratios
marine insurance
nationalization
national savings
no-claim discount
non-contributory
non-profit making
personal pension
political
  science (16)
preference bonds
preference share
preference stock

preferred shares
public ownership
public relations
purchasing power
rationalization
redemption yield
reducing balance
reserve currency
secured creditor
service industry
sleeping partner
sterling balance
supply and demand
suspense account
unissued capital

CLOTHES AND MATERIALS

3	hem	tee	cape	fold
	kid	tie	clog	frog
aba	kit	top	coat	garb
abb	lap	wig	coif	gear
alb	lei	zip	comb	geta
bag	mac		cony	gimp
bib	nap	**4**	cope	gore
boa	net		cord	gown
bra	obi	band	cowl	haik
cap	pin	barb	cuff	heel
cop	PVC	batt	dart	hide
cut	rag	bead	down	hood
dye	rep	belt	drag	hoop
fez	rig	bias	duck	hose
fur	tag	boot	duds	jama
hat	tam	brim	felt	jute
		burr		

képi	slip	chain	jeans	rayon
kilt	sock	chaps	jupon	robes
knot	sole	chino	kapok	romal
lace	spur	cloak	karam	ruche
lamé	stud	clogs	khaki	rumal
lawn	suit	cloth	lacet	sable
leno	tank	clout	lapel	sabot
list	toga	cotta	Levis	sagum
mask	togs	crape	linen	satin
maud	topi	crash	liner	scarf
maxi	trim	crêpe	lisle	serge
mesh	tuck	cymar	lungi	shako
midi	tutu	denim	lurex	shawl
mini	vamp	dhoti	manta	sheer
mink	veil	dicky	mitre	shift
mitt	vent	dress	mitts	shirt
mode	vest	drill	moiré	shoes
muff	warp	ducks	mufti	skirt
mule	wear	ephod	mules	slops
mull	weft	fanon	mutch	smock
peak	wool	fichu	nappy	snood
pelt	wrap	fogle	ninon	spats
poke	yarn	frill	nylon	stays
pump	yoke	frock	Orlon	stock
repp		gauze	orris	stole
ring	**5**	get-up	pants	stuff
robe		gilet	parka	suede
ruff	amice	glove	pique	surah
sack	baize	guimp	plaid	tabby
sari	batik	gunny	plait	tails
sark	beige	habit	pleat	talma
sash	beret	hanky	plume	tammy
seam	boots	heels	plush	terry
shag	braid	ihram	print	thong
shoe	burka	inkie	pumps	thrum
silk	busby	jabot	purse	tiara

Tibet
toile
topee
toque
train
trews
tulle
tunic
tweed
twill
V-neck
voile
weeds
welly
wigan

6

afghan
alpaca
angora
anklet
anorak
armlet
attire
banian
barège
barret
basque
beaver
bertha
biggin
bikini
blazer
blouse
boater
bob-wig

bodice
bolero
bonnet
bootee
bouclé
bowler
bow tie
braces
briefs
brogan
brogue
brolly
buckle
bum bag
burlap
burnet
buskin
bustle
button
byssus
caftan
calash
calico
camlet
canvas
capote
castor
cestus
chimer
chinos
chiton
choker
chopin
cilice
cloche

coatee
collar
collet
corset
cotton
cravat
crepon
crewel
curler
Dacron
damask
denier
denims
diadem
diaper
dimity
dirndl
domett
domino
dowlas
duffel
ear-cap
edging
ermine
fabric
fag-end
faille
fedora
ferret
fillet
flares
fleece
fox-fur
frieze
fringe
gaiter

galosh
garter
girdle
gurrah
gusset
hankie
hatpin
helmet
humhum
insole
jacket
jerkin
jersey
jilbab
joseph
jubbah
jumper
kaftan
kersey
kimono
kirtle
lappet
lining
livery
madras
mantle
mantua
merino
mitten
mobcap
mohair
moreen
muslin
nankin
nutria
nylons

Oxford
Panama
parure
patent
patten
peltry
peplum
peruke
pleats
pomade
pompon
poncho
pongee
poplin
puttee
PVC mac
raglan
ratine
rebato
reefer
riband
ribbon
rigout
rochet
ruffle
russet
samite
sandal
sarong
satara
sateen
sendal
sequin
serape
shades
sheath

shoddy
shorts
shroud
ski cap
slacks
sleeve
smalls
sunhat
T-shirt
tabard
tartan
thibet
thread
tiepin
tights
tippet
tissue
top-hat
topper
torque
toupee
toupet
Tricel
tricot
trilby
trunks
tucker
turban
tussah
tuxedo
tweeds
ulster
velure
velvet
visite
waders

wampus
weeper
whites
wimple
wincey
woolly

7

Acrilan
acrylic
alamode
apparel
armband
art-silk
baldric
bandeau
batiste
biretta
blanket
blucher
bottine
brocade
brogans
buckram
burnous
cagoule
calotte
cambric
capuche
cassock
casuals
challis
chamois
chapeau
chaplet
chemise

chiffon
chimere
chlamys
civvies
clobber
clothes
coating
cockade
compact
coronet
corsage
costume
couture
cow-hide
crochet
culotte
cut-away
delaine
doeskin
doublet
drabbet
drawers
drip-dry
elastic
epaulet
falsies
felt hat
felting
fig leaf
filibeg
flannel
flat hat
flounce
foulard
frounce
fur coat

fustian
G-string
gaiters
galloon
gambado
garment
gingham
grogram
guipure
gumboot
gymslip
handbag
hat-band
hessian
hoggers
hogskin
holland
homburg
hopsack
hosiery
jaconet
lasting
latchet
layette
leather
legging
leghorn
leotard
loafers
Mae West
maniple
Mechlin
miniver
modiste
monocle
montero

morocco
mozetta
mudpack
muffler
nacarat
nankeen
necktie
new look
nightie
non-iron
oilskin
organdy
organza
Orleans
orphrey
outsize
overall
padding
paisley
pajamas
paletot
pallium
panties
parasol
partlet
pattens
pegtops
pelisse
percale
periwig
petasus
pigskin
pillbox
pork-pie
puggree
puttees

pyjamas
raiment
rompers
rosette
rubbers
sacking
satinet
sayette
scarlet
silesia
silk hat
singlet
slicker
slip-ons
slipper
soutane
spencer
sporran
stammel
stetson
suiting
sunsuit
surcoat
surtout
sweater
tabaret
tabinet
taffeta
tank top
tarbush
tatting
tea-gown
textile
ticking
tiffany
top boot

top coat
top-knot
topless
tricorn
tunicle
turn-ups
tussore
twinset
undress
uniform
vandyke
velours
vesting
vesture
webbing
wellies
wetsuit
wiggery
woollen
worsted
yashmak
y-fronts

8

aigrette
appliqué
babouche
Balmoral
barracan
bathrobe
bearskin
bed linen
bedsocks
berretta
black tie
bloomers

bluchers	dalmatic	high heel	osnaburg
boat-neck	day dress	hipsters	overalls
bobbinet	deerskin	homespun	overcoat
body-belt	diamanté	hot pants	overshoe
bonelace	djellaba	jackboot	paduasoy
bootlace	drilling	Jacquard	peignoir
bottines	dungaree	jodhpurs	pelerine
breeches	dustcoat	jump suit	pinafore
brodekin	earmuffs	kerchief	playsuit
buckskin	ensemble	knickers	plumelet
Burberry	eyeshade	knitwear	polo-neck
camisole	facepack	lambskin	ponyskin
capuchin	Fair Isle	leggings	prunella
cardigan	fatigues	lingerie	puggaree
cashmere	fillibeg	lustring	pullover
Celanese	flannels	mackinaw	rag trade
chasuble	footwear	mantelet	raincoat
chausses	frilling	mantilla	reticule
chenille	frippery	material	sandshoe
cincture	frontlet	menswear	sarcenet
cloaking	froufrou	mocassin	scapular
cloth cap	furbelow	moccasin	sealskin
clothing	galoshes	moleskin	shagreen
coiffure	gambeson	moquette	shalloon
collaret	gambroon	muffatee	Shantung
coonskin	gauntlet	muslinet	sheeting
corduroy	glad rags	musquash	shirring
cordwain	gold lace	nainsook	shirting
corporal	gold lamé	neckband	shoe horn
corsage	gossamer	neckline	shoelace
corselet	gumboots	negligée	shot silk
cosmetic	gymshoes	nightcap	ski boots
creepers	half-hose	nose ring	ski pants
cretonne	hand-knit	oilcloth	skullcap
crew-neck	headband	opera hat	slippers
culottes	headgear	organdie	smocking

snap brim
sneakers
snowshoe
sombrero
soutache
spun silk
spun yarn
stocking
straw hat
sundress
sunshade
surplice
swanskin
swimsuit
tabbinet
tailcoat
tapestry
tarboosh
tarlatan
Terylene
trimming
trousers
two-piece
umbrella
vestment
wardrobe
war paint
whipcord
white tie
woollens
wristlet
zoot suit

9

Alice band
ankle-boot

astrakhan
baby linen
balaclava
ball dress
bandolier
beachwear
bedjacket
billycock
blond lace
blue jeans
bombazine
bowler hat
brassiere
broadbrim
bushshirt
calamanco
camelhair
caparison
cassimere
cerecloth
chantilly
charmeuse
chaussure
cheongsam
chinstrap
clump boot
coat-tails
cocked hat
comforter
Courtelle
crinoline
Cuban heel
cufflinks
dalmatica
décolleté
djellabah

dog collar
drainpipe
dress coat
dress suit
duffel bag
dungarees
epaulette
fermillet
fingering
fleshings
flipflops
floss silk
forage cap
frockcoat
full dress
full skirt
fur collar
gabardine
gaberdine
gambadoes
garibaldi
gauntlets
georgette
Glengarry
greatcoat
grenadine
grosgrain
haircloth
hairpiece
hairshift
headdress
headscarf
high heels
hip pocket
hoop skirt
horsehair

housecoat
huckaback
Inverness
jack boots
jockey cap
justi-coat
kid gloves
kirby grip
knee socks
lambswool
levantine
linen mesh
loincloth
longcloth
long dress
long skirt
long socks
macintosh
millinery
miniskirt
moiré silk
muffettee
neckcloth
nightgown
nightwear
off the peg
organzine
overdress
overshoes
panama hat
pantalets
pantaloon
panty hose
paramatta
patchwork
pea jacket

10

peaked cap
percaline
persienne
petersham
petticoat
piccadill
pina cloth
pinstripe
pixie hood
plimsolls
plus-fours
point lace
polonaise
polo shirt
polyester
pompadour
pourpoint
press stud
ready made
redingote
round-neck
sackcloth
sack dress
safety pin
sailcloth
sailor hat
sanbenito
sartorial
satinette
scapulary
school cap
scoop-neck
separates
sharkskin
sheepskin
shell suit

shirt-band
shirt-tail
shovel hat
shower cap
siren suit
sloppy joe
slouch hat
snowshoes
sou'wester
stockinet
stockings
stomacher
strapless
suede coat
sunbonnet
sun helmet
swansdown
sweatband
sword belt
tarpaulin
towelling
track suit
trilby hat
trousseau
undervest
underwear
velveteen
vestments
waistband
waistcoat
wedge heel
whalebone
wide-awake
wristband
zucchetto

ankle socks
balbriggan
ballet shoe
bathing cap
beaverteen
Berlin wool
black dress
blanketing
bobbin lace
bobbysocks
boiler suit
bombazette
broadcloth
brocatelle
bushjacket
buttonhole
candlewick
canonicals
chatelaine
chemisette
chinchilla
collarette
collar stud
court dress
court shoes
coverchief
crêpe soles
cricket cap
cummerbund
déshabillé
dishabille
diving suit
drainpipes
dressmaker
dress shirt

dress shoes
duffel coat
embroidery
empire line
epauletted
Eton collar
Eton jacket
fancy dress
fascinator
fearnought
feather boa
flak jacket
florentine
flying suit
foresleeve
foundation
fustanella
Geneva gown
gold thread
grass cloth
grass skirt
habiliment
hair ribbon
halterneck
hodden-grey
hook and eye
horsecloth
Irish linen
jersey silk
jersey wool
kerseymere
khaki drill
life jacket
lounge suit
mackintosh
mess jacket

mock velvet
monk's habit
mousseline
needlecord
new clothes
nightdress
nightshirt
old clothes
opera cloak
overblouse
Oxford bags
pantaloons
parramatta
party dress
piccadilly
pilot-cloth
pinstripes
pith helmet
plastic mac
poke bonnet
powder puff
print dress
riding-hood
romper suit
roquelaure
sailor suit
scratch wig
seersucker
shirt front
shoe buckle
shoestring
sleeveless
slingbacks
solar topee
sportscoat
sportshirt

sportswear
string vest
suede shoes
Sunday best
sunglasses
suspenders
sweatshirt
three piece
thrown silk
toilinette
trench coat
trousering
turtle-neck
tussah silk
under linen
underpants
undershirt
waterproof
windjammer
wing collar
wraparound

11

Anthony Eden
Aran sweater
baseball cap
bathing suit
battledress
bellbottoms
best clothes
black patent
boiled shirt
boutonnière
bovver boots
boxer shorts
candystripe

canvas shoes
cap and bells
cheesecloth
clodhoppers
cloth-of-gold
contact lens
crash-helmet
dark glasses
décolletage
deerstalker
diving dress
Dolly Varden
dreadnought
dressmaking
dress shield
espadrilles
evening gown
farthingale
flannelette
flared skirt
football cap
formal dress
hammer cloth
hand-me-downs
Harris tweed
herringbone
hobble skirt
Honiton lace
Kendal green
lawn sleeves
leather coat
leatherette
leg of mutton
leopardskin
matinée coat
Mechlin lace

middy blouse
morning coat
mortarboard
neckerchief
nettlecloth
pantalettes
panty girdle
Persian lamb
Phrygian cap
pilot jacket
ready-to-wear
regimentals
riding habit
shawl collar
shell jacket
shirt button
shoe leather
shoulder bag
slumberwear
spatterdash
stiff collar
suede jacket
swallowtail
tam-o'-shanter
tennis dress
tennis skirt
torchon lace
trencher cap
trouser suit
tussore silk
watered silk
wellingtons
white collar
widow's weeds
wind breaker
windcheater

Windsor knot
work clothes
yachting cap

12

acrylic fibre
bathing dress
billycock hat
birthday suit
body stocking
bolting cloth
bomber jacket
breast pocket
business suit
cardinal's hat
cavalry twill
chastity belt
chesterfield
circassienne
clothes horse
collar and tie
college scarf
combinations
crêpe-de-chine
dinner jacket
divided skirt
Donegal tweed
donkey jacket
dress clothes
dressing gown
dress uniform
Easter bonnet
evening dress
fatigue dress
full mourning
galligaskins

haberdashery
handkerchief
haute couture
Hessian boots
Indian cotton
knee breeches
leather skirt
lumber jacket
moiré antique
monkey jacket
morning dress
Paisley shawl
plain clothes
pleated skirt
pressure suit
raglan sleeve
reach-me-downs
salwar kameez
service dress
shirtwaister
sleeping suit
sports jacket
stovepipe hat
underclothes
wedding dress

13

Bermuda shorts
cashmere shawl
casual clothes
chinchilla fur
cocktail dress
football boots
football scarf
hacking jacket

Hawaiian skirt
Highland dress
Inverness cape
leather jacket
linsey-woolsey
made to measure
matinee jacket
Norfolk jacket
patent leather
period costume
pinafore dress
platform soles
Russia leather
shalwar kameez
shoulder strap
smoking jacket
spatterdashes
sports clothes
swaddling band
underclothing

14

afternoon dress
antiperspirant
artificial silk
bathing costume
cardigan jacket
chamois leather
clerical collar
collar-attached
double-breasted
Fair Isle jumper
fully fashioned
hobnailed boots
knickerbockers

Morocco leather
off the shoulder
riding breeches
Shetland jumper
shooting jacket
three-piece suit
undress uniform
winter woollies

15

balaclava helmet
cardigan sweater
civilian clothes
crease-resistant
maribou feathers
mourning clothes
ostrich feathers
sheepskin jacket
swimming
    costume
tarpaulin jacket
wellington boots

COINS AND CURRENCY

2 AND 3

as
at
bit
bob
cob
dam
ecu
far
fen
fil
fin
jon
lac
lat
lek
leu
lev
mag
mil
mna
oof
öre
pie
pul
pya
red
ree
rei
sen
sho
sol
sou

tin
won
yen
zac
zuz

4

anna
baht
bean
beka
biga
buck
cash
cedi
cent
chip
chon
daum
dawm
dime
doit
dong
dosh
duro
euro
geld
joey
kick
kran
kuna
kyat
lipa
lira

lire
loot
lwei
mail
mark
merk
mina
mite
note
obol
para
peag
peak
peso
pice
pony
punt
quid
rand
real
reis
rial
riel
ryal
tael
taka
tein
thou
unik
yuan
zack

5

agora

angel
asper
aurei
belga
betso
boole
brass
bread
chiao
colón
conto
copec
crore
crown
daric
dinar
dobra
dough
ducat
eagle
fanam
fiver
franc
grand
groat
haler
koban
kopek
krona
krone
kroon
leone
liard
libra

litas
livre
locho
lolly
louis
lucre
maneh
medio
mohar
mohur
moola
naira
noble
obang
ochre
oncer
paisa
paolo
pence
pengo
penny
piece
plack
pound
ready
rhino
riyal
royal
ruble
rupee
rupia
sceat
scudi
scudo
semis
soldi

soldo
sucre
sugar
sycee
tenge
tical
ticcy
tizzy
toman
uncia
unite
verso
zloty

6

amania
aureus
balboa
bawbee
bezant
bodole
boodle
change
condor
copang
copeck
copper
couter
deaner
décime
denier
dirham
dirhem
doblon
dollar
drachm

escudo
florin
forint
fuorte
gourde
groszy
guinea
gulden
halala
heller
kobang
kopeck
koruna
kwanza
lepton
markka
monkey
nickel
obolus
pagoda
pagode
peseta
pesewa
rosser
rouble
rupiah
sceatt
sequin
shekel
souran
specie
stater
stiver
talari
talent
tanner

tenner
tester
teston
thaler
tickey
tizzie
tomaun
valuta
zechin

7

afghani
angelot
bolivar
carolus
centava
centavo
centime
cordoba
crusado
denarii
drachma
exergue
guaraní
guilder
ha'penny
jacobus
kopiyka
lempira
manilla
millime
milreis
moidore
ngusang
nummary
obverse

pfennig
piastre
pistole
quarter
quetzal
reverse
ringgit
sawbuck
sextans
smacker
solidus
stooter
testoon
testril
thrymsa
unicorn

8

ambrosin
assignat
australe
cruzeiro
denarius
didrachm
doubloon
ducatoon
farthing
florence
groschen
half anna
half mark
imperial
johannes
kreutzer
louis d'or
maravedi

megabuck
napoleon
new pence
ngultrum
picayune
planchet
portague
qïndarka
quadrans
quetzale
sesterce
shilling
sixpence
stotinka
twopence
zecchino

9

boliviano
centésimo
cuartillo
didrachma
dupondius
fourpence
gold broad
gold noble
gold penny
half ackey
half angel
half broad
halfcrown
half eagle
half groat
halfpenny
lilangeni
pistareen

rixdollar
rose-noble
schilling
sestertii
sovereign
spur royal
yellow boy

10

broad piece
crown piece
easterling
emalangeni
first brass
gold stater
half florin
half guinea
half laurel
quadrussis
Reichsmark
sestertium
silverling
stour-royal
threepence
tripondius
venezolano

11

Deutschmark
double crown
double eagle
george noble
guinea piece
half guilder
half thistle
silver penny

spade guinea
tetradrachm
twelvepenny

12 AND 13

antoninianus (12)
Deutsche Mark (12)
double sequin (12)
folding money (12)
half farthing (12)
half rose-noble (13)
half sovereign (13)
mill sixpence (12)
piece of eight (12)
quarter angel (12)
quarter dollar (13)
quarter florin (13)
quarter laurel (13)
quarter noble (12)

silver dollar (12)
silver-stater (12)
sixpenny piece (13)
threepenny bit (13)
twenty dollars (13)
two-pound coin (12)
twopence piece (13)

14 AND OVER

fifty-pence piece (15)
five-guinea piece (15)
Hong Kong dollar (14)
Maria Theresa dollar (18)
three farthings (14)
threepenny piece (15)
twenty shillings (15)
two-guilder piece (15)
two-guinea piece (14)

COMPUTERS
Computer terms

1 AND 2	bit	DPI	LSI
	bot	DSP	MSB
AI	bug	DTE	MSI
C	CAD	DTP	PDA
CD	CAV	DVD	PIN
IT	CAM	FSK	POP
PC	COM	FTP	RAM
WP	CPL	GIF	ROM
	CPU	IDE	tab
	cut	ISP	UPS
3	DMA	LCD	URI
ADA	DOS	LSB	URL

USB	MIDI	key in	insert
VDU	poll	log off	JOVIAL
VGA	port	log on	keypad
WAN	quit	macro	laptop
web	read	micro	memory
zap	save	modem	nibble
zip	scan	mouse	output
	SCSI	octal	PASCAL
	sort	PILOT	Prolog
4	view	pixel	QWERTY
	WIMP	pop-up	reboot
baud	word	queue	return
boot	WORM	slave	sample
burn	wrap	store	screen
byte		tools	scroll
cell	**5**	virus	sector
chip		write	server
code	Algol		upload
copy	alias	**6**	window
core	ASCII		
data	BASIC	access	**7**
disk	block	back up	
drag	CD-ROM	binary	address
dump	clock	boot up	archive
edit	clone	buffer	barcode
exit	COMAL	busbar	bundled
file	CORAL	coding	carrier
find	crash	cursor	circuit
font	debug	decode	command
GIGO	drive	delete	compile
GIPS	enter	dongle	console
help	EPROM	escape	corrupt
icon	erase	export	default
ISDN	field	format	density
JAVA	FORTH	hacker	desktop
loop	G-byte	header	display
menu	input	import	end user

Fortran	firewall	assembler
garbage	firmware	backspace
imaging	gigabyte	bootstrap
menu bar	graphics	cartridge
monitor	hard disk	character
printer	hardware	clipboard
program	internet	cyberpunk
readout	joystick	data entry
scanner	keyboard	digitizer
sorting	key punch	directory
sort key	kilobyte	disk drive
storage	language	dot matrix
tool kit	light pen	downgrade
upgrade	low-level	flowchart
virtual	megabyte	hypertext
zip disk	password	interface
	printout	mainframe
8	real time	microchip
	recovery	multisync
arrow key	register	null modem
baud rate	retrieve	overwrite
beta test	shift key	pop-up menu
capacity	shut down	processor
caps lock	software	QuickTime
check sum	space bar	range left
compiler	spooling	repeat key
computer	start bit	shareware
core dump	terminal	smart card
databank	typeface	sound card
database	wild card	word break
digitize	zip drive	
diskette		**10**
document	**9**	
download		access time
emulator	algorithm	alphameric
encoding	alternate	attachment
feedback	antivirus	contiguous

core memory
daisy wheel
encryption
file server
floppy disk
Java Script
memory bank
numeric pad
peripheral
processing
programmer
range right
serial data
spellcheck
standalone
throughput
wraparound

11

application
circuit card
compact disk
compression
cut and paste
data capture
diagnostics
display mode
display unit
file sharing
function key
input device
interactive
line printer
machine code
motherboard
multiplexer

optical disk
print server
programming
silicon chip
spreadsheet
time-sharing
Trojan Horse
visual BASIC
work station

12

addition time
alphanumeric
assembly code
bubble memory
circuit board
control panel
direct access
housekeeping
laser printer
multitasking
opto isolator
output device
parallel data
random access
response time
spell checker
user-friendly

13

barcode reader
compatibility
display screen
double density
expansion slot
fragmentation

ink-jet printer
justified text
microcomputer
neural network
supercomputer
virtual memory
word processor

14

computer dating
copy protection
data processing
data protection
electronic mail
microprocessor
read-only memory
system operator
systems analyst
word processing

15

acoustic coupler
batch processing
computerization
computer science
data compression
error correction
machine language
multiprocessing
storage capacity
systems analysis
systems operator

16

assembly language
bubble-jet printer

compiled language
computer engineer
computer graphics
computer language
computer literacy
computer-literate
computer operator
dot-matrix printer
low-level language
personal computer

daisywheel printer (17)
desktop publishing (17)
high-level language (17)
integrated circuit (17)
integrated package (17)
non-volatile memory (17)
password protection (18)
personal organizer (17
random-access memory (18)

17 AND 18

assembler language (17)

The Internet

3

AOL
BBS
bot
DOS
FAQ
GIF
GUI
hit
IRC
ISP
PDF
PPP

4 AND 5

ASDL
blog
cache
chat

email
HTML
HTTP
in-box
ISDN
spam
surf
Yahoo

6

browse
cookie
dial-up
domain
Google
hacker
newbie
online
portal

router
server
sign on
stream
upload
weblog

7

addware
blogger
browser
malware
offline
spammer
spyware
surfing
website

8

anti-spam
blogspot
chat room
homepage
image map
Internet
Netscape
phishing
protocol
spam site

9

Ask Jeeves
broadband
cybercafé
hyperlink
hypertext
newsgroup

shareware
webmaster

10 AND OVER

access provider (14)
acrobat reader (13)
attachment (10)
cyber police (11)

cyberspace (10)
electronic mail (14)
encryption (10)
Internet Explorer (16)
netiquette (10)
online service (13)
search engine (12)
worldwide web (12)

DANCES AND BALLET TERMS

3

bop
fan
hay
hop
jig
pas

4

ball
clog
coda
frug
haka
hula
jeté
jive
jota
juba
plié
reel
step

5

barre
bebop
brizé
caper
conga
fling
galop
gigue
gopak
limbo
mambo
pavan
pavin
polka
rumba
samba
sauté
shake
stomp
tango
twist
valse

volta
waltz

6

adagio
Apache
bolero
boston
canary
cancan
cha-cha
chassé
épaulé
flurry
gallop
minuet
morris
pavane
penché
pointe
redowa
relevé
rhumba

shimmy
valeta
veleta

7

beguine
bourrée
carioca
choctaw
czardas
forlana
fouetté
fox-trot
gavotte
Helston
hoedown
lancers
ländler
la volta
leotard
madison
mazurka
measure

morisco
one-step
planxty
roundel
sardana
shuffle
two-step
watutsi

8

bunny-hug
cachucha
cake-walk
capriole
chaconne
coryphée
courante
fan-dance
fandango
flamenco
galliard
glissade
habanera
hay-de-guy
hornpipe
hulahula
lindy-hop
notation
rigadoon
saraband
tap-dance

9

allemande
arabesque
barn dance

bossa nova
cha-cha-cha
clog dance
cotillion
écossaise
eightsome
entrechat
farandole
folkdance
gallopade
grand jeté
jitterbug
line dance
pas de chat
pas de deux
paso doble
passepied
Paul Jones
pirouette
polonaise
poussette
quadrille
quickstep
raccourci
rock 'n' roll
siciliana
tambourin
tripudium
zapateado

10

boston reel
break dance
charleston
demi-pointe
Gay Gordons

hay-de-guize
hokey-cokey
pas d'action
saltarello
strathspey
sword-dance
tarantella
torch dance
tour en l'air
turkey-trot

11

black bottom
contredanse
floral dance
Lambeth Walk
morris dance
palais glide
rock and roll

rond de jambe
schottische
square dance
varsovienne

12

country dance
maypole dance

13 AND OVER

Boston two-step (13)
divertissement (14)
eightsome reel (13)
Helston flurry
    dance (13)
Highland fling (13)
military
    two-step (15)
pas d'élévation (13)

DRINK (WINES, SPIRITS, NON-ALCOHOLIC BEVERAGES, ETC.)

3

ale	rye	bols	hock	ouzo
cha	sip	brut	kava	port
dop	sup	café	krug	raki
fix	tea	char	kvas	rosé
gin	tot	coke	lush	sack
jar	vat	cola	marc	sake
kir		dram	maté	saki
mum	**4**	fine	mead	slug
nip	arak	fino	mild	soda
nog	Bass	fizz	milk	swig
rum	beer	flip	Moët	wine
	bock	grog	Mumm	wort

5

booze
broth
Byrrh
cider
cocoa
cream
cuppa
drink
Evian
glass
hooch
hyson
Irish
Jerez
joram
julep
kvass
lager
latte
Macon
Médoc
mocha
negus
noyau
oopak
pekoe
perry
pinta
plonk
punch
quass
Rioja
shrub
sirup
sling

smash
snort
soave
stout
toddy
Tokay
tonic
Vichy
vodka
water

6

alegar
Alsace
amrita
arrack
Barsac
Beaune
bishop
bitter
Bovril
brandy
bubbly
bumper
canary
cassis
caudle
chicha
claret
coffee
Cognac
congou
double
egg-nog
elixir
entire

geneva
grappa
Graves
hootch
kirsch
kumiss
kümmel
liquor
Malaga
muscat
nectar
noggin
oolong
pastis
Pernod
plotty
poison
porter
posset
poteen
potion
ptisan
pulque
Ribena
rickey
saloop
Saumur
Scotch
shandy
sherry
single
spirit
squash
stingo
Strega
swipes

tiffin
tipple
tisane
treble
Volnay
wallop
wherry
whisky

7

absinth
alcohol
aquavit
Bacardi
beef tea
bitters
bourbon
Campari
catawba
Chablis
Chandon
Chianti
cobbler
collins
cordial
curaçao
draught
dry wine
egg-flip
Falerno
gin fizz
gin sour
iced tea
koumiss
limeade
liqueur

low wine
mace ale
Madeira
Malmsey
Marsala
martini
mineral
Moselle
new wine
oloroso
Orvieto
pale ale
Perrier
pilsner
pink gin
Pomerol
Pommard
Pommery
Pouilly
ratafia
real ale
red wine
retsina
rosolio
Sangria
sherbet
sidecar
sloe gin
snifter
spirits
stinger
tequila
twankay
Vouvray
whiskey

8

absinthe
Adam's ale
advocaat
alcopops
alicante
anisette
aperitif
beeswing
beverage
bock-beer
Bordeaux
brick tea
Burgundy
champers
China tea
ciderkin
Clicquot
Coca-Cola
cocktail
daiquiri
dog's nose
Drambuie
dry wines
Dubonnet
eau-de-vie
espresso
Florence
Frascati
fruit cup
fruit tea
gin-and-it
gin-sling
green tea
Guinness
herb beer

highball
Hollands
Horlicks
hydromel
lemonade
montilla
muscadel
near beer
nightcap
pekoe tea
pilsener
pink lady
Pol Roger
port wine
Punt y Mes
red biddy
red wines
Riesling
root beer
rosé wine
rosoglio
ruby port
rum punch
rum toddy
sack-whey
St Julien
sangaree
Sauterne
schnapps
sillabub
skim-milk
small ale
souchong
sour milk
spritzer
strong ale

syllabub
tia maria
tincture
verjuice
vermouth
vin blanc
wish-wash

9

altar wine
Angostura
applejack
aqua vitae
badminton
bitter ale
black beer
Bollinger
Buck's fizz
Budweiser
cappucino
Carlsberg
Ceylon tea
champagne
chocolate
claret cup
clary wine
Cointreau
Cuba libre
dry sherry
elder wine
Falernian
firewater
ginger ale
ginger pop
grenadine
gunpowder

Hall's wine
Heidsieck
Hermitage
hippocras
iced water
Indian tea
lager beer
lamb's wool
Lambrusco
limejuice
Manhattan
metheglin
Meursault
milk punch
milkshake
mint julep
Mochacino
moonshine
mulled ale
muscadine
oolong tea
orangeade
Rhine wine
St Emilion
St Raphael
Sauternes
Scotch ale
slivovitz
slivowitz
small beer
soda water
soft drink
sundowner
tarragona
tawny port
white lady

white port
white wine
Wincarnis

10

barley wine
Beaujolais
bitter beer
black-strap
bloody Mary
Bull's Blood
buttermilk
café-au-lait
caffe latte
canned beer
cappuccino
Chambertin
Chartreuse
clary-water
Constantia
cowslip tea
dry martini
Frontignac
ginger beer
ginger wine
horse's neck
iced drinks
Jamaica rum
lemon juice
malt liquor
malt whisky
malted milk
Manzanilla
maraschino
Mateus Rosé
Mickey Finn

Montrachet
Moselle cup
mulled wine
Munich beer
pale sherry
piña colada
raisin wine
Rhine wines
Rhône wines
rye whiskey
sack posset
shandygaff
soft drinks
spruce beer
still wines
stirrup cup
sweet wines
tanglefoot
Tom Collins
tonic water
twankay tea
usquebaugh
Vichy Water
vinho verde
whisky sour
white wines

11

aguardiente
amontillado
apple brandy
barley-water
Bénédictine
black coffee
black velvet
bottled beer

Bristol milk
cider-brandy
citron water
Courvoisier
cowslip wine
doch-an-doris
draught beer
Earl Grey tea
Irish coffee
John Collins
lemon squash
mountain dew
Niersteiner
orange juice
orange pekoe
peach brandy
Plymouth gin
potash water
Saint Julien
screwdriver
scuppernong
soda and milk
souchong tea
spring water
sweet sherry
tomato juice
vin de Graves
vintage wine
white coffee

12

champagne cup
cherry brandy
Côtes-du-Rhône
crème de cacao
Cyprus sherry

Fernet-Branca
ginger brandy
Grand Marnier
gunpowder tea
hot chocolate
ice-cream soda
India Pale Ale
Irish whiskey
kirschwasser
Malvern water
mulled claret
old fashioned
orange brandy
orange squash
peach bitters
Perrier-Jouet
red wine punch
Rhenish wines
Saint Emilion
Saint Raphael
sarsaparilla
Scotch whisky
seltzer water
supernaculum
treacle water
Valpolicella
vin ordinaire

13

aerated waters
apricot brandy
blended whisky
Château d'Yquem
Château Lafite
Château Latour
cooking sherry

crème de menthe
dandelion wine
Darjeeling tea
Entre Deux Mers
Falernian wine
ginger cordial
instant coffee
Liebfraumilch
liqueur brandy
liqueur whisky
mild and bitter
mineral waters
Moët et Chandon
orange bitters
pink champagne
planters' punch
Pouilly Fuissé
prairie oyster
Seidlitz water
sherry cobbler
sparkling hock
sparkling wine
Veuve Clicquot

14

champagne cider
champagne punch
Château Margaux
elderberry wine
espresso coffee
French vermouth
Johannisberger
Napoleon brandy
pineapple juice
Piper-Heidsieck
sparkling wines

vermouth cassis
white wine punch

15

champagne-cognac
grapefruit juice

green Chartreuse
Italian vermouth
lapsang souchong
martini cocktail
sacramental wine
sparkling waters

FAMOUS PEOPLE
The world of entertainment

Theatre, opera, ballet, films, the circus, television, radio,
music (classical, jazz, folk, pop, etc.)

3 AND 4

Baez, Joan
Ball, Lucille
Ball, Zoë
Bass, Alfie
Bilk, Acker
Bird, John
Bow, Clara
Bron, Eleanor
Bull, Deborah
Butt, Dame Clara
Cash, Johnny
Cobb, Lee J.
Coco (clown)
Cole, George
Cole, Nat King
Cook, Peter
Day, Doris
Day, Sir Robin
Dean, James
Dors, Diana
Duse, Eleonora

Fame, Georgie
Ford, John
Ford, Harrison
Fry, Stephen
Fury, Billy
Gaye, Marvin
Getz, Stan
Gish, Lillian
Gwyn, Nell
Hall, Henry
Hall, Sir Peter
Hay, Will
Hess, Dame Myra
Hill, Benny
Hird, Dame Thora
Hope, Bob
Joad, Cyril
John, Sir Elton
Kaye, Danny
Kean, Edmund
Kerr, Deborah
Ladd, Alan
Lahr, Bert

Lang, Fritz
Law, Jude
Lean, Sir David
Lee, Bruce
Lee, Christopher
Lee, Gypsy Rose
Lee, Peggy
Lent, Alfred
Lind, Jenny
Lynn, Dame Vera
Monk, Thelonious
More, Kenneth
Muir, Frank
Nunn, Trevor
Peck, Gregory
Piaf, Edith
Ray, Satyajit
Reed, Sir Carol
Reed, Oliver
Reid, Beryl
Rice, Sir Tim
Rigg, Dame Diana
Rix, Brian

Ross, Annie
Ross, Diana
Sher, Sir Antony
Sim, Alastair
Swan, Donald
Tati, Jacques
Thaw, John
Took, Barrie
Tree, Sir Herbert
Vigo, Jean
Wark, Kirsty
West, Mae
Wise, Ernie
Wise, Robert
Wood, Sir Henry
Wood, Natalie
York, Michael
York, Susannah

5

Adler, Larry
Allen, Chesney
Allen, Dave
Allen, Woody
Arden, John
Arrau, Claudio
Askey, Arthur
Badel, Alan
Baker, Dame Janet
Baker, Sir Stanley
Basie, Count
Bates, Alan
Benny, Jack
Berry, Chuck
Björk
Black, Cilla

Blair, Lionel
Bloom, Clair
Boult, Sir Adrian
Bowie, David
Boyer, Charles
Bragg, Melvyn
Brain, Dennis
Brand, Jo
Bream, Julian
Brice, Fanny
Brook, Peter
Brown, Pamela
Bruno, Walter
Bryan, Dora
Bülow, Hans von
Caine, Sir Michael
Capra, Frank
Carné, Marcel
Clair, René
Clark, Lord
  Kenneth
Clark, Petula
Clary, Julian
Clift, Montgomery
Cline, Patsy
Close, Glenn
Cooke, Alistair
Crowe, Russell
Cukor, George
Dando, Jill
Davis, Bette
Davis, Sir Colin
Davis, Miles
Davis, Sammy
Dench, Dame Judi
Dolin, Anton

Du Pré, Jacqueline
Dylan, Bob
Elton, Ben
Evans, Chris
Evans, Dame Edith
Evans, Sir Geraint
Evans, Gill
Faith, Adam
Feltz, Vanessa
Finch, Peter
Flynn, Errol
Fonda, Henry
Fonda, Jane
Frost, Sir David
Gabin, Jean
Gable, Clark
Gabor, Zsa Zsa
Gance, Abel
Garbo, Greta
Gibson, Mel
Gigli, Beniamino
Gobbi, Tito
Gould, Elliott
Gould, Glenn
Grade, Lew
Grant, Cary
Grant, Hugh
Greco, Juliette
Green, Hughie
Greer, Germaine
Grove, Sir George
Haley, Bill
Hallé, Sir Charles
Handl, Dame Irene
Handy, W.C.
Hanks, Tom

Teyte, Dame Maggie
Topol, Chaim
Tracy, Spencer
Tutin, Dorothy
Tynan, Kenneth
Vitti, Monica
Wajda, Andrzej
Wayne, John
Welch, Raquel
Wogan, Terry
Worth, Irene
Zappa, Frank

6

Adrian, Max
Antoine, André
Arnaud, Yvonne
Artaud, Antonin
Ashton, Sir Frederick
Atkins, Eileen
Bacall, Lauren
Balcon, Sir Michael
Barber, Chris
Bardot, Brigitte
Barnum, P.T.
Bassey, Dame Shirley
Battle, Kathleen
Baylis, Lilian
Beatty, Warren
Bechet, Sidney
Benson, Sir Frank
Bogart, Humphrey
Boulez, Pierre
Braden, Bernard
Brando, Marlon
Briers, Richard

Bryant, Michael
Buñuel, Luis
Burney, Fanny
Burton, Richard
Cagney, James
Callas, Maria
Callow, Simon
Cantor, Eddie
Caruso, Enrico
Casals, Pablo
Casson, Sir Lewis
Charles, Ray
Cibber, Colley
Cleese, John
Cobain, Kurt
Colman, Ronald
Colyer, Ken
Cooper, Gary
Cooper, Dame Gladys
Cortot, Alfred
Coward, Sir Noël
Cranko, John
Crosby, Bing
Cruise, Tom
Curran, Charles
Curtis, Tony
Curzon, Sir Clifford
Cusack, Cyril
De Niro, Robert
de Sica, Vittorio
Devine, George
Disney, Walt
Domino, Fats
Dowell, Anthony
Draper, Ruth
Dreyer, Carl

Duncan, Isadora
Fields, Dame Gracie
Fields, W.C.
Finney, Albert
Fokine, Mikhail
Forman, Milos
Formby, George
Foster, Jodie
French, Dawn
Galway, James
Garcia, Jerry
Garson, Greer
Geldof, Bob
Godard, Jean-Luc
Gong Li
Goring, Marius
Graham, Martha
Greene, Sir Hugh
Groves, Sir Charles
Guitry, Sacha
Harlow, Jean
Herzog, Werner
Heston, Charlton
Hiller, Dame Wendy
Hislop, Ian
Hobson, Harold
Hotter, Hans
Howard, Leslie
Howard, Trevor
Howerd, Frankie
Hupert, Isabelle
Irving, Sir Henry
Izzard, Eddie
Jacobi, Sir Derek
Jacobs, David
Jagger, Mick

Jarman, Derek
Jolson, Al
Joplin, Janis
Joplin, Scott
Jouvet, Louis
Keaton, Buster
Kemble, Fanny
Kendal, Felicity
Kenton, Stan
Kidman, Nicole
Kramer, Stanley
Lauder, Sir Harry
Lemmon, Jack
Lennon, John
Lillie, Beatrice
Lipman, Maureen
Maazel, Lorin
McKern, Leo
Marley, Bob
Martin, Mary
Massey, Daniel
Massey, Raymond
Mayall, Rik
Merman, Ethel
Miller, Glenn
Miller, Jonathan
Mingus, Charlie
Monroe, Marilyn
Moreau, Jeanne
Morley, Robert
Morton, Jelly Roll
Mostel, Zero
Mutter, Anne Sophie
Nerina, Nadia
Newman, Nanette
Newman, Paul

Norden, Denis
Norman, Jessye
Oliver, King
O'Toole, Peter
Pacino, Al
Parker, Charlie
Parker, Dorothy
Parton, Dolly
Paxman, Jeremy
Powell, Dilys
Powell, Michael
Previn, André
Quayle, Sir Anthony
Rattle, Sir Simon
Remick, Lee
Renoir, Jean
Robson, Dame Flora
Rogers, Ginger
Rooney, Mickey
Savile, Sir Jimmy
Seeger, Peggy
Seeger, Pete
Sharif, Omar
Sibley, Antoinette
Sinden, Sir Donald
Spacey, Kevin
Steele, Tommy
Streep, Meryl
Suzman, Janet
Talbot, Godfrey
Tauber, Richard
Taylor, Dame Elizabeth
Temple, Shirley
Tilley, Vesta
Turner, Lana
Turner, Tina

Waller, Fats
Waring, Eddie
Warner, David
Waters, Muddy
Welles, Orson
Wilder, Billy
Wilder, Gene
Wolfit, Sir Donald
Wonder, Stevie
Zanuck, Darryl F.

7

Andress, Ursula
Andrews, Eamon
Andrews, Dame Julie
Astaire, Fred
Auteuil, Daniel
Baillie, Dame Isobel
Beckham, Victoria
Beecham, Sir Thomas
Bennett, Alan
Bennett, Jill
Bentine, Michael
Bentley, Dick
Bergman, Ingmar
Bergman, Ingrid
Bergner, Elisabeth
Berkoff, Steven
Bogarde, Sir Dirk
Branagh, Kenneth
Bremner, Rory
Brendel, Alfred
Bresson, Robert
Burbage, Richard
Caballé, Montserrat
Campion, Jane

Chabrol, Claude
Chaplin, Sir Charles
Chester, Charlie
Clapton, Eric
Cochran, Eddie
Cocteau, Jean
Colbert, Claudette
Coleman, Ornette
Collins, Joan
Compton, Fay
Connery, Sir Sean
Coppola, Francis Ford
Corbett, Harry
Cushing, Peter
Delfont, Bernard
De Mille, Cecil B.
Deneuve, Catherine
Domingo, Plácido
Donegan, Lonnie
Donovan
Douglas, Kirk
Douglas, Michael
Durante, Jimmy
Edwards, Jimmy
Elliott, Denholm
Feldman, Marty
Fellini, Federico
Ferrier, Kathleen
Fiennes, Ralph
Fonteyn, Dame Margot
Forsyth, Bruce
Garland, Judy
Garrick, David
Gielgud, Sir John
Gingold, Hermione
Giulini, Carlo Maria

Goldwyn, Sam
Goodman, Benny
Guthrie, Sir Tyrone
Guthrie, Woody
Haitink, Bernard
Hammond, Dame Joan
Hancock, Sheila
Hancock, Tony
Handley, Tommy
Harding, Gilbert
Hawkins, Jack
Hendrix, Jimi
Hepburn, Audrey
Hepburn, Katharine
Hoffman, Dustin
Holiday, Billie
Hopkins, Sir Anthony
Hordern, Sir Michael
Ingrams, Richard
Jackson, Glenda
Jackson, Mahalia
Jackson, Michael
Jacques, Hattie
Johnson, Dame Celia
Karajan, Herbert von
Karloff, Boris
Kennedy, Sir Ludovic
Kubelik, Rafael
Kubrick, Stanley
Langtry, Lillie
Lehmann, Lilli
Lehmann, Lotte
Lympany, Moira
MacColl, Ewan
Madonna
Malcolm, George

Marceau, Marcel
Markova, Dame Alicia
Massine, Léonide
McQueen, Steve
Menuhin, Yehudi
Mercury, Freddie
Mitchum, Robert
Montand, Yves
Monteux, Pierre
Murdoch, Richard
Nilsson, Birgit
Novello, Ivor
Nureyev, Rudolf
Olivier, Laurence
Paltrow, Gwyneth
Pavlova, Anna
Paxinou, Katina
Pickles, Wilfred
Plummer, Christopher
Poitier, Sidney
Portman, Eric
Presley, Elvis
Quilley, Denis
Rambert, Dame Marie
Rantzen, Esther
Redding, Otis
Redford, Robert
Richard, Sir Cliff
Richter, Hans
Roberts, Julia
Robeson, Paul
Rodgers, Joan
Rodgers, Richard
Rushton, William
Russell, Jane
Russell, Ken

Sargent, Sir Malcolm
Secombe, Sir Harry
Segovia, Andrés
Sellers, Peter
Seymour, Lynn
Shankar, Ravi
Shearer, Moira
Sherrin, Ned
Siddons, Sarah
Simmons, Jean
Sinatra, Frank
Solomon (Solomon Cutner)
Steiger, Rod
Stevens, Cat
Stewart, James
Stewart, Rod
Swanson, Gloria
Tarrant, Chris
Thibaud, Jacques
Ulanova, Galina
Ustinov, Sir Peter
Vaughan, Frankie
Vaughan, Sarah
Wheldon, Sir Huw
Whicker, Alan
Winfrey, Oprah
Winters, Shelley
Withers, Googie
Wynette, Tammy

8

Anderson, Dame Judith
Anderson, Lindsay
Anderson, Marian
Ansermet, Ernest
Ashcroft, Dame Peggy

Atkinson, Rowan
Baddeley, Hermione
Bakewell, Joan
Bancroft, Anne
Bankhead, Tallulah
Barrault, Jean-Louis
Beerbohm, Sir Max
Belmondo, Jean-Paul
Berkeley, Busby
Boulting, John
Boulting, Roy
Brambell, Wilfrid
Brasseur, Pierre
Buchanan, Jack
Bygraves, Max
Calloway, Cab
Campbell, Mrs Patrick
Carreras, José
Christie, Julie
Clements, John
Coltrane, John
Connolly, Billy
Crawford, Joan
Crawford, Michael
Davidson, Jim
de Valois, Dame Ninette
Dietrich, Marlene
Dimbleby, Sir Richard
Eastwood, Clint
Flagstad, Kirsten
Flanagan, Bud
Flanders, Michael
Fletcher, Cyril
Franklin, Aretha
Goossens, Leon
Grenfell, Joyce

Grierson, John
Grimaldi, Joseph
Guinness, Sir Alec
Harrison, George
Harrison, Sir Rex
Hayworth, Rita
Helpmann, Sir Robert
Hoffnung, Gerard
Holloway, Stanley
Horowitz, Vladimir
Iglesias, Julio
Kreisler, Fritz
Kurosawa, Akira
Lansbury, Angela
Laughton, Charles
Lawrence, Gertrude
Leighton, Margaret
Liberace
Lockwood, Margaret
McDonald, Sir Trevor
McGregor, Ewan
McKellen, Sir Ian
Marsalis, Wynton
Matthews, Jessie
Melchior, Lauritz
Mercouri, Melina
Milligan, Spike
Milstein, Nathan
Mitchell, Joni
Morrison, Jim
Morrison, Van
Mulligan, Gerry
Nijinsky, Vaslav
Oistrakh, David
Oistrakh, Igor
Paganini, Niccolò

Peterson, Oscar
Pfeiffer, Michelle
Pickford, Mary
Polanski, Roman
Rampling, Charlotte
Rathbone, Basil
Redgrave, Corin
Redgrave, Lynn
Redgrave, Sir Michael
Redgrave, Vanessa
Reynolds, Burt
Robinson, Edward G.
Robinson, Robert
Schnabel, Artur
Schumann, Elisabeth
Scofield, Paul
Scorsese, Martin
Selznick, David O.
Stephens, Sir Robert
Streeter, Fred
Stroheim, Erich von
Te Kanawa, Dame Kiri
Thompson, Emma
Travolta, John
Truffaut, François
Visconti, Luchino
Whitelaw, Billie
Williams, Andy
Williams, Hank
Williams, John
Williams, Kenneth
Ziegfeld, Florenz

9

Almodóvar, Pedro
Antonioni, Michelangelo

Armstrong, Louis
Ashkenazy, Vladimir
Bacharach, Burt
Barenboim, Daniel
Barrymore, Ethel
Barrymore, John
Barrymore, Lionel
Belafonte, Harry
Beriosova, Svetlana
Bernhardt, Sarah
Betterton, Thomas
Brannigan, Owen
Cardinale, Claudia
Chaliapin, Fyodor
Chevalier, Maurice
Christoff, Boris
Courtenay, Tom
Dankworth, John
Davenport, Bob
Depardieu, Gérard
Diaghilev, Serge
Dolmetsch, Arnold
Du Maurier, Sir Gerald
Ellington, Duke
Fairbanks, Douglas
Fernandel
Feuillère, Edwige
Gillespie, Dizzy
Grappelli, Stéphane
Halliwell, Geri
Hampshire, Susan
Hitchcock, Sir Alfred
Humphries, Barry
Klemperer, Otto
Lancaster, Burt
Landowska, Wanda

Lyttelton, Humphrey
McCartney, Sir Paul
McCartney, Stella
Mackerras, Sir Charles
MacMillan, Sir Kenneth
Monkhouse, Bob
Morecambe, Eric
Nicholson, Jack
Parkinson, Michael
Pavarotti, Luciano
Peckinpah, Sam
Pleasence, Donald
Plowright, Joan
Preminger, Otto
Reinhardt, Django
Reinhardt, Max
Spielberg, Steven
Sternberg, Joseph von
Stokowski, Leopold
Streisand, Barbra
Tarantino, Quentin
Tarkovsky, Andrei
Thorndike, Dame Sybil
Tortelier, Paul
Toscanini, Arturo
Valentino, Rudolf
Zellweger, Renée
Zinnemann, Fred

10

Balanchine, George
Barbirolli, Sir John
Bertolucci, Bernardo
Boucicault, Dion
Carmichael, Hoagy
Carmichael, Ian

Courtneige, Dame Cicely
Cunningham, Merce
D'Oyly Carte, Richard
Eisenstein, Sergei
Fassbinder, Rainer
Fitzgerald, Ella
Galli-Curci, Amelita
Lanchester, Elsa
Littlewood, Joan
Mengelberg, William
Michelmore, Cliff
Muggeridge, Malcolm
Paderewski, Ignacy
Richardson, Ian
Richardson, Sir Ralph
Rossellini, Roberto
Rubinstein, Arthur
Rutherford, Dame Margaret
Stradivari, Antonio
Sutherland, Dame Joan
Tetrazzini, Luisa
Zeffirelli, Franco

11 AND OVER

Attenborough, David (12)
Attenborough, Richard (12)
Beiderbecke, Bix (11)
Buffalo Bill (11)
De Havilland, Olivia (11)
Ffrangcon-Davies, Gwen
  (15)
Fischer-Dieskau, Dietrich
  (14)
Forbes-Robertson,
  Sir Johnston (15)
Furtwängler, Wilhelm (11)

Granville-Barker, Harley (15)
Hammerstein, Oscar (11)
Laurel and Hardy (14)
Mac Liammóir, Micheál (11)
Marx Brothers (12)
Mastroianni, Marcello (11)
Mistinguett (11)

Schlesinger, John (11)
Schwarzkopf, Elisabeth (11)
Springfield, Dusty (11)
Stanislavsky, Konstantin (12)
Stradivarius, Antonio (12)
Terry Thomas (11)

Sports and games

(ath.)=athletics; box.= boxing; (ch.)=chess; (crc.)=cricket; (fb.)=football; (gf.)=golf; (gym.)=gymastics; (hr.)=horseracing; (mr.)=motor-racing; (mt.)=mountaineering; (sj.)=showjumping; (sw.)= swimming; (ten.)=tennis; (yt.)=yachting

3 AND 4

Ali, Muhammad (box.)
Ashe, Arthur (ten.)
Best, George (fb.)
Borg, Björn (ten.)
Cash, Pat (ten.)
Cobb, Ty (baseball)
Coe, Sebastian (Lord) (ath.)
Cram, Steve (ath.)
Duke, Geoffrey (motor-cycling)
Endo, Yukio (gym.)
Fox, Uffa (yt.)
Graf, Steffi (ten.)
Hill, Damon (mr.)
Hill, Graham (mr.)
Hoad, Lew (ten.)
Hunt, James (mr.)

Hunt, Sir John (mt.)
John, Barry (rugby)
Khan, Imran (crc.)
Khan, Jahangir (squash)
Kim, Nellie (gym.)
King, Billie Jean (ten.)
Lara, Brian (crc.)
Law, Denis (fb.)
Lock, Tony (crc.)
Lomu, Jonah (rugby)
Lyle, Sandy (gf.)
May, Peter (crc.)
Moss, Sir Stirling (mr.)
Pelé (fb.)
Read, Phil (motor-cycling)
Ruth, 'Babe' (baseball)
Snow, John (crc.)
Wade, Virginia (ten.)
Webb, Matthew (sw.)

5

Amiss, Dennis (crc.)
Banks, Gordon (fb.)
Blyth, Chay (yt.)
Brown, Joe (mt.)
Bruno, Frank (box.)
Budge, Don (ten.)
Bueno, Maria (ten.)
Busby, Sir Matthew (fb.)
Clark, Jim (mr.)
Close, Brian (crc.)
Court, Margaret (ten.)
Curry, John (skating)
Davis, Fred (billiards)
Davis, Joe (billiards)
Evans, Godfrey (crc.)
Evert, Chris (ten.)
Faldo, Nick (gf.)
Gooch, Graham (crc.)
Grace, W.G. (crc.)
Greig, Tony (crc.)
Hagen, Walter (gf.)
Hobbs, Sir John (crc.)
Hogan, Ben (gf.)
Jeeps, Dickie (rugby)
Jones, Ann (ten.)
Jones, Bobby (gf.)
Knott, Alan (crc.)
Laker, Jim (crc.)
Lauda, Niki (mr.)
Laver, Rod (ten.)
Lendl, Ivan (ten.)
Lewis, Carl (ath.)
Lewis, Lennox (box.)
Lloyd, Clive (crc.)
Louis, Joe (box.)

Meade, Richard (sj.)
Moore, Bobby (fb.)
Nurmi, Paavo (ath.)
Ovett, Steve (ath.)
Owens, Jesse (ath.)
Perry, Fred (ten.)
Pirie, Gordon (ath.)
Prost, Alain (mr.)
Revie, Don (fb.)
Roche, Stephen (cycling)
Seles, Monica (ten.)
Senna, Ayrton (mr.)
Smith, Harvey (sj.)
Smith, Stan (ten.)
Spitz, Mark (sw.)
Tyson, Mike box.
Wills, Helen (ten.)
Woods, Tiger (gf.)

6

Agassi, André (ten.)
Becker, Boris (ten.)
Bedser, Alec (crc.)
Benaud, Richie (crc.)
Border, Allan (crc.)
Botham, Ian (crc.)
Broome, David (sj.)
Brough, Louise (ten.)
Bugner, Joe (box.)
Carson, Willie (hr.)
Cawley, Evonne (ten.)
Cooper, Henry (box.)
Cruyff, Johan (fb.)
Dexter, Ted (crc.)
Drobny, Jaroslav (ten.)
Edberg, Stefan (ten.)

Edrich, John (crc.)
Fangio, Juan (mr.)
Finney, Tom (fb.)
Foster, Brendan (ath.)
Fraser, Dawn (sw.)
Gibson, Althea (ten.)
Hadlee, Sir Richard (crc.)
Henman, Tim (ten.)
Holmes, Dame Kelly (ath.)
Hutton, Sir Len (crc.)
Kanhai, Rohan (crc.)
Karpov, Anatoly (ch.)
Keegan, Kevin (fb.)
Korbut, Olga (gym.)
Lillee, Dennis (crc.)
Liston, Sonny (box.)
Merckx, Eddy (cycling)
Norman, Greg (gf.)
Palmer, Arnold (gf.)
Peters, Mary (ath.)
Player, Gary (gf.)
Ramsey, Sir Alf (fb.)
Rhodes, Wilfred (crc.)
Robson, Bryan (fb.)
Rooney, Wayne (fb.)
Shankly, Bill (fb.)
Sheene, Barry (motor-cycling)
Smythe, Pat (sj.)
Sobers, Sir Gary (crc.)
Stolle, Fred (ten.)
Taylor, Roger (ten.)
Thoeni, Gustavo (skiing)
Titmus, Fred (crc.)
Tunney, Gene (box.)
Turpin, Randolph (box.)
Wilkie, David (sw.)

Wright, Billy (fb.)

7

Beckham, David (fb.)
Boycott, Geoffrey (crc.)
Brabham, Sir Jack (mr.)
Bradman, Sir Donald (crc.)
Cantona, Eric (fb.)
Carling, Will (rugby)
Carnera, Primo (box.)
Compton, Denis (crc.)
Connors, Jimmy (ten.)
Cowdrey, Sir Colin (crc.)
Dempsey, Jack (box.)
Elliott, Herb (ath.)
Emerson, Roy (ten.)
Eusebio, Silva (fb.)
Ferrari, Enzio (mr.)
Fischer, Bobby (ch.)
Foreman, George (box.)
Fosbury, Richard (ath.)
Frazier, Joe (box.)
Greaves, Jimmy (fb.)
Gunnell, Sally (ath.)
Hammond, Wally (crc.)
Higgins, Alex (snooker)
Hillary, Sir Edmund (mt.)
Hopkins, Thelma (hockey)
Jacklin, Tony (gf.)
Johnson, Earvin (basketball)
Johnson, Jack (box.)
Larwood, Harold (crc.)
Lenglen, Suzanne (ten.)
Lineker, Gary (fb.)
McBride, Willie (rugby)
McEnroe, John (ten.)

Mansell, Nigel (mr.)
Mottram, Buster (ten.)
Nastase, Ilie (ten.)
Paisley, Bob (fb.)
Piggott, Lester (hr.)
Pinsent, Matthew (rowing)
Reardon, Ray (snooker)
Sampras, Pete (ten.)
Shilton, Peter (fb.)
Souness, Graeme (fb.)
Spassky, Boris (ch.)
Stewart, Jackie (mr.)
Surtees, John (motor-cycling, mr.)
Trevino, Lee (gf.)
Trueman, Freddy (crc.)
Whymper, Edward (mt.)
Winkler, Hans (sj.)
Worrell, Sir Frank (crc.)
Zatopek, Emil (ath.)

8

Abrahams, Harold (ath.)
Agostini, Giacomo (motor-cycling)
Atherton, Michael (crc.)
Brinkley, Brian (sw.)
Campbell, Sir Malcolm (mr.)
Campbell, Donald (mr.)
Chappell, Greg (crc.)
Chappell, Ian (crc.)
Charlton, Sir Bobby (fb.)
Charlton, Jack (fb.)
Christie, Linford (ath.)
Comaneci, Nadia (gym.)
Connolly, Maureen (ten.)

Dalglish, Kenny (fb.)
DiMaggio, Joe (baseball)
Docherty, Tommy (fb.)
Elvstrom, Paul (yt.)
Ferguson, Sir Alec (fb.)
Gligoric, Svetozar (ch.)
Graveney, Tom (crc.)
Hailwood, Mike (motor-cycling)
Hawthorn, Mike (mr.)
Kapil Dev (crc.)
Kasparov, Gary (ch.)
Korchnoi, Viktor (ch.)
Latynina, Larissa (gym.)
Lindwall, Ray (crc.)
McLaren, Bruce (mr.)
Maradona, Diego (fb.)
Marciano, Rocky (box.)
Matthews, Sir Stanley (fb.)
Mortimer, Angela (ten.)
Newcombe, John (ten.)
Nicklaus, Jack (gf.)
Redgrave, Sir Stephen (rowing)
Richards, Viv (crc.)
Robinson, Sugar Ray (box.)
Rosewall, Ken (ten.)
Rusedski, Greg (ten.)
Thompson, Daley (ath.)
Williams, Serena (ten.)
Williams Venus (ten.)

9

Bannister, Sir Roger (ath.)
Bonington, Sir Chris (mt.)
Botvinnik, Mikhail (ch.)

Davenport, Lindsay (ten.)
D'Oliveira, Basil (crc.)
Gascoigne, Paul (fb.)
Goolagong, Evonne (ten.)
Llewellyn, Harry (sj.)
MacArthur, Dame Ellen (yt.)
Patterson, Floyd (box.)
Schmeling, Max (box.)
Scudamore, Peter (hr.)
Sharapova, Maria (ten.)
Shoemaker, Willie (hr.)
Sutcliffe, Herbert (crc.)
Underwood, Derek (crc.)
Whitbread, Fatima (ath.)
Wilkinson, Jonny (rugby)

10 AND OVER

Ballesteros, Severiano (gf.) (11)
Barrington, Jonah (squash) (10)
Beckenbauer, Franz (fb.) (11)
Blanchflower, Danny (fb.) (12)
Capablanca, José (ch.) (10)
Carpentier, Georges (box.) (10)
Chichester, Sir Francis (yt.) (10)

Constantine, Sir Learie (crc.) (11)
Culbertson, Ely (bridge) (10)
Fittipaldi, Emerson (mr.) (10)
Fitzsimmons, Bob (box.) (11)
Illingworth, Ray (crc.) (11)
Knox-Johnston, Sir Robin (yt.) (12)
Kournikova, Anna (ten.) (10)
Lonsbrough, Anita (sw.) (10)
Navratilova, Martina (ten.) (10)
Oosterhuis, Peter (gf.) (10)
Ranjitsinhji, Prince (crc.) (12)
Schockemöhle, Paul (sj.) (12)
Schumacher, Michael (mr.) (10)
Tenzing Norgay (mt.) (13)
Torvill and Dean (ice skating) (14)
Turisheva, Ludmila (gym) (10)
Weissmuller, Johnny (sw.) (11)
Wills Moody, Helen (ten.) (10)

Other prominent people

3 AND 4

Ayer, A.J. (Eng. philosopher)
Beit, Alfred (S. African financier)
Cid, El (Spanish hero)

Eddy, Mary Baker (US founder of Christian Science)
Fox, George (Eng. preacher)
Fry, Elizabeth (Eng. social reformer)

Hall, Marshall (Eng. physiologist)

Hill, Octavia (Eng. social reformer)

Hill, Sir Rowland (Eng. pioneer in postal services)

Hume, David (Sc. philosopher)

Huss, Jan (Bohemian religious reformer)

Jung, Carl Gustav (Swiss psychoanalyst)

Kant, Immanuel (Ger. philosopher)

Kidd, William (Sc. pirate)

Knox, John (Sc. religious reformer)

Kun, Bela (communist leader in Hungary)

Lee, Ann (Eng. founder of Society of Shakers)

Low, Sir David (N.Z.-born cartoonist)

Luce, Clare Booth (US journalist and politician)

Luce, Henry Robinson (US publisher)

Marx, Karl (Ger. philosopher and social theorist)

Mond, Ludwig (Ger.-born chemist)

Nash, Beau (Eng. social arbiter)

Penn, William (Eng. Quaker, founder of Pennsylvania)

Polo, Marco (It. explorer)

Salk, Jonas Edward (US scientist)

5

Acton, Lord (Eng. historian)

Adams, Henry (US historian)

Adler, Alfred (Austrian psychologist)

Amati, Nicolò (Italian violin-maker)

Astor, Jacob (US millionaire)

Astor, Nancy (first woman to sit in Br. House of Commons)

Bacon, Roger (Eng. philosopher)

Baird, John Logie (Sc. pioneer in TV)

Banks, Joseph (Eng. naturalist)

Barth, Karl (Swiss theologian)

Booth, William (founder of the Salvation Army)

Botha, Louis (Boer leader)

Clive, Robert (Eng. colonial administrator)

Freud, Sigmund (Austrian psychoanalyst)

Hegel, Friedrich (Ger. philosopher)

Herzl, Theodor (Hung.-born founder of Zionism)

Karsh, Yousuf (Armenian-born photographer)

Keble, John (Eng. divine)

Zeiss, Carl (Ger. optical instrument maker)

6

Alcock, Sir John William (Eng. pioneer aviator)

Attila (ruler of the Huns)

Barker, Sir Herbert Atkinson (Eng. specialist in manipulative surgery)

Baruch, Bernard Mannes (US financier)

Batten, Jean (N.Z. aviator)

Beeton, Isabella (Eng. cookery writer)

Besant, Annie (Eng. theosophist)

Boehme, Jakob (Ger. theosophist)

Butler, Josephine (Eng. social reformer)

Calvin, John (Fr. theologian)

Capone, Al (US gangster)

Caslon, William (Eng. typefounder)

Cavell, Nurse Edith (Eng. patriot)

Caxton, William (first Eng. printer)

Childe, Vere Gordon (Australian archaeologist)

Cicero, Marcus Tullius (Roman statesman and writer)

Dunant, Henri (Swiss founder of International Red Cross)

Fawkes, Guy (Eng. conspirator)

Fokker, Anton (Dutch aviation pioneer)

Graham, Billy (US evangelist)

Halley, Edmond (Eng. astronomer)

Hearst, William Randolph (US newspaper publisher)

Hobbes, Thomas (Eng. philosopher)

Keynes, John Maynard (Eng. economist)

Loyola, St Ignatius (Sp. founder of Jesuit order)

Luther, Martin (Ger. church reformer)

Mellon, Andrew William (US financier)

Mesmer, Friedrich Franz (Ger. hypnotist)

Morgan, John Pierpont (US financier)

Murrow, Edward R. (US journalist and broadcaster)

Petrie, William Flinders (Eng. archaeologist)

Pitman, Sir Isaac (Eng. inventor of shorthand)

Planck, Max (Ger. physicist; formulated quantum theory)

Reuter, Paul Julius (Ger. founder of Reuters news agency)

Sandow, Eugene (Ger. strong man)

Sartre, Jean-Paul (Fr. writer and philosopher)

Stopes, Dr Marie (Eng. pioneer in family planning)

Tagore, Rabindranath (Indian poet and philosopher)

Teresa, Mother (Albanian-born Catholic missionary in India)

Turpin, Dick (Eng. highwayman)

Wesley, John (Eng. founder of Methodism)

Wright, Orville (US pioneer aviator)

Wright, Wilbur (US pioneer aviator)

7

Abelard, Peter (Fr. philosopher)

Aga Khan (Ismaili leader)

Agassiz, Jean (Swiss-born US palaeontologist)

Aquinas, St Thomas (It. philosopher and theologian)

Atatürk, Kemal (Turkish soldier and statesmen)

Blériot, Louis (Fr. aviator)

Blondin, Charles (Fr. acrobat)

Boyd-Orr, John, Baron (Sc. nutritionist)

Buchman, Frank (US founder of Moral Rearmament)

Cassini, Giovanni Domenico (It. astronomer)

Celsius, Anders (Sw. inventor of Centigrade thermometer)

Cuvier, Georges (Fr. anatomist)

Earhart, Amelia (US aviator)

Ehrlich, Paul (Ger. bacteriologist)

Erasmus, Desiderius (Dutch religious reformer and theologian)

Eysenck, Hans (Ger.-born psychologist)

Haeckel, Ernest Heinrich (Ger. naturalist)

Houdini, Harry (Erich Weiss) (Hung.-born magician and escapologist)

Johnson, Amy (Eng. aviator)

Leblanc, Nicolas (Fr. chemist)

Lesseps, Ferdinand de (Fr. engineer and diplomat)

Linacre, Thomas (Eng. founder of Royal College of Physicians)

Lumière, August and Louis (Fr. pioneers of cinematography)

MacEwen, Sir William (Sc. surgeon)

Marcuse, Herbert (Ger.-born political philosopher)

Murdoch, Rupert (Australian-born US media proprietor)

Russell, Bertrand (Eng. philosopher)

Russell, William Howard (Eng. journalist)

Spencer, Herbert (Eng. philosopher)

Spinoza, Benedict (Dutch philosopher)

Steiner, Rudolf (Hung.-born philosopher and educationalist)

Tussaud, Marie (Swiss-born modeller in wax)

Wheeler, Sir Mortimer (Eng. archaeologist)

Woolley, Leonard (Eng. archaeologist)

8

Averroës (Arab philosopher)

Avicenna (Arab philosopher)

Baedeker, Karl (Ger. publisher of travel guides)

Bancroft, George (US historian)

Berkeley, George (Irish philosopher)

Carnegie, Andrew (Sc.-born philanthropist)

Cousteau, Jean-Jacques (Fr. oceanographer)

Foucault, Michel (Fr. philosopher)

Gollancz, Victor (Eng. publisher)

Grimaldi, Joseph (Eng. clown)

Larousse, Pierre-Athanase (Fr. encyclopedist)

Mercator, Gerardus (Flemish geographer)

Negretti, Enrico (It.-born instrument-maker)

Nuffield, William Richard Morris, Viscount (Eng. motor manufacturer and philanthropist)

Scribner, Charles (US publisher)

Sheraton, Thomas (Eng. cabinet-maker)

Socrates (Gr. philosopher)

Wedgwood, Josiah (Eng. potter)

Wycliffe, John (Eng. religious reformer)

9

Arbuthnot, Alexander (printer of first bible, 1579, in Scotland)

Aristotle (Gr. philosopher)

Arkwright, Sir Richard (inventor)

Blackwell, Elizabeth (first registered woman doctor in Eng. and US)

Blavatsky, Helena (Russian-born theosophist)

Courtauld, Samuel (Eng. silk manufacturer)

Descartes, René (Fr. philosopher)

Gutenberg, Johannes (Ger. founder of movable type)

Heidegger, Martin (Ger. philosopher)

Lindbergh, Charles (US aviator)

Lucretius (Roman philosopher and poet)

MacGregor, Robert 'Rob Roy' (Sc. rebel)

Max-Müller, Friedrich (Ger.-born philologist and orientalist)

Nietzsche, Friedrich (Ger. philosopher)

Pankhurst, Emmeline (Eng. suffragette)

Santayana, George (Spanish-born US philosopher)

Guggenheim, Meyer (US financier)

Kraft-Ebing, Richard von (Ger. psychiatrist)

Macpherson, Aimée Semple (US evangelist)

Montessori, Maria (It. founder of Montessori educational method)

Richthofen, Manfred von (Ger. air ace)

Rothermere, Harold Sidney Harmsworth, Viscount (Eng. newspaper publisher)

Rothschild, Meyer Amschel (Ger. financier)

Rutherford, Daniel (Sc. discoverer of nitrogen)

Schweitzer, Albert (Ger. musician and medical missionary)

Stradivari, Antonio (It. violin-maker)

Swedenborg, Emanuel (Sw. theologian)

Vanderbilt, Cornelius (US financier)

10

Bernadotte, Jean-Baptiste (Fr. general and king of Sweden)

Cagliostro, Alessandro (It. adventurer)

Flammarion, Camille (Fr. astronomer)

11

Aristarchos (Gr. astronomer)

Beaverbrook, William Maxwell Aitken, 1st Baron (Canadian-born newspaper publisher)

Chippendale, Thomas (Eng. furniture designer)
Hippocrates (Gr. physician)
Kierkegaard, Søren (Danish philosopher)
Machiavelli, Niccolò (It. political reformer)
Montesquieu, Charles de (Fr. writer and philosopher)
Nightingale, Florence (Eng. pioneer in training nurses)
Northcliffe, Alfred Harmsworth, Viscount (Irish-born newspaper owner)
Shaftesbury, Anthony Ashley

Cooper, 7th Earl (Eng. philanthropist)
Wilberforce, Samuel (Eng. divine)
Wilberforce, William (Eng. abolitionist)

12

Krishnamurti, Jiddu (Indian mystic)
Schopenhauer, Arthur (Ger. philosopher)
Wittgenstein, Ludwig (Austrian-born philosopher)

Presidents of the United States

4 AND 5

Adams, John
Adams, John Quincy
Bush, George H.
Bush, George W.
Ford, Gerald
Grant, Ulysses S.
Hayes, Rutherford B.
Nixon, Richard M.
Polk, James K
Taft, William
Tyler, John

6

Arthur, Chester A.
Carter, Jimmy
Hoover, Herbert
Monroe, James
Pierce, Franklin
Reagan, Ronald
Taylor, Zachary
Truman, Harry S
Wilson, Woodrow

7

Clinton, William J.
Harding, Warren G.

Jackson, Andrew
Johnson, Andrew
Johnson, Lyndon B.
Kennedy, John F.
Lincoln, Abraham
Madison, James

8

Buchanan, James
Coolidge, Calvin
Fillmore, Millard
Garfield, James A.
Harrison, Benjamin

Harrison, William
McKinley, William
Van Buren, Martin

9

Cleveland, Grover
Jefferson, Thomas
Roosevelt, Franklin D.
Roosevelt, Theodore

10

Eisenhower, Dwight
Washington, George

Prime ministers of Great Britain

4 AND 5

Blair, Tony
Bute, John Stuart
Derby, 14th Earl of
Eden, Sir Anthony
Grey, Henry George
Heath, Edward
Major, John
North, Frederick
Peel, Sir Robert
Pitt, William (the Younger)

6

Attlee, Clement
Pelham, Henry
Wilson, Sir Harold

7

Asquith, Herbert
Baldwin, Stanley
Balfour, Arthur
Canning, George
Chatham, Lord (William Pitt
    the Elder)
Grafton, 3rd Duke of
Russell, Lord John
Walpole, Sir Robert

8

Aberdeen, 4th Earl of
Bonar Law, Andrew
Disraeli, Benjamin
Perceval, Spencer
Portland, Duke of
Robinson, Frederick

Rosebery, 5th Earl of
Thatcher, Margaret

9

Addington, Henry
Callaghan, James
Churchill, Sir Winston
Gladstone, William
Grenville, George
Grenville, William
Liverpool, 2nd Earl of
MacDonald, Ramsay
Macmillan, Harold
Melbourne, 2nd Viscount
Newcastle, Duke of
Salisbury, 3rd Marquis of

Shelburne, 2nd Earl of

10

Devonshire, Duke of
Palmerston, 3rd Viscount
Rockingham, 2nd Marquis of
Wellington, Duke of
Wilmington, Earl of

11 AND OVER

Beaconsfield, Lord (12)
Campbell-Bannerman, Sir
  Henry (17)
Chamberlain, Neville (11)
Douglas-Home, Sir Alec (11)
Lloyd George, David (11)

FIRST NAMES
Boys' names

Including abbreviations, nicknames and some common
foreign names.

2 AND 3

	Col	Gil	Jed	Lee
Abe	Cy	Gus	Jem	Len
Al	Dai	Guy	Jim	Leo
Alf	Dan	Hal	Job	Les
Ali	Dee	Hay	Joe	Lew
Art	Del	Hew	Jon	Lex
Asa	Des	Huw	Jos	Lou
Bat	Don	Ian	Kay	Lyn
Ben	Dud	Ira	Ken	Mac
Bob	Ed	Ivo	Kid	Mat
Boy	Eli	Jan	Kim	Max
Bud	Ely	Jay	Kit	Mel

Nat	Aldo	Dana	Hans	Kris
Ned	Alec	Dave	Herb	Kurt
Nye	Aled	Davy	Huey	Kyle
Pat	Alex	Dean	Hugh	Lars
Pip	Algy	Dewi	Hugo	Leon
Rab	Ally	Dick	Hume	Liam
Ray	Alun	Dion	Hyam	Loel
Reg	Amos	Dirk	Iain	Ludo
Rex	Andy	Doug	Ifor	Luke
Rob	Axel	Drew	Igor	Lyle
Rod	Bald	Duff	Ikey	Lyle
Ron	Bart	Duke	Iohn	Marc
Roy	Beau	Earl	Ivan	Mark
Sam	Bert	Eben	Ivor	Matt
Seb	Bill	Eddy	Jack	Merv
Sid	Bing	Eden	Jake	Mick
Sim	Boyd	Emil	Jean	Mike
Stu	Brad	Eric	Jeff	Milo
Syd	Bram	Erik	Jess	Mort
Tam	Bret	Erle	Jock	Moss
Ted	Bryn	Esau	Joel	Muir
Tel	Buck	Esme	Joey	Neal
Tex	Burt	Esra	John	Neil
Tim	Cain	Euan	José	Nero
Tom	Carl	Evan	Josh	Nick
Vic	Cary	Ewan	Joss	Noah
Vin	Cass	Ewen	Juan	Noel
Wal	Ceri	Eyre	Judd	Norm
Wat	Chad	Ezra	Jude	Olaf
Win	Chas	Fred	Kane	Olav
Zak	Chay	Gary	Karl	Omar
	Ciro	Gene	Keir	Orme
4	Clem	Glen	Kemp	Ossy
	Cole	Glyn	Kent	Otho
Abel	Curt	Gwyn	King	Otis
Adam	Dale	Hank	Kirk	Otto
Alan				

Owen	Wynn	Baron	Cecil
Page	Yves	Barry	Chris
Paul	Zack	Barty	Chuck
Pete	Zane	Basie	Clark
Phil		Basil	Claud
Rafe	**5**	Benjy	Cliff
René		Benny	Clint
Rhys	Aaron	Berny	Clive
Rich	Abdul	Berty	Clyde
Rick	Abner	Bevis	Colin
Rolf	Abram	Billy	Conan
Rory	Adolf	Bjorn	Cosmo
Ross	Aidan	Blair	Craig
Rudy	Alain	Blake	Cuddy
Russ	Alban	Bobby	Cyril
Ryan	Aldis	Bonar	Cyrus
Saul	Aldus	Booth	Damon
Sean	Alfie	Boris	Danny
Seth	Algie	Brent	Dante
Shaw	Alick	Brett	Darcy
Stan	Allan	Brian	Daryl
Theo	Allen	Brice	David
Toby	Alvar	Brock	Davie
Todd	Alvis	Bruce	Denis
Tony	Alwin	Bruno	Denny
Trev	Alwyn	Bryan	Denys
Troy	Amand	Bryce	Derby
Vane	Amyas	Bunny	Derek
Vere	André	Byron	Derry
Vick	Angus	Caius	Deryk
Wade	Anson	Caleb	Dicky
Walt	Anton	Calum	Digby
Ward	Archy	Carey	Donal
Wilf	Arden	Carlo	Donny
Will	Athol	Carol	Dylan
Winn	Aubyn	Casey	Eamon
	Aymar		

Earle	Geoff	Jared	Mitch
Eddie	Gerry	Jason	Monty
Edgar	Giles	Jemmy	Moray
Edwin	Glenn	Jerry	Moses
Edwyn	Glynn	Jesse	Moshe
Eldon	Govan	Jimmy	Mungo
Elias	Grant	Johan	Myles
Elihu	Gregg	Jonah	Neill
Eliot	Guido	Jonas	Niall
Ellis	Gyles	Jules	Nicky
Elmer	Hardy	Karol	Nicol
Elvin	Harry	Keith	Nigel
Elvis	Haydn	Kenny	Ogden
Elwyn	Hebel	Kevin	Olave
Emery	Henri	Kirby	Ollie
Emile	Henry	Lance	Orson
Emlyn	Heron	Larry	Orval
Emrys	Hervé	Leigh	Oscar
Enoch	Hiram	Leroy	Osman
Ernie	Homer	Lewin	Oswyn
Ernst	Humph	Lewis	Pablo
Errol	Hyman	Lisle	Paddy
Ethan	Hymie	Lloyd	Paolo
Ewart	Hywel	Louie	Parry
Felix	Idris	Louis	Pedro
Fidel	Inigo	Lucas	Perce
Floyd	Innes	Luigi	Percy
Franc	Irvin	Lyall	Perry
Frank	Irwin	Madoc	Peter
Franz	Isaac	Manny	Piers
Frith	Jabez	Marco	Punch
Fritz	Jacky	Mario	Ralph
Fulke	Jacob	Marty	Ramon
Garry	Jaime	Micah	Raoul
Garth	James	Micky	Ricki
Gavin	Jamie	Miles	Ricky

Roald	Uriah	Aubrey	Denzil
Robin	Vince	August	Dermot
Roddy	Waldo	Austin	Deryck
Roger	Wally	Aylmer	Dickie
Rolfe	Wayne	Aylwin	Dickon
Rollo	Willy	Balbus	Donald
Romeo	Wolfe	Barney	Dorian
Rowan	Wyatt	Bennie	Dougal
Rufus	Wynne	Bertie	Dudley
Ryder	Yorke	Blaise	Dugald
Sacha		Braham	Duggie
Sammy	**6**	Brodie	Duncan
Sandy		Brutus	Dustin
Saxon	Adolph	Bryden	Dwayne
Scott	Adrian	Bulwer	Edmond
Serge	Aeneas	Caesar	Edmund
Shane	Alaric	Calvin	Eduard
Shaun	Albert	Carlos	Edward
Shawn	Aldous	Caspar	Egbert
Silas	Aldred	Cedric	Eldred
Simon	Aldwin	Cicero	Elijah
Solly	Aldwyn	Claude	Ellery
Starr	Alexis	Connor	Elliot
Steve	Alfred	Conrad	Ernest
Storm	Alonzo	Conway	Erroll
Tabor	Alston	Cormac	Ervine
Taffy	Alured	Dafydd	Esmond
Teddy	Andrew	Dallas	Eugene
Terry	Angelo	Damian	Evelyn
Timmy	Anselm	Damien	Fabian
Titus	Antony	Daniel	Fergal
Tommy	Archer	Darren	Fergus
Tudor	Archie	Darryl	Finlay
Ulick	Armand	Declan	Forbes
Ulric	Arnold	Delroy	Fraser
Upton	Arthur	Dennis	Freddy
	Ashley		

Gareth	Herman	Julian	Morgan
Garnet	Hervey	Julien	Moritz
Garret	Hilary	Julius	Morris
Gaspar	Hilton	Justin	Morvyn
Gaston	Hobart	Kelvin	Mostyn
Gawain	Holden	Kendal	Murray
George	Holman	Kenelm	Nathan
Gerald	Horace	Kersey	Nelson
Gerard	Howard	Kieran	Nevile
Gideon	Howell	Kirwan	Nevill
Gilroy	Hubert	Launce	Ninian
Giulio	Hughie	Lauren	Norman
Godwin	Hylton	Leslie	Norris
Gonvil	Ignace	Lionel	Norton
Gordon	Illtyd	Loftus	Nowell
Graeme	Irvine	Lonnie	Oliver
Graham	Irving	Lucian	Osbert
Gregan	Isaiah	Lucien	Osmond
Gregor	Israel	Ludwig	Oswald
Grover	Jackie	Luther	Pelham
Gunter	Jacomb	Lyndon	Philip
Gustav	Japhet	Magnus	Pierre
Gwilym	Jarred	Malory	Powell
Hallam	Jarvis	Manuel	Prince
Hamish	Jasper	Marcel	Rabbie
Hamlet	Jeremy	Marcus	Rafael
Hamlyn	Jerome	Marius	Ramsay
Harley	Jervis	Marten	Ramsey
Harold	Jethro	Martin	Ranald
Hassan	Johann	Marvin	Randal
Hayden	Johnny	Melvin	Rayner
Haydon	Jolyon	Melvyn	Reggie
Hector	Jordan	Merlin	Rendle
Hedley	Joseph	Mervyn	Reuben
Henryk	Joshua	Mickey	Rhodes
Herbie	Josiah	Milton	Robbie

Robert	Vivian	Baldwin	Diggory
Rodger	Vyvyan	Balfour	Dillwyn
Rodney	Wallis	Barclay	Dominic
Roland	Walter	Barnaby	Donovan
Ronald	Warner	Barnard	Douglas
Ronnie	Warren	Beaufoi	Edouard
Rowley	Wesley	Bernard	Elliott
Royden	Wilbur	Bertram	Emanuel
Rudolf	Willem	Botolph	Emilius
Rupert	Willie	Brandon	Ephraim
Russel	Willis	Brendan	Etienne
St John	Wystan	Burnard	Eustace
Samson	Xavier	Calvert	Everard
Samuel	Yehudi	Cameron	Ezekiel
Seamus		Caradoc	Faraday
Sefton	**7**	Carlton	Feargus
Selwyn		Carlyon	Fielder
Sergei	Absalom	Charles	Fitzroy
Seumas	Adolphe	Charley	Florian
Shafto	Ainsley	Charlie	Francis
Sholto	Aladdin	Chester	Frankie
Sidney	Alberic	Clayton	Freddie
Simeon	Alfonso	Cledwyn	Gabriel
Sinbad	Alister	Clement	Garrett
Steven	Almeric	Clifton	Gaspard
Stevie	Amadeus	Clinton	Gaylord
Stuart	Ambrose	Compton	Geoffry
Sydney	Anatole	Connell	Georgie
Taylor	Andreas	Crispin	Geraint
Thomas	Andries	Cyprian	Gervais
Tobias	Aneurin	Dalziel	Gervase
Travis	Anthony	Darrell	Gilbert
Trefor	Antoine	Denholm	Gilmour
Trevor	Antonio	Denison	Gladwyn
Vernon	Artemus	Derrick	Gloster
Victor	Auberon	Desmond	Godfrey
	Auguste		

Goronwy
Grahame
Gregory
Gunther
Gustave
Gwynfor
Hadrian
Hartley
Herbert
Hermann
Hewlett
Hilaire
Hildred
Hillary
Horatio
Humbert
Humphry
Ibrahim
Ichabod
Isidore
Jackson
Jacques
Jeffrey
Joachim
Jocelyn
Johnnie
Justice
Kenneth
Lachlan
Lambert
Lazarus
Leander
Lennard
Leonard
Leopold
Lincoln

Lindsay
Lindsey
Lorenzo
Lorimer
Lucifer
Ludovic
Malachy
Malcolm
Mallory
Matthew
Maurice
Maxwell
Maynard
Merrick
Michael
Montagu
Neville
Nicolas
Norbert
Orlando
Orpheus
Orville
Osborne
Padraic
Padraig
Paladin
Patrick
Perseus
Phineas
Pierrot
Quentin
Quintin
Randall
Ranulph
Raphael
Raymond

Raymund
Redvers
Reynard
Ricardo
Richard
Roderic
Rodolph
Rodrigo
Romulus
Rowland
Royston
Rudolph
Rudyard
Russell
Sampson
Sergius
Seymour
Sheldon
Sigmund
Solomon
Spencer
Spenser
Stanley
Stephen
Steuart
Stewart
Tancred
Terence
Tertius
Timothy
Torquil
Travers
Tristan
Ughtred
Ulysses
Umberto

Vaughan
Vincent
Wallace
Warwick
Wendell
Westley
Wilfred
Wilfrid
Wilhelm
Willard
William
Windsor
Winston
Woodrow
Wyndham
Zachary
Zebedee

8

Adolphus
Alasdair
Alastair
Algernon
Alisdair
Alistair
Aloysius
Alphonse
Alphonso
Annesley
Antonius
Aristide
Augustin
Augustus
Aurelius
Barnabas
Bartlemy

Beaumont	Garfield	Marshall	Thaddeus
Bedivere	Geoffrey	Matthias	Theobald
Benedict	Geoffroy	Melville	Theodore
Benjamin	Giovanni	Meredith	Thornton
Bernhard	Giuseppe	Montague	Thurstan
Berthold	Greville	Mortimer	Trelawny
Bertrand	Gustavus	Napoleon	Tristram
Boniface	Hamilton	Nehemiah	Vladimir
Campbell	Hannibal	Nicholas	Winthrop
Carleton	Harcourt	Octavian	Wolseley
Champion	Harrison	Octavius	
Charlton	Havelock	Oliphant	**9**
Christie	Herbrand	Oughtred	
Clarence	Hercules	Paulinus	Abernethy
Claudius	Hereward	Perceval	Abimeleck
Clemence	Hezekiah	Percival	Alaistair
Clements	Horatius	Peregrin	Alexander
Clifford	Humphrey	Peterkin	Alphonsus
Constant	Ignatius	Philemon	Ambrosius
Courtney	Immanuel	Randolph	Arbuthnot
Crispian	Jephthah	Randulph	Archibald
Crauford	Jeremiah	Reginald	Aristotle
Crawford	Jonathan	Robinson	Armstrong
Cuthbert	Joscelyn	Roderick	Athelstan
Diarmaid	Josephus	Ruaraidh	Augustine
Dominick	Kingsley	Sandford	Balthasar
Ebenezer	Lancelot	Secundus	Bartimeus
Emmanuel	Laurence	Septimus	Beauchamp
Ethelred	Lawrance	Sheridan	Broderick
FitzHugh	Lawrence	Sherlock	Christian
Florizel	Leighton	Siegmund	Christmas
François	Leonhard	Sinclair	Constable
Franklin	Leonidas	Spensley	Cornelius
Frederic	Llewelyn	Stafford	Courtenay
Fredrick	Llywelyn	Stirling	Courteney
Gamaliel	Maitland	Sylvanus	Creighton
			Demetrius

Dionysius	Rupprecht	Barrington (10)
Ethelbert	Sackville	Bartholomew (11)
Ferdinand	Salvatore	Cadwallader (11)
Francesco	Sebastian	Carmichael (10)
Francisco	Siegfried	Christopher (11)
Frederick	Sigismund	Constantine (11)
Gascoigne	Stanislas	Hieronymus (10)
Glanville	Sylvester	Hildebrand (10)
Granville	Thaddaeus	Hippolytus (10)
Josceline	Theodoric	Maximilian (10)
Launcelot	Valentine	Montgomery (10)
Llewellyn	Valentino	Sacheverell (11)
Mackenzie	Wilbraham	Somerville (10)
Marcellus	Zachariah	Stanislaus (10)
Marmaduke	Zechariah	Theodosius (10)
Nathaniel		Theophilus (10)
Peregrine	**10 AND OVER**	Washington (10)
Philibert	Athanasius (10)	Willoughby (10)
Rodriguez	Athelstane (10)	

Girls' names

Including abbreviations, nicknames and some common
foreign names.

	Deb	Eve	Jan	Lot
2 AND 3	Dee	Fay	Jay	Lou
	Di	Flo	Jen	Mae
Ada	Dot	Gay	Joy	May
Amy	Eda	Gus	Kay	Meg
Ann	Em	Ida	Kim	Mia
Ava	Ena	Ina	Kit	Nan
Bea	Eth	Isa	Lil	Pam
Bee	Eva	Ivy	Liz	Pat
Bel				

Peg	Clem	Ilse	Lucy	Sile
Pen	Cleo	Inez	Lulu	Sita
Pia	Cora	Inge	Lynn	Suky
Pru	Dawn	Iona	Mair	Suzy
Rae	Dido	Iris	Mara	Tess
Ria	Dora	Irma	Mary	Tina
Ros	Edie	Isla	Maud	Toni
Sal	Edna	Isma	Meta	Trix
Sam	Ella	Jade	Mimi	Vera
Sue	Elle	Jane	Mina	Vida
Una	Elma	Jean	Moll	Vita
Val	Elsa	Jess	Mona	Viva
Vi	Else	Jill	Myra	Wynn
Viv	Emma	Joan	Nell	Zara
Win	Emmy	Jody	Nena	Zena
Zoë	Enid	Judi	Neva	Zita
	Erna	Judy	Niki	
4	Esmé	June	Nina	**5**
Abby	Etta	Kate	Nita	
Alex	Etty	Kath	Nona	Abbie
Alix	Evie	Katy	Nora	Adela
Ally	Faye	Kaye	Olga	Adele
Alma	Fern	Keri	Oona	Aggie
Alva	Fifi	Lala	Pola	Agnes
Alys	Fran	Leah	Poll	Ailsa
Anna	Gaby	Lena	Prue	Aimée
Anne	Gail	Lila	Rena	Alana
Anya	Gale	Lily	Rene	Alexa
Avis	Gaye	Lina	Rita	Alice
Babs	Gert	Lisa	Rosa	Aline
Bess	Gina	Lita	Rose	Altha
Beth	Gwen	Liza	Rosy	Amber
Cary	Gwyn	Lois	Ruby	Angel
Cath	Hebe	Lola	Ruth	Angie
Ceri	Hedy	Lori	Sara	Anita
Ciss	Hope	Lorn	Sian	Annie
				Anona

Aphra	Circe	Evita	Janie	Lydia
April	Cissy	Faith	Janis	Lynne
Arbel	Clair	Fanny	Jayne	Mabel
Ariel	Clara	Filia	Jemma	Madge
Astra	Clare	Fiona	Jenny	Maeve
Avice	Coral	Flavia	Joann	Magda
Avril	Daisy	Fleur	Jodie	Maggy
Beata	Delia	Flora	Joely	Mamie
Becky	Della	Freda	Josie	Mandy
Bella	Diana	Freya	Joyce	Manon
Belle	Diane	Gemma	Julia	Marge
Berta	Dilys	Gerda	Julie	Margo
Beryl	Dinah	Gerry	Karen	Maria
Bessy	Dodie	Gerty	Karin	Marie
Betsy	Dolly	Ginny	Kathy	Marni
Bette	Donna	Grace	Katie	Matty
Betty	Doris	Greer	Kelly	Maude
Biddy	Dulce	Greta	Kerry	Mavis
Bobby	Edith	Gussy	Kitty	Megan
Bonny	Effie	Hazel	Kylie	Mercy
Bride	Eilsa	Hedda	Laila	Merle
Brita	Elena	Heidi	Laura	Merry
Britt	Elfie	Helen	Leila	Meryl
Bunny	Elisa	Helga	Letty	Milly
Bunty	Elise	Henny	Libby	Minna
Candy	Eliza	Hetty	Lilia	Mitzi
Carey	Ellen	Hilda	Lilly	Moira
Carla	Ellie	Holly	Linda	Molly
Carly	Elsie	Honor	Lindy	Morag
Carol	Emily	Hulda	Lizzy	Moyna
Cathy	Emmie	Hylda	Lorna	Moyra
Cecil	Erica	Ilona	Lorne	Myrna
Celia	Essie	Irene	Lotte	Nadia
Chloe	Ethel	Jacky	Lotty	Nancy
Cilla	Ethne	Janet	Lucia	Nanny
Cindy	Ettie	Janey	Lucie	Naomi

Nelly	Rhian	Venus	Astrid	Cecile
Nerys	Rhoda	Vesta	Athene	Cecily
Nessa	Rhona	Vicki	Audrey	Celina
Nesta	Robin	Viola	Auriol	Celine
Netta	Robyn	Wanda	Aurora	Cherie
Nicky	Rosie	Wendy	Averil	Cherry
Nikky	Sadie	Willa	Barbie	Cicely
Ninie	Sally	Wilma	Barbra	Cissie
Ninny	Sandy	Xenia	Beatie	Claire
Niobe	Sarah	Zelda	Benita	Connie
Noele	Selma	Zelma	Bertha	Dagmar
Norah	Shena		Bessie	Danuta
Norma	Shona	**6**	Bethan	Daphne
Nuala	Sonia		Bettie	Davina
Nyree	Sonja	Agatha	Beulah	Deanna
Odile	Sophy	Agneta	Bianca	Debbie
Olive	Sukey	Aileen	Biddie	Denise
Olwen	Susan	Alexia	Binnie	Dorcas
Oriel	Susie	Alexis	Birdie	Doreen
Pansy	Sybil	Alicia	Birgit	Dorice
Patsy	Tammy	Alison	Blanch	Dorita
Patti	Tania	Althea	Bobbie	Dulcie
Patty	Tanis	Amabel	Bonita	Eartha
Paula	Tansy	Amalie	Bonnie	Editha
Pearl	Tanya	Amanda	Brenda	Edwina
Peggy	Terri	Amelia	Bridie	Edythe
Penny	Terry	Amelie	Brigid	Egeria
Petra	Tessa	Aminta	Briony	Eileen
Phebe	Thora	Anabel	Candis	Elaine
Pippa	Tilda	Andrea	Carina	Elinor
Pixie	Tonia	Andrée	Carmen	Elissa
Polly	Topsy	Angela	Carola	Eloise
Poppy	Tracy	Annika	Carole	Elvira
Queen	Trudy	Annwen	Carrie	Emilia
Raine	Unity	Anthea	Cassie	Esther
Renée	Valda	Armyne	Catrin	Eunice

Evadne	Honora	Lilian	Mollie
Evelyn	Honour	Lilias	Monica
Fannie	Ileana	Lilith	Muriel
Fatima	Imelda	Lillah	Myrtle
Felice	Imogen	Lillie	Nadine
Franca	Ingrid	Lizzie	Nellie
Franny	Ioanna	Lolita	Nerina
Frieda	Isabel	Lorina	Nessie
Galena	Ishbel	Lottie	Nettie
Gerrie	Isobel	Louisa	Nicola
Gertie	Isolde	Louise	Nicole
Gisela	Jackie	Luella	Noelle
Gisele	Jacqui	Maggie	Noreen
Gladys	Janice	Maidie	Odette
Glenda	Jeanie	Maisie	Olivia
Glenys	Jeanne	Marcia	Oonagh
Gloria	Jemima	Margie	Oriana
Glynis	Jennie	Margot	Paddie
Godiva	Jessie	Marian	Pamela
Goldie	Joanna	Marina	Pattie
Gracie	Joanne	Marion	Pegeen
Gretel	Joleen	Marisa	Peggie
Grizel	Jolene	Marnie	Pepita
Gussie	Judith	Marsha	Petula
Gwenda	Juliet	Martha	Phoebe
Gwynne	Kirsty	Marthe	Portia
Haidee	Lalage	Mattie	Psyche
Hannah	Lallie	Maxine	Rachel
Hattie	Laurel	Melita	Ramona
Hayley	Lauren	Mercia	Regina
Hedwig	Lavina	Meriel	Renata
Helena	Leanne	Mignon	Rhonda
Helene	Leonie	Millie	Richie
Hermia	Lesley	Mimosa	Robina
Hester	Leslie	Minnie	Roisin
Hilary	Lettie	Miriam	Rosita

Rowena	Ursula	Babette	Damaris
Roxana	Verity	Barbara	Davinia
Roxane	Verona	Barbary	Deborah
Sabina	Vickie	Beatrix	Deirdre
Sabine	Violet	Bedelia	Delilah
Salome	Vivian	Belinda	Delysia
Sandie	Vivien	Bernice	Diamond
Sandra	Vyvyan	Bethany	Dolores
Sappho	Wallis	Bettina	Dorinda
Selina	Winnie	Billy Jo	Dorothy
Seonad	Xanthe	Blanche	Dulcima
Serena	Yvette	Blodwen	Dymphna
Sharon	Yvonne	Blossom	Eleanor
Sheena	Zandra	Bridget	Elfreda
Sheila		Caitlin	Elfrida
Silvia	**7**	Camilla	Ellenor
Simone		Candice	Ellinor
Sophia	Abigail	Candida	Elspeth
Adeline	Adeline	Carolyn	Emerald
Sophie	Adriana	Cecilia	Emiline
Sorcha	Ainsley	Celeste	Estelle
Stella	Alberta	Charity	Eudoxia
Stevie	Alethea	Charley	Eugenia
Sybell	Alfrida	Charlie	Eugenie
Sylvia	Allegra	Chrissy	Eulalia
Tamsin	Allison	Christy	Evaline
Teresa	Ameline	Clarice	Eveline
Tertia	Annabel	Claudia	Fabiana
Tessie	Annette	Clodagh	Felicia
Thalia	Anouska	Colette	Fenella
Thelma	Anstice	Colleen	Feodora
Tootie	Antonia	Coralie	Florrie
Tracey	Ariadne	Corinna	Flossie
Tricia	Arianna	Crystal	Frances
Trisha	Athenia	Cynthia	Frannie
Trixie	Augusta	Darlene	Georgia
Ulrica	Aurelia		

Gertrud
Gillian
Giselle
Grainne
Gwladys
Gwynedd
Gwyneth
Harriet
Heather
Héloïse
Hillary
Honoria
Horatia
Hypatia
Isadora
Janette
Jasmine
Jeannie
Jessica
Jillian
Jocasta
Jocelyn
Johanna
Josette
Juanita
Juliana
Kathryn
Katrina
Kirsten
Kristen
Kristin
Laraine
Larissa
Lavinia
Leonora
Letitia

Lettice
Lillian
Lillias
Lindsay
Lisbeth
Lisette
Lizbeth
Loraine
Loretta
Lorinda
Lucasta
Lucilla
Lucille
Lucinda
Lucrece
Lurleen
Mahalia
Manuela
Margery
Marilyn
Marjory
Martina
Martine
Matilda
Maureen
Meirion
Melanie
Melinda
Melissa
Michèle
Mildred
Minerva
Mirabel
Miranda
Modesty
Monique

Myfanwy
Nanette
Natalia
Natalie
Natasha
Nerissa
Nigella
Ninette
Octavia
Olympia
Ophelia
Ottilie
Palmyra
Pandora
Paulina
Pauline
Perdita
Phillis
Phyllis
Queenie
Rafaela
Rebecca
Rebekah
Rhodena
Ricarda
Roberta
Rosalia
Rosalie
Rosanna
Rosetta
Sabrina
Sheilah
Shelagh
Shelley
Shirley
Sibilla

Sidonia
Sidonie
Silvana
Siobhan
Susanna
Susanne
Suzanne
Suzette
Sybilla
Tabitha
Tatiana
Theresa
Thérèse
Tiffany
Titania
Valerie
Valetta
Vanessa
Venetia
Yolanda
Yolande
Zenobia
Zuleika

8

Adelaide
Adelheid
Adrienne
Angelica
Angelina
Angeline
Angharad
Antonina
Arabella
Araminta
Atalanta

Beatrice	Ellaline	Marianne	Theodora
Berenice	Emanuela	Mariette	Veronica
Beverley	Emmeline	Marigold	Victoria
Birgitta	Euphemia	Marjorie	Violetta
Brigitta	Evelinda	Mercedes	Violette
Brigitte	Everalda	Meredith	Virginia
Calliope	Felicity	Michaela	Vivienne
Callista	Filomena	Michelle	Wilfrida
Carlotta	Florence	Mireille	Winifred
Carolina	Francine	Morwenna	
Caroline	Georgina	Murielle	**9**
Cathleen	Germaine	Nathalie	Albertina
Catriona	Gertrude	Patience	Albertine
Charlene	Gretchen	Patricia	Alexandra
Charmian	Grizelda	Paulette	Amaryllis
Chrissie	Grizelle	Penelope	Ambrosine
Christie	Hepzibah	Perpetua	Anastasia
Chrystal	Hermione	Petronel	Angelique
Clarinda	Hortense	Philippa	Annabella
Clarissa	Isabella	Phyllida	Annabelle
Claudine	Jeanette	Primrose	Anneliese
Clemency	Jennifer	Prudence	Artemisia
Clotilda	Julianne	Prunella	Bathsheba
Consuelo	Julietta	Raymonde	Britannia
Cordelia	Juliette	Rhiannon	Cassandra
Cornelia	Kathleen	Rosalind	Catherine
Cressida	Kimberly	Rosamond	Celestine
Daniella	Laetitia	Rosamund	Charlotte
Danielle	Lavender	Roseanna	Charmaine
Delphine	Lorraine	Rosemary	Christina
Dorothea	Lucretia	Samantha	Christine
Drusilla	Madeline	Sapphire	Cleopatra
Dulcinia	Magdalen	Sheelagh	Clothilde
Eleanora	Marcella	Stefanie	Columbine
Eleanore	Marcelle	Susannah	Constance
Elfriede	Margaret	Tallulah	Desdemona

Dorabella
Eglantine
Elisabeth
Elizabeth
Emmanuela
Ermengard
Ernestine
Esmeralda
Esperance
Esperanza
Francesca
Francisca
Frederica
Gabrielle
Georgiana
Geraldine
Ghislaine
Guglielma
Guinivere
Gwendolen
Harriette
Henrietta
Henriette
Hildegard
Hippolyta
Hortensia
Hyacinthe
Iphigenia
Josephine
Kathailin
Katharine
Katherine
Kimberley
Madeleine
Magdalena

Magdalene
Margareta
Margarita
Melisande
Millicent
Mirabelle
Philomena
Pierrette
Pollyanna
Priscilla
Rosabelle
Rosalinda
Rosemarie
Seraphina
Sophronia
Stephanie
Theodosia
Thomasina
Valentine
Véronique
Victorine
Winefride

10 AND 11

Alexandrina (11)
Antoinette (10)
Berengaria (10)
Bernadette (10)
Christabel (10)
Christiana (10)
Christiania (11)
Christobel (10)
Cinderella (10)
Clementina (10)
Clementine (10)

Constantia (10)
Dulcibella (10)
Ermintrude (10)
Ethelwynne (10)
Evangelina (10)
Evangeline (10)
Fredericka (10)
Gwendoline (10)
Hildegarde (10)
Irmentrude (10)
Jacqueline (10)
Margaretta (10)
Margherita (10)
Marguerite (10)
Petronella (10)
Philippina (10)
Wilhelmina (10)

FOOD

3 AND 4

bap
bean
beef
blin
bran
Brie
bun
cake
chop
chow
cob
curd
dal
dhal
dip
Edam
egg
fare
fat
feta
fish
flan
fool
fowl
game
ghee
grub
ham
hare
hash
herb
ice

jam
junk
kai
kale
lamb
lard
lean
leg
loaf
loin
lung
meal
meat
menu
milk
mint
mush
nan
Oxo
paté
pie
poi
pork
puff
rice
roe
roll
roti
roux
rusk
sago
side
soup
soy

soya
stew
suet
tart
tuna
veal
whey
yolk

5

aioli
aspic
bacon
bagel
blini
blood
board
bombe
borsh
brawn
bread
brose
broth
cakes
candy
capon
chips
clove
cream
crêpe
crumb
crust
curds
curry

dough
dulse
filet
flank
flour
fruit
fudge
gigot
glaze
Gouda
gravy
gruel
gumbo
heart
honey
icing
jelly
joint
juice
kebab
korma
liver
lolly
lunch
manna
matzo
melba
melts
mince
offal
pasta
paste
pasty
patty

pilaf
pilau
pilaw
pitta
pizza
prune
pulse
purée
roast
salad
salep
salmi
sauce
scoff
scone
scrag
shank
shape
snack
spice
split
steak
stock
sugar
sushi
sweet
syrup
table
taffy
tansy
toast
torte
tripe
viand

wafer
yeast

6

almond
banger
batter
biffin
blintz
bonbon
borsch
Bovril
brains
breast
brunch
burger
butter
canapé
casein
catsup
caviar
cereal
cheese
chilli
coburg
collop
comfit
cookie
cornet
course
croute
crowdy
crumbs
cutlet
dainty
dinner

dragée
éclair
entrée
faggot
fillet
flitch
fodder
fondue
fumado
gammon
garlic
gateau
gelato
giblet
ginger
grease
greens
grouse
haggis
hot dog
hotpot
humbug
hummus
jujube
junket
kidney
kipper
leaven
lights
mousse
muffin
mutton
noodle
nougat
noyeau
nut oil

oliver
omelet
oxtail
paella
panada
pastry
pepper
pickle
pilaff
pillau
polony
potage
potato
quiche
rabbit
ragout
raisin
rasher
relish
saddle
salami
samosa
sea pie
simnel
sorbet
sowens
sponge
squash
staple
sundae
supper
sweets
tiffin
titbit
toffee
tongue

trifle
viands
waffle
walnut
yogurt

7

aliment
baklava
bannock
banquet
Bath bun
beef tea
biltong
biriani
biryani
biscuit
bloater
bloomer
borscht
botargo
bouilli
Boursin
brioche
brisket
broiler
brownie
cabbage
calipee
caramel
catchup
caviare
chapati
cheddar
chicken
chicory

chiffon
chowder
chutney
compote
confect
corncob
cracker
crumble
crumpet
cupcake
currant
custard
dessert
faggots
falafel
fig cake
fritter
galette
game pie
gelatin
giblets
glucose
gnocchi
goulash
Gruyère
gumdrop
haricot
haslets
jam roll
jam tart
ketchup
lasagne
Madeira
Marmite
matzoth
meat pie

mustard
oatcake
oatmeal
pancake
paprika
pavlova
pickles
plum jam
plum pie
polenta
popcorn
pork pie
pottage
poultry
praline
pretzel
pudding
ramekin
rarebit
ratafia
ravioli
rhubarb
rice bun
ricotta
risotto
rissole
rum baba
sapsago
sausage
saveloy
savoury
seafood
sherbet
sirloin
soufflé
Stilton

strudel
sucrose
Tabasco
tapioca
tartlet
teacake
treacle
truffle
venison
vinegar
yoghurt
yule log

8

acid drop
allspice
ambrosia
angelica
apple jam
apple pie
baguette
Bath chap
béchamel
Bel Paese
bouillon
bull's eye
chapatti
chestnut
chop suey
chow mein
clambake
coleslaw
conserve
consommé
coq au vin
couscous

cracknel
cream bun
cross bun
croutons
dainties
date roll
déjeuner
delicacy
doughnut
dressing
dripping
dumpling
Emmental
escalope
flapjack
flummery
fried egg
frosting
fruit pie
frumenty
hardbake
hazelnut
hung beef
ice cream
iced cake
Julienne
kedgeree
kickshaw
lamb chop
loblolly
loin chop
lollipop
luncheon
macaroni
macaroon
marzipan

meatball
meatloaf
meringue
mince pie
mishmash
molasses
moussaka
mushroom
olive oil
omelette
Parmesan
pastrami
pemmican
peperoni
plum cake
plum duff
poppadum
pork chop
porridge
pot roast
preserve
ramequin
rice cake
rigatoni
rock cake
rollmops
roly poly
rye bread
salad oil
salpicon
salt beef
salt junk
salt pork
sandwich
scrag-end

seedcake
shoulder
skim milk
slapjack
soda cake
soy sauce
squab pie
steak pie
stuffing
syllabub
takeaway
tiramisu
tortilla
turnover
undercut
victuals
vindaloo
yoghourt
zwieback

9

angel cake
antipasto
appetizer
arrowroot
banquette
beefsteak
boiled egg
breakfast
bridecake
bubblegum
Camembert
cassareep
casserole
cassoulet
chipolata

chocolate
chump chop
comfiture
condiment
confiture
corn bread
corn salad
crackling
cream cake
cream puff
croissant
croquette
drop scone
Easter egg
enchilada
entremets
fairy cake
fettucine
forcemeat
fricassee
fried eggs
fried fish
fried rice
fruit cake
fruit tart
galantine
Genoa cake
giblet pie
gravy soup
hamburger
honeycomb
Irish stew
lemon curd
loafsugar
lobscouse
lump sugar

macedoine
madeleine
marchpane
margarine
marmalade
mincemeat
mint sauce
mutton ham
mutton pie
nutriment
petit four
pigeon pie
Port Salut
potato pie
potpourri
pound cake
puff paste
raccahout
rillettes
Roquefort
rump steak
sage Derby
schnitzel
Scotch egg
seasoning
shellfish
shortcake
soda bread
sour cream
sourdough
spaghetti
spare ribs
stirabout
succotash
sugarloaf
sugarplum

sweetmeat
Swiss roll
tipsy cake
vol-au-vent
white meat
wholemeal
wild honey

10

apple sauce
apricot jam
baked beans
Bath oliver
bêche-de-mer
beefburger
blancmange
blanquette
Bombay duck
breadfruit
bread sauce
breadstuff
bridescake
brown bread
buttermilk
Caerphilly
candy floss
cannelloni
cheesecake
Chelsea bun
comestible
confection
corned beef
cornflakes
cottage pie
crispbread
currant bun

custard pie
Danish blue
delicacies
Eccles cake
egg custard
fig pudding
frangipane
French loaf
fricandeau
fruit salad
garlic salt
giblet soup
ginger cake
girdle cake
Gloucester
Gorgonzola
grape sugar
ground rice
guava jelly
ham and eggs
hodge-podge
hotch-potch
ice pudding
Indian corn
jugged hare
lamb cutlet
maple sugar
marrowbone
mascarpone
mayonnaise
minced meat
minestrone
mock turtle
mortadella
mozzarella
mutton chop

peach Melba
pepper cake
peppermint
piccalilli
pitta bread
poached egg
Pontefract
potted fish
potted meat
provisions
pudding pie
puff pastry
raisin loaf
rhubarb pie
rolled oats
saccharine
salmagundi
sauerkraut
shish kebab
shortbread
shortcrust
silverside
simnel cake
sponge cake
stewed meat
sugar candy
sweetbread
tea biscuit
temse bread
tenderloin
tinned food
tortellini
turtle soup
veal cutlet
vermicelli
water gruel

white bread
white sauce
zabaglione

11

baked Alaska
baked potato
banana split
Banbury cake
barley sugar
basmati rice
black pepper
bonne bouche
brandy sauce
cassava cake
chiffon cake
chilli sauce
comestibles
cottage loaf
cream cheese
curry powder
dressed crab
frankfurter
French bread
gammon steak
garlic bread
gingerbread
golden syrup
green pepper
griddle cake
ham sandwich
hollandaise
hors d'oeuvre
hot cross bun
iron rations
jam turnover

leg of mutton
Madeira cake
marshmallow
meat pudding
medlar jelly
milk pudding
olla podrida
oyster patty
pattisserie
peppermints
petits fours
plum pudding
potato crisp
potato salad
profiterole
raisin bread
refreshment
rice biscuit
rice pudding
roast potato
sago pudding
sausage roll
Scotch broth
short pastry
side of bacon
sliced bread
smörgasbord
spotted dick
stewed fruit
suet pudding
tagliatelle
tomato sauce
treacle tart
vichyssoise
wedding cake
Welsh mutton

Welsh rabbit
Wensleydale
wheaten loaf
wine biscuit

12

apfelstrudel
apple crumble
apple fritter
Bakewell tart
birthday cake
black pudding
brandy butter
breast of lamb
brown Windsor
burnt almonds
butterscotch
cheeseburger
chicken tikka
chip potatoes
clotted cream
corn-on-the-cob
Cornish pasty
creme caramel
curds and whey
Danish pastry
Dunmow flitch
eggs and bacon
finnan haddie
fromage frais
guarana bread
hasty pudding
julienne soup
liver sausage
lobster patty
luncheon meat

maid of honour
millefeuille
mulligatawny
nutmeg butter
peanut butter
pease pudding
pickled onion
plum porridge
potato crisps
pumpernickel
quartern loaf
refreshments
Russian salad
salted butter
scrambled egg
shepherd's pie
sherry trifle
ship's biscuit
smoked salmon
steak pudding
sweet and sour
taramasalata
tripe de roche
Waldorf salad
water biscuit
Welsh rarebit

13

apple dumpling
apple fritters
apple turnover
béchamel sauce
bouillabaisse
Cheddar cheese
cheese biscuit
chili con carne

Christmas cake
confectionery
cottage cheese
crêpes suzette
custard-coffin
flitch of bacon
French mustard
German sausage
gigot de mouton
ginger pudding
Gruyère cheese
Oxford sausage
pease porridge
roll and butter
salad dressing
scrambled eggs
sirloin of beef
sponge pudding
Stilton cheese
summer pudding
toad-in-the-hole
veal-and-ham pie

14

almond hardbake
apple charlotte
banana fritters
beef stroganoff
bologna sausage
bread and butter
bread and cheese
caramel custard
charlotte russe
Cheshire cheese
French dressing
haunch of mutton

macaroni cheese
mashed potatoes
mock-turtle soup
Parmesan cheese
Pontefract cake
saddle of mutton
toasted teacake
treacle pudding
tripe and onions
Turkish delight
wholemeal bread
Worcester sauce

15

Bakewell pudding
bubble and squeak
chicken Maryland
chocolate éclair
Devonshire cream
haunch of venison
ploughman's lunch
sausages and mash

FURNITURE, FITTINGS AND PERSONAL EFFECTS

3

bag
bar
bed
bin
can
cot
fan
hod
ink
mat
nib
nog
pad
ped
pen
pew
pin
rug
urn
vat

4

ambo
bath
bowl
bulb
bunk
butt
case
cask
cist

comb
crib
desk
door
etui
ewer
form
gong
hi-fi
lamp
mull
plug
poke
rack
sack
safe
seal
seat
sofa
tank
tape
tray
vase
wick

5

apron
arras
basin
bench
besom
bidet
blind

board
broom
chair
chest
china
cigar
clock
cloth
coign
couch
cover
crate
cruse
diner
divan
doily
duvet
flask
futon
glass
globe
grate
guard
Jesse
jorum
label
light
linen
mural
panel
paper
piano
poker

pouch
purse
quill
quilt
radio
razor
scrip
shade
shelf
slate
spill
stand
stool
stoup
strop
suite
swing
table
tapis
tongs
tools
torch
towel
traps
trunk
twine
vesta
watch

6

air-bed
ash-bin
ashcan

awning
basket
boiler
box-bed
bunker
bureau
burner
camera
candle
carafe
carboy
carpet
carver
casket
caster
castor
cheval
chowry
coffer
cradle
damper
day-bed
drawer
duster
fender
forfex
gas tap
geyser
goblet
goglet
hamper
handle
hat-box

hearth
heater
hookah
hussif
ice-box
inkpot
jordan
kitbag
ladder
locker
log bin
loofah
lowboy
mirror
mobile
napery
napkin
needle
noggin
pallet
patera
pelmet
pencil
piggin
pillow
plaque
pomade
pottle
pouffe
punkah
punnet
red ink
rocker
salver
scales
sconce

screen
settee
settle
shower
siphon
socket
sponge
switch
syphon
tablet
teapot
teapoy
teaset
tea urn
thread
tinder
toy box
tripod
trophy
valise
wallet
window

7

adaptor
amphora
andiron
armoire
ashtray
baggage
bathmat
bathtub
bedding
beeswax
bellows
bibelot

blanket
blotter
bolster
brasier
bunk bed
cabinet
camp bed
canteen
chalice
chamois
charpoy
cistern
coaster
coir mat
commode
compact
console
counter
cue-rack
curtain
cushion
cutlery
deed box
doormat
drapery
dresser
drugget
dustbin
dustpan
epergne
fire-dog
flannel
flasket
fly-rail
fuse-box
gas fire

gas ring
hair-oil
hammock
hassock
heating
highboy
hip bath
holdall
ink-horn
keyhole
lagging
lantern
lectern
lighter
matches
matting
monocle
oil-lamp
ottoman
padlock
pannier
parquet
pianola
picture
pincase
playpen
pomatum
pot-hook
roaster
rush mat
sadiron
samovar
sampler
sand-box
satchel
scraper

shelves
shoebox
soap-box
sofabed
stopper
stopple
syringe
tallboy
tambour
tankard
tea-cosy
tea-tray
tent-bed
Thermos
thimble
toaster
tobacco
tool kit
trammel
trolley
truckle
tumbler
tun-dish
twin-bed
valance
whatnot
whisket
woodcut
work-bag
workbox
yulelog

8

ale bench
Ansafone
armchair

baluster
banister
barbecue
bassinet
bed cover
bed linen
bed quilt
bedstead
bird-bath
bird-cage
bookcase
bookends
card-case
cashbook
CD player
cellaret
chair-bed
chair leg
chattels
cigar box
clay pipe
coat-hook
computer
coverlet
crockery
cupboard
curtains
cuspidor
decanter
demi-john
ditty-box
divan bed
doorbell
doorknob
doorstep
endirons

eyeglass
fauteuil
field-bed
firewood
fly paper
foot-bath
fuse wire
gallipot
gas meter
handbell
hangings
hat-brush
hatstand
heirloom
hi-fi unit
hip flask
holdfast
inkstand
jalousie
jewel box
knapsack
lamp-wick
lanthorn
latchkey
linoleum
lipstick
loo table
love seat
matchbox
mattress
nail-file
notebook
oak chest
oilcloth
ornament
penknife

pipe-rack
postcard
pot plant
press-bed
quill-pen
radiator
reticule
scissors
sea chest
shoehorn
shoelace
showcase
sitz-bath
slop bowl
slop pail
snuffbox
soap dish
speculum
spittoon
stair-rod
stairway
suitcase
sun-blind
table leg
table-mat
table top
tabouret
tantalus
tape-line
tapestry
tea-caddy
tea-chest
tea-table
triptych
tweezers
umbrella

vestiary
wall-safe
wardrobe
watch-key
water bed
water-pot
wax cloth
wax light
wine rack
wineskin
wireless

9

barometer
bathtowel
bedspread
black-jack
bookshelf
book-stand
boot-brush
bric-à-brac
cakestand
camp stool
cane chair
card table
carpet-bag
carpeting
carpet rod
china bowl
chinaware
cigarette
club chair
coffee-cup
coffee-pot
container
corkscrew

davenport
deckchair
directory
dish-cover
dog-basket
dog-collar
dog-kennel
double-bed
dust cloth
dust-sheet
Dutch oven
easy chair
eiderdown
face cloth
face towel
faldstool
fire-board
fire-brick
fire-guard
fire-irons
fireplace
flower-pot
foot-board
footstool
girandole
gold plate
hairbrush
hair tonic
hall stand
hall table
hand-towel
haversack
high chair
horsewhip
housewife
inventory

jack-towel
jewel case
lamp-shade
lampstand
letterbox
lightbulb
loving-cup
marquetry
master-key
mouse-trap
muffineer
music book
nail brush
newspaper
nick-nacks
notepaper
ornaments
palliasse
paper clip
parchment
pewter pot
pier-glass
pier-table
piggy-bank
plate-rack
porringer
portfolio
pot-hanger
potpourri
pounce-box
powder-box
punchbowl
punkah fan
radiogram
rush-light
safety-pin

secretary
serviette
shakedown
shoe-brush
shower-cap
sideboard
side-light
side-table
single bed
slop-basin
sponge-bag
sprinkler
stair rods
steel wool
stopwatch
sword-cane
table lamp
tableware
telephone
timepiece
timetable
tinder-box
toothpick
underfelt
vanity box
wallpaper
washbasin
washstand
water-butt
water-tank
wax candle
wax polish
windowbox
wine glass
wing chair
worktable

10

air-cushion
alarm clock
alarm watch
bedclothes
biscuit-box
boot polish
broomstick
brown paper
buck-basket
bucket seat
calefactor
candelabra
canterbury
ceiling fan
chandelier
chessboard
chiffonier
clothes peg
clothes pin
coal bucket
coal bunker
coat hanger
crumb-brush
crumb cloth
curtain rod
dumb-waiter
elbow-chair
escritoire
feather bed
finger-bowl
fire-basket
fire-bucket
fire-escape
firescreen
fire-shovel

floor-cloth
flower bowl
flycatcher
flyswatter
folding bed
foot-warmer
fourposter
garbage-can
gas-bracket
gas-lighter
gramophone
grand piano
hair lotion
humidifier
jardinière
lead pencil
letter-rack
loose cover
marking ink
musical box
music-stand
music-stool
napkin ring
needle-book
needle-case
needlework
nightlight
nutcracker
opera glass
overmantel
pack-thread
paperknife
paper-stand
pencilcase
pewter dish
photograph

piano stool
pianoforte
pile carpet
pillowcase
pillowslip
pincushion
plate-glass
pocket-book
pouncet-box
prayer-book
razor-strop
riding-whip
scatter rug
sealing-wax
secretaire
shower-bath
soda syphon
spectacles
spirit lamp
stamp-album
stationery
step-ladder
strip light
tablecloth
table linen
television
thermostat
time-keeper
time-switch
tobacco-jar
toilet roll
toothbrush
toothpaste
transistor
truckle-bed
typewriter

upholstery
vapour-bath
warming-pan
wassail-cup
watch-chain
watch-glass
watch-guard
window-seat
wine bottle
wine-cooler
work basket
wristwatch

11

account book
address book
attaché case
basket chair
bed-hangings
billiard-cue
bolster-case
book matches
bookshelves
butter-print
butter-stamp
button-stick
candelabrum
candlestick
centrepiece
chafing-dish
cheeseboard
cheval-glass
clothes-line
coal-scuttle
coffee table
counterpane

curtain hook
curtain rail
curtain ring
dining chair
dining table
dinner table
dispatch-box
dredging box
firelighter
first-aid box
floor polish
fountain-pen
gaming-table
garden chair
hearth brush
king-size bed
knick-knacks
lamp-chimney
leather case
linen basket
mantelpiece
minute glass
minute watch
mosquito net
music centre
nutcrackers
ormolu clock
paperweight
picture-rail
pipe-lighter
pocket flask
pocket-glass
pocket-knife
portmanteau
primus stove
pumice-stone

reading lamp
rolltop desk
safety-razor
shopping bag
slate-pencil
stair-carpet
straw pillow
studio couch
table napkin
table-runner
tape-measure
tea-canister
thermometer
tissue paper
tobacco pipe
toilet-cover
toilet-table
tooth-powder
vacuum flask
wash-leather
water heater
watering-can
wicker chair
window blind
work station
work surface
writing-desk

12

adhesive tape
antimacassar
bedside light
bedside table
blotting book
bottle-opener
candle-sconce

candleholder
carpetbeater
chaise longue
chesterfield
churchwarden
clothesbrush
clothes drier
clotheshorse
console table
cottage piano
cup and saucer
dessertspoon
dispatch-case
dressing-case
drinking-horn
electric bulb
electric fire
electric iron
electric lamp
extractor fan
field-glasses
fitted carpet
fitted sheets
flower-basket
folding stool
gate-leg table
Gladstone bag
hot-water tank
ironing board
kitchen table
kneehole desk
leather chair
light fitting
looking-glass
nail scissors
nest of tables

nutmeg-grater
opera-glasses
paraffin lamp
picnic basket
place setting
playing cards
postage stamp
reading glass
record-player
rocking chair
rocking horse
serving hatch
sheepskin rug
standard lamp
straw bolster
sweating-bath
table lighter
table service
tallow candle
tape recorder
Thermos flask
tin-lined case
toasting-fork
tobacco pouch
toilette case
trestle table
turkey carpet
upright piano
visitors' book
walking-staff
Welsh dresser
wicker basket
Windsor chair
wine decanter
writing paper
writing table

13

billiard balls
billiard table
blotting paper
carpet sweeper
carriage clock
clothes basket
cribbage board
dinner service
dressing-table
drinks cabinet
drop-leaf table
electric clock
electric razor
feather pillow
feeding bottle
filing cabinet
Florence flask
folding screen
four-poster bed
medicine chest
newspaper rack
Persian carpet
petrol-lighter
pingpong table
quizzing-glass
roulette table
sewing-machine
Sheraton chair
smoothing-iron
storage heater
straw mattress
styptic pencil
television set
umbrella stand
vacuum cleaner

Venetian blind
video recorder
visiting-cards
wash-hand basin
wash-hand stand

14

airing-cupboard
Anglepoise lamp
billiard marker
breakfast table
central heating
chest of drawers
cocktail-shaker

electric geyser
electric shaver
feather bolster
glove-stretcher
hot-water bottle
hot-water septum
insulating tape
meerschaum pipe
Queen Anne chair
reclining chair
tobacco stopper
Venetian blinds

15

cocktail cabinet
dining-room table
electric blanket
feather mattress
garden furniture
gate-legged table
Japanese lantern
knitting needles
occasional table
photograph album
pneumatic pillow
weighing machine

GEOGRAPHY
Abbreviations for geographical lists

Adr. Adriatic Sea
Aeg. Aegean Sea
Af. Africa
Afghan. Afghanistan
Alb. Albania
Alg. Algeria
Am. America
Ang. Angola
Antarc. Antarctic (Ocean)
Arab. Arabia, Arabian Sea
Arc. Arctic (Ocean)
Arg. Argentina
Arm. Armenia
Asia M. Asia Minor
Atl. Atlantic Ocean
Aust. Austria
Austral. Australia

Azer. Azerbaijan
Balt. Baltic (Sea)
Bangla. Bangladesh
Bela. Belarus
Belg. Belgium
Boliv. Bolivia
Bos. Bosnia-Herzegovina
Braz. Brazil
Bulg. Bulgaria
Bur. Burundi
Burk. Burkina Faso
C. Am. Central America
Can. Canada
Cen. Af. Rep. Central African
   Republic
Ch. Is. Channel Islands
Col. Colombia

Congo, Dem. Rep. Democratic Republic of the Congo
Congo, Rep. of Republic of the Congo
Cors. Corsica
Cro. Croatia
Cze. Czech Republic
Den. Denmark
E. Af. East Africa
E.I. East Indies
Eng. England
Est. Estonia
Eth. Ethiopia
Eur. Europe
Fin. Finland
Fr. France
Geo. Georgia
Ger. Germany
Gr. Greece
Green. Greenland
Him. Himalayas
Hung. Hungary
Ind. India; Indian Ocean
Indo. Indonesia
Ire. Ireland; Republic of Ireland
Isr. Israel
It. Italy
Jam. Jamaica
Jap. Japan
Jord. Jordan
Kaz. Kazakhstan
Kyr. Kyrgyzstan
Lat. Latvia
Lith. Lithuania

Lux. Luxembourg
Mac. Macedonia
Mad. Madagascar
Malay. Malaysia
Med. Mediterranean (Sea)
Mex. Mexico
Mold. Moldova; Moldavia
Mon. Mongolia
Monte. Montenegro
Moroc. Morocco
Moz. Mozambique
N.Af. North Africa
N.Am. North America
N.Guin. New Guinea
N.I. Northern Ireland
N. Pac. North Pacific
N.Z. New Zealand
Nam. Namibia
Nep. Nepal
Neth. Netherlands
Nig. Nigeria
Nor. Norway
Oc. Oceania
Pac. Pacific Ocean
Pak. Pakistan
Pal. Palestine
Papua Papua New Guinea
Philip. Philippines
Pol. Poland
Port. Portugal
Pyr. Pyrenees
Red S. Red Sea
Rom. Romania
Rus. Russia
SA South Africa
S.Am. South America

S.Pac. South Pacific
Sard. Sardinia
Saudi Saudi Arabia
Scot. Scotland
Serb. Serbia
Serb. and Monte. Serbia and
  Montenegro
Sib. Siberia
Sic. Sicily
Slov. Slovakia
Sloven. Slovenia
Sp. Spain
Sri Sri Lanka
Swed. Sweden
Swit. Switzerland
Taj. Tajikistan
Tanz. Tanzania

Tas. Tasmania
Thai. Thailand
Trin. Trinidad
Tun. Tunisia
Turk. Turkey
Turkmen. Turkmenistan
UAE United Arab Emirates
Ukr. Ukraine
Uru. Uruguay
US United States of America
Uzbek. Uzbekistan
Venez. Venezuela
Viet. Vietnam
W.Af. West Africa
W.I. West Indies
Zam. Zambia
Zim. Zimbabwe

Bays, bights, firths, gulfs, sea lochs, loughs and harbours

(B.)=Bay; (Bi.)=Bight; (F.)=Firth; (Fi.)=Fiord; (G.)=Gulf;
(Har.)=Harbour; (L.)=Loch (Scottish); (Lou.)=Lough (Irish);
(S.)=Sea

2–4

Acre, B. of (Isr.)
Aden, G. of (Arab.)
Awe, L. (Scot.)
Clew B. (Ire.)
Ewe, L. (Scot.)
Fyne, L. (Scot.)
Gilp, L. (Scot.)
Goil, L. (Scot.)

Ise B. (Jap.)
Kiel, B. (Ger.)
Long, L. (Scot.)
Lorn, F. of (Scot.)
Luce B. (Scot.)
Lyme B. (Eng.)
Ob, G. of (Rus.)
Pigs, B. of (Cuba)
Riga, G. of (Lat.)
Siam, G. of (Asia)

Suez, G. of (Red S.)
Tay, F. of (Scot.)
Tees B. (Eng.)
Tor B. (Eng.)
Vigo, B. of (Sp.)
Wash, The (Eng.)

Paria, G. of (S.Am.)
Table B. (SA)
Tampa B. (USA)
Tokyo B. (Jap.)
Tunis, G. of (N.Af.)
Vlöre B. (Alb.)

5

Algoa B. (S.A.)
Aqaba, G. of (Red. S.)
Benin, Bi. of (W.Af.)
Blind B. (N.Z.)
Broom, L. (Scot.)
Cadiz, B. of (Sp.)
Casco B. (USA)
Clyde, F. of (Scot.)
Dvina B. (Rus.)
Enard B. (Scot.)
Evans B. (N.Z.)
False B. (SA)
Forth, F. of (Scot.)
Foyle, Lou. (Ire.)
Fundy, B. of (Can.)
Genoa, G. of (It.)
Hawke B. (N.Z.)
Izmir, G. of (Turk.)
James B. (Can.)
Kutch, G. of (Ind.)
Leven, L. (Scot.)
Lyons, G. of (Med.)
Milne B. (Papua)
Moray F. (Scot.)
Omura B. (Jap.)
Osaka B. (Jap.)
Otago Har. (N.Z.)
Papua, G. of (N.Guin.)

6

Aegina, G. of (Gr.)
Alaska, G. of (USA)
Ariake B. (Jap.)
Aylort, L. (Scot.)
Baffin B. (Can.)
Bantry B. (Ire.)
Bengal, B. of (Ind.)
Biafra, Bi. of (W.Af.)
Biscay, B. of (Fr., Sp.)
Botany B. (Austral.)
Broken B. (Austral.)
Callao. B. of (Peru)
Cambay, G. of (Ind.)
Cloudy B. (N.Z.)
Colwyn B. (Wales)
Danzig G. of (Pol.)
Darien, G. of (S.Am.)
Denial B. (Austral.)
Dingle B. (Ire.)
Drake's B. (USA)
Dublin B. (Ire.)
Galway B. (Ire.)
Gdansk, G. of (Pol.)
Guinea, G. of (W.Af.)
Hervey B. (Austral.)
Hudson B. (Can.)
Jervis B. (Austral.)
Linnhe, L (Scot.)

Lobito B. (Ang.)
Lübeck B. (Ger.)
Manaar, G. of (Ind.)
Mexico, G. of (Mex.)
Mobile B. (USA)
Mounts B. (Eng.)
Naples, B. of (It.)
Panama, G. of (C.Am.)
Plenty, B. of (N.Z.)
Ramsey B. (Eng.)
St Malo, G. of (Fr.)
Sharks B. (Austral.)
Smyrna, G. of (Turk.)
Solway F. (Scot.)
Sunart, L. (Scot.)
Swilly, Lou. (Ire.)
Sydney Har. (Austral.)
Tasman B. (N.Z.)
Tonkin, G. of (S.China S.)
Toyama B. (Jap.)
Tralee B. (Ire.)
Ungava B. (Can.)
Venice, G. of (It.)
Walvis B. (SA)
Zuider S. (Neth.)

7

Aboukir B. (Med.)
Argolis, G. of (Gr.)
Belfast Lou. (N.I)
Boothia, G. of (Can.)
Bothnia, G. of (Swed.)
Bustard B. (Austral.)
Cape Cod B. (USA)
Chaleur B. (Can.)
Delagoa B. (SA)

Donegal B. (Ire.)
Dornoch F. (Scot.)
Dundalk B. (Ire.)
Finland, G. of (Eur.)
Florida B. (USA)
Fortune B. (Can.)
Halifax B. (Austral.)
Hudson's B. (Can.)
Kaipara Har. (N.Z.)
Khambat, G. of (Ind.)
Killala B. (Ire.)
Lepanto, G. of (Gr.)
Montego B. (Jam.)
Moreton B. (Austral.)
Pegasus B. (N.Z.)
Persian G. (Asia)
Poverty B. (N.Z.)
Salerno, G. of (It.)
Setúbal, B. of (Port.)
Snizort, L. (Scot.)
Swansea B. (Wales)
Taranto, G. of (It.)
Tarbert, L. (Scot.)
Thunder B. (Can.)
Trieste, G. of (Adr.)
Trinity B. (Can.)
Wexford B. (Ire.)
Wigtown B. (Scot.)
Youghal B. (Ire.)

8

Biscayne B. (USA)
Buzzards B. (USA)
Cagliari, G. of (It.)
Campeche, B. of (Mex.)
Cardigan B. (Wales)

Cochinos, B. of (Cuba)
Cromarty F. (Scot.)
Delaware B. (USA)
Dunmanus B. (Ire.)
Georgian B. (Can.)
Hammamet, G. of (Tun.)
Hangzhou B. (China)
Honduras, G. of (C.Am.)
Liaodong, G. of (China)
Martaban, G. of (Burma)
Pentland F. (Scot.)
Plymouth Har. (Eng.)
Portland B. (Austral.)
Portland Har. (Eng.)
Quiberon B. (Fr.)
St Bride's B. (Wales)
Salonika, G. of (Gr.)
San Jorge, G. of (S.Am.)
San Pablo B. (USA)
Spencer's G. (Austral.)
Thailand, G. of (Asia)
Tongking, G. of (S. China S.)
Tremadog B. (Wales)
Weymouth B. (Eng.)

9

Admiralty B. (N.Z.)
Broughton B. (Austral.)
Cambridge G. (Austral.)
Discovery B. (Austral.)
Encounter B. (Austral.)
Famagusta B. (Cyprus)
Frobisher B. (Can.)
Galveston B. (USA)
Gweebarra B. (Ire.)
Hermitage B. (Can.)

Inverness F. (Scot.)
Liverpool B. (Eng.)
Mackenzie B. (Can.)
Magdalena B. (Mex.)
Morecambe B. (Eng.)
Notre Dame B. (Can.)
Placentia B. (Can.)
St Austell B. (Eng.)
St George's B. (Can.)
St George's B. (S.Am.)
Saint Malo, B. of (Fr.)
St Vincent G. (Austral.)
San Matías, G. of (S.Am.)
Van Diemen G. (Austral.)
Venezuela, G. of (S.Am.)

10 AND OVER

Ballyteige B. (Ire.) (10)
Barnstaple B. (Eng.) (10)
Bridgwater B. (Eng.) (10)
Bridlington B. (Eng.) (11)
Caernarfon B. (Wales) (10)
Caernarvon B. (Wales) (10)
California, G. of (Mex.) (10)
Carmarthen B. (Wales) (10)
Canterbury Bi. (N.Z.) (10)
Carpentaria, G. of (Austral.) (11)
Chesapeake B. (USA) (10)
Christiania Fi. (Nor.) (11)
Conception B. (Can.) (10)
Corpus Christi B. (USA) (13)
Espíritu Santo, B. of (Mex.) (13)
Great Australian Bi. (Austral.) (15)
Guantánamo B. (Cuba) (10)
Heligoland Bi. (Ger.) (10)

Lutzow-Holm B. (Antarc.) (10)
Massachusetts B. (USA) (13)
Narragansett B. (USA) (12)
Pomeranian B. (Baltic S.) (10)
Port Jackson B. (Austral.) (11)
Port Philip B. (Austral.) (10)
Portsmouth Har. (Eng.) (10)
Princess Charlotte B.
  (Austral.) (17)
Ringkøbing Fi. (Den.) (10)
Robin Hood's B. (Eng.) (10)
St Lawrence, G. of (Can.) (10)
Saint Vincent, G. (Austral.) (12)
San Francisco B. (USA) (12)
Southampton Water
  (Eng.) (16)
Tehuantepec, G. of (Mex.) (11)

Capes, headlands, points, etc.

C.=Cape; Hd.=Head or Headland; N.=Ness; Pt.=Point

3 AND 4

Aird Pt. (Scot.)
Ann, C. (USA)
Ayre Pt (Eng.)
Baba, C. (Turk.)
Bon, C. (N.Af.)
Busa, C. (Crete)
Cod, C. (USA)
Cruz, C. (S.Am.)
East C. (N.Z.)
East Pt (Can.)
Farr Pt (Scot.)
Fear, C. (USA)
Fife N. (Scot.)
Fogo, C. (Can.)
Frio, C. (Braz.)
Frio, C. (W.Af.)
Hoe Pt (Scot.)
Horn, C. (S.Am.)
Howe, C. (Austral.)
Icy C. (Can.)

Krio, C. (Crete)
Loop Hd. (Ire.)
May, C. (USA)
Mink, C. (W.Af.)
Nao, C. (It.)
Naze, The (Eng.)
Naze, The (Nor.)
Nord, C. (Nor.)
Noss Hd. (Scot.)
Nun, C. (W.Af.)
Race, C. (Can.)
Roxo, C. (Can.)
Sima, C. (Jap.)
Slea Hd. (Ire.)
Soya, C. (Jap.)
Sur Pt (S.Am.)
Toe Hd. (Scot.)
Turn N. (Scot.)
York, C. (Austral.)

5

Adieu, C. (Austral.)

Amber, C. (E.Af.)
Aniva, C. (Rus.)
Bauer, C. (Austral.)
Brims N. (Scot.)
Byron, C. (Austral.)
Clare, C. (Ire.)
Clark Pt (Can.)
Corso, C. (Cors.)
Creus, C. (Sp.)
Gallo, C. (Gr.)
Gaspé C. (Can.)
Lopez, C. (W.Af.)
Malia, C. (Gr.)
Negro, C. (W.Af.)
North C. (N.Z.)
North C. (Nor.)
Orme's Hd. (Wales)
Otway, C. (Austral.)
Quoin Pt (SA)
Roray Hd. (Scot.)
Sable, C. (Can.)
Sable, C. (USA)
Sandy C. (Austral.)
San Ho, C. (Viet.)
Sheep Hd. (Ire.)
Slade Pt (Austral.)
Sleat Pt (Scot.)
Slyne Hd. (Ire.)
South C. (China)
Spurn Hd. (Eng.)
Start Pt (Eng.)
Tavoy Pt (Burma)
Troup Hd. (Scot.)
Verde, C. (W. Af.)
Wiles, C. (Austral.)
Worms Hd. (Wales)

Wrath, C. (Scot.)
Yakan, C. (Sib.)

6

Andres Pt (S.Am.)
Bantam, C. (Indo.)
Barren, C. (Austral.)
Beachy Hd. (Eng.)
Blanco, C. (N.Af.)
Blanco, C. (S.Am.)
Branco, C. (S.Am.)
Breton, C. (Can.)
Buddon N. (Scot.)
Burrow Hd. (Scot.)
Burrow Pt (Scot.)
Carmel, C. (Isr.)
Castle Pt (N.Z.)
Comino, C. (Sard.)
Cuvier, C. (Austral.)
De Gata, C. (Spain)
De Roca, C. (Port)
Dodman Pt (Eng.)
Dunnet Hd. (Scot.)
Egmont, C. (N.Z.)
Formby Hd. (Eng.)
Friars Pt (USA)
Galley Hd. (Ire.)
Gallon Hd. (Scot.)
Glossa, C. (Turk.)
Lizard, The (Eng.)
Orford N. (Eng.)
Palmas, C. (W.Af.)
Prawle Pt (Eng.)
Recife, C. (SA)
Rhynns Pt (Scot.)
St Abb's Hd. (Scot.)

St Bees Hd. (Eng.)
St Mary, C. (Can.)
St Paul, C. (W.Af.)
Sambro, C. (Can.)
Sanaig Pt (Scot.)
Sidero, C. (Crete)
Soreli, C. (Austral.)
Tarbat, N. (Scot.)
Tarifa, C. (Sp.)
Tolsta Hd. (Scot.)
Wad Nun, C. (N.Af.)
Whiten Hd. (Scot.)
Yerimo, C. (Jap.)

7

Agulhas, C. (SA)
Arisaig Pt (Scot.)
Bengore Hd. (N.I.)
Bismark, C. (Green.)
Bizzuto, C. (It.)
Blanche C. (Austral.)
Charles C. (USA)
Clogher Hd. (Ire.)
Colonna, C. (Gr.)
Comorin, C. (Ind.)
De Palos, C. (Sp.)
De Penas, C. (Sp.)
De Sines, C. (Port.)
Formosa C. (W.Af.)
Gregory, C. (Can.)
Gris-Nez, C. (Fr.)
Kataska, C. (Jap.)
Kennedy, C. (USA)
Leeuwin, C. (Austral.)
Matapan, C. (Gr.)
Milazzo, C. (Sic.)

Mondego, C. (Port.)
Mumbles Hd. (Wales)
Needles, The (Eng.)
Negrais, C. (Burma)
Orlando, C. (Sic.)
Ortegal, C. (Sp.)
Rattray Hd. (Scot.)
Romania, C. (Malay.)
Runaway, C. (N.Z.)
St Lucia, C. (SA)
San Bias, C. (USA)
São Tomé, C. (Braz.)
Spartel, C. (Moroc.)
Strathy Pt (Scot.)
Tegupan Pt (Mex.)
Teulada, C. (Sard.)
The Horn (S.Am.)
The Naze (Eng.)
The Naze (Nor.)
Toe Head (Scot.)
Upstart, C. (Austral.)
Vincent, C. (USA)

8

Bathurst, C. (Can.)
Cambodia Pt (Thai.)
Cap, Haïtien (Haiti)
East Cape (N.Z.)
Espicher, C. (Port.)
Fairhead, C. (N.I.)
Farewell, C. (Green.)
Farewell, C. (N.Z.)
Fife Ness (Scot.)
Flattery, C. (USA)
Foreland, The (Eng.)
Gallinas Pt (S.Am.)

Good Hope, C. of (SA)
Greenore Pt (Ire.)
Hangklip, C. (SA)
Hartland Pt (Eng.)
Hatteras, C. (USA)
Kaliakra, C. (Bulg.)
Kinnaird Hd. (Scot.)
Land's End (Eng.)
Loop Head (Ire.)
Maranhao, C. (Braz.)
Melville, C. (Austral.)
Palliser, C. (N.Z.)
Palmyras Pt (Ind.)
St Albans Hd. (Eng.)
St David's Hd. (Wales)
St George, C. (Can.)
St-Gildas, Pointe du (Fr.)
St Gowan's Hd. (Wales)
San Diego, C. (S.Am.)
San Lucas, C. (Mex.)
São Roque, C. (Braz.)
Sidmouth, C. (Austral.)
Slea Head (Ire.)
Sordwana Pt (SA)
Strumble Hd. (Wales)
Sumburgh Hd. (Scot.)
Sur Point (USA)
Thorsden, C. (Arc.)
Turn Ness (Scot.)
Vaticano, C. (It.)

Claremont Pt (Austral.)
De la Hague, C. (Fr.)
De Talbert Pt (Fr.)
Dungeness (Eng.)
East Point (Can.)
Esquimaux, C. (Can.)
Farr Point (Scot.)
Girardeau, C. (USA)
Granitola, C. (Sic.)
Inishowen Hd. (Ire.)
Mendocino, C. (USA)
Murchison, C. (Can.)
Nash Point (Wales)
North Cape (N.Z.)
North Cape (Nor.)
Ormes Head (Wales)
Roray Head (Scot.)
Saint Abb's Hd. (Scot.)
Saint Bees Hd. (Eng.)
St Francis, C. (Can.)
Saint Mary, C. (Can.)
Saint Paul, C. (Ghana)
St Vincent, C. (Port.)
Sand Patch Pt (Austral.)
Sandy Cape (Tas.)
Santo Vito, C. (Sic.)
Sheep Head (Ire.)
Slyne Head (Ire.)
South Cape (Hawaii)
Spurn Head (Eng.)
Streedagh Pt (Ire.)
The Lizard (Eng.)
Trafalgar, C. (Sp.)
Troup Head (Scot.)
Vaternish Pt (Scot.)
Worms Head (Wales)

9

Bonavista, C. (Can.)
Brims Ness (Scot.)
Canaveral, C. (USA)
Carvoeira, C. (Port.)

10

Beachy Head (Eng.)
Breakheart Pt (Can.)
Buddon Ness (Scot.)
Burrow Head (Scot.)
Clark Point (Can.)
Conception Pt (USA)
Duncansbay Hd. (Scot.)
Dunnet Head (Scot.)
Finisterre, C. (Sp.)
Galley Head (Ire.)
Gallon Head (Scot.)
Great Ormes Hd. (Wales)
Greenstone Pt (Scot.)
Orford Ness (Eng.)
Palmerston, C. (Austral.)
Quoin Point (SA)
Rayes Point (S.Am.)
Saint Lucia, C. (SA)
St Margaret Pt (Can.)
St Matthieu Pt (Fr.)
San Antonio Pt (Mex.)
San Lorenzo, C. (S.Am.)
Santa Maria, C. (Port.)
Selsey Bill (Eng.)
Slade Point (Austral.)
Sleat Point (Scot.)
Snettisham Pt (Can.)
Start Point (Eng.)
Tarbat Ness (Scot.)
Tavoy Point (Burma)
The Needles (Eng.)
Tolsta Head (Scot.)
Walsingham, C. (Can.)
Washington, C. (Arc.)
Whiten Head (Scot.)

11

Andrés Point (S.Am.)
Bengore Head (N.I.)
Bridgewater, C. (Austral.)
Castle Point (N.Z.)
Catastrophe, C. (Austral.)
Clogher Head (Ire.)
Dodman Point (Eng.)
Downpatrick Hd. (N.I.)
Flamborough Hd. (Eng.)
Friars Point (USA)
Little Ormes Hd. (Wales)
Lizard Point (Eng.)
Mumbles Head (Wales)
Murraysburg, C. (SA)
Prawle Point (Eng.)
Rattray Head (Scot.)
Rhynns Point (Scot.)
Saint Albans Hd. (Eng.)
Saint David's Hd. (Wales)
Saint Gowan's Hd. (Wales)
Sanaig Point (Scot.)
The Foreland (Eng.)
Three Points, C. (W.Af.)
Tribulation, C. (Austral.)

12 AND OVER

Ardnamurchan Pt (Scot.) (12)
Arisaig Point (Scot.) (12)
Breakheart Point (Can.) (15)
Cape of Good Hope (SA) (14)
Cayenne Point (E.Af.) (12)
Claremont Point (Austral.) (14)

Conception Point (USA) (15)
Downpatrick Head (N.I.) (15)
Duncansbay Head (Scot.) (14)
Flamborough Head (Eng.) (15)
Gracias a Dios, C. (C.Am.) (12)
Inishowen Head (Ire.) (13)
North Foreland (Eng.) (13)
Northumberland, C. (Austral.) (14)

Palmuras Point (Ind.) (13)
Portland Bill (Eng.) (12)
Saint Margaret Pt. (Can.) (13)
San Francisco, C. (S.Am.) (12)
Sand Patch Point (Austral.) (14)
Strumble Head (Wales) (12)
Sumburgh Head (Scot.) (12)
Tegupan Point (Mex.) (12)

Capital cities of the world

3 AND 4

Apia (Samoa)
Baku (Azer.)
Dili (East Timor)
Doha (Qatar)
Kiev (Ukr.)
Lima (Peru)
Lomé (Togo)
Male (Maldives)
Oslo (Nor.)
Riga (Latvia)
Rome (It.)
Suva (Fiji)

5

Abuja (Nig.)
Accra (Ghana)
Agana (Guam)
Ajman (Ajman)
Amman (Jordan)

Berne (Swit.)
Cairo (Egypt)
Dakar (Senegal)
Dhaka (Bangla.)
Dubai (Dubai)
Hanoi (Viet.)
Kabul (Afghan.)
La Paz (Boliv.)
Macao (Macao)
Minsk (Bela.)
Paris (Fr.)
Praia (Cape Verde)
Quito (Ecuador)
Rabat (Moroc.)
Sana'a (Yemen)
Seoul (S. Korea)
Sofia (Bulg.)
Sucre (Boliv.)
Tokyo (Jap.)
Tunis (Tunis.)
Vaduz (Liechtenstein)

Yaren (Nauru)

6

Akmola (Kaz.)
Ankara (Turk.)
Asmara (Eritrea)
Athens (Gr.)
Bamako (Mali)
Bangui (Cen. Af. Rep.)
Banjul (Gambia)
Beirut (Lebanon)
Berlin (Ger.)
Bissau (Guinea-Bissau)
Bogotá (Colombia)
Dodoma (Tanz.)
Dublin (Ire.)
Harare (Zimbabwe)
Havana (Cuba)
Hobart (Tasmania)
Kigali (Rwanda)
Kuwait (Kuwait)
Lisbon (Port.)
London (UK)
Luanda (Angola)
Lusaka (Zambia)
Madrid (Sp.)
Malabo (Equatorial Guinea)
Manama (Bahrain)
Manila (Philip.)
Maputo (Mozambique)
Maseru (Lesotho)
Monaco (Monaco)
Moroni (Comoro Is.)
Moscow (Russia)
Muscat (Oman)
Nassau (Bahamas)

Niamey (Niger)
Ottawa (Can.)
Prague (Cze.)
Riyadh (Saudi)
Roseau (Dominica)
Skopje (Mac.)
Taipei (Taiwan)
Tarawa (Kiribati)
Tehran (Iran)
Tirana (Albania)
Vienna (Aust.)
Warsaw (Pol.)
Yangon (Burma)
Zagreb (Cro.)

7

Algiers (Alg.)
Almaata (Kaz.)
Baghdad (Iraq)
Bairiki (Kiribati)
Bangkok (Thai.)
Beijing (China)
Belfast (N. Ire.)
Bishkek (Kyr.)
Caracas (Venez.)
Cardiff (Wales)
Cayenne (Fr. Guiana)
Colombo (Sri)
Conakry (Guinea)
Douglas (Isle of Man)
El Aaiún (W. Sahara)
Honiara (Solomon Islands)
Jakarta (Indo.)
Kampala (Uganda)
Managua (Nicaragua)
Mbabane (Swaziland)

Nairobi (Kenya)
Nicosia (Cyprus)
Palikir (Micronesia)
Papeete (Fr. Polynesia)
Rangoon (Myanmar)
St John's (Antigua and
    Barbuda)
San José (Costa Rica)
San Juan (Puerto Rico)
São Tomé (São Tomé and
    Principe)
Sharjah (Sharjah)
Stanley (Falkland Is.)
Tallinn (Est.)
Tbilisi (Geo.)
Teheran (Iran)
Thimphu (Bhutan)
Tripoli (Libya)
Vilnius (Lith.)
Yaoundé (Cameroon)
Yerevan (Arm.)

8

Abu Dhabi (UAE)
Ashgabat (Turkmen.)
Asunción (Paraguay)
Belgrade (Serb.)
Belmopan (Belize)
Brasilia (Braz.)
Brussels (Belg.)
Budapest (Hung.)
Canberra (Austral.)
Cape Town (SA)
Castries (St Lucia)
Chisinau (Mold.)
Damascus (Syria)

Djibouti (Djibouti)
Dushanbe (Taj.)
Freetown (Sierra Leone)
Fujairah (Fujairah)
Gabarone (Botswana)
Hamilton (Bermuda)
Helsinki (Fin.)
Khartoum (Sudan)
Kingston (Jamaica)
Kinshasa (Dem. Rep. of
    Congo)
Kishiner (Mold.)
Lilongwe (Malawi)
Lubijana (Sloven.)
Monrovia (Liberia)
N'Djaména (Chad)
New Delhi (Ind.)
Plymouth
    (Montserrat)
Port Vila (Vanuatu)
Pretoria (SA)
Reykavik (Iceland)
Santiago (Chile)
St Helier (Jersey)
Sarajevo (Bos.)
Tashkent (Uzbek.)
Valletta (Malta)
Victoria (Seychelles)
Windhoek (Namibia)

9

Amsterdam (Neth.)
Bucharest (Rom.)
Bujumbura (Burundi)
Denpassar (Bali)
Edinburgh (Scot.)

Fongafale (Tuvalu)
Grand Turk (Turks and Caicos Is.)
Islamabad (Pak.)
Jamestown (St Helena)
Jerusalem (Israel)
Kathmandu (Nepal)
Kingstown (St Vincent and the Grenadines)
Ljubljana (Sloven.)
Mogadishu (Somalia)
Nuku'alofa (Tonga)
Phnom Penh (Cambodia)
Port Louis (Mauritius)
Porto Novo (Benin)
Pyongyang (N. Korea)
St George's (Grenada)
San Marino (San Marino)
Singapore (Singapore)
Stockholm (Swed.)
The Valley (Anguilla)
Ulan Bator (Mon.)
Vientiane (Laos)

10

Addis Ababa (Eth.)
Basseterre (Guadeloupe)
Bratislava (Slov.)
Bridgetown (Barbados)
Copenhagen (Den.)
George Town (Guyana)
Georgetown (Cayman Is.)
Kuwait City (Kuwait)

Libreville (Gabon)
Luxembourg (Lux.)
Mexico City (Mexico)
Montevideo (Uruguay)
Nouakchott (Mauritania)
Oranjestad (Arulsa)
Panama City (Panama)
Paramaribo (Surinam)
Washington (USA)
Wellington (NZ)

11 AND OVER

Andorra la Vella (Andorra) (14)
Antananarivo (Mad.) (12)
Bandar Seri Begawan (Brunei) (17)
Bloemfontein (SA) (12)
Brazzaville (Dem. Rep. of Congo) (11)
Buenos Aires (Arg.) (11)
Dalap-Uliga-Darrit (Marshall Islands) (16)
Guatemala City (Guatemala) (13)
Kuala Lumpur (Malay.) (11)
Ouagadougou (Burk.) (11)
Port-au-Prince (Haiti) (12)
Port Moresby (Papua New Guinea) (11)
Port of Spain (Trinidad and Tobago) (11)
Ras al-Khaimah (Ras al-Khaimah) (12)
St Peter Port (Guernsey) (11)

San Salvador (El Salvador)
(11)

Santo Domingo
(Dominican Rep.) (12)

Tegucigalpa
(Honduras) (11)

Umm al-Qaiwain (Umm al-
Qaiwain) (12)

Vatican City
(Vatican City) (11)

Yamoussoukro
(Ivory Coast) (12)

Channels, passages, sounds and straits

Ch.=Channel; P.=Passage; Sd=Sound; St(s)=Strait(s)
Note The land references are to give a general idea as to
location

3 AND 4

Bass St (Austral.)
Coll, P. of (Scot.)
Cook St (N.Z.)
Fox Ch. (Can.)
Jura Sd (Scot.)
Mona P. (W.I.)
Nore, The (Eng.)
Palk St (Ind.)

5

Cabot St (Can.)
Davis St (Can.)
Dover, Sts of (Eng.)
Johor, Sts of (Malay.)
Kerch St (Ukr., Rus.)
Korea St (Jap.)
Menai Sts (Wales)
Minch, The (Scot.)
North Ch. (Scot.)
Puget Sd (USA)
Sleat, Sd of (Scot.)

Smith Sd (Can.)
Sound, The (Swed.)
Sumba St (Indo.)
Sunda, St of (Indo.)
Tatar St (Rus.)

6

Achill Sd (Ire.)
Bangka St (Indo.)
Barrow St (Can.)
Bering St (Pac.)
Hainan St (China)
Harris, St of (Scot.)
Hecate St (Can.)
Hormuz, St of (Iran)
Hudson St (Can.)
Lombok St (Indo)
Madura St (Indo.)
Nootka Sd (Can.)
Panama Canal (C.Am.)
Queen's Ch (Austral.)
Solent, The (Eng.)
Taiwan St (China)

Torres St (Austral.)
Tromsø Sd (Nor.)

7

Bristol Ch. (Eng.)
Denmark St (Green.)
Dolphin St (Can.)
English Ch. (Eng.)
Florida St (USA)
Foveaux St (N.Z.)
Georgia, St of (Can.)
Le Maire St (Arg.)
Malacca St (Malaya)
Malacca, St of (Indo.)
Messina, St of (It.)
Molucca P. (E.I.)
Øresund (Swed., Den.)
Otranto, St of (It.)
Pamlico Sd (USA)
The Nore (Eng.)
Yucatán Ch. (Mex.)

8

Colonsay, P. of (Scot.)
Kattegat (Den.)
Mackinac, Sts of (USA)
Magellan, St of (S.Am.)
Makassar Sts (Indo.)
Plymouth Sd (Eng.)
Spithead (Eng.)
The Minch (Scot.)
The Sound (Swed.)
Windward P. (W.I.)

9

Belle Isle, St of (Can.)

Bonifacio, St of (Med.)
Bosphorus, The (Turk.)
Gibraltar, Sts of (Spain)
Great Belt, The (Den.)
Lancaster Sd (Can.)
La Pérouse St (Jap., Rus.)
St George's Ch. (Eng.)
Scapa Flow (Scot.)
Skagerrak (Nor. and Den.)
Suez Canal (Egypt)
The Solent (Eng.)

10

Dogger Bank (N.Sea)
Golden Gate (USA)
Golden Horn (Turk.)
Juan de Fuca, St of (Can.,
USA)
Kilbrennan Sd (Scot.)
King George Sd (Austral.)
Little Belt, The (Den.)
Mozambique Ch. (Moz.)

11 AND OVER

Bab-el-Mandeb St (Red S.)
(11)
Caledonian Canal (Scot.)
(15)
Corinth Canal (Gr.) (12)
Dardanelles, The (Turk.) (11)
Goodwin Sands (Eng.) (12)
Grand Union Canal (Eng.)
(15)
Hampton Roads (USA) (12)
Northumberland St (Can.)
(14)

Pas de Calais (Fr.) (11)	The Bosphorus (Turk.) (12)
Queen Charlotte Sd (Can.) (14)	The Dardanelles (Turk.) (14)
	The Great Belt (Den.) (12)
Saint George's Ch. (Eng.) (12)	The Little Belt (Den.) (13)

Counties: United Kingdom and the Republic of Ireland

(E)=England; (Ire.)=Republic of Ireland; (N.I.)=Northern Ireland; (S.)=Scotland; (W.)=Wales
Note As the names of some counties are commonly used in shortened form, both full and shortened names are given in this list, which also includes county names no longer officially in use.

3 AND 4

Avon (E.)
Ayr (S.)
Beds (E.)
Bute (S.)
Cork (Ire.)
Down (N.I.)
Fife (S.)
IOW (E.)
Kent (E.)
Leix (Ire.)
Mayo (Ire.)
Oxon (E.)
Ross (S.)

5

Angus (S.)
Banff (S.)

Berks (E.)
Bucks (E.)
Cavan (Ire.)
Clare (Ire.)
Clwyd (W.)
Derby (E.)
Devon (E.)
Dyfed (W.)
Elgin (S.)
Essex (E.)
Flint (W.)
Gwent (W.)
Hants (E.)
Herts (E.)
Hunts (E.)
Kerry (Ire.)
Lancs (E.)
Laois (Ire.)
Leics (E.)

Lincs (E.)
Louth (Ire.)
Meath (Ire.)
Moray (S.)
Nairn (S.)
Notts (E.)
Perth (S.)
Powys (W.)
Salop (E.)
Sligo (Ire.)
Wilts (E.)
Yorks (E.)

6

Antrim (N.I.)
Argyll (S.)
Armagh (N.I.)
Brecon (W.)
Carlow (Ire.)

Dorset (E.)
Dublin (Ire.)
Durham (E.)
Forfar (S.)
Galway (Ire.)
Gloucs. (E.)
Lanark (S.)
London (E.)
N. Yorks (E.)
Offaly (Ire.)
Orkney (S.)
Oxford (E.)
Radnor (W.)
Surrey (E.)
Sussex (E.)
Tyrone (N.I.)

7

Bedford (E.)
Berwick (S.)
Borders (S.)
Central (S.)
Cumbria (E.)
Denbigh (W.)
Donegal (Ire.)
Gwynedd (W.)
Kildare (Ire.)
Kinross (S.)
Leitrim (Ire.)
Lincoln (E.)
Norfolk (E.)
Peebles (S.)
Renfrew (S.)
Rutland (E.)
Selkirk (S.)
Suffolk (E.)

Tayside (S.)
Warwick (E.)
Wexford (Ire.)
Wicklow (Ire.)
Wigtown (S.)

8

Aberdeen (S.)
Anglesey (W.)
Ayrshire (S.)
Cardigan (W.)
Cheshire (E.)
Cornwall (E.)
Cromarty (S.)
Dumfries (S.)
Grampian (S.)
Hereford (E.)
Hertford (E.)
Highland (S.)
Kilkenny (Ire.)
Laoighis (Ire.)
Limerick (Ire.)
Longford (Ire.)
Monaghan (Ire.)
Monmouth (E.)
Pembroke (W.)
Roxburgh (S.)
Somerset (E.)
Stirling (S.)

9

Berkshire (E.)
Caithness (S.)
Cambridge (E.)
Cleveland (E.)
Connaught (Ire.)

Dunbarton (S.)
Edinburgh (S.)
Fermanagh (N.I.)
Glamorgan (W.)
Hampshire (E.)
Inverness (S.)
Leicester (E.)
Merioneth (W.)
Middlesex (E.)
Northants (E.)
Roscommon (Ire.)
Tipperary (Ire.)
Waterford (Ire.)
Westmeath (Ire.)
Wiltshire (E.)
Worcester (E.)
Yorkshire (E.)

10

Banffshire (S.)
Buckingham (E.)
Caernarvon (W.)
Carmarthen (W.)
Cumberland (E.)
Derbyshire (E.)
Devonshire (E.)
East Sussex (E.)
Flintshire (W.)
Gloucester (E.)
Haddington (E.)
Humberside (E.)
Huntingdon (E.)
Inverclyde (S.)
Kincardine (S.)
Lancashire (E.)
Linlithgow (S.)

Merseyside (E.)
Midlothian (S.)
Montgomery (W.)
Perthshire (S.)
Shropshire (E.)
Sutherland (S.)
West Sussex (E.)

11 AND 12

Argyllshire (S.) (11)
Bedfordshire (E.) (12)
Berwickshire (S.) (12)
Clackmannan (S.) (11)
Denbighshire (W.) (12)
East Ayrshire (S.) (12)
East Lothian (S.) (11)
Forfarshire (S.) (11)
Isle of Wight (E.) (11)
Kircudbright (S.) (12)
Lanarkshire (S.) (11)
Lincolnshire (E.) (12)
Londonderry (N.I.) (11)
Mid Glamorgan (W.) (12)
Oxfordshire (E.) (11)
Radnorshire (W.) (11)
Renfrewshire (S.) (12)
Strathclyde (S.) (11)
Tyne and Wear (E.) (11)
Warwickshire (E.) (12)
Western Isles (S.) (12)
West Lothian (S.) (11)
West Midlands (E.) (12)
Westmorland (E.) (11)

13 AND 14

Aberdeenshire (S.) (13)

Argyll and Bute (S.) (13)
Brecknockshire (W.) (14)
Cambridgeshire (E.) (14)
Cardiganshire (W.) (13)
Clackmannanshire (S.) (16)
Dumfriesshire (S.) (13)
Dunbartonshire (S.) (14)
East Renfrewshire (S.) (16)
Greater London (E.) (13)
Herefordshire (E.) (13)
Hertfordshire (E.) (13)
Inverness-shire (S.) (14)
Leicestershire (E.) (14)
Merionethshire (W.) (14)
Monmouthshire (E.) (13)
North Ayrshire (S.) (13)
North Lanarkshire (S.) (16)
North Yorkshire (E.) (14)
Northumberland (E.) (14)
Orkney Islands (S.) (13)
Pembrokeshire (W.) (13)
Perth and Kinross (S.) (15)
Scottish Borders (S.) (15)
Shetland Islands (S.) (15)
South Ayrshire (S.) (13)
South Glamorgan (W.) (14)
South Lanarkshire (S.) (16)
South Yorkshire (E.) (14)
Staffordshire (E.) (13)
West Glamorgan (W.) (13)
West Yorkshire (E.) (13)
Worcestershire (E.) (14)

15 AND 16

Buckinghamshire (E.) (15)
Caernarvonshire (W.) (15)

Carmarthenshire (W.) (15)
Gloucestershire (E.) (15)
Huntingdonshire (E.) (15)
Montgomeryshire (W.) (15)

Northamptonshire (E.) (16)
Nottinghamshire (E.) (15)
Ross and Cromarty (S.) (15)

Countries and continents

Note This list includes the names of former countries

3 AND 4

Asia
Bali (Asia)
CIS (Asia, Eur.)
Chad (Af.)
Cuba (W.I.)
DDR (E. Ger.)
Eire (Eur.)
FDR (W. Ger.)
Fiji (S.Pac.)
GDR (E. Ger.)
Guam (Pac.)
Iran (Asia)
Iraq (Asia)
Java (Asia)
Laos (Asia)
Mali (Af.)
Nejd (Arab.)
Oman (Arab.)
Peru (S.Am.)
Siam (Asia)
Togo (Af.)
UAR (Af.)
USA (N.Amer.)
USSR (Asia, Eur.)

5

Annam (Asia)
Assam (Asia)
Benin (Af.)
Burma (Asia)
Chile (S.Am.)
China (Asia)
Congo (Af.)
Egypt (Af.)
Fiume (Eur.)
Gabon (Af.)
Ghana (Af.)
Haiti (W.I.)
India (Asia)
Italy (Eur.)
Japan (Asia)
Kandy (Asia)
Kenya (Af.)
Khmer (Asia)
Korea (Asia)
Libya (Af.)
Lydia (Asia)
Macao (Asia)
Macáu (Asia)
Malta (Med.)
Natal (Af.)

Nauru (Pac.)
Nepal (Asia)
Niger (Af.)
Papua (E.I.)
Qatar (Arab.)
Samoa (Oc.)
Spain (Eur.)
Sudan (Af.)
Syria (Asia)
Tchad (Af.)
Tibet (Asia)
Timor (Indo.)
Tonga (Oc.)
Tunis (Af.)
Wales (Eur.)
Yemen (Arab.)
Zaïre (Af.)

6

Africa
Angola (Af.)
Arabia (Asia)
Azores (Atl.)
Belize (C.Am.)
Bhutan (Asia)
Brazil (S.Am.)
Brunei (E.I.)

Canada (N.Am.)
Cathay (Asia)
Ceylon (Asia)
Cyprus (Med.)
Epirus (Eur.)
Europe
France (Eur.)
Gambia (Af.)
Greece (Eur.)
Guinea (Af.)
Guyana (S.Am.)
Hawaii (Pac.)
Israel (Asia)
Johore (Asia)
Jordan (Asia)
Kuwait (Arab.)
Latvia (Eur.)
Malawi (Af.)
Malaya (Asia)
Mexico (N.Am.)
Monaco (Eur.)
Muscat (Asia)
Norway (Eur.)
Panama (C.Am.)
Persia (Asia)
Poland (Eur.)
Ruanda (Af.)
Russia (Eur., Asia)
Rwanda (Af.)
Serbia (Eur.)
Sicily (Eur.)
Sikkim (Asia)
Soudan (Af.)
Sweden (Eur.)
Taiwan (Asia)
Tobago (W.I.)

Turkey (Eur.,
   Asia)
Tuvalu (Oc.)
Uganda (Af.)
Ulster (Eur.)
Zambia (Af.)

7

Albania (Eur.)
Algeria (Af.)
America
Andorra (Eur.)
Antigua (W.I.)
Armenia (Asia)
Ashanti (Af.)
Assyria (Asia)
Austria (Eur.)
Bahamas (W.I.)
Bahrain (Arab.)
Bavaria (Eur.)
Belarus (Eur.)
Belgium (Eur.)
Bermuda (Atl.)
Bohemia (Eur.)
Bolivia (S. Am.)
Britain (Eur.)
Burkina (Af.)
Burundi (Af.)
Comoros (Eur.)
Croatia (Eur.)
Dahomey (Af.)
Denmark (Eur.)
Ecuador (S.Am.)
England (Eur.)
Eritrea (Af.)
Estonia (Eur.)

Faeroes (Atl.)
Finland (Eur.)
Formosa (Asia)
Georgia (Eur.)
Germany (Eur.)
Grenada (W.I.)
Holland (Eur.)
Hungary (Eur.)
Iceland (Eur.)
Ireland (Eur.)
Jamaica (W.I.)
Lebanon (Asia)
Lesotho (Af.)
Liberia (Af.)
Livonia (Eur.)
Macedon (Eur.)
Moldova (Eur.)
Morocco (Af.)
Myanmar (Asia)
Namibia (Af.)
Nigeria (Af.)
Prussia (Eur.)
Romania (Eur.)
Rumania (Eur.)
St Kitts (W.I.)
St Lucia (W.I.)
São Tomé (Atl.)
Sarawak (Asia)
Senegal (Af.)
Somalia (Af.)
Sumatra (E.I.)
Sumeria (Asia)
Surinam (S.Am.)
Tangier (Af.)
Tartary (Asia)
Tripoli (Af.)

Tunisia (Af.)
Ukraine (Eur.)
Uruguay (S.Am.)
Vanuatu (Oc.)
Vatican (Eur.)
Vietnam (Asia)

8

Barbados (W.I.)
Botswana (Af.)
Bulgaria (Eur.)
Burgundy (Eur.)
Cambodia (Asia)
Cameroon (Af.)
Colombia (S.Am.)
Djibouti (Af.)
Dominica (W.I.)
Ethiopia (Af.)
Honduras (C.Am.)
Hong Kong (Asia)
Kiribati (S.Pac.)
Malagasy (Af.)
Malaysia (Asia)
Maldives (Ind.)
Moldavia (Eur.)
Mongolia (Asia)
Pakistan (Asia)
Paraguay (S.Am.)
Portugal (Eur.)
Rhodesia (Af.)
Roumania (Eur.)
St Helena (Atl.)
St Vincent (W.I.)
Salvador (C.Am.)
Sardinia (Med.)
Scotland (Eur.)

Slovakia (Eur.)
Slovenia (Eur.)
Suriname (S. Am)
Tanzania (Af.)
Tasmania (Austral.)
Thailand (Asia)
Togoland (Af.)
Trinidad (W.I.)
Zanzibar (Af.)
Zimbabwe (Af.)
Zululand (Af.)

9

Argentina (S.Am.)
Argentine, The (S.Am.)
Australia
Babylonia (Asia)
Caledonia (Eur.)
Cameroons (Af.)
Cape Verde (Af.)
Costa Rica (C.Am.)
East Timor (E.I.)
Gibraltar (Eur.)
Greenland (Arc.)
Guatemala (C.Am.)
Hindustan (Asia)
Indochina (Asia)
Indonesia (E.I.)
Kampuchea (Asia)
Kirghizia (Asia)
Lithuania (Eur.)
Luxemburg (Eur.)
Macedonia (Eur.)
Manchuria (Asia)
Mauritius (Af.)
New Guinea (E.I.)

Nicaragua (C.Am.)
Nyasaland (Af.)
Palestine (Asia)
Pondoland (Af.)
San Marino (Eur.)
Singapore (Asia)
Swaziland (Af.)
Transvaal (Af.)
Venezuela (S. Am.)

10

Antarctica
Azerbaijan (Asia)
Bangladesh (Asia)
Basutoland (Af.)
Belorussia (Eur.)
California (N.Am.)
Cape Colony (Af.)
Damaraland (Af.)
El Salvador (C.Am.)
Hispaniola (W.I.)
Ivory Coast (Af.)
Kazakhstan (Asia)
Kyrgyzstan (Asia)
Luxembourg (Eur.)
Madagascar (Af.)
Mauretania (Af.)
Mauritania (Af.)
Micronesia (Oc.)
Montenegro (Eur.)
Montserrat (W.I.)
Mozambique (Af.)
New Zealand (Pac.)
North Korea (Asia)
Seychelles (Af.)
Shan States (Asia)

Somaliland (Af.)
South Korea (Asia)
South Yemen (Asia)
Tajikistan (Asia)
Tanganyika (Af.)
Upper Volta (Af.)
Uzbekistan (Asia)
Yugoslavia (Eur.)

11

Afghanistan (Asia)
Australasia
Baluchistan (Asia)
Burkina Faso (Af.)
Byelorussia (Eur.)
Cochin China (Asia)
Cook Islands (Pac.)
Côte d'Ivoire (Af.)
Dutch Guiana (S.Am.)
East Germany (Eur.)
French Congo (Af.)
Malay States (Asia)
Mashonaland (Af.)
Mesopotamia (Asia)
Namaqualand (Af.)
Netherlands (Eur.)
New Hebrides (Pac.)
Philippines (Asia)
Saudi Arabia (Arab.)
Sierra Leone (Af.)
South Africa (Af.)
Soviet Union (Asia, Eur.)
Switzerland (Eur.)
Transjordan (Asia)
Vatican City (Eur.)
West Germany (Eur.)

12

Bechuanaland (Af.)
Belgian Congo (Af.)
Cocos Islands (Ind.)
Faroe Islands (Atl.)
French Guiana (S.Am.)
Great Britain (Eur.)
Guinea-Bissau (Af.)
Indian Empire (Asia)
Matabeleland (Af.)
Newfoundland (N. Am.)
North America
North Vietnam (Asia)
Ruanda-Urundi (Af.)
South America
South Vietnam (Asia)
Tadzhikistan (Asia)
Turkmenistan (Asia)
United States (N.Am.)
Western Samoa (Oc.)

13

Afars and Issas (Af.)
Barbary States (Af.)
Cayman Islands (W.I.)
Comoro Islands (Af.)
Czech Republic (Eur.)
Khmer Republic (Asia)
Liechtenstein (Eur.)
Norfolk Island (Pac.)
Trucial States (Asia)
United Kingdom (Eur.)
Western Sahara (Af.)

14

Cape of Good Hope (Af.)
Congo Free State (Af.)
Czechoslovakia (Eur.)
Gilbert Islands (Pac.)
Irish Free State (Eur.)
Leeward Islands (W.I.)
Maldive Islands (Ind.)
Mariana Islands (Pac.)
Papua New Guinea (Oc.)
Pitcairn Island (Pac.)
Society Islands (Pac.)
Solomon Islands (Oc.)

15

British Honduras (C. Am.
Caroline Islands (Pac.)
Christmas Island (Pac.)
Falkland Islands (Atl.)
Holy Roman Empire (Eur.)
Marshall Islands (N. Pac)
Northern Ireland (Eur.)
Northern Nigeria (Af.)
Orange Free State (Af.)
Republic of Congo (Af.)
South-West Africa (Af.)
Southern Nigeria (Af.)

16 AND OVER

Antigua and Barbuda
   (W.I.) (17)
Bosnia-Herzegovina (Eur.) (17)
Cape Verde Islands (Af.) (16)
Dominican Republic
   (W.I.) (17)
Equatorial Guinea (Af.) (16)

Malagasy Republic (Af.) (16)
São Tomé and Principé
  (Af.) (18)
Trinidad and Tobago
  (W.I.) (17)

United Arab Emirates
  (Asia) (18)
United Arab Republic
  (Af., Asia) (18)
Vatican City State (Eur.) (16)

Geographical terms

2 AND 3

alp
alt
as
bay
ben
bog
cay
col
cwm
dam
dun
fen
lea
lin
map
mud
ria
sea
sod
tor
voe

4

aber
bank

beck
belt
berg
bill
bore
brae
burn
bush
cape
cave
city
clay
comb
dale
deli
dene
dike
doab
down
dune
dyke
east
eyot
firn
floe

flow
ford
fork
foss
ghat
gill
glen
gulf
head
hill
holm
holt
hook
inch
isle
kaim
kame
lake
land
lane
limb
linn
loam
loch
lock
marl
mead

mere
mesa
midi
mire
moor
mull
naze
neck
ness
névé
park
pass
peak
peat
plat
pole
pond
pool
port
race
reef
rift
rill
road
rock
sand
scar

seam
seat
sial
sike
silt
sima
soil
spit
spur
sudd
tarn
town
tump
vale
vega
veld
wadi
wash
weir
well
west
wind
wold
wood
wynd
zone

5

abyss	esker	mound	
alley	falls	mount	
atlas	fault	mouth	
atoll	field	north	
banat	fiord	oasis	
bayou	firth	ocean	
beach	fjord	oxbow	
bight	flats	plain	
bluff	flood	point	
bough	fosse	polar	
bourn	geoid	poles	
broad	ghaut	reach	
brook	ghyll	rhine	
butte	glade	ridge	
canal	globe	river	
chart	gorge	sands	
chasm	grove	sault	
chine	gully	scarp	
cliff	haven	scree	
clime	heath	shelf	
coast	hithe	shire	
combe	hurst	shoal	
coomb	hythe	shore	
copse	inlet	slade	
creek	islet	slope	
crest	karoo	sound	
croft	kloof	south	
delta	knoll	state	
ditch	kopje	swale	
donga	lande	swamp	
downs	levee	sward	
drift	llano	talus	
duchy	loess	tract	
dunes	magma	veldt	
erode	marsh	weald	
	monte	wilds	

6

alpine	inning
Arctic	island
boreal	isobar
broads	jungle
canton	karroo
canyon	lagoon
cavern	maldan
clough	margin
colony	massif
colure	meadow
common	morass
corrie	nullah
coulee	orient
county	pampas
course	parish
crater	plains
cuesta	polder
defile	rapids
desert	ravine
dingle	region
divide	riding
domain	rillet
empire	runlet
eyalet	runnel
feeder	sarsen
forest	schist
geyser	seaway
glacis	sierra
grotto	sinter
gulley	skerry
hamlet	source
harbor	spinny
icecap	spruit
icicle	steppe
inland	strait
	strath

stream
street
suburb
summit
tropic
trough
tundra
upland
valley
warren

7

alluvia
austral
bogland
caldera
channel
clachan
commune
compass
conduit
conflux
contour
country
crevice
cuffing
deltaic
drought
eastern
enclave
eparchy
equator
estuary
exclave
georama
glacier

habitat
harbour
highway
hillock
hilltop
hornito
hummock
hundred
iceberg
ice-floe
icepack
incline
insular
isthmus
kingdom
lakelet
lowland
midland
new town
oceanic
plateau
polders
prairie
rivulet
saltpan
satrapy
savanna
seaport
seaside
straits
subsoil
thicket
topsoil
torrent
tropics
village

volcano
western

8

affluent
alluvial
alluvium
altitude
brooklet
cantonal
cataract
causeway
crevasse
currents
district
dominion
downland
dustbowl
easterly
eastward
effluent
eminence
eminency
environs
eruption
foreland
fracture
frontier
headland
highland
high road
hillside
icefield
interior
isostasy
isthmian

landmark
landslip
latitude
lava flow
littoral
lowlands
mainland
midlands
monticle
moorland
mountain
neap-tide
northern
occident
oriental
prospect
province
quagmire
republic
riparian
river bed
riverine
salt lake
sandbank
sand dune
seaboard
seacoast
sea level
seashore
sediment
shallows
sheading
snow-line
southern
sub-polar
telluric

toparchy
township
tropical
undertow
volcanic
westerly
westward
woodland

9

Antarctic
antipodal
antipodes
avalanche
backwater
backwoods
billabong
boondocks
cadastral
catchment
cisalpine
cliff face
coalfield
coastline
continent
coral reef
epicentre
everglade
fleet-dike
foothills
foreshore
geography
heathland
highlands
landscape
landslide

longitude
marshland
midstream
monticule
northeast
northwest
northerly
northward
peneplain
peninsula
precipice
rainwater
rockbound
salt-marsh
sandbanks
sand dunes
shore-line
snowdrift
snowfield
southeast
southerly
southmost
southward
southwest
streamlet
sub-alpine
tableland
territory
tetrarchy
tidal flow
trade wind
tributary
up country
wapentake
waste land
waterfall

water-hole
watershed
waterside
westwards
whirlpool

10

co-latitude
confluence
cordillera
county town
depression
earthquake
equatorial
escarpment
fluviatile
fresh water
frigid zone
garden city
geographer
Gulf Stream
headstream
headwaters
hemisphere
high ground
hinterland
landlocked
margravate
market town
meridional
metropolis
no-man's-land
occidental
palatinate

peninsular
plantation
polar-angle
population
presidency
projection
promontory
quicksands
rain forest
rift valley
river basin
sandy beach
seismology
spring tide
stratiform
subsidence
substratum
tidal creek
torrid zone
water spout
water table
wilderness

11

archipelago
back country
bergschrund
circumpolar
cisatlantic
continental
conurbation
coral island
countryside
earth tremor
equinoctial
mountainous

northwardly
polar circle
polar region
river course
river valley
septentrion
subtropical
territorial
tetrarchate
tidal waters
transalpine
transmarine
ultramarine
watercourse

12

Arctic Circle
equatorially
geographical
geomagnetism
glacial drift
glacial epoch
landgraviate
magnetic pole
mean sea level
mountain pass
mountain peak
northeastern
northwestern
principality
protectorate
rising ground
southeastern
southernmost
southwestern
stratosphere

subcontinent
subterranean
tropical zone
ultramontane
virgin forest

13

above sea level
active volcano
deltafication
drainage basin
eastnortheast
eastsoutheast
extratropical
geotechtonics
intertropical
magnetic north
Mediterranean
mother country
neighbourhood
northeasterly
northeastward
northwesterly
northwestward
polar distance
septentrional

southeasterly
southeastward
southwesterly
southwestward
temperate zone
transatlantic
virgin country
watering place

14 AND 15

acclimatization (15)
Antarctic Circle (15)
circummeridian (14)
circumnavigate (14)
irrigation canal (15)
magnetic equator (15)
Mercator's chart (14)
north frigid zone (15)
northeastwards (14)
south frigid zone (15)
southeastwards (14)
tropic of Cancer (14)

17

tropic of Capricorn

Islands

Arch.=Archipelago; I.=Island; Is.=Islands; (v.)=volcanic

2–4

Adi (Pac.)
Amoy (China)
Aran (Ire.)

Arru Is. (Indo.)
Bali (Indo.)
Bay Is. (C.Am.)
Be (Mad.)
Bere (Ire.)

Brac (Adr.)
Bua (Adr.)
Buru (Indo.)
Bute (Scot.)
Cebu (Philip.)

Ceos (Gr.)
Coil (Scot.)
Cook Is. (Pac.)
Cos (Gr.)
Cres (Cro.)
Cuba (W.I.)
Dago (Fin.)
Dogs, I. of (Eng.)
Eigg (Scot.)
Elba (Med.)
Ewe (Scot.)
Farm Is. (Eng.)
Faro (Balt.)
Fiji Is. (Pac.)
Fohr (Ger.)
Gozo (Med.)
Guam (Pac.)
Hall Is. (Pac.)
Herm (Ch.Is.)
High I. (Ire.)
Holy I. (Scot.)
Hoy (Scot.)
Hvar (Cro.)
Idra (Gr.)
Iona (Scot.)
Java (Indo.)
Jura (Scot.)
Kea (Gr.)
Kei Is. (Indo.)
Kish (Iran)
Low Arch. (Pac.)
Man, I. of (British Is.)
May, I. of (Scot.)
Milo (Gr.)
Moen (Den.)

Muck (Scot.)
Mull, I. of (Scot.)
Oahu (Pac.)
Paxo (Gr.)
Pine I. (USA)
Rat Is. (Pac.)
Ré (Fr.)
Rum (Scot.)
Saba (W.I.)
Sark (Ch.Is.)
Scio (Gr.)
Skye (Scot.)
Sulu Is. (Indo.)
Sylt (Ger.)
Syra (Gr.)
Tory (Ire.)
Uist (Scot.)
Ulva (Scot.)
Unst (Scot.)
Yap (Pac.)
Yell (Scot.)
Yezo (Jap.)
Zea (Gr.)
Zebu (Indo.)

5

Abaco (W.I.)
Aland Is. (Balt.)
Albay (Indo.)
Ambon (Indo.)
Arran (Scot.)
Bahía Is. (C. Am.)
Banca (Malay.)
Banda (Indo.)
Banks (S.Pac.)
Barra (Heb.)

Bioko (W.Af.)
Bonin Is. (Pac.)
Brach (Adr.)
Caldy (Wales)
Canna (Scot.)
Capri (It.)
Ceram (Indo.)
Cheja (Korea)
Chios (Gr.)
Clare (Ire.)
Clear (Ire.)
Cocos Is. (Ind.)
Corfu (Gr.)
Corvo (Atl.)
Crete (Med.)
Delos (Gr.)
Devon I. (Arc.)
Eagle I. (Ire.)
Ellis I. (USA)
Farne Is. (Eng.)
Fayal (Atl.)
Ferro (Atl.)
Foula (Scot.)
Funen (Den.)
Goree (Atl.)
Haiti (W.I.)
Hart's I. (USA)
Hondo (Jap.)
Hydra (Gr.)
Ibiza (Med.)
Irian (Indo.)
Islay (Scot.)
Iviza (Med.)
Leros (Gr.)
Lewis (Scot.)
Leyte (Philip.)

Lissa (Adr.)
Lobos Is. (S.Am.)
Lundy I. (Eng.)
Luzon (Philip.)
Malta (Med.)
Matsu (China)
Melos (Gr.)
Milos (Gr.)
Mores (Atl.)
Nauru (Pac.)
Naxos (Gr.)
Nevis (W.I.)
Oesel (Est.)
Ormuz (Iran)
Panay (Philip.)
Parry Is. (Arc.)
Pearl Is. (Pac.)
Pemba (Af.)
Perim (Af.)
Pines, I. of (Cuba)
Pines, I. of (Pac.)
Rhode I. (USA)
Rugen (Ger.)
Sable I. (Can.)
Samar (Philip.)
Samoa (Oc.)
Samos (Gr.)
Samsø (Den.)
Spice Is. (Indo.)
Sunda Is. (Indo.)
Texel (Neth.)
Thera (Gr.)
Timor (Indo.)
Tiree (Scot.)
Tonga (Oc.)
Turk's I. (W.I.)

Voorn (Neth.)
Wight, I. of (Eng.)
Zante (Gr.)

6

Achill (Ire.)
Aegina (Gr.)
Albany (Austral.)
Andros (Gr.)
Baffin I. (Can.)
Bahama Is. (W.I.)
Banana Is. (Atl.)
Bissau (Atl.)
Borkum (Ger.)
Borneo (Indo.)
Bounty Is. (N.Z.)
Brazza (Adr.)
Burray (Scot.)
Caicos I. (W.I.)
Canary Is. (Atl.)
Candia (Med.)
Cayman Is. (W.I.)
Cerigo (Gr.)
Cherso (Cro.)
Chiloé (Chile)
Chusan (China)
Comoro Is. (Af.)
Crozet Is. (Ind.)
Cyprus (Med.)
Djerba (Tun.)
Dursey (Ire.)
Easter I. (Pac.)
Ellice Is. (Pac.)
Euboea (Aeg.)
Faroes (Atl.)
Flores (Atl.)

Flores (Indo.)
Gilolo (Indo.)
Gomera (Can.)
Hainan (China)
Harris (Scot.)
Hawaii (Pac.)
Honshu (Jap.)
Hormuz (Iran)
Imbros (Turk.)
Inagna Is. (W.I.)
Ionian Is. (Med.)
Ischia (It.)
Ithaca (Med.)
Iturup (Rus.)
Jaluit (Pac.)
Jersey (Ch.Is.)
Jethou (Ch.Is.)
Kadavu (Oc.)
Kodiak (Alaska)
Kurile Is. (Pac.)
Kyushu (Jap.)
Labuan (Malay.)
Lambay (Ire.)
Lemnos (Aeg.)
Lesbos (Aeg.)
Lesina (Cro.)
Limnos (Gr.)
Lipari Is. (v.) (It.)
Lombok (v.)
   (Indo.)
Madura (Indo.)
Mahore Is. (Af.)
Maluka Is. (Indo.)
Marajó (S. Am.)
Negros (Philip.)
Oléron (Fr.)

Orkney Is. (Scot.)
Patmos (Aeg.)
Penang (Malay.)
Quemoy (Taiwan)
Rhodes (Aeg.)
Robben I. (SA)
St John (W.I.)
St Paul (Alaska)
Sangir Is. (Indo.)
Savai'i I. (Pac.)
Scarba (Scot.)
Scilly Is. (Eng.)
Sicily (Med.)
Skyros (Aeg.)
Staffa (Scot.)
Staten I. (USA)
Stroma (Scot.)
Tahiti (Pac.)
Taiwan (China)
Thanet, I. of (Eng.)
Tholen (Neth.)
Tobago (W.I.)
Tromsø (Nor.)
Tubuai Is. (Pac.)
Usedom (Ger.)
Ushant (Fr.)
Virgin Is. (W.I.)

7

Aeolian Is. (v.) (It.)
Amboina (Indo.)
Ameland (Neth.)
Anambas Is. (Indo.)
Andaman Is. (Ind.)
Antigua (W.I.)
Austral Is. (Pac.)

Bahamas (W.I.)
Bahrain (Arab.)
Balleny Is. (Antarc.)
Barents (Arc.)
Bermuda (Atl.)
Bernera (Scot.)
Bonaire (W.I.)
Cabrera (Med.)
Capraia (Med.)
Celebes (Indo.)
Channel Is. (Eng.)
Chatham Is. (Pac.)
Chinmen (Taiwan)
Comoros (Af.)
Corsica (Med.)
Curaçao (W.I.)
Curzola (Cro.)
Cythera (Gr.)
Dampier Is. (Austral.)
Eivissa (Med.)
Eriskay (Scot.)
Faeroes (Atl.)
Falster (Balt.)
Fanning (Pac.)
Fehmarn (Balt.)
Flannan Is. (Scot.)
Formosa (China)
Frisian Is. (N.Sea)
Gambier Is. (Pac.)
Gilbert Is. (Pac.)
Gotland (Balt.)
Grenada (W.I.)
Hayling I. (Eng.)
Iceland (v.) (Atl.)
Ireland
Jamaica (W.I.)

Kalamos (Gr.)
Kamaran (Red S.)
Keeling Is. (Ind.)
Korcula (Cro.)
Kythira (Gr.)
Leeward Is. (W.I.)
Lefkada (Gr.)
Lofoten Is. (Nor.)
Lolland (Den.)
Loyalty Is. (Pac.)
Madeira (Atl.)
Majorca (Med.)
Maldive Is. (Ind.)
Mariana Is. (Pac.)
Massowa (Red S.)
Mayotte Is. (Af.)
Mindoro (Philip.)
Minicoy Is. (Ind.)
Minorca (Med.)
Molokai (Pac.)
Mombasa (Af.)
Mykonos (Gr.)
Nicobar Is. (Ind.)
Norfolk I. (Austral.)
Nossi Bé (v.) (Mad.)
Oceania (Pac.)
Okinawa (Jap.)
Orkneys (Scot.)
Palawan (Philip.)
Phoenix Is. (Pac.)
Purbeck, I. of (Eng.)
Rathlin (N.I.)
Réunion (Ind.)
Roanoke (USA)
Rockall (Atl.)
Rotumah (Pac.)

St Agnes (Eng.)
St Kilda (Scot.)
St Kitts (W.I.)
St Lucia (W.I.)
Salamis (Gr.)
São Tomé (W.Af.)
Serifos (Gr.)
Sheppey, I. of (Eng.)
Sherbro (W. Af.)
Shikoku (Jap.)
Society Is. (Pac.)
Socotra (Yemen)
Solomon Is. (Pac.)
Stewart I. (N.Z.)
Sumatra (Indo.)
Sumbawa (Indo.)
Ternate (Indo.)
Tortola (W.I.)
Tortuga (W.I.)
Tuamotu (Pac.)
Watling I. (W.I.)
Whalsay (Scot.)
Wrangel I. (Arc.)

8

Alderney (Ch.Is.)
Aleutian Is. (Pac.)
Amirante Is. (Ind.)
Andamans (Ind.)
Anglesey (Wales)
Antilles Is. (W.I.)
Auckland Is. (N.Z.)
Balearic Is. (Med.)
Barbados (Is.) (W.I.)
Belitung (Indo.)
Belle Ile (Fr.)

Bermudas (Atl.)

Berneray (Scot.)

Billiton (Indo.)

Bismarck Arch. (Pac.)

Bissagos Is. (W.Af.)

Bornholm (Den.)

Campbell I. (N.Z.)

Canaries (Atl.)

Caroline Is. (Pac.)

Colonsay (Scot.)

Copeland I. (N.I.)

Cyclades Is. (Gr.)

Desertas Is. (Atl.)

Dominica (W.I.)

Dugi Otok (Cro.)

Fair Isle (Scot.)

Falkland Is. (Atl.)

Flinders (Austral.)

Friendly Is. (Pac.)

Furneaux Is. (Austral.)

Gökçeada (Turk.)

Guernsey (Ch.Is.)

Hebrides (Scot.)

Hokkaido (Jap.)

Hong Kong (China)

Jan Mayen (Arc.)

Juventud, I. de la (Cuba)

Kangaroo Is. (Austral.)

Kermadec Is. (Pac.)

Krakatoa (v.) (Indo.)

Ladrones (Pac.)

Lord Howe Is. (Austral.)

Magerøya (Arc.)

Mallorca (Med.)

Manihiki Is. (Pac.)

Marianas (Pac.)

Marshall Is. (Pac.)

Melville I. (Austral.)

Melville I. (Can.)

Mindanao (Philip.)

Miquelon (Can.)

Mitylene (Gr.)

Moluccas (Indo.)

Mustique (W.I.)

Pitcairn Is. (Pac.)

Portland, I. of (Eng.)

Pribilov Is. (Pac.)

Príncipe (W.Af.)

Quelpart (S. Korea)

St Helena (Atl.)

St Martin (W.I.)

St Thomas (W.I.)

Sakhalin (Rus.)

Sandwich Is. (Pac.)

Sardinia (Med.)

Scillies, Is. of (Eng.)

Seriphos (Gr.)

Shetland Is. (Scot.)

Skopelos (Gr.)

Somerset I. (Arc.)

Sri Lanka (Asia)

Starbuck (Pac.)

Sulawesi (Indo.)

Tasmania (Austral.)

Tenerife (v.) (Atl.)

Thousand Is. (N.Am.)

Tortugas Is. (W.I.)

Trinidad (W.I.)

Unalaska (USA)

Valencia I. (Ire.)

Victoria I. (Can.)

Viti-Levu (Fiji)

Vlieland (Neth.)
Watlings I. (W.I.)
Windward Is. (W.I.)
Zanzibar (E.Af.)

9

Admiralty Is. (Pac.)
Anticosti, Ile d' (Can.)
Ascension (Atl.)
Benbecula (Scot.)
Cape Verde Is. (Atl.)
Caribbees Is. (W.I.)
Carolines (Pac.)
Christmas I. (Pac.)
Christmas I. (Ind.)
Elephanta I. (Ind.)
Eleuthera (W.I.)
Ellesmere I. (Can.)
Erromango (Pac.)
Falklands (Atl.)
Galápagos Is. (v.) (Pac.)
Greenland (Arc.)
Halmahera (Indo.)
Inchkeith (Scot.)
Inishturk (Ire.)
Isle of May (Scot.)
Karpathos (Gr.)
Kerguelen Is. (Ind.)
Lampedusa (Med.)
Langeland (Den.)
Lanzarote (Atl.)
Louisiade Arch. (Pac.)
Manhattan (USA)
Margarita (W.I.)
Marquesas Is. (Pac.)
Marshalls (Pac.)

Mauritius (Ind.)
Melanesia (Pac.)
Nantucket (U.S.A.)
New Guinea (E.I.)
New Ireland (Pac.)
Norderney (Ger.)
Polynesia (Pac.)
Rarotonga (Pac.)
Rodrigues (Ind.)
Saint John (W.I.)
St Nicolas (Atl.)
Saint Paul I. (Pac.)
St Vincent (W.I.)
Santa Cruz (Pac.)
Santa Cruz (Mex.)
Santa Cruz. I. (USA)
Santa Cruz Is. (Pac.)
Santorini (v.) (Gr.)
Scarpanto (Gr.)
Shetlands (Scot.)
Singapore (Asia)
Stromboli (v.) (Med.)
Tabuaeran (Pac.)
Vancouver I. (Can.)
Vanua Levu (Fiji)
Walcheren (Neth.)
Wellesley Is. (Austral.)

10

Ailsa Craig (Scot.)
Bay Islands (C.Am.)
Calamianes (Indo.)
Cape Barren I. (Austral.)
Cape Breton I. (Can.)
Cephalonia (Gr.)
Dirk Hartog I. (Austral.)

Dodecanese (Med.)
Fernando Po (W.Af.)
Formentera (Med.)
Grenadines (W.I.)
Guadeloupe (W.I.)
Heligoland (N.Sea)
Hispaniola (W.I.)
Holy Island (Eng.)
Isle of Dogs (Eng.)
Isle of Mull (Scot.)
Isle of Skye (Scot.)
Kuria Muria Is. (Arab.)
Laccadives (Ind.)
Long Island (USA)
Madagascar (Af.)
Manitoulin I. (Can.)
Martinique (W.I.)
Micronesia (Pac.)
Montserrat (W.I.)
New Britain (Pac.)
New Zealand (Pac.)
North Devon I. (Arc.)
Philippine Is. (Asia)
Puerto Rico (W.I.)
Saint Agnes (Eng.)
Saint Kilda (Scot.)
Saint Kitts (W.I.)
Saint Lucia (W.I.)
Sandlewood I. (Malay.)
Seychelles (Ind.)
West Indies (Caribbean)

Gran Canaria (Atl.)
Grand Canary (Atl.)
Guadalcanal (Pac.)
Hall Islands (Pac.)
Hart's Island (USA)
Isle of Pines (Cuba)
Isle of Pines (Pac.)
Isle of Wight (Eng.)
Isola Grossa (Cro.)
Lakshadweep Is. (Ind.)
Lindisfarne (Eng.)
Lundy Island (Eng.)
Mascarene Is. (Ind.)
Montecristo (It.)
New Hebrides (Pac.)
New Siberian Is. (Arc.)
North Island (N.Z.)
Pantelleria (Med.)
Philippines (Asia)
Rhode Island (USA)
Rottumeroog (Neth.)
Sable Island (Can.)
Saint Helena (Atl.)
Saint Thomas (W.I.)
Sainte Marie (Mad.)
San Salvador (W.I.)
Scilly Isles (Eng.)
Sint Maarten (W.I.)
South Island (N.Z.)
Southampton I. (Can.)
Spitsbergen (Arc.)

11

Axel Heiberg (Arc.)
Cook Islands (Pac.)
Eagle Island (Ire.)

12

Baffin Island (Arc.)
Bougainville (Pac.)
British Isles

Devil's Island (S.Am.)
Easter Island (Pac.)
Great Britain (UK)
Isle of Thanet (Eng.)
Marie-Galante (W.I.)
New Caledonia (Pac.)
Newfoundland (Can.)
Novaya Zemlya (Arc.)
Prince Edward I. (Can.)
Puffin Island (Wales)
Saint Vincent (W.I.)
Savai'i Island (Pac.)
South Georgia (Atl.)
St. Barthélemy (W.I.)
Staten Island (USA)
Turks' Islands (W.I.)

13 AND OVER

D'Entrecasteaux Is.
  (Austral.) (14)
Friendly Islands (Pac.) (15)
Isle of Portland (Eng.) (14)
Isle of Purbeck (Eng.) (13)

Isle of Sheppey (Eng.) (13)
Juan Fernandez Is. (Pac.) (13)
Martha's Vineyard (USA)
  (15)
Norfolk Island (Pac.) (13)
Prince Edward Island
  (Can.) (18)
Prince of Wales I. (Malay.) (13)
Prince of Wales I. (Arc.) (13)
Prince Patrick I. (Arc.) (13)
Queen Charlotte Is. (Can.) (14)
St Bartholomew (W.I.) (13)
St Christopher (W.I.) (13)
Saint Eustatius (W.I.) (14)
St Michael's Mount
  (Eng.) (15)
Santa Catalina (Mex.) (13)
South Shetlands (Atl.) (13)
Stewart Island (N.Z.) (13)
Tierra del Fuego (Chile) (14)
Tristan da Cunha (Atl.) (14)
Watling Island (Atl.) (13)

Lakes, inland seas, lochs, loughs, etc.

3 AND 4

Aral (Kaz. and
  Uzbek.)
Ard (Scot.)
Awe (Scot.)
Bala (Wales)
Bear (USA)
Bear (Can.)

Biwa (Jap.)
Chad (Af.)
Como (It.)
Dall (USA)
Derg (N.I.)
Dore (Can.)
Earn (Scot.)
Eil (Scot.)
Erie (Can. and

USA)
Erne (N.I.)
Ewe (Scot.)
Eyre (Austral.)
Há Há (Can.)
Iseo (It.)
Key (Ire.)
Kivu (Af.)
Long (Scot.)

Mask (Ire.)
Mead (USA)
Nemi (It.)
Ness (Scot.)
Oahe (USA)
Ryan (Scot.)
Tana (Eth.)
Tay (Scot.)
Thun (Swit.)
Utah (USA)
Van (Turk.)
Zug (Swit.)

5

Abaya (Eth.)
Baker (Can.)
Clark (USA)
Elton (Rus.)
Etive (Scot.)
Foyle (N.I.)
Frome (Austral.)
Garda (It.)
Hamun (Afghan.)
Honey (USA)
Huron (Can. and USA)
Ilmen (Rus.)
Kossu (Af.)
Kyoga (Af.)
Leech (USA)
Léman (Swit.)
Leven (Scot.)
Lochy (Scot.)
Loyal (Scot.)
Mälar (Swed.)
Maree (Scot.)

Minto (Can.)
Mjøsa (Nor.)
Moore (Austral.)
Morar (Scot.)
Mweru (Cen.Af.)
Neagh (N.I.)
Nevis (Scot.)
Nyasa (Cen.Af.)
Onega (Rus.)
Payne (Can.)
Rainy (Can.)
Rainy (USA)
Shiel (Scot.)
Takoe (USA)
Taupo (N.Z.)
Tumba (Dem. Rep. of Congo)
Urmia (Iran)
Volta (Ghana)

6

Albert (Cen.Af.)
Arkaig (Scot.)
Assynt (Scot.)
Austin (Austral.)
Baikal (Sib.)
Biwako (Jap.)
Chilka (Ind.)
Chilwa (Malawi)
Corrib (Ire.)
Edward (E.Af.)
Ennell (Ire.)
Geneva (Swit.)
George (Uganda)
George (USA)
IJssel (Neth.)

Indian (USA)
Itasca (USA)
Kariba (Af.)
Khanka (Asia)
Kossou (Ivory Coast)
Ladoga (Rus.)
Lomond (Scot.)
Lop Nor (China)
Lugano (Swit.)
Malawi (Cen.Af.)
Martin (USA)
Nasser (Egypt)
Natron (Tanz.)
Nyanza (Bur.)
Oneida (USA)
Peipus (Est. and Rus.)
Placid (USA)
Poyang (China)
Quoich (Scot.)
Rideau (Can.)
Rudolf (Kenya)
St-Jean (Can.)
St John (USA)
Shasta (USA)
Shirwa (Malawi)
Simcoe (Can.)
Stuart (Can.)
Te Anau (N.Z.)
Tuz Göl (Turk.)
Vänern (Swed.)
Viedma (Arg.)
Vyrnwy (Wales)
Wanaka (N.Z.)
Zürich (Swit.)

7

Abitibi (Can.)
Balaton (Hung.)
Belfast (N.I.)
Benmore (N.Z.)
Blanche (Austral.)
Caspian (Asia)
Chapala (Mex.)
Chilika (Ind.)
Dead Sea (Isr. and Jord.)
Etawney (Can.)
Fannich (Scot.)
Galilee (Isr.)
Hickory (USA)
Hirakud (Ind.)
Hjalmar (Swed.)
Idi Amin (Af.)
Iliamna (USA)
Katrine (Scot.)
Koko Nor (China)
La Croix (Can. and USA)
Loch Eil (Scot.)
Loch Tay (Scot.)
Lucerne (Swit.)
Muskoka (Can.)
Nipigon (Can.)
Nu Jiang (China and Burma)
Ontario (Can. and USA)
Perugia (It.)
Pyramid (USA)
Qinghai (China)
Quesnel (Can.)
Rannoch (Scot.)
Rosseau (Can.)
Rutland (Eng.)
Rybinsk (Rus.)

St Clair (Can. and USA)
Sheelin (Ire.)
Tezcuco (Mex.)
Torrens (Austral.)
Turkana (Kenya)
Tyrrell (Austral.)
Ugashik (USA)

8

Balkhash (Kaz.)
Bear Lake (USA)
Becharof (USA)
Chiemsee (Ger.)
Chowilla (Austral.)
Clywedog
  (Wales)
Coniston (Eng.)
Dongting (China)
Drummond (USA)
Gairdner (Austral.)
Grasmere (Eng.)
Hirfanli (Turk.)
Humboldt (USA)
Issyk-Kul (Kyr.)
Kakhovka (Ukr.)
Kawartha (Can.)
Kootenay (Can.)
Loch Ness (Scot.)
Loch Ryan (Scot.)
Luichart (Scot.)
Maggiore (It.)
Manitoba (Can.)
Menindee (Austral.)
Michigan (USA)
Reindeer (Can.)
Seaforth (Scot.)

Stefanie (E.Af.)
Superior (USA)
Tarawera (N.Z.)
Titicaca (Peru)
Tonle Sap (Cambodia)
Tungtin'g (China)
Victoria (Cen.Af.)
Wakatipu (N.Z.)
Winnipeg (Can.)

9

Argentino (S.Am.)
Athabasca (Can.)
Bangweulu (Zamb.)
Champlain (Can. and USA)
Constance (Swit.)
Ennerdale (Eng.)
Great Bear (Can.)
Great Lake (Austral.)
Great Salt (USA)
Hindmarsh (Austral.)
Honey Lake (USA)
Killarney (Ire.)
Kuibyshev (Rus.)
Loch Leven (Scot.)
Loch Maree (Scot.)
Loch Nevis (Scot.)
Mai-Ndombe (Dem. Rep. of Congo)
Maracaibo (Venez.)
Mille Lacs (USA)
Moosehead (USA)
Neuchâtel (Swit.)
Nicaragua (C.Am.)
Nipissing (Can.)
Rutanzige (E.Af.)

Salton Sea (USA)
Sempacher (Swit.)
Teshekpuk (USA)
Thirlmere (Eng.)
Trasimeno (It.)
Tustumena (USA)
Ullswater (Eng.)
Wast Water (Eng.)
Winnebago (USA)
Wollaston (Can.)

10

Brokopondo (S.Am.)
Buttermere (Eng.)
Great Lakes (Can. and USA)
Great Slave (Can.)
Haweswater (Eng.)
IJsselmeer (Neth.)
Indian Lake (USA)
Loch Lomond (Scot.)
Lough Neagh (N.I.)
Michigamme (Can.)
Mistassini (Can.)
Okeechobee (USA)
Rydal Water (Eng.)
Serpentine (Eng.)
Strangford (N.I.)
Tanganyika (E.Af.)
Windermere (Eng.)
Xochimilco (Mex.)

11 AND OVER

Albert Edward Nyanza (Af.) (18)
Albert Nyanza (Af.) (12)
Bassenthwaite (Eng.) (13)

Bitter Lakes (Egypt) (11)
Cabora Bassa (Af.) (11)
Coniston Water (Eng.) (13)
Derwent Water (Eng.) (12)
Diefenbaker (Can.) (11)
Grand Coulee (USA) (11)
Great Salt Lake (USA) (13)
Great Slave Lake (Can.) (14)
Lake of the Woods (Can. and
    USA) (14)
Lesser Slave Lake (Can.) (15)
Loch Katrine (Scot.) (11)
Neusiedler See (Aust. and
    Hung.) (13)

Pend Oreille (USA) (11)
Pontchartrain (USA) (13)
The Cooroong (Austral.) (11)
Timiskaming (Can.) (11)
Upper Klamath (USA) (12)
Victoria Nyanza (Af.) (14)
Vierwaldstättersee
    (Swit.) (18)
Virginia Water (Eng.) (13)
Winnibigoshish (USA) (14)
Winnipegosis (Can.) (12)
Yellowstone (USA) (11)

Mountains

H.=Hill; Hs.=Hills; M.=Mountain (commonly used *after*
name); Ms.=Mountains; Mt.=Mount, Monte, or Mont
(commonly used *before* name); (v.)=volcanic

2–4

Abu, Mt. (Ind.)
Adam, Mt.
    (Falkland Is.)
Alps (Eur.)
Blue Ms. (Austral.)
Blue Ms.(USA)
Caha Ms. (Ire.)
Cook, Mt. (N.Z.)
Ebal, Mt. (Jord.)
Etna, Mt. (v.) (Sic.)
Fuji, Mt. (v.) (Jap.)
Harz Ms. (Ger.)

Ida, Mt. (Crete)
Iron M. (USA)
Jura Ms. (Eur.)
K2 (Him.)
Kea (v.) (Hawaii)
Kibo, Mt. (Tanz.)
Meru, Mt. (Tanz.)
Naga Hs. (Ind.)
Ore Ms. (Ger.)
Ossa, Mt.
    (Austral.)
Ossa, Mt. (Gr.)
Ural Ms. (Rus.)
Zug M. (Ger.)

5

Adams, Mt. (USA)
Altai Ms. (Him.)
Andes (S.Am.)
Aripo M. (Trin.)
Athos, Mt. (Gr.)
Atlas Ms. (Af.)
Black Ms. (USA)
Black Ms. (Wales)
Blanc, Mt. (Alps)
Brown, Mt.
    (Austral.)
Cenis, Mt. (Alps)

Coast Ms. (Can.)
Djaja, Mt. (Indo.)
Downs, The (Eng.)
Eiger (Swit.)
Elgon, Mt. (Uganda)
Galty Ms. (Ire.)
Ghats, The (Ind.)
Green Ms. (USA)
Hekla (v.) (Iceland)
Kenya, Mt. (E.Af.)
Logan, Mt. (Can.)
Maipo (v.) (Arg.)
Minto, Mt. (Antarc.)
Ochil Hs. (Scot.)
Ozark Ms. (USA)
Pelée, Mt. (v.) (W.I.)
Potro M. (Chile)
Rocky Ms. (Can. and USA)
Sinai, Mt. (Egypt)
Snowy Ms. (Austral.)
Table M. (SA)
Tabor, Mt. (Isr.)
Tatra Ms. (Slov. and Pol.)
Urals (Rus.)
White Ms. (USA)
Wolds, The (Eng.)

6

Ararat, Mt. (Turk.)
Balkan Ms. (Eur.)
Bogong, Mt. (Austral.)
Bonete, Mt. (Arg.)
Carmel, Mt. (Isr.)
Darwin Ms. (Chile)
Elbert, Mt. (USA)
Elbrus, Mt. (Rus. and Geo.)

Elburz Ms. (Iran)
Erebus, Mt. (v.) (Antarc.)
Hermon, Mt. (Syria)
Hoggar Ms. (Alg.)
Juncal (v.) (Chile)
Katmai, Mt. (v.) (Alaska)
Kazbek, Mt. (Geo.)
Koryak Ms. (Rus.)
Lennox Hs. (Scot.)
Lhotse, Mt. (Him.)
Makalu, Mt. (Him.)
Masaya (v.) (C.Am.)
Mendip Hs. (Eng.)
Mourne Ms. (Ire.)
Muztag (China)
Olives, Mt. of (Isr.)
Ortles (It.)
Ozarks (USA)
Pamirs (Asia)
Pelion, Mt. (Gr.)
Pindus Ms. (Gr.)
Pissis, Mt. (Arg.)
Robson, Mt. (Can.)
Sidlaw Hs. (Scot.)
Sidley, Mt. (Antarc.)
Taunus Ms. (Ger.)
Taurus Ms. (Turk.)
Vosges Ms. (Fr.)
Zagros Ms. (Iran)

7

Belukha (Kaz.)
Ben More (Scot.)
Bermina (It.)
Big Horn Ms. (USA)
Brocken, Mt. (Ger.)

Cascade Ms. (USA)
Cheviot Hs. (Eng. and Scot.)
Dapsang, Mt. (Him.)
Darling Ms. (Austral.)
Estrela (Ms.) (Port.)
Everest, Mt. (Him.)
Helicon, Mt. (Gr.)
Hoffman, Mt. (USA)
Illampu, Mt. (Boliv.)
Jaintia Ms. (Assam)
Kilauea (v.) (Pac.)
Lebanon, Mt. (Leb.)
Malvern Hs. (Eng.)
Mendips (Eng.)
Nan Ling Ms. (China)
Nan Shan Ms. (China)
Nilgiri Hs. (Ind.)
Olympus, Mt. (Gr.)
Orizaba (v.) (Mex.)
Palomar, Mt. (USA)
Preseli Ms. (Wales)
Rainier, Mt. (USA)
Rhodope Ms. (Turk.)
Rockies (Can. and USA)
Roraima, Mt. (S.Am.)
Ruahine Ms. (N.Z.)
Ruapehu, Mt. (N.Z.)
St Elias Ms. (Can. and USA)
St Elias, Mt. (Alaska)
San Juan Ms. (USA)
Siwalik Hs. (Ind.)
Skiddaw, Mt. (Eng.)
Snowdon, Mt. (Wales)
Stanley, Mt. (Uganda and
    Dem. Rep. of Congo)
Sudetes (Cze. and Pol.)

Triglav, Mt. (Sloven.)
Vindhya Ms. (Ind.)
Whitney, Mt. (USA)

8

Aravalli Ms. (Ind.)
Ben Nevis (Scot.)
Ben Venue (Scot.)
Ben Wyvis (Scot.)
Cambrian Ms. (Wales)
Cameroon, Mt. (Cameroon)
Catskill Ms. (USA)
Caucasus Ms. (Eur.)
Cévennes (Fr.)
Cheviots (Eng. and Scot.)
Chiltern Hs. (Eng.)
Cotopaxi (v.) (Ecuad.)
Cotswold Hs. (Eng.)
Cumbrian Ms. (Eng.)
Damavand, Mt. (Iran)
Flinders (Ms.) (Austral.)
Fujiyama (v.) (Jap.)
Goat Fell (Mt.) (Scot.
Hualapei Ms. (USA)
Illimani, Mt. (v.) (Bol.)
Jaya Peak (Indo.)
Jungfrau (Swit.)
Katahdin, Mt. (USA)
Kinabalu (v.) (Born.)
Krakatoa (v.) (Indo.)
McKinley, Mt. (USA)
Mitchell, Mt. (USA)
Mulhacén (Sp.)
Pennines (Eng.)
Pentland Hs. (Scot.)
Pyrenees Ms. (Eur.)

Quantock Hs. (Eng.)
Rajmahal Hs. (Ind.)
Rushmore, Mt. (USA)
Snaefell, Mt. (IOM)
Sulaiman Ms. (Pak.)
Tarawera, Mt. (N.Z.)
The Downs (Eng.)
The Ghats (Ind.)
The Wolds (Eng.)
Tien Shan Ms. (Asia)
Vesuvius (v.) (It.)
Whitmore Ms. (Antarc.)
Wrangell, Mt. (USA)

9

Aconcagua (v.) (Arg.)
Adam's Peak (Sri)
Allegheny Ms. (USA)
Annapurna (Him.)
Apennines (It.)
Ben Lawers (Scot.)
Black Dome (USA)
Blue Ridge Ms. (USA)
Carstensz (Indo.)
Chilterns (Eng.)
Cleveland Hs. (Eng.)
Communism (Taj.)
Cotswolds (Eng.)
Dolomites (It.)
Grampians (Scot.)
Helvellyn, Mt. (Eng.)
Himalayas (Asia)
Hindu-Kush (Asia)
Huascarán (v.) (Peru)
Karakoram (Asia)
Kosciusko, Mt. (Austral.)

Lafayette, Mt. (USA)
Lenin Peak (Kyr.)
Liverpool (Austral.)
Mont Blanc (Alps)
Mont Cenis (Alps)
Monte Rosa (Alps)
Naga Hills (Ind.)
Parnassus, Mt. (Gr.)
Pic du Midi (Pyr.)
Pikes Peak (USA)
Rakaposhi (Ind.)
Ras Dashan (Eth.)
Ruwenzori Ms. (Uganda and
    Dem. Rep. of Congo)
Solfatara (v.) (It.)
Stromboli (v.) (Med.)
Thian-Shan Ms. (Asia)
Tirich Mir (Mt.) (Pak.)
Tongariro, Mt. (v.) (N.Z.)
Tupungato (v.) (Arg.)
Weisshorn (Swit.)
Yablonovy (Rus.)
Zugspitze (Ger.)

10

Adirondack Ms. (USA)
Arakan Yoma Ms. (Burma)
Baker Butte (v.) (USA)
Ben Macdhui (Scot.)
Cader Idris (Wales)
Cairngorms (Scot.)
Cantabrian Ms. (Sp.)
Carpathian Ms. (Eur.)
Chimborazo (v.) (Ecuad.)
Dent du Midi (Swit.)
Dhaulagiri, Mt. (Him.)

Diablerets, Mt. (Swit.)
Erzgebirge (Ger.)
Graian Alps (Eur.)
Khyber Pass (Afghan., Pak.)
Kuh-i-Taftan (v.) (Iran)
Kunlun Shan Ms. (China)
Lammermuir Hs. (Scot.)
Laurentian Ms. (Can.)
Matterhorn (Alps)
Moel Fammau, Mt. (Wales)
Monte Corno (It.)
Ochil Hills (Scot.)
Pinlimmon, Mt. (Wales)
Pobeda Peak
    (China and Kyr.)
Saint Elias (Alaska)
Saint Elias Ms. (Can. and
    USA)
Wetterhorn (Swit.)

11

Adirondacks (USA)
Alleghenies (USA)
Appalachian Ms. (USA)
Bernese Alps (Swit.)
Brenner Pass (Aust. and It.)
Brooks Range (USA)
Carpathians (Eur.)
Coast Ranges (Can.)
Corno Grande (It.)
Descabezado (v.) (Chile)
Dinaric Alps (Eur.)
Drachenfels (Ger.)
Drakensberg Ms. (SA)
Drakenstein, Mt. (SA)
Hochstetter, Mt. (N.Z.)

Kilimanjaro, Mt. (Tanz.)
Koryak Range (Rus.)
La Soufrière (v.) (W.I.)
Livingstone Ms. (Tanz.)
Livingstone Ms. (N.Z.)
Mendip Hills (Eng.)
Nanga Parbat (Him.)
Ortler Spitz (It.)
Owen Stanley (Papua)
Pennine Alps (Eur.)
Scafell Pike (Eng.)
Sierra Madre Ms.
    (Mex.)
Simplon Pass (Alps)
Splügen Pass (Swit.)
Swabian Alps (Ger.)
Vatnajökull (Iceland)

12

Appalachians (USA)
Cheviot Hills
    (Eng. and Scot.)
Citlaltépetl (Mex.)
Godwin Austen, Mt.
    (Him.)
Gran Paradiso (It.)
Ingleborough, Mt. (Eng.)
Kanchenjunga, Mt. (Him.)
Kinchinjunga, Mt. (Him.)
Malvern Hills (Eng.)
Maritime Alps (Fr., It.)
Monte Cassino (It.)
Nilgiri Hills (Ind.)
Peak District (Eng.)
Pennine Chain (Eng.)
Popocatépetl (v.) (Mex.)

Roncesvalles (v) (Pyr.)
Saint Gothard, Mt. (Swit.)
Schiehallion, Mt. (Scot.)
Sierra Nevada Ms. (Sp.)
Siwalik Hills (Ind.)
Slieve Donard (N.I.)
Tinguiririca (v.) (Chile)

13 AND OVER

Black Dome Peak
  (USA) (13)
Blue Mountains
  (Austral.) (13)
Blue Mountains (USA) (13)
Brecon Beacons (Wales)
  (13)
Carrauntuohil, Mt. (Ire.)
  (13)
Cerro de Mulhacén (Sp.) (14)
Cerro del Potro (Chile) (13)
Chiltern Hills (Eng.) (13)
Chirripó Grande
  (Costa Rica) (14)
Coast Mountains (Can.) (14)
Communism Peak (Taj.) (13)
Cotswold Hills (Eng.) (13)
Fichtelgebirge Ms. (Ger.) (14)
Finsteraahorn, Mt. (Swit.)
  (13)
Flinders Ranges (Austral.)
  (14)
Grossglockner (Aust.) (13)
Knockmealdown Ms.
  (Ire.) (13)
Macgillicuddy's Reeks
  (Ire.) (19)

Margherita Peak (Uganda
  and Dem. Rep. of Congo)
  (14)
Massif Central (Fr.) (13)
Mont Aux Sources
  (Lesotho) (14)
Mount of Olives (Isr.) (13)
Ojos del Salado (v.) (Chile
  and Arg. 13)
Pentland Hills (Scot.) (13)
Pidurutalagala (Sri) (14)
Rocky Mountains
  (Can. and USA) (14)
St Bernard Pass (Swit.) (13)
St Golthard Pass (Swit.) (14)
Serra de Estrela (Ms.) (Port.)
  (14)
Sierra Maestra (Ms.)
  (Cuba) (13)
Stanovoy Range (Rus.) (13)
Sudeten Mountains (Cze. and
  Pol.) (16)
Table Mountain (SA) (13)
Tabor Mountain (Isr.) (13)

Oceans and seas

3 AND 4

Aral S. (Kaz., Uzbek.)
Azov, S. of (Ukr., Rus.)
Dead S. (Jord., Isr.)
Java S. (Indo.)
Kara S. (Rus.)
Red S. (Egypt, Arab.)
Ross S. (Antarc.)
Savu S. (Indo.)
Sulu S. (Philip.)

5

Banda S. (Indo.)
Black S. (Eur., Turk.)
Ceram S. (Indo.)
China S. (China)
Coral S. (Indo.)
Irish S. (Brit. Isles)
Japan, S. of (Jap.)
North S. (Eur.)
Timor S. (Indo.)
White S. (Rus.)

6

Aegean S. (Gr., Turk.)
Arctic O.
Baltic S. (N. Eur.)
Bering S. (Pac.)
Flores S. (Indo.)
Indian O.
Ionian S. (Gr.)
Laptev S. (Rus.)
Tasman S. (Austral.)

Yellow S. (China)

7

Andaman S. (Indo.)
Arabian S. (Ind.)
Arafura S. (Austral.)
Barents S. (Rus.)
Caspian S. (Eur., Asia)
Celebes S. (Indo.)
Marmora, S. of (Turk.)
Molucca S. (Indo.)
Okhotsk, S. of (Rus.)
Pacific O.
Weddell S. (Antarc.)

8

Adriatic S. (Med.)
Amundsen S. (Antarc.)
Atlantic O.
Beaufort S. (Can.)
Bismarck S. (Pac.)
Ligurian S. (It.)
Sargasso S. (Atl.)
Sulawesi S. (Indo.)

9

Antarctic O.
Caribbean S. (Am.)
East China S. (China)
Greenland S. (Green.)
Norwegian S. (Nor.)
Waddenzee (Neth.)
Zuider Zee (Neth.)
Zuyder Zee (Neth.)

10 AND OVER

Bellingshausen S.
 (Antarc.) (14)
East Siberian S. (Rus.) (12)

Mediterranean S. (Eur., Af.,
 Asia) (13)
South China S. (China) (10)
Tyrrhenian S. (Med.) (10)

Ports

3 AND 4

Acre (Isr.)
Aden (Yemen)
Akko (Isr.)
Baku (Azer.)
Bar (Monte.)
Bari (It.)
Cebu (Philip.)
Cobh (Ire.)
Cork (Ire.)
Deal (Eng.)
Elat (Isr.)
Erie (USA)
Hull (Eng.)
Ilo (Peru)
Kiel (Ger.)
Kobe (Jap.)
Lüda (China)
Okha (Rus.)
Oran (Alg.)
Oslo (Nor.)
Para (Braz.)
Pula (Cro.)
Riga (Latvia.)
Rye (Eng.)
Safi (Moroc.)
Suez (Egypt)

Tain (Scot.)
Tema (Ghana)
Wick (Scot.)

5

Akyab (Burma)
Amboy (USA)
Arica (Chile)
Barry (Wales)
Basra (Iraq)
Beira (Moz.)
Belém (Braz.)
Brest (Fr.)
Cadiz (Sp.)
Canea (Gr.)
Ceuta (Moroc.)
Colón (Panama)
Corfu (Gr.)
Dakar (Senegal)
Delft (Neth.)
Dover (Eng.)
Dubai (Dubai)
Eilat (Isr.)
Emden (Ger.)
Gaeta (It.)
Galle (Sri.)
Genoa (It.)
Haifa (Isr.)

Hanko (Fin.)
Havre, Le (Fr.)
Izmir (Turk.)
Kerch (Ukr.)
Kochi (Jap.)
Kotor (Monte.)
Lagos (Nig.)
Larne (N. Ire.)
Leith (Scot.)
Lulea (Swed.)
Mahón (Minorca)
Malmö (Swed.)
Mocha (Yemen)
Osaka (Jap.)
Ostia (It.)
Palma (Sp.)
Palos (Sp.)
Poole (Eng.)
Pusan (S. Korea)
Rabat (Moroc.)
Reval (Est.)
Scapa (Scot.)
Split (Cro.)
Tiksi (Rus.)
Trani (It.)
Tunis (Tun.)
Turku (Fin.)
Varna (Bulg.)
Visby (Swed.)
Yaita (Ukr.)
Ystad (Swed.)

6

Agadir (Moroc.)
Ancona (It.)
Ashdod (Isr.)

Balboa (Panama)
Bastia (Cors.)
Beirut (Lebanon)
Bergen (Nor.)
Bilbao (Sp.)
Bombay (Ind.)
Boston (USA)
Bremen (Ger.)
Calais (Fr.)
Callao (Peru)
Cannes (Fr.)
Chefoo (China)
Cochin (Ind.)
Dairen (China)
Danzig (Pol.)
Darwin (Austral.)
Dieppe (Fr.)
Douala (Cameroon)
Dunbar (Scot.)
Dundee (Scot.)
Durban (SA)
Fdérik (Mauritania)
Fuzhou (China)
Gdansk (Pol.)
Gdynia (Pol.)
Haldia (Ind.)
Hankow (China)
Hobart (Tas.)
Izmail (Ukr.)
Jeddah (Saudi)
Kalmar (Swed.)
Kuwait (Kuwait)
Larvik (Nor.)
Lisbon (Port.)
Lobito (Angola)
London (Eng.)

Luanda (Ang.)
Lüshun (China)
Madras (Ind.)
Málaga (Sp.)
Manila (Philip.)
Matadi (Dem. Rep. of Congo)
Mtwara (Tanz.)
Mumbai (Ind.)
Naples (It.)
Narvik (Nor.)
Nelson (N.Z.)
Odense (Den.)
Odessa (Ukr.)
Oporto (Port.)
Ostend (Belg.)
Padang (Indo.)
Patras (Gr.)
Penang (Malay.)
Ramsey (IOM)
Recife (Braz.)
Rhodes (Gr.)
Rijeka (Cro.)
Santos (Braz.)
Sittwe (Burma)
Skikda (Alg.)
Smyrna (Turk.)
Suakin (Sudan)
Sydney (Austral.)
Tainan (Taiwan)
Tetuán (Moroc.)
Toulon (Fr.)
Tromsø (Nor.)
Venice (It.)
Weihai (China)
Wismar (Ger.)
Yantai (China)

7

Aalborg (Den.)
Abidjan (Ivory Coast)
Ajaccio (Cors.)
Algiers (Alg.)
Antwerp (Belg.)
Bangkok (Thai.)
Belfast (N.I.)
Bushehr (Iran)
Cardiff (Wales)
Cattaro (Monte.)
Cayenne (Fr. Guiana)
Chatham (Eng.)
Colombo (Sri)
Corunna (Sp.)
Cotonou (Benin)
Dampier (Austral.)
Detroit (USA)
Donegal (Ire.)
Dundalk (Ire.)
Dunkirk (Fr.)
Foochow (China)
Funchal (Port.)
Geelong (Austral.)
Gotland (Swed.)
Grimsby (Eng.)
Guaymas (Mex.)
Halifax (Can.)
Hamburg (Ger.)
Harwich (Eng.)
Hodeida (Yemen)
Horsens (Den.)
Houston (USA)
Izmayil (Ukr.)
Jakarta (Indo.)
Karachi (Pak.)

Keelung
  (Taiwan)
Kitimat (Can.)
Kowloon (Hong Kong)
La Plata (Arg.)
Larnaca (Cyprus)
Leghorn (It.)
Le Havre (Fr.)
Livorno (It.)
Marsala (It.)
Melilla (Moroc.)
Messina (It.)
Mogador (Moroc.)
Mombasa (Kenya)
New York (USA)
Norfolk (USA)
Okhotsk (Rus.)
Palermo (It.)
Petsamo (Fin.)
Piraeus (Gr.)
Rangoon (Burma)
Rosario (Arg.)
Rostock (Ger.)
Salerno (It.)
San Juan
  (Puerto Rico)
Seattle (USA)
Shantou (China)
Stettin (Pol.)
Swansea (Wales)
Tallinn (Est.)
Tangier (Moroc.)
Tianjin (China)
Tilbury (Eng.)
Trapani (It.)
Trieste (It.)

Tripoli (Libya)
Yingkou (China)
Youghal (Ire.)

8

Abu Dhabi (Abu Dhabi)
Adelaide (Austral.)
Alicante (Sp.)
Arrecife (Sp.)
Auckland (N.Z.)
Benghazi (Libya)
Bordeaux (Fr.)
Boulogne (Fr.)
Brindisi (It.)
Brisbane (Austral.)
Budapest (Hung.)
Calcutta (Ind.)
Cape Town (SA)
Cocanada (Ind.)
Coquimbo (Chile)
Cuxhaven (Ger.)
Damietta (Egypt)
Djibouti (Djibouti)
Dunleary (Ire.)
El Ferrol (Sp.)
Elsinore (Den.)
Falmouth (Eng.)
Flushing (Neth.)
Freetown (Sierra Leone)
Gisborne (N.Z.)
Göteborg (Swed.)
Greenock (Scot.)
Hakodate (Jap.)
Halmstad (Swed.)
Hangzhou (China)
Helsinki (Fin.)

Holyhead (Wales)
Honfleur (Fr.)
Hong Kong (China)
Honolulu (Hawaii)
Istanbul (Turk.)
Kakinada (Ind.)
Kingston (Jam.)
La Coruña (Sp.)
La Guaira (Venez.)
Llanelli (Wales)
Macassar (Indo.)
Makassar (Indo.)
Montreal (Can.)
Moulmein (Burma)
Murmansk (Rus.)
Nagasaki (Jap.)
Nakhodka (Rus.)
Newhaven (Eng.)
Newhaven (USA)
Nyköping (Swed.)
Pechenga (Rus.)
Pembroke (Wales)
Penzance (Eng.)
Plymouth (Eng.)
Portland (Eng.)
Port Said (Egypt)
Rosslare (Ire.)
St Helier (Ch. Is.)
Sandwich (Eng.)
Shanghai (China)
Szczecin (Pol.)
Taganrog (Rus.)
Takoradi (Ghana)
Tamatave (Mad.)
Tientsin (China)
Veracruz (Mex.)

Weymouth (Eng.)
Yokohama (Jap.)

9

Algeciras (Sp.)
Amsterdam (Neth.)
Archangel (Rus.)
Ardrossan (Scot.)
Avonmouth (Eng.)
Baltimore (USA)
Barcelona (Sp.)
Cartagena (Col.)
Cartagena (Sp.)
Cherbourg (Fr.)
Churchill (Can.)
Cristóbal (Panama)
Devonport (Eng.)
Dubrovnik (Cro.)
Ermoupoli (Gr.)
Esquimalt (Can.)
Essaouira (Moroc.)
Europoort (Neth.)
Fishguard (Wales)
Flensburg (Ger.)
Fremantle (Austral.)
Galveston (USA)
Gravesend (Eng.)
Guayaquil (Ecuador)
Helsingör (Den.)
Hiroshima (Jap.)
Inhambane (Moz.)
Kagoshima (Jap.)
Kaohsiung (Taiwan)
King's Lynn (Eng.)
Kolobrzeg (Pol.)
Las Palmas (Sp.)

Leningrad (Rus.)
Liverpool (Eng.)
Lyttelton (N.Z.)
Melbourne (Austral.)
Mossel Bay (SA)
Nantucket (USA)
Newcastle (Austral.)
Newcastle (Eng.)
Owen Sound (Can.)
Pensacola (USA)
Port Klang (Malay.)
Port Louis (Mauritius)
Port Mahon (Sp.)
Port Natal (SA)
Port Royal (Jam.)
Port Sudan (Sudan)
Portmadoc (Wales)
Porto Novo (Benin)
Rotterdam (Neth.)
Scapa Flow (Scot.)
Sheerness (Eng.)
Singapore (Singapore)
Stavanger (Nor.)
Stockholm (Swed.)
Stornoway (Scot.)
Toamasina (Mad.)
Trondheim (Nor.)
Vancouver (Can.)
Zeebrugge (Belg.)

10

Alexandria (Egypt)
Barnstaple (Eng.)
Bridgeport (USA)
Casablanca (Moroc.)
Charleston (USA)

Chittagong (Ind.)
Constantza (Rom.)
Copenhagen (Den.)
East London (SA)
Felixstowe (Eng.)
Folkestone (Eng.)
George Town (Malay.)
Gothenburg (Swed.)
Hammerfest (Nor.)
Hartlepool (Eng.)
Jersey City (USA)
La Rochelle (Fr.)
Los Angeles (USA)
Marseilles (Fr.)
Montego Bay (Jam.)
Montevideo (Uruguay)
New Bedford (USA)
New Orleans (USA)
Nouadhibou (Mauritania)
Pernambuco (Braz.)
Port Arthur (China)
Port Kelang (Malay.)
Portsmouth (Eng.)
Rock Harbor (USA)
San Juan Bay (Peru)
Simonstown (SA)
Sunderland (Eng.)
Teignmouth (Eng.)
Travemünde (Ger.)
Valparaíso (Chile)
Vlissingen (Neth.)
Whitstable (Eng.)

11

Bremerhaven (Ger.)
Buenos Aires (Arg.)

Cinque Ports (Eng.)
Dar es Salaam (Tanz.)
Grangemouth (Scot.)
Helsingborg (Swed.)
Hermoupolis (Gr.)
Pearl Harbor (Hawaii)
Pondicherry (Ind.)
Port Glasgow (Scot.)
Port Jackson (Austral.)
Port Moresby (Papua)
Port of Spain (Trinidad)
Saint Helier (Ch.Is.)
St Peter Port (Ch.Is.)
Shimonoseki (Jap.)
Southampton (Eng.)
Trincomalee (Sri)
Vladivostok (Rus.)

12

Barranquilla (Col.)
Buenaventura (Col.)
Dun Laoghaire (Ire.)
Kota Kinabalu (Malay.)

Kristiansund (Nor.)
Masulipatnam (Ind.)
Milford Haven (Wales)
North Shields (Eng.)
Port Adelaide (Austral.)
Port Harcourt (Nig.)
Port Sunlight (Eng.)
Rio de Janeiro (Braz.)
St Petersburg (Rus.)
San Francisco (USA)

13 AND 14

Constantinople (Turk.) (14)
Frederikshavn (Den.) (13)
Machilipatnam (Ind.) (13)
Middlesbrough (Eng.) (13)
Petropavlovsk (Kaz.) (13)
Port Elizabeth (SA) (13)
Puerto Cabello (Venez.) (13)
Puerto de Hierro (Venez.) (14)
Santiago de Cuba (Cuba) (14)
Trois-Rivières (Can.) (13)
Wilhelmshaven (Ger.) (13)

Provinces, cantons, districts, regions, dependent states, etc.

3 AND 4

ACT (Austral.)	Bern (Swit.)	Goa (Ind.)
Aceh (Indo.)	Cher (Fr.)	Ica (Peru)
Ain (Fr.)	Diu (Ind.)	Iowa (USA)
Aube (Fr.)	Eure (Fr.)	Jaén (Sp.)
Aude (Fr.)	Fars (Iran)	Java (Indo.)
Bali (Indo.)	Gard (Fr.)	Jura (Fr.)
Bari (It.)	Gaza (Moz.)	Kano (Nig.)
	Gers (Fr.)	Komi (Rus.)

León (Sp.)
Lima (Peru)
Lodz (Pol.)
Lot (Fr.)
Lugo. (Sp.)
Nord (Fr.)
Ohio (USA)
Oise (Fr.)
Ondo (Nig.)
Orne (Fr.)
Oudh (Ind.)
Pará (Braz.)
Pegu (Burma)
Perm (Rus.)
Pisa (It.)
Qom (Iran)
Qum (Iran)
Saar (Ger.)
Sind (Pak.)
Tarn (Fr.)
Tuva (Rus.)
Uri (Swit.)
Utah (USA)
Var (Fr.)
Vaud (Swit.)
Zug (Swit.)

5

Achin (Indo.)
Adana (Turk.)
Aisne (Fr.)
Altai (Rus.)
Anhui (China)
Anjou (Fr.)
Assam (Ind.)
Baden (Ger.)

Bahía (Braz.)
Banat (Eur.)
Basel (Swit.)
Basle (Swit.)
Bauchi (Nig.)
Béarn (Fr.)
Beira (Port.)
Benue (Nig.)
Berne (Swit.)
Berry (Fr.)
Bihar (Ind.)
Cadiz (Sp.)
Ceará (Braz.)
Daman (Ind.)
Delhi (Ind.)
Doubs (Fr.)
Drome (Fr.)
Eifel (Ger.)
Gansu (China)
Gilon (Iran)
Goiás (Braz.)
Hamar (Nor.)
Hebei (China)
Hejaz (Saudi)
Henan (China)
Herat (Afghan.)
Hesse (Ger.)
Honan (China)
Hopeh (China)
Hunan (China)
Hupeh (China)
Idaho (USA)
Indre (Fr.)
Isère (Fr.)
Jilin (China)
Johor (Malay.)

Judea (Isr.)
Jujuy (Arg.)
Kansu (China)
Karoo (SA)
Khiva (Asia)
Kirin (China)
Kwara (Nig.)
Lagos (Nig.)
La Paz (Boliv.)
Lazio (It.)
Liège (Belg.)
Loire (Fr.)
Maine (Fr.)
Maine (USA)
Marne (Fr.)
Meuse (Fr.)
Morea (Gr.)
Namur (Belg.)
Nubia (Sudan)
Opole (Pol.)
Oruro (Boliv.)
Otago (N.Z.)
Perak (Malay.)
Posen (Pol.)
Puglia (It.)
Rhône (Fr.)
Sabah (Malay.)
Sahel (Af.)
Salta (Arg.)
Savoy (Fr.)
Seine (Fr.)
Sivas (Turk.)
Somme (Fr.)
Tacna (Peru)
Texas (USA)
Tibet (China)

Tigre (Eth.)
Tomsk (Rus.)
Tyrol (Aust.)
Viseu (Port.)
Weald (The) (Eng.)
Yonne (Fr.)
Yukon (Can.)

6

Aargau (Swit.)
Adygea (Rus.)
Alaska (USA)
Allier (Fr.)
Alsace (Fr.)
Anhwei (China)
Apulia (It.)
Aragón (Sp.)
Ariège (Fr.)
Artois (Fr.)
Baffin (Can.)
Bengal (Bangla.)
Bengal (Ind.)
Borneo (Indo.)
Cracow (Pol.)
Creuse (Fr.)
Crimea (Ukr.)
Dakota (USA)
Danzig (Pol.)
Darfur (Sudan)
Emilia (It.)
Epirus (Gr.)
Faiyum (Egypt)
Fujian (China)
Fukien (China)
Gdansk (Pol.)

Geneva (Swit.)
Gerona (Sp.)
Ghilan (Iran)
Glarus (Swit.)
Guiana (S.Am.)
Hawaii (USA)
Huelva (Sp.)
Huesca (Sp.)
Johore (Malay.)
Judaea (Isr.)
Kansas (USA)
Karroo (S.A.)
Kerala (Ind.)
Kerman (Iran)
Kielce (Pol.)
Ladakh (Ind.)
Landes (Fr.)
Latium (It.)
Lérida (Sp.)
Levant (Sp.)
Loiret (Fr.)
Lozère (Fr.)
Lublin (Pol.)
Madrid (Sp.)
Madras (Ind.)
Madura (Indo.)
Málaga (Sp.)
Manche (Fr.)
Mari El (Rus.)
Mercia (Eng.)
Mergui (Burma)
Molise (It.)
Murcia (Sp.)
Mysore (Ind.)
Nelson (N.Z.)
Nevada (USA)

Nièvre (Fr.)
Novara (It.)
Oaxaca (Mex.)
Oregon (USA)
Orense (Sp.)
Orissa (Ind.)
Oviedo (Sp.)
Pahang (Malay.)
Pampas (S.Am.)
Paraná (Braz.)
Poitou (Fr.)
Potosí (Boliv.)
Poznán (Pol.)
Punjab (Ind.)
Punjab (Pak.)
Quebec (Can.)
Rivers (Nig.)
Sahara (Af.)
St Gall (Swit.)
Sarthe (Fr.)
Saxony (Ger.)
Scania (Swed.)
Schwyz (Swit.)
Seyhan (Turk.)
Shansi (China)
Shanxi (China)
Shensi (China)
Sicily (It.)
Sikkim (Ind.)
Sokoto (Nig.)
Sonora (Mex.)
Styria (Aust.)
Swabia (Ger.)
Tasman (N.Z.)
Tehran (Iran)
Thrace (Gr.)

Ticino (Swit.)
Toledo (Sp.)
Tyumen (Rus.)
Ulster (N.I.)
Umbria (It.)
Upsala (Swed.)
Valais (Swit.)
Vendée (Fr.)
Veneto (It.)
Viborg (Den.)
Vienne (Fr.)
Vosges (Fr.)
Warsaw (Pol.)
Wessex (Eng.)
Yunnan (China)
Zamora (Sp.)
Zurich (Swit.)

7

Abruzzi (It.)
Alabama (USA)
Alagoas (Braz.)
Alberta (Can.)
Algarve (Port.)
Almería (Sp.)
Antwerp (Belg.)
Arizona (USA)
Aveyron (Fr.)
Bavaria (Ger.)
Bohemia (Cze.)
Bokhara (Uzbek.)
Brabant (Belg.)
Bukhara (Uzbek.)
Cáceres (Sp.)
Castile (Sp.)
Chiapas (Mex.)

Córdoba (Sp.)
Córdoba (Arg.)
Corrèze (Fr.)
Côte-d'Or (Fr.)
Drenthe (Neth.)
Durango (Mex.)
Fergana (Uzbek.)
Florida (USA)
Galicia (Sp.)
Galicia (Pol.)
Galicia (Ukr.)
Galilee (Isr.)
Gascony (Fr.)
Gauteng (SA)
Georgia (USA)
Gotland (Swed.)
Granada (Sp.)
Grisons (Swit.)
Guienne (Fr.)
Guizhou (China)
Gujarat (Ind.)
Hanover (Ger.)
Haryana (Ind.)
Hérault (Fr.)
Hidalgo (Mex.)
Holland (Neth.)
Huánuco (Peru)
Indiana (USA)
Iquique (Chile)
Jalisco (Mex.)
Jiangsu (China)
Jiangxi (China)
Jutland (Den.)
Karelia (Rus.)
Kashmir (Ind.)
Kashmir (Pak.)

Katsina (Nig.)
Kiangsi (China)
Kiangsu (China)
Lapland (Eur.)
La Rioga (Sp.)
Liguria (It.)
Limburg (Neth.)
Limburg (Belg.)
Lucerne (Swit.)
Malacca (Malay.)
Manipur (Ind.)
Marches (It.)
Mayenne (Fr.)
Mendoza (Arg.)
Montana (USA)
Moravia (Cze.)
Munster (Ire.)
Navarra (Sp.)
Navarre (Sp.)
New York (USA)
Ontario (Can.)
Ossetia (Rus.)
Paraíba (Braz.)
Perugia (It.)
Picardy (Fr.)
Prussia (Ger.)
Qinghai (China)
Ravenna (It.)
Riviera, The (Fr.
  and It.)
Santa Fé (Arg.)
Sarawak (Malay.)
Segovia (Sp.)
Sennaar (Sudan)
Sergipe (Braz.)
Sevilla (Sp.)

Seville (Sp.)
Shaanxi (China)
Siberia (Rus.)
Sichuan (China)
Silesia (Pol.)
Sinaloa (Mex.)
Sondrio (It.)
Sumatra (Indo.)
Tabasco (Mex.)
Tanjore (Ind.)
Teheran (Iran)
Thurgau (Swit.)
Trabzon (Turk.)
Tripura (Ind.)
Tucuman (Arg.)
Tuscany (It.)
Uppsala (Swed.)
Utrecht (Neth.)
Venetia (It.)
Vermont (USA)
Vizcaya (Sp.)
Waikato (N.Z.)
Wroclaw (Pol.)
Wyoming (USA)
Yakutia (Rus.)
Yucatán (Mex.)
Zeeland (Neth.)

8

Alentejo (Port.)
Alicante (Sp.)
Amazonas (Braz.)
Anatolia (Turk.)
Ardennes (Fr.)
Arkansas (USA)
Asturias (Sp.)

Auckland (N.Z.)
Brittany (Fr.)
Bukovina (Eur.)
Burgundy (Fr.)
Buryatia (Rus.)
Calabria (It.)
Calvados (Fr.)
Campania (It.)
Campeche (Mex.)
Carniola (Sloven.)
Carolina (USA)
Caucasus (Rus., Geo., Arm.
  and Azer.)
Charente (Fr.)
Chechnya (Rus.)
Chekiang (China)
Coahuila (Mex.)
Colorado (USA)
Columbia (USA)
Dagestan (Rus.)
Dalmatia (Cro.)
Dauphiné (Fr.)
Delaware (USA)
Dordogne (Fr.)
Ferghana (Uzbek.)
Finnmark (Nor.)
Flanders (Belg.)
Florence (It.)
Fribourg (Swit.)
Girgenti (It.)
Gisborne (N.Z.)
Guerrero (Mex.)
Hainault (Belg.)
Hannover (Ger.)
Haut Rhin (Fr.)
Holstein (Ger.)

Illinois (USA)
Kandahar (Afghan.)
Kemerovo (Rus.)
Kentucky (USA)
Khorasan (Iran)
Kordofan (Sudan)
Kweichow (China)
Labrador (Can.)
Leinster (Ire.)
Liaoning (China)
Limbourg (Belg.)
Limousin (Fr.)
Lombardy (It.)
Lorestan (Iran)
Lorraine (Fr.)
Lothians, The (Scot.)
Lowlands (Scot.)
Lyonnais (Fr.)
Manitoba (Can.)
Maranhão (Braz.)
Maryland (USA)
Michigan (USA)
Missouri (USA)
Moldavia (Rom.)
Morbihan (Fr.)
Nagaland (Ind.)
Nebraska (USA)
Normandy (Fr.)
Oberland (Swit.)
Oklahoma (USA)
Palencia (Sp.)
Parahiba (Braz.)
Peshawar (Ind.)
Piacenza (It.)
Piedmont (It.)
Provence (Fr.)

Roumelia (Turk.)
Ruthenia (Ukr.)
Saarland (Ger.)
Salonika (Gr.)
Salzburg (Aust.)
São Paulo (Braz.)
Sardinia (It.)
Shandong (China)
Shantung (China)
Sinkiang (China)
Slavonia (Cro.)
Szechwan (China)
Taranaki (N.Z.)
Tarapaca (Chile)
Tasmania (Austral.)
Thessaly (Gr.)
Tlaxcala (Mex.)
Tongking (Asia)
Trentino (It.)
Tsinghai (China)
Udmurtia (Rus.)
Valdivia (Chile)
Valencia (Sp.)
Vaucluse (Fr.)
Veracruz (Mex.)
Victoria (Austral.)
Vila Real (Port.)
Virginia (USA)
Wallonia (Belg.)
Westland (N.Z.)
Xinjiang (China)
Zaragoza (Sp.)
Zhejiang (China)

9

Agrigento (It.)

Alto Adige (It.)
Andalusia (Sp.)
Appenzell (Swit.)
Aquitaine (Fr.)
Archangel (Rus.)
Asia Minor (Asia)
Astrakhan (Rus.)
Cantabria (Sp.)
Carinthia (Aust.)
Catalonia (Sp.)
Champagne (Fr.)
Chihuahua (Mex.)
Chuvashia (Rus.)
Connaught (Ire.)
Entre Ríos (Arg.)
Franconia (Ger.)
Free State (SA)
Friesland (Neth.)
Gaza Strip (Pal.)
Groningen (Neth.)
Guangdong (China)
Guipúzcoa (Sp.)
Hadramaut (Arab.)
Hawkes Bay (N.Z.)
Highlands (Scot.)
Kamchatka (Rus.)
Karnataka (Ind.)
Khuzestan (Iran)
Krasnodar (Rus.)
Kwangtung (China)
Languedoc (Fr.)
Louisiana (USA)
Macedonia (Gr.)
Meghalaya (Ind.)
Melanesia (Pac.)
Michoacán (Mex.)

Minnesota (USA)
Mordvinia (Rus.)
Neuchâtel (Swit.)
New Forest (Eng.)
New Guinea (Indo.)
New Jersey (USA)
New Mexico (USA)
Nivernais (Fr.)
North-West (SA)
Northland (N.Z.)
Nuevo León (Mex.)
Oldenburg (Ger.)
Palestine (Asia)
Patagonia (S.Am.)
Polynesia (Pac.)
Pomerania (Ger.)
Pomerania (Pol.)
Potteries, The (Eng.)
Querétaro (Mex.)
Rajasthan (Ind.)
Rajputana (Ind.)
Rhineland (Ger.)
Saint Gall (Swit.)
Salamanca (Sp.)
Samarkand (Asia)
Saragossa (Sp.)
Schleswig (Ger.)
Southland (N.Z.)
Stavropol (Rus.)
Tamil Nadu (Ind.)
Tarragona (Sp.)
Tatarstan (Rus.)
Tennessee (USA)
Thuringia (Ger.)
Transvaal (SA)
Trebizond (Turk.)

Turkestan (Asia)
Turkistan (Asia)
Turkmenia (Asia)
Villa Real (Port.)
Wallachia (Rom.)
West Coast (N.Z.)
West Irian (Indo.)
Wisconsin (USA)
Zacatecas (Mex.)

10

Basilicata (It.)
Bessarabia (Mold. and Ukr.)
Burgenland (Aust.)
California (USA)
Canterbury (N.Z.)
East Africa
East Anglia (Eng.)
Gelderland (Neth.)
Griqualand (SA)
Guanajuato (Mex.)
Haute-Loire (Fr.)
Haute-Marne (Fr.)
Haute-Saône (Fr.)
Ingushetia (Rus.)
Khabarovsk (Rus.)
Lambayeque (Peru)
Loir-et-Cher (Fr.)
Mazandaran (Iran)
Micronesia (Pac.)
Montenegro (Serb. and
   Monte.)
New Castile (Sp.)
Nova Scotia (Can.)
Old Castile (Sp.)
Overijssel (Neth.)

Palatinate (Ger.)
Pernambuco (Braz.)
Pontevedra (Sp.)
Queensland (Austral.)
Roussillon (Fr.)
Saxe-Coburg (Ger.)
Senegambia (Af.)
Slave Coast (Af.)
Sverdlovsk (Rus.)
Tamaulipas (Mex.)
Tenasserim (Burma)
Valladolid (Sp.)
Valparaíso (Chile)
Vorarlberg (Aust.)
Washington (USA)
Waziristan (Pak.)
West Africa
West Bengal (Ind.)
West Indies (Carib.)
Westphalia (Ger.)

11

Arkhangelsk (Rus.)
Baluchistan (Pak.)
Bay of Plenty (N.Z.)
Bourbonnais (Fr.)
Brandenburg (Ger.)
Buenos Aires (Arg.)
Connecticut (USA)
Côtes-du-Nord (Fr.)
Eastern Cape (SA)
Eure-et-Loire (Fr.)
Extremadura (Sp.)
Great Karroo (SA)
Guadalajara (Sp.)
Haute-Savoie (Fr.)

Haute-Vienne (Fr.)
Hautes-Alpes (Fr.)
Hercegovina (Bos.)
Hesse-Nassau (Ger.)
Ile-de-France (Fr.)
Krasnoyarsk (Rus.)
Lower Saxony (Ger.)
Maharashtra (Ind.)
Marlborough (N.Z.)
Matto Grosso (Braz.)
Mecklenburg (Ger.)
Minas Gerais (Braz.)
Mississippi (USA)
North Africa
North Dakota (USA)
Northumbria (Eng.)
Pas de Calais (Fr.)
Peloponnese (Gr.)
Pondicherry (Ind.)
Quintana Roo (Mex.)
Rhode Island (USA)
Schwarzwald (Ger.)
South Dakota (USA)
Sudetenland (Cze.)
The Lothians (Scot.)
Unterwalden (Swit.)
Upper Karroo (SA)
Valle d'Aosta (It.)
Western Cape (SA)
White Russia
Württemberg (Ger.)

12

British Isles (Eur.)
Franche-Comté (Fr)
Haute-Garonne (Fr.)

Heilongjiang (China)
Hohenzollern (Ger.)
Huancavelica (Peru)
Ile-et-Vilaine (Fr.)
Indre-et-Loire (Fr.)
KwaZulu-Natal (SA)
Latin America
Little Karroo (SA)
Little Russia
Lot-et-Garonne (Fr.)
Lower Austria (Aust.)
New Brunswick (Can.)
Newfoundland (Can.)
New Hampshire (USA)
North Brabant (Neth.)
Northern Cape (SA)
North Holland (Neth.)
Pennsylvania (USA)
Rio de Janeiro (Braz.)
Saskatchewan (Can.)
Schaffhausen (Swit.)
Seine-et-Marne (Fr.)
South Holland (Neth.)
Transylvania (Rom.)
Upper Austria (Aust.)
Uttar Pradesh (Ind.)
West Virginia (USA)

13

Andhra Pradesh (Ind.)
Bashkortostan (Rus.)
Canary Islands (Sp.)
Emilia-Romagna (It.)
Espírito Santo (Braz.)
Inner Mongolia (China)
Madhya Pradesh (Ind.)

Massachusetts (USA)
New South Wales (Austral.)
North Carolina (USA)
Rhondda Valley (Wales)
Romney Marshes (Eng.)
San Luis Potosí (Mex.)
Santa Catarina (Braz.)
Saxe-Altenberg (Ger.)
Saxe-Meiningen (Ger.)
South Carolina (USA)
Tarn-et-Garonne (Fr.)
Witwatersrand (SA)

14 AND OVER

Alpes-Maritimes (Fr.) (14)
Alsace-Lorraine (Fr.) (14)
Baden-Württemberg
  (Ger.) (16)
Balearic Islands (Sp.) (15)
Basque Provinces (Sp.) (15)
Bihar and Orissa (Ind.) (14)
British Columbia (Can.) (15)
Castilla-La Mancha (Sp.)
  16)
Central America (14)
Channel Islands (UK) (14)
District of Columbia
  (USA) (18)
Entre-Douro-e-Minho
  (Port.) (16)
Griqualand West (SA) (14)
Hautes-Pyrénées (Fr.) (14)
Himachal Pradesh (Ind.) (15)
Jammu and Kashmir (15)
Loire-Atlantique (Fr.) (15)
Lower California (Mex.) (15)

Manawatu-Wanganui (N.Z.)
  (16)
North Rhine-Westphalia
  (Ger.) (20)
North-West Frontier
  (Pak.) (17)
Northern Ireland (UK) (15)
Northern Territory
  (Austral.) (17)
Northwest Territories
  (Can.) (20)
Orange Free State (SA) (15)
Prince Edward Island
  (Can.) (18)
Rhenish Prussia (Ger.) (14)
Rio Grande do Sul (Braz.) (14)
Santa Catharina (Braz.) (14)
Saxe-Coburg-Gotha (Ger.) (15)
Schaumberg-Lippe (Ger.) (15)
Schleswig-Holstein (Ger.) (17)
South Australia (Austral.)
  (14)
Southern Africa (14)
United Provinces (Ind.) (15)
United Provinces (Neth.)15
Western Australia
  (Austral.) (16)
Yukon Territory (Can.) (14)

Rivers

R.=River and is inserted where the word River commonly
follows the name

1–3

Aar (Swit.)
Ain (Fr.)
Aln (Eng.)
Axe (Eng.)
Bug (Pol. and Ukr.)
Cam (Eng.)
Dee (Wales)
Dee (Scot.)
Don (Scot.)
Don (Rus.)
Ems (Ger.)
Esk (Scot.)
Esk (Eng.)
Exe (Eng.)
Fal (Eng.)
Fly (Papua)
Han (China)
Ili (Asia)
Ill (Fr.)
Inn (Aust.)
Ket (Sib.)
Kwa (Dem. Rep. of Congo)
Lea (Eng.)
Lee (Ire.)
Lek (Neth.)
Lot (Fr.)
Lys (Fr. and Belg.)
Nen (Eng.)

Ob (Sib.)
Oka (Rus.)
Po (It.)
Red R. (USA)
Rur (Ger. and Neth.)
Rye (Eng.)
Sid (Eng.)
Syr (Kaz.)
Taw (Eng.)
Tay (Scot.)
Tom (Sib.)
Ure (Eng.)
Usa (Rus.)
Usk (Wales)
Vah (Slov.)
Var (Fr.)
Vis (Nam. and SA)
Wey (Eng.)
Wye (Eng.)
Wye (Wales)
Yeo (Eng.)
Yug (Rus.)
Zab (Turk.)

4

Adda (It.)
Adda (Sudan)
Adur (Eng.)
Aire (Eng.)
Alma (Ukr.)
Amur (Asia)

Arno (It.)
Arun (Eng.)
Avon (Eng.)
Bann (N.I.)
Beas (Ind.)
Bobr (Bela.)
Bobr (Pol.)
Bure (Eng.)
Cher (Fr.)
Cole (Eng.)
Dart (Eng.)
Doon (Scot.)
Earn (Scot.)
Ebro (Sp.)
Eden (Eng.)
Elbe (Ger.)
Emba (Kaz.)
Enns (Aust.)
Erne (Ire.)
Fish R. (Nam. and SA)
Geba (W.Af.)
Gila (USA)
Gota (Swed.)
Isar (Aust. and Ger.)
Isis (Eng.)
Juba (E.Af.)
Kama (Rus.)
Kura (Asia)
Kwai (Thai.)
Lähn (Pol.)

Lech (Aust. and Ger.)
Leie (Fr. and Belg.)
Lena (Sib.)
Loir (Fr.)
Lune (Eng.)
Maas (Neth.)
Main (Ger.)
Main (Ire.)
Milk R. (Jam.)
Milk R. (USA)
Miño (Sp.)
Mole (Eng.)
Neva (Rus.)
Nida (Pol.)
Nile (Af.)
Nith (Scot.)
Nith (Can.)
Oder (Cze. Ger. and Pol.)
Ohio (USA)
Oise (Fr.)
Ouse (Eng.)
Oxus (Asia)
Peel (Can.)
Pegu R. (Burma)
Prut (SE Eur.)
Ravi (Ind. and Pak.)
Rede (Eng.)
Roer (Ger. and Neth.)
Ruhr (Ger.)
Saar (Fr. and Ger.)
Salt R. (USA)

Sava (SE Eur.)
Save (Fr.)
Save (Moz. and Zim.)
Slov (Hung.)
Spey (Scot.)
Styr (Bel. and Ukr.)
Suck (Ire.)
Suir (Ire.)
Swan (Can.)
Taff (Wales)
Tajo (Sp.)
Tana (Kenya)
Tapi (Ind.)
Tara (Serb. and Monte.)
Tarn (Fr.)
Tees (Eng.)
Tefé (Braz.)
Teif (Wales)
Tejo (Port.)
Test (Eng.)
Thur (Swit.)
Tisa (SE Eur.)
Towy (Wales)
Tyne (Eng.)
Uele (Dem. Rep. of Congo)
Ural (Rus. and Kaz.)
Vaal (SA)
Vire (Fr.)
Waal (Neth.)
Wash (Eng.)
Wear (Eng.)

Wlén (Pol.)
Yalu (China and N. Korea)
Yana (Sib.)
Yare (Eng.)

5

Adige (It.)
Adour (Fr.)
Agout (Fr.)
Aisne (Fr.)
Aller (Ger.)
Argun (Rus. and China)
Avoca R. (Austral.)
Awash (Eth.)
Benue (W. Af.)
Bío-Bío (Chile)
Black R. (USA)
Blood R. (SA)
Boyne (Ire.)
Camel (Eng.)
Chari (Cen.Af.)
Clyde (Scot.)
Colne (Eng.)
Congo (Af.)
Deben (Eng.)
Desna (Rus.)
Donau (Eur.)
Douro (Port. and Sp.)
Dovey (Wales)
Drava (Cen.Eur.)
Drave (Hung.)
Drina (Bos.)
Duero (Sp.)

Dvina (Rus.)
Dvina (Rus., Bela. and Lat.)
Eider (Ger.)
Feale (Ire.)
Fleet (Eng.)
Forth (Scot.)
Foyle (Ire.)
Frome (Eng.)
Grand R. (Can.)
Grand R. (USA)
Green R. (USA)
Gumti (Ind.)
Havel (Ger.)
Huang (China)
Hugli (Ind.)
Hunza (Pak.)
Ikopa (E.Af.)
Indus (Asia)
Isère (Fr.)
Ishim (Kaz.)
James R. (USA)
Jumna (Ind.)
Juruá (Braz. and Peru)
Kabul (Afghan.)
Kafue (Zam.)
Karun (Iran)
Kasai (Ang. and Dem. Rep. of Congo)
Katun (Sib.)
Koros (Hung.)
Lagan (N.Ire.)
Lagan (Swed.)
Lagen (Nor.)

Liard (Can.)
Lippe (Ger.)
Loire (Fr.)
Marne (Fr.)
Maros (Rom. and Hung.)
Memel (NE Eur.)
Meuse (Belg.)
Minho (Port.)
Moose (Can.)
Moose R. (USA)
Mosel (Fr., Lux. and Ger.)
Mures (Rom. and Hung.)
Neath (Wales)
Negro (S.Am.)
Neman (NE Eur.)
Neuse R. (USA)
Niger (W.Af.)
Nitra (Slov.)
Oglio (It.)
Onega (Rus.)
Osage R. (USA)
Otter (Eng.)
Peace R. (Can.)
Peace R. (USA)
Pearl R. (China)
Pecos R. (USA)
Perak (Malay.)
Piave (It.)
Plate (S.Am.)
Pruth (Rom.)
Pungo (USA)
Purus (S.Am.)

Rance (Fr.)
Reuss (Swit.)
Rhine (Ger., Neth. and Swit.)
Rhône (Fr. and Swit.)
Saale (Ger.)
Saone (Fr.)
Sarre (Fr. and Ger.)
Seine (Fr.)
Shari (Cen.Af.)
Shire (SE Af.)
Siang (S.Asia)
Siret (Rom. and Ukr.)
Snake R. (USA)
Snowy R. (Austral.)
Somme (Fr.)
Spree (Ger.)
Stour (Eng.)
Swale (Eng.)
Tagus (Port.)
Tamar (Eng.)
Tamis (Rom. and Serb.)
Tapti (Ind.)
Tarim (China)
Teifi (Wales)
Teign (Eng.)
Teith (Scot.)
Tiber (It.)
Tinto (Sp.)
Tisza (SE Eur.)
Traun (Aust.)

Trent (Can.)
Trent (Eng.)
Tweed (Scot.)
Usuri (China and Rus.)
Vitim (Rus.)
Volga (Rus.)
Volta (W.Af.)
Warta (Pol.)
Welle (Dem. Rep. of Congo)
Werra (Ger.)
Weser (Ger.)
White R. (USA)
Xingú (S.Am.)
Yonne (Fr.)
Yssel (Neth.)
Yukon (Can.)
Yuruá (Braz. and Peru)
Zaïre (Cen.Af.)

6

Agogna (It.)
Alagón (Sp.)
Albany (Can.)
Allier (Fr.)
Amazon (S.Am.)
Angara (Rus.)
Arinos (Braz.)
Atbara (NE Af.)
Barrow (Ire.)
Barwon R. (Austral.)
Beauly (Scot.)
Bolsas (Mex.)
Brazos R. (USA)
Buller (N.Z.)
Calder (Eng.)
Caroni (S.Am.)

Caroni R. (Trin.)
Carron (Scot.)
Chenab (Ind.)
Coquet (Eng.)
Crouch (Eng.)
Cuanza (Ang.)
Danube (Eur.)
Dihang (Ind.)
Donets (Rus. and Ukr.)
Elster (Cze. and Ger.)
Escaut (Belg. and Neth.)
Finlay (Can.)
Fraser (Can.)
French R. (Can.)
Gambia R. (W.Af.)
Gandak (Ind.)
Ganges (Ind.)
Glomma (Nor.)
Gomati (Ind.)
Grande (Bol.)
Grande (USA and Mex.)
Grande (Braz.)
Hawash (E.Af.)
Hudson (USA)
Humber (Eng.)
Hunter (Austral.)
Hunter (N.Z.)
IJssel (Neth.)
Irtish (Kaz. and Rus.)
Irwell (Eng.)
Itchen (Eng.)
Japura (Braz.)
Javari (Braz. and Peru)
Jhelum (Ind.)
Jordan (Isr., Jord. and Syria)
Kagera (Rwanda and Tan.)

Kaveri (Ind.)
Kennet (Eng.)
Kistna (Ind.)
Kolyma (Rus.)
Komati (E.Af.)
Kwanza (Ang.)
Leitha (Aust. and Hung.)
Liffey (Ire.)
Loddon (Austral.)
Lomami (Dem. Rep. of Congo)
Mamoré (S.Am.)
Medina (USA)
Medina R. (Rus.)
Medway (Eng.)
Mekong (Asia)
Mersey (Eng.)
Mincio (It.)
Mobile R. (USA)
Modder R. (SA)
Mohawk R. (USA)
Moldau (Cze.)
Monnow (Eng.)
Morava (Cze.)
Moskva (Rus.)
Muluya (Moroc.)
Murray R. (Austral.)
Neckar (Ger.)
Neisse (Ger. and Pol.)
Nelson (Can.)
Neutra (Slov.)
Niemen (NE Eur.)
Orange (SA)
Orwell (Eng.)
Ottawa (Can.)
Paraná (S.Am.)

Parret (Eng.)
Platte R. (USA)
Porali (Pak.)
Pungoè (Moz.)
Pungwe (Moz.)
Racket (USA)
Ribble (Eng.)
Roding (Eng.)
Rother (Eng.)
Rovuma (Moz. and Tanz.)
Rufiji (E.Af.)
Sabine R. (USA)
Salado (Arg.)
Sambre (Belg. and Fr.)
Santee R. (USA)
Sarthe (Fr.)
Scioto (USA)
Sereth (Rom. and Ukr.)
Severn (Can.)
Severn (Eng. and Wales)
Shilka (Rus.)
Slaney (Ire.)
Struma (Bulg. and Gr.)
Sunday (SA)
Sutlej (Ind. and Pak.)
Swilly (Ire.)
Tamega (Port. and Spain)
Tanaro (It.)
Teviot (Scot.)
Thames (Can.)
Thames (Eng.)
Theiss (SE Eur.)
Ticino (Swit.)
Tigris (Iraq and Turk.)
Tormes (Sp.)
Tornio (Fin. and Swed.)

Tugela (SA)
Tummel (Scot.)
Ubangi (Cen.Af.)
Ussuri (China and Rus.)
Vienne (Fr.)
Vilyay (Rus.)
Vltava (Cze.)
Wabash (USA)
Waihou (N.Z.)
Wandle (Eng.)
Warthe (Pol.)
Weaver (Eng.)
Wharfe (Eng.)
Wipper (Ger.)
Witham (Eng.)
Yavarí (Braz. and Peru)
Yellow R. (China)
Yellow R. (USA)

7

Abitibi (Can.)
Akagera (Rwanda and Tanz.)
Alabama (USA)
Berbice (Guyana)
Big Blue R. (USA)
Bighorn R. (USA)
Buffalo (USA)
Catawba (USA)
Cauvery (Ind.)
Chambal (Ind.)
Chelmer (Eng.)
Cubango (SA)
Darling (Austral.)
Derwent (Eng.)
Deveron (Scot.)
Dnieper (E.Eur.)

Dubawnt (Can.)
Dunajec (Pol.)
Durance (Fr.)
Ettrick (Scot.)
Feather R. (USA)
Fitzroy (Austral.)
Garonne (Fr.)
Genesee R. (USA)
Gilbert (Austral.)
Glenelg (Austral.)
Glommen (Nor.)
Guaporé (Bol. and Braz.)
Han Shui (China)
Helmand (Afghan.)
Hooghly (Ind.)
Huang He (China)
Juniata R. (USA)
Kanawha (USA)
Krishna (Ind.)
Lachlan (Austral.)
La Plata (Arg.)
Limpopo (SE Af.)
Lualaba (Cen.Af.)
Luangwa (Moz. and Zam.)
Lugenda (Moz.)
Madeira (Braz.)
Marañón (Peru)
Maritsa (S. Eur.)
Mattawa (Can.)
Mayenne (Fr.)
Meklong (Thail.)
Moselle (Fr., Lux. and Ger.)
Murghob (Taj.)
Narmada (Ind.)
Niagara (Can.)
Orinoco (S.Am.)

Orontes (Leb. and Syria)
Paraíba (Braz.)
Paraná (S.Am.)
Pechora (Rus.)
Potomac (USA)
Roanoke (Ind.)
Rubicon (It.)
St Clair (Can. and USA)
Salween (Tibet and Burma)
San Juan (S.Am.)
San Juan (Mex.)
San Juan R. (USA)
Sankuru (Af.)
Schelde (Belg. and Neth.)
Scheldt (Belg. and Neth.)
Selenga (Asia)
Semliki (Uganda and Dem.
  Rep. of Congo)
Senegal (W.Af.)
Shannon (Ire.)
Spokane R. (USA)
Sungari (China)
Tapajós (S.Am.)
Thomsen (Can.)
Trinity R. (USA)
Tsangpo (S.Asia)
Ucayali (Peru)
Uruguay (S.Am.)
Vistula (Pol.)
Waikato (N.Z.)
Waitaki (N.Z.)
Warrego R. (Austral.)
Washita R. (USA)
Waveney (Eng.)
Welland (Eng.)
Wichita R. (USA)

Yangtze (China)
Yarkand (China)
Yenisei (Sib.)
Zambezi (S.Af.)

8

Amu Darya (Cen. Asia)
Arkansas R. (USA)
Beaulieu (Eng.)
Berezina (Bela.)
Big Black R. (USA)
Big Sandy R. (USA)
Big Sioux R. (USA)
Blue Nile (Eth. and Sudan)
Cape Fear R. (USA)
Cherweli (Eng.)
Cheyenne R. (USA)
Chindwin (Burma)
Clarence R. (Austral.)
Colorado R. (USA)
Columbia (Can. and USA)
Delaware R. (USA)
Demerara R. (Guyana)
Dniester (Ukr. and Mold.)
Dordogne (Fr.)
Eastmain (Can.)
Evenlode (Eng.)
Flinders R. (Austral.)
Gatineau (Can.)
Godavari (Ind.)
Goulburn R. (Austral.)
Great Kei (SA)
Guadiana (Sp. and Port.)
Huallaga (Peru)
Humboldt R. (USA)
Illinois R. (USA)

Itimbiri (Dem. Rep. of Congo)
Kankakee R. (USA)
Kelantan (Malay.)
Kennebec R. (USA)
Klondike R. (Can.)
Kootenai (Can. and USA)
Mahanadi (Ind.)
Manawatu (N.Z.)
Mazaruni R. (Guyana)
Missouri (USA)
Mitchell R. (Austral.)
Moulouya (Moroc.)
Nebraska (USA)
Okavango (SA)
Olifants (Nam.)
Olifants (SA)
Paraguay (S.Am.)
Parnaíba (Braz.)
Putumayo (S.Am.)
Red River (USA)
Rio Negro (S.Am.)
Rio Tinto (Sp.)
Saguenay (Can.)
St Claire (Can.)
Santiago (Peru)
Savannah (USA)
Suwannee R. (USA)
Syr Daria (Kaz.)
Torridge (Eng.)
Wanganui (N.Z.)
Winnipeg (Can.)

9

Allegheny R. (USA)
Athabaska (Can.)

Byerezino (Bela.)
Chambeshi (Zamb.)
Churchill (Can.)
Crocodile R. (SA)
East River (USA)
Essequibo (Guyana)
Euphrates (Iraq., Turk. and Syria)
Gala Water (Scot.)
Great Ouse (Eng.)
Guadalete (Sp.)
Han Chiang (China)
Indigirka (Rus.)
Irrawaddy (Burma)
Kalamazoo R. (USA)
Mackenzie (Can.)
Macquarie R. (Austral.)
Macquarie R. (Tas.)
Magdalena (Col.)
Merrimack R. (USA)
Murchison R. (Austral.)
Paranaíba (Braz.)
Penobscot R. (USA)
Pilcomayo (S.Am.)
Porcupine R. (Can.)
Rede River (Eng.)
Rio Grande (Braz.)
Rio Grande (USA and Mex.)
Rio Grande (Bol.)
Saint John (Can. and USA)
Saint Paul (W.Af.)
Salt River (USA)
Tennessee R. (USA)
Tocantins (Braz.)
White Nile (Uganda and Sudan)

Wisconsin R. (USA)
Yarkant He (China)

10

Black River (USA)
Blackwater (Eng.)
Blackwater (Ire.)
Chang Jiang (China)
Chao Phraya (Thai.)
Dora Baltea (It.)
Frome Creek (Austral.)
Green River (USA)
Kizil Irmak (Turk.)
Manzanares (Sp.)
Missinaibi (Can.)
Mississagi (Can.)
Qezel Owzan (Iran)
Republican R. (USA)
Sacramento (USA)
Saint John's R. (USA)
St Lawrence (Can.)
San Joaquin R. (USA)
Shenandoah R. (USA)
Snake River (USA)
Torneälven (Fin. and Swed.)
Torniojoki (Fin. and Swed.)
White River (USA)

11 AND OVER

Assiniboine (Can.) (11)
Big Black River (USA) (13)
Big Blue River (USA) (12)
Bighorn River (USA) (12)
Big Sandy River (USA) (13)
Big Sioux River (USA) (13)
Bonaventure (Can.) (11)

Brahmaputra (S.Asia) (11)
Desaguadero (Bol. and Peru) (11)
Dora Riparia (It.) (11)
Great Kanawka (USA) (12)
Guadalquivir (Sp.) (12)
Mississippi (USA) (11)
Modder River (SA) (11)
Murrumbidgee (Austral.) (12)
Paraíba do Sul (Braz.) (12)
Rappahannock R. (USA) (12)
Río de la Plata (Arg.) (12)
Saint Claire (Can.) (11)
Saint Lawrence (Can.) (13)
São Francisco (Braz.) (12)
Saskatchewan (Can.) (12)
Shatt al-Arab (Iraq) (11)
Songhua Jiang (China) (12)
Susquehanna R. (USA) (11)
Upper Paraná (S.Am.) (11)
Yangtse Kiang (China) (12)
Yarrowwater (Scot.) (11)
Yellow River (China) (11)
Yellowstone R. (USA) (11)

Towns and cities: United Kingdom

(E.)=England; (N.I.)=Northern Ireland; (S.)=Scotland;
(W.)=Wales

3 AND 4

Alva (S.)
Ayr (S.)
Bala (W.)
Barr (S.)
Bath (E.)
Bray (E.)
Bude (E.)
Bury (E.)
Clun (E.)
Deal (E.)
Diss (E.)
Duns (S.)
Elie (S.)
Ely (E.)
Eton (E.)
Eye (E.)
Holt (E.)
Holt (W.)
Hove (E.)
Hull (E.)
Hyde (E.)
Ince (E.)
Kirn (S.)
Leek (E.)
Looe (E.)
Luss (S.)
Lydd (E.)
Mold (W.)
Nigg (S.)
Oban (S.)

Pyle (W.)
Reay (S.)
Rhyl (W.)
Ross (E.)
Ryde (E.)
Rye (E.)
Shap (E.)
Stow (E.)
Uig (S.)
Usk (E.)
Ware (E.)
Wark (E.)
Wem (E.)
Wick (S.)
Wick (S.)
Yarm (E.)
York (E.)

5

Acton (E.)
Alloa (S.)
Alton (E.)
Annan (S.)
Avoch (S.)
Ayton (S.)
Bacup (E.)
Banff (S.)
Beith (S.)
Blyth (E.)
Brora (S.)
Busby (S.)
Caine (E.)

Ceres (S.)
Chard (E.)
Cheam (E.)
Chirk (W.)
Clova (S.)
Colne (E.)
Corby (E,)
Cowes (E.)
Crail (S.)
Crewe (E.)
Cupar (S.)
Denny (S.)
Derby (E.)
Doagh (N.I.)
Dover (E.)
Egham (E.)
Elgin (S.)
Ellon (S.)
Epsom (E.)
Errol (S.)
Filey (E.)
Flint (W.)
Fowey (E.)
Frome (E.)
Fyvie (S.)
Glynn (N.I.)
Goole (E.)
Govan (S.)
Grays (E.)
Hawes (E.)
Hurst (E.)
Hythe (E.)

Insch (S.)
Keady (N.I.)
Keiss (S.)
Keith (S.)
Kelso (S.)
Lairg (S.)
Largs (S.)
Larne (N.I.)
Leeds (E.)
Leigh (E.)
Leith (S.)
Lewes (E.)
Louth (E.)
Louth (N.I.)
Luton (E.)
March (E.)
Nairn (S.)
Neath (W.)
Newry (N.I.)
Olney (E.)
Omagh (N.I.)
Otley (E.)
Perth (S.)
Poole (E.)
Reeth (E.)
Ripon (E.)
Risca (W.)
Rugby (E.)
Salen (S.)
Sarum (E.)
Selby (E.)
Stoke (E.)

Stone (E.)	Bo'Ness (S.)	Edzell (S.)	Malton (E.)
Tebay (E.)	Bodmin (E.)	Epping (E.)	Marlow (E.)
Tenby (W.)	Bognor (E.)	Exeter (E.)	Masham (E.)
Thame (E.)	Bolton (E.)	Findon (S.)	Meigle (S.)
Towyn (W.)	Bootle (E.)	Forfar (S.)	Moffat (S.)
Tring (E.)	Boston (E.)	Forres (S.)	Morley (E.)
Troon (S.)	Bourne (E.)	Girvan (S.)	Naseby (E.)
Truro (E.)	Brecon (W.)	Glamis (S.)	Nelson (E.)
Wells (E.)	Bruton (E.)	Goring (E.)	Neston (E.)
Wendy (E.)	Buckie (S.)	Hanley (E.)	Newark (E.)
Wergs (E.)	Bungay (E.)	Harlow (E.)	Newent (E.)
Wigan (E.)	Burton (E.)	Harrow (E.)	Newlyn (E.)
	Buxton (E.)	Havant (E.)	Newton (E.)
6	Carron (S.)	Hawick (S.)	Newton (S.)
	Caston (E.)	Henley (E.)	Norham (E.)
Aboyne (S.)	Clunes (S.)	Hexham (E.)	Oakham (E.)
Alford (E.)	Cobham (E.)	Higham (E.)	Oldham (E.)
Alford (S.)	Comber	Howden (E.)	Ossett (E.)
Alston (E.)	(N.I.)	Huntly (S.)	Oundle (E.)
Amlwch (W.)	Comrie (S.)	Ilkley (E.)	Oxford (E.)
Antrim (N.I.)	Conway (W.)	Irvine (S.)	Penryn (E.)
Ashton (E.)	Crieff (S.)	Jarrow (E.)	Pewsey (E.)
Augher (N.I.)	Cromer (E.)	Kendal (E.)	Pinner (E.)
Bangor (W.)	Cullen (S.)	Killin (S.)	Pladda (S.)
Bangor (N.I.)	Darwen (E.)	Lanark (S.)	Pudsey (E.)
Barnet (E.)	Dollar (S.)	Lauder (S.)	Putney (E.)
Barrow (E.)	Dudley (E.)	Leslie (S.)	Ramsey (E.)
Barton (E.)	Dunbar (S.)	Leyton (E.)	Redcar (E.)
Barvas (S.)	Dundee (S.)	Linton (E.)	Reston (S.)
Batley (E.)	Dunlop (S.)	Lochee (S.)	Rhynie (S.)
Battle (E.)	Dunnet (S.)	London (E.)	Ripley (E.)
Bawtry (E.)	Dunoon (S.)	Ludlow (E.)	Romney (E.)
Beauly (S.)	Durham (E.)	Lurgan (N.I.)	Romsey (E.)
Bedale (E.)	Dysart (S.)	Lynton (E.)	Rosyth (E.)
Belcoo (N.I.)	Ealing (E.)	Lytham (E.)	Rothes (S.)
Belper (E.)	Eccles (E.)	Maldon (E.)	Ruabon (W.)
Biggar (S.)			

Rugely (E.)
Ruthin (W.)
St Ives (E.)
Seaham (E.)
Seaton (E.)
Selsey (E.)
Settle (E.)
Shotts (S.)
Slough (E.)
Snaith (E.)
Strood (E.)
Stroud (E.)
Sutton (E.)
Thirsk (E.)
Thorne (E.)
Thurso (S.)
Tongue (S.)
Totnes (E.)
Walmer (E.)
Walton (E.)
Watton (E.)
Welwyn (E.)
Weston (E.)
Whitby (E.)
Widnes (E.)
Wigton (E.)
Wilton (E.)
Wishaw (S.)
Witham (E.)
Witney (E.)
Woking (E.)
Wooler (E.)
Wormit (S.)
Yarrow (S.)
Yeovil (E.)

7

Airdrie (S.)
Alnwick (E.)
Andover (E.)
Appleby (E.)
Arundel (E.)
Ashford (E.)
Aylsham (E.)
Balfron (S.)
Balloch (S.)
Bampton (E.)
Banavie (S.)
Banbury (E.)
Barking (E.)
Beccles (E.)
Bedford (E.)
Belfast (N.I.)
Belford (E.)
Belleek (N.I.)
Berwick (E.)
Bewdley (E.)
Bexhill (E.)
Bilston (E.)
Bourton (E.)
Bowmore (S.)
Braemar (S.)
Brandon (E.)
Brechin (S.)
Bristol (E.)
Brixham (E.)
Brodick (S.)
Bromley (E.)
Burnley (E.)
Burslem (E.)
Caistor (E.)
Caledon (N.I.)

Carbost (S.)
Cardiff (W.)
Carluke (S.)
Carrick (N.I.)
Catford (E.)
Cawston (E.)
Charing (E.)
Chatham (E.)
Cheadle (E.)
Cheddar (E.)
Chesham (E.)
Chester (E.)
Chorley (E.)
Clacton (E.)
Clifton (E.)
Clogher (N.I.)
Crathie (S.)
Crawley (E.)
Croydon (E.)
Culross (S.)
Cumnock (S.)
Cwmbran (W.)
Datchet (E.)
Dawlish (E.)
Denbigh (W.)
Denholm (S.)
Dervock (N.I.)
Devizes (E.)
Dorking (E.)
Douglas (E.)
Douglas (S.)
Dundrum (N.I.)
Dunkeld (S.)
Dunmore (N.I.)
Dunning (S.)
Dunster (E.)

Elstree (E.)
Enfield (E.)
Epworth (E.)
Evanton (S.)
Everton (E.)
Evesham (E.)
Exmouth (E.)
Fairlie (S.)
Falkirk (S.)
Fareham (E.)
Farnham (E.)
Feltham (E.)
Fintona (N.I.)
Galston (S.)
Gifford (S.)
Gilford (N.I.)
Glasgow (S.)
Glenarm (N.I.)
Glencoe (S.)
Glossop (E.)
Golspie (S.)
Gosport (E.)
Gourock (S.)
Granton (S.)
Grimsby (E.)
Halifax (E.)
Halkirk (S.)
Hampton (E.)
Harwich (E.)
Haworth (E.)
Helston (E.)
Heywood (E.)
Hitchin (E.)
Honiton (E.)
Hornsea (E.)
Hornsey (E.)

Horsham (E.)
Ipswich (E.)
Ixworth (E.)
Jesmond (E.)
Kenmore (S.)
Keswick (E.)
Kilmory (S.)
Kilmuir (S.)
Kilsyth (S.)
Kington (E.)
Kinross (S.)
Kintore (S.)
Lamlash (S.)
Lancing (E.)
Langton (E.)
Larbert (S.)
Ledbury (E.)
Leyburn (E.)
Lincoln (E.)
Lisburn (N.I.)
Lybster (S.)
Macduff (S.)
Maesteg (W.)
Malvern (E.)
Margate (E.)
Matlock (E.)
Maybole (S.)
Melrose (S.)
Melvich (S.)
Meridan (E.)
Methven (S.)
Monikie (S.)
Moreton (E.)
Morpeth (E.)
Mossley (E.)
Mossley (N.I.)

Muthill (S.)
New Quay (W.)
Newbury (E.)
Newport (E.)
Newport (W.)
Newport (S.)
Newquay (E.)
Newtown (W.)
Norwich (E.)
Oldbury (E.)
Ormesby (E.)
Overton (E.)
Overton (W.)
Padstow (E.)
Paisley (S.)
Peebles (S.)
Penrith (E.)
Polmont (S.)
Poolewe (S.)
Portree (S.)
Portsoy (S.)
Poulton (E.)
Prescot (E.)
Preston (E.)
Rainham (E.)
Reading (E.)
Redhill (E.)
Redruth (E.)
Reigate (E.)
Renfrew (S.)
Retford (E.)
Romford (E.)
Royston (E.)
Runcorn (E.)
Saddell (S.)
St Asaph (W.)

St Neots (E.)
Salford (E.)
Saltash (E.)
Sandown (E.)
Sarclet (S.)
Saxilby (E.)
Scourie (S.)
Seaford (E.)
Selkirk (S.)
Shifnal (E.)
Shipley (E.)
Shipton (E.)
Silloth (E.)
Skipton (E.)
Spilsby (E.)
Staines (E.)
Stanley (E.)
Stanley (E.)
Stilton (E.)
Strathy (S.)
Sudbury (E.)
Sunbury (E.)
Swanage (E.)
Swansea (W.)
Swindon (E.)
Swinton (E.)
Swinton (S.)
Tarbert (S.)
Tarland (S.)
Taunton (E.)
Tayport (S.)
Telford (E.)
Tenbury (E.)
Tetbury (E.)
Thaxted (E.)
Tilbury (E.)

Torquay (E.)
Tranent (S.)
Turriff (S.)
Twyford (E.)
Ventnor (E.)
Walsall (E.)
Waltham (E.)
Wantage (E.)
Wareham (E.)
Warwick (E.)
Watchet (E.)
Watford (E.)
Weobley (E.)
Wickwar (E.)
Windsor (E.)
Winslow (E.)
Winster (E.)
Wisbech (E.)
Worksop (E.)
Wrexham (W.)

8

Aberavon (W.)
Aberdare (W.)
Aberdeen (S.)
Abergele (W.)
Aberlady (S.)
Abingdon (E.)
Abington (S.)
Ahoghill (N.I.)
Alfreton (E.)
Alnmouth (E.)
Amersham (E.)
Amesbury (E.)
Ampthill (E.)
Arbroath (S.)

Armadale (S.)
Arrochar (S.)
Auldearn (S.)
Aviemore (S.)
Axbridge (E.)
Bakewell (E.)
Ballater (S.)
Bamburgh (E.)
Banchory (S.)
Barmouth (W.)
Barnsley (E.)
Barrhill (S.)
Bearsden (S.)
Beattock (S.)
Bedworth (E.)
Berkeley (E.)
Beverley (E.)
Bicester (E.)
Bideford (E.)
Blantyre (S.)
Bolsover (E.)
Brackley (E.)
Bradford (E.)
Brampton (E.)
Bridgend (W.)
Bridport (E.)
Brighton (E.)
Bromyard (E.)
Broseley (E.)
Burghead (S.)
Caerleon (W.)
Camborne (E.)
Canonbie (S.)
Cardigan (W.)
Carlisle (E.)
Carnwath (S.)

Caterham (E.)
Chepstow (E.)
Chertsey (E.)
Clevedon (E.)
Clovelly (E.)
Coventry (E.)
Crediton (E.)
Creetown (E.)
Cromarty (S.)
Dalkeith (S.)
Dalmally (S.)
Dartford (E.)
Daventry (E.)
Debenham (E.)
Dedworth (E.)
Deptford (E.)
Dewsbury (E.)
Dingwall (S.)
Dirleton (S.)
Dolgelly (W.)
Dufftown (S.)
Dumfries (S.)
Dunbeath (S.)
Dunblane (S.)
Dungiven (N.I.)
Dunscore (S.)
Earlston (S.)
Ebbw Vale (W.)
Egremont (E.)
Eversley (E.)
Eyemouth (S.)
Fakenham (E.)
Falmouth (E.)
Findhorn (S.)
Fortrose (S.)
Foulness (E.)

Glenluce (S.)
Grantham (E.)
Grantown (E.)
Greenlaw (S.)
Greenock (S.)
Hadleigh (E.)
Hailsham (E.)
Halstead (E.)
Hamilton (S.)
Hastings (E.)
Hatfield (E.)
Hawarden (W.)
Helmsley (E.)
Hereford (E.)
Herne Bay (E.)
Hertford (E.)
Hilltown (N.I.)
Hinckley (E.)
Holbeach (E.)
Holyhead (W.)
Holywell (W.)
Holywell (E.)
Hunmanby (E.)
Ilkeston (E.)
Inverury (S.)
Jedburgh (S.)
Keighley (E.)
Kidwelly (W.)
Kilbride (S.)
Kilniver (S.)
Kilrenny (S.)
Kinghorn (S.)
Kingston (E.)
Kirkwall (S.)
Knighton (W.)
Lampeter (W.)

Langholm (S.)
Latheron (S.)
Lavenham (E.)
Lechlade (E.)
Leuchars (S.)
Leyland (E.)
Liskeard (E.)
Llanelli (W.)
Llanrwst (W.)
Loanhead (S.)
Longtown (E.)
Lynmouth (E.)
Markinch (S.)
Marykirk (S.)
Maryport (E.)
Maryport (S.)
Midhurst (E.)
Minehead (E.)
Moniaive (S.)
Monmouth (E.)
Montrose (S.)
Monymusk (S.)
Muirkirk (S.)
Nantwich (E.)
Neilston (S.)
Newburgh (S.)
Newhaven (E.)
Newmilns (S.)
Nuneaton (E.)
Ormskirk (E.)
Oswestry (E.)
Paignton (E.)
Pembroke (W.)
Penicuik (S.)
Penzance (E.)
Pershore (E.)

Peterlee (E.)
Petworth (E.)
Pevensey (E.)
Plaistow (E.)
Plymouth (E.)
Portrush (N.I.)
Pwllheli (W.)
Ramsgate (E.)
Redditch (E.)
Rhayader (W.)
Richmond (E.)
Ringwood (E.)
Rochdale (E.)
Rothbury (E.)
Rothesay (S.)
St Albans (E.)
St Fergus (S.)
St Helens (E.)
Saltburn (E.)
Sandgate (E.)
Sandwich (E.)
Sedbergh (E.)
Shanklin (E.)
Shipston (E.)
Sidmouth (E.)
Skegness (E.)
Sleaford (E.)
Solihull (E.)
Southend (E.)
Spalding (E.)
Stafford (E.)
Stamford (E.)
Stanhope (E.)
Stanhope (S.)
Stanwell (E.)
Stirling (S.)

Stockton (E.)
Strabane (N.I.)
Stratton (E.)
Strichen (S.)
Surbiton (E.)
Swaffham (E.)
Talgarth (W.)
Tamworth (E.)
Thetford (E.)
Thornaby (E.)
Tiverton (E.)
Tredegar (W.)
Tregaron (W.)
Tunstall (E.)
Uckfield (E.)
Ullapool (S.)
Uxbridge (E.)
Wallasey (E.)
Wallsend (E.)
Wanstead (E.)
Westbury (E.)
Wetheral (E.)
Wetherby (E.)
Weymouth (E.)
Whithorn (S.)
Woodford (E.)
Woolwich (E.)
Worthing (E.)
Yarmouth (E.)

9

Aberaeron (W.)
Aberdovey (W.)
Aberfeldy (S.)
Aberffraw (W.)
Aberfoyle (S.)

Aldbrough (E.)
Aldeburgh (E.)
Aldershot (E.)
Allendale (E.)
Ambleside (E.)
Ardrossan (S.)
Ashbourne (E.)
Ashburton (E.)
Ashington (E.)
Avonmouth (E.)
Axminster (E.)
Aylesbury (E.)
Ballymena (N.I.)
Banbridge (N.I.)
Beaumaris (W.)
Bebington (E.)
Beckenham (E.)
Bettyhill (S.)
Blackburn (E.)
Blackburn (E.)
Blackpool (E.)
Blandford (E.)
Blisworth (E.)
Bracadale (S.)
Bracknell (E.)
Braintree (E.)
Brentford (E.)
Brentwood (E.)
Brighouse (E.)
Broadford (S.)
Broughton (E.)
Broughton (S.)
Broughton (W.)
Buckhaven (S)
Bushmills (N.I.)
Callander (S.)

Cambridge (E.)
Carnarvon (W.)
Carnforth (E.)
Carstairs (S.)
Castleton (E.)
Chingford (E.)
Clitheroe (E.)
Coleraine (N.I.)
Colwyn Bay (W.)
Congleton (E.)
Cookstown (N.I.)
Craigavon (N.I.)
Cranbrook (E.)
Crewkerne (E.)
Criccieth (W.)
Cricklade (E.)
Cuckfield (E.)
Dartmouth (E.)
Devonport (E.)
Doncaster (E.)
Donington (E.)
Droitwich (E.)
Dronfield (E.)
Dumbarton (S.)
Dungannon (N.I.)
Dungeness (E.)
Dunstable (E.)
Edinburgh (S.)
Ellesmere (E.)
Faversham (E.)
Fishguard (W.)
Fleetwood (E.)
Fochabers (S.)
Gateshead (E.)
Godalming (E.)
Gravesend (E.)

Greenwich (E.)
Guildford (E.)
Halesowen (E.)
Harrogate (E.)
Haslemere (E.)
Haverhill (E.)
Hawkhurst (E.)
Holmfirth (E.)
Ilchester (E.)
Immingham (E.)
Inveraray (S.)
Inverness (S.)
Johnstone (S.)
Kettering (E.)
King's Lynn (E.)
Kingswear (E.)
Kingussie (S.)
Kircubbin (N.I.)
Kirkcaldy (S.)
Lambourne (E.)
Lancaster (E.)
Leadhills (S.)
Leicester (E.)
Lichfield (E.)
Liverpool (E.)
Llanberis (W.)
Llandudno (W.)
Llangadog (W.)
Lochgelly (S.)
Lochinver (S.)
Lockerbie (S.)
Longridge (E.)
Lowestoft (E.)
Lyme Regis (E.)
Lymington (E.)
Maidstone (E.)

Mansfield (E.)
Mauchline (S.)
Middleton (E.)
Milngavie (S.)
Moneymore (N.I.)
Morecambe (E.)
Newcastle (E.)
Newcastle (N.I.)
Newmarket (E.)
New Radnor (W.)
New Romney (E.)
Northwich (E.)
Otterburn (E.)
Pembridge (E.)
Penistone (E.)
Penkridge (E.)
Peterhead (S.)
Pickering (E.)
Pitlochry (S.)
Pontypool (E.)
Portadown (N.I.)
Port Ellen (S.)
Porthcawl (W.)
Portmadoc (W.)
Prestwick (S.)
Rasharkin (N.I.)
Riccarton (S.)
Rochester (E.)
Rostrevor (N.I.)
Rotherham (E.)
St Andrews (S.)
St Austell (E.)
St Fillans (S.)
Salisbury (E.)
Saltfleet (E.)
Sevenoaks (E.)

Sheerness (E.)
Sheffield (E.)
Sherborne (E.)
Shieldaig (S.)
Slamannan (S.)
Smethwick (E.)
Southgate (E.)
Southport (E.)
Southwell (E.)
Southwold (E.)
Starcross (E.)
Stevenage (E.)
Stewarton (S.)
Stockport (E.)
Stokesley (E.)
Stornoway (S.)
Stourport (E.)
Stranraer (S.)
Stratford (E.)
Strathdon (S.)
Stretford (E.)
Strontian (S.)
Tarporley (E.)
Tavistock (E.)
Tenterden (E.)
Thornhill (S.)
Tobermore (N.I.)
Tobermory (S.)
Todmorden (E.)
Tomintoul (S.)
Tonbridge (E.)
Tovermore (N.I.)
Towcester (E.)
Tynemouth (E.)
Ulverston (E.)
Upminster (E.)

Uppingham (E.)
Uttoxeter (E.)
Wainfleet (E.)
Wakefield (E.)
Welshpool (W.)
Westerham (E.)
Weybridge (E.)
Wimbledon (E.)
Wincanton (E.)
Wokingham (E.)
Woodstock (E.)
Worcester (E.)
Wymondham (E.)

10

Abbotsford (S.)
Accrington (E.)
Achnasheen (S.)
Altrincham (E.)
Anstruther (S.)
Applecross (S.)
Ardrishaig (S.)
Auchinleck (S.)
Ballantrae (S.)
Ballyclare (N.I.)
Ballymoney (N.I.)
Ballyronan (N.I.)
Barnstaple (E.)
Beaminster (E.)
Bedlington (E.)
Bellingham (E.)
Berriedale (S.)
Billericay (E.)
Birkenhead (E.)
Birmingham (E.)
Bridgnorth (E.)

Bridgwater (E.)
Bromsgrove (E.)
Broxbourne (E.)
Buckingham (E.)
Caernarfon (W.)
Caerphilly (W.)
Carnoustie (S.)
Canterbury (E.)
Carmarthen (W.)
Carshalton (E.)
Carsphairn (S.)
Castlederg (N.I.)
Castletown (S.)
Castletown (E.)
Chelmsford (E.)
Cheltenham (E.)
Chichester (E.)
Chippenham (E.)
Chulmleigh (E.)
Coatbridge (S.)
Coggeshall (E.)
Colchester (E.)
Coldingham (S.)
Coldstream (S.)
Cranbourne (E.)
Cullompton (E.)
Cushendall (N.I.)
Dalbeattie (S.)
Darlington (E.)
Donaghadee (N.I.)
Dorchester (E.)
Drumlithie (S.)
Dukinfield (E.)
East Linton (S.)
Eastbourne (E.)
Eccleshall (E.)

Farningham (E.)
Ffestiniog (W.)
Folkestone (E.)
Freshwater (E.)
Galashiels (S.)
Gillingham (E.)
Glenrothes (S.)
Gloucester (E.)
Haddington (S.)
Halesworth (E.)
Hartlepool (E.)
Haslingden (E.)
Heathfield (E.)
Horncastle (E.)
Hornchurch (E.)
Hungerford (E.)
Hunstanton (E.)
Huntingdon (E.)
Ilfracombe (E.)
Johnshaven (S.)
Kenilworth (E.)
Kilcreggan (S.)
Kilmarnock (S.)
Kilwinning (S.)
Kincardine (S.)
Kingsbarns (S.)
Kingsclere (E.)
Kirkmaiden (S.)
Kirkoswald (E.)
Kirkoswald (S.)
Kirriemuir (S.)
Launceston (E.)
Leamington (E.)
Lennoxtown (S.)
Leominster (E.)
Lesmahagow (S.)

Letchworth (E.)
Linlithgow (S.)
Littleport (E.)
Livingston (S.)
Llandovery (W.)
Llanfyllin (W.)
Llangollen (W.)
Llanidloes (W.)
Maidenhead (E.)
Malmesbury (E.)
Manchester (E.)
Markethill (N.I.)
Mexborough (E.)
Middlewich (E.)
Mildenhall (E.)
Milnathort (S.)
Montgomery (W.)
Motherwell (S.)
Nailsworth (E.)
Nottingham (E.)
Okehampton (E.)
Pangbourne (E.)
Patrington (E.)
Peacehaven (E.)
Pittenweem (S.)
Pontefract (E.)
Pontypridd (W.)
Portaferry (N.I.)
Portishead (E.)
Portobello (E.)
Portsmouth (E.)
Port Talbot (W.)
Potter's Bar (E.)
Presteigne (W.)
Ravenglass (E.)
Rutherglen (S.)

Saintfield (N.I.)
St Leonards (E.)
Saltcoates (S.)
Saxmundham (E.)
Scunthorpe (E.)
Shepperton (E.)
Sheringham (E.)
Shrewsbury (E.)
Stalbridge (E.)
Stonehaven (S.)
Stonehouse (S.)
Stoneykirk (S.)
Stowmarket (E.)
Strangford (N.I.)
Sunderland (E.)
Tanderagee (N.I.)
Teddington (E.)
Teignmouth (E.)
Tewkesbury (E.)
Thamesmead (E.)
Torrington (E.)
Trowbridge (E.)
Tweedmouth (S.)
Tweedsmuir (S.)
Twickenham (E.)
Warminster (E.)
Warrington (E.)
Washington (E.)
Wednesbury (E.)
Wellington (E.)
West Calder (S.)
Westward Ho! (E.)
Whitchurch (E.)
Whitehaven (E.)
Whitstable (E.)
Whittlesey (E.)

Willenhall (E.)
Winchelsea (E.)
Winchester (E.)
Windermere (E.)
Wirksworth (E.)
Withernsea (E.)
Wolsingham (E.)
Woodbridge (E.)
Workington (E.)

11

Aberchirder (S.)
Abergavenny (E.)
Aberystwyth (W.)
Ballycastle (N.I.)
Ballygawley (N.I.)
Balquhidder (S.)
Bannockburn (S.)
Basingstoke (E.)
Berkhamsted (E.)
Bickley Moss (E.)
Blairgowrie (S.)
Bognor Regis (E.)
Bournemouth (E.)
Bridlington (E.)
Builth Wells (W.)
Buntingford (E.)
Campbeltown (S.)
Carrickmore (N.I.)
Charlestown (S.)
Cirencester (E.)
Cleethorpes (E.)
Cockermouth (E.)
Crickhowell (W.)
Crossmaglen (N.I.)
Cumbernauld (S.)

Downpatrick (N.I.)
Draperstown (N.I.)
Dunfermline (S.)
East Dereham (E.)
East Molesey (E.)
East Retford (E.)
Ecclefechan (S.)
Enniskillen (N.I.)
Farnborough (E.)
Fettercairn (S.)
Fort William (S.)
Fraserburgh (S.)
Glastonbury (E.)
Grangemouth (S.)
Great Dunmow (E.)
Guisborough (E.)
Haltwhistle (E.)
Hampton Wick (E.)
Hatherleigh (E.)
Helensburgh (S.)
High Wycombe (E.)
Ingatestone (E.)
Invergordon (S.)
Kirkmichael (S.)
Leytonstone (E.)
Littlestone (E.)
Llantrisant (W.)
Londonderry (N.I.)
Lossiemouth (S.)
Lostwithiel (E.)
Ludgershall (E.)
Lutterworth (E.)
Mablethorpe (E.)
Machynlleth (W.)
Magherafelt (N.I.)
Manningtree (E.)

Market Rasen (E.)
Marlborough (E.)
Maxwelltown (S.)
Much Wenlock (E.)
Musselburgh (S.)
New Brighton (E.)
Newton Abbot (E.)
Northampton (E.)
Oystermouth (W.)
Petersfield (E.)
Pocklington (E.)
Port Glasgow (S.)
Portglenone (N.I.)
Portmeirion (W.)
Port Patrick (S.)
Prestonpans (S.)
Pultneytown (S.)
Randalstown (N.I.)
Rathfriland (N.I.)
Rawtenstall (E.)
St Margaret's (E.)
Scarborough (E.)
Shaftesbury (E.)
South Molton (E.)
Southampton (E.)
Stalybridge (E.)
Stourbridge (E.)
Strathblane (S.)
Toome Bridge (N.I.)
Wallingford (E.)
Walthamstow (E.)
Westminster (E.)
West Molesey (E.)
Woodhall Spa (E.)

12

Attleborough (E.)
Auchterarder (S.)
Ballachulish (S.)
Beaconsfield (E.)
Bexhill-on-Sea (E.)
Burnham-on-Sea (E.)
Castledawson (N.I.)
Castlewellan (N.I.)
Chesterfield (E.)
Christchurch (E.)
East Kilbride (S.)
Fivemiletown (N.I.)
Fort Augustus (S.)
Gainsborough (E.)
Garelochhead (S.)
Great Grimsby (E.)
Great Malvern (E.)
Hillsborough (N.I.)
Huddersfield (E.)
Innerleithen (S.)
Inverkeithny (S.)
Long Stratton (E.)
Loughborough (E.)
Macclesfield (E.)
Milton Keynes (E.)
North Berwick (S.)
North Shields (E.)
North Walsham (E.)
Ottery St Mary (E.)
Peterborough (E.)
Portmahomack (S.)
Port Sunlight (E.)
Shoeburyness (E.)
Skelmersdale (E.)
South Shields (E.)

Stewartstown (N.I.)
Stoke-on-Trent (E.)
Strathpeffer (S.)
Tenbury Wells (E.)
Tillicoultry (S.)
West Bromwich (E.)
Wrotham Heath (E.)

13

Allendale Town (E.)
Auchtermuchty (S.)
Barnard Castle (E.)
Bishop's Castle (E.)
Boroughbridge (E.)
Brightlingsea (E.)
Brookeborough (N.I.)
Burnham Market (E.)
Bury St Edmunds (E.)
Carrickfergus (N.I.)
Castle Douglas (S.)
Chipping Ongar (E.)
Cockburnspath (S.)
Dalmellington (S.)
Derrygonnelly (N.I.)
East Grinstead (E.)
Godmanchester (E.)
Great Yarmouth (E.)
Haverfordwest (W.)
Higham Ferrers (E.)
Inverkeithing (S.)
Inverkeithnie (S.)
Kidderminster (E.)
Kirkby Stephen (E.)
Kirkcudbright (S.)
Kirkintilloch (S.)
Knaresborough (E.)

Leamington Spa (E.)
Littlehampton (E.)
Lytham St Anne's (E.)
Market Deeping (E.)
Market Drayton (E.)
Melcombe Regis (E.)
Melton Mowbray (E.)
Merthyr Tydfil (W.)
Middlesbrough (E.)
Newton Stewart (S.)
Northallerton (E.)
Rothiemurchus (S.)
Saffron Walden (E.)
Shepton Mallet (E.)
Wolverhampton (E.)

14

Ashby de la Zouch (E.)
Bishop Auckland (E.)
Bishops Waltham (E.)
Chipping Barnet (E.)
Chipping Norton (E.)
Grantown-on-Spey (S.)
Hemel Hempstead (E.)
Kirkby Lonsdale (E.)
Market Bosworth (E.)
Mortimer's Cross (E.)
Newton Aycliffe (E.)
Newtown Stewart (N.I.)
Stockton-on-Tees (E.)
Stony Stratford (E.)
Sutton Courtney (E.)
Thornaby-on-Tees (E.)
Tunbridge Wells (E.)
Wellingborough (E.)
West Hartlepool (E.)

Wootton Bassett (E.)

15

Ashton-under-Lyne (E.)
Barrow-in-Furness (E.)
Burnham-on-Crouch (E.)
Burton upon Trent (E.)
Clifton-upon-Teme (E.)
Leighton Buzzard (E.)
Shipston-on-Stour (E.)

Sutton Coldfield (E.)
Weston-super-Mare (E.)

16

Bishop's Stortford (E.)
Berwick-upon-Tweed (E.)
Littlestone-on-Sea (E.)
Saltburn-by-the-Sea (E.)
Welwyn Garden City (E.)

Towns and cities: United States

4	Salem	Fresno	Warren	Laramie
	Selma	Irvine	**7**	Lincoln
Erie	Tempe	Irving		Livonia
Gary	Tulsa	La Mesa	Abilene	Lubbock
Mesa	Utica	Laredo	Anaheim	Lynwood
Reno		Lowell	Atlanta	Madison
Troy	**6**	Mobile	Boulder	Memphis
Waco		Monroe	Buffalo	Modesto
Yuma	Albany	Nassau	Chicago	New York
	Aurora	Newark	Concord	Norfolk
5	Austin	Orange	Detroit	Oakland
	Bangor	Oxnard	El Monte	Ontario
Akron	Biloxi	Peoria	Fremont	Orlando
Boise	Boston	Pomona	Garland	Palm Bay
Bronx	Camden	Queens	Hampton	Phoenix
Butte	Canton	Racine	Hayward	Pontiac
Flint	Dallas	St Paul	Hialeah	Raleigh
Macon	Dayton	Tacoma	Hoboken	Reading
Miami	Denver	Toledo	Houston	Roanoke
Ogden	Duluth	Topeka	Jackson	Saginaw
Omaha	Durham	Tucson	Key West	St Louis
Ozark	El Paso	Urbana	Lansing	Salinas
Plano	Eugene			

San Jose
Seattle
Spokane
Vallejo
Wichita
Yonkers

8

Amarillo
Ann Arbor
Beaumont
Berkeley
Chandler
Columbia
Columbus
Dearborn
Glendale
Green Bay
Hannibal
Hartford
Honolulu
Lakeland
Lakewood
Las Vegas
Longview
Mesquite
Monterey
New Haven
Oak Ridge
Palo Alto
Pasadena
Paterson
Portland
Richmond
Rockford
San Diego

Santa Ana
Savannah
Scranton
Stamford
Stockton
Syracuse
Torrance
Wheeling
Whittier

9

Allentown
Anchorage
Annapolis
Arlington
Baltimore
Bethlehem
Cambridge
Champaign
Charlotte
Cleveland
Des Moines
Elizabeth
Escondido
Fairbanks
Fort Wayne
Fort Worth
Fullerton
Galveston
Henderson
Hollywood
Inglewood
Johnstown
Kalamazoo
Knoxville
Lafayette

Lancaster
Lexington
Long Beach
Manhattan
Milwaukee
Nashville
New London
Northeast
Oceanside
Pawtucket
Pine Bluff
Princeton
Rapid City
Riverside
Rochester
Santa Rosa
Sioux City
South Bend
Tombstone
Vicksburg
Waterbury
Worcester
Ypsilanti

10

Alexandria
Baton Rouge
Birmingham
Bridgeport
Charleston
Chesapeake
Chula Vista
Cincinnati
Evansville
Greensboro
Greenville

Harrisburg
Huntsville
Jersey City
Kansas City
Little Rock
Long Branch
Los Angeles
Louisville
Miami Beach
Montgomery
Naperville
New Bedford
New Orleans
Pittsburgh
Portsmouth
Providence
Richardson
Sacramento
Saint Louis
San Antonio
Scottsdale
Shreveport
Sioux Falls
Terre Haute
Tuscaloosa
Washington
Youngstown

11

Albuquerque
Bakersfield
Brownsville
Cedar Rapids
Chattanooga
Garden Grove
Grand Rapids

Lake Charles
Midwest City
Minneapolis
Newport News
Palm Springs
Schenectady
Springfield
Tallahassee

12 AND OVER

Atlantic City (12)
Beverly Hills (12)
Colorado Springs (15)
Corpus Christi (13)
Fayetteville (12)
Fort Lauderdale (14)
Huntington Beach (15)
Independence (12)
Indianapolis (12)
Jacksonville (12)
Lexington-Fayette (16)
Moreno Valley (12)
New Brunswick (12)
Newport Beach (12)
Niagara Falls (12)
Oklahoma City (12)
Overland Park (12)
Philadelphia (12)
Pompano Beach (12)
Poughkeepsie (12)
Rancho Cucamonga (15)
St Petersburg (12)
Salt Lake City (12)
San Bernardino (13)
San Francisco (12)
Santa Barbara (12)

Santa Clarita (12)
Saratoga Springs (15)
Staten Island (12)
Sterling Heights (15)

Thousand Oaks (12)
Virginia Beach (13)
West Palm Beach (13)

Towns and cities: rest of the world

3 AND 4

Agra (Ind.)
Aix (Fr.)
Albi (Fr.)
Bâle (Swit.)
Bari (It.)
Bonn (Ger.)
Bray (Ire.)
Brno (Cze.)
Caen (Fr.)
Cali (Col.)
Cobh (Ire.)
Cork (Ire.)
Fez (Moroc.)
Gaza (Pal.)
Gera (Ger.)
Giza (Egypt)
Graz (Aust.)
Györ (Hung.)
Hama (Syria)
Homs (Syria)
Hue (Viet.)
Jaén (Sp.)
Jos (Nig.)
Juba (Sudan)
Kano (Nig.)
Kiel (Ger.)

Kobe (Jap.)
Köln (Ger.)
Kota (Ind.)
Lamu (Kenya)
Laon (Fr.)
Linz (Aust.)
Lodz (Pol.)
Lüda (China)
Lund (Swed.)
Lviv (Ukr.)
Lvov (Ukr.)
Lyon (Fr.)
Metz (Fr.)
Mons (Belg.)
Naas (Ire.)
Nice (Fr.)
Nis (Yug.)
Omsk (Rus.)
Oran (Alg.)
Orel (Rus.)
Osh (Kyr.)
Pará (Braz.)
Pau (Fr.)
Pécs (Hung.)
Pegu (Burma)
Perm (Rus.)
Pisa (It.)
Pune (Ind.)

Puno (Peru)
Sian (China)
Suez (Egypt)
Suhl (Ger.)
Tour (Fr.)
Troy (Asia M.)
Tula (Rus.)
Tver (Rus.)
Tyre (Lebanon)
Ufa (Rus.)
Vigo (Sp.)
Xian (China)
Yazd (Iran)

5

Adana (Turk.)
Ajmer (Ind.)
Akyab (Burma)
Alwar (Ind.)
Aosta (It.) .
Arbil (Iraq)
Arles (Fr.)
Arras (Fr.)
Aswan (Egypt)
Asyut (Egypt)
Avila (Sp.)
Basel (Swit.)
Basle (Swit.)

Basra (Iraq)
Beira (Moz.)
Belém (Braz.)
Boyle (Ire.)
Braga (Port.)
Breda (Neth.)
Brest (Fr.)
Brest (Bela.)
Bursa (Turk.)
Cadiz (Sp.)
Cavan (Ire.)
Cuzco (Peru)
Davao (Phil.)
Delhi (Ind.)
Dijon (Fr.)
Ennis (Ire.)
Enugu (Nig.)
Essen (Ger.)
Evian (Fr.)
Fayum (Egypt)
Galle (Sri)
Genoa (It.)
Ghent (Belg.)
Gomel (Bela.)
Gorky (Rus.)
Haifa (Isr.)
Halle (Ger.)
Haora (Ind.)
Herat (Afghan.)
Izmir (Turk.)
Jaffa (Isr.)
Jinau (China)
Kabwe (Zamb.)
Kandy (Sri)
Kazan (Rus.)
Kells (Ire.)

Kirov (Rus.)
Konya (Turk.)
Kursk (Rus.)
Kyoto (Jap.)
Liège (Belg.)
Lille (Fr.)
Luxor (Egypt)
Lyons (Fr.)
Macon (Fr.)
Mainz (Ger.)
Malmö (Swed.)
Mbeya (Tanz.)
Mecca (Saudi)
Medan (Indo.)
Memel (Lith.)
Milan (It.)
Mosul (Iraq)
Namen (Belg.)
Namur (Belg.)
Nancy (Fr.)
Ndola (Zamb.)
Nîmes (Fr.)
Osaka (Jap.)
Ostia (It.)
Padua (It.)
Parma (It.)
Patna (Ind.)
Perth (Austral.)
Pinsk (Bela.)
Piura (Peru)
Poona (Ind.)
Posen (Pol.)
Pskov (Rus.)
Pusan (S. Korea)
Ramla (Isr.)
Reims (Fr.)

Rieti (It.)
Rouen (Fr.)
Sidon (Lebanon)
Siena (It.)
Simla (Ind.)
Sligo (Ire.)
Sohag (Egypt)
Split (Cro.)
Surat (Ind.)
Taegu (S. Korea)
Talca (Chile)
Tanta (Egypt)
Tomsk (Rus.)
Tours (Fr.)
Trent (It.)
Trier (Ger.)
Turin (It.)
Tuzla (Bos.)
Varna (Bulg.)
Vlöre (Alb.)
Worms (Ger.)
Wuhan (China)
Yalta (Ukr.)
Ypres (Belg.)

6

Aachen (Ger.)
Aarhus (Den.)
Abadan (Iran)
Agadir (Moroc.)
Aizawl (Ind.)
Aleppo (Syria)
Amiens (Fr.)
Ancona (It.)
Anshan (China)
Arklow (Ire.)

Arnhem (Neth.)
Bantry (Ire.)
Baroda (Ind.)
Bauchi (Nig.)
Bayeux (Fr.)
Berber (Sudan)
Bergen (Nor.)
Bhopal (Ind.)
Bilbao (Sp.)
Bochum (Ger.)
Bombay (Ind.)
Bremen (Ger.)
Bruges (Belg.)
Bukavu (Dem.
  Rep. of Congo)
Burgos (Sp.)
Calais (Fr.)
Callao (Peru)
Cannes (Fr.)
Canton (China)
Carlow (Ire.)
Cashel (Ire.)
Cassel (Ger.)
Chonju (S. Korea)
Cracow (Pol.)
Dairen (China)
Dalian (China)
Da Nang (Viet.)
Danzig (Pol.)
Darwin (Austral.)
Dieppe (Fr.)
Dinant (Belg.)
Dodoma (Tanz.)
Durban (SA)
Durrës (Alb.)
Erfurt (Ger.)

Fushun (China)
Galway (Ire.)
Gdansk (Pol.)
Geneva (Swit.)
Grodno (Bela.)
Harbin (China)
Hobart (Austral.)
Hohhot (China)
Howrah (Ind.)
Hrodna (Bela.)
Huambo (Ang.)
Huelva (Sp.)
Huesca (Sp.)
Ibadan (Nig.)
Ilorin (Nig.)
Imphal (Ind.)
Indore (Ind.)
Jaffna (Sri)
Jaipur (Ind.)
Jeddah (Saudi)
Jhansi (Ind.)
Jiddah (Saudi)
Juárez (Mex.)
Kaduna (Nig.)
Kalyan (Ind.)
Kanpur (Ind.)
Kassel (Ger.)
Kaunas (Lith.)
Khulna (Bangla.)
Kirkuk (Iraq)
Kisumu (Kenya)
Kohima (Ind.)
Kosice (Slov.)
Kraków (Pol.)
Kurgan (Rus.)
Lahore (Pak.)

Leiden (Neth.)
Le Mans (Fr.)
Leyden (Neth.)
Lobito (Angola)
Lübeck (Ger.)
Lublin (Pol.)
Lüshun (China)
Madras (Ind.)
Málaga (Sp.)
Manaus (Braz.)
Manisa (Turk.)
Medina (Saudi)
Meerut (Ind.)
Meknès (Moroc.)
Modena (It.)
Mostar (Bos.)
Mukden (China)
Multan (Pak.)
Mumbai (Ind.)
Munich (Ger.)
Murcia (Sp.)
Mutare (Zim.)
Mwanza (Tanz.)
Mysore (Ind.)
Nagoya (Jap.)
Nagpur (Ind.)
Nakuru (Ken.)
Nantes (Fr.)
Napier (N.Z.)
Naples (It.)
Nelson (N.Z.)
Oaxaca (Mex.)
Odense (Den.)
Odessa (Ukr.)
Oporto (Port.)
Orange (Fr.)

Ostend (Belg.)
Panaji (Ind.)
Paraná (Arg.)
Patras (Gr.)
Pilsen (Cze.)
Poznán (Pol.)
Puebla (Mex.)
Quebec (Can.)
Quetta (Pak.)
Rampur (Ind.)
Recife (Braz.)
Reggio (It.)
Regina (Can.)
Rheims (Fr.)
Rostov (Rus.)
St Gall (Swit.)
St Malo (Fr.)
Samara (Rus.)
Samsun (Turk.)
Sendai (Jap.)
Shiraz (Iran)
Sittwe (Burma)
Smyrna (Turk.)
Sokoto (Nig.)
Soweto (SA)
Sparta (Gr.)
Sydney (Austral.)
Szeged (Hung.)
Tabora (Tanz.)
Tabriz (Iran)
Taejon (S. Korea)
Thebes (Gr.)
Thebes (Egypt)
Tobruk (Libya)
Toledo (Sp.)
Toulon (Fr.)

Toyota (Jap.)
Tralee (Ire.)
Trento (It.)
Trèves (Ger.)
Tromsø (Nor.)
Tsinan (China)
Tudmur (Syria)
Urumqi (China)
Venice (It.)
Verdun (Fr.)
Verona (It.)
Viborg (Den.)
Vyatka (Rus.)
Zurich (Swit.)
Zwolle (Neth.)

7

Aalborg (Den.)
Ajaccio (Cors.)
Alençon (Fr.)
Alkmaar (Neth.)
Antalya (Turk.)
Antwerp (Belg.)
Athlone (Ire.)
Avignon (Fr.)
Babylon (Iraq.)
Badajoz (Sp.)
Bandung (Indo.)
Bassein (Burma)
Bayonne (Fr.)
Benares (Ind.)
Bergamo (It.)
Bologna (It.)
Bolzano (It.)
Brescia (It.)
Breslau (Pol.)

Bryansk (Rus.)
Bushehr (Iran)
Calabar (Nig.)
Calgary (Can.)
Carrick (Ire.)
Catania (It.)
Chengdu (China)
Chongju (S. Korea)
Clonmel (Ire.)
Coblenz (Ger.)
Coimbra (Port.)
Cologne (Ger.)
Córdoba (Sp.)
Córdoba (Arg.)
Corinth (Gr.)
Corunna (Sp.)
Cottbus (Ger.)
Donetsk (Ukr.)
Dongola (Sudan)
Dresden (Ger.)
Dundalk (Ire.)
Dunedin (N.Z.)
Dunkirk (Fr.)
Elbasan (Alb.)
El Obeid (Sudan)
Entebbe (Ug.)
Erzerum (Turk.)
Ferrara (It.)
Fukuoka (Jap.)
Funchal (Port.)
Gangtok (Ind.)
Granada (Sp.)
Gwalior (Ind.)
Haarlem (Neth.)
Halifax (Can.)

Hamburg (Ger.)
Hanover (Ger.)
Hitachi (Jap.)
Holguín (Cuba)
Homburg (Ger.)
Homyyel (Bela.)
Irkutsk (Rus.)
Isfahan (Iran)
Jericho (Pal.)
Jodhpur (Ind.)
Kalinin (Rus.)
Karachi (Pak.)
Karbela (Iraq.)
Kenitra (Moroc.)
Kharkiv (Ukr.)
Kharkov (Ukr.)
Kildare (Ire.)
Koblenz (Ger.)
Kunming (China)
La Plata (Arg.)
Lanchow (China)
Lanzhou (China)
Latakia (Syria)
Le Havre (Fr.)
Leipzig (Ger.)
Lemberg (Ukr.)
Liepaja (Lat.)
Lifford (Ire.)
Limoges (Fr.)
Logroño (Sp.)
Lourdes (Fr.)
Lucerne (Swit.)
Lucknow (Ind.)
Malines (Belg.)
Mansura (Egypt)
Maramba (Zam.)

Mashhad (Iran)
Massawa (Eritrea)
Memphis (Egypt)
Mendoza (Arg.)
Messina (It.)
Miskolc (Hung.)
Mogilev (Bela.)
Mombasa (Kenya)
Morelia (Mex.)
München (Ger.)
Mycenae (Gr.)
Nanjing (China)
Nanking (China)
Nanning (China)
Nicosia (Cyprus)
Novi Sad (Yug.)
Orléans (Fr.)
Ostrava (Cze.)
Palermo (It.)
Palmyra (Syria)
Perugia (It.)
Pescara (It.)
Piraeus (Gr.)
Plovdiv (Bulg.)
Pompeii (It.)
Potsdam (Ger.)
Ravenna (It.)
Rosario (Arg.)
Rostock (Ger.)
St John's (Can.)
Salerno (It.)
Santa Fe (Arg.)
San Remo (It.)
Sapporo (Jap.)
Setúbal (Port.)
Seville (Sp.)

Taiyuan (China)
Tangier (Moroc.)
Tel Aviv (Isr.)
Tétouan (Moroc.)
Tianjin (China)
Toronto (Can.)
Trieste (It.)
Tripoli (Leb.)
Tripoli (Libya)
Tucumán (Arg.)
Uppsala (Swed.)
Utrecht (Neth.)
Vitebsk (Bela.)
Vitoria (Sp.)
Wexford (Ire.)
Wicklow (Ire.)
Wroclaw (Pol.)
Yakutsk (Rus.)
Youghal (Ire.)
Zagazig (Egypt)

8

Acapulco (Mex.)
Adelaide (Austral.)
Agartala (Ind.)
Alicante (Sp.)
Amritsar (Ind.)
Auckland (N.Z.)
Augsburg (Ger.)
Benguela (Ang.)
Besançon (Fr.)
Biarritz (Fr.)
Bordeaux (Fr.)
Boulogne (Fr.)
Brisbane (Austral.)
Bulawayo (Zim.)

Cagliari (It.)
Calcutta (Ind.)
Camagüey (Cuba)
Carthage (Tun.)
Cawnpore (Ind.)
Changsha (China)
Changzhi (China)
Chartres (Fr.)
Chemnitz (Ger.)
Chonqing (China)
Clontarf (Ire.)
Curitiba (Braz.)
Damietta (Egypt)
Debrecen (Hung.)
Dortmund (Ger.)
Drogheda (Ire.)
Edmonton (Can.)
El Faiyum (Egypt)
Florence (It.)
Göteborg (Swed.)
Grenoble (Fr.)
Haiphong (Viet.)
Hakodate (Jap.)
Hamilton (Can.)
Hannover (Ger.)
Ismailia (Egypt)
Istanbul (Turk.)
Jamalpur (Ind.)
Kandahar (Afghan.)
Karlstad (Swed.)
Kawasaki (Jap.)
Kilkenny (Ire.)
Kingston (Can.)
Klaipeda (Lith.)
Lausanne (Swit.)
Limerick (Ire.)

Listowel (Ire.)
Longford (Ire.)
Ludhiana (Ind.)
Mafeking (SA)
Mahilyou (Bela.)
Mandalay (Burma)
Mannheim (Ger.)
Matanzas (Cuba)
Mechelen (Belg.)
Medellín (Col.)
Monaghan (Ire.)
Montreal (Can.)
Murmansk (Rus.)
Nagasaki (Jap.)
Nazareth (Isr.)
Novgorod (Rus.)
Nürnberg (Ger.)
Omdurman (Sudan)
Pamplona (Sp.)
Peshawar (Pak.)
Port Said (Egypt)
Przemysl (Pol.)
Rajshahi (Bangla.)
Rathdrum (Ire.)
St Tropez (Fr.)
Salonica (Gr.)
Salvador (Braz.)
Salzburg (Aust.)
São Paulo (Braz.)
Schwerin (Ger.)
Semarang (Indo.)
Shanghai (China)
Shenyang (China)
Shillong (Ind.)
Shymkent (Kaz.)
Smolensk (Rus.)

Soissons (Fr.)
Srinagar (Ind.)
Surabaya (Indo.)
Syracuse (It.)
The Hague (Neth.)
Tientsin (China)
Timbuktu (Mali)
Toulouse (Fr.)
Vadodara (Ind.)
Valencia (Sp.)
Varanasi (Ind.)
Veracruz (Mex.)
Victoria (Can.)
Vladimir (Rus.)
Voronezh (Rus.)
Winnipeg (Can.)
Yokohama (Jap.)
Zanzibar (Tanz.)
Zaragoza (Sp.)

9

Abbeville (Fr.)
Agrigento (It.)
Ahmadabad (Ind.)
Allahabad (Ind.)
Archangel (Rus.)
Astrakhan (Rus.)
Bangalore (Ind.)
Banja Luka (Bos.)
Barcelona (Sp.)
Beersheba (Isr.)
Benin City (Nig.)
Brunswick (Ger.)
Byzantium (Turk.)
Cartagena (Sp.)
Cartagena (Col.)

Castlebar (Ire.)
Changchun (China)
Changzhou (China)
Cherbourg (Fr.)
Cherkessk (Rus.)
Chungking (China)
Connemara (Ire.)
Darmstadt (Ger.)
Dordrecht (Neth.)
Eindhoven (Neth.)
El Mansura (Egypt)
Fortaleza (Braz.)
Frankfurt (Ger.)
Gazientep (Turk.)
Gibraltar (Eur.)
Groningen (Neth.)
Guangzhou (China)
Guayaquil (Ecuador)
Heraklion (Gr.)
Hiroshima (Jap.)
Hyderabad (Ind.)
Hyderabad (Pak.)
Innsbruck (Aust.)
Jalalabad (Afghan.)
Kaohsiung (Taiwan)
Karaganda (Kaz.)
Killarney (Ire.)
Kimberley (SA)
Kisangani (Dem. Rep. of
   Congo)
Krivoi Rog (Ukr.)
Kryvyy Rig (Ukr.)
Kuibyshev (Rus.)
Ladysmith (SA)
Las Palmas (Sp.)
Leningrad (Rus.)

Linköping (Swed.)
Ljubljana (Sloven.)
Magdeburg (Ger.)
Maiduguri (Nig.)
Maracaibo (Venez.)
Marrakech (Moroc.)
Marrakesh (Moroc.)
Marseille (Fr.)
Matsuyama (Jap.)
Melbourne (Austral.)
Montauban (Fr.)
Monterrey (Mex.)
Mullingar (Ire.)
Newcastle (Austral.)
Nuremberg (Ger.)
Palembang (Indo.)
Perpignan (Fr.)
Podgorica (Monte.)
Roscommon (Ire.)
Rotterdam (Neth.)
St Étienne (Fr.)
Samarkand (Uzbek.)
Santander (Sp.)
Saragossa (Sp.)
Saskatoon (Can.)
Stavanger (Nor.)
Stavropol (Rus.)
Stuttgart (Ger.)
Tipperary (Ire.)
Trondheim (Nor.)
Tullamore (Ire.)
Vancouver (Can.)
Volgograd (Rus.)
Waterford (Ire.)
Wiesbaden (Ger.)
Wuppertal (Ger.)

Yaroslavl (Rus.)
Zamboanga (Phil.)
Zhengzhou (China)
Zonguldak (Turk.)

10

Alexandria (Egypt)
Baden Baden (Ger.)
Bad Homburg (Ger.)
Casablanca (Moroc.)
Chandigarh (Ind.)
Chittagong (Bangla.)
Concepción (Chile)
Cuernavaca (Mex.)
Darjeeling (Ind.)
Daugavpils (Lat.)
Diyarbakir (Turk.)
Düsseldorf (Ger.)
Faisalabad (Pak.)
Gothenburg (Swed.)
Gujranwala (Pak.)
Heidelberg (Ger.)
Jamshedpur (Ind.)
Kitakyushu (Jap.)
Klagenfurt (Aust.)
Königsberg (Rus.)
Lubumbashi (Dem. Rep. of
Congo)
Maastricht (Neth.)
Marseilles (Fr.)
Montélimar (Fr.)
Port Arthur (China)
Port Laoise (Ire.)
Portoviejo (Ecuador)
Qaraghandy (Kaz.)
Rawalpindi (Pak.)

Sevastopol (Ukr.)
Shillelagh (Ire.)
Simonstown (SA)
Stalingrad (Rus.)
Strasbourg (Fr.)
Sverdlovsk (Rus.)
Thunder Bay (Can.)
Trivandrum (Ind.)
Valladolid (Sp.)
Valparaíso (Chile)
Versailles (Fr.)
Whitehorse (Can.)

11

Armentières (Fr.)
Bahia Blanca (Arg.)
Ballymurphy (Ire.)
Bandar Abbas (Iran)
Bhubaneswar (Ind.)
Campo Grande (Braz.)
Chelyabinsk (Rus.)
Dar es Salaam (Tanz.)
Fredericton (Can.)
Grahamstown (SA)
Guadalajara (Mex.)
Guadalajara (Sp.)
Helsingborg (Swed.)
Kaliningrad (Rus.)
Khorramabad (Iran)
Lillehammer (Nor.)
Montpellier (Fr.)
Novosibirsk (Rus.)
Porto Alegre (Braz.)
Puerto Montt (Chile)
Punta Arenas (Chile)
Rostov-on-Don (Rus.)

Saarbrücken (Ger.)
Sharpeville (SA)
Trincomalee (Sri)
Vladivostok (Rus.)
Yellowknife (Can.)

12

Alice Springs (Austral.)
Barranquilla (Col.)
Bloemfontein (SA)
Braunschweig (Ger.)
Cagayan de Oro (Phil.)
Christchurch (N.Z.)
Dun Laoghaire (Ire.)
Johannesburg (SA)
Niagara Falls (Can.)
Port Harcourt (Nig.)
Rio de Janeiro (Braz.)
St Petersburg (Rus.)
San Sebastian (Sp.)
Thessaloniki (Gr.)

13 AND OVER

Aix-la-Chapelle (Ger.) (13)
Banská Bystrica (Slov.) (14)
Belo Horizonte (Braz.) (13)
Carrick-on-Shannon (Ire.) (16)
Ceske Budejovice (Cze.) (15)
Charlottetown (Can.) (13)
Clermont-Ferrand (Fr.) (15)
Constantinople (Turk.) (14)
Dnepropetrovsk (Ukr.) (14)
Karl-Marx-Stadt (Ger.) (13)
Nizhny Novgorod (Rus.) (14)
Pietermaritzburg (SA) (16)
Port Elizabeth (SA) (13)

Reggio di Calabria (It.) (16)
Reggio nell'Emilia (It.) (16)
Santiago de Cuba (Cuba) (14)

s'-Hertogenbosch (Neth.) (14)
Yekaterinburg (Rus.) (13)

Waterfalls: the largest

Angel (Venez.) (5)
Churchill (Can.) (9)
Gavarnie (Fr.) (8)
Giessbach (Swit.) (9)
Guaira (Braz.) (6)
Hamilton (Can.) (8)
Krimml (Aust.) (6)
Multnomah (USA) (9)
Niagara (Can.–USA) (7)
Ribbon (USA) (6)

Roraima (Guyana) (7)
Sete Quedas (Braz.) (10)
Stanley (Dem. Rep. of Congo) (7)
Sutherland (N.Z.) (10)
Trümmelbach (Swit.) (11)
Vettisfos (Nor.) (9)
Victoria (Zambia–Zimbabwe) (8)
Yosemite (USA) (8)

Weather

3 AND 4	gust	snow	cirri	north
	haar	sun	cloud	rainy
bise	hail	thaw	dusty	sleet
bora	haze	tide	Eurus	snowy
calm	hazy	veer	flood	south
cold	heat	warm	foehn	storm
cool	hoar	west	foggy	sunny
damp	hot	wet	front	windy
dark	ice	wind	frost	
dry	icy		gusty	6
dull	mild	5	heavy	Aeolus
east	mist	blast	humid	arctic
fog	rain	blowy	light	aurora
föhn	rime	buran	misty	auster
gale	smog	chill	muggy	boreal

Boreas
breeze
breezy
brumal
chilly
cirrus
clouds
cloudy
colder
corona
degree
deluge
floods
freeze
frosty
haboob
hot day
isobar
isohel
mizzle
mizzly
nimbus
normal
red sky
samiel
serein
shower
simoom
solano
squall
starry
stormy
stuffy
sultry
torrid
trades

vortex
warmer
wet day
winter
wintry
zephyr

7

air-mass
aureole
backing
blowing
blue sky
bluster
chinook
clement
climate
clouded
cold air
cold day
coldish
cumulus
current
cyclone
drizzle
drizzly
drought
element
etesian
fogbank
freshen
fresher
freshet
gregale
grey sky
hailing

hottish
ice-cold
icy wind
isohyet
khamsin
meltemi
mistral
monsoon
pampero
pea soup
rainbow
raining
set fair
showery
sirocco
sizzler
snowing
squally
stratus
sub-zero
summery
sunspot
tempest
thunder
tornado
typhoon
veering
warm day
warmish
weather
wintery

8

autumnal
Beaufort
black ice

blizzard
clear day
climatic
cloud cap
cold wave
cold wind
cyclonic
dead calm
dewpoint
doldrums
downpour
east wind
easterly
elements
etesian
favonian
fireball
forecast
freezing
haziness
headwind
heat haze
heatwave
high wind
humidity
isothere
isotherm
levanter
libeccio
low cloud
lowering
meteoric
moderate
nubilous
occluded
overcast

pressure
rain belt
raindrop
rainfall
rainless
rainy day
scirocco
scorcher
snowfall
sunburst
sunlight
sunshine
thundery
tropical
westerly
west wind
wind cone
windless
windsock
windvane

9

anemology
barometer
below zero
blue skies
cloud bank
cloud over
cold front
corposant
drizzling
dry season
dust storm
fogginess
frostbite
gale force

hailstone
hailstorm
hard frost
harmattan
heavy rain
hoarfrost
hurricane
inclement
light rain
lightning
midday sun
mild spell
mistiness
moonlight
nor'easter
north wind
northeast
northerly
northwest
nor'wester
occlusion
overcloud
pea souper
raincloud
rain gauge
rainstorm
sandstorm
sea breeze
snowflake
snowstorm
south wind
southeast
southerly
southwest
sou'-wester
starlight

tidal wave
trade wind
turbulent
unclouded
unsettled
warm front
weak front
whirlwind
wind gauge
windstorm

10

anemograph
arctic cold
bitter cold
black frost
changeable
cloudburst
cloudiness
cool breeze
depression
euroclydon
freshening
frostbound
hailstones
hot climate
hot weather
hygrometer
icy patches
land breeze
light winds
March winds
patchy rain
pouring-wet
Scotch mist
sharp frost

stormcloud
strong wind
sweltering
turbulence
waterspout
wet weather
white frost

11

altocumulus
altostratus
anticyclone
cats and dogs
cold climate
cold weather
driving rain
dull weather
etesian wind
foul weather
fresh breeze
gale warning
ground frost
harvest moon
low pressure
lowering sky
mackerel sky
meteorology
mild weather
monsoon wind
northeaster
northwester
patchy cloud
pouring rain
precipitate
rain or shine
rainy season

showery rain
stiff breeze
summer cloud
temperature
tempestuous
thermometer
thunderbolt
thunderclap
warm weather
weathercock
weathervane
wind backing
wind veering

12

anticyclonic
April showers
atmospherics
bitterly cold
cirrocumulus
cirrostratus
cumulonimbus
easterly wind
equinoctials
freezing cold
freezing rain
high pressure
Indian summer
microclimate
nimbostratus
offshore wind
shooting star
storm brewing
storm signals
thundercloud
thunderstorm

tropical heat
tropical rain
warm sunshine
weather chart
weather glass
westerly wind
wind velocity
windy weather

13 AND 14

aurora borealis (14)
autumn weather (13)
Beaufort scale (13)
cumulostratus (13)
frosty weather (13)
further outlook (14)
meteorological (14)
meteorologist (13)
moonlight night (14)
northeast wind (13)
northerly wind (13)
northwest wind (13)

sheet lightning (14)
southeast wind (13)
southerly wind (13)
southwest wind (13)
starlight night (14)
stratocumulus (13)
summer weather (13)
thunder-shower (13)
torrential rain (14)
weather prophet (14)
weather report (13)
weather station (13)
wintry weather (13)

15

forked lightning
meteoric showers
prevailing winds
summer lightning
tropical climate
weather forecast

JEWELLERY, GEMS, ETC.

3 AND 4

bead
clip
gaud
gem
gold
jade
jet
onyx
opal

ring
ruby
sard
stud
torc

5

agate
aglet
amber
badge

beads
beryl
bezel
bijou
bugle
cameo
carat
charm
clasp
coral
crown

ivory
jewel
lapis
links
nacre
paste
pearl
tiara
topaz
watch

6

albert
amulet
anklet
armlet
augite
bangle
bauble
brooch
corals
diadem
enamel
fibula
garnet
gewgaw
iolite
jargon
locket
olivet
pearls
pyrope
quartz
sequin
signet
silver
spinel
tiepin
torque
wampum
zircon

7

abraxas
adamant
annulet
armilla

asteria
cat's eye
chaplet
coronet
crystal
diamond
eardrop
earring
emerald
euclase
girasol
jacinth
jewelry
olivine
pendant
peridot
regalia
ringlet
sardine
sardius
sceptre
spangle
telesia
trinket

8

adularia
aigrette
amethyst
bracelet
carcanet
corundum
crucifix
filigree
fire opal
gemstone

hallmark
hyacinth
intaglio
ligurite
necklace
pectoral
platinum
sapphire
sardonyx
scarf-pin
sparkler
sunstone

9

balas ruby
black onyx
black opal
breast-pin
brilliant
carbuncle
carnelian
cornelian
cufflinks
gold watch
grossular
jadestone
jewellery
marcasite
medallion
moonstone
moss agate
paillette
press stud
rubellite
seed pearl
solitaire

starstone
thumb ring
trinketry
turquoise
water opal

10

amber beads
aquamarine
black pearl
bloodstone
chalcedony
chrysolite
coral beads
glass beads
lucky charm
rhinestone
signet ring
topazolite
tourmaline
watch-chain
watchstrap
wristwatch

11

aiguillette
alexandrite
cameo brooch
chalcedonyx
chrysoberyl
chrysoprase
crocidolite
lapis lazuli
wedding-ring

12 AND OVER

bead necklace (12)
chain bracelet (13)
charm bracelet (13)
coral necklace (13)
crystal necklace (15)
engagement ring (14)
eternity ring (12)
link bracelet (12)
mother-of-pearl (13)
mourning brooch (14)
mourning ring (12)
pearl necklace (13)
precious stone (13)

JOURNALISM, PRINTING AND PUBLISHING

2	pi	box	imp	run
	sc	cap	ink	set
ad	wf	crc	mat	sub
em		cub	OCR	web
en	3	cut	out	
MS	ads	die	pie	4
op	bed	DTP	pot	back

body	ruby	forme	tilde
bold	rule	fount	title
book	sewn	gloss	verso
bulk	sink	grain	widow
case	slug	index	xerox
caps	stet	inset	
comp	take	leads	**6**
copy	trim	libel	
crop	type	linen	author
cyan	word	litho	back-up
dash		metal	banner
demy	**5**	paper	binder
edit		pearl	blow up
etch	align	plate	boards
face	beard	point	ceriph
film	black	press	cicero
flap	bleed	print	cliché
font	block	proof	coated
grid	blurb	punch	cock-up
hack	cameo	quire	column
ISBN	canon	quote	dagger
lead	caret	recto	delete
leaf	cased	reset	design
limp	chase	roman	editor
line	chill	rough	em-dash
matt	cloth	royal	en-dash
mode	clump	run-on	errata
news	cover	scoop	flimsy
open	crown	serif	format
page	daily	sigla	galley
pica	devil	solid	glossy
puff	Didot	sorts	gutter
pull	draft	spike	indent
quad	dummy	spine	italic
read	extra	stone	jacket
ream	flong	story	keep up
	folio		layout

			8
leaded	uncial	heading	abridged
leader	weekly	imprint	addendum
linage	weight	in print	art board
lock up		italics	ascender
makeup	**7**	journal	bad break
margin		justify	biweekly
mark up	acetate	leading	bleeding
marked	article	literal	boldface
masked	artwork	masking	book club
matrix	binding	measure	bookends
matter	bled off	minion	bookmark
minion	brevier	monthly	bookshop
mock-up	bromide	mortice	city desk
morgue	bumping	net sale	co-author
octavo	capital	overrun	colophon
offset	capsule	overset	contents
ozalid	caption	paste-up	contract
period	cast off	pen-name	cut flush
précis	cedilla	preface	cuttings
quarto	chapter	prelims	database
quotes	clicker	printer	dateline
random	collate	profile	deadline
review	desk-top	publish	designer
revise	diamond	reissue	endpaper
rotary	display	release	foolscap
run off	edition	reprint	footnote
screen	English	rewrite	fudge box
serial	engrave	royalty	full stop
series	erratum	section	gatefold
set-off	etching	sits vac	graphics
sketch	feature	subedit	hairline
spiked	flyleaf	tabloid	halftone
splash	fold-out	typeset	handbook
spread	Fraktur	woodcut	hardback
stereo	full out	wordage	headband
umlaut	gravure		
	gripper		

9

headline
hot metal
imperial
intaglio
keyboard
laminate
ligature
linotype
longhand
magazine
misprint
monotype
obituary
offprint
paginate
photoset
print run
printers
printing
register
reporter
slipcase
softback
streamer
stringer
subtitle
tailband
text area
textbook
turnover
type area
typeface
type size
verbatim
vignette
woodpulp

ampersand
art editor
bimonthly
bookplate
bookstall
bookstore
book trade
bourgeois
box number
brilliant
broadside
casebound
character
clippings
co-edition
collating
collotype
columnist
condensed
copypaper
copyright
crossword
descender
editorial
end matter
end papers
exclusive
facsimile
freelance
furniture
half title
hard cover
idiot tape
keystroke
laminated

late extra
lightface
lineblock
line break
loose leaf
lower case
make ready
marked set
marking up
necrology
newspaper
newsprint
nonpareil
overprint
page proof
paperback
paragraph
photocopy
photostat
pressroom
print shop
proofread
pseudonym
publisher
quarterly
sans serif
shorthand
signature
small caps
small pica
soft cover
stonehand
subeditor
symposium
tear sheet
the morgue

title page
underline
upper case
watermark
web-offset
woodblock
wrong font

10

annotation
assembling
blockmaker
body matter
bookbinder
bookseller
broadsheet
casting box
casting-off
catch title
city editor
compositor
copy edition
copyholder
copytaster
copywriter
correction
dead matter
dirty proof
feuilleton
film critic
four colour
house style
imposition
impression
imprimatur
interleave

jacket copy
journalese
journalism
journalist
lamination
leader page
lithograph
long primer
manuscript
metal plate
microfiche
monochrome
news agency
news editor
nom-de-plume
out of print
overmatter
pagination
paraphrase
periodical
plagiarism
press agent
proof stage
publishing
ranged left
reverse out
separation
short story
stereotype
subheading
supplement
syndication
title verso
trade paper
typescript
typesetter

typography
vignetting
wrong fount
xerography

11

advance copy
advertising
agony column
chapter head
circulation
copy-editing
copy-fitting
crown octavo
cub reporter
display type
drama critic
filmsetting
fortnightly
front matter
galley proof
ghostwriter
great primer
gutter press
half measure
hyphenation
late edition
letterpress
line drawing
line spacing
lithography
night editor
platemaking
printer's ink
proofreader
publication

rotary press
rotogravure
running
   head
section-sewn
special sort
superscript
unjustified

12

advance proof
bibliography
block letters
book reviewer
centrespread
contents list
cross heading
double-column
early edition
facing matter
feature story
first edition
fourth estate
frontispiece
illustration
introduction
keep standing
leader writer
London editor
magazine page
newspaperman
perfect bound
photogravure
press release
repagination
running title

saddle stitch
single column
sports editor
telegraphese
transparency
works manager

13

advertisement
composing room
cylinder press
editor-in-chief
foreign editor
foreign rights
justification
literary agent
litho printing
pocket edition
spiral binding
stop press news
typographical
wire stitching

14 AND OVER

banner headline (14)
calendered paper (15)

camera-ready copy (15)
coffee table book (15)
colour separation (16)
colour supplement (16)
cross-reference (14)
desk-top publishing (17)
double-page
    spread (16)
features editor (14)
half-title verso (14)
leading article (14)
limited edition (14)
line illustration (16)
literary editor (14)
managing editor (14)
offset printing (14)
perfect binding (14)
personal column (14)
photolithography (16)
picture research (15)
printer's error (14)
proof correcting (15)
proof correction (15)
running headline (15)
silk-screen printing (18)

LAW AND GOVERNMENT
Legal terms

2	3 AND 4		
JP	abet	bail	bribe
KC	act	bar	case
QC	aka	bars	dock
	aver	beak	DPP
		bond	fair

fee	**5**	order	bailee
feu	abate	overt	bigamy
fine	adopt	parol	breach
gbh	alias	penal	caveat
gaol	alibi	petty	censor
IOU	alien	plead	charge
jail	arson	poach	commit
jury	award	prize	convey
law	bench	proof	cy pres
lien	brief	quash	deceit
life	bylaw	right	decree
m'lud	cause	rules	de jure
nisi	claim	steal	delate
not	clerk	swear	delict
oath	costs	tenor	depose
plea	covin	thief	devise
quit	court	title	dictum
rape	crime	trial	disbar
rent	crook	trust	domain
rob	demur	usher	duress
rule	devil	usury	elegit
seal	estop	valid	enjoin
silk	false	venue	entail
soke	felon		equity
stay	feoff	**6**	escrow
sue	forge	adjure	estate
suit	fraud	access	felony
term	grant	action	fiscal
tort	guilt	affirm	forger
try	in rem	affray	guilty
use	judge	amerce	Hilary
veto	juror	appeal	holdup
ward	lease	arrest	incest
will	legal	assets	indict
writ	libel	asylum	injury
	mulct	attorn	insult

junior	tender	coroner	juryman
jurist	trover	counsel	justice
kidnap	warder	cruelty	larceny
lawful		custody	law lord
lawyer	**7**	damages	lawless
legacy		damnify	lawsuit
legist	abscond	de facto	legatee
lessee	accused	default	legator
lessor	accuser	defence	licence
lethal	adjourn	delator	marshal
malice	alimony	demesne	mens rea
master	amnesty	deodand	movable
mayhem	arbiter	devolve	neglect
motion	arraign	dies non	non suit
motive	assault	divorce	offence
murder	assizes	engross	penalty
nonage	autopsy	escheat	perjury
on oath	bailiff	estreat	precept
outlaw	battery	ex parte	probate
pardon	bencher	foreman	proctor
parole	bequest	forfeit	relator
piracy	binding	forgery	release
police	borstal	garnish	replevy
prison	bribery	grantee	reserve
puisne	burglar	hanging	Riot Act
relief	capital	harming	robbery
remand	case law	hearing	sheriff
remise	cashier	hearsay	sine die
repeal	caution	illegal	slander
robber	charter	illicit	statute
ruling	chattel	impeach	summary
script	circuit	implead	summons
socage	codicil	inquest	suspect
suitor	commute	inquiry	swear in
surety	connive	John Doe	tenancy
tenant	consent	joinder	testate
	convict		

testify
treason
trustee
verdict
warrant
witness

8

abeyance
absolute
abstract
act of God
advocate
advowson
allodium
amortize
attorney
avulsion
barratry
bequeath
bottomry
burglary
canon law
chancery
civil law
coercion
contempt
contract
copyhold
covenant
criminal
decedent
deed poll
demurrer
deponent
detainee

detainer
disorder
disseize
distrain
distress
domicile
drafting
embezzle
entailed
estoppel
estovers
eviction
evidence
executor
felo de se
feme sole
fidelity
findings
forensic
foul play
genocide
gravamen
guardian
homicide
hung jury
in camera
indecent
informer
innocent
instruct
jailbird
jeopardy
jointure
judgment
judicial
law agent

law court
law lords
legal aid
licensee
litigant
litigate
majority
mandamus
mistrial
mittimus
mortmain
murderer
novation
nuisance
offender
peculate
penal law
penology
perjuror
petition
pleading
preamble
prisoner
promisee
promisor
rebuttal
rebutter
receiver
recorder
replevin
reprieve
Salic law
sedition
sentence
Shops Act
stealing

subpoena
sui juris
testator
test case
tipstaff
tortious
trespass
tribunal
Truck Act
true bill
unlawful
validity
war crime

9

abatement
abduction
accession
accessory
acquittal
ademption
affidavit
agreement
alienable
allotment
annulment
appellant
appellate
attainder
bailiwick
barrister
blackmail
bona fides
bound over
care order
champerty

code of law
collusion
common law
copyright
courtroom
coverture
defendant
desertion
de son tort
discharge
discovery
dismissal
disseisin
distraint
doli capax
embezzler
embraceor
embracery
endowment
equitable
execution
executory
executrix
exonerate
extortion
fee simple
felonious
feoffment
Gaming Act
garnishee
good faith
grand jury
guarantee
guarantor
high court
income tax

indemnity
innocence
intestacy
intestate
judiciary
jurywoman
justiciar
libellant
litigious
loitering
mala fides
mandatory
matricide
murderous
nisi prius
not guilty
not proven
objection
Old Bailey
open court
parricide
penal code
petty jury
pilfering
plaintiff
precatory
precedent
privilege
probation
procedure
pronounce
prosecute
receiving
refresher
registrar
remission

represent
reprimand
residuary
restraint
sanctions
servitude
smuggling
solicitor
statement
statutory
sub judice
subrogate
summing up
surrender
testament
testatrix
testimony
title deed
vexatious

10

actionable
admissible
alienation
appearance
assessment
assignment
attachment
attornment
bank robber
bankruptcy
breath test
certiorari
cessionary
child abuse
civil wrong

co-executor
cognizance
competence
confession
connivance
conspiracy
contraband
contravene
conveyance
conviction
copyholder
corruption
court of law
court order
crime sheet
crown court
decree nisi
deed of gift
defamation
delinquent
deposition
disclaimer
disinherit
duty of care
enticement
estate duty
executrix
eye witness
feme covert
finance act
forfeiture
fratricide
fraud squad
fraudulent
free pardon
gaming acts

gun licence
hard labour
illegality
impediment
in chambers
indictment
injunction
inter vivos
judicature
justiciary
King's Bench
land tenure
Law Society
legal right
legitimacy
limitation
liquor laws
litigation
magistrate
martial law
misconduct
misprision
negligence
next friend
nonjoinder
out of court
personalty
petty theft
pickpocket
post mortem
prima facie
prize court
procurator
prosecutor
respondent
revocation

separation
settlement
shoplifter
soliciting
spoliation
statute law
submission
title deeds
trespasser
ultra vires
witness box

11

advancement
affiliation
appointment
arbitration
assize court
attestation
Children Act
civil wrongs
class action
Common Pleas
composition
concealment
condonation
coparcenary
county court
criminal law
death duties
debtors' acts
deportation
dissolution
disturbance
enabling act
encumbrance

enforcement
engrossment
escheatment
examination
extenuating
extradition
fair comment
false arrest
fingerprint
fieri facias
foreclosure
garnishment
high treason
higher court
house arrest
impeachment
incriminate
infanticide
issue of writ
King's Pardon
law merchant
legal tender
libel action
locus standi
maintenance
malpractice
market overt
mayor's court
misfeasance
obstruction
open verdict
prerogative
prosecution
puisne judge
Queen's
    Bench

quo warranto
requisition
restitution
root of title
royal assent
scire facias
sequestrate
sheriff's act
shoplifting
stamp duties
stipendiary
subornation
subrogation
suicide pact
third degree
trespassing
trial by jury
under arrest
Vagrancy Act
vesting deed
ward of court

12

adjudication
age of consent
amicus curiae
bill of rights
bona vacantia
breathalyzer
case of thorns
causa proxima
caution money
caveat emptor
charter party
chattels real
chief justice

circuit judge
Companies Act
compensation
compurgation
condemnation
confiscation
constabulary
conveyancing
co-respondent
court martial
cross-examine
crown witness
death penalty
disaffection
divorce court
embezzlement
encroachment
express trust
ferae naturae
first offence
force majeure
grand assizes
guardianship
habeas corpus
hereditament
imprisonment
infringement
inherent vice
interpleader
intimidation
jail sentence
joint tenancy
jurisdiction
kerb crawling
King's Counsel
legal fiction

life sentence
Lord Advocate
lord of appeal
manslaughter
mensa et thoro
misbehaviour
misdemeanour
misdirection
obiter dictem
oral evidence
pendente lite
petty larceny
prescription
privy council
prostitution
Queen's Pardon
ratification
royal charter
royal warrant
sheriff clerk
supreme court
taxing master
testamentary

13

administrator
ancient lights
apportionment
appropriation
breach of trust
burden of proof
charging order
citizen's arrest
common assault
consideration
coroner's court

corpus delecti
court of appeal
Court of Arches
criminal libel
cross-question
damage feasant
ejection order
eminent domain
Ground Game Act
hereditaments
housebreaking
illegal action
impersonation
interlocutory
judge advocate
justification
juvenile court
kangaroo court
letters patent
lord president
nolle prosequi
parliamentary
petty sessions
public trustee
quantum meruit
Queen's Counsel
recognizances
right of appeal
search warrant
sharp practice
sitting tenant
statute barred
treasure trove
trial by combat
trial by ordeal
Witchcraft Act

14

act of indemnity
Admiralty Court
choses in action
civil liberties
common nuisance
common sergeant
conjugal rights
county judgment
court of inquiry
court of justice
criminal damage
criminal record
decree absolute
default summons
double jeopardy
ejusdem generis
exclusion order
false pretences
identification
identity parade
legally binding
lord chancellor
naturalization
penal servitude
plea bargaining
public nuisance
Queen's evidence
special licence
wrongful arrest

15

act of bankruptcy
act of Parliament
Act of Settlement
attorney-general

autrefois acquit
benefit of clergy
breach of promise
charitable trust
compound a felony
confidence trick
consistory court
contempt of court
coroner's inquest
detention centre
disorderly house
emergency powers
hearsay evidence
indecent assault
latent ambiguity
majority verdict
marriage licence
oyer and terminer
power of attorney
protection money
quarter sessions
stay of execution

Parliamentary and political terms

2	Diet	clerk	decree	7
EC	DORA	count	divide	
EU	Duma	draft	enosis	adjourn
MP	EFTA	edict	Fabian	al Fatah
PM	gain	elect	Führer	al-Qa'ida
UN	left	enact	govern	Althing
	lord	forum	heckle	anarchy
3	mace	house	Labour	barrack
	NATO	junta	leader	borough
ANC	Nazi	legal	Majlis	boycott
act	noes	lobby	Maoism	cabinet
bar	oath	Nazis	member	canvass
BNP	pact	order	motion	censure
CBI	pass	paper	nation	chamber
CIA	peer	party	picket	closure
DUP	poll	Provo	policy	cold war
EEC	rump	purge	putsch	Comecon
ETA	seat	rally	quorum	Commons
gag	SDLP	right	recess	commune
IRA	Sejm	SEATO	record	council
KGB	Tory	sit-in	reform	deficit
OAU	UKIP	valid	report	détente
PLO	veto	voter	ruling	dissent
red	vote		satrap	elector
SNP	Whig	6	secede	embargo
sit	whip		senate	fascism
TUC	writ	assent	sirkar	fascist
tax		backer	speech	federal
	5	ballot	strike	finance
4		budget	summon	gallery
	agent	caucus	swaraj	Hansard
ayes	amend	clause	tariff	heckler
bill	Boule	colony	teller	hot line
coup	bylaw	commie	tyrant	Knesset
Dáil	chair	Cortes		

liberal
lock out
mandate
Marxism
neutral
new left
opening
outvote
pairing
passage
politic
poor law
premier
primary
prolong
radical
reading
recount
re-elect
re-enact
Riksdag
senator
session
speaker
statute
Toryism
tribune
Tynwald
tyranny
vacancy
Zionism
Zionist

8

assembly
autarchy

autocrat
Black Rod
blockade
caudillo
chairman
Chiltern
   (Hundreds)
commissar
commoner
Congress
democrat
dictator
dissolve
division
dominion
ecclesia
election
elective
feminism
free vote
Gerousia
home rule
hustings
left-wing
Lok Sabha
majority
minister
ministry
minority
national
official
oligarch
politics
prorogue
republic
rollback

schedule
Sinn Féin
Sobranie
Storting
suffrage
Tanaiste
Treasury
triumvir
unionism
unionist
Whiggery
woolsack

9

amendment
anarchism
apartheid
autocracy
ballot box
Barebone's
bicameral
Bundesrat
Bundestag
coalition
Cominform
Comintern
committee
communism
communist
democracy
deterrent
Eduskunta
exchequer
first lord
Folketing
legislate

New Labour
oligarchy
ombudsman
politburo
Poujadist
president
red guards
Reichstag
right-wing
sanctions
secretary
shire-moot
show trial
socialism
socialist
Stalinism
Taoiseach
terrorism

10

aristocrat
block grant
by-election
capitalism
chancellor
collective
conference
devolution
federalism
filibuster
government
Greenpeace
guillotine
invalidate
monarchism
Monday Club

opposition
parliament
Plaid Cymru
plebiscite
psephology
radicalism
Rajya Sabha
referendum
republican
resolution
revolution
scrutineer
sitting day
Third Reich
Third World
trade union
Trotskyism
unicameral
Warsaw Pact
White House
white paper

11

adjournment
aristocracy
backbencher
ballot-paper
casting vote
coexistence
congressman
constituent
containment
co-operative
demarcation
dissolution
divine right

enfranchise
finance bill
front runner
imperialist
independent
legislation
legislative
legislature
McCarthyism
nationalist
Nationalrat
package deal
party leader
prerogative
private bill
reactionary
revisionism
statute book
suffragette
syndicalism
syndicalist
Tamil Tigers
Tammany Hall
Witenagemot
yeoman-usher

12

commissioner
Common Market
Commonwealth
Conservative
constituency
constitution
dictatorship
domino theory
favourite son

federal union	home secretary	House of
House of Lords	international	Commons
house of peers	lord president	lord chancellor
invalidation	lord privy seal	representative
lord advocate	National Front	sergeant-at-arms
lord chairman	prime minister	social democrat
privy council	shadow cabinet	
reading clerk	single chamber	**15**
snap division	States General	
snap election	trade unionist	attorney-general
ways and means	United Nations	cabinet minister
welfare state	vote of censure	clerk of the house
		general election
13	**14**	Liberal Democrat
		Marxist-Leninist
demonstration	constitutional	minister of state
deputy speaker	deputy chairman	people's republic
disengagement	deputy premier	personality cult
division lobby	deputy sergeant	social democracy
free-trade area	gerrymandering	totalitarianism

LITERATURE
Literary terms

2 AND 3	**4**	form	play	song
lay	agon	gest	plot	stem
MS	anon	hack	poem	text
No.	bard	hymn	poet	tone
ode	book	iamb	puff	verb
pen	case	idyl	quip	weak
pun	coda	mime	read	word
saw	copy	mode	rime	yarn
set	dual	mood	root	
tag	epic	muse	rule	**5**
wit	epos	myth	rune	
	foot	noun	saga	acute
		past	scan	adage
				affix

argot
blurb
canto
caret
carol
codex
colon
comma
diary
dirge
ditty
drama
elegy
elide
envoi
envoy
epode
essay
fable
farce
folio
genre
geste
ghost
gloss
gnome
háček
haiku
humor
ictus
idiom
idyll
image
index
Ionic
irony

lyric
maxim
metre
motif
novel
octet
paean
parse
poesy
proem
prose
prosy
quill
quote
rebus
recto
rhyme
rondo
runic
scald
scene
sci fi
shift
skald
slang
stich
story
study
style
summa
tense
theme
tilde
tract
triad
usage

verse
verso
vowel

6

abrégé
accent
active
adonic
adverb
Aeneid
alcaic
annals
annual
anthem
aorist
aperçu
author
ballad
bathos
caesura
chorus
clause
cliché
climax
comedy
copula
crisis
critic
dactyl
dative
define
derive
dictum
diesis
digest

dipody
ending
epopee
errata
etymon
eulogy
exposé
finite
future
gender
genius
gerund
gnomic
govern
heroic
hiatus
homily
hubris
humour
hymnal
hyphen
iambic
iambus
jacket
jargon
lacuna
lament
legend
lyrist
macron
mantra
memoir
monody
neuter
number
object

octave
parody
pathos
period
person
phrase
pidgin
plural
poetic
poetry
précis
prefix
primer
résumé
review
rhythm
riddle
rondel
satire
school
series
sestet
simile
sketch
sonnet
stanza
stress
strong
suffix
symbol
syntax
thesis
umlaut
verbal
zeugma

7

abridge
adjunct
anagram
analogy
analyse
anapest
antonym
apocope
apology
article
ballade
berhyme
bucolic
cadence
caesura
cantata
cedilla
chanson
collate
content
context
couplet
decline
descant
dialect
diction
digraph
distich
eclogue
edition
elegiac
elision
epicene
epigram
epistle

epitaph
euphony
extract
fabliau
fantasy
fiction
georgic
grammar
harmony
Homeric
homonym
idyllic
imagery
inflect
introit
journal
jussive
lampoon
leonine
lexicon
library
literal
litotes
lyrical
memoirs
metonym
mimesis
mystery
nemesis
novella
paradox
parsing
passage
passive
pen-name
perfect

phoneme
playlet
poetess
poetics
poetize
polemic
preface
present
pronoun
prosaic
prosody
proverb
psalter
pyrrhic
realism
refrain
regular
requiem
romance
rondeau
Sapphic
sarcasm
scholia
sestina
setting
sextain
spondee
stichic
strophe
subject
subplot
summary
syncope
synonym
systole
tiercet

tragedy
trilogy
triolet
triplet
trochee
versify
virelay
vocable
western

8

ablative
absolute
abstract
acrostic
allegory
allusion
alphabet
amoebean
analects
analysis
anapaest
anaphora
anecdote
anti-hero
antiphon
aphorism
apodosis
apologia
apothegm
appendix
archaism
assonant
asterisk
Augustan
bacchius

balladry	handbook	relative	whodunit
brackets	Horatian	revision	word play
caesural	hornbook	rhapsody	yearbook
Calliope	language	rhetoric	
canticle	laureate	romantic	**9**
chiasmus	libretto	root word	
choriamb	ligature	satirist	accidence
clerihew	limerick	scanning	acrostics
construe	logogram	scansion	adjective
contrast	lyricism	scenario	adverbial
critique	madrigal	scholium	ambiguity
dactylic	metaphor	sentence	amoebaean
definite	metonomy	singular	ampersand
dialogue	metrical	solecism	anacrusis
didactic	modifier	spelling	anapestic
dieresis	morpheme	stanzaic	Anglicism
discrete	narrator	suspense	annotator
doggerel	negative	swan song	anonymous
dramatic	nonsense	syllable	anthology
ellipsis	novelist	synopsis	antinovel
enclitic	optative	synoptic	apocopate
epic poem	opuscule	systolic	archetype
epigraph	Ossianic	temporal	assonance
epilogue	oxymoron	textbook	authoress
essayist	paradigm	thematic	autograph
euphuism	particle	threnody	biography
exegesis	pastoral	thriller	broadside
eye rhyme	personal	treatise	burlesque
fabulist	phonetic	tribrach	cacophony
feminine	Pindaric	trimeter	catalogue
folktale	pleonasm	trochaic	catharsis
footnote	poetical	trouvère	chronicle
full stop	positive	unpoetic	classical
genitive	prologue	versicle	comic book
glossary	quantity	vignette	conjugate
guttural	quatrain	vocative	consonant
			copyright

criticism	melodrama	semantics
diaeresis	metaplasm	semicolon
diphthong	minor poet	semivowel
dithyramb	monometer	soliloquy
dramatist	monorhyme	sonneteer
elegiacal	monostich	syllabary
epic verse	narration	syllepsis
etymology	narrative	symbolism
euphemism	neologism	symposium
exegetics	nonce word	symptosis
facsimile	novelette	synalepha
fairy tale	objective	syntactic
fictional	octameter	terza rima
flashback	pararhyme	tetrapody
formative	parataxis	trimetric
free verse	partitive	verse form
Gallicism	past tense	versifier
gazetteer	philippic	Virgilian
gerundive	philology	vulgarism
guidebook	phonemics	whodunnit
hemistich	platitude	
hendiadys	poetaster	**10**
hexameter	potboiler	
hexastich	potential	accusative
hypallage	predicate	adjectival
hyperbole	preterite	amphibrach
hypotaxis	privative	amphimacer
idiomatic	prolepsis	anapaestic
imperfect	prose poem	anarthrous
inflexion	prosodist	anastrophe
inversion	pseudonym	Anglo-Saxon
irregular	quotation	antepenult
leitmotiv	recension	anticlimax
love story	reflexive	antithesis
lyric poem	rhymester	apostrophe
masculine	roundelay	apposition
		avant-garde

bestseller	infinitive	synaloepha
blank verse	inflection	synecdoche
bowdlerize	intonation	tetracolon
caricature	involution	tetrameter
choriambus	lexicology	tetrastich
circumflex	linguistic	transitive
colloquial	manuscript	unpoetical
common noun	metathesis	vernacular
comparison	miscellany	vocabulary
compendium	mock heroic	
declension	morphology	**11**
definition	naturalism	
definitive	neuter verb	abridgement
denouement	nom de plume	acute accent
derivation	nominative	Alexandrine
derivative	non-fiction	amphibology
dissonance	noun clause	anachronism
disyllabic	ottava rima	anacoluthon
disyllable	palindrome	antiphrasis
epenthesis	paraphrase	antistrophe
epenthetic	participle	aposiopesis
epic poetry	pentameter	association
fairy story	Petrarchan	ballad style
figurative	picaresque	bibliomancy
finite verb	plagiarism	catachresis
ghost story	pleonastic	catastrophe
government	pluperfect	chansonette
grammarian	possessive	cliff-hanger
heptameter	pronominal	comic relief
hexametric	proper noun	comparative
hyphenated	reciprocal	compilation
imperative	short story	concordance
impersonal	similitude	conditional
incunabula	spoonerism	conjugation
indefinite	subjective	conjunction
indicative	synaeresis	conjunctive
		connotation

Writers, poets and dramatists

3 AND 4

Agee	Gide	Muir	West	Butor
Amis	Glyn	Nash	Wood	Byatt
Asch	Gray	Nin	Wren	Byron
Ayer	Grey	Okri	Zola	Cable
Baum	Gunn	Ovid		Caine
Bede	Hall	Owen	**5**	Camus
Behn	Hare	Paz	Acton	Capek
Bell	Hart	Poe	Adams	Carew
Benn	Hay	Pope	Aesop	Clare
Blok	Hogg	Pugh	Agate	Colum
Böll	Home	Pym	Aiken	Corvo
Bolt	Hood	Read	Albee	Couch
Bond	Hook	Reid	Arden	Crane
Buck	Hope	Rhys	Arlen	Croce
Cary	Hugo	Roth	Auden	Dante
Coke	Hunt	Rowe	Babel	Darío
Cole	King	Ruck	Bacon	Defoe
Cruz	Knox	Reúz	Barry	Donne
Dahl	Kyd	Sade	Barth	Doyle
Dana	Lamb	Saki	Bates	Dumas
Dane	Lang	Sala	Behan	Duras
Day	Lear	Sand	Bembo	Eliot
Dell	Lee	Seth	Benda	Ellis
Eco	Levi	Shaw	Benét	Elyot
Eden	Livy	Sims	Betti	Evans
Elia	Loos	Snow	Beyle	Field
Eyre	Loti	Sue	Blake	Frame
Ford	Lyly	Tate	Bloom	Frayn
Foxe	Lynd	Urfé	Blunt	Freud
Fry	Mais	Vane	Bowen	Frost
Fyfe	Mann	Vega	Brink	Genet
Gay	Marx	Wain	Bruce	Gibbs
	Mill	Ward	Burke	Gogol
	More	Webb	Burns	Gorki

Gosse	Lorca	Queen	Wolfe	Besant
Gower	Lowry	Raine	Woolf	Bierce
Grass	Lucan	Reade	Wyatt	Binchey
Green	Lucas	Rilke	Yeats	Binyon
Greer	Mamet	Rolfe	Yonge	Blixen
Grimm	Marot	Sagan	Young	Blyton
Halle	Marsh	Scott	Zweig	Borges
Hardy	Martí	Seton		Borrow
Harte	Mason	Shute	**6**	Braine
Hašek	Milne	Smart		Brecht
Heine	Moore	Smith	Adamov	Breton
Henry	Murry	Spark	Adcock	Bridie
Henty	Musil	Staël	Alcott	Brontë
Herzl	Nashe	Stark	Aldiss	Brooke
Hesse	Noyes	Stein	Algren	Brophy
Heyer	Odets	Stowe	Ambler	Browne
Homer	O'Dowd	Svevo	Andric	Bryant
Hulme	O'Hara	Swift	Anstey	Buchan
Ibsen	Opitz	Synge	Aragon	Bunyan
Innes	Orczy	Taine	Arnold	Burney
Irwin	Orton	Tasso	Ascham	Burton
James	Otway	Twain	Asimov	Butler
Jarry	Ouida	Tynan	Atwood	Caesar
Jeans	Paine	Tzara	Aubrey	Camões
Jones	Pater	Udall	Austen	Capote
Joyce	Paton	Varro	Azorin	Carter
Kafka	Peake	Verne	Balzac	Cather
Keats	Peele	Vidal	Barham	Cavafy
Keith	Péguy	Vigny	Barnes	Céline
Kesey	Pepys	Waley	Baroja	Chopin
Keyte	Perse	Walsh	Barrès	Cibber
Lewis	Plath	Waugh	Barrie	Cicero
Loach	Plato	Wells	Beeton	Clarke
Locke	Pliny	Welty	Bellay	Clough
Lodge	Pound	White	Belloc	Conrad
Logue	Powys	Wilde	Bellow	Cooper
			Benson	

Coward	Harris	Mannin	Ruskin
Cowley	Haynes	Martyn	Sandys
Cowper	Heaney	Miller	Sapper
Crabbe	Heller	Milton	Sappho
Cronin	Hemans	Molnár	Sardou
Darwin	Henley	Morgan	Sartre
Daudet	Hesiod	Mörike	Savage
Davies	Hilton	Morris	Sayers
Dekker	Hobbes	Motion	Scribe
Dowson	Holmes	Munthe	Seneca
Dryden	Holtby	Murray	Sidney
Dunbar	Horace	Musset	Silone
Duncan	Howitt	Necker	Singer
Empson	Hughes	Neruda	Sontag
Ennius	Ibañez	Nerval	Steele
Ervine	Irving	Nesbit	Sterne
Evelyn	Jacobs	O'Brien	Stoker
Fichte	Jerome	O'Casey	Storey
Finlay	Jonson	Ogilvy	Strabo
Fowles	Kaiser	O'Neill	Surrey
France	Keller	Orwell	Symons
Frazer	Kleist	Parker	Tagore
Frisch	Laclos	Petöfi	Taylor
Froude	Landor	Pindar	Thomas
Fugard	Lao-Tse	Pinero	Thorne
Fuller	Larkin	Pinter	Thrale
George	Lawler	Piozzi	Toller
Gibbon	Lawson	Plumer	Traven
Godwin	Le Fanu	Porter	Trevor
Goethe	Le Sage	Potter	Updike
Gordon	London	Powell	Uttley
Graeme	Lowell	Proust	Valéry
Graves	Ludwig	Racine	Villon
Greene	Lytton	Rohmer	Virgil
Hallam	Mailer	Rowley	Walker
Hamsun	Malozy	Runyon	Waller

Walton	Boswell	Drabble	Herbert
Warren	Bridges	Drayton	Herrick
Watson	Brodsky	Dreiser	Heywood
Weldon	Büchner	Duhamel	Hichens
Werfel	Bunting	Dunsany	Hocking
Wesker	Burgess	Durrell	Hopkins
Weyman	Caedmon	Emerson	Housman
Wilcox	Calvino	Erasmus	Howells
Wilder	Camoens	Feydeau	Ibn Ezra
Wilson	Carlyle	Firbank	Ionesco
Wotton	Carroll	Flecker	Jiménez
Wright	Chapman	Fleming	Johnson
	Chaucer	Fontane	Juvenal
7	Cheever	Forster	Kastner
	Chekhov	Forsyth	Kaufman
Abelard	Chénier	Foscolo	Kerouac
Addison	Cheyney	Frankau	Kinross
Aelfric	Claudel	Freeman	Kipling
Alarcón	Clayton	Fuentes	Kundera
Alfieri	Clemens	Galileo	Lardner
Angelou	Cobbett	Gallico	Laxness
Anouilh	Cocteau	Gardner	Layamon
Aquinas	Coetzee	Garnett	Leacock
Ariosto	Colette	Gaskell	Le Carré
Balchin	Collins	Gautier	Lehmann
Baldwin	Corelli	Gilbert	Le Queux
Ballard	Crashaw	Gissing	Lessing
Beckett	Da Ponte	Glossop	Lindsay
Beddoes	Deeping	Golding	Machaut
Beeding	Delaney	Goldoni	Mahfouz
Belasco	Dickens	Haggard	Malamud
Bennett	Diderot	Hakluyt	Malraux
Bentham	Dinesen	Hammett	Manning
Bentley	Dodgson	Hartley	Manzoni
Birrell	Doughty	Hazlitt	Marlowe
Blunden	Douglas	Hellman	Marquez
Boileau			

Marryat
Marston
Martial
Marvell
Maugham
Mauriac
Maurois
Maurras
Mencken
Mérimée
Meynell
Mishima
Mistral
Mitford
Molière
Montagu
Moravia
Murdoch
Nabokov
Naevius
Naipaul
Narayan
Newbolt
Novalis
O'Connor
Ogilvie
Osborne
Patmore
Peacock
Plautus
Prévert
Pushkin
Pynchon
Queneau
Ransome
Régnier

Renault
Rendell
Richler
Richter
Rimbaud
Rolland
Romains
Ronsard
Rostand
Rowling
Rushdie
Rushkin
Russell
Sadleir
Sarasin
Saroyan
Sassoon
Scarron
Seferis
Service
Shaffer
Shelley
Simenon
Simonov
Sitwell
Skelton
Southey
Soyinka
Spencer
Spender
Spenser
Spinoza
Stevens
Strauss
Surtees
Tacitus

Terence
Thomson
Thoreau
Thurber
Tolkien
Tolstoy
Tutuola
Vaughan
Vicente
Wallace
Walpole
Webster
Wharton
Whitman

8

Anacreon
Andersen
Anderson
Andreyev
Apuleius
Asturias
Aumonier
Banville
Barbusse
Beaumont
Beauvoir
Beckford
Beerbohm
Benchley
Béranger
Bernanos
Berryman
Betjeman
Bjørnson
Bradbury

Brentano
Brookner
Browning
Bushnell
Calderón
Campbell
Cartland
Catullus
Chambers
Chandler
Chodorov
Christie
Congreve
Conquest
Constant
Crichton
Crockett
Crompton
Cummings
Davenant
Day Lewis
Deighton
De la Mare
De Musset
Disraeli
Donleavy
Drummond
Du Bellay
Etherege
Farquhar
Faulkner
Fielding
Firdausi
Flaubert
Fletcher
Fontaine

Forester	Mitchell	Suckling	Cervantes
Ginsberg	Morrison	Tennyson	Charteris
Goncourt	Mortimer	Thompson	Churchill
Gordimer	Nekrasov	Tibullus	Coleridge
Grierson	Oliphant	Tourneur	Corneille
Hamilton	Palgrave	Traherne	D'Annunzio
Han Suyin	Pattison	Trilling	De la Roche
Heinlein	Perelman	Trollope	De Quincey
Henryson	Perrault	Turgenev	Descartes
Hochhuth	Petrarch	Vanbrugh	Dickinson
Hoffmann	Plutarch	Verlaine	Doolittle
Huysmans	Proudhon	Voltaire	Dos Passos
Ishiguro	Quennell	Vonnegut	Dudintsev
Jean Paul	Rabelais	Wedekind	Du Maurier
Keneally	Radiguet	Wheatley	Eddington
Kingsley	Rattigan	Whittier	Edgeworth
Koestler	Remarque	Williams	Ehrenberg
Kotzebue	Richards	Xenophon	Euripides
Laforgue	Rossetti	Zangwill	Froissart
Lagerlöf	Rousseau		Giraudoux
Langland	Sabatini	**9**	Goldsmith
Lawrence	Salinger	Aeschylus	Goncharov
Leopardi	Sandburg	Ainsworth	Greenwood
Lonsdale	Sarraute	Akhmatova	Hall Caine
Lovelace	Schiller	Aldington	Hauptmann
Macaulay	Schlegel	Alec Waugh	Hawthorne
McCarthy	Shadwell	Allingham	Heidegger
MacNeice	Sheridan	Anita Loos	Hemingway
Malherbe	Sillitoe	Ayckbourn	Herodotus
Mallarmé	Sinclair	Blackmore	Highsmith
Melville	Smollett	Blackwood	Hölderlin
Menander	Spillane	Boccaccio	Isherwood
Meredith	Stendhal	Bottomley	Jefferies
Merriman	Stoppard	Bret Harte	Kaye-Smith
Michelet	Strachey	Burroughs	Klopstock
Michener	Sturgess	Callaghan	La Bruyère

La Fayette
Lamartine
Lampedusa
Leigh Hunt
Lermontov
Linklater
Llewellyn
Lomonosov
Lord Byron
Lucretius
McCullers
Mackenzie
Macrobius
Malaparte
Mansfield
Mark Twain
Martineau
Masefield
Massinger
Middleton
Mitchison
Montaigne
O'Flaherty
Pasternak
Priestley
Pritchett
Quasimodo
Radcliffe
Robertson
Rochester
Sackville
Sax Rohmer
Schreiner
Shenstone
Sholokhov
Sophocles

Steinbeck
Stevenson
Sturluson
Suetonius
Swinburne
Thackeray
Tomlinson
Trevelyan
Turgeniev
Van Druton
Verhaeren
Wodehouse
Wycherley
Yourcenar

10

Bainbridge
Ballantyne
Baudelaire
Brett Young
Chatterton
Chesterton
Conan Doyle
Don Marquis
Dostoevsky
Drinkwater
Dürrenmatt
Elinor Glyn
Emil Ludwig
Fitzgerald
Galsworthy
Hungerford
Hutchinson
Jack London
Jane Austen
John Buchan

Jules Verne
La Fontaine
Lagerkvist
Longfellow
Lope de Vega
Lord Lytton
MacDiarmid
McGonagall
Mandelstam
Maupassant
Mayakovsky
Mickiewicz
Mrs. Gaskell
Noël Coward
Oscar Wilde
Phillpotts
Pierre Loti
Pirandello
Propertius
Pryce-Jones
Quintilian
Richardson
Ronaldshay
Saint-Simon
Saintsbury
Schnitzler
Sean O'Casey
Strindberg
Tarkington
Theocritus
Thucydides
Van der Post
Williamson
Wordsworth

11

Abbé Prévost
Apollinaire
Callimachus
Demosthenes
Dostoievski
García Lorca
Grillparzer
Kazantzakis
Kierkegaard
Lautréamont
Maeterlinck
Montesquieu
Montherlant
Omar Khayyam
Pérez Galdós
Ravenscroft
Sainte-Beuve
Shakespeare
Sienkiewicz
Streatfeild
Tocqueville
Vargas Llosa
Watts-Dunton
Yevtushenko

12

Aristophanes
Beaumarchais
Blasco Ibañez
Bulwer Lytton
Chesterfield
De Selincourt
Feuchtwanger
Hans Andersen
Hergesheimer
Hofmannsthal
López de Ayala
Martin du Gard
Matthew Paris
Quiller-Couch
Rider Haggard
Robbe-Grillet
Rose Macaulay
Saint-Exupéry
Solzhenitsyn
Storm Jameson
Wittgenstein
Wyndham Lewis

13

Andrew Marvell
Arnold Bennett
Baroness Orczy
Bertran de Born
Cecil Day Lewis
Chateaubriand
Edgar Allan Poe
Ford Madox Ford
Hilaire Belloc
Jeffrey Farnol
Jerome K. Jerome
Marie de France
Sackville-West
Sinclair Lewis
Stacy Aumonier
Upton Sinclair
Wilkie Collins

14

Agatha Christie
Compton-Burnett

Leconte de Lisle
Marcus Aurelius
Middleton Murry
Oehlenschläger
Rafael Sabatini
Rudyard Kipling
Warwick Deeping
Wollstonecraft

15 AND 16

Booth Tarkington (15),
Chrétien de Troyes (16)
Christine de Pisan (16)
Granville Barker (15)
La Rochefoucauld (15)
Millington Synge (15)
Pierre de Ronsard (15)
Somerset Maugham (15)
Washington Irving (16)

MEDICINE

2 AND 3

CJD	pox	bubo	duct	jowl
ear	pr	burn	dumb	knee
ECG	pus	burp	face	lame
ECT	rib	calf	falx	limb
EEG	sty	cast	flux	lint
ENT	tic	cell	foot	lips
eye	toe	chin	gall	lisp
fat	VD	clap	game	lobe
fit	wen	clot	gene	lung
flu		cold	germ	maim
gum	**4**	coma	gout	mole
gut	ache	corn	grip	mute
hip	acne	cure	guts	nail
HIV	ACTH	cusp	hair	nape
ill	ague	cyst	hand	neck
jaw	AIDS	deaf	head	noma
leg	axon	derm	heal	nose
lip	back	diet	heel	numb
LSD	balm	disc	hips	oral
ME	bile	dope	hurt	otic
MS	bleb	dose	hypo	ovum
pm	boil	drip	ilia	pain
	bone	drug	iris	palm

pang	womb	cheek	heart	piles
pica	X-ray	chest	helix	pinna
pill	yaws	chill	hilum	plate
pock	**5**	chyle	hyoid	plica
pore		chyme	ictus	polio
râle	acute	cilia	ileum	polyp
rash	agony	colic	iliac	probe
rest	algid	colon	ilium	pulse
rete	algor	cough	incus	pupil
ribs	aloes	cramp	joint	purge
roof	ancon	crick	lance	quack
root	angst	croup	leech	rabid
scab	ankle	death	leper	renal
scan	anvil	decay	liver	rheum
scar	aorta	donor	locum	rigor
shin	apnea	drain	lungs	salts
sick	ataxy	dress	lupus	salve
SIDS	aural	drops	lymph	scald
skin	belch	edema	lysis	scalp
sole	belly	elbow	mania	scurf
sore	birth	ether	medic	semen
spot	blain	faint	molar	senna
stye	bleed	femur	mouth	serum
swab	blend	fetus	mucus	shock
tent	blind	fever	mumps	sight
tolu	blood	fibre	nasal	sinew
turn	bolus	flesh	navel	sinus
ulna	borax	flush	nerve	skull
vein	botch	fossa	nurse	sleep
vena	bowel	gauze	opium	sling
wale	brace	gland	orbit	spasm
wall	brain	gonad	organ	sperm
ward	bulla	graft	ovary	spine
wart	bursa	graze	palsy	sprue
weal	canal	gumma	penis	stall
welt	chafe	gyrus	phial	sting

stoma	**6**	cervix	foment
stone	addict	chorea	fornix
stool	ailing	clinic	gargle
stupe	albino	clonic	goitre
sweat	amytal	clonus	gravel
swoon	anemia	coccyx	gripes
tabes	anemic	comedo	grippe
talus	angina	concha	growth
teeth	antrum	corium	gullet
thigh	apnoea	cornea	healer
thumb	areola	cortex	health
tibia	armpit	coryza	hernia
tonic	arnica	costal	heroin
tooth	artery	cowpox	herpes
torso	asthma	crisis	hiccup
toxin	ataxia	crutch	idiocy
tract	aurist	deflux	immune
treat	autism	dengue	infect
trunk	axilla	dental	infirm
truss	balsam	dermis	injury
tummy	bedpan	doctor	insane
ulcer	bellon	dorsal	intern
ulnar	benign	dosage	iodine
unfit	biceps	dropsy	iritis
urine	biopsy	eczema	kidney
uvula	bowels	elixir	labium
vagus	breath	embryo	labour
valve	bruise	emetic	larynx
virus	bunion	eschar	lesion
vomit	caecum	eyelid	lotion
vulva	callus	fascia	lumbar
waist	cancer	fester	lunacy
wound	canker	fibula	maimed
wrist	caries	finger	malady
X-rays	carpus	flexor	maniac
	cavity	foetus	matron

matter
megrim
morbid
morula
mucous
muscle
myopia
myopic
oedema
opiate
oxygen
palate
pelvis
pepsin
peptic
perone
phenol
phenyl
phobia
pimple
plague
plasma
pleura
poison
potion
quinsy
rabies
radium
ranula
reflex
remedy
retina
sacrum
saliva
scurvy
sepsis

septic
sister
spinal
spleen
splint
sprain
squint
stitch
stroke
stupor
suture
tablet
taenia
tampon
tannin
tartar
temple
tendon
tetany
thorax
throat
thrush
ticker
tissue
tongue
tonsil
torpor
trance
trauma
tremor
trepan
troche
tumour
typhus
unwell
uterus

vagina
vomica

7

abdomen
abscess
acidity
aconite
adenoid
adipose
adrenal
ailment
albumen
allergy
amnesia
anaemia
anaemic
analyst
anatomy
anodyne
antacid
anthrax
antigen
aphasia
aseptic
aspirin
atrophy
autopsy
bandage
bedsore
bifocal
bilious
bladder
blister
booster
boracic

bromide
bubonic
bulimia
calomel
capsule
cardiac
cascara
catarrh
caustic
cautery
chafing
chancre
chloral
choking
cholera
chronic
cocaine
cochlea
colitis
coroner
cranium
culture
cupping
curable
cuticle
deltoid
dentist
dietary
dieting
disease
dissect
earache
eardrum
endemic
enteric
eupepsy

eyewash
fasting
febrile
femoral
fibroid
filling
fistula
forceps
forearm
formula
gastric
glottis
gumboil
harelip
healing
healthy
heparin
hormone
hospice
humerus
hygiene
illness
inhaler
insulin
invalid
jugular
kneecap
knuckle
lanolin
leprosy
leprous
linctus
lockjaw
lozenge
lumbago
Luminal

lunatic
malaria
massage
masseur
mastoid
measles
medical
menthol
microbe
mixture
morphia
myalgia
nervous
nostrum
obesity
occiput
oculist
operate
organic
ossicle
otalgia
otology
palsied
panacea
patella
patient
pharynx
pillbox
pink-eye
placebo
plaster
podagra
polypus
pustule
pyaemia
pyretic

quinine
recover
relapse
rickets
roseola
rubella
rupture
sarcoma
scabies
scalpel
scanner
seasick
seizure
sick-bay
sickbed
spastic
stamina
stammer
sterile
sternum
steroid
stertor
stomach
stunned
styptic
sunburn
surgeon
surgery
symptom
syncope
syringe
tetanus
theatre
therapy
thyroid
tonsils

trachea
triceps
typhoid
tympana
urethra
vaccine
variola
Veronal
verruca
vertigo
vitamin
wet-pack
whitlow
wryneck

8

abnormal
abortion
abrasion
accident
acidosis
adenoids
adhesion
allergic
alopecia
amputate
aneurysm
antibody
antidote
aperient
apoplexy
appendix
appetite
Asian flu
asphyxia
atheroma

atropine	diabetes	hip joint	narcosis
backache	diagnose	hospital	narcotic
bacteria	dialyser	hot flush	neonatal
baldness	diseased	hygienic	neuritis
beri beri	disorder	hypnotic	neurotic
bile duct	diuretic	hysteria	ointment
blackout	dressing	immunity	oncology
blue pill	drop-foot	impetigo	otoscope
botulism	dropsied	impotent	overdose
caffeine	druggist	incision	paranoia
carditis	dyslexia	infected	paranoic
casualty	emulsion	inflamed	paranoid
cataract	epidemic	insanity	paroxysm
catheter	epilepsy	insomnia	pellagra
cervical	excision	iodoform	pharmacy
clinical	eyedrops	iron lung	phthisis
club foot	eye salve	irritant	placenta
cold sore	eye tooth	jaundice	pleurisy
collapse	fainting	lameness	poisoned
comatose	feverish	laudanum	poultice
compress	first aid	laxative	pregnant
coronary	flat feet	lethargy	prenatal
critical	forehead	ligament	progeria
cyanosis	formalin	ligature	prostate
cystitis	fracture	liniment	ptomaine
dandruff	freckles	lobotomy	pulmonic
deafness	fumigate	lordosis	recovery
deathbed	ganglion	magnesia	Red Cross
debility	gangrene	malarial	remedial
deceased	glaucoma	mal de mer	rest cure
deformed	grand mal	medicine	revivify
delirium	hard drug	melanoma	ringworm
delivery	hay fever	membrane	sanitary
demented	headache	mescalin	schizoid
dementia	heat spot	migraine	sciatica
dentures	hiccough	morphine	scrofula

9

sedation
sedative
senility
shingles
shoulder
sickness
sickroom
smallpox
sneezing
soft drug
specific
specimen
speculum
stitches
subacute
surgical
swelling
syphilis
tapeworm
terminal
the bends
thoracic
tincture
toxaemia
trachoma
traction
ulcerous
uric acid
varicose
vertebra
vomiting
wet nurse
wheezing
windpipe

admission
adrenalin
aetiology
alleviate
allopathy
Alzheimer
ambulance
analgesic
angiogram
ankylosis
antalkali
antenatal
antitoxin
arthritis
asthmatic
bedridden
bilharzia
birthmark
blackhead
blindness
blood test
breakdown
Caesarean
carbuncle
carcinoma
cartilage
castor oil
catalepsy
catatonic
catharsis
cauterize
chilblain
cirrhosis
cold cream
colostomy

complaint
condition
conscious
contagion
contusion
cortisone
curvature
deformity
delirious
dentistry
deodorant
diagnosis
diaphragm
diarrhoea
diathermy
dietetics
dietetist
dietician
digestion
digestive
discharge
disinfect
dislocate
doctoring
dropsical
dysentery
dyspepsia
dystrophy
emaciated
emergency
emollient
emphysema
epileptic
eye lotion
eyestrain
faintness

frost-bite
funnybone
gastritis
gathering
geriatric
germicide
giddiness
glandular
glycerine
halitosis
hartshorn
healthful
heartburn
hepatitis
histamine
hunchback
hygienist
hypnotism
hypnotist
hysterics
ill health
impaction
incubator
incurable
infection
infirmary
infirmity
influenza
inoculate
in-patient
in plaster
invalided
isolation
isoniazid
leukaemia
liquorice

10

Listerism	prescribe	amputation	disability
liver spot	psoriasis	anti-poison	dispensary
long sight	psychosis	antibiotic	dispensing
malignant	psychotic	antiseptic	dissecting
medicated	pulmonary	apoplectic	dissection
medicinal	pulsation	apothecary	drug addict
menopause	purgative	astralagus	Ebola fever
midwifery	pyorrhoea	aureomycin	emaciation
milk teeth	radiology	barium meal	enervation
mongolism	rheumatic	blood count	epidemical
mouthwash	rock-fever	blood donor	epiglottis
nappy rash	sclerosis	blood group	Epsom salts
narcotics	secretion	brain death	erysipelas
nebulizer	silicosis	brain fever	eucalyptus
nephritis	sinusitis	breastbone	euthanasia
nerve cell	skin graft	bronchitis	extraction
neuralgia	soporific	cardiogram	false teeth
nostalgia	squinting	chicken pox	fibrositis
Novocaine	sterilize	chloroform	flatulence
nutrition	stiff neck	collar bone	fumigation
nux vomica	stiffness	concussion	gingivitis
nystagmus	still-born	congestion	gonorrhoea
open-heart	stimulant	consultant	hearing aid
operation	stone deaf	contagious	heat stroke
osteopath	stretcher	convalesce	hemorrhage
pacemaker	sunstroke	convulsion	homoeopath
paralysis	toothache	cotton wool	hydropathy
paralytic	treatment	cough syrup	hypodermic
pathology	umbilicus	cystectomy	incubation
phlebitis	unhealthy	depressant	indisposed
physician	urticaria	depression	infectious
pneumonia	vaccinate	dermatitis	inhalation
poisoning	vasectomy	diagnostic	insanitary
porphyria	water cure	diphtheria	interferon
pregnancy		dipsomania	ionization
premature			kiss of life

knock-kneed
laparotomy
laryngitis
Lassa fever
lung cancer
mastectomy
medicament
meningitis
metabolism
metacarpal
metatarsal
nettle rash
neuropathy
night nurse
obstetrics
oesophagus
ophthalmia
optic nerve
orthocaine
osteopathy
out-patient
oxygen mask
oxygen tent
paediatric
painkiller
palliative
paraplegic
penicillin
pestilence
pharmacist
post mortem
presbyopia
preventive
psychiatry
quarantine
recuperate

relaxation
rheumatism
salmonella
sanatorium
sanitarium
scarlatina
short sight
sickle-cell
sore throat
specialist
spinal cord
staff nurse
stammering
starvation
sterilizer
strychnine
stuttering
thrombosis
tourniquet
toxic shock
tracheitis
transplant
urethritis
wheel chair

11

abnormality
acupuncture
albuminuria
aminobutene
amphetamine
anaesthetic
angioplasty
anti-pyretic
asthmatical
astigmatism

bactericide
bandy-legged
barbiturate
beta blocker
biliousness
bloodstream
blood vessel
brucellosis
Calabar bean
cardiograph
case history
chiropodist
cholesterol
circulation
cleft palate
cod-liver oil
colour-blind
confinement
consumption
consumptive
contact lens
corn plaster
dengue fever
dermatology
disablement
dislocation
double-blind
embrocation
examination
expectorant
face-lifting
fatty tissue
fibre optics
finger stall
fluoroscope
fomentation

frostbitten
gall bladder
gastrectomy
gerontology
gynaecology
haemoglobin
haemophilia
haemorrhage
heart attack
homoeopathy
hospitalize
hydrophobia
hypothermia
indigestion
inoculation
intercostal
intravenous
jungle fever
kwashiorkor
miscarriage
mustard bath
nursing home
observation
obstruction
orthopaedic
palpitation
pathologist
peptic ulcer
peritonitis
perspiration
pharyngitis
plaster cast
prickly heat
probationer
proctoscope
prophylaxis

psittacosis
radiography
restorative
rigor mortis
sal volatile
seasickness
septicaemia
skin disease
spina bifida
stethoscope
stomach ache
stomach-pump
suppuration
temperature
thalidomide
therapeutic
thermometer
tonsillitis
torticollis
tracheotomy
transfusion
trench fever
typhus fever
unconscious
vaccination
vasodilator
vivisection
wisdom tooth
yellow fever

12

alexipharmic
anaesthetist
appendectomy
appendicitis
aquapuncture

athlete's foot
auscultation
carbolic acid
casualty ward
chemotherapy
chiropractor
complication
constipation
consultation
convalescent
cough mixture
court plaster
critical list
day blindness
decongestant
degeneration
disinfectant
disinfection
Dover's powder
encephalitis
enteric fever
faith healing
fallen arches
family doctor
friar's balsam
gastric fever
group therapy
growing pains
heart disease
heart failure
homoeopathic
hospital case
hypertension
hysterectomy
immune system
immunization

inflammation
malnutrition
menstruation
mesothelioma
neurasthenia
obstetrician
orthodontics
osteoporosis
palpitations
parasitology
pharmaceutic
pharmacology
prescription
preventative
prophylactic
psychiatrist
radiotherapy
recuperation
recuperative
reflex action
sarsaparilla
scarlet fever
sclerodermia
shaking palsy
short-sighted
skin-grafting
sleeping pill
slimming diet
spinal column
streptococci
streptomycin
student nurse
subcutaneous
surgical boot
takadiastase
talcum powder

tartar emetic
tertian fever
thyroid gland
tuberculosis
typhoid fever
varicose vein
Weil's disease
zinc ointment

13

anticoagulant
antihistamine
anti-spasmodic
blood pressure
bubonic plague
cardiac arrest
Chagas' disease
clearing station
contraception
convalescence
Crohn's disease
dental surgery
Down's syndrome
duodenal ulcer
elephantiasis
eucalyptus oil
fever hospital
gamma globulin
gentian violet
German measles
group practice
gynaecologist
health service
health visitor
heat treatment
hydrocephalus

indisposition
intensive care
kidney machine
lead poisoning
malarial fever
materia medica
medical school
medicine glass
mononucleosis
mortification
non-contagious
ophthalmology
osteomyelitis
paediatrician
pharmaceutics
pharmacopoeia
physiotherapy
poliomyelitis
St Vitus's dance
schizophrenia
shooting pains
shoulder blade
smelling salts
social disease
speech therapy
sterilization
stretcher case
styptic pencil
tonsillectomy
tranquilliser
varicose veins
whooping cough

14

Achilles tendon
blood poisoning

Bright's disease
bulimia nervosa
carcinogenesis
cardiovascular
conjunctivitis
corticosteroid
corticotrophin
cross-infection
cystic fibrosis
family planning
floating kidney
glandular fever
Gregory's powder
hallucinations
hallucinogenic
hole in the heart
housemaid's knee
hypersensitive
Kaposi's sarcoma
keyhole surgery
medical officer
medical student
medicine bottle
mucous membrane
mustard plaster
night blindness
operating table
pasteurization
patent medicine
phenobarbitone
plastic surgery
pneumoconiosis
psychoanalysis
rheumatic fever
Seidlitz powder
smelling bottle

surgical spirit	blackwater fever	locomotor ataxia
15	counter-irritant	manic depression
	delirium tremens	morning sickness
Addison's disease	dressing station	physiotherapist
adhesive plaster	endocrine glands	sticking plaster
alimentary canal	Eustachian tubes	vasoconstrictor
anorexia nervosa	gastroenteritis	venereal disease
antenatal clinic	general practice	
aversion therapy	Hodgkin's disease	

MUSIC
Composers

3–5

Adam	Byrd	Kern	Suk	Cardew
Adams	Cage	Lalo	Suppé	Carter
Alkan	Cowen	Lasso	Tye	Chopin
Arne	Cui	Lehar	Verdi	Clarke
Auber	D'Indy	Liszt	Weber	Coates
Auric	Dufay	Locke	Weill	Coward
Bach	Dukas	Lully	Weir	Cowell
Balfe	Dupré	Mayr	Widor	Czerny
Bart	Durey	Nono	Wirén	Davies
Bax	Elgar	Orff	Wolf	Delius
Berg	Falla	Parry	Ysaye	Duparc
Berio	Fauré	Pärt	Zorn	Dussek
Bizet	Field	Peri		Dvořák
Bliss	Finck	Ravel	**6**	Enesco
Bloch	Friml	Reger	Arnold	Eötvös
Blow	Glass	Reich	Barber	Flotow
Boito	Gluck	Rossi	Bartok	Foster
Boyce	Grieg	Satie	Berlin	Franck
Brian	Haydn	Senfl	Bishop	German
Bruch	Henze	Smyth	Boulez	Glinka
Bull	Holst	Sor	Brahms	Gounod
Bush	Ibert	Sousa	Bridge	Grétry
	Ives	Spohr	Busoni	Halévy

	7		**8**
Handel		Lutyens	
Harris	Albéniz	Machaut	Berkeley
Hummel	Allegri	Martinu	Boughton
Kodály	Antheil	Menotti	Bruckner
Krenek	Arriaga	Milhaud	Chabrier
Lassus	Babbitt	Nicolai	Cimarosa
Léonin	Bantock	Nielsen	Clementi
Liadov	Bellini	Novello	Couperin
Ligeti	Bennett	Obrecht	Dohnanyi
Mahler	Berlioz	Pérotin	Fletcher
Marais	Berners	Poulenc	Gabrieli
Moeran	Berwald	Puccini	Gershwin
Morley	Blacher	Purcell	Gesualdo
Mozart	Borodin	Quilter	Giordano
Muffat	Britten	Rodgers	Glazunov
Parker	Caccini	Rodrigo	Grainger
Piston	Campion	Rossini	Granados
Pleyel	Cavalli	Roussel	Honegger
Porter	Copland	Ruggles	Kreisler
Quantz	Corelli	Salieri	Maconchy
Rameau	Debussy	Schuman	Marcabru
Rubbra	Delibes	Smetana	Marcello
Scelsi	Dowland	Stainer	Marenzio
Schütz	Feldman	Stamitz	Mascagni
Searle	Frankel	Strauss	Massenet
Seiber	Fricker	Tartini	Messager
Stuart	Galuppi	Tavener	Messiaen
Tallis	Gibbons	Thomson	Monckton
Taylor	Górecki	Tippett	Musgrave
Varèse	Ireland	Torelli	Ockeghem
Viotti	Janácek	Vivaldi	Paganini
Vitali	Joachim	Warlock	Palmgren
Wagner	Ketelby	Weelkes	Panufnik
Walton	Lambert	Wellesz	Petrassi
Webern	Landini	Xenakis	Pizzetti
Wesley	Litolff		Respighi

Schnabel
Schubert
Schumann
Scriabin
Sessions
Sibelius
Sondheim
Stanford
Sullivan
Svendsen
Taverner
Telemann
Victoria
Wagenaar

9 AND 10

Addinsell (9)
Andriessen (10)
Balakirev (9)
Beethoven (9)
Bernstein (9)
Birtwistle (10)
Boccherini (10)
Boieldieu (9)
Boulanger (9)
Buxtehude (9)
Carissimi (9)
Cherubini (9)
Donizetti (9)
Dunstable (9)
Dutilleux (9)
Hindemith (9)
Kabalevsky (10)
Locatelli (9)
MacDowell (9)
Malipiero (9)

Manfredini (10)
Meyerbeer (9)
Monteverdi (10)
Mussorgsky (10)
Offenbach (9)
Pachelbel (9)
Paisiello (9)
Palestrina (10)
Penderecki (10)
Pergolesi (9)
Ponchielli (10)
Praetorius (10)
Prokofiev (9)
Rawsthorne (10)
Rubinstein (10)
Saint-Saëns (10)
Scarlatti (9)
Schnittke (9)
Schoenberg (10)
Schönberg (9)
Sciarrino (9)
Skalkottas (10)
Stravinsky (10)
Sweelinck (9)
Vieuxtemps (10)
Villa-Lobos (10)
Waldteufel (10)

11

Butterworth
Charpentier
Dimitriesen
Dittersdorf
Ferneyhough
Frescobaldi
Humperdinck

Leoncavallo
Lloyd Webber
Lutoslawski
Mendelssohn
Moussorgsky
Rachmaninov
Stockhausen
Szymanowski
Tailleferre
Tchaikovsky
Wolf-Ferrari

12 AND OVER

Coleridge Taylor (15)

Dallapiccola (12)
Hildegard of Bingen (17)
Jaques-Dalcroze (14)
Josquin Desprez (14)
Khachaturian (12)
Lennox Berkeley (14)
Maxwell Davies (13)
Rachmaninoff (12)
Racine Fricker (13)
Richard Strauss (14)
Rimsky Korsakov (14)
Shostakovich (12)
Sterndale Bennett (16)
Vaughan Williams (15)

Music, musical instruments and terms

1–3	hum	si	base	horn
	jig	soh	bass	hymn
air	key	sol	beat	jazz
alt	kit	ten	bell	koto
bar	la	tie	brio	lead
bis	lah	ud	clef	Lied
bow	lay	ut	coda	lilt
cue	mf	va	drum	lute
dim.	mi	vox	duet	lyre
do	p	zel	echo	mass
doh	più		fife	mode
duo	pop	**4**	fine	mood
f	pp	alta	flat	mort
fa	ray	alto	fret	mute
fah	re	arco	glee	node
ff	rit	aria	gong	note
gli	run	ayre	harp	oboe
gu	sax	band	high	opus
gue	sf	bard	hold	part

peal	arsis	ditty	neume	shawm
pean	assai	dolce	nodal	sitar
pipe	atone	drone	nonet	sixth
poco	aulos	duple	notes	slide
port	banjo	elegy	octet	snare
raga	basso	étude	opera	soave
rall	basta	fifer	organ	sol-fa
reed	baton	flute	paean	sound
reel	bebop	folia	pause	staff
rest	bells	forte	pavan	stave
root	blare	fugal	pedal	Strad
sign	blues	fugue	piano	strum
sing	bones	galop	pieno	study
slur	brass	gamba	piper	suite
solo	breve	gamut	pitch	swell
song	buffo	gigue	pluck	swing
stop	bugle	grace	polka	tabla
tace	canon	grave	primo	tabor
time	canto	jodel	proms	tacet
tone	carol	knell	psalm	tanto
trio	cello	kyrie	quill	tardo
tuba	cento	largo	rebec	tempo
tuck	chang	lento	reeds	tenor
tune	chant	lyric	regal	theme
vamp	chime	major	resin	third
vina	choir	march	rondo	thrum
viol	chord	metre	round	tonic
vivo	cornu	mezzo	scale	tonus
voce	crook	minim	scena	triad
wind	croon	minor	score	trill
wood	crowd	molto	segno	tritone
	crwth	mosso	segue	trope
5	dance	motet	senza	tuned
	dauli	motif	shake	tuner
adapt	dirge	naker	shalm	tutti
ad lib	disco	nebel	sharp	twang
album				

valse
valve
vibes
viola
vocal
voice
volta
volti
waits
waltz
wrest
yodel
zheng
zinke

6

accent
adagio
al fine
anthem
arghul
arioso
atabal
atonal
attune
aubade
ballad
ballet
bolero
bridge
bugler
cadent
cantor
catgut
chimes
chiuso

choral
choric
chorus
cither
citole
cornet
contra
cymbal
da capo
damper
design
diesis
duetto
dulcet
eighth
encore
fading
fiddle
figure
finale
fluter
fugato
gallop
giusto
ground
guitar
hammer
intone
Ionian
jingle
kettle
kinnor
legato
Lieder
litany
lutist

Lydian
manual
medley
melody
minuet
monody
motive
nobile
oboist
octave
off-key
pavane
phrase
piston
plagal
player
presto
quaver
rattan
rattle
rebeck
record
reggae
rhythm
ritard
rubato
sancho
scales
second
sempre
sennet
septet
serial
sestet
sextet
shanty

shofar
singer
sonata
spinet
stanza
string
subito
syrinx
tabour
tabret
tam-tam
tenuto
tercet
thesis
tierce
timbal
timbre
tirade
tom-tom
treble
trigon
troppo
tucket
tune up
tuning
tymbal
unison
up-beat
vamper
veloce
ventil
vielle
violin
vivace
volume
warble

zincke
zither

7

agitato
allegro
alphorn
al segno
alt-horn
amoroso
andante
angelot
animato
arietta
ariette
Ars Nova
attacca
attuned
bagpipe
ballade
bandore
baroque
baryton
bassist
bassoon
battuta
bazooka
bellows
bitonal
bravura
cadence
cadency
cadenza
calando
calypso
cantata

canzona
canzone
caprice
celeste
cellist
cembalo
chamade
chanson
chanter
chantry
chorale
cithara
cittern
clapper
clarion
clavier
codetta
con brio
concert
conduct
cornett
counter
courant
Cremona
crooner
cymbals
czardas
descant
descend
descent
diagram
discord
distune
dolente
drummer
episode

euphony
fagotto
fanfare
fantasy
fermata
fiddler
flatten
flutist
furioso
gavotte
giocoso
gittern
G-string
harmony
harpist
hautboy
juke-box
karaoke
keynote
kithara
Locrian
lullaby
maestro
maracas
marimba
mazurka
measure
mediant
melisma
melodic
middle C
mistune
mordent
musette
musical
natural

ocarina
octette
offbeat
organum
pan-pipe
pandora
pesante
pianist
pianola
pibroch
piccolo
piffaro
pomposo
pop song
pop tune
posaune
prelude
quartet
quintet
ragtime
recital
refrain
reprise
requiem
rescore
ripieno
romance
rondeau
rondino
rosalia
roulade
sackbut
sambuca
samisen
sarangi
saxhorn

scherzo	vespers	cavatina	eleventh
sciolto	vibrato	chaconne	ensemble
scoring	vihuela	cheville	entr'acte
serpent	violist	choirboy	euphonic
seventh	violone	cimbalon	exercise
sfogato	warbler	clappers	faburden
singing	wassail	clarinet	falsetto
sistrum	whistle	clarsach	fandango
skiffle	zithern	clavecin	fantasia
slurred		clavicor	fantasie
soloist	**8**	col legno	flautist
soprano		composer	folk-song
sordino	absonant	con amore	forzando
spinnet	addition	con anima	galliard
stopped	altoclef	concerto	gemshorn
stretto	alto horn	con fuoco	glee club
strophe	antiphon	continuo	grazioso
sub-bass	arch-lute	courante	half-note
subject	arpeggio	cromorne	handbell
syncope	autoharp	crotales	harmonic
taboret	bagpiper	crotchet	harp-lute
tambour	bagpipes	crumhorn	hornpipe
theorbo	baritone	dal segno	interval
timbrel	bass clef	demi-tone	intonate
timpani	bass drum	diapason	isotonic
timpano	bass-horn	diatonic	jew's harp
toccata	bass note	diminish	jongleur
tone-row	bass oboe	ding-dong	keyboard
tremolo	bass viol	distance	key bugle
triplet	beat time	doloroso	lentando
trumpet	bell harp	dominant	libretto
tuneful	berceuse	down beat	ligature
ukelele	canticle	drumbeat	lutanist
ukulele	canzonet	drum-head	lutenist
upright	carillon	duettist	madrigal
up-tempo	castanet	dulcimer	maestoso

major key	recorder	tonality	bombardon
mandolin	reed pipe	tone down	bow-string
melodeon	register	tone poem	brass band
melodics	resonant	triangle	brillante
melodist	response	trichord	bugle-horn
melodize	rhapsody	trigonon	cacophony
minor key	rigadoon	trombone	cantabile
minstrel	ritenuto	trouvere	cantilena
mirliton	Romantic	tympanum	capriccio
miserere	saraband	vigoroso	castanets
moderato	semitone	virginal	celestina
modulate	septette	virtuosi	charivari
monotone	sequence	virtuoso	chromatic
movement	serenade	vocalion	clarionet
musician	serenata	vocalist	classical
nocturne	sestetto	warbling	coach-horn
notation	sextette	woodwind	conductor
notturno	sforzato	zambomba	contralto
operatic	shamisen		cornemuse
operetta	side drum	**9**	cornopean
oratorio	smorzato		crescendo
organist	sonatina	accordion	crookhorn
ostinato	song book	acoustics	cymbalist
overture	songster	adagietto	danceband
pan-pipes	spiccato	alla breve	dead-march
partbook	spinette	allemande	decachord
part-song	staccato	alto viola	deep-toned
pastoral	subtonic	andamento	dissonant
phorminx	symphony	andantino	dithyramb
phrasing	syntonic	antiphony	drone-pipe
Phrygian	tabouret	arabesque	drumstick
pianette	tamboura	atonality	elbow-pipe
plectrum	tenorino	bagatelle	euphonium
post horn	terzetto	balalaika	extempore
psaltery	threnody	banjolele	fiddle-bow
quantity	timoroso	banjoline	flageolet
		barcarole	

flute-stop	monochord	serialism
gallopade	monophony	sforzando
generator	monotonic	Siciliana
glissando	mouth harp	signature
grace-note	music-book	slow march
gradation	nose flute	snaredrum
grandioso	obbligato	soft pedal
Gregorian	octachord	solfeggio
guitarist	orchestra	sopranino
half-shift	orpharion	sostenuto
hand organ	part music	sottovoce
harmonica	pastorale	sound-post
harmonics	pitch-pipe	spiritoso
harmonium	pizzicato	spiritual
harmonize	plainsong	succentor
hexachord	polonaise	symphonic
high pitch	polychord	syncopate
high-toned	polyphony	tablature
homophony	polytonal	tail-piece
impromptu	quadrille	tambourin
improvise	quartette	tenor clef
in harmony	quintette	tenor horn
interlude	recording	tenor tuba
inversion	reed organ	tenor viol
irregular	rehearsal	tessitura
jazz music	resonance	theorbist
lagrimoso	rhythmics	time-table
larghetto	ricercare	timpanist
leger-line	roundelay	trumpeter
leitmotif	sarabande	tympanist
mandoline	saxophone	union pipe
melodious	semibreve	untunable
metronome	semitonic	variation
mezza-voce	septimole	violinist
microtone	seraphina	voluntary
modulator	seraphine	vox humana

whistling
whole tone
xylophone
xylorimba

10

accidental
adaptation
affettuoso
alla caccia
allargando
allegretto
antiphonal
appoggiato
arpeggione
attunement
background
bandmaster
barcarolle
bass guitar
basset-horn
bassoonist
bull fiddle
cantillate
canzonetta
chitarrone
chorus girl
clairseach
clarabella
clavichord
coloratura
concertina
con spirito
continuato
contrabass
cor anglais

cornettist
dance-music
didgeridoo
diminuendo
discordant
disharmony
dissonance
dissonancy
dolcemente
double bass
double time
embouchure
enharmonic
Eolian harp
Eolian mode
euphonicon
euphonious
flügelhorn
folk singer
fortissimo
French horn
gramophone
grand opera
grand piano
ground bass
harmonicon
harp-string
homophonic
hurdy-gurdy
incidental
instrument
intermezzo
intonation
kettledrum
lentamente
light opera

major chord
major scale
melismatic
mezzoforte
microtonal
minimalism
minor chord
minor scale
minstrelsy
modulation
monotonous
mouth-organ
mouthpiece
musica viva
musicology
nobilmente
opera buffa
opera music
ophicleide
orchestral
pentachord
percussion
pianissimo
pianoforte
plainchant
polychoral
polyphonic
prima donna
recitative
ritardando
ritornello
scherzando
semiquaver
sousaphone
Stradivari
strathspey

298 MUSIC, MUSICAL INSTRUMENTS AND TERMS

strepitoso
string-band
stringendo
submediant
supertonic
suspension
symphonist
syncopated
tambourine
tarantella
tetrachord
tin whistle
tonic sol-fa
triple time
trombonist
troubador
tuning fork
twelve-tone
undulation
vibraphone
vocal music
Zumpe piano

11

accelerando
Aeolian harp
Aeolian mode
arrangement
ballad opera
barrel-organ
broken chord
canned music
capriccioso
church music
clarion note
composition

concertante
contratenor
counterpart
decrescendo
demi-cadence
diatessaron
discordance
discordancy
extemporize
fiddlestick
figured bass
finger-board
first violin
harmonizing
harpsichord
high-pitched
hunting-horn
incantation
madrigalist
mandolinist
minnesinger
music master
nickelodeon
opera bouffe
orchestrate
passing note
piano player
polyphonism
polyphonist
prestissimo
progression
quarter note
quarter-tone
rallentando
rock and roll
sacred music

saxophonist
senza rigore
solmization
subsemitone
symphonious
syncopation
synthesizer
transposing
tridiapason
viola d'amore
violoncello
vivacissimo
voce di petto
voce di testa
volti subito

12

accordionist
acoustic bass
allegrissimo
allegro assai
appassionata
appoggiatura
augmentation
bass baritone
boogie-woogie
cembal d'amour
chamber music
chromaticism
clarinettist
clavicembalo
comedy ballet
concert grand
concert pitch
conservatory
contrapuntal

cottage piano
countertenor
counterpoint
divertimento
dotted quaver
double-octave
extravaganza
false cadence
fiddle string
funeral march
glockenspiel
instrumental
key signature
leggeramente
marcatissimo
mezzo-soprano
military band
musicologist
natural notes
opéra comique
orchestrator
organ-grinder
organ recital
pandean pipes
passion music
penny whistle
philharmonic
philomusical
Phrygian mode
polytonality
pralltriller
repercussion
sesquialtera
Stradivarius
thoroughbass
tuning hammer

viola da gamba
vocalization

13

accompaniment
acoustic guitar
alto saxophone
bagpipe player
basso continuo
choral singing
conservatoire
contrabassoon
cornet-à-piston
disharmonious
harmonic chord
Kapellmeister
music festival
musical comedy
neoclassicism
operatic music
orchestration
piano concerto
Postmodernism
ranz des vaches
slide trombone
sol-fa notation
staff notation
string quartet
string quintet
superdominant
swanee whistle
symphonic poem
terpsichorean
time signature
transposition
unaccompanied

violin concerto (14)
violoncellist

14 AND OVER

Ambrosian chant (14)
brass instrument(s) (15, 16)
chromatic scale (14)
classical music (14)
concerto grosso (14)
demisemiquaver (14)
direct interval (14)
double stopping (14)
double-tonguing (14)
electric guitar (14)
electronic music (15)
fife-and-drum band (15)
fiute-flageolet (14)
Gregorian chant (14)
Highland bagpipe (15)
incidental music (15)

instrumentalist (15)
instrumentation (15)
inverted mordent (15)
Lowland bagpipe (14)
musique concrète (15)
piano accordion (14)
promenade concert (16)
reed instrument (14)
regimental band (14)
string orchestra (15)
symphony concert (15)
tintinnabulary (14)
tintinnabulate (14)
tintinnabulation (16)
triple-tongueing (15)
twelve-note music (15)
twelve-tone music (15)
wind instrument(s)
(14, 15)

NATURAL HISTORY – LIVING CREATURES
Birds

2 AND 3	hen	poe	anas	crax
	jay	ree	ayes	crow
auk	kae	roc	barb	dodo
cob	kea	ruc	bird	dove
daw	mew	tit	bubo	duck
emu	moa	tui	chat	erne
ern	owl	**4**	cock	eyas
fop	pen		coly	fowl
fum	pie	alca	coot	gier

guan	teal	junco	skite	condor
gull	tern	larus	snipe	corbie
hawk	tody	lowan	solan	corvus
hern	wren	macaw	spink	coucal
huia	yite	madge	squab	cuckoo
ibis	yunx	mavis	stilt	culver
kaka		merle	stint	curlew
kite	**5**	miner	stork	cushat
kiwi	agami	murre	strix	cygnet
knot	ajaia	mynah	swift	cygnus
koel	amzel	nandu	terek	darter
lark	ardea	noddy	twite	dipper
loom	biddy	ornis	urubu	drongo
loon	booby	ousel	veery	dunlin
lory	brant	ouzel	vireo	eaglet
lung	brent	owlet	wader	falcon
mina	capon	pewet	wavey	fulmar
myna	chick	pewit	whaup	gambet
otus	crake	picus		gander
pavo	crane	pipit	**6**	gannet
pern	didus	pitta	alcedo	garrot
pica	diver	poaka	alcyon	godwit
piet	drake	poult	ancona	gooney
poll	eagle	quail	anklet	gorhen
rail	egret	raven	argala	goslet
rhea	eider	reeve	avocet	grakle
rook	finch	robin	avoset	grouse
ruff	galah	rodge	bantam	hoopoe
shag	geese	saker	barbet	howlet
skua	glede	scaup	brolga	jabiru
smew	goose	scops	bulbul	jacana
sora	goura	scray	canary	jaeger
sord	grebe	senex	chewet	jerkin
spot	harpy	serin	chough	kakapo
swan	heron	shama	chukar	lanner
taha	hobby	sitta	citril	leipoa

linnet
loriot
magpie
martin
merlin
missel
mistle
mopoke
motmot
musket
nestor
oriole
osprey
parrot
pavone
peahen
pecker
peewit
petrel
pigeon
plover
pouter
puffin
pullet
pygarg
quelea
quezal
ratite
redcap
roller
runner
scobby
scoter
sea-bar
sea-cob
seamew

sea-pie
shrike
simurg
siskin
sultan
takabe
tercel
thrush
tirwit
tomtit
toucan
tringa
trogon
turaco
turbit
turdus
turkey
turner
weaver
whydah
wigeon
willet
yaffle
yowley
zivola

7

apteryx
awl-bird
babbler
barn owl
bee-bird
bittern
bluecap
bluetit
boobook

buceros
bullbat
bunting
buphaga
bustard
buzzard
cariama
cat-bird
cheeper
chicken
ciconia
coaltit
cobswan
colibri
columba
corella
cotinga
courlan
courser
cow-bird
creeper
cropper
dorhawk
dorking
dottrel
dovekie
dovelet
dum bird
dunnock
egg-bird
emu wren
fantail
fen duck
fern owl
finfoot
gadwall

galeeny
gobbler
gorcock
gorcrow
goshawk
gosling
grackle
grallae
greyhen
greylag
griffin
haggard
halcyon
harrier
hawk owl
hickway
hoatzin
horn owl
ice-bird
impeyan
jacamar
jackass
jackdaw
jacobin
kamichi
kestrel
killdee
kinglet
lapwing
largopus
leghorn
lich-owl
limpkin
mallard
manakin
manikin

marabou
martlet
migrant
minivet
moorhen
motacil
moth owl
mudlark
oil bird
ortolan
oscines
ostrich
pandeon
partlet
peacock
peafowl
pelican
penguin
percher
phoenix
pinnock
pintado
pintail
poe-bird
poshard
poultry
puttock
quetzal
redpoll
redwing
rooster
rosella
ruddock
sakaret
sawbill
sea-crow

sea-dove
sea-duck
sea-fowl
seagull
sea-hawk
seriema
sirgang
skimmer
skylark
sparrow
squacco
staniel
sunbird
swallow
tadorna
tanager
tarrock
tattler
tiercel
tinamou
titlark
titling
titmice
touraco
tree tit
trochil
tumbler
vulture
vulturn
wagtail
wapacut

8

accentor
adjutant
aigrette

amadavat
avadavat
barnacle
bee-eater
bellbird
blackcap
bluebird
boat-bill
bobolink
bob-white
brancher
bush hawk
caracara
cardinal
cockatoo
cockerel
curassow
cursores
dabchick
dandy-hen
didapper
dinornis
dipchick
dotterel
duck hawk
duckling
dun-diver
eagle-owl
fauvette
fern-bird
fish-hawk
flamingo
gairfowl
game-bird
gamecock
gang-gang

garefowl
garganey
great auk
great tit
greenlet
grey duck
grey teal
grosbeak
guacharo
hamerkop
hawfinch
hemipode
hernshaw
hickwall
hornbill
hula-bird
killdeer
kingbird
landrail
langshan
lanneret
laverock
lorikeet
love-bird
lyrebird
mandarin
marabout
marsh tit
megapode
mire crow
moorbird
moorcock
moorfowl
moorgame
morillon
musk duck

mute swan
myna bird
nestling
nightjar
notornis
nuthatch
ovenbird
oxpecker
parakeet
paraquet
peesweep
peetweet
phaethon
pheasant
podargus
popinjay
prunella
puff bird
redshank
redstart
reedling
reed wren
ricebird
rifleman
ringdove
ringtail
rock dove
sagecock
sakabula
screamer
scrub-tit
sea-drake
sea-eagle
shelduck
shoebill
shoveler

snowbird
snowy owl
songbird
songlark
songster
starling
struthio
swamphen
tantalus
tawny owl
tercelet
thrasher
throstle
titmouse
tomnoddy
tragopan
umbrette
waterhen
wheatear
whimbrel
whinchat
whistler
white-eye
wildfowl
woodchat
woodcock
wood ibis
woodlark
wood wren
yeldring
yoldring
zopilote

9

accipiter
aepyornis

albatross
ant-thrush
bald eagle
Baltimore
bean goose
beccafico
beefeater
black cock
black swan
blackbird
blacktail
bower-bird
brambling
broadbill
bullfinch
campanero
cassowary
chaffinch
chatterer
church owl
cockatiel
columbine
cormorant
corncrake
crossbill
currawong
dandy-cock
dowitcher
eagle-hawk
eider duck
field-duck
fieldfare
field wren
firecrest
fledgling
francolin

friar-bird
fringilla
frogmouth
gallinazo
gallinule
gerfalcon
gier-eagle
goldcrest
goldeneye
goldfinch
goosander
great skua
grenadier
grey goose
grey heron
grossbeak
guillemot
guinea-hen
gyrfalcon
hammerkop
heathbird
heathcock
heath-fowl
heath-game
horned owl
jacksnipe
jenny-wren
jerfalcon
kittiwake
lint-white
little auk
macartney
mallee hen
mallemuck
marsh bird
marsh hawk

marsh wren
merganser
merulidan
mousebird
natatores
night hawk
ossifrage
paradisea
partridge
passerine
peregrine
phalarope
ptarmigan
quail-call
quail-hawk
razorbill
redbreast
red grouse
rifle-bird
ring-ouzel
rossignol
salangane
sandpiper
scaup duck
scrub-bird
scrub-fowl
scrub-wren
sedge-bird
sedge-wren
shearbill
sheldrake
shorebird
shoveller
shrike-tit
silver-eye
skunk-bird

snake-bird
snow goose
sooty tern
spinebill
spoonbill
stilt-bird
stock-dove
stonechat
storm-bird
strigidae
swamp-hawk
talegalla
tetraonid
thickhead
thornbill
tiercelet
trochilus
trumpeter
turnstone
waterbird
waterfowl
water-rail
wedgebill
wheat-bird
whiteface
whitetail
widow-bird
wild goose
willow tit
windhover
woodspite
wyandotte

10

aberdevine
ant-catcher

Arctic skua
Arctic tern
bearded tit
bell-magpie
bird of prey
blight-bird
blue-throat
boobook owl
Brent goose
bronzewing
budgerigar
burrow-duck
butter-bird
canary bird
canvasback
chiffchaff
crested tit
demoiselle
didunculus
dishwasher
dusky minah
dusky robin
ember goose
eurylaimus
fledgeling
flycatcher
fratercula
goatmilker
goatsucker
grassfinch
greenfinch
greenshank
grey falcon
grey parrot
grey plover
ground dove

ground lark
guinea-fowl
hammerhead
harpy eagle
hen-harrier
honeyeater
honey-guide
hooded crow
jungle-fowl
kingfisher
king parrot
kookaburra
magpie-lark
mallee bird
mallee-fowl
meadowlark
mutton-bird
night heron
night raven
nutcracker
parson-bird
prairie hen
pratincole
ramphastos
regent-bird
rockjumper
rock parrot
rock pigeon
rock thrush
sacred ibis
saddleback
sagegrouse
sanderling
sandgrouse
sandmartin
screech-owl

sea-swallow
shearwater
sheathbill
shovelbill
silver gull
solan goose
song thrush
sun-bittern
tailor-bird
tit-warbler
tree-runner
tropic-bird
turkey-cock
turtle dove
water crake
water-ouzel
wattlebird
weaverbird
whidah-bird
white egret
whydah-bird
willow wren
wonga-wonga
woodgrouse
woodpecker
wood-pigeon
yellow-bird
yellowlegs
zebra finch

11

apostle-bird
banded stilt
barn swallow
black falcon
black grouse

black martin
bonebreaker
booby gannet
brush-turkey
bush-creeper
butcher-bird
button quail
Canada goose
carrion crow
chanticleer
citril finch
cochinchina
cock-sparrow
corn bunting
dentiroster
Dorking fowl
dragoon-bird
fairy martin
flock pigeon
frigate-bird
fruit-pigeon
golden eagle
grallatores
grey wagtail
ground robin
herring gull
house martin
humming-bird
king penguin
king vulture
lammergeier
lammergeyer
leatherhead
leptodactyl
lily-trotter
magpie-goose

meadow-pipit
mocking-bird
Muscovy duck
nightingale
pied wagtail
pintail duck
procellaria
reed babbler
reed bunting
reed sparrow
reed warbler
rhamphastos
rock warbler
scarlet ibis
scissor-beak
scissor-bill
scissor bird
scissor tail
screech hawk
sea-pheasant
snow-bunting
song sparrow
sparrowhawk
stilt plover
stone curlew
stone plover
tenuiroster
tree-creeper
tree sparrow
wall-creeper
whitethroat
whooper swan
wood-swallow
wood warbler

12

adjutant bird
burrowing-owl
capercaillie
capercailzie
cardinal-bird
collared dove
common turkey
crested grebe
Dentirostres
fairy penguin
Fissirostres
golden oriole
golden plover
grass warbler
greater skaup
ground thrush
hedge sparrow
honey-buzzard
house sparrow
mandarin duck
marsh harrier
marsh warbler
missel-thrush
mistle-thrush
mourning-dove
pink cockatoo
red-head finch
sea cormorant
sedge warbler
serpent-eater
stone-chatter
stormy petrel
swamp sparrow
swamp-harrier
tenuirosters

turbit-pigeon
umbrella bird
water-wagtail
wattle turkey
whippoorwill
white goshawk
yellowhammer

13

Adélie penguin
adjutant crane
adjutant stork
American eagle
argus pheasant
Baltimore bird
barnacle goose
carrier pigeon
crested pigeon
crocodile bird
fantail pigeon
harlequin duck
little bustard
long-tailed tit
northern diver
oystercatcher
plain-wanderer
recurviroster
screech martin
secretary bird
spider-catcher
swallow-shrike
tumbler-pigeon
turkey-buzzard
turkey vulture
whistling duck
whistling swan

willow warbler
yellow bunting
yellow wagtail

14

bearded vulture
bird of paradise

canvasback duck
emperor penguin
golden pheasant
griffon vulture
horned screamer
king-lory parrot
Manx shearwater

prairie-chicken
red-headed finch
rhinoceros-bird
Rhode Island Red
robin redbreast
tawny frogmouth
whistling eagle

Dogs

3 AND 4

chow
cur
peke
pom
pug
pup
Skye
tike
toy
tyke

5

bitch
boxer
brach
cairn
corgi
dhole
dingo
hound
husky
pooch
puppy

shock
spitz
whelp

6

Afghan
bandog
barbet
basset
beagle
borzoi
bowwow
canine
cocker
collie
Eskimo
gundog
jowler
kelpie
lapdog
pariah
poodle
pugdog
pye-dog
ranger

ratter
saluki
setter
shough
talbot
toy dog

7

basenji
bird-dog
brachet
bulldog
clumber
griffon
harrier
lurcher
Maltese
mastiff
mongrel
pointer
samoyed
sheltie
spaniel
terrier
tumbler

whippet
wolf-dog

8

Aberdeen
Airedale
Alsatian
Blenheim
chowchow
coachdog
Doberman
elkhound
foxhound
hound-dog
housedog
keeshond
Labrador
otter dog
papillon
Pekinese
Sealyham
sheepdog
spitz dog
Springer
turnspit

watchdog
water-dog

9

badger dog
boarhound
buckhound
chihuahua
dachshund
Dalmatian
deerhound
Eskimo dog
gazehound
Great Dane
greyhound
Kerry blue
limehound
lyamhound
Pekingese
police dog
red setter
retriever
St Bernard
schnauzer
staghound
wolfhound

10

Bedlington
bloodhound
Clydesdale
fox terrier
Maltese dog
otter hound
Pomeranian
Rottweiler

schipperke
Weimaraner
Welsh corgi

11

Afghan hound
basset hound
bull mastiff
bull terrier
carriage dog
Irish setter
Jack Russell
King Charles
shepherd dog
Skye terrier

12

Belvoir hound
Border collie
cairn terrier
Gordon setter
Irish terrier
Newfoundland
Saint Bernard
water spaniel
Welsh terrier

13

Border terrier
Boston terrier
cocker spaniel
Dandie Dinmont
English setter
Scotch terrier
Sussex spaniel

14 AND OVER

Aberdeen terrier (15)
Airedale terrier (15)
Blenheim spaniel (15)
Clumber spaniel (14)
English springer (15)
German shepherd (14)
golden retriever (15)
Highland terrier (15)

Irish wolfhound (14)
Lakeland terrier (15)
Norfolk spaniel (14)
pitbull terrier (14)
Pyrenean mastiff (15)
Scottish terrier (15)
Shetland sheepdog (16)
springer spaniel (15)
Tibetan mastiff (14)

Fish, crustaceans, etc.

3 AND 4	fugu	parr	angel	murry
	gar	peal	apode	nacre
amia	ged	pike	blain	nurse
barb	goby	pope	bleak	perch
bass	grig	pout	bleck	pogge
bib	hag	ray	bream	porgy
blay	hake	roe	brill	powan
brit	huso	rudd	charr	prawn
cale	huss	ruff	cisco	reeve
carp	ide	sapo	cobia	roach
char	jack	sar	cohoe	roker
chub	kelt	scad	cuddy	ruffe
cod	keta	scar	doree	salmo
coho	ling	shad	dorse	sargo
crab	lox	snig	elver	saury
cusk	luce	sole	fluke	scrod
dab	lump	tau	gaper	sepia
dace	mako	tope	grunt	sewin
dory	mold	tuna	guppy	shark
drum	mort		laker	skate
eel	opah	**5**	loach	smelt
esox	orca	ablen	molly	smolt
fin	orfe	ablet	moray	snoek

snook	doctor	sauger	anchovy
solen	dorado	saurel	asterid
sprag	ellops	scampi	batfish
sprat	finnan	scarus	bergylt
sprod	gadoid	sea-ape	bloater
squid	ganoid	sea-bat	box-fish
tench	gardon	sea-cat	bubbler
tetra	garvie	sea-eel	bummalo
togue	ginkin	sea-egg	capelin
torsk	goramy	sea-fox	cat-fish
trout	grilse	sea-hog	chimera
tunny	groper	sea-owl	cichild
umber	gunnel	sea-pad	cod-fish
whiff	gurnet	sea-pig	codling
witch	hermit	sephen	cow-fish
	kipper	shanny	croaker
6	launce	shiner	crucian
	maigre	shrimp	cusk eel
alevin	marlin	sucker	cyprine
anabas	milter	tarpon	dog-fish
angler	minnow	tautog	dun-fish
barbel	mud-eel	tomcod	echinus
belone	mullet	trygon	eel-fare
beluga	plaice	turbot	eel-pout
blenny	pollan	twaite	fiddler
bonito	puffer	wapper	garfish
bowfin	quahog	weever	garpike
burbot	red-eye	wirrah	garvock
caplin	remora	wrasse	gourami
caranx	robalo	zander	grouper
cheven	rochet	zingel	grunter
chevin	runner		gudgeon
comber	saithe	**7**	gurnard
conger	salmon		gwyniad
cuttle	samlet	acaleph	haddock
darter	sardel	actinia	hagfish
Diodon		alewife	

halibut	rat-tail	Asterias	glass-eel
herling	red-fish	asteroid	goatfish
herring	rock-cod	band-fish	goldfish
hogfish	rotifer	barnacle	graining
homelyn	sand eel	bill fish	grayling
houting	sardine	blue fish	green eel
icefish	sawfish	blue-gill	gymnotus
jewfish	Scomber	boarfish	halfbeak
keeling	sculpin	brisling	halosaur
lampern	sea-bass	bullhead	horn-beak
lamprey	sea-fish	calamary	horn-fish
latchet	sea-hare	cavefish	John Dory
lobster	sea-lion	characin	king crab
mahseer	sea-moth	chimaera	king-fish
merling	sea-pike	clupeoid	lancelet
monodon	sea-slug	coalfish	land crab
moon-eye	sea-wolf	corkwing	lemon dab
morwong	Silurus	cowshark	lump-fish
mud-fish	snapper	crawfish	lung-fish
Muraena	sock-eye	crayfish	mackerel
murexes	sterlet	dealfish	manta ray
oar-fish	sunfish	dragonet	menhaden
octopus	sweeper	drum-fish	milkfish
old-wife	teleost	eagle-ray	monkfish
osseter	top-knot	eulachon	moon-fish
pegasus	torgoch	filefish	moray eel
pen-fish	torpedo	fire-fish	nannygai
piddock	vendace	flatfish	numbfish
pig-fish	whiting	flathead	ophidion
pike eel	worm-eel	flounder	Physalla
piranha		forktail	pickerel
pollack	**8**	fox-shark	pigmy-eel
pollock		gamefish	pilchard
polypus	albacore	Ganoidei	pipefish
pompano	Anguilla	gillaroo	polyneme
ragfish	arapaima	gilt-head	poor-John
	ascidian		

red perch
redbelly
reedfish
rock-bass
rock-fish
rockling
sail-fish
salt-fish
sand-fish
sardelle
saw-shark
scombrid
scopelid
sea-acorn
sea bream
sea-devil
sea-horse
sea-lemon
sea-louse
sea perch
sea-raven
sea robin
sea snipe
siscowet
skipjack
soapfish
sparling
spelding
spiny eel
springer
starfish
sting-ray
stomapod
sturgeon
swamp-eel
tarwhine

teraglin
testacea
thrasher
thresher
toad-fish
trevally
troutlet
tuna fish
wolf-fish
zoophyte

9

acalephae
angelfish
argentine
barracuda
black drum
blackfish
blue nurse
blue shark
brandling
bullshark
bulltrout
ceratodus
chaetodon
cling-fish
conger eel
coralfish
crampfish
crustacea
cycloidei
devil fish
dimyarian
Dover sole
echinidan
finny-scad

fire-flair
fish-louse
frost-fish
ganoidean
garden eel
globe-fish
goldsinny
goosefish
grenadier
grey nurse
gulper eel
hippodame
houndfish
jaculator
jellyfish
jollytail
lemon sole
loach goby
mango fish
Murray cod
pike perch
pilot fish
placoderm
porbeagle
pycnodont
razor fish
red mullet
red salmon
ribbon eel
river crab
sand shark
sand-lance
schnapper
sea-mullet
sea-needle
sea-nettle

sheat-fish
silver-eel
snipefish
spear-fish
stargazer
stingaree
stockfish
stomapoda
stone fish
stone-bass
surfperch
surmullet
sweetfish
sword-tail
swordfish
thornback
threadfin
tiger-barb
tigerfish
tittlebat
toothcarp
top minnow
troutling
trumpeter
trunkfish
tunny fish
whitebait
whitefish
wobbegong
yellowfin
zebra fish

10

angelshark
angler fish
archer fish

barracouta
basket fish
black bream
black whale
blue groper
Bombay duck
bottle-nose
brown trout
butterfish
candlefish
Cestracion
clouded eel
clown loach
cock-paddle
coelacanth
coral trout
cornet fish
ctenoidans
cuttlefish
cyclostome
damselfish
doctor fish
dragon-fish
dwarf shark
echinoderm
fingerling
five-finger
flying fish
ganoideans
ghost-shark
great skate
grey mullet
groundling
guitarfish
hammerfish
hammerhead

hermit crab
Holothuria
lizardfish
loggerhead
lumpsucker
maskanonge
maskinonge
midshipman
mirror carp
mudskipper
needlefish
nurse shark
paddlefish
parrot-fish
periwinkle
pufferfish
pycnodonts
pygmy perch
rapier fish
red gurnard
red snapper
ribbon-fish
robber-crab
rudderfish
sand-hopper
sand-launce
sand-mullet
scleroderm
Scopelidae
sea catfish
silver carp
silver dory
silverfish
silverside
squeteague
sucker-fish

surf scoter
tiger shark
tongue-sole
trout perch
tub gurnard
turkey fish
turret-fish
whale-shark
white shark
yellow-tail
zebra shark

11

balance-fish
black-angler
blue catfish
bluefin tuna
blue-pointer
bridled goby
brineshrimp
brown groper
carpet-shark
common skate
crested goby
electric eel
electric ray
fiddler crab
fiddler fish
flying squid
golden trout
gurnet perch
hatchet fish
hippocampus
holothurian
jackass-fish
javelin-fish

lantern fish
lepidosiren
orange perch
peacock-fish
peacock-sole
plectognath
prickleback
rainbow-fish
red fire-fish
salmon-trout
scleroderms
sea-cucumber
sea-elephant
sea-hedgehog
sea-scorpion
silver perch
soldier-crab
soldier-fish
stickleback
surgeon-fish
torpedo fish
trigger fish
trumpet-fish

12

basking shark
cucumber-fish
dogfish shark
European pike
fan-tailed ray
four-eyed fish
Pacific saury
rainbow trout
requiem shark
river garfish
rock flathead

scarlet bream
scorpion fish
sentinel crab
silver mullet
sixgill sharp
spiny lobster
squirrelfish
thornback ray
worm pipefish

13

barred garfish
blacktip shark
butterfly fish
climbing perch
finnan haddock
flying gurnard
giant boar-fish
gilthead bream
greater weaver
horse-mackerel
leafy seahorse
leatherjacket
long-finned eel
mackerel shark
ox-eyed herring
Pacific salmon
porcupine fish
saltwater fish
scarlet angler
snub-nosed dart
sockeye salmon
spiny flathead
spiny seahorse
striped angler
thresher shark

tiger-flathead
zebra firefish

14

banded sea-perch
black stingaree
blue-spotted ray
great barracuda
Greenland whale
Macquarie perch
many-banded sole
purple sea-perch
red gurnet-perch
river blackfish
short-finned eel
shovel-nosed ray
smooth flathead
spotted dogfish
spotted whiting
striped catfish
striped gudgeon
striped sea-pike
white horse-fish
zebra angelfish

15

Australian perch
Australian smelt
beaked coral-fish
blue-spot rock-cod
common stingaree
crusted flounder
electric catfish
frigate mackerel
hairback herring
long-finned perch

marbled flathead	smooth stingaree	spotted eagle-ray
painted dragonet	spangled grunter	spotted pipefish
short sucker-fish	Spanish mackerel	white-spotted ray
small-headed sole	spotted cat-shark	

Fossils, shells, etc.

(f.s.)=fossil shell; (s.)=shell

4 AND 5

amber
auger
baler
chama (s.)
chank (s.)
conch (s.)
cone (s.)
cowry
drill (s.)
gaper (s.)
murex (s.)
nacre
ormer
peuce
razor (s.)
snail (s.)
tooth (s.)
tulip (s.)
whelk (s.)

6

buckie (s.)
chiton (s.)
cockle (s.)

cowrie
fornix (s.)
helmet (s.)
jingle (s.)
limpet (s.)
macoma (s.)
matrix
mussel (s.)
natica (s.)
nerite (s.)
Ogygia
olenus
oyster (s.)
quahog (s.)
seaear
tellin (s.)
triton (s.)
trivea (s.)
turban (s.)
volute (s.)
winkle (s.)

7

abalone (s.)
crabite
crinoid

discoid (s.)
muscite
neptune (s.)
ovulite
piddock (s.)
scallop (s.)
zoolite

8

ammonite (f.s.)
argonaut (s.)
ark shell (s.)
balanite
buccinum (s.)
capstone
ceratite
choanite
cololite
conchite (f.s.)
dogwhelk (s.)
ear shell (s.)
echinite
epiornis
escallop (s.)
fig shell (s.)
galerite

janthina (s.)
mangelia (s.)
muricite
mytilite
nautilus (s.)
penshell (s.)
ram's horn (f.s.)
retinite
scaphite (f.s.)
seashell
sea snail
solenite (f.s.)
strombid (s.)
testacel (s.)
topshell (s.)
trochite
tunshell (s.)
volulite (f.s.)
volutite (f.s.)

9

Aepyornis
alcyonite
belemnite
buccinite (f.s.)
cancerite
carpolite
clam shell (s.)
cone shell (s.)
coprolite
corallite
crow stone
dicynodon
encrinite
favosites
foot shell (s.)

frog shell (s.)
giant clam (s.)
harp shell (s.)
hippurite
horn shell (s.)
lima shell (s.)
lithocarp
lithophyl
marsupite
miliolite (f.s.)
moon shell (s.)
moon snail (s.)
muscalite (f.s.)
nautilite
nummulite
ostracite (f.s.)
palmacite
patellite (f.s.)
reliquiae
rock-borer (s.)
serpulite (f.s.)
slip shell (s.)
star shell (s.)
stone lily
strombite (f.s.)
tellinite (f.s.)
trilobite
turbinate (f.s.)
turrilite (f.s.)
tusk shell (s.)

10

agate shell
batrachite
canoe shell (s.)
confervite

dendrolite
dicynodont
entomolite
entrochite
gyrogonite
mosasaurus
odontolite
periwinkle (s.)
razor shell (s.)
screw shell (s.)
snake stone (f.s.)
tiger shell (s.)
tubiporite
ulodendron
wentletrap (s.)
wing oyster (s.)
xanthidium

11

amphibolite
asterolepis
cetotolites
dinotherium
fairy stones
finger shell (s.)
finger stone
furrowshell (s.)
gongiatites (f.s.)
helmet shell (s.)
ichthyolite
madreporite
margin shell
milleporite
mohair shell (s.)
needle shell (s.)
needle whelk (s.)

ornitholite
oyster drill (s.)
rhyncholite
sting winide (s.)
strobilites
sunset shell (s.)
tiger cowrie (s.)
trough shell (s.)
turtle shell (s.)

12

brocade shell (s.)
Chinaman's
  hat (s.)
holoptychis
Hungarian cap (s.)
lantern shell (s.)
macrotherium
megalichthys
pandora shell (s.)
pelican's foot (s.)
pentacrinite
saddle oyster (s.)

serpentstone
slipper shell (s.)
spindle shell (s.)
sundial shell (s.)
trumpet conch
trumpet shell (s.)
zamiostrobus

13 AND 14

bothrodendron (13)
carboniferous (13)
conchyliaceous (f.s.) (14)
dolichosaurus (13)
lepidodendron (13)
lithoglyphite (13)
nacreous shells (s.) (14)
necklace shell (s.) (13)
palaeontology (13)
porphyry shell (s.) (13)
staircase shell (s.) (14)
syringodendron (14)
woodcock shell (s.) (13)

Insects, etc.

3 AND 4			5	
	flea	mite		comma
	fly	moth		culex
ant	frit	nit	acera	drake
bee	gnat	pupa	aphid	drone
bot	grig	slug	aphis	egger
bug	grub	tick	borer	emmet
cleg	ked	wasp	brize	fluke
cob	lice	worm	cerci	gaster
dor	mawk	zimb	cimex	imago

larva
louse
midge
musca
pulex
satyr

6

acarid
acarus
ant cow
bedbug
bee fly
beetle
blatta
botfly
breeze
burnet
buzzer
caddis
capsid
chafer
chigoe
chinch
cicada
cicala
cigala
coccus
cocoon
dayfly
dobson
earwig
elater
gadfly
hop-fly
hopper

hornet
Io moth
jigger
lappet
larvae
locust
looper
maggot
mantis
maybug
mayfly
mygale
sawfly
scarab
sow-bug
sphinx
spider
termes
thrips
Tipula
tsetse
weevil
worker
woubit

7

annelid
antenna
ant-hill
ant-lion
aphides
army ant
bagworm
bean fly
beehive
bee moth

blowfly
boat fly
cestoid
chalcid
chigger
cricket
culicid
cutworm
daphnia
Diptera
epizoon
firefly
frit-fly
gallfly
greyfly
hexapod
June bug
katydid
lady-cow
lobworm
lugworm
mawworm
microbe
monarch
noctuid
peacock
pismire
pyralid
rose-bug
rotifer
sandfly
satyrid
skipper
stylops
termite
tortrix

Vanessa
wasp bee
wasp-fly
wax-moth
wood-ant

8

acaridan
alder-fly
antennae
arachnid
army worm
blackfly
bookworm
caseworm
cheilfer
cinnabar
cocktail
cranefly
dipteran
doglouse
drone-fly
ephemera
firebrat
flatworm
flesh-fly
fossores
fruitfly
gall-wasp
geometer
glow worm
goat-moth
greenfly
hawkmoth
honey-bee
hop-louse

horntail
horsefly
housefly
hoverfly
Isoptera
itch-mite
lacewing
ladybird
luna moth
mason
  bee
mealworm
mealy bug
mosquito
multiped
myriapod
night-fly
nocturna
parasite
pedipalp
Pupipara
puss moth
queen-bee
rotifera
sand-flea
sand-wasp
sandworm
scolytus
scorpion
sheep ked
shipworm
silkworm
stone-fly
tapeworm
tetrapod
water-bug

water-fly
wheat-fly
white ant
white-fly
wireworm
wood wasp
woodlice

9

acaridean
Amazon ant
Anopheles
Arachnida
arthropod
atlas moth
auger worm
bloodworm
book louse
brimstone
bumble-bee
burnet fly
butterfly
caddis fly
canker fly
cantharis
centipede
cheesefly
chinch bug
chrysalis
clavicorn
cochineal
cockroach
coleopter
corn borer
crab-louse
cynipides

damsel fly
dorbeetle
dragonfly
driver-ant
dumbledor
earthworm
egger moth
ephemerid
ephemeron
flying-ant
forest-fly
gall louse
gall-midge
geometrid
ghost-moth
gipsy moth
hemiptera
hornet fly
humble-bee
ichneumon
isopteran
lac insect
longicorn
millipede
Myriapoda
nymphalid
oil beetle
orange tip
owlet moth
plant-lice
potato bug
robber fly
saturniid
screw worm
sheep-lice
sheep-tick

shield bug
squash-bug
sugar-mite
tarantula
thysanura
tiger moth
tumblebug
turnip-fly
warble-fly
water-flea
wax-insect
wheat-moth
whirligig
wood-borer
wood-louse
worker ant
worker bee

10

arachnidan
arthropods
bark-beetle
bird-spider
black widow
blister-fly
bluebottle
boll-weevil
bombardier
burnet moth
cabbage-fly
caddice fly
caddisworm
cankerworm
carpet moth
chalcid fly
cheese-mite

coccinella
cockchafer
Coleoptera
corn-beetle
corn-weevil
crab spider
cuckoospit
death's-head
death-watch
digger wasp
dolphin-fly
dorr-beetle
drosophila
dumbledore
dung beetle
entomolite
flea-beetle
fritillary
froghopper
gall insect
green-drake
hairstreak
harvest bug
harvest man
hessian-fly
June beetle
lantern-fly
lappet moth
leaf beetle
leaf cutter
leaf hopper
leaf-insect
looper-moth
musk beetle
Neuroptera
Orthoptera

palmerworm
phylloxera
pine-weevil
plant-louse
pond skater
potter wasp
red admiral
ribbonworm
rice-weevil
rose beetle
rosechafer
rove beetle
saltigrade
scarabaeus
sheep-louse
silverfish
soldier ant
Spanish fly
spider wasp
spittlebug
springtail
stag beetle
thysanuran
timber-moth
treehopper
trichopter
turnip-flea
wasp beetle
web-spinner
wheat-midge
wolf-spider
woolly-bear
xylophagan

11

arachnidans

assassin bug
atlas beetle
auger beetle
bagworm moth
balm-cricket
beehawk moth
black beetle
bloodsucker
bristletail
bush cricket
cabbage moth
cabbage worm
cantharides
camel spider
capharis bug
caterpillar
chalcia wasp
click beetle
clothes moth
codling moth
coprophagan
drumbledore
emperor moth
entomophaga
Ephemeridae
flour weevil
grain beetle
grasshopper
Hymenoptera
Lepidoptera
mole-cricket
noctuid moth
painted lady
pyralid moth
saprophagan
scale insect

scolopendra
scorpion-fly
snout-beetle
stick-insect
swallow-tail
tetrapteran
thysanurans
tiger-beetle
Trichoptera
tussock-moth
vine-fretter
water beetle
water spider
wood-fretter

12

bent-wing moth
book-scorpion
cabbage white
carpenter ant
carpenter bee
carpet beetle
cecropia moth
cinnabar moth
clerid-beetle
diadem spider
diving beetle
flower-beetle
geometer moth
ground beetle
horned clerid
horse-stinger
ichneumon fly
money-spinner
nightcrawler

potato beetle
Rhynchophera
scarab beetle
sexton beetle
spruce sawfly
sycamore moth
trichopteran
walking-stick
water-boatman
water-strider
white admiral

13

blister beetle
burying beetle
carpenter moth
clearwing moth
clouded yellow
daddy-long-legs
diamond beetle
elm bark beetle
fig-leaf beetle
giant wood-moth
goliath beetle
green wood-moth
ichneumon-wasp
leaf-cutter ant
leaf-cutter bee
leather-jacket
praying mantis
purple emperor
saturniid moth
soldier beetle
tortoiseshell
underwing moth

water scorpion

14

ambrosia beetle
cabbage-root fly
Colorado beetle
death's-head moth
elephant-beetle
Hercules beetle
ironbark sawfly

15

funnel-web spider
serricorn beetle
striped hawkmoth
wheel-animalcule
whirligig beetle

Mammals

2 AND 3

ai
ape
ass
bat
cat
cob
cow
cub
cur
dam
doe
dog
dso
dzo
elk
ewe
fox
gam
gnu
goa
hob
hog
kid
kob
man
mog
nag
orc
ox
pad
pig
pod
pug
ram
rat
roe
sal
seg
sow
teg
tit
tod
tom
tup
ure
wat
yak
zho
zo

4

anoa
Arab
arni
barb
bear
beef
boar
buck
bull
calf
cavy
colt
cony
coon
deer
douc
dray
euro
eyra
fawn
foal
gaur
goat
hack
hare
hart
hind
ibex
jade
joey
kine
kudu
lamb
lion
lynx
mare
mhor
mice
mink
moke
mole
mule
musk
mutt
neat
nowt
oryx
oxen
paca
paco
pard
pika
pony
prad
puma
puss
quey
roan
runt
rusa
saki
seal
sika
stag
stot
stud
suni
tahr
tait
tatu
tike
titi
topi
tyke
unau
urus
vole
wolf
zati
zebu
zobo

5

addax
ammon
apery
ariel
beast
bidet
billy
biped
bison
bongo
brach
brock
bruin
bubal
bunny
burro
camel
caple
capra
capul
cavey
civet
coati
coney
coypu
crone
cuddy
daman
dhole
dicky
dingo

dogie	manis	sheep	zibet	colugo
drill	manul	shire	zoril	cosset
eland	maral	shoat	zorra	cougar
equus	meles	shote	zorro	coyote
fauna	moggy	shott		cuscus
felis	moose	shrew	**6**	dassie
filly	morse	simia		desman
fitch	mount	skunk	agouti	dickey
fossa	mouse	sloth	aliped	dik-dik
gayal	nagor	sorel	alpaca	dobbin
genet	nandu	sorex	Angora	dog fox
goral	nanny	spitz	aoudad	dogape
grice	nyala	steed	argali	donkey
grise	okapi	steer	aye-aye	entire
hinny	oribi	stirk	baboon	ermine
hippo	otter	stoat	badger	farrow
horse	ounce	swine	bandog	fennec
hound	panda	tabby	barrow	ferret
husky	pekan	takin	bayard	fisher
hutia	phoca	talpa	beagle	fox bat
hyena	pinto	tapir	beaver	galago
hyrax	pongo	tatou	beeves	garron
indri	pooch	taxel	bharal	gelada
izard	potto	tayra	bobcat	gerbil
jocko	puppy	tiger	boomer	gibbon
jumbo	pussy	tigon	bovine	ginnet
kaama	rasse	urial	bronco	gopher
kiang	ratel	urson	brumby	grison
koala	rhino	ursus	castor	grivet
kulan	royal	vixen	catalo	guenon
kyloe	sable	waler	cattle	hacker
lemur	saiga	whale	cayuse	he goat
liger	sajou	whelp	cervus	heifer
llama	sasin	yapok	chacma	hogget
loris	screw	zebra	chetah	howler
magot	serow	zerda	coaiti	hunter
			cocker	

hyaena	ovibos	taurus	bulldog
hybrid	padnag	teledu	bullock
impala	poodle	tenrec	Burmese
inyala	porker	thamin	bushcat
jackal	possum	theave	bushpig
jaguar	pugdog	tomcat	cane rat
jennet	pyedog	tupaia	caracal
jerboa	pygarg	tusker	caribou
Jersey	quagga	urchin	cattalo
jument	quokka	vermin	cervine
kalong	rabbit	vervet	cetacea
kelpie	racoon	vicuña	chamois
kitten	ranger	walrus	charger
Kodiak	red fox	wapiti	cheetah
koodoo	reebok	weasel	Cheviot
langur	renard	wether	clumber
lapdog	rhesus	wisent	colobus
lechwe	roarer	wombat	courser
lionet	rodent	wow-wow	dasyure
litter	saluki	yapock	dinmont
macaco	sambar		dolphin
mammal	sambur	**7**	echidna
margay	sea cow		ermelin
marmot	serval	acouchi	fatling
marten	setter	ant-bear	finback
mataco	shammy	aurochs	fitchew
merino	she ass	banteng	foumart
monkey	shelty	bettong	fur seal
morkin	simian	bighorn	gazelle
mouser	sleuth	blesbok	gelding
musk ox	sorrel	blue cat	gemsbok
musmon	suslik	blue fox	gerenuk
nilgai	taguan	Bovidae	giraffe
ocelot	talbot	brawner	glutton
olingo	tanrec	brocket	gorilla
onager	tarpan	bubalis	grampus
		buffalo	

griffon
grizzly
grysbok
guanaco
hackney
hamster
harrier
huanaco
hystrix
jacchus
jackass
jumbuck
karakul
lambkin
lemming
leopard
leveret
linsang
lioness
lurcher
macaque
mammoth
manatee
Manx cat
mariput
markhor
marmose
marmoset
meerkat
megamys
mole-rat
mongrel
moon rat
moschus
mouflon
muntjak
musk-rat

mustang
mustela
narwhal
nasalis
noctule
nylghai
nylghau
opossum
pack rat
palfrey
panther
peccary
polecat
potoroo
prancer
pricket
primate
procyon
raccoon
red deer
rietbok
roe buck
roe deer
rorqual
saimiri
sapajou
sassaby
sciurus
sea-bear
sea-calf
sea-lion
sheltie
siamang
Siamese
spaniel
spanker

sumpter
tamarau
tamarin
tarsier
tatouay
terrier
testudo
thiller
tigress
toxodon
trotter
twinter
urocyon
vampire
viverra
wallaby
wart-hog
wheeler
wild ass
wildcat
wild dog
wistiti
wolf-dog
zamouse
zorilla

8

aardvark
aardwolf
anteater
antelope
axis deer
babirusa
Bactrian
behemoth
bontebok

brown rat
bull-calf
bushbaby
bushbuck
cachalot
capuchin
capucine
capybara
carcajou
cariacou
cavebear
cavicorn
chipmunk
civet-cat
Cotswold
creodont
cricetus
dormouse
duckbill
elephant
entellus
eohippus
foxhound
Galloway
gin-horse
grey wolf
grysbock
Guernsey
hair seal
hedgehog
hoggerel
hylobate
kangaroo
kinkajou
kolinsky
lamantin

landrace
macropus
Mammalia
mandrill
mangabey
mantiger
marmoset
mastodon
maverick
meriones
mongoose
moufflon
milch-cow
musk deer
musquash
ouistiti
pack mule
pangolin
physeter
platypus
polo pony
porkling
porpoise
pteropus
reedbuck
reindeer
river-hog
Rodentia
ruminant
sea-otter
sei whale
serotine
sewellel
sewer-rat
shorling
sirenian

springer
squirrel
staggard
stallion
steenbok
suilline
suricate
tabby-cat
talapoin
tamandua
tetrapod
tiger cat
twinling
ungulata
viscacha
wallaroo
wanderoo
war-horse
warrigal
water-hog
water-rat
weanling
wild boar
wild goat
yeanling
yearling

9

Angora cat
arctic fox
armadillo
babacoote
babirussa
bandicoot
bezantler
binturong

black bear
black buck
blue whale
brood-mare
brown bear
buckhound
carnivore
cart-horse
catamount
chevrotin
chickaree
dachshund
deer-mouse
desert rat
Didelphys
Didelphia
Dinoceras
draught-ox
dray-horse
dromedary
dziggetai
eared seal
flying~fox
glyptodon
golden cat
greyhound
grimalkin
ground-hog
gruntling
guinea-pig
hamadryad
honey-bear
ichneumon
lagomorph
leviathan
livestock

malt-horse
marsupial
monotreme
mouse-hare
mousedeer
orang-utan
pachyderm
pack-horse
palm civet
percheron
petaurist
phalanger
pipistrel
polar bear
porcupine
post-horse
predacean
prongbuck
pronghorn
prosimian
quadruped
racehorse
retriever
rock hyrax
rosinante
rosmarine
shearling
shorthorn
shrew-mole
silver fox
sitatunga
sloth-bear
solenodon
southdown
springbok
steerling

steinbock
stud-horse
thylacine
tragelaph
tree hyrax
tree shrew
waterbuck
watermole
watervole
white bear
wild horse
wolverene
wolverine
woodchuck
woodshock
youngling
zoophagan

10

Angora goat
angwantibo
anthropoid
babiroussa
barasingha
Barbary ape
bloodhound
bottlenose
buckjumper
cacomistle
camelopard
catarrhine
chevrotain
chimpanzee
chinchilla
Chiroptera
chousingha

Clydesdale
coach-horse
coatimundi
cottontail
dolichotis
fallow deer
fieldmouse
giant panda
hartebeest
honey mouse
hooded seal
housemouse
human being
jack rabbit
Kodiak bear
Malay tapir
marsupials
monotremes
muscardine
musk beaver
otter shrew
paddymelon
pantheress
paradoxure
Persian cat
pichiciago
pilot whale
pine marten
prairie dog
pygmy shrew
quadricorn
quadrumane
raccoon dog
rhinoceros
right whale
river horse

rock badger
rock rabbit
Ruminantia
saki monkey
sea-unicorn
shrew-mouse
sperm whale
springhaas
timber wolf
vampire bat
water shrew
white whale
wildebeest

11

American elk
barbastelle
brown hyaena
bull terrier
Cape buffalo
Cheiroptera
digitigrade
douroucouli
flying lemur
Grevy's zebra
grizzly bear
harbour seal
horned horse
Insectivora
jumping deer
kangaroo dog
kangaroo rat
killer whale
Megatherium
mountain cat
orang-outang

pipistrelle
prairie wolf
Pterodactyl
red kangaroo
red squirrel
sea elephant
sleuthhound
snow leopard
vespertilio
wishtonwish

12

Angora rabbit
Barbary sheep
catamountain
cinnamon bear
draught horse
elephant seal
flittermouse
goat antelope
grey squirrel
harvest mouse
hippopotamus
horseshoe bat
howler monkey
jumping mouse
klipspringer
mountain goat
mountain ibex
mountain lion
Pachydermata
Paleotherium
pouched mouse
rhesus monkey
rock squirrel
Shetland pony

snowshoe hare
spider monkey
spotted hyena
striped hyena
tree kangaroo
water buffalo
water spaniel

13

Abyssinian cat
Australian cat
Bactrian camel
carriage horse
Chapman's zebra
European bison
Galeopithecus
golden hamster
Indian buffalo
laughing hyena
mountain sheep
Palaeotherium
Parry's wallaby
ring-tail coati
sable antelope
Semnopithecus
shorthorn bull
spiny anteater
sulphur bottom
Tasmanian wolf
tree porcupine

14

bridled wallaby
Burchell's zebra
capuchin monkey
crab-eating seal

flying squirrel
ground squirrel
hunting leopard
Indian elephant
Indian pangolin
laughing hyaena
Patagonian cavy
snowshoe rabbit
Tasmanian devil

15

African elephant
American buffalo
American leopard
Bennett's wallaby
flying phalanger
laughing jackass
ring-tailed coati
sabretooth tiger
springer spaniel
Tasmanian possum
Thomson's gazelle
white rhinoceros

Marine growths, etc.

4–6

algae (5)
astrea (6)
coral (5)
dulse (5)
fungia (6)
kelp (4)
laver (5)
limpet (6)
mussel (6)
polyp (5)
sponge (6)
tang (4)
tangle (6)
varec (5)
ware (4)
wrack (5)

7 AND 8

actinia (7)
agar agar (8)
alcyonic (8)
astraea (7)
badioga (7)
blubber (7)
calycle (7)
eschara (7)
fungite (7)
gulf weed (8)
naiades (7)
polypary (8)
porifera (8)
red algae (8)
red coral (8)
sea moss (7)
seaweed (7)
seawrack (8)
tubipora (8)
zoophyte (8)

9

Alcyoneae
alcyonite
bathybius
blue algae
blue coral
carrageen
ecardines
Irish moss

madrepore
millepore
nullipore
pink coral
sea nettle

10 AND OVER

abrotanoid (10)
acorn barnacle (13)
Alcyonacea (10)
alva marina (10)
animal flower (12)
bladder kelp (11)
bladderwrack (12)
brown algae (10)
carragheen (10)
coral zoophytes (14)
goose barnacle (13)
lithodendron (12)
lithogenous (11)
lithophyte (10)
marine plants (12)
sea anemone (10)
tubiporite (10)
utricularia (11)

Molluscs, tunicates, etc.

3–5

bulla
chank
clam
clio
ensis
fusus
gaper
helix
murex
mya
naiad
sepia
slug
snail
solen
spat
Unio
venus

whelk

6

anodon
buckie
chiton
cockle
cuttle
dodman
dolium
limpet
loligo
mantle
mussel
naiads
nerite
ostrea
oyster
pecten
quahog
sea ear
teredo
triton
volute
winkle

7

acerans
actaeon
aplysia
balanus
bivalve
diceras
eschera
etheria
glaucus

mollusc
mytilus
octopus
patella
piddock
polyzoa
purpura
quahaug
scallop
scollop
sea hare
spirula
taccata
teffina
toheroa

8

argonaut
ascidian
buccinum
decapoda
limnaeid
Mollusca
nautilus
pedireme
pteropod
sea lemon
sea snail
shipworm
spirifer
strombus
teredine
tridacna

9

acephalan

gastropod
giant clam
heteropod
hodmandod
lithodome
ostracean
pteropods
rock borer
scaphopod
shellfish
spondylus

10

acorn shell
amphineura
amphitrite
brachiopod
cephalopod
conchifera
cuttlefish
date-mussel
Haliotidae
Heteropoda
periwinkle
razorshell
stone borer
stone eater

11

dragon shell
fasciolaria
Gasteropoda
pearl oyster
river oyster
rock scallop
terebratula

12 AND OVER

boring mussel (12)
cyclobranchiata (15)
entomostomata (13)

lamellibranch (13)
pelican's foot (12)
spindleshell (12)
tectibranchiata (15)

Reptiles and amphibians

3–5

adder
agama
anole
apod
asp
aspic
boa
cobra
draco
eft
ernys
frog
gecko
guana
hydra
krait
kufi
mamba
newt
olm
pipa
rana
seps
siren
skink
snake

toad
tokay
viper
worm

6

anolis
caiman
cayman
dipsas
dragon
gavial
iguana
lizard
moloch
mugger
python
Sauria
taipan
triton
turtle
uraeus
worral
zonure

7

agamids
axolotl

coluber
gharial
ghavial
hicatee
lacerta
monitor
ophidia
paddock
rattler
reptile
saurian
scincus
serpent
snapper
tadpole
testudo
tuatara
urodele
varanus

8

amphibia
anaconda
asp viper
basilisk
bullfrog
cerastes
chelonia

Congo eel
dinosaur
hiccatee
keelback
lachesis
matamata
moccasin
mud puppy
ophidian
pit viper
platanna
rat snake
ringhals
scincoid
seasnake
slow-worm
terrapin
tortoise
treefrog
typhlops

9

alligator
amphibian
batrachia
blind-worm
blue krait
boomslang

box turtle
caecilian
chameleon
chelonian
coach-whip
corn snake
crocodile
dart snake
eyed skink
galliwasp
giant frog
giant toad
green toad
hairy frog
hamadryad
hawk's-bill
iguanodon
horned asp
king cobra
king snake
marsh frog
ophidians
pine snake
pterosaur
puff adder
ring snake
rock snake
spadefoot
stegosaur
tree snake
vine snake
wall gecko
whip snake
wolf snake

10

allosaurus
ankylosaur
black mamba
black snake
blind snake
bushmaster
chuckwalla
clawed frog
cockatrice
Congo snake
copperhead
coral snake
death adder
diplodocus
eyed lizard
fer-de-lance
glass snake
grass snake
green anole
green mamba
green snake
hellbender
horned frog
horned toad
mosasaurus
natterjack
plesiosaur
pond turtle
river snake
rock python
salamander
sand lizard
sea serpent
sidewinder
tiger snake

wall lizard
water snake
worm lizard

11

amphisbaena
banded krait
black cayman
black iguana
bloodsucker
carpet snake
cottonmouth
crested newt
diamondback
draco lizard
flying snake
forest cobra
Gaboon viper
gartersnake
gila monster
goliath frog
gopher snake
green lizard
green turtle
horned snake
horned viper
ichthyosaur
leatherback
midwife toad
pterodactyl
rattlesnake
royal python
smooth snake
stegosaurus
Surinam toad
thorny devil

triceratops

12

brontosaurus
chicken snake
flying lizard
herpetofauna
horned lizard
Komodo dragon
leopard gecko
marine iguana
megalosaurus
pond tortoise
spring lizard

13 AND OVER

alligator lizard (15)
bearded dragon (13)
blue-tongued skink (16)
boa constrictor (14)
brachiosaurus (13)
brown tree snake (14)
coach-whip snake (14)
cobra de capello (14)
dolichosaurus (14)
egg-eating snake (14)
fire salamander (14)
five-lined snake (14)
frilled lizard (13)
giant tortoise (13)
golden tree frog (14)
golden tree snake (15)
green pit viper (13)
green tree frog (13)
hawk's-bill turtle (15)

Himalayan viper (14)
hog-nosed snake (13)
horn-nosed viper (14)
ichthyosaurus (13)
legless lizard (13)
long-nosed viper (14)
mangrove snake (13)
Nile crocodile (13)
painted terrapin (15)
painted turtle (13)
rat-tailed snake (14)
rhinoceros viper (15)
ringhals cobra (13)
Russell's viper (13)
snapping turtle (14)
spadefoot toad (13)
stump-tailed skink (16)
tiger salamander (15)
Tyrannosaurus (13)
water moccasin (13)

NATURAL HISTORY – PLANTS
Cereals, etc.

3 AND 4

bere
bran
corn
dari
dohl
dura
far
gram
malt
meal
oats
oca
poar
rabi
rice
rye
sago
teff
zea

5

bajra
bajri
brank
brigg
durra
durum
emmer
ervum
fundi
grain

grama
grist
grout
maize
paddy
panic
pulse
rivet
short
spelt
straw
typha
wheat

6 AND 7

barley (6)
cassava (7)
corncob (7)
dhurra (6)
farina (6)
groats (6)
hominy (6)
mealie (6)
meslin (6)
millet (6)
muesli (6)
nocake (6)
raggee (6)
rokeage (7)
sorghum (7)
tapioca (7)
wild oat (7)
Zea mays (7)

8 AND 9

arrowroot (9)
buckwheat (9)
espiotte (8)
garavance (9)
mangcorn (8)
middlings (9)
pearl rice (9)
pot barley (9)
seed corn (8)
seed grain (9)
semolina (8)
sweetcorn (9)
wild rice (8)

10 AND OVER

barleycorn (10)
barleymeal (10)
basmati rice (11)
cracked wheat (12)
German millet (12)
gramma grass (11)
Guinea corn (10)
Indian corn (10)
Indian meal (10)
Indian millet (12)
Indian rice (10)
long-grain rice (13)
mountain rice (12)
pearl barley (11)
pearl millet (11)
Scotch barley (12)

spring wheat (11)   winter barley (12)
summer wheat (11)   winter wheat (11)
turkey wheat (11)

Flowers

3 AND 4	daisy	yucca	iberis	zinnia
	erica	yulan	kochia	
aloe	faham		lupine	7
arum	flora	6	lychis	
balm	gilia	acacia	madder	aconite
flag	gorse	acaena	mallow	alonsoa
geum	gowan	acorus	malope	aloysia
iris	henna	alisma	mimosa	althaea
ixia	lilac	alpine	myrtle	alyssum
lei	linum	alsike	nerine	anchusa
lily	lotus	arnica	nuphar	anemone
may	lupin	azalea	opulus	begonia
musk	orris	balsam	orchid	blawort
pink	ox-eye	bellis	orchis	blewert
rose	oxlip	bennet	oxalis	blossom
sego	padma	borage	paigle	bouquet
weld	pagle	cactus	privet	bugloss
whin	pansy	camass	reseda	campion
wold	peony	cistus	rocket	candock
5	petal	clover	salvia	catmint
	phlox	coleus	scilla	chaplet
agave	poppy	cosmea	sesame	chelone
aspic	sepal	cosmos	silene	chicory
aster	spray	crants	sundew	clarkia
avens	stock	crocus	thrift	cowslip
blite	tansy	dahlia	torana	cup rose
briar	thyme	datura	violet	cytisus
broom	tulip	fennel	wattle	day lily
canna	viola	henbit	yarrow	deutzia
				dittany

dog rose
festoon
figwort
freesia
fuchsia
gazania
genista
gentian
gerbera
godetia
heather
honesty
jasmine
jessamy
jonquil
kingcup
lantana
linaria
lobelia
lupinus
marybud
may-lily
melissa
milfoil
mimulus
nelumbo
nemesia
nigella
nosegay
opuntia
papaver
petunia
picotee
primula
ragwort
rambler

rampion
sea-pink
seringa
spiraea
statice
succory
syringa
tagetes
tea rose
thistle
tritoma
ursinia
verbena
vervain
witloof

8

abutilon
acanthus
achillea
ageratum
amaranth
angelica
arum lily
asphodel
auricula
bear's ear
bedstraw
bignonia
bindweed
bluebell
buddleia
calamint
camellia
camomile
capsicum

catchfly
cattleya
clematis
cockspur
cornflag
crowfoot
cyclamen
daffodil
dianthus
dicentra
dropwort
erigeron
feverfew
fleabane
foxglove
gardenia
geranium
gladiola
gladioli
glaucium
gloriosa
gloxinia
goat's rue
hare's ear
harebell
hawkweed
helenium
hepatica
hibiscus
hottonia
hyacinth
japonica
laburnum
larkspur
lavatera
lavender

lent-lily
magnolia
marigold
martagon
moss rose
musk rose
myosotis
nenuphar
noisette
nymphaea
oleander
phacelia
phormium
plumbago
pond lily
primrose
rock-rose
scabious
sea-heath
skull-cap
snowdrop
stapelia
starwort
sweet-pea
tigridia
toad-flax
trillium
tuberose
turnsole
valerian
veronica
viscaria
wild rose
wistaria
wisteria
woodbind

woodbine
wood sage
xanthium

9

Aaron's-rod
achimines
amaryllis
anagallis
aquilegia
aubrietia
bear's foot
buttercup
calendula
campanula
candytuft
carnation
carthamus
celandine
cherry pie
China rose
cineraria
clove pink
cockscomb
colchicum
colt's foot
columbine
composite
coreopsis
corn-poppy
dandelion
digitalis
dog violet
dove's foot
edelweiss
eglantine

forsythia
gelsemium
gladiolus
golden rod
hellebore
hollyhock
hydrangea
jessamine
kniphofia
ladysmock
lotus lily
mayflower
meadowrue
moneywort
monkshood
moon daisy
naked lady
narcissus
nemophila
oenothera
pimpernel
polygonum
pyrethrum
remontant
rudbeckia
saxifrage
snowflake
speedwell
spikenard
sunflower
tiger lily
twayblade
verbascum
wake robin
water flag
waterlily

wolf's-bane

10

agapanthus
amaranthus
aspidistra
belladonna
bell flower
blue-bottle
burnet rose
caffre lily
calliopsis
China aster
chionodoxa
cinquefoil
coquelicot
corncockle
cornflower
corn violet
crane's-bill
crow flower
cuckoopint
damask rose
delphinium
Easter lily
fritillary
gaillardia
gelder rose
goat's-beard
golden drop
gypsophila
heart's-ease
helianthus
heliophila
heliotrope
immortelle

king's spear
lady's-smock
limnanthes
marguerite
mayblossom
mignonette
mock orange
montbretia
moonflower
nasturtium
nightshade
orange lily
ox-eye daisy
passiflora
pennyroyal
pentstemon
periwinkle
poinsettia
polyanthus
potentilla
ranunculus
snapdragon
spiderwort
stork's bill
sweetbriar
sweetbrier
thalictrum
wallflower
white poppy
willow herb
wind flower
wood sorrel
yellow wort

11

Aaron's beard

antirrhinum
bittersweet
bladderwort
blood flower
cabbage rose
calandrinia
calceolaria
cheiranthus
convallaria
convolvulus
cotoneaster
everlasting
fig marigold
forget-me-not
gillyflower
globeflower
green dragon
guelder rose
heather bell
helichrysum
honey-flower
honeysuckle
Indian cress
kidney-vetch
lady's mantle
London pride
loosestrife
love-in-a-mist
Madonna lily
meadowsweet
Nancy pretty
night flower
pelargonium
pepper elder
poppy mallow
ragged robin

rambler rose
red-hot poker
rose campion
St John's wort
schizanthus
sea lavender
spear flower
sweet rocket
sweet sultan
tiger flower
wild flowers
wood anemone
xeranthemum

12

apple blossom
autumn crocus
bougainvilia
century plant
cuckoo-flower
heather bells
Iceland poppy
Jacob's ladder
lady's slipper
morning glory
none-so-pretty
old man's-beard
orange flower
pasque flower
peach blossom
pheasant's eye
rhododendron
rose of Sharon
salpiglossis
Shirley poppy
snow-in-summer

Solomon's seal
sweet william
tradescantia
virgin's bower

13

African violet
alpine flowers
blanket flower
bleeding heart
bougainvillea
Bristol flower
cherry blossom
Christmas rose
chrysanthemum
creeping jenny
crown imperial
eschscholtzia
grape-hyacinth
huntsman's horn
marsh marigold

meadow saffron
orange blossom
passion flower
sweet calabash
traveller's joy
trumpet flower
water hyacinth

14 AND 15

bougainvillaea (14)
Canterbury bell (14)
cardinal flower (14)
Christmas flower (15)
evening primrose (15)
lily of the valley (15)
lords-and-ladies (14)
love-in-idleness (14)
Michaelmas daisy (15)
shepherd's purse (14)
star of Bethlehem (15)

Fruit

3 AND 4	hep	pepo	agava	grape
akee	hip	plum	agave	grout
bito	kaki	pome	akena	guava
Cox's	kiwi	rasp	anana	lemon
crab	lime	skeg	apple	lichi
date	mare	sloe	arnot	mango
fig	mast	ugli	betel	melon
gage	musa	uva	carob	merry
gean	nut	**5**	cubeb	morel
haw	ogen	abhal	drupe	morus
	pear		eleot	naras

olive
papaw
peach
pecan
prune
regma
ribes
rubus
whort
whurt

6

achene
almond
ananas
banana
biffin
cashew
cedrat
cherry
citron
citrus
cobnut
colmar
damson
drupel
durian
egriot
elk nut
ginger
groser
lichee
linden
longan
loquat
lychee

mammee
medlar
narras
nelies
nutmeg
orange
papaya
pawpaw
peanut
pignut
pippin
pomelo
prunus
punica
quince
raisin
rennet
russet
samara
squash
tomato
walnut
zapote

7

apricot
avocado
bilimbi
bramble
buckeye
bullace
capulin
cassava
catawba
cedrate
cheston

coconut
codling
corinth
costard
cumquat
currant
deal-nut
dessert
dogwood
etaerio
filbert
genipap
golding
hautboy
hog-plum
karatas
kumquat
litchee
mahaleb
mayduke
mineola
morello
naartje
pompion
pumpkin
quashey
rizzart
rosehip
satsuma
soursop
sultana
tangelo
wilding
winesap

8

allspice
barberry
bayberry
beechnut
bergamot
betel-nut
bilberry
breadnut
buckmast
calabash
cat's-head
chestnut
citrange
coquilla
cream-nut
date-plum
dewberry
dogberry
drupelet
earthnut
earthpea
fenberry
fig-apple
fox grape
hastings
hazelnut
japonica
jonathan
mandarin
may apple
minneola
mulberry
muscadel
muscatel
musk pear

nonesuch
oleaster
pearmain
plantain
prunello
quandong
queening
rambutan
shaddock
spondias
sweeting
tamarind
Valencia
whitsour
windfall

9

alkekengi
apple-john
aubergine
beechmast
blueberry
brazil nut
butternut
cantaloup
canteloup
carmelite
cherimoya
chokepear
corozo nut
crab-apple
cranberry
crowberry
damascene
drupaceae
elvas plum

greengage
groundnut
haanepoot
king apple
kiwi fruit
melocoton
mirabelle
monkey nut
muscadine
muskapple
muskmelon
nectarine
nonpareil
Ogen melon
ortanique
oxycoccus
persimmon
pineapple
pistachio
raspberry
redstreak
sapodilla
sorbapple
star-apple
tangerine
ugli fruit
victorine
Worcester

10

adam's apple
bird-cherry
blackberry
blackheart
breadfruit
cantaloupe

charentais
china berry
chokeberry
cider apple
clementine
clingstone
cream-fruit
damask plum
dried fruit
elderberry
florentine
gooseberry
granadilla
grapefruit
Indian date
loganberry
Madeira nut
mangosteen
marking nut
orange musk
pompelmous
queen-apple
redcurrant
stone fruit
strawberry
waterlemon
watermelon
wild cherry
winter pear

11

anchovy pear
bitter apple
blood orange
boysenberry
candleberry

China orange
chokecherry
coquilla nut
French berry
granny smith
huckleberry
hurtleberry
Jaffa orange
leathercoat
mammee apple
monkey bread
myrtleberry
navel orange
pomegranate
quarrington
russet apple
scuppernong
winter apple
winter berry

12

bitter almond
blackcurrant
chaumontelle
Chester grape
chocolate nut

cooking apple
custard apple
mammee-sapota
passion fruit
pistachio nut
serviceberry
Victoria plum
white currant
whortleberry
winter cherry
winter citron

13 AND OVER

alligator pear (13)
Barbados cherry (14)
Blenheim orange (14)
Cape gooseberry (14)
Catherine pear (13)
conference pear (14)
cornelian cherry (16)
golden delicious (15)
mandarin orange (14)
morello cherry (13)
preserved fruit (14)
Seville orange (13)
water chestnut (13)

Herbs and spices

3–5	chive	mace	senna	6
ani se	clary	mint	tansy	bennet
balm	clove	myrrh	thyme	betony
basil	cress	rape	woad	borage
bay	cumin	rue		burnet
	dill	sage		

capers
chilli
chives
cicely
cloves
endive
fennel
galega
garlic
ginger
hyssop
isatis
lovage
lunary
nutmeg
orpine
pepper
rocket
savory
sesame
simple
sorrel

7

aconite
burdock
caraway
catmint
cayenne
chervil
chicory
comfrey
dittany
frasera
gentian
henbane

juniper
lettuce
milfoil
mustard
oregano
panicum
paprika
parsley
pimento
pot herb
rampion
saffron
salsify
spigel
succory
tabasco
turpeth
vanilla
zedoary

8

agrimony
allspice
angelica
camomile
cardamom
centaury
cinnamon
costmary
feverfew
fumitory
hog's-bean
lavender
lungwort
marigold
marjoram

mouse ear
origanum
plantain
purslane
reedmace
rosemary
samphire
spicknel
tarragon
turmeric
waybread
wormwood

9

baneberry
bear's foot
chickweed
colocynth
coriander
coronopus
dittander
eyebright
fenugreek
fever-root
finocchio
goose foot
groundsel
hellebore
horehound
liquorice
patchouli
sea fennel
spearmint
sweet herb
tormentil

10

asafoetida
cassumunar
lemon thyme
motherwort
penny royal
peppermint
watercress
willow herb

11

dog's cabbage
dragon's head
hedge hyssop
horseradish
hyoscyamine
oyster plant
pot marigold

pot marjoram
sweet rocket
swine's cress
winter cress
wintergreen

12 AND OVER

adder's tongue (12)
Florence fennel (14)
medicinal herb (13)
mournful widow (13)
mustard and cress (15)
southernwood (12)
summer savory (12)
sweet marjoram (13)
thoroughwort (12)
winter savory (12)

Plants

3	poa	anil	crab	geum
	rue	arum	culm	hemp
box	rye	balm	dari	herb
cos	seg	bean	dill	holm
ers	tea	beet	diss	ilex
fog	tod	bent	dock	iris
hay	yam	bigg	doob	jute
hop	zea	bulb	dora	kale
ivy		cane	ecad	kali
nep	**4**	coca	fern	kans
oat		coco	flag	leek
oca	aira	coix	flax	ling
pea	akee	cole	gale	mint
pia	alfa	corn	gama	moly
	aloe			

moss	woad	dicot	musci	tamus
musa	wort	dryas	napal	tansy
musk		dulse	olive	thorn
nard	**5**	durra	orach	thyme
okra	abaca	dwale	orpin	trapa
peat	agave	erica	orris	tucum
pipi	ajuga	eruca	oryza	urena
ragi	algae	ficus	oshac	vetch
rape	alpia	fitch	osier	vicia
reed	anise	fucus	oxlip	vinca
rhea	apium	fungi	paddy	viola
rice	arnut	furze	palas	vitis
root	aspic	glaux	palea	wahoo
rush	aster	goman	panic	wapon
sage	avena	gorse	poker	wheat
sago	basil	gourd	radix	whort
sida	brake	grama	ramie	withy
sium	brank	grass	reate	wrack
sloe	briar	grias	rheum	yerba
soma	broom	henna	roosa	yucca
star	bugle	holly	rubia	yupon
tara	cacao	hosta	rubus	zamia
tare	calla	kunai	runch	
taro	camas	ledum	savin	**6**
teff	canna	liana	savoy	acorus
thea	chive	liane	scrog	agaric
tree	cicer	lotus	sedge	albino
tule	clary	loufa	shrub	alisma
turf	clote	lupin	sison	amomum
tutu	clove	madia	solah	aninga
ulex	couch	maize	starr	annual
vine	cress	medic	stipa	arabis
wald	cumin	morel	stole	aralia
weed	cycad	moril	sumac	azalea
weld	dagga	mucor	swede	bamboo
whin	daisy	mudar	tacca	barley

batata	filago	marram	rattan
bejuco	fiorin	matico	redtop
betony	frutex	medick	reseda
biblus	fucoid	milium	rocket
borage	fungus	millet	ruscus
bryony	funkia	mimosa	sabine
burnet	gallum	myrica	savine
cactus	garlic	myrtle	savory
caltha	garrya	nardoo	scilla
camass	gervan	nerium	secale
cassia	gnetum	nettle	sesame
catnip	gromel	nostoc	sesban
cicely	guills	nubbin	seseli
cicuta	hedera	oilnut	smilax
cissus	henbit	orache	sorrel
cistus	hervea	orchid	spurge
clover	hyssop	orchis	spurry
cockle	iberis	origan	squash
conium	indigo	orpine	squill
conyza	jawari	osmund	stolon
cosmos	jujube	oxalis	styrax
cotton	juncus	paigle	sumach
cowage	kalmia	pampas	sundew
croton	kiekie	peanut	teasel
cynara	knawel	peplis	teazel
darnel	kousso	pepper	thrift
daphne	lichen	phleum	tutsan
dodder	locust	potato	twitch
elaeis	lolium	privet	urtica
endive	lupine	protea	viscum
eringo	luzula	quinoa	yamboo
exogen	madder	quitch	yarrow
fathen	maguey	radish	
fennel	mallee	raffia	**7**
ferula	mallow	raggee	
fescue	manioc	ramson	absinth
			aconite

alcanna
alecost
alfalfa
alhenna
alkanet
all-good
all-heal
althaea
amanita
aquatic
arabine
arbutus
awlwort
azarole
barilla
bartram
begonia
bistort
bogbean
bogmass
bogrush
bracken
bramble
bugloss
bugwort
bulbule
bulrush
burdock
bur-reed
calamus
caltrop
calypso
campion
canella
cannach
caraway

carduus
carline
cassada
cassado
cassava
cat's-ear
catmint
chicory
clarkia
clotbur
columba
comfrey
cowbane
cowhage
cow-itch
cowslip
cow-weed
creeper
crottle
cudbear
cudweed
cup moss
curcuma
cytisus
dasheen
dionaea
dittany
dogbane
dog's rue
ear-wort
ehretia
elatine
epacris
esparto
eugenia
euryale

euterpe
felwort
festuca
ficaria
figwort
fitweed
foxtail
frogbit
fumaria
funaria
genista
gentian
gerbera
ginseng
gladwyn
guayule
gunnera
gutwort
hardock
hawkbit
heather
hemlock
henbane
hogweed
honesty
hop-bind
hop-bine
hop-vine
humulus
ipomaea
jasmine
Jew's ear
jonquil
juniper
karatas
kedlack

lobelia
lucerne
lychnis
lycopod
madwort
mahonia
melilot
milfoil
monocot
mudwort
munjeet
mustard
nonsuch
opuntia
oregano
osmunda
panicum
papyrus
pareira
parella
parelle
parsley
pinguin
primula
pumpion
pumpkin
quamash
ragwort
rambler
rampion
redroot
rhatany
rhubarb
saffron
saguaro
saligot

salsify	zalacca	cassweed	dolichos
salsola	zanonia	cat's foot	downweed
sampire	zizania	cat's tail	dropwort
sanicle		catchfly	duckmeat
sarcina	**8**	centaury	duckweed
sawwort		cerealia	dumb-cane
sea tang	abutilon	cetraria	earth nut
seaweed	acanthus	charlock	earth-pea
sencion	adiantum	cinchona	echinops
senecio	agrimony	cleavers	eelgrass
seringa	air plant	clematis	eggplant
solanum	amaranth	clubmoss	eglatere
sonchus	amphigen	clubrush	eleusine
sorghum	angelica	cocculus	epiphyte
sourock	anthemis	cockspur	erigeron
soybean	asphodel	cockweed	erisimum
spignel	banewort	conferva	feverfew
spiraea	barometz	cornflag	finochio
sporule	bearbind	cornrose	fireweed
statice	bear's ear	costmary	flaxweed
syringa	bedstraw	cowberry	fleabane
tagetes	bellwort	cowgrass	fleawort
talipot	bignonia	cow-wheat	flixweed
tannier	bindweed	crithmum	foalfoot
thistle	blueweed	crow silk	foxglove
tobacco	bogberry	cunjevoi	fragaria
trefoil	bogwhort	danewort	fussball
truffle	boxthorn	death-cap	garcinia
turpeth	brassica	death-cup	gillenia
uncaria	buckweed	dewberry	glory pea
vanilla	bullweed	diadelph	gloxinia
verbena	bullwort	diandria	glumales
vervain	calamint	dicentra	glumella
vetiver	camomile	dog briar	glyceria
waratah	cannabis	dog grass	goutweed
wcorara	capsicum	dog's bane	goutwort
	carraway		

gratiola
gromwell
gulfweed
hagtaper
harebell
hare's ear
hartwort
hawkweed
hawthorn
hepatica
hibiscus
hockherb
ice plant
iochroma
knapweed
knotweed
laceleaf
ladyfern
larkspur
lavender
lungwort
lustwort
male fern
mandrake
marjoram
mat grass
matfelon
may bloom
mezereon
milkweed
milkwort
monocarp
moonseed
moonwort
mulewort
mushroom

myosotis
nut grass
oenanthe
oleander
orchanet
oreganum
paspalum
peat moss
phormium
pillwort
pinkroot
plantlet
plantule
plumbago
pokeweed
polygala
pond weed
prunella
puffball
purslane
putchock
red algae
reedrace
rib grass
roccella
rock-rose
rockweed
rosebush
rosemary
rye grass
sainfoin
saltwort
samphire
sargasso
scammony
sea holly

seawrack
seedling
sengreen
septfoil
shamrock
simaruba
skull-cap
smallage
soapwort
stapelia
starwort
sun-plant
sweetsop
tara fern
tarragon
tea plant
tentwort
tickweed
toad-flax
tree-fern
tremella
triticum
tuberose
turk's cap
turmeric
turnsole
valerian
veratrum
veronica
victoria
wait-a-bit
wall-moss
wall-wort
wartwort
water-poa
wild oats

wild rose
wind seed
wistaria
wisteria
with-wine
woodbine
woodroof
woodruff
woodsage
woodwart
wrightia
xanthium
zingiber

9

abrotanum
aerophyte
alpargata
amaryllis
arbor-vine
arracacha
arrowhead
arrowroot
artemisia
asclepiad
balsamine
basil weed
bean caper
bearberry
beech fern
bent grass
bird's foot
birthwort
bloodroot
bloodwort
blue algae

blue grass	cuckoo bud	glasswort	lyme grass
bog myrtle	culver key	golden cup	mare's tail
brooklime	cup lichen	golden rod	marsh fern
brookmint	cyclamine	goose corn	meadow rue
brookweed	decagynia	goosefoot	milk vetch
broomcorn	decandria	gramineae	mistletoe
broomrape	desert rod	grapewort	monk's-hood
burstwort	didynamia	grasspoly	moschatel
butterbur	digitalis	greenweed	mousetail
candytuft	digitaria	ground ivy	navelwort
canebrake	dittander	groundnut	nelumbium
caprifole	dockcress	groundsel	nepenthes
cardamine	doob grass	hair grass	nicotiana
carrageen	duck's foot	hellebore	patchouli
catchweed	duck's meat	helophyte	pellitory
celandine	dulcamara	hoarhound	pennywort
cetrarine	dyer's weed	holly fern	penstemon
chickweed	earthstar	holy-grass	pilularia
cineraria	eglantine	honeywort	pimpernel
club-grass	elaeagnus	horehound	planticle
coal plant	entophyte	horsefoot	poison ivy
cockscomb	equisetum	horsetail	polygonum
cock's head	euphorbia	houseleek	portulaca
colchicum	euphrasia	hypericum	pyracanth
colocynth	evergreen	Indian fig	pyrethrum
colt's foot	evolvulus	Irish moss	quillwort
columbine	eyebright	jessamine	rafflesia
coralwort	fenugreek	Job's tears	red clover
coriander	fever root	kite's foot	red pepper
corn poppy	feverwort	knee holly	reed-grass
corn salad	fly agaric	knotgrass	rocambole
cotyledon	forsythia	ladysmock	rockcress
crabgrass	galingale	lark's heel	rock-plant
cramp-bark	gama grass	laserwort	royal fern
crosswort	gelanthus	liquorice	safflower
crowberry	germander	liverwort	saintfoin

saxifrage
sea-tangle
smartweed
snakeroot
snakeweed
snowberry
soap plant
socotrine
spearmint
spearwort
speedwell
spikenard
spirogyra
spoonwort
stellaria
stinkweed
stonecrop
sugar cane
sugarbeet
sun spurge
sweet flag
sweet gale
sweet john
sweet rush
taraxacum
thallogen
theobroma
toadstool
toothwort
tormentil
trifolium
twayblade
villarsia
wakerobin
wall cress
waterlath

waterlily
waterweed
waterwort
wax myrtle
whitecrop
widow wail
wincopipe
wolfsbane
wolf's claw
wormgrass
woundwort
xanthosia

10

Adam's apple
Adam-and-Eve
adder grass
agrostemma
alabastrus
alexanders
amaranthus
ampelopsis
angiosperm
arbor vitae
arrow grass
asarabacca
aspidistra
beard grass
beccabunga
belladonna
bitterwort
brome grass
brown algae
butterbush
butterweed
butterwood

butterwort
Canada lily
candelilla
cassumunar
cellulares
cinquefoil
cloudberry
corn rocket
corncockle
cotton rose
cottonweed
couch grass
cow parsley
cow parsnip
crake berry
crotalaria
cuckoopint
dead nettle
devil's club
dog's fennel
dog's poison
dog's tongue
dracontium
elaeococca
elecampane
eriocaulon
eriophoron
escallonia
eupatorium
fimble-hemp
friar's cowl
fritillary
gaultheria
globe daisy
globularia
goat's-beard

golden seal
goldenhair
goldilocks
goose grass
granadilla
grass-wrack
green algae
gymnosperm
heart's-ease
helianthus
hemp nettle
herb robert
herds grass
honey stalk
Indian corn
Indian hemp
Indian reed
Indian shot
Jew's mallow
jimson weed
kidney-wort
king's spear
lemon grass
lycopodium
maidenhair
mandragora
manila hemp
may blossom
mock orange
mock privet
motherwort
muscardine
nasturtium
nightshade
nipplewort
panic grass

passiflora
penny-cress
pennyroyal
pentstemon
peppermint
pepperwort
periwinkle
poker plant
potentilla
race ginger
ranunculus
rest harrow
rhein berry
rhinanthus
rose mallow
salicornia
sand-binder
saprophyte
sarracenia
sea lettuce
setterwort
shave grass
shield fern
silver weed
sneezewort
sow thistle
Spanish nut
speargrass
spiderwort
spleenwort
stavesacre
stitchwort
stonebreak
stork's bill
sweetbriar
sweetbrier

swine bread
swinecress
swinegrass
swordgrass
thalecress
throatwort
tiger's foot
touch-me-not
tragacanth
tropaeolum
tumbleweed
Venus's comb
wall pepper
water plant
way thistle
whitethorn
wild indigo
willow herb
willow weed
witch hazel
wolf's peach
wood sorrel
yellow-root
yellow wort

11

Adam's needle
bear's breech
bell heather
bishop's weed
blackbonnet
bottle gourd
brank ursine
bur marigold
calceolaria
calycanthus

canary grass
chanterelle
chive garlic
coffee plant
contrayerva
convolvulus
corn parsley
cotton grass
cotton plant
crest marine
cuckoo's meat
dame's violet
dog's cabbage
dog's mercury
dracunculus
dragon's head
dragon's wort
Dutch clover
dyer's rocket
erythronium
everlasting
false acacia
fescue grass
fig marigold
finger grass
fuller's weed
gentianella
giant cactus
giant fennel
gramma grass
green dragon
guelder rose
hart's tongue
holy thistle
honeysuckle
horseradish

humble plant
Iceland moss
Indian berry
Indian cress
indigo plant
ipecacuanha
kidney vetch
lady's-finger
latticeleaf
laurustinus
London pride
marram grass
marsh mallow
meadowsweet
melon cactus
milk thistle
millet grass
moon trefoil
moving plant
myoporaceae
oyster plant
pampas grass
pedicedaris
pelargonium
pepper grass
prickly pear
red-hot poker
ribbon grass
ripple grass
Roman nettle
rubber plant
scurvy grass
sea lavender
sea milkwort
sempervivum
serpentaria

snail clover
snail flower
sparrow wort
spergularia
stagger bush
star thistle
sulphur-wort
swallow wort
swallow-wort
sweet cicely
sweet cistus
sweet potato
thorough wax
tonquin bean
tree creeper
tussac grass
twitch grass
viper's grass
water-nymph
water pepper
water radish
water violet
welwitschia
white clover
white darnel
winter berry
winter bloom
winter cress
wintergreen
wood anemone
xanthoxylum

12

adder's-tongue
adderstoupie
aerial plants

bladderwrack
buffalo grass
Christ's thorn
compass plant
corn marigold
cow's lungwort
deadly carrot
echinocactus
erythroxylon
esparto grass
feather grass
fennel flower
fool's parsley
German millet
globe thistle
hemp agrimony
hound's tongue
Indian millet
Indian turnip
Jacob's ladder
leopard's bane
mangel wurzel
marsileaceae
melon thistle
palma christi
pickerel weed
pitcher plant
poison sumach
quaking grass
reindeer moss
rhododendron
sarsaparilla
sheep's fescue
skunk cabbage
snail trefoil
Solomon's seal

southern wood
Spanish broom
Spanish grass
sparrow-grass
spear thistle
strangleweed
swine thistle
telentospore
timothy grass
tobacco plant
torch thistle
tussock grass
Venus flytrap
Venus's sumach
vinegar plant
virgin's bower
water hemlock
water milfoil
water parsnip
water pitcher
water soldier
white campion
whitlow grass
whortleberry
wild williams
winter cherry
xanthorrhiza
yellow rattle

13

chrysanthemum
crown imperial
dog's-tail grass
elephant grass
elephant's foot
eschscholtzia

flowering fern
flowering rush
globe amaranth
golden thistle
horse mushroom
Indian tobacco
lady's bedstraw
meadow saffron
noli-me-tangere
raspberry bush
Scotch thistle
spike lavender
stag's-horn moss
summer cypress
sweet marjoram
traveller's joy
Venus's flytrap
vervain mallow
viper's bugloss
wall pellitory
wall pennywort
water calamint
water crowfoot
water hyacinth
wayfaring tree

14

blackberry bush
blue couch grass
carline thistle
distaff thistle
fuller's thistle
giant groundsel
golden lungwort
golden mouse-ear

gooseberry bush
lords and ladies
mountain sorrel
prince's feather
reindeer lichen
sensitive plant
shepherd's pouch
shepherd's purse
shepherd's staff
snake's-head iris
Spanish bayonet
starch hyacinth
treacle mustard

15

golden saxifrage
Italian rye grass
shepherd's needle
Venus's navelwort
Virginia creeper
woody nightshade

Trees, shrubs, etc.

2 AND 3

asa
ash
bay
bel
ben
bo
box
dan
elm
fig
fir
gum
haw
hip
hop
ita
ivy
kin
may
nut
oak
sal
sap
tea
ti
tod
yew

4

acer
akee
aloe

amla
arar
arum
atap
athe
bael
balm
bark
bass
bast
bead
beam
bhel
bito
bixa
bole
bosk
bush
cone
cork
dari
date
deal
dhak
dita
doob
holm
huon
hura
ilex
jaca
kina
lana
leaf

lime
milk
mowa
nipa
ombu
palm
pear
pine
pipe
plum
pole
rata
rimu
roan
root
rose
shea
sloe
sorb
teak
teil
toon
tree
twig
ulex
upas
vine
whin

5

abele
abies
acorn
afara

agave
agila
alder
algum
almug
amber
anise
anona
apple
arbor
areca
Argan
aspen
assai
balsa
Banga
beech
belah
belar
birch
bough
briar
brier
brush
bunya
butea
cacao
caper
carob
cedar
clove
copse
coral
cubeb

durio
dwarf
ebony
elder
fagus
fruit
furze
glade
gorse
grove
guava
hazel
henna
holly
hurst
iroko
jambu
judas
karri
kauri
kokra
kunal
larch
lemon
lilac
mahwa
mango
maple
mulga
myall
myrrh
ngaio
nyssa
olive

6

osier	abroma	coffee	obeche
palas	acacia	cornel	orange
palay	acajou	daphne	papaya
papaw	alerce	deodar	pawpaw
peach	almond	durian	pepper
pecan	antiar	durion	pinery
picea	aralla	elaeis	platan
pinon	aralla	emblic	poplar
pipal	arbute	fustet	privet
plane	arolla	fustic	quince
plank	balsam	gatten	red bud
quina	bamboo	ginkgo	red fir
roble	banana	gomuti	red gum
roots	banyan	gomuto	ricker
rowan	baobab	illipe	rubber
salal	bo-tree	jarool	sallal
salix	bog-oak	jarrah	sallow
sally	bombax	jujube	sapota
saman	bottle	kalmia	sappan
sapan	branch	kittul	saxaul
scrog	brazil	kumbuk	she-oak
shrub	buriti	kunari	sissoo
sumac	busket	laurel	sorrel
taxus	butter	lignum	souari
thorn	button	linden	spruce
tilia	carapa	locust	sumach
tingi	carica	loquat	sylvan
trunk	cashew	macoya	tallow
tsuga	catkin	mallee	tamanu
tuart	caudex	manuka	tewart
ulmus	cedrat	mastic	timber
walan	cembra	medlar	titoki
yucca	cerris	mimosa	touart
yulan	cerrus	miriti	tupelo
zamia	cherry	myrtle	veneer
	citron	nargil	vinery

walnut
wampee
wattle
wicken
willow
yampon

7

ailanto
ambatch
amboyna
aniseed
arbutus
ash tree
avocado
banksia
bay tree
bebeeru
blossom
blue gum
boxwood
bubinga
buckeye
bullace
bursera
cabbage
cajaput
camphor
camwood
catalpa
champac
coconut
conifer
coppice
coquito
cork-oak

corylus
cowtree
cypress
daddock
dammara
determa
deutzia
dogwood
dottard
duramen
elk-wood
elm tree
emblica
enterpe
fan palm
fig tree
fir cone
fir tree
genipap
gum tree
hemlock
hickory
hog palm
holm oak
hop tree
jugians
juniper
king gum
lentisk
logwood
lumbang
madroña
madroño
margosa
mastich
mesquit

moriche
moringa
nut palm
nut pine
oakling
oak tree
oil palm
orchard
palmyra
pinetum
pollard
quercus
quillai
red pine
redwood
robinia
saksaul
sandbox
sanders
sapling
sapwood
sequoia
seringa
service
shallon
shittah
shittim
silk oak
snow-gum
sour-sop
spindle
sundari
syringa
tanghin
tea-tree
varnish

wallaba
wax palm
wax tree
wych-elm

8

agalloch
agalwood
alburnum
algaroba
allspice
arbuscle
ash grove
barberry
bass wood
beachnut
beam tree
beef-wood
benjamin
berberis
berberry
bilberry
black gum
box elder
bud-scale
calabash
carnauba
castanea
chestnut
cinchona
coco-palm
coco-tree
coolabah
cork tree
crab-tree
date palm

date plum
date-tree
doom-palm
eucalypt
euonymus
fraxinus
gardenia
giant gum
glory pea
groo-groo
guaiacum
hardbeam
hardwood
hawthorn
hemp palm
holly-oak
hornbeam
ironbark
ironwood
jack tree
jack wood
kingwood
laburnum
lacebark
lavender
lima wood
long jack
magnolia
mahogany
mangrove
manna-ash
mezereon
milk tree
mulberry
musk wood
mustaiba

oiticica
oleander
oleaster
palm tree
palmetto
pandanus
pear tree
piassava
pichirim
pinaster
pine cone
pine tree
pistacia
plantain
pockwood
quillaia
raintree
red cedar
red maple
rosemary
rosewood
royal oak
sago palm
sandarac
sapindus
scrub-oak
searwood
seedling
shadbush
silky oak
softwood
sugar gum
swamp oak
sweet-bay
sweet gum
sweet sop

sycamine
sycamore
tamarack
tamarind
tamarisk
taxodium
teil-tree
toon-wood
tungtree
upas tree
viburnum
white ash
white fir
white gum
white oak
wistaria
witch-elm

9

adansonia
ailanthus
algarroba
aloes wood
alpine fir
Andromeda
angophora
araucaria
areca palm
balsam fir
blackwood
bodhi tree
brown pine
buckthorn
bully tree
butternut
calambour

caliatour
caliature
casuarina
chaparral
China tree
chincapin
coniferae
courbaril
crab apple
crowberry
Cupressus
deciduous
dwarf tree
eaglewood
erythrine
evergreen
forest oak
forsythia
fruit tree
grapevine
greenwood
ground ash
ground oak
hackberry
hydrangea
ivory palm
jacaranda
Judas tree
Juneberry
kokra wood
lance wood
lentiscus
lilac tree
macaw tree
maracauba
mustahiba

paper bark
paulownia
persimmon
pistachio
pitchpine
plane tree
poison oak
pyracanth
quebracho
quickbeam
rose apple
rowan tree
royal palm
sagebrush
sandarach
sapan wood
sapodilla
saskatoon
sassafras
satinwood
Scotch elm
Scotch fir
Scots pine
screw-pine
scrogbush
shade tree
shell-bark
silver fir
sloethorn
smoke tree
snake-wood
snowberry
soapberry
sour-gourd
spicewood
star anise

stonepine
suradanni
sweetwood
terebinth
thorn tree
tigerwood
toothwort
touch-wood
tulip tree
wax myrtle
white pine
whitebeam
whitewood
woodlayer
wych-hazel
yacca wood
zebrawood

10

African oak
agollochum
almond tree
artocarpus
balaustine
blackthorn
blue spruce
bottle tree
brazilwood
breadfruit
bunji-bunji
bunya-bunya
burra-murra
butter tree
button bush
button tree
buttonwood

chinquapin
coastal-tea
coccomilia
coniferous
cotton tree
cottonwood
Douglas fir
dragon tree
durmast oak
eucalyptus
fiddle wood
flindersia
flooded gum
garlic-pear
goat's thorn
gomuti palm
greenheart
ground pine
hackmatack
holly berry
Indian date
japati palm
kunai grass
laurustine
letter wood
lilly-pilly
locust tree
manchineel
mangosteen
orange-ball
orange wood
palisander
paper birch
pine needle
prickly ash
quercitron

362 TREES, SHRUBS, ETC.

rain forest
redsanders
rose acacia
sandalwood
sand-cherry
sand-myrtle
sappanwood
Scotch pine
silverbell
sneeze-wood
Spanish fir
strawberry
sugar-maple
swamp maple
tallow tree
tall wattle
thyine wood
tree of life
weeping ash
white cedar
whitethorn
wild cherry
witch-hazel
woolly butt
yellow-wood

11

African teak
Algerian fir
bald cypress
bean trefoil
black walnut
black wattle
black willow
bladder tree
blue-gum tree

bottle-brush
cabbage palm
cabbage tree
camel's thorn
camphor tree
cedar wattle
chrysobalan
coconut palm
cootamundra
copper beech
cotoneaster
cypress pine
elaeocarpus
eriodendron
glory flower
golden chain
golden mohur
hoary poplar
honey locust
Japan laurel
juniper tree
laurustinus
leper-wattle
lignum vitae
mountain ash
pandanaceae
phoenix-palm
pomegranate
pussy willow
quicken tree
red mahogany
red-iron bark
sandbox tree
sea-purslane
service tree
sideroxylon

silver birch
slippery elm
spindle tree
stringybark
sweet willow
varnish tree
white poplar
white spruce
white willow
xanthozylum
zygophyllum

12

almond willow
balsam poplar
balsam spruce
benjamin-tree
betel-nut palm
calabash tree
caryophyllus
chestnut tree
Christ's-thorn
crow's-foot elm
cucumber tree
custard apple
flowering ash
golden wattle
monkey-puzzle
Norway spruce
rhododendron
sea buckthorn
serviceberry
silver-wattle
Spanish broom
Spanish cedar
spurge laurel

tree of heaven
umbrella tree
virgin's-bower
weeping birch
welllngtonia
white cypress
winter cherry
xylobalsamum

13 AND OVER

bird's-eye maple (13)
campeachy wood (13)
Cedar of Lebanon (14)
Christmas tree (13)
cornus florida (13)
dog-wood wattle (13)
galactodendron (14)

horse-chestnut (13)
Japanese cedar (13)
Lombardy poplar (14)
maidenhair tree (14)
partridge wood (13)
red sandalwood (13)
Spanish chestnut (15)
strawberry shrub (15)
sweet chestnut (13)
sunshine wattle (14)
toothache tree (13)
toxicodendron (13)
trembling poplar (15)
turpentine tree (14)
weeping willow (13)
white sandalwood (15)

Vegetables

3 AND 4

bean
beet
cole
corn
faba
kale
leek
lima
neep
oca
okra
pea
sage

slaw
spud
tuber
urd
yam

5

caper
chard
chick
chive
cibol
cress
cubeb
fitch

maize
navew
onion
orach
pease
pulse
savoy
swede

6

borage
carrot
celery
chilli
cowpea

daucus
endive
fennel
garlic
girkin
greens
legume
lentil
marrow
murphy
nettle
orache
porret
potato
pratie

radish
rocket
runner
savory
sprout
squash
tomato
turnip

7

batatas
bay leaf
blewits
cabbage
cardoon
chervil
chicory
collard
frijole
gherkin
haricot
hasting
hotspur
lactuca
lettuce
mustard
parsley
parsnip
pea bean
peppers
pimento
pumpkin
salsify
seakale
shallot
skirret

soybean
spinach
sprouts
zanonia

8

allspice
beetrave
beetroot
borecole
brassica
broccoli
capsicum
celeriac
chickpea
coleslaw
colewort
cucumber
eggplant
eschalot
kohlrabi
lima bean
mirepoix
mushroom
plantain
rutabaga
scallion
smallage
soyabean
split pea
tickbean
zucchini

9

aduki bean
artichoke

asparagus
aubergine
broad bean
calabrese
courgette
curly kale
dandelion
dried peas
green peas
horsebean
mangetout
marrowfat
new potato
radicchio
red pepper
split peas
sweetcorn
turban-top
turnip top

10

adsuki bean
alexanders
beet radish
butter bean
cos lettuce
cow parsnip
French bean
green beans
kidney bean
King Edward
petits pois
red cabbage
runner bean
salad onion
sauerkraut

scorzonera
stringbean
turnip tops
watercress
Welsh onion

11

cauliflower
French beans
green pepper
haricot bean
horseradish
ratatouille
scarlet bean
spinach beet
sweet potato
water radish

12

bamboo shoots
chilli pepper
corn on the cob
giant shallot

lamb's lettuce
savoy cabbage
Spanish onion
spring greens
spring onions
white cabbage

13 AND OVER

broccoli sprouts (15)
Brussels sprouts (15)
Chinese cabbage (14)
globe artichoke (14)
green vegetables (15)
horse cucumber (13)
ladies' fingers (13)
marrowfat peas (13)
purple broccoli (14)
scarlet runner (13)
spring cabbage (13)
tankard turnip (13)
vegetable marrow (15)
water chestnut (13)

OFFICIALS (INCLUDING TITLES AND RELIGIOUS DESIGNATIONS)

2–4	beak	doge	imam	MC
	bey	don	inca	miss
abbé	CEO	duce	JP	MP
aga	cid	duke	khan	page
agha	curé	earl	king	peer
aide	czar	emir	lady	pope
amir	dean	Graf	lama	rani
babu	dey	head	lord	rex

shah
sir
sire
tsar
tzar
ward
whip

5

abbot
agent
ameer
baboo
baron
bedel
begum
board
boyar
calif
canon
chair
chief
count
dewan
divan
donna
doyen
edile
elder
emeer
envoy
ephor
friar
hakim
imaum
judge

junta
junto
jurat
laird
laity
liege
macer
mahdi
mayor
mufti
mulla
nabob
nawab
nizam
noble
pacha
padre
pasha
porte
prior
queen
rabbi
rajah
ranee
reeve
ruler
sahib
sheik
staff
suite
synod
thane
title
vakil
vicar
wazir

witan

6

abbess
aedile
alcade
archon
ataman
bailie
barony
bashaw
beadle
bigwig
bishop
brehon
bursar
caesar
caliph
cantor
censor
childe
consul
curate
custos
datary
deacon
deputy
despot
donzel
duenna
dynast
eparch
ephori
exarch
Führer
gauger

hakeem
herald
hetman
judger
Kaiser
keeper
khalif
knight
legate
lictor
mikado
misses
mullah
nuncio
police
préfet
pretor
primus
prince
puisne
rabbin
ranger
rector
regent
sachem
satrap
senate
serang
sexton
sheikh
sherif
shogun
sirdar
squire
sultan
syndic

tanist	empress	prelate	Black Rod
umpire	equerry	premier	burgrave
verger	equites	primate	canoness
vestry	esquire	proctor	cardinal
vizier	Fuehrer	prophet	caudillo
warden	Gaekwar	provost	chairman
warder	Gestapo	referee	chaplain
	grandee	regency	cicerone
7	hangman	retinue	co-bishop
	head boy	sea-king	co-regent
alcaide	headman	Sea Lord	czarevna
alcalde	hidalgo	senator	deemster
apostle	infanta	shereef	delegate
armiger	infante	sheriff	dictator
attaché	jemadar	skipper	diocesan
bailiff	justice	speaker	diplomat
baronet	khalifa	steward	director
bellman	khedive	subadar	douanier
bencher	kinglet	subdean	duumviri
burgess	maestro	sultana	duumvirs
cacique	magnate	supremo	emeritus
caloyer	mahatma	tribune	emissary
commère	majesty	tsarina	ethnarch
compère	marquis	tzarina	guardian
consort	marshal	vaivode	head girl
coroner	monarch	vavasor	headsman
council	muezzin	viceroy	heptarch
curator	nomarch	voivode	hierarch
czarina	notable		highness
dauphin	officer	**8**	hospodar
dowager	paladin		imperial
duchess	peeress	adjutant	interrex
duumvir	podestà	alderman	laureate
effendi	pontiff	archduke	lawgiver
elector	praetor	autocrat	lawmaker
embassy	prefect	banneret	lay elder
emperor		baroness	

legation
licenser
life peer
lordling
maharaja
manciple
mandarin
margrave
marquess
marquise
martinet
mayoress
minister
monocrat
myrmidon
nobility
nobleman
noblesse
official
oligarch
overlord
overseer
Padishah
palatine
placeman
pontifex
princess
prioress
quaestor
recorder
register
resident
sagamore
seigneur
seignior
summoner

suzerain
tetrarch
tipstaff
triarchy
tribunal
triumvir
tsarevna
tzarevna
verderer
viscount
zamindar
zemindar

9

archdruid
authority
bodyguard
Carmelite
castellan
catchpole
celebrant
cellarist
centurion
chevalier
chief whip
chieftain
chiliarch
commander
commodore
constable
Cordelier
cupbearer
custodian
czarevich
Dalai Lama
deaconess

decemviri
diaconate
dictatrix
dignitary
diplomate
Directory
dominator
drum major
electress
escheator
estafette
exciseman
executive
Gold Stick
grand duke
incumbent
inspector
Jack Ketch
justiciar
landgrave
lifeguard
liveryman
lord mayor
magnifico
maharajah
majordomo
mandatary
mandatory
matriarch
moderator
monsignor
oligarchy
ombudsman
Orangeman
palsgrave
patriarch

patrician
pendragon
pentarchy
policeman
portreeve
potentate
precentor
presbyter
president
pretender
principal
proconsul
registrar
rural dean
sacristan
secretary
seneschal
sovereign
statesman
subdeacon
suffragan
timocracy
town clerk
town crier
treasurer
tsarevich
vestryman
waldgrave
whipper-in

10

aide-de-camp
ambassador
archbishop
archdeacon
archflamen

archpriest
Areopagite
bumbailiff
camerlengo
chancellor
chatelaine
commandant
commissary
controller
corporator
corregidor
coryphaeus
councillor
covenanter
crown agent
czarevitch
dauphiness
delegation
designator
doorkeeper
enumerator
episcopate
excellency
headmaster
hierophant
high master
high priest
inquisitor
institutor
justiciary
lay brother
legislator
lieutenant
lower house
mace-bearer
magistracy

magistrate
margravine
marquisate
midshipman
ministrant
noblewoman
postmaster
praeposter
prebendary
presbytery
procurator
prolocutor
proscriber
pursuivant
ringmaster
sea captain
upper house
vice-consul
vice-regent
vicegerent
war council

11

archduchess
aristocracy
burgomaster
cardinalate
chamberlain
comptroller
court jester
crown prince
diplomatist
directorate
earl-marshal
ecclesiarch
executioner

flag officer
functionary
grandmaster
grand vizier
gymnasiarch
intercessor
internuncio
landgravine
legislatrix
lord provost
marchioness
monseigneur
papal legate
papal nuncio
policewoman
prince royal
protonotary
puisne judge
queen mother
school board
squirearchy
stadtholder
subordinate
sword-bearer
tax assessor
tax gatherer
town council
triumvirate
viscountess
witenagemot

12

agent-general
ambassadress
armour-bearer
chief justice

chief of staff
churchwarden
civil servant
commissioner
constabulary
ecclesiastic
field officer
headmistress
heir apparent
House of Lords
inspectorate
jack-in-office
legislatress
lord temporal
maid of honour
mastersinger
metropolitan
notary-public
office-bearer
parish priest
peace officer
poet laureate
prince-bishop
Privy Council
prothonotary
queen-consort
queen-dowager
queen-regnant
remembrancer
staff officer
tax collector
vicar-general

13

administrator
archimandrite

army commander
consul-general
count palatine
county council
district judge
Elder Brethren
generalissimo
grand seigneur
high constable
judge-advocate
lord spiritual
mounted police
police officer
prime minister
Prince of Wales
Princess Royal
public trustee
states-general
vice-president

14

auditor-general
camp commandant
chief constable
chief inspector
dowager duchess
gentleman-usher
high court judge
House of Commons
king's messenger
lord chancellor
lord lieutenant
lord of the manor
lords spiritual
medical officer
political agent

provost-marshal
revenue officer
superintendent
town councillor
vicar-apostolic
vice-chancellor

15

advocate-general
astronomer-royal
attorney-general
cabinet minister
chargé d'affaires
district officer
election auditor
governor-general
heir-presumptive
lords lieutenant
parliamentarian
plenipotentiary
privy councillor
queen's messenger
sheriff's officer
suffragan bishop
surveyor-general
vice-chamberlain

PEOPLES AND LANGUAGES
African peoples

3

Edo
Ewe
Fon
Ibo
Ijo
Iru
Luo
Rif
San
Suk
Tiv
Vai
Yao

4

Afar
Agni
Alut
Anyi
Baga
Bena
Bete
Bini
Bisa
Bubi
Efik
Fang
Fula
Guro
Haya
Hehe

Hirna
Hutu
Igbo
Ijaw
Khoi
Lala
Lozi
Mali
Meru
Nama
Nupe
Nyao
Oran
Pedi
Riff
Teso
Toro
Yako
Ziba
Zulu

5

Anuak
Bamum
Bantu
Bassa
Baule
Bemba
Chaga
Chewa
Chopi
Dinka
Dogon

Dyula
Galla
Ganda
Gissi
Grebo
Hausa
Iraqu
Kamba
Luhya
Lulua
Lunda
Lwena
Makua
Mande
Masai
Mende
Mongo
Mossi
Nandi
Ngoni
Nguni
Nguru
Oromo
Pygmy
Rundi
Shona
Sotho
Swazi
Tonga
Tussi
Tutsi
Xhosa

6

Acholi
Angoni
Anywak
Awemba
Bakota
Balega
Bamoun
Bapedi
Basuto
Bateke
Batusi
Batoro
Bayaka
Berber
Chagga
Fulani
Griqua
Herero
Ibibio
Kikuyu
Kpwesi
Lumbwa
Luvale
Malozi
Maravi
Murozi
Ngqika
Ngwato
Rolong
Sambaa
Senufo

Somali
Sukuma
Thonga
Tlokwa
Tsonga
Tswana
Tuareg
Veddah
Wahaya
Warega
Yoruba

7

Ashanti
Baganda
Bakweii
Bambara
Bangala
Bapende
Barotse
Barundi
Basonge

Batonka
Berbers
Bunduka
Bushmen
Dagamba
Dagomba
Gcaleka
Haranga
Kalanga
Khoisan
Kipsigi
Makonde
Malinde
Manyika
Mashona
Namaqua
Ndebele
Nilotes
Samburu
Shilluk
Songhai
Soninke

Turkana
Watutsi

8

Bergdama
Bushongo
Kipsikis
Mamprusi
Mandingo
Matabele
Nyakyusa
Nyamwezi
Tallensi
Vhavenda

9 AND OVER

Bangarwanda (11)
Bathlaping (10)
Hottentots (10)
Karamojong (10)
Karimojong (10)
Kgalagedi (9)

Languages, nationalities and races

2 AND 3

Dan
Edo
Ewe
Fon
Fur
Ga
Gur
Ha

Hun
Ibo
Ido
Ijo
Ila
Jew
Kam
Kru
Kua
Kui

Kwa
Lao
Li
Luo
Mam
Mon
Pai
Pho
San
Shi

Sui
Tem
Tho
Tiv
Twi
Vai
Wa
Wu
Yao
Zan

4

Afar
Akan
Alur
Ambo
Anyi
Arab
Avar
Bali

Bari	Ijaw	Nuer	Wend
Basa	Kafa	Nung	Zend
Beja	Kelt	Nupe	Ziba
Bena	Khmu'	Pali	Zulu
Bete	Kisi	Palu	
Bini	Ko'ho	Pedi	**5**
Bisa	Komi	Pict	Akoli
Bobo	Kono	Pole	Aleut
Bodo	Kota	Puyi	Aryan
Boer	Koya	Remi	Asian
Buja	Krio	Riff	Attic
Bulu	Kurd	Samo	Azeri
Buol	Laki	Scot	Banda
Caga	Lala	Sena	Bantu
Celt	Lapp	Serb	Bare'e
Chad	Lari	Sgaw	Bargu
Cham	Lett	Shan	Bassa
Ciga	Lisi	Sikh	Batak
Copt	Lobi	Slav	Bemba
Dane	Loma	Sobo	Benga
Efik	Lore	Soga	Berta
Embo	Lozi	Sora	Bhili
Enga	Luba	Susu	Bikol
Erse	Lubu	Tara	Bulom
Eton	Luwu'	Teke	Burra
Fang	Madi	Teso	Bussi
Finn	Mame	Thai	Carib
Garo	Mano	Toba	Chaga
Gaul	Manx	Toda	Chopi
Gaya	Mero	Toro	Croat
Ge'ez	Miao	Tswa	Cuban
Gogo	Moor	Tulu	Cymry
Gola	Moxu	Tupí	Czech
Gond	Naga	Turk	Dagur
Grig	Naha	Tuva	Dayak
Igbo	Nuba	Urdu	Dinka

Diola	Kadai	Munda	Swazi
Dogon	Kafir	Mwera	Swede
Doric	Kamba	Nandi	Swiss
Duala	Karen	Naron	Tajik
Dutch	Kazak	Negro	Tamil
Dyold	Khasi	Ngaju	Tatar
Dyula	Khmer	Ngala	Temne
Fante	Kisii	Ngoni	Tigré
Farsi	Konde	Nguni	Tikar
Frank	Kongo	Nkore	Tonga
Galla	Konzo	Norse	Uigur
Ganda	Krahn	Nyole	Uzbek
Gbari	Kumyk	Nyong	Venda
Gbaya	Kurku	Nyoro	Welsh
Gipsy	Kusal	Oirat	Wolof
Gondi	Kweni	Ordos	Xhosa
Greek	Lahya	Oriya	Yupik
Gurma	Lamba	Oromo	Zande
Gusii	Lango	Oscan	
Gwere	Latin	Otomi	**6**
Gypsy	Lenda	Punic	Abkhaz
Hadya	Lendu	Roman	Acholi
Hadza	Lenge	Ronga	Aeolic
Hausa	Limba	Rundi	Afghan
Hindi	Lomwe	Sango	Altaic
Iɗoma	Makua	Santa	Arabic
Igala	Malay	Saudi	Arawak
Iloko	Malvi	Saxon	Argive
Indic	Mande	Scots	Aymará
Inuit	Maori	Serer	Baltic
Ionic	Margi	Shilh	Bangba
Iraqi	Masai	Shluh	Baoule
Iraqw	Meude	Shona	Basque
Irish	Mongo	Sinic	Berber
Jarai	Mossi	Songe	Bihari
Kabre	Mu'òng	Sotho	Bokmal

Bolewa	Ibanag	Mumuye	Slavic
Brahui	Ibibio	Navaho	Slovak
Breton	Indian	Ndandi	Somali
Briton	Ingush	Ndonga	Soviet
Bulgar	Inupik	Neners	Sranan
Bungku	Ionian	Nepali	Sukuma
Buryat	Italic	Newari	Syriac
Celtic	Jewess	Ngbaka	Syrian
Chamba	Jewish	Ngombe	Talysh
Chimbu	Judaic	Norman	Tangsa
Chokwe	Kabyle	Nsenga	Telugu
Ciokwe	Kaffir	Nubian	Teuton
Coptic	Kalmuk	Nyanja	Theban
Creole	Kalmyk	Ostman	Thonga
Cymric	Kanuri	Papuan	Tobote
Dagari	Kazakh	Parian	Tongan
Daghur	Kekchí	Parsee	Trojan
Danish	Khalka	Pashto	Tsonga
Dargwa	Kikuyu	patois	Tswana
Derasa	Kirgiz	Polish	Tuareg
Dorian	Korean	Pushto	Tungus
Eskimo	Kosali	Pushtu	Turkic
Fijian	Kpelle	Quiché	Tuscan
Frafra	Kpessi	Rajput	Udmurt
French	Kurukh	Romaic	Uighur
Fulani	Lahnda	Romany	Uralic
Gaelic	Libyan	Ruguru	Viking
Gagauz	Lobiri	Rwanda	Votyak
Gallic	Luvale	Ryukyu	Walamo
Gambai	Maasai	Saamia	Yankee
Gascon	Magahi	Sabine	Yemeni
German	Manchu	Samoan	Yoruba
Gothic	Masaba	Senari	Zenaga
Gurage	Mbundu	Sérère	Zigula
Hebrew	Mixtec	Sidamo	
Herero	Mongol	Sindhi	

7

	Dalicad	Lappish	Pahlavi
Acadian	dialect	Latvian	Palaung
African	English	Linear B	Panjabi
Amharic	Finnish	Lingala	Persian
Angolan	Fleming	Loinang	Prakrit
Arabian	Flemish	Lombard	Punjabi
Aramaic	Frisian	Losengo	Quechua
Aramean	Gambian	Lugbara	Quekchí
Armoric	Gaulish	Maduran	Redjang
Asiatic	Guaraní	Makonde	Romance
Avestan	Haitian	Malinka	Romansh
Bagirmi	Hamitic	Malinke	Russian
Balanta	Hebraic	Maltese	Rwandan
Balochi	Hessian	Mandyak	Samiote
Baluchi	Hittite	Manxman	Samoyed
Bambara	Iberian	Marathi	Sandawe
Banggai	Igbirra	Masalit	Santali
Bashkir	Illongo	Meithei	Sebuano
Bedouin	Ilocano	Mexican	Semitic
Belgian	Iranian	Moorish	Serbian
Bengali	Israeli	Mordvin	Shambaa
Bisayan	Italian	Morisco	Shilluk
Bislama	Kambata	Mozareb	Siamese
British	Kannada	Mulatto	Slovene
Burmese	Karanga	Mundari	Songhai
Bushmen	Khoisan	Nahuatl	Soninke
Butung	Khorcin	Nauruan	Sorbian
Catalan	Kikamba	Ndebele	Spanish
Chechen	Kirghiz	Negrito	Spartan
Chilean	Konkani	Ngbandi	Swahili
Chinese	Kumauni	Nilamba	Swedish
Chuvash	Kurdish	Nilotic	Tadzhik
Cornish	Kuwaiti	Nynorsk	Tagalog
Cypriot	Lampung	Occitan	Tibetan
Dagbani	Laotian	Ossetic	Tigrina
Dagomba	Laotien	Ottoman	Tinombo

Totonac	Bohemian	Irishman	Old Norse
Tripuri	Bolivian	Japanese	Old Saxon
Turkana	Cambrian	Javanese	Parthian
Turkish	Canadian	Kanarese	Pelasgic
Turkmen	Chaldaic	Karachay	Peruvian
Ugandan	Chaldean	Karelian	Phrygian
Umbrian	Chamorro	Kashmiri	Prussian
Umbundu	Cheremis	Kasimbar	Romanian
Venetic	Cherokee	Kerintji	Romansch
Walloon	Chingpaw	Kimbundu	Rumanian
Yiddish	Corsican	Kingwana	Sanskrit
Zairese	Cushitic	Konkomba	Scotsman
Zambian	Cyrenaic	Kuki-Chin	Scottish
Zapotec	Delphian	Kukuruku	Sicilian
	Dutchman	Kwanyama	Slavonic
8	Dzongkha	Lebanese	Spaniard
	Egyptian	Lezghian	Sudanese
Abderite	Estonian	Liberian	Sumerian
Achinese	Ethiopic	Madurese	Tamashek
Akkadian	Etruscan	Maithili	Taungthu
Albanian	Eurasian	Makassar	Teutonic
Algerian	Filipino	Malagasy	Tigrinya
American	Frankish	Malawian	Tunisian
Andorran	Friulian	Mandarin	Turanian
Antiguan	Gallican	Mandingo	Turkomen
Aramaean	Garhwali	Mandinka	Tuvinian
Armenian	Georgian	Mangbetu	Vandalic
Assamese	Germanic	Memphian	Visigoth
Assyrian	Ghanaian	Moroccan	Welshman
Austrian	Gujarati	Moru-Madi	
Balantak	Guyanese	Neǧrillo	**9**
Balinese	Hawaiian	Nepalese	
Bamileke	Hellenic	Nigerian	Abkhazian
Bavarian	Helvetic	Nyamwesi	Afrikaans
Bermudan	Honduran	Nyankole	Afrikaner
Bhojpuri	Illyrian	octoroon	Afro-Asian
Biginese			Anatolian

Armorican
Barbadian
Bengalese
Brazilian
Bulgarian
Byzantian
Byzantine
Cambodian
Cantonese
Caucasian
Ceylonese
Cimmerian
Colombian
Congolese
Dravidian
Esperanto
Ethiopian
Frenchman
Gorontalo
Hanseatic
Hibernian
Hottentot
Hungarian
Icelander
Icelandic
Israelite
Jordanian
Kabardian
Kannarese
Khandeshi
Low German
Malayalam
Malaysian
Maldivian
Mauritian
Mongolian

Norwegian
Ostrogoth
Pakistani
Provençal
Red Indian
Rhodesian
Roumanian
Samaritan
Sardinian
Sinhalese
Sri Lankan
Sundanese
Taiwanese
Tanzanian
Tocharian
Ukrainian
Uruguayan

10

Abyssinian
Algonquian
Amerindian
Anglo-Saxon
Araucanian
Australian
autochthon
Babylonian
Cakchiquel
Circassian
Costa Rican
Ecuadorian
Englishman
Finno-Ugric
Florentine
Guatemalan
High German

Hindustani
Indonesian
Karakalpak
Karamojong
Lithuanian
Macedonian
Melanesian
Monegasque
Neapolitan
Nicaraguan
Nicobarese
Panamanian
Pangasinan
Paraguayan
Patagonian
Philippine
Philistine
Phoenician
Polynesian
Pomeranian
Portuguese
Rajasthani
Scots Irish
Senegalese
Serbo-Croat
Singhalese
Venezuelan
vernacular
Vietnamese

11

Argentinian
Azerbaijani
Bangladeshi
Belorussian
Greenlander

Indo-Hittite
Indo-Iranian
Irish Gaelic
Mauretanian
Minangkabau
Palestinian
Scots Gaelic
Sino-Tibetan
Trinidadian

12

Afro-American
basic English
Byelorussian
Chattis-garhi
Indo-European
King's English
Luxemburgish
Moru-Mangbetu
mother tongue
New Zealander

Plattdeutsch
Scandinavian
Tibeto-Burman

13

Irish American
pidgin English
Queen's English
Rhaeto-Romanic
Serbo-Croatian

Native American peoples

3 AND 4

Cree
Crow
Fox
Hopi
Hupa
Inca
Iowa
Maya
Mold
Pima
Sac
Sauk
Ute
Yuma
Zuñi

5

Aztec
Blood

Caddo
Campa
Carib
Creek
Haida
Huron
Kansa
Kiowa
Konza
Lipan
Miami
Moqui
Nahua
Omaha
Osage
Piman
Sioux
Teton
Wappo
Yaqui
Yuchi

Yunca

6

Abnaki
Apache
Aymara
Aztecs
Biloxi
Caribs
Cayuga
Cocopa
Dakota
Dogrib
Kichai
Mandan
Micmac
Mixtec
Mohave
Mohawk
Navaho
Navajo

Nootka
Ojibwa
Oneida
Ostiak
Ottawa
Paiute
Pawnee
Pequot
Pericu
Piegan
Pueblo
Quakaw
Salish
Santee
Sarcee
Seneca
Toltec
Warrau

7

Amerind

Arapaho
Arikara
Catawba
Chilcal
Chinook
Choctaw
Hidatsa
Mapuche
Mohegan
Mohican
Nahuatl
Naskapi
Natchez
Ojibway
Orejone
Quechua
Serrano
Shawnee
Stonies
Tlingit
Tlinkit

Tonkawa	Muskogee	Winnebago
Wichita	Nez Percé	
Wyandot	Onondaga	**10**
Yucatec	Powhatan	
	Seminole	Amerindian
8	Shoshone	Araucanian
	Shushwap	Assiniboin
Aguaruna		Athabascan
Algonkin	**9**	Bella Coola
Cherokee		Leni-Lenapé
Cheyenne	Algonquin	Minnetaree
Chippewa	Apalachee	Montagnais
Comanche	Ashochimi	Shoshonean
Delaware	Blackfoot	
Flathead	Chickasaw	**11** AND OVER
Illinois	Karankawa	
Iroquois	Menominee	Narragansett (12)
Kickapoo	Muskogean	Passamaquoddy
Kootenay	Penobscot	(13)
Kwakiutl	Tuscarora	Root-diggers (11)
Menomini	Wappinger	Susquehanna (11)

Slang words

2 AND **3**	con	gob	nut	sod
	cop	guv	OD	tit
Abo	cow	ham	oik	top
ace	cut	ice	oof	yob
bat	dig	jag	pc	zap
b.f.	dip	job	pig	zit
bog	do	jug	pop	
bug	erk	kip	pot	**4**
bum	fag	kit	rap	
can	fix	lay	sad	AC/DC
cat	fly	mug	sap	acid
cod	gas	nit	s.o.b.	Afro
				alky

arse
babe
baby
bang
bash
beak
bean
beat
belt
bent
berk
biff
bike
bilk
Bill, the
bind
bint
bird
blab
blag
bona
bonk
boob
buck
bull
bumf
buzz
camp
chop, the
clap
coke
come
cool
cove
crap
cred

crud
cunt
dago
dame
deck
dyke
fart
fave
fink
fist
flab
flip
frig
Frog
frot
funk
fuzz
gaff
gaga
gash
geek
glop
gong
goof
goon
goth
hack
horn
hunk
hype
jack
john
junk
kook
leak

lush
make
mega
mick
moll
mule
naff
nark
neat
nerd
nick
nosh
nuts
perv
poke
poof
pouf
poxy
pull
punk
push
quid
ramp
rock
rook
rush
sack
scam
shop
skim
skin
slag
snog
snow
soak
spin

stir
suck
surf
swag
tart
tool
trip
turd
tush
weed
wick
wino
yack
yuck
zonk
ziff

5

aggro
angel
barmy
batty
beano
beaut
bevvy
bilge
bimbo
binge
blast
blind
bogey
botty
broad
butch
buy it
caned

chick
choky
clean
clink
combo
crack
crash
creep
croak
cutie
dekko
detox
dimbo
dippy
dishy
ditsy
dumbo
dweeb
fairy
fence
flash
fruit
funky
gismo
glass
goner
goose
grass
grind
grope
hairy
heavy
honky
horny
jerry
joint

Kraut	troll	cruise	sheila
Limey	trots, the	crusty	sleaze
loony	twerp	deejay	snotty
Mr Big	upper	dog-end	sod off
nance	wally	do over	squeal
nancy	yikes	dosser	stoned
nimby	yobbo	downer	sucker
nonce	yonks	fat cat	toerag
nooky	yucky	floozy	turkey
patsy		gasbag	turn on
pokey	**6**	groovy	verbal
pommy		grotty	wallop
ponce	anorak	gut-rot	wasted
pooch	bandit	gutted	winkle
porky	banger	hang-up	wicked
quack	barney	hit man	Yardie
queen	big bug	hooker	zonked
queer	blimey	hooter	
rhino	bog off	johnny	**7**
rocks	boodle	junkie	
saddo	bottle	kick in	airhead
score	bovver	minder	apehead
skunk	bugger	moggie	bad trip
slick	bummer	mucker	baggage
smack	bum rap	nutter	baloney
snort	canned	pecker	bawl out
snout	cheapo	pick-up	big-shot
spiel	cock-up	pizazz	big time
spook	con-man	pusher	blackie
sprog	cookie	rapper	Blighty
stiff	cooler	ratbag	boloney
sting	cop-out	ratted	bogroll
stuff	corker	reefer	bolshie
tacky	corpse	rip-off	bonkers
tramp	cowboy	rookie	bonking
trick	cruddy	rot-gut	booze-up
			bouncer

carry-on
carve-up
cat's-paw
charlie
chocker
chuck it
chuffed
chunder
clanger
clobber
conchie
cop-shop
cottage
cracked
crumpet
dogging
ecstasy
flapper
flasher
floozie
flutter
gangsta
goolies
groupie
hard nut
hit list
hustler
jankers
knock up
louse up
marbles
mugging
mug shot
nymphet
Old Bill
pillock

plonker
quids in
right on
scarper
schmuck
scumbag
shebang
sloshed
smashed
sniffer
snot-rag
snuff it
sod's law
stinker
stoolie
swinger
tea-leaf
trolley
whopper
wrinkly

8

acid-head
acid trip
bad-mouth
base-head
beefcake
Big Apple
big house
big-mouth
bimbette
blue funk
bonehead
boob-tube
bullshit
bum's rush

caboodle
cake-hole
cat-house
chill out
crackers
crash-pad
freak-out
freebase
gang-bang
half-inch
knockers
knock off
lunch-box
mainline
man-eater
nut-house
plug-ugly
porridge
scrubber
stitch up
whopping
work over

9

arty-farty
bay window
bovver boy
clip-joint
doss-house
easy-peasy
flop-house
funny farm
ginormous
plastered
screwball
skin-flick

smart-arse
spaced out
speakeasy

10

back-hander
basket case
bit of fluff
bit of skirt
bog standard
bog trotter
booby-hatch
clapped out
copper shop
freeloader

glasshouse
gold-digger
headbanger
rough trade
switched-on

11 AND 12

Bible basher (11)
bit on the side (12)
bog standard (11)
brewer's droop (12)
cat's pyjamas (11)
cat's whiskers (12)
limp-wristed (11)
watering-hole (12)

PROFESSIONS, TRADES AND OCCUPATIONS

2–4	GP	PA	vet	clown
	grip	page	ward	coach
alma	gyp	PC	whip	comic
amah	hack	peon		crier
ayah	hand	pimp	**5**	crimp
babu	head	PM	actor	curer
bard	herd	poet	ad-man	daily
boss	hind	pro	agent	dhobi
char	lead	PRO	augur	envoy
chef	magi	rep	baker	extra
cook	maid	ryot	bobby	fakir
crew	mate	seer	bonze	fence
diva	MD	serf	boots	fifer
doc	mime	spy	bosun	filer
don	MO	syce	caddy	flier
dyer	mole	thug	choir	gipsy
gang	mule	tout	clerk	gluer

groom	tuner	canner	fowler	lender
guard	tutor	carman	framer	loader
guide	ulmah	carter	fuller	lumper
guild	usher	carver	gaffer	master
gypsy	valet	casual	ganger	matron
hakim		clergy	gaoler	medico
heavy	**6**	cleric	gaucho	mender
helot	airman	coiner	gauger	menial
hirer	archer	con man	gilder	mentor
leech	artist	coolie	gillie	mercer
mason	aurist	cooper	glazer	milker
medic	author	copper	glover	miller
miner	bagman	coster	graver	minter
model	bailee	cowboy	grocer	monger
navvy	bailor	cowman	gunner	mummer
nurse	bandit	critic	hatter	mystic
oiler	banker	cutler	hawker	notary
payer	barber	cutter	healer	oboist
pilot	bargee	dacoit	hitman	oilman
piper	barker	dancer	hodman	orator
pupil	barman	dealer	hooper	ostler
quack	batman	digger	hosier	packer
reeve	bearer	docker	hunter	pander
scout	beggar	doctor	intern	parson
sewer	binder	dowser	issuer	pastor
shoer	boffin	draper	jailer	pedant
slave	bookie	driver	jailor	pedlar
smith	bowman	drover	jobber	penman
sower	brewer	editor	jockey	picker
staff	broker	factor	joiner	pieman
swami	bugler	farmer	jurist	pirate
sweep	bursar	fellah	keeper	pitman
tamer	busker	fisher	lackey	plater
taxer	butler	fitter	lascar	porter
thief	cabbie	flayer	lawyer	potboy
tiler	cabman	forger	lector	potter

priest	skivvy	waiter	bottler
pruner	slaver	warden	bouncer
purser	slavey	warder	brigand
querry	sleuth	weaver	builder
ragman	snarer	weeder	burglar
ranger	sorter	welder	butcher
ratter	souter	whaler	buttons
reader	squire	worker	callboy
reaper	stager	wright	cambist
rector	stoker	writer	carrier
regent	storer		cashier
relief	sutler	**7**	cateran
renter	tailor		caterer
rigger	tanner	abigail	caulker
robber	taster	acolyte	cellist
roofer	teller	acrobat	chanter
rozzer	tester	actress	chapman
runner	tiller	actuary	chemist
sailor	tinker	alewife	cleaner
salter	tinman	almoner	clicker
salvor	tinner	analyst	clippie
sartor	touter	Arabist	co-agent
sawyer	tracer	arbiter	coalman
scribe	trader	artisan	cobbler
sea-dog	troupe	artiste	collier
sealer	turner	assayer	co-pilot
seaman	tycoon	auditor	copyist
seiner	typist	aviator	coroner
seizor	usurer	bailiff	corsair
seller	vacher	barmaid	counsel
server	vanman	bellboy	courier
setter	vassal	bellhop	cowherd
sexton	vender	birdman	cowpoke
shrink	vendor	blender	crofter
shroff	verger	boatman	cropper
singer	viewer	bondman	curator
		bookman	

currier	hackler	palmist	skinner
danseur	harpist	peddler	skipper
dentist	haulier	pianist	smelter
ditcher	herbist	picador	socager
dominie	herdman	planner	soldier
doorman	higgler	planter	soloist
drayman	hogherd	pleader	spencer
dresser	hostler	plumber	spinner
drummer	indexer	poacher	spotter
dustman	inlayer	poetess	stamper
exegete	janitor	pop star	stapler
famulus	juggler	postboy	statist
farrier	junkman	postman	steerer
fiddler	knacker	presser	steward
fireman	knitter	printer	surgeon
flesher	laborer	puddler	swabber
florist	linkboy	rancher	sweeper
flunkey	linkman	realtor	taborer
flutist	mailman	refiner	tallier
footboy	maltman	rentboy	tapster
footman	manager	riveter	taxi-man
footpad	marbler	roadman	teacher
foreman	mariner	rustler	tipster
founder	marshal	saddler	tracker
friseur	matador	sampler	trainer
frogman	matelot	samurai	trapper
furrier	midwife	scourer	trimmer
gateman	milkman	servant	trucker
glazier	modiste	settler	trustee
gleaner	moulder	sharper	tumbler
gleeman	newsboy	shearer	turnkey
grafter	oculist	shipper	vintner
granger	orderly	shopboy	violist
grazier	packman	shopman	wagoner
grinder	pageboy	showman	warrior
gymnast	painter	shunter	webster

weigher
whetter
wireman
woodman
woolman
workman
wrapper

8

aeronaut
analyser
annalist
aphorist
apiarist
arborist
armorist
armourer
assessor
attorney
bagpiper
bandsman
bargeman
bedmaker
bleacher
boatsman
bondmaid
bondsman
boniface
brewster
cabin boy
callgirl
cellarer
ceramist
chandler
choirboy
clothier

coachman
co-author
codifier
collator
comedian
compiler
composer
conclave
conjurer
conjuror
coryphée
courtier
coxswain
croupier
cutpurse
dairyman
danseuse
deckhand
designer
director
domestic
doughboy
dragoman
druggist
editress
educator
embalmer
emissary
employee
employer
engineer
engraver
enroller
epic poet
essayist
examiner

exorcist
explorer
exporter
fabulist
factotum
falconer
farmhand
ferryman
figurant
film star
fishwife
flatfoot
flautist
fletcher
forester
gangster
gardener
gendarme
glassman
goatherd
governor
guardian
gunsmith
hammerer
handmaid
handyman
hatmaker
haymaker
head cook
headsman
helmsman
henchman
herdsman
hired man
hireling
home help

hotelier
houseboy
huckster
huntsman
importer
improver
inkmaker
inventor
japanner
jet pilot
jeweller
jongleur
kipperer
labourer
landgirl
landlady
landlord
lapidary
Latinist
leadsman
lecturer
linesman
magician
magister
maltster
maniple
masseuse
mechanic
medalist
melodist
merchant
milkmaid
millgirl
millhand
milliner
minister

minstrel
mistress
modeller
muleteer
musician
neatherd
newshawk
novelist
operator
optician
ordinand
organist
outrider
overseer
pargeter
parodist
penmaker
perfumer
peterman
pewterer
picaroon
picklock
pinmaker
plagiary
polisher
portress
potmaker
preacher
pressman
procurer
promoter
prompter
psalmist
publican
pugilist
purveyor

quarrier
raftsman
ranchero
rapparee
receiver
recorder
regrater
repairer
reporter
restorer
retailer
retainer
reviewer
rewriter
romancer
rugmaker
salesman
satirist
sawbones
scullion
sculptor
sea-rover
seamster
seedsman
sempster
servitor
shepherd
ship's boy
shipmate
shopgirl
showgirl
sidesman
sketcher
smuggler
soldiery
sorcerer

spaceman
spearman
speedcop
spurrier
stockman
storeman
stripper
stuntman
supplier
surveyor
swindler
tabourer
tallyman
taverner
teamster
thatcher
thespian
thresher
tin miner
tinsmith
tipstaff
toymaker
tripeman
truckman
tutoress
unionist
valuator
vintager
virtuoso
vocalist
waitress
walker-on
wardress
warrener
watchman
waterman

wet nurse
whaleman
wigmaker
winnower
wool-dyer
workfolk
wrestler

9

alchemist
anatomist
annotator
announcer
arbitress
archeress
architect
archivist
art critic
art dealer
artificer
astronaut
attendant
authoress
balladeer
ballerina
bank agent
barrister
barrow boy
beefeater
beekeeper
berserker
biologist
Boanerges
boatswain
bodyguard
boilerman

bondslave	cracksman	felt-maker	historian
bondwoman	craftsman	figurante	homeopath
bookmaker	crayonist	film actor	hop-picker
bootblack	cymbalist	film extra	hosteller
bootmaker	daily help	film-maker	housemaid
buccaneer	dairymaid	financier	hygienist
bus driver	decorator	fire-eater	hypnotist
cab driver	decretist	fish-curer	incumbent
café owner	desk clerk	fish-woman	innholder
cameraman	detective	fisherman	inscriber
caretaker	die-sinker	flag-maker	inspector
carpenter	dietitian	flyfisher	intendant
catechist	directrix	freelance	ironsmith
cellarman	dispenser	freighter	itinerant
chanteuse	dissector	fruiterer	kennelman
charwoman	distiller	furbisher	lacemaker
chauffeur	doctoress	furnisher	lacquerer
cheapjack	draftsman	gas fitter	lady's maid
chorister	dramatist	gazetteer	lampooner
clergyman	drysalter	gem-cutter	land agent
clinician	ecologist	geologist	lap dancer
clogmaker	embezzler	gladiator	larcenist
coalminer	enameller	gluemaker	launderer
collector	engineman	goldsmith	laundress
colourist	engrosser	gondolier	legionary
columnist	errand boy	gospeller	librarian
comprador	estimator	governess	linotyper
concierge	examinant	guitarist	lion-tamer
conductor	exchanger	gun-runner	liveryman
conserver	exciseman	harlequin	loan agent
cosmonaut	executive	harpooner	lockmaker
cost clerk	exorcizer	harvester	locksmith
costumier	eye doctor	herbalist	log-roller
courtesan	fabricant	herb-woman	lumberman
couturier	fan dancer	hired hand	machinist
cowkeeper	fashioner	hired help	major-domo

male model	planisher	rum-runner	swordsman
male nurse	plasterer	sacristan	syndicate
man-at-arms	ploughboy	safemaker	tablemaid
mannequin	ploughman	sailmaker	tactician
medallist	pluralist	sailor	tailoress
mendicant	poetaster	scavenger	tap dancer
mercenary	pointsman	scenarist	tea-taster
mesmerist	policeman	scholiast	tentmaker
messenger	pontonier	schoolman	test pilot
metrician	pop artist	scientist	therapist
middleman	porteress	scrivener	theurgist
mill-owner	portrayer	sea-robber	tire-woman
modelgirl	postilion	secretary	toolsmith
mortician	postwoman	ship's mate	town clerk
muffin-man	poulterer	shipowner	town crier
musketeer	precentor	shoeblack	tradesman
musketoon	preceptor	shoemaker	tragedian
navigator	predicant	signalman	traveller
negotiant	prelector	Sinologue	treasurer
net-surfer	priestess	soapmaker	trepanner
newsagent	privateer	solicitor	trumpeter
nursemaid	professor	sonneteer	tympanist
odd job man	publicist	sorceress	usherette
office boy	publisher	soubrette	varnisher
operative	pulpiteer	space crew	versifier
orchestra	puppeteer	spiderman	vexillary
osteopath	quarryman	stableboy	violinist
otologist	racketeer	stableman	voltigeur
outfitter	railmaker	stagehand	washerman
pantaloon	recruiter	stationer	waxworker
part-timer	rehearser	steersman	winemaker
paymaster	ribbonman	stevedore	zookeeper
pedagogue	roadmaker	subeditor	zoologist
performer	ropemaker	subworker	zootomist
physician	roundsman	succentor	
physicist	ruddleman	swineherd	
		switchman	

10

able seaman	blacksmith	comedienne	forecaster
accoucheur	blockmaker	compositor	frame-maker
accountant	bluejacket	contractor	freebooter
advertiser	bombardier	controller	fund raiser
aerologist	bondswoman	copyholder	gamekeeper
agrologist	bonesetter	copywriter	game warden
agronomist	bookbinder	cordwainer	geisha girl
air hostess	bookkeeper	counsellor	geneticist
air steward	bookseller	customs man	geographer
algebraist	bootlegger	cytologist	glee-singer
amanuensis	bricklayer	delineator	gold-beater
apothecary	bureaucrat	directress	gold-digger
apple-woman	butterwife	disc jockey	grammarian
apprentice	career girl	dishwasher	gunslinger
arbalester	cartoonist	dispatcher	hall porter
arbalister	cartwright	dockmaster	handmaiden
arbitrator	cat breeder	dog breeder	harvestman
astrologer	cat burglar	dog-fancier	head porter
astronomer	ceramicist	doorkeeper	head waiter
auctioneer	chargehand	dramaturge	highwayman
audit clerk	charioteer	dressmaker	horn player
ballet girl	chirurgeon	drummer-boy	horologist
balloonist	chorus girl	dry cleaner	house agent
ballplayer	chronicler	enamellist	huckstress
bandmaster	chucker-out	epitaphist	husbandman
bank robber	circuiteer	evangelist	inoculator
bassoonist	clapper boy	eye-servant	institutor
beadswoman	clockmaker	fell monger	instructor
beautician	clog dancer	fictionist	ironmonger
bell-ringer	cloth maker	film editor	ironworker
bibliopole	coachmaker	firemaster	journalist
bill-broker	coalheaver	fishmonger	journeyman
billposter	co-assessor	flight crew	kennelmaid
biochemist	coastguard	flowergirl	land-holder
biographer	cold-caller	folk-dancer	laundryman
	colporteur	folk singer	law officer

legislator	panegyrist	saleswoman	technocrat
librettist	pantrymaid	schoolmarm	theologian
lighterman	park-keeper	scrutineer	theologist
lime-burner	pastry-cook	sculptress	timekeeper
linotypist	pathfinder	sea-captain	tractarian
liquidator	pawnbroker	seamstress	trade union
lobsterman	pearl-diver	seminarist	traffic cop
lock-keeper	pedicurist	serving-man	trafficker
lumberjack	penologist	sexologist	tram-driver
magistrate	perruquier	ship-broker	translator
management	pharmacist	shipmaster	trawlerman
manageress	philologer	shipwright	treasuress
manicurist	piano tuner	shopfitter	troubadour
manservant	pickpocket	shopkeeper	typesetter
matchmaker	platelayer	shopwalker	undertaker
meat-hawker	playwright	signwriter	veterinary
medical man	politician	silk-mercer	victualler
militiaman	postillion	silk-weaver	vinegrower
millwright	postmaster	Sinologist	vivandiere
missionary	prima donna	slop seller	wage-earner
moonshiner	private eye	sneak thief	wainwright
naturalist	procurator	spin doctor	watchmaker
nautch girl	programmer	staff nurse	wharfinger
negotiator	proprietor	stewardess	wholesaler
newscaster	prospector	stocktaker	wine-waiter
news editor	quiz-master	stonemason	winegrower
newsreader	railwayman	strategist	wireworker
newsvendor	ratcatcher	superviser	woodcarver
night nurse	recitalist	symphonist	woodcutter
nosologist	researcher	tally clerk	woodworker
nurseryman	ringmaster	taskmaster	wool-carder
obituarist	roadmender	taxi-dancer	wool-comber
oil painter	rope dancer	taxi-driver	wool-grower
orchardist	roughrider	tea-blender	wool-sorter
osteologer	safeblower	tea planter	wool-trader
overlooker	sales force	technician	wool-worker

workfellow
working man
workmaster
workpeople
yardmaster
zinc-worker
zymologist

11

accompanist
accoucheuse
acoustician
adjudicator
allopathist
annunciator
antiquarian
apple-grower
arbitratrix
army officer
arquebusier
artillerist
audio typist
auscultator
bag-snatcher
bank cashier
bank manager
bargemaster
basketmaker
beachcomber
bell-founder
Benedictine
bill-sticker
bird-catcher
bird-fancier
birdwatcher
boatbuilder

body servant
boilermaker
boilersmith
bondservant
broadcaster
bullfighter
businessman
candlemaker
car salesman
cat's-meat-man
cattle thief
chair-mender
chalk-cutter
chambermaid
chiffonnier
chiromancer
chiropodist
choirmaster
chronologer
coffin-maker
cognoscente
condisciple
condottiere
conductress
confederate
congressman
consecrator
conservator
constituent
conveyancer
coppersmith
cosmogonist
cosmologist
crane driver
cub reporter
cypher clerk

day-labourer
delivery man
demographer
dhobi wallah
dispensator
draughtsman
duty officer
electrician
embroiderer
entertainer
estate agent
ethnologist
etymologist
executioner
extortioner
face-painter
factory hand
faith healer
field worker
filing clerk
fire brigade
fire insurer
flax-dresser
fourbisseur
fruit picker
funambulist
galley-slave
genealogist
ghostwriter
glass-bender
glass-blower
glass-cutter
glass-worker
gouvernante
grass-cutter
gravedigger

greengrocer
haberdasher
hagiologist
hairdresser
hair stylist
head foreman
hierologist
histologist
horse doctor
horse trader
hospitaller
hotel-keeper
housekeeper
housemaster
housemother
hymnologist
illuminator
illusionist
illustrator
infantryman
interpreter
interviewer
iron-founder
ivory-carver
ivory-worker
kitchenmaid
lamplighter
land steward
laundrymaid
leading lady
ledger clerk
lifeboatman
lightkeeper
linen draper
lithologist
lithotomist

lollipop man
lorry driver
madrigalist
maidservant
master baker
mechanician
medicine man
memorialist
metal worker
miniaturist
money-broker
money-lender
monographer
mule-skinner
music critic
music master
mythologist
necrologist
necromancer
needlewoman
neurologist
night porter
night sister
nightworker
nomenclator
numismatist
office staff
onion-seller
opera singer
ophiologist
orientalist
orthopedist
osteologist
pamphleteer
panel-beater
pantomimist

paperhanger
parish clerk
parlourmaid
pathologist
pearl fisher
pedobaptist
penny-a-liner
petrologist
pettifogger
philatelist
philologist
phonologist
phytologist
piece worker
polyphonist
pork butcher
portraitist
preceptress
print-seller
probationer
promulgator
proofreader
property man
proprietrix
quacksalver
radiologist
rag merchant
rhetorician
roadsweeper
safebreaker
sandwich man
saxophonist
scoutmaster
scrapdealer
secret agent
seditionary

servant girl
serving-maid
share-broker
sheepfarmer
shepherdess
ship's master
shipbreaker
shipbuilder
shop steward
silversmith
slaughterer
slave-driver
slaveholder
slave-trader
smallholder
sociologist
stake-holder
steeplejack
stereotyper
stipendiary
stockbroker
stockjobber
stonecutter
storekeeper
stripteaser
taxidermist
telegrapher
telephonist
ticket agent
toastmaster
tobacconist
topographer
torch-bearer
town planner
toxophilite
tragedienne

train-bearer
transcriber
transporter
travel agent
type-founder
typographer
underletter
underwriter
upholsterer
versemonger
vinedresser
washerwoman
watchkeeper
wax-chandler
wheelwright
witch-doctor
woman doctor
wool-stapler
xylophonist

12

accordionist
actor manager
ambulance man
anaesthetist
archeologist
artilleryman
artist's model
ballad-monger
ballad singer
ballet dancer
ballet master
bantamweight
bibliologist
bibliopegist
bibliopolist

body-snatcher
booking clerk
bus conductor
cabinet-maker
calligrapher
camp follower
caricaturist
carpet-bagger
carpet-fitter
cartographer
casual labour
cerographist
cheesemonger
chief cashier
chimney-sweep
chiropractor
chronologist
churchwarden
circuit rider
civil servant
clarinettist
clerk of works
cloth-shearer
coach-builder
coleopterist
commissioner
conchologist
confectioner
corn chandler
cosmographer
costermonger
craniologist
cryptogamist
dance hostess
deep-sea diver
demonologist

demonstrator
dendrologist
dramaturgist
ecclesiastic
Egyptologist
electionist
engine-driver
entomologist
entrepreneur
escapologist
ethnographer
experimenter
family doctor
farm labourer
film director
film producer
first officer
flying doctor
footplateman
geometrician
geriatrician
glass-grinder
glossologist
greasemonkey
gynecologist
hagiographer
harness-maker
head gardener
headshrinker
homeopathist
horse-breaker
hotel manager
housebreaker
housepainter
house steward
house surgeon

hydrographer
hydropathist
hypothecator
immunologist
instructress
invoice clerk
jerry-builder
joint-trustee
jurisconsult
juvenile lead
king's counsel
knife-grinder
knife-thrower
labouring man
leader-writer
legal adviser
lexicologist
lithographer
lollipop lady
longshoreman
loss adjuster
maître d'hôtel
make-up artist
malacologist
man of letters
manual worker
manufacturer
mass producer
master singer
metallurgist
mezzo-soprano
microscopist
mineralogist
miscellanist
money-changer
monographist

morris dancer
musicologist
mythographer
newspaperman
notary public
nutritionist
obstetrician
office junior
oneirocritic
orchestrator
organ-grinder
orthodontist
orthographer
ovariotomist
papyrologist
pattern-maker
pediatrician
photographer
phrenologist
physiologist
plant manager
ploughwright
plumber's mate
pornographer
postmistress
practitioner
press officer
prison warder
prize-fighter
professional
propagandist
proprietress
psychiatrist
psychologist
publicity man
pupil-teacher

puppet-master
pyrotechnist
quarry master
racing driver
radiographer
receptionist
remembrancer
restaurateur
riding-master
right-hand man
sales manager
scene-painter
scene-shifter
schoolmaster
screenwriter
scriptwriter
scullery-maid
seafaring man
seed-merchant
seismologist
sharecropper
sharpshooter
ship chandler
ship's husband
shoe-repairer
silver-beater
site engineer
slaughterman
snake-charmer
social worker
soil mechanic
special agent
speechwriter
spice-blender
sportscaster
sportswriter

stage manager
statistician
steel erector
stenographer
stonebreaker
stonedresser
street-trader
street-walker
sugar-refiner
tax-collector
technologist
telegraph boy
telegraphist
test engineer
therapeutist
thief-catcher
timber trader
toll-gatherer
tourist agent
toxicologist
tradespeople
transplanter
trichologist
trick cyclist
undermanager
underservant
veterinarian
waiting-woman
warehouseman
water diviner
wine merchant
wood-engraver
works manager
zincographer

13

administrator
agriculturist
antique dealer
arachnologist
archaeologist
arithmetician
articled clerk
Assyriologist
barber-surgeon
bibliographer
calico-printer
campanologist
chicken-farmer
choreographer
chronographer
civil engineer
clearstarcher
coffee-planter
contortionist
contrabandist
cotton-spinner
counterfeiter
cryptographer
dancing master
dental surgeon
dermatologist
diagnostician
diamond-cutter
district nurse
draughtswoman
drawing-master
dress designer
drill sergeant
electroplater
encyclopedist

epigrammatist
estate manager
exhibitionist
family butcher
fencing-master
fortune-teller
freight-broker
glossographer
gynaecologist
harbour master
health visitor
hieroglyphist
hospital nurse
ichthyologist
industrialist
intelligencer
joint-executor
lady in waiting
lexicographer
lift attendant
lighthouse-man
maid-of-all-work
master builder
master mariner
mathematician
melodramatist
metaphysician
meteorologist
music mistress
night-watchman
office manager
old-clothes-man
ornithologist
orthographist
park attendant
pharmaceutist

physiognomist
physiographer
police officer
poultry farmer
printer's devil
prison visitor
privateersman
process-server
psalmographer
psychoanalyst
pteridologist
public speaker
queen's counsel
racing-tipster
rag and bone man
revolutionary
revolutionist
rubber-planter
sailing master
schoolteacher
science master
scrap merchant
ship's chandler
shop assistant
singing-master
station-master
stenographist
stereoscopist
stethoscopist
street-sweeper
sub-contractor
superintender
supernumerary
thaumaturgist
thimble-rigger
toll collector

trade unionist
traffic warden
tram conductor
tramcar-driver
ventriloquist
violoncellist
window-cleaner
window-dresser
woollen-draper

14

administratrix
anthropologist
autobiographer
bacteriologist
ballet mistress
billiard-player
black marketeer
casual labourer
charcoal burner
chimney-sweeper
citizen-soldier
classics master
clerical worker
colour sergeant
commissionaire
dancing partner
discount-broker
ecclesiologist
educationalist
encyclopaedist
exchange-broker
features editor
gentleman usher
grammaticaster
handicraftsman

heresiographer
horticulturist
house decorator
house furnisher
king's messenger
language master
leather-dresser
maintenance man
manual labourer
market-gardener
marriage broker
medical officer
mining engineer
miscellanarian
mother-superior
music publisher
nursing officer
pharmacologist
pneumatologist
prison governor
psalmographist
reception clerk
representative
schoolmistress
ship's-carpenter
siderographist
spectacle-maker
spectroscopist
sports reporter
station manager
store detective
street musician
superintendent
systems analyst
tallow chandler
troubleshooter

turf accountant
water-colourist
weather prophet

15

arboriculturist
assistant master
Bow Street runner
crossing-sweeper
crustaceologist
customs official
dancing mistress
diamond merchant
domestic servant
forwarding agent
funeral director
gentleman-farmer
gossip columnist
hackney coachman
heart specialist
helminthologist
hierogrammatist
historiographer
instrumentalist
insurance broker
jack-of-all-trades
musical director
numismatologist
ophthalmologist
palaeontologist
planning officer
platform-speaker
police constable
police inspector
portrait-painter
prestidigitator

professional man
programme seller
queen's messenger
railway engineer
resurrectionist
shorthand typist
sleeping partner
stretcher-bearer
ticket collector
tightrope walker
tonsorial artist
undercover agent

RELIGION AND MYTHOLOGY
Biblical characters

3

Asa
Eve
God
Ham
Job
Lot

4

Abel
Adam
Agag
Ahab
Amos
Baal
Boaz
Cain
Esau
Ezra
Jael
Jehu
Joab
Joel
John
Jude
Leah
Levi
Luke
Magi, the
Mark
Mary
Moab

Noah
Paul
Ruth
Saul
Shem

5

Aaron
Annas
Caleb
David
Demas
Devil, the
Elihu
Enoch
Herod
Hiram
Hosea
Isaac
Jacob
James
Jesse
Jesus
Joash
Jonah
Judah
Judas
Laban
Linus
Micah
Moses
Nahum
Naomi

Peter
Satan
Sihon
Silas
Simon
Titus
Uriah
Uriel
Zadok

6

Abijah
Andrew
Balaam
Christ
Daniel
Darius
Dorcas
Elijah
Elisha
Esther
Festus
Gehazi
Gideon
Haggai
Isaiah
Jahweh
Jairus
Jethro
Joseph
Joshua
Judith
Kohath

Martha
Miriam
Naaman
Naboth
Nathan
Philip
Pilate
Rachel
Reuben
Salome
Samson
Samuel
Simeon
Sisera
Thomas
Uzziah
Yahweh

7

Abraham
Absalom
Ananias
Azariah
Clement
Delilah
Eleazar
Ephraim
Ezekiel
Gabriel
Goliath
Ishmael
Japheth
Jehovah

Jezebel
Joiakim
Lazarus
Lucifer
Malachi
Matthew
Meshach
Michael
Obadiah
Pharaoh
Raphael
Rebekah
Shallum
Solomon
Stephen
Thadeus
Timothy
Zebulun

8

Abednego
Barnabas
Barrabas
Benjamin
Caiaphas
Gamaliel
Habakkuk

Hezekiah
Issachar
Jeremiah
Jeroboam
Jonathan
Matthias
Mordecai
Nehemiah
Philemon
Rehoboam
Sapphira
Shadrach
Thaddeus
Zedekiah

9

Abimelech
Ahasuerus
Bathsheba
Jehoiakim
Maccabees
Nathanael
Nicodemus
Thaddaeus
Zacchaeus
Zachariah
Zacharias

Zechariah
Zephaniah

10

Bartimaeus
Belshazzar
Holofernes
Methuselah
Theophilus

11

Bartholomew
Jehoshaphat
Melchizedek
Sennacherib

13 AND 14

Herod the
  Great (13)
John the
  Baptist (14)
Judas Iscariot (13)
Mary Magdalene
  (13)
Nebuchadnezzar
  (14)
Pontius Pilate (13)

Mythology

2 AND 3	Ali	As	Bes	Ea
	Amt	Ask	Bor	elf
Aah	Ana	Ate	Con	Ens
Aea	Anu	Aya	Cos	Eos
Ahi	Aon	Bel	Dis	Eru

fay	Ran	Anit	Dido	Iole
Fum	Roc	Ankh	Dike	Iris
Ge	Roe	Annu	Dino	Irus
Geb	Seb	Anpu	Donu	Isis
god	Set	Apia	Duse	Issa
Gog	Shu	Apis	Dwyn	Itys
Heh	Sif	Area	Echo	Iynx
Hel	Sol	Ares	Eden	jinn
hob	Sri	Argo	Elli	Jove
Höd	Sua	Asia	Enna	Juno
Ida	Tiw	Askr	Enyo	Kali
imp	Tum	Aten	Eros	Kama
Io	Tyr	Atys	Esus	Kami
Ira	Ull	Auge	Fama	Lear
Kay	Uma	Baal	Fate	Leda
Lar	Urd	Bakh	Faun	Leto
Ler	Urt	Bali	Frey	Llyr
Lif	Van	Bast	Fury	Lofn
Lot	Ve	Beda	Gaea	Loki
Lug	Ziu	Beli	Gerd	Ludd
Mab		Bias	gods	Maat
Min	**4**	Bilé	Gwyn	Maia
mo	Abae	Bran	Gyes	Mana
Mot	Abas	Buri	Hapi	Mara
Mut	Abia	Buto	Hebe	Mark
Neo	Abii	Ceto	hell	Mars
Nix	Acis	Ceyx	Heno	Math
Nox	Adad	Chac	Hera	Medb
Nun	Agni	Chin	hero	Moly
Nut	Ajax	Clio	Hest	Mont
On	Amam	Core	Idas	Mors
Ops	Amen	Dana	Idun	muse
Orc	Amor	Danu	Iila	myth
Pan	Amsi	Deva	Ikto	Nabu
Pax	Amsu	Devi	Ilus	Naga
Ra	Amun	Dice	Inar	Nebu

Nick	Tiki	Aesop	Barce	Delos
Nike	Tros	Aetna	Belus	demon
Nila	Troy	Agave	Bennu	Deuce
Nubu	Tupa	Ahura	Beroe	Deuse
Nudd	Tyro	Alope	Bitol	devas
Odin	Upis	Amata	Biton	devil
Ogma	Vali	Ament	Boann	Diana
ogre	Vata	Ammon	Bogie	Dione
Pasi	Vayu	Amset	Borvo	Dirce
Peri	Vili	Anava	Bragi	djinn
Pero	Wasi	angel	Butis	Dolon
pixy	Xulu	Anher	Byrsa	Donar
Ptah	Yama	Anhur	Cacus	Doris
Puck	Yeti	Anius	Cales	Dorus
Rahu	Yggr	Antea	Canis	dryad
Raji	Ymir	Anxor	Capra	Durga
Rama	Yoga	Anxur	Capys	dwarf
Rhea	Yuga	Apepi	Caria	Dyaus
Roma	yule	Arawn	Carna	Dylan
saga	Zemi	Arcas	Carpo	Dymas
Sati	Zeus	Arete	Ceres	Edoni
Selk	Zume	Arges	Chaos	Egypt
Shai		Argos	Cilix	elfin
Shri	**5**	Argus	Circe	elves
Sita	Abila	Ariel	Coeus	Embla
Siva	Acron	Arimi	Creon	Enlil
Soma	Actor	Arion	Crete	Epeus
Spes	Aditi	Armes	Crius	Epona
Styx	Aedon	Artio	Cupid	Erato
Surt	Aegir	Ashur	Cyane	Estas
Susa	Aegis	Asius	Dagda	Etana
tabu	Aegle	Atlas	Dagon	Eurus
Tadg	Aello	Atman	Damon	Evius
Tara	Aenea	Attis	Danaë	faery
Thia	Aesir	Aulis	Dares	fairy
Thor	Aeson	Bacis	deity	Fates

Fauna	Honor	Laius	Nandi	Rimac
Fides	Horae	Lamia	Neheh	Rudra
fiend	Horta	Lamus	Nemon	Sakra
Flora	Horus	lares	Nerio	Sakti
Freya	houri	Lethe	Niobe	Salus
Freyr	Hydra	Liber	Nisus	Santa
Frigg	Hylas	Linus	Nixie	Satan
Frija	Hymen	Lludd	Njord	satyr
Fulla	Hymir	Lotis	Norna	Sebek
Gades	Iamus	Lugus	norns	Seker
Galar	Iapyx	Lycus	Notus	Sesha
Galli	Iason	Macar	Nuada	Shiva
Garme	Iasus	Macha	nymph	Sibyl
Gauri	Ichor	Maera	Ogina	Sinis
genie	Idmon	Magog	Orcus	Sinon
Gerda	Idyia	Manes	Oread	Siren
Getae	Ilama	Maron	Orion	Skuld
ghost	Iliad	Mazda	Paean	Sulis
ghoul	Ilium	Medea	Pales	Supay
giant	Indra	Medon	Panes	Surya
Gibil	Ionia	Melia	Paris	sylph
gnome	Iphis	Metis	Pavan	Syren
golem	Irene	Midas	Perse	Ta-urt
Gorge	Istar	Mimas	Phaon	taboo
Grail	Iulus	Mimir	Phyto	Tages
Gwyar	Ixion	Minos	Picus	Talos
Gyges	Janus	Mitra	pigmy	Tanen
Gymir	Jason	Moira	pisky	tarot
Hadad	Jorth	Molus	Pitys	Theia
Hades	Jotun	Momus	pixie	Thoas
Harpy	Kaboi	Monan	Pluto	Thoth
Heket	Kabul	Mothi	Poeas	Thrym
Helen	Khnum	Mullo	Preta	Thule
Helle	Khons	Muses	Priam	Thyia
Herse	Kurma	naiad	Pwyll	Thyus
Homer	Ladon	Nanda	Remus	Titan

Tohil
Tonan
totem
Troad
Troll
Tyche
Uazit
Uller
Urien
Ushas
Uther
Vanir
Venti
Venus
Vesta
Vidar
Wodan
Woden
Wotan
Xquiq
Yasna
Zarnna
Zelia
Zetes

6

Abaris
Abdera
Abeona
Abydos
Acamus
Achaei
Achaia
Actaea
Admeta
Adonai

Adonis
Aeacus
Aeetes
Aegeus
Aegina
Aegypt
Aeneas
Aeneid
Aeolus
Aerope
Aethra
Africa
Agenor
Aglaia
Agrius
Aithea
Alecto
Aletes
Aleuas
Aloeus
Amazon
Amen-Ra
Amon-Ra
Ampyse
Amrita
Amycus
Amydon
Anapus
Andros
Angont
Antium
Anubis
Anukit
Aphaca
Apollo
Aquila

Araxes
Arctos
Arjuna
Arthur
Asgard
Asopus
Athena
Athene
Athens
Atreus
Augeas
Aurora
Avalon
avatar
Baalim
Bacabs
Balder
Baldur
Balius
Battus
Baucis
Befana
Bendis
Benshi
Bestla
Bitias
Boanna
Boreas
Brahma
Brigit
Buddha
Byblis
Byblus
Cabiri
Cadmus
Calais

Canens
Cardea
Caryae
Castor
Caurus
Celeus
Charis
Charon
cherub
Chione
Chiron
Chryse
Clotho
Clytie
Codrus
Comana
Consus
Cratos
Creios
Creusa
Crissa
Crocus
Cronos
Cybele
Cycnus
Cyrene
daemon
Damona
Danaus
Daphne
Daulis
Daunus
Dea Dia
Delius
Delphi
Dictys

Dipsas	Fornax	Hestia	Latona
Dirona	Freyja	Heyoka	Lilith
Dodona	Frigga	Hoenir	Locris
dragon	Furies	Hroptr	Lucina
Dryads	Furnia	Huginn	Lycaon
Dryope	Galeus	Hyades	Lyceus
Dumuzi	Ganesa	Hygeia	Maenad
Durinn	Garuda	Hyllus	Mamers
dybbuk	Gawain	Hypnos	Mammon
Echion	Gemini	Ianthe	Manasa
Egeria	genius	Iarbas	Marduk
Egesta	Geryon	Iasion	Marica
Eirene	Ghanna	Iasius	Matsya
Elaine	Glance	Icarus	Medusa
Elatus	goblin	Ilaira	Megara
Elymus	Gobniu	Iliona	Memnon
Empusa	Gorgon	Inferi	Mentor
Eostre	Graces	Iolaus	Merlin
Eponae	Graeae	Iolcus	merman
Erebus	Haemon	Iphias	Merope
Erinys	Haemus	Iseult	Merops
Euneus	Hafgan	Ishtar	Mestra
Europa	Hamhit	Ismene	Mictla
Evadne	Haokah	Isolde	Milcom
Evenus	Hathor	Italus	Miming
faerie	heaven	Ithaca	Mintha
Fafnir	Hebrus	Ithunn	Minyas
Faunus	Hecale	Itonia	Mithra
Febris	Hecate	Khensu	Moccos
Fenrir	Hector	Khepri	Modred
Fenris	Hecuba	Kobold	Moerae
fetish	Helice	Kraken	Moirae
Fidius	Helios	Kronos	Moloch
Fimila	Hellen	Kubera	Mopsus
Fjalar	Hermes	Kvasir	Munnin
Foliot	Hesiod	Larvae	Mygdon

Myrrha	Ossian	Pythia	Sphinx
mythic	Palici	Python	spirit
naiads	Pallas	Ravana	sprite
Narada	Pallos	Renpet	Stheno
Natose	Panope	Rhenea	sun god
nectar	Paphus	Rhesus	Syrinx
Neleus	Parcae	Rhodes	Talaus
Nereid	Peleus	Rhodos	Tammuz
Nereus	Pelias	Rumina	Tarvos
Nergal	Pelion	Safekh	Tefnut
Nessus	Pelops	Samana	Tellus
Nestor	Peneus	Sancus	Tereus
Ninlil	Perdix	Sappho	Tethys
Nireus	Peryda	Saturn	Teucer
Niskai	Phenix	Satyrs	Thalia
Nomius	Phocis	Sciron	Thallo
Nornas	Phoebe	Scylla	Theano
nymphs	Pholus	Scyros	Themis
Oberon	Phylas	sea god	Thetis
Oeneus	Pirene	Selene	Thisbe
Oenone	Pistor	Selket	Thunor
Oeonus	Plutus	Semele	Thyone
Ogmios	Polias	Semnai	Tiamat
ogress	Pollux	Seshat	Titans
Ogyges	Pomona	Sestus	Tlaloc
Ogygia	Pontus	Sethon	Tmolus
Oileus	Pothos	Sibyls	Triton
Olenus	Prithi	Sigeum	Tydeus
Ondine	Prithu	Simois	Typhon
Ophion	Pronax	Sirens	Ulixes
oracle	Psyche	Sirius	Umbria
Ormuzd	Puchan	Sirona	Undine
Orphic	Pulaha	Skanda	Upuaut
Orthia	Pulhas	sky god	Urania
Orthus	Pushan	Somnus	Uranus
Osiris	Pyrrha	Sothis	Utgard

Utopia
Vacuna
Valkyr
Vamana
Varaha
Varuna
Vishnu
Vulcan
Xangti
Xelhua
Xolotl
Xuthus
Yaksha
Zancle
Zethus
zombie

7

Abderus
Acarnam
Acastus
Acerbas
Acestes
Achaeus
Achates
Acheron
Acoetes
Actaeon
Admetus
Aegaeon
Aegiale
Aenaria
Aepytus
Aesacus
Aetolus
Agamede

Agyieus
Ahriman
Alastor
Alcides
Alcmene
Alcyone
Alpheus
Aluberi
Amathus
Amazons
Ampelus
Amphion
Ampycus
Amymone
Amyntor
Anaburn
Anagnia
Anaphae
Anaurus
Ancaeus
Angitia
Anigrus
Antaeus
Antenor
Anteros
Anthene
Antiope
Antissa
Aphetae
Aphytos
Arachne
Arcadia
Arestor
Argolis
Ariadne
Arsinoë

Artemis
Asathor
Astarte
Asteria
Astraea
Astrope
Ataguju
Athamas
Atropos
Audumla
Autonoë
Auxesia
Avallon
avatars
Avernus
Bacchae
Bacchus
banshee
banshie
Behdety
Belenos
Bellona
Beltane
Bifrost
Bochica
bogyman
Bona Dea
Brahman
Branwen
Brauron
Briseis
Bromius
Brontes
brownie
Busiris
Cabeiri

Caeneus
Calchas
Calypso
Camelot
Camenae
Camilla
Canopus
Capella
Caranus
Carneus
Cecrops
Celaeno
centaur
Cepheus
Cercyon
Cessair
Chelone
chimera
Chloris
Chryses
Cinyras
Cleobis
Clymene
Cocytus
Copreus
Coronis
Creteus
Curetes
Cyaneae
Cyclops
Cythera
Dactyls
Danaids
Daphnis
Delphus
Demeter

demi-god	Galleus	Icarius	Maenads
Diomede	Gargara	Idalium	Maponos
Discord	Gelanor	Idothea	Marsyas
Dwynwen	Glaucus	Iguvium	Megaera
Echemus	Gnossos	Imhotep	Menippe
Echidna	goddess	Inarime	Mercury
Ehecatl	Goibniu	incubus	mermaid
Electra	Gordius	Inferno	Metylto
Eleusis	Gorgons	Iobates	Michabo
Elicius	Grannus	Ioskeha	Michael
Elpenor	gremlin	Ismenos	Midgard
Elysian	Grendel	Itzamna	Minerva
Elysium	griffin	Iztal Ix	Mithras
Epaphus	Grimnir	Iztat Ix	Mjolnir
Epigoni	gryphon	Jocasta	Mordred
Erginus	Gungnir	Jupiter	Morrigu
Erigone	Halesus	Juturna	Musaeus
erl-king	Hamoneu	Khepera	Myrddin
Eumaeus	Hanuman	Krishna	Nauplia
Eumelus	Harpies	Laeradh	Nemesis
Eunomia	Harpina	Laertes	Nephele
Euryale	Helenus	Lakshmi	Neptune
Eurybia	Helicone	Laocoon	Nereids
Eurytus	Hesione	Laodice	Niflhel
Euterpe	Hilaira	Lapiths	Nokomis
Evander	Himeros	Larunda	Nycteus
evil eye	Hor-Amen	Latinus	Nysaeus
Exadius	Hun-Ahpu	Lavinia	Oceanus
Februus	Hunbatz	Leander	Ocyrhoe
Feronia	Hurakan	Lemures	Oeagrus
Formiae	Hydriad	Limnads	Oedipus
Fortuna	Hygieia	Lorelei	Ogygian
Fylgjur	Hylaeus	Lothurr	Old Nick
Gabriel	Iacchus	Lynceus	Olympia
Galahad	Ialemus	Macaria	Olympus
Galatea	Iapetus	Machaon	Omphale

Onniont
oracles
Orestes
Ormenus
Orphean
Orpheus
Orthrus
Ortygia
Ouranos
Pandion
Pandora
Parvati
Pegasus
Penates
Perseis
Perseus
Petasus
Phaedra
Phegeus
Phemius
Phineus
Phoebus
Phorcys
Phrixus
Phyllis
Pierian
Pleiads
Pleione
Plouton
Pluvius
Polites
Priapus
Procles
Procris
Proetus

Proteus
Pryderi
Purusha
Pylades
Pyramus
Pyrrhus
Pythias
Qabanil
Racumon
rain god
Raphael
Renenet
Rhamnus
Rhoecus
Rhoetus
Rig-Veda
Robigus
Romulus
Rubicon
Rukmini
Samblin
Saranya
Savitar
Savitri
Scandea
Scaptia
Scheria
Scythia
Segesta
Sekhmet
Selleis
Serapis
serpent
Sesheta
Setebos
Shamash

Sicinus
Sigmund
Silenus
Skirnir
Soranus
Spright
sprites
Stentor
Stimula
sylphid
Talarea
Taueret
Taygete
Telamon
Telemus
Temenus
Thaumas
Theonoe
Theseus
Thialfi
Titania
Triopas
Tristan
Troilus
Ubertas
Ubitina
Ulysses
unicorn
Unktahe
vampire
Veionis
Venilia
vestals
Vintios
Virbius
Vitharr

Walkyrs
Wayland
Wieland
wood god
Xanthus
Xibalba
Xmucane
Yakshas
Yolcuat
Zagreus
Zipacna

8

Abantias
Absyrtus
Academus
Achelous
Achilles
Acidalla
Aconteus
Acontius
Acrisius
Adrastia
Adrastus
Aeacides
Aegimius
Aegyptus
Aeneades
Agamedes
Aganippe
Aglauros
Aidoneus
Alberich
Albiorix
Alcathoe
Alcestis

Alcimede	Avernian	Cocidius	Eteocles
Alcinous	Baba Yaga	Coroebus	Eteoclus
Alcmaeon	basilisk	Cretheus	Eumolpus
Alsaeids	Bebryces	Crommyon	Euphemus
Amaethon	Bedivere	Cyclades	Euryabus
Amaithea	Belisama	Cyclopes	Euryclea
ambrosia	Bhairavi	Cyllarus	Eurydice
Anacreon	bogeyman	Cynosura	Eurynome
Anatarho	Bolthorn	Cytherea	Faesulae
Anchiale	Branchus	Daedalus	Farbauti
Anchises	Briareus	Damascus	Favonius
Anemotis	Brynhild	Damastes	folklore
Angharad	Bubastis	Damocles	Fornjotr
Antemnae	Bylazora	Dardanus	Ganymede
Anthedon	caduceus	Delanira	giantess
Anthemus	Caeculus	demiurge	Gigantes
Anthylla	Calliope	Dervones	Gilgames
Anticlea	Callisto	Despoena	good folk
Antigone	Camaxtli	Diomedes	Govannon
Antiphus	Camazotz	Dionysos	Gucumatz
Apaturia	Carmenta	Dionysus	Halcyone
Apidonus	Castalla	Dioscuri	Harmonia
Apollyon	Celaenae	Dodonian	Haroeris
Appareus	centaurs	Doybayba	Heimdall
Arcesius	Centeotl	Draupnir	Heliadae
Arethusa	Cephalus	El Dorado	Heracles
Argonaut	Cerberus	Elivager	Hercules
Arianrod	Cercopes	Endymion	Hermione
Ascanius	Chalybes	Enigorio	Hersilia
Asmodeus	Chantico	Entellus	Hesperus
Asterion	Charites	Enyalius	Hyperion
Astraeus	Chimaera	Epicaste	Ilithyia
Astyanax	Chrysaor	Epidanus	Illatici
Ataensic	Chryseis	Eriphyle	Iphicles
Atalanta	Cimmeril	Erynnyes	Jarnsaxa
Atlantis	Cipactli	Eretheis	Jurupari

Juventas	Nephthys	Pierides	Srikanta
Kalevala	Nibelung	Pilumnus	Steropus
Keridwen	Niflheim	Pisander	succubus
Kukulcan	Nin-Lilla	Pittheus	Summanus
Labdacus	Oceanids	Pleiades	Talassio
Lachesis	Odysseus	Podarces	talisman
Lampetie	Oenomaus	Polyxena	Tantalus
Lancelot	Olympian	Porthaon	Tartarus
Laodamas	Orithyia	Portunus	Tecmessa
Laodamia	Othrerir	Poseidon	Telephus
Laomedon	Pacarina	Prithivi	Terminus
Lapithae	Palaemon	Proximae	Thamyris
Iardanes	Pandarus	Psamathe	Thanatos
Lupercus	Panopeus	Pulastya	Theogony
Lycurgus	Pantheon	Queen Mab	Thyestes
Maeander	Panthous	Quiateot	Tiresias
Mama Nono	paradise	Quirinal	Tithonus
Manannan	Parjanya	Quirinus	Tonatiuh
Marpessa	Pasiphaë	Ragnarok	Tristram
Megareus	Pasithea	Rakshasa	Tvashtar
Melampus	Pelasgus	Rhiannon	Ucalegon
Meleager	Pelopids	Rhodopis	Valhalla
Menelaus	Penelope	Rosmerta	Valkyrie
Merodach	Pentheus	Rubezahl	Vasudeva
Merseger	Pephredo	Sabazius	Verdandi
Meshkent	Perceval	Sahadeva	Vesuvius
Messenia	Percival	Sarawati	Victoria
Minotaur	Periphas	Sarpedon	Virginia
Morpheus	Perseids	Schedius	Visvampa
Mulciber	Pessinus	Sciathus	Wakinyan
Myrtilus	Phaethon	Seriphos	water god
Narayana	Philemon	Silvanus	Waukkeon
Nauplius	Phintias	Sipontum	werewolf
Nausicaa	Phlegyas	Sisyphus	Xpiyacoc
Nefertum	Phoronis	Sleipnir	Yadapati
Nekhebit	Picumnus	Sparsana	Zalmoxis

Zephyrus

9

Achilleum
Acmonides
Adsullata
Aegialeus
Aegisthus
Aethiopia
Agamemnon
Agathyrsi
Akha-Kanet
Alcathous
Alcyoneus
Amalivaca
Ambrosial
Amphrysus
Anaxarete
Andraemon
Androclus
Androgeus
Andromeda
Antandrus
Antevorta
Aphrodite
Areithous
Areopagus
Argonauts
Aristaeus
Ascalabus
Asclepios
Asclepius
Ashtoreth
Assoracus
Autolycus
Automeden

Aventinus
Bacchante
Bosphorus
Brunhilde
Bucentaur
Byzantium
Cassandra
Cephissus
Cerberean
Cernunnos
Chalcodon
Charybdis
Chthonius
Clitumnus
Coatilcue
Cockaigne
Concordia
Cytherean
Davy Jones
Deianeira
Deiphobus
Demophoon
Deucalion
Dian Cécht
Diespiter
Dionysius
Domdaniel
Enceladus
Epidaurus
Eumenides
Euphorbus
Eurybates
Eurypylus
Eurysaces
Excalibur

Fabia Gens
fairy tale
Fairyland
Faustulus
Ferentina
Feretrius
Fjawrgynn
Friar Tuck
Gagurathe
Gargaphin
Ghisdubar
Gilgamesh
Guinivere
Hamadryad
Harakhtes
Harmakhis
Harsaphes
Heimdallr
Hippocoon
Hippolyta
Hippolyte
hobgoblin
Holy Grail
Hypsipyle
Idacanzas
Idomeneus
Ilmarinen
Immortals
Indigetes
Iphigenia
Iphimedia
Ixiomides
Jotunheim
labyrinth
Launcelot
Lycomedes

Lyonnesse
Melanthus
Melisande
Melpomene
Menoeceus
Menoetius
Mertseger
Metaneira
Missibizi
Mnemosyne
Mnestheus
Myrmidons
Nanahuatl
Narasimha
Narcissus
Noncomala
Nyctimene
Oceanides
orgiastic
Palamedes
Pandareus
Pandrosos
Parnassus
Patroclus
Pelopidae
Periander
Philammon
Philomela
Phoroneus
Pied Piper
Pirithous
Polydamas
Polydorus
Polynices
Polyphron
Portumnus

Postvorta
Prajapati
Pudicitia
Pygmalion
Quahootze
Rakshasas
Rediculus
Rigasamos
Robin Hood
Sagittary
Salmoneus
Samavurti
Sarasvati
Saturnius
Scamander
Scyllaeum
Sibylline
Siegfried
Sthenelus
Strophius
Taranucus
Tawiscara
Teichines
Teiresias
Telegonus
Thersites
Thymoetes
Tisamenus
Tisiphone
Toutiorix
tree nymph
Trojan War
Tyndareus
Uxellimus
Valkyrean
Valkyries

Vasishtha
Vertumnus
Walpurgis
white lady
wood nymph
Xbakiyalo
Xbalanque
Yggdrasil
Zacynthus
Zerynthus

10

Abantiades
Achillides
Aetholides
Ahsonnutli
Ahura Mazda
Ambisagrus
Amisodarus
Amnisiades
Amphiaraus
Amphictyon
Amphitrite
Amphitryon
Andromache
Antilochus
Antitaurus
Arcesilaus
Archemoros
Asclepiads
Bacchantes
Berecyntia
Bussumarus
Callirrhoe
Cassiopeia
changeling

Chryssipus
Cihuacoatl
cockatrice
compitalia
cornucopia
Corybantes
Cretan Bull
Cyparissus
Delphinium
Eileithyia
Eldhrimnir
Electryone
Emathiades
Epimenides
Epimetheus
Erechtheum
Erechtheus
Erymanthus
Euphrosyne
Eurystheus
Fisher King
Galinthias
Gandharvas
Gwenhwyvar
Hamadryads
Heliopolis
Hephaestus
Hesperides
Hippocrene
Hippodamia
hippogriff
Hippolytus
Hippomedon
Hippothous
Horbehutet
Hyacinthus

Jabberwock
Jagannatha
Juggernaut
Kaneakeluh
Karttikeya
King Arthur
leprechaun
Lifthrasir
little folk
Little John
Maid Marian
Mama Quilla
Melanippus
Melanthius
Melicertes
Menestheus
mundane egg
Nausithous
Necessitas
Nemean lion
Nilmadhava
Onocentaur
Pachacamac
Palladinus
Pallantids
Parnassian
Periphetes
Persephone
Phlegethon
Phosphorus
Pigwidgeon
Plisthenes
Polydectes
Polydeuces
Polyhymnia
Polymestor

Polyneices
Polyphemus
Porphyrion
Prajapatis
Procrustes
Prometheus
Proserpina
Qebhsennuf
Rhea Silvia
Round Table
Sakambhari
salamander
Samothrace
Santa Claus
Saturnalia
sea serpent
Strophades
Talthybius
Telemachus
Tiepolemus
Trophonius
Utgardloki
Vardhamana
Visvakarma
Visvamitra
Vrihaspati
Vukub-Cakix
water nymph
Wonderland
Yajneswara
Yoganindra

11

Aesculapius
Alaghom Naom
Alalcomenae

Amphilochus
Amphisbaena
Anna Perenna
Antaeopolis
Anthesteria
Aphrodisias
Apocatequil
Arimaspians
Atius Tirawa
Awonawilona
Bellerophon
Britomartis
canopic jars
Cueravaperi
Eileithyias
Enigohatgea
Erysichton
Eurysthenes
Finn MacCool
Ginnungagap
Gladsheimir
Harpocrates
Helen of Troy
Heracleidae
hippocampus
moon goddess
Morgan Le Fay
mythologist
mythologize
Nantosvelta
Neoptolemus
Pandora's box
Penthesilea
Philoctetes
Polyphontes
Protesilaus

Saptajihiva
Savitripati
Scamandrius
Skidbladnir
Sraddhadeva
Symplegades
Terpsichore
Thrasymedes
Three Graces
Triptolemus
troglodytes
Ultima Thule
Vishnamvara

12

Acca Larentia
Achaemenides
Acroceraunia
Agathodaemon
Aius Locutius
Ancus Martius
Bandersnatch
Belatucadrus
Chrysothemis
Clytemnestra
Erichthonius
Gigantomachy
golden apples
Golden Fleece
Hippocentaur
Hyperboreans
Hypermnestra
Jormundgandr
Kittanitowit
Lernean Hydra
Mount Olympus

Muspellsheim
mythographer
mythological
Pallas Athene
Periclymenus
Purushattama
Quetzalcoatl
Rhadamanthus
Tezcatlipoca
Theoclymenus
Trismegistus
Wandering Jew
white goddess
Xochiquetzal
Yohualticiti
Yudhishthira

13 AND OVER

Achilleus Dromos (15)
Apochquiahuayan (15)
Apple of Discord (14)
Augean stables (13)
Calydonian Hunt (14)
Ceryneian Hind (13)
Colonus Hippius (14)
Damocles' sword (13)
Elysian Fields (13)
Father Christmas (15)
Halirrhathius (13)
Hermaphroditus (14)
Huitzilopochtli (15)
Itsikamahidis (13)
Jupiter Elicius (14)
Jupiter Pluvius (14)
Jupiter Victor (13)
Laestrygonians (14)

Lernaean Hydra (13)
Llew Llaw Gyffes (14)
Mayan mythology (14)
Never Never Land (14)
Oonawieh Unggi (13)
Phoebus Apollo (13)
Quetzalcohuatl (14)
Robin Goodfellow (15)
Stymphalian Birds (16)

Sword of Damocles (15)
Thesmophoriae (13)
Tioque Nahuaque (14)
Tonacatecutli (14)
Tuatha De Danann (14)
Uther Pendragon (14)
Walpurgis Night (14)
Wayland the Smith (15)
Yoalli Ehecati (13)

Religious terms, movements and orders

2–4	dean	IHS	pyre	Zion
	Ebor	imam	pyx	
abbé	Eden	INRI	RIP	**5**
alb	Eve	Jah	rite	abbey
alms	evil	Jain	robe	abbot
ambo	ewer	Jew	rood	agape
amen	fane	joss	sect	aisle
apse	fast	kirk	see	Allah
ark	font	lama	seer	Alpha
ave	God	lay	sext	altar
Baal	goy	Lent	sin	ambry
bema	guni	mass	Siva	amice
bier	guru	monk	soul	Amish
bon	haj	naos	Sufi	angel
bull	haji	nave	text	apron
cant	hajj	nun	Toc H	Arian
cell	halo	obit	tomb	banns
chan	hell	pall	Veda	beads
cope	holy	pew	veil	Bible
Copt	host	pie	vow	bigot
cowl	hymn	pome	Xmas	bless
curé	icon	pope	yoga	burse
dana	idol	pray	Zen	canon

420 RELIGIOUS TERMS, ETC.

carol	grave	piety	beadle	Elohim
cella	guild	pious	Beguin	embalm
chant	Hades	prior	Belial	Essene
chela	hafiz	psalm	bishop	Exodus
choir	hajji	purim	Brahma	Father
cotta	Hindu	rabbi	Buddha	ferial
credo	image	relic	burial	flamen
creed	Islam	saint	cantor	friary
cross	Jewry	Satan	casket	Gloria
cruet	Kaaba	selah	censer	Gospel
crypt	karma	stole	chapel	gradin
curia	knell	stoup	cherub	hallow
Dagon	Koran	stupa	chimer	hearse
deify	laity	Sudra	chrism	heaven
deism	lauds	Sunna	Christ	Hebrew
deist	laver	Sunni	church	Hegira
deity	limbo	sutra	cierge	heresy
demon	Logos	synod	clergy	hermit
devil	Magus	taboo	cleric	homily
dirge	Maker	terce	coffin	hymnal
dogma	manna	Torah	corban	I-ching
druid	manse	tract	Culdee	intone
dulia	matin	Vedic	curacy	Israel
elder	Mecca	vicar	curate	Jesuit
ephod	mitre	vigil	datary	Jewess
exeat	morse		deacon	Jewish
faith	motet	**6**	decani	Jordan
fakir	myrrh		deific	Judaic
fanon	nones	abbacy	devout	keblah
friar	Omega	abbess	dharma	latria
glebe	padre	Advent	diadem	lavabo
glory	paean	adytum	divine	lector
godly	pagan	anoint	dossal	legate
goyim	papal	anthem	double	Levite
grace	pasch	ashram	Dunker	litany
Grail	paten	aumbry	Easter	living
		Babism		

mantra
martyr
matins
maundy
missal
Mormon
mosaic
Moslem
mosque
mullah
Muslim
mystic
nimbus
novena
novice
nuncio
oblate
octave
office
ordain
orders
orison
pagoda
painim
palace
palmer
papacy
papism
papist
parish
Parsee
parson
pastor
popery
prayer
preach

priest
primus
priory
proper
psalms
pulpit
purana
Quaker
rector
repent
ritual
rochet
rosary
rubric
sacred
Saddhu
santon
schism
scribe
sedile
seraph
sermon
server
sexton
Shaker
shaman
Shiite
Shinto
shrine
shrive
shroud
sinful
sinner
sister
solemn
spirit

stalls
Sufism
Sunday
suttee
tablet
Talmud
tantra
Taoism
Te Deum
temple
theism
tierce
tippet
trance
triune
verger
vestry
virgin
Vishnu
voodoo
votive
Wahabi
zealot

7

Aaronic
Abaddon
acolyte
Adamite
advowee
Alcoran
Alkoran
almoner
ampulla
angelic
Angelus

animism
apostle
atheism
atheist
Bahaism
baptism
baptist
baptize
beatify
Beghard
Beguine
bigotry
biretta
blessed
Brahman
Brahmin
brother
cabbala
calotte
calvary
capuche
cassock
chalice
chancel
chantry
chaplet
chapter
charity
chrisom
Cluniac
collect
complin
confirm
convent
convert
crosier

crozier	heathen	nocturn	sainted
crusade	heretic	nunnery	saintly
dataria	hexapla	oratory	sanctum
deanery	holy day	ordinal	Saracen
decanal	hosanna	orphrey	satanic
defrock	impiety	Our Lady	Saviour
deified	impious	pallium	secular
dervish	incense	parable	sedilia
diocese	infidel	paschal	serpent
diptych	introit	penance	service
diviner	Jainism	peshito	Shakers
Elohist	Jehovah	pietism	Shaster
epistle	jubilee	pietist	Shastra
Essenes	Judaism	pilgrim	Sivaism
eternal	Judaize	piscina	Sivaist
evangel	Lady Day	pontiff	Sivaite
exegete	lamaism	prayers	soutane
faculty	Lateran	prebend	steeple
fanatic	lectern	prelate	stipend
fasting	lection	prester	sub-dean
frontal	liturgy	primacy	Sunnite
Galilee	Lollard	primate	synodal
gaudete	low mass	profane	Tantric
Gehenna	madonna	prophet	Tempter
Genesis	maniple	Psalter	tonsure
Genevan	mattins	Puritan	Trinity
gentile	Messiah	Quakers	tunicle
glorify	mid-Lent	Ramadan	unction
gnostic	minaret	rebirth	unfrock
goddess	minster	rectory	Vatican
godhead	miracle	requiem	Vedanta
godless	mission	reredos	vespers
gradine	muezzin	retable	Vulgate
gradual	mystics	retreat	worship
gremial	narthex	Sabbath	Xmasday
hassock	nirvana	sacring	Zionism

8

ablution
aceldama
acephali
advowson
agnostic
Agnus Dei
alleluia
almighty
anathema
anchoret
Anglican
anointed
antiphon
antipope
apostasy
apostate
Arianism
Arminian
Ave Maria
basilica
beadroll
beadsman
beatific
bedesman
believer
benifice
bénitier
biblical
blessing
brethren
breviary
Buddhism
Buddhist
canonize
canticle

cantoris
capuchin
cardinal
catacomb
Catholic
celibacy
cemetery
cenobite
cenotaph
chaplain
chasuble
cherubim
chimere
choirboy
chrismal
christen
ciborium
cincture
clerical
cloister
compline
conclave
corporal
covenant
creation
credence
crucifer
crucifix
Crusader
dalmatic
deaconry
devotion
diaconal
Dies Irae
diocesan
disciple

ditheism
ditheist
divinity
divinize
doctrine
Donatism
Donatist
doxology
druidess
druidism
Ebionism
Ebionite
elements
Ember Day
embolism
Emmanuel
epiphany
epistler
Erastian
Essenian
eternity
Eusebian
evensong
exegesis
exorcism
exorcist
faithful
feretory
frontlet
futurist
God's acre
Good Book
Hail Mary
hallowed
hellfire
hierarch

high mass
holiness
holy city
Holy Land
holy rood
Holy Week
Holy Writ
Huguenot
hymn book
idolater
idolatry
Immanuel
immortal
Jesuitic
Jesuitry
Judaizer
lamasery
laywoman
libation
lichgate
literate
Lord's Day
Lutheran
lychgate
marabout
mass book
menology
minister
ministry
Minorite
Miserere
Mohammed
monachal
monastic
Moravian
mozzetta

nativity
Nazarene
neophyte
obituary
oblation
offering
ordinary
orthodox
paganism
pantheon
papistry
Paradise
pardoner
parousia
Passover
penitent
Pharisee
pontifex
preacher
predella
prie-dieu
priestly
prioress
prophecy
prophesy
Proverbs
province
psalmist
psalmody
psaltery
Puseyism
Puseyite
quietism
quietist
Ramadhan
recollet

Redeemer
religion
response
reverend
reverent
rogation
Romanism
Romanist
Romanize
rood loft
sacristy
Sadducee
sanctify
sanctity
satanism
scapular
sequence
seraphic
seraphim
Shepherd
sidesman
skullcap
Socinian
suffrage
superior
surplice
synoptic
Tantrism
Tenebrae
theology
thurible
thurifer
transept
Trimurti
triptych
unbelief

venerate
versicle
vestment
viaticum
vicarage
Wesleyan
zoolatry

9

ablutions
adoration
Adventist
All Saints
alleluiah
allelujah
anchorite
anointing
antipapal
Apocrypha
apostolic
archangel
archenemy
archfiend
Ascension
atonement
Ayatollah
baldachin
baldaquin
baptismal
barbarian
beatitude
Beelzebub
beneficed
bishopric
bismillah
black mass

blasphemy
born-again
cabbalism
Calvinism
Calvinist
Candlemas
canonical
Carmelite
catechism
cathedral
celebrant
celestial
cerecloth
cerements
Christian
Christmas
churching
claustral
clergyman
cloisters
coadjutor
co-eternal
communion
confessor
converted
Cordelier
credendum
cremation
dalmatica
Dalai Lama
damnation
deaconess
Decalogue
dedicated
Dei gratia
desecrate

devotions
diaconate
dissenter
dissident
dog collar
Dominican
Easter Day
Ember days
Ember week
episcopal
epistoler
Eucharist
godfather
godliness
godmother
godparent
good works
gospeller
Gregorian
hagiarchy
hagiology
Halloween
hereafter
Hexateuch
hierarchy
hierogram
hierology
High Altar
Holocaust
Holy Ghost
Holy Grail
holy water
incumbent
induction
interdict
interment

Jansenism
Jansenist
Jesuitism
joss-stick
Lamb of God
Lammas Day
last rites
lay reader
Levitical
Leviticus
Low Church
Low Sunday
Magdalene
Mahomedan
Maronites
martyrdom
Methodism
Methodist
moderator
monachism
monastery
Monsignor
Mormonism
Mosaic Law
mundatory
Mussulman
mysticism
Nestorian
obeisance
offertory
orthodoxy
ostensory
pantheism
pantheist
papal bull
Paraclete

Parseeism
patriarch
Pentecost
pharisaic
plainsong
prayer mat
prayer rug
preaching
precentor
presbyter
priestess
profanity
proselyte
prothesis
purgatory
Quakerism
reconvert
religieux
religious
reliquary
repentant
responses
reverence
righteous
ritualism
ritualist
rural dean
sabbatism
Sabellian
sackcloth
sacrament
sacrarium
sacrifice
sacrilege
sacristan
sainthood

salvation
sanctuary
scapegoat
scapulary
Scripture
semi-Arian
sepulchre
shamanism
Shintoist
solemnity
solemnize
spiritual
sub-beadle
subdeacon
subrector
succentor
suffragan
sutteeism
synagogue
synergism
synodical
teleology
Testament
Theatines
theocracy
theomachy
theopathy
theophany
theosophy
triforium
tritheism
unfrocked
Unitarian
venerable
vestments
Waldenses

Yom Kippur
zucchetto

10

absolution
abstinence
Albigenses
All Hallows
almsgiving
altar bread
altar cloth
altar front
altarpiece
altar plate
altar rails
altar table
amen corner
Anabaptism
Anabaptist
anointment
Antichrist
Apocalypse
apostolate
apotheosis
archbishop
archdeacon
archflamen
archimagus
arch-priest
Armageddon
Assumption
Athanasian
baldachino
baptistery
bar mitzvah
Benedicite

Bernardine
bible class
black friar
Brahminism
Buddhistic
canonicals
Carthusian
catechumen
ceremonial
Church Army
church bell
churchgoer
churchyard
Cistercian
clearstory
clerestory
cloistered
confession
conformist
consecrate
consistory
conversion
Covenanter
dedication
devotional
diaconicon
ditheistic
divination
doctrinism
Dominicans
dragonnade
Eastertide
ecumenical
Eleusinian
Ember weeks
encyclical

episcopacy
episcopate
episcopize
evangelism
evangelist
evangelize
Evil Spirit
fellowship
Franciscan
free chapel
Free Church
Geneva gown
gnosticism
God-fearing
golden calf
Good Friday
gospel side
gymnosophy
hagiolatry
halleluiah
hallelujah
heathenism
heliolater
heliolatry
Heptateuch
hierocracy
hierophant
High Church
high priest
holy orders
Holy Spirit
House of God
hylotheism
hyperdulia
iconoclasm
iconoclast

iconolater
iconolatry
idolatress
idolatrous
impanation
incumbency
indulgence
infallible
invocation
irreligion
irreverent
juggernaut
Lady chapel
Last Supper
lay brother
lectionary
Magnificat
Mariolatry
meditation
ministrant
missionary
Mohammedan
monotheism
monotheist
monstrance
omnipotent
ophiolatry
ordination
Palm Sunday
papal court
papal cross
Passionist
Pentateuch
pharisaism
phylactery
pilgrimage

pontifical
prayer book
prayer flag
prebendary
presbytery
priesthood
procession
prophetess
Protestant
Providence
puritanism
rectorship
redemption
repentance
revelation
rock temple
Roman Curia
rood screen
sacerdotal
sacrosanct
sanctified
sanctifier
schismatic
scholastic
scriptural
Scriptures
Septuagint
sepulchral
Sexagesima
Shrovetide
subdeanery
syncretism
tabernacle
temptation
theologian
Tridentine

unanointed
unbaptized
unbeliever
unorthodox
veneration
visitation
white friar
Whit Sunday
worshipper
Zend-Avesta

11

abbreviator
agnosticism
All Souls' Day
altar screen
antependium
antiphonary
apologetics
apotheosize
arch-heretic
arch-prelate
archdiocese
Arches Court
Arminianism
aspergillum
aspersorium
Augustinian
Benedictine
benediction
benedictory
bibliolatry
bibliomancy
blasphemous
Bodhisattva
burning bush

Catholicism
celebration
chrismatory
Christendom
christening
church house
commandment
commination
communicant
consecrator
conventicle
convocation
creationism
creationist
crematorium
crucifixion
decanal side
deification
desecration
devotionist
divine light
doxological
ecclesiarch
epistle side
Erastianism
eschatology
eternal life
evangelical
evening hymn
everlasting
exhortation
fire-worship
freethinker
Geneva bands
Geneva Bible
genuflection

graven image
hagiography
hagiologist
Hare Krishna
hierarchism
hierography
humeral veil
immortality
incarnation
Inquisition
intercessor
investiture
irreligious
irreverence
Judgment Day
Latin Church
lawn sleeves
Lord of Hosts
Lord's Prayer
Lord's Supper
Lutheranism
miracle play
Mohammedism
Nicene Creed
oecumenical
original sin
parish clerk
parishioner
paschal lamb
passing bell
Passion play
Passion Week
paternoster
patron saint
pedobaptism
pharisaical

pontificals
pontificate
prayer wheel
priestcraft
Prodigal Son
proselytism
proselytize
protomartyr
purificator
Rastafarian
Reformation
religionary
religionism
religionist
religiosity
requiem mass
reservation
ritualistic
Roman Church
Sabbatarian
sacramental
sacring bell
Sadduceeism
saintliness
Sanctus bell
sarcophagus
Scientology
Socinianism
theosophist
Trinitarian
triple crown
unbeneficed
uncanonical
unorthodoxy
unrighteous
vicar forane

Wesleyanism
Whitsuntide
Zen Buddhism
Zoroastrian

12

All Saints' Day
altar frontal
Annunciation
Apostolic See
archdeaconry
Ascension Day
Ash Wednesday
Augustinians
Bible Society
bishop's court
chapel of ease
chapterhouse
Charterhouse
choir service
chosen people
Christianity
Christmas Day
Christmas Eve
church living
church parade
churchwarden
confessional
confirmation
Confucianism
congregation
consecration
consistorial
Coptic Church
denomination
devil worship

Disciplinant
disestablish
dispensation
ditheistical
Easter Sunday
Ecclesiastes
ecclesiastic
ecclesiology
enthronement
Episcopalian
evangelicism
frankincense
Good Shepherd
hagiographer
hot gospeller
image worship
intercession
interdiction
Jacob's ladder
Last Judgment
Low Churchman
Major Prophet
metropolitan
Minor Prophet
mission house
New Testament
Nunc Dimittis
Old Testament
omnipresence
paedobaptism
Presbyterian
Promised Land
purification
Quadragesima
reconsecrate
reconversion

red letter day
Redemptorist
residentiary
Resurrection
Rogation days
Sabellianism
sacrilegious
Salvationist
Sanctus bell
Second Coming
Septuagesima
spiritualism
Sunday school
superfrontal
thanksgiving
Three Wise Men
Tower of Babel
ultramontane
Unitarianism
Universalism
Universalist
unscriptural
vicar-general

13

Allhallowmass
Allhallows Eve
Allhallowtide
Anglo-Catholic
Antichristian
antiepiscopal
Apostles' Creed
archbishopric
archdeaconate
beatification
bidding prayer

burial service
burnt offering
canonical hour
church service
confessionary
convocational
coreligionist
Corpus Christi
Court of Arches
credence table
Day of Judgment
devotionalist
divine service
Eastern Church
ecumenicalism
eschatology
excommunicate
glorification
High Churchman
holy innocents
Last Judgement
Lord Spiritual
miracle worker
mission church
Mohammedanism
morning prayer
Nonconformist
Nonconformity
paschal candle
pectoral cross
prayer-meeting
Protestantism
Quinquagesima
reincarnation
Roman Catholic
Sacerdotalism

Salvation Army
scripturalist
Shrove Tuesday
Swedenborgian
Tractarianism
Trinity Sunday
unconsecrated
Vicar of Christ
way of the cross
Zarathustrian

14

Anglican Church
antiscriptural
archiepiscopal
church assembly
communion table
crutched friars
denominational
Easter offering
ecclesiastical
Ecclesiasticus
ecclesiologist
eschatological
evangelicalism
evangelization
extreme unction
fire-worshipper
fundamentalism
fundamentalist
Gregorian chant
high priesthood
intercommunion
Maundy Thursday
morning service
mother superior

Orthodox Church
Oxford Movement
psilanthropism
psilanthropist
Rastafarianism
reconsecration
Recording Angel
Reformed Church
Revised Version
Rogation Sunday
Sabbatarianism
Sacramentarian
sanctification
sign of the cross
Society of Jesus
transmigration
Tridentine Mass
Trinitarianism
vicar apostolic
Zoroastrianism

15

anticlericalism
antitrinitarian
archiepiscopate
articles of faith
Athanasian Creed
cardinal virtues
chapter and verse
Church of England
Episcopalianism
excommunication
General Assembly
harvest festival
infernal regions
Jehovah's Witness

metropolitanate
Moral Rearmament
Mothering Sunday
Presbyterianism

suffragan bishop
Ten Commandments
Transfiguration

Saints

3 AND 4	5	Andrew	7
Abb	Agnes	Anselm	Ambrose
Anne	Aidan	Ansgar	Anthony
Bede	Alban	Blaise	Austell
Bee	Amand	Cosmas	Barbara
Bega	Asaph	Fabian	Bernard
Chad	Basil	Fergus	Bridget
Cyr	Bride	George	Casimir
Ebba	Bruno	Heiler	Cecilia
Eloi	Clare	Helena	Charles
Gall	Cyril	Hilary	Clement
Joan	David	Hubert	Crispin
John	Denis	Jerome	Dominic
Jude	Elias	Joseph	Dorothy
Leo	Genny	Justin	Dunstan
Luce	Giles	Magnus	Eustace
Lucy	Hilda	Martha	Francis
Luke	James	Martin	Gregory
Mark	Kilda	Maurus	Isidore
Mary	Louis	Michel	Joachim
Olaf	Lucia	Monica	Leonard
Paul	Peter	Philip	Matthew
Roch	Simon	Teresa	Maurice
Rose		Thomas	Michael
Zeno	**6**	Ursula	Pancras
	Albert	Xavier	Patrick
	Andrea		Raphael

Raymond
Romuald
Saviour
Stephen
Swithin
Swithun
Thérèse
Vincent
William

8

Aloysius
Barnabas
Benedict
Boniface
Cuthbert
Damianus
Donatian
Eusebius
Germanus
Hyacinth
Ignatius
Lawrence
Longinus
Mamertus
Margaret
Nicholas
Paulinus
Polycarp
Veronica
Walpurga
Winifred
Zenobius

9

Apollonia

Augustine
Catherine
Demetrius
Elizabeth
Exuperius
Fredewith
Joan of Arc
Sebastian
Servatius
Sylvester
Valentine
Walpurgis

10 AND 11

Apollinaris (11)
Athanasius (10)
Bartholomew (11)
Bonaventura (11)
Christopher (11)
Ethelburga (10)
Eustathius (10)
Gallo Abbato (11)
Gaudentius (10)
Hippolytus (10)
Jeanne d'Arc (10)
Mercuriale (10)
Peter Martyr (11)
Philip Neri (10)
Scholastica (11)
Thomas More (10)
Zaccharias (10)

12 AND OVER

Anthony of Padua (14)
Bridget of Sweden (15)
Catherine of Siena (16)

SCIENCE AND TECHNOLOGY
Biology, biochemistry, botany and zoology

2 AND 3

ADH
ADP
ATP
bud
CNS
cud
DNA
ear
egg
ER
eye
FAD
fin
gel
gum
gut
IAA
jaw
lip
NAD
ova
pod

rib
RNA
rod
sac
sap
sex

4

alar
anal
anus
apex
axil
axon
bark
bile
bird
body
bone
bulb
burr
cell
claw

cone
cork
corm
cyst
food
foot
gall
gene
germ
gill
haem
hair
hand
head
hoof
host
iris
leaf
lens
life
limb
lung
milk

NADH
NADP
neck
node
ovum
palp
pith
pome
pore
root
salt
seed
skin
stem
tail
urea
vein
wilt
wing
wood
yolk

5

actin
akene
algae
aorta
aster
auxin
berry
bifid
birth
bract
bursa
calyx
chyle
chyme
cilia
class
clime
clone
codon
colon
cutin
cycad

cycle	order	touch	caudal	hyphae
cyton	organ	trunk	chaeta	joints
death	ovary	tuber	chitin	labial
digit	ovate	urine	climax	labium
drupe	ovoid	vagus	cloaca	labrum
druse	ovule	villi	coccus	lacuna
fauna	penis	virus	coccyx	lamina
femur	petal	whorl	cocoon	larynx
fibre	phage	wrist	coelum	leaves
flora	plant	xylem	colony	lignin
fruit	pubic	zooid	cornea	lipase
gemma	pubis		cortex	lysine
genus	pupil	**6**	dermis	mammal
gland	ramus		dormin	mantle
gonad	resin	achene	embryo	marrow
graft	scale	aerobe	enamel	mucous
group	semen	agamic	energy	muscle
heart	sense	albino	enzyme	mutant
hilum	sepal	allele	facial	nastic
humus	shell	amnion	faeces	nectar
hymen	shoot	amoeba	family	nekton
hypha	sinus	animal	fibril	neural
ileum	skull	annual	fibrin	neuron
imago	slide	anther	fibula	oocyte
labra	smell	apical	floral	oogamy
larva	sperm	artery	flower	ovisac
latex	spine	atrium	foetus	palate
linin	spore	biceps	forest	palpus
liver	stoma	biotic	fusion	pappus
lymph	style	biotin	gamete	pectin
lysin	sweat	botany	gemmae	pelvic
molar	taste	branch	genome	pelvis
mouth	taxis	bulbil	girdle	phloem
mucus	testa	caecum	growth	phylum
nasal	thigh	canine	gullet	pistil
nerve	tibia	carpal	hybrid	plasma
		carpet		

pollen	adenine	creeper	mammary
purine	adipose	cristae	maxilla
rachis	adrenal	culture	medulla
radius	aerobic	cuticle	meiosis
rectum	albumen	cutting	mitosis
retina	albumin	diploid	myotome
runner	amylase	dormant	nectary
sacrum	anatomy	ecdysis	neurone
sexual	annulus	ecology	nostril
spinal	antenna	elastin	nucleus
spleen	antigen	enteron	obovate
stamen	asexual	entozoa	obovoid
stigma	atavism	epiboly	oogonia
stolon	auricle	epigeal	organic
sucker	benthos	gastric	osmosis
tactic	biology	genital	oviduct
tannin	biotope	gizzard	ovulate
telome	bipolar	gliadin	oxidase
tendon	bladder	glottis	papilla
tensor	blubber	habitat	pedicel
testis	bronchi	haploid	pedicle
thorax	cambium	hearing	petiole
tissue	capsule	hepatic	pharynx
tongue	cardiac	histone	pigment
turgor	carotid	hormone	pinnate
ureter	cell sap	humerus	plastid
uterus	chaetae	incisor	plumule
vagina	chalaza	insulin	protein
vessel	chiasma	isogamy	pyloric
vision	chorion	jejunum	radicle
zygote	cochlea	keratin	rhachis
zymase	conifer	lactase	rhizoid
	cordate	lacteal	rhizome
7	corolla	lamella	root cap
	cranial	lignose	species
abdomen	cranium	linkage	spindle
acyclic			

sternum	allogamy	ectoderm	muscular
stomach	alveolus	efferent	mutation
stomata	amitosis	egestion	mycelium
suberin	amoeboid	endoderm	mycology
synapse	anaerobe	entozoon	nerve net
syncarp	antibody	epiblast	nucellus
synergy	apospory	feedback	ontogeny
syngamy	appendix	flagella	oogonium
systole	auditory	flatworm	organism
tapetum	autogamy	follicle	pancreas
tap root	bacteria	ganglion	papillae
teleost	basidium	genetics	parasite
tetanus	biennial	genitals	pectoral
thallus	bile duct	genotype	perianth
thyroid	biomorph	geotaxis	pericarp
trachea	bisexual	germ cell	perineum
triceps	blastema	holdfast	placenta
trophic	blastula	holozoic	plankton
tropism	brachial	homodont	polarity
trypsin	carapace	homogamy	polysome
urethra	carotene	hypogeal	pregnant
vacuole	cellular	inner ear	prop root
viscera	cell wall	involute	prophase
vitamin	cerebral	isotropy	protozoa
yolk sac	cerebrum	lamellae	receptor
zoogamy	chordate	lenticel	ribosome
zoology	clavicle	life span	root hair
	cleavage	ligament	ruminant
8	clitoris	mast cell	sclereid
	coenzyme	maxillae	seedling
abductor	collagen	membrane	skeleton
abscisin	cytology	meristem	spiracle
acoelous	demersal	mesoderm	symbiont
acrosome	dendrite	midbrain	synapsis
adductor	diastase	moulting	syncarpy
aeration	duodenum	movement	taxonomy
alkaloid			

tegument
tentacle
thalamus
thiamine
tracheid
tympanum
vascular
vertebra
virology
xenogamy
zoospore

9

adrenalin
allantois
amino acid
anabolism
anaerobic
aneuploid
anisogamy
antennule
appendage
arteriole
atavistic
autonomic
basal body
bifarious
bionomics
biorhythm
branchial
branching
capillary
carnivore
cartilage
cellulase
cellulose

centriole
chiasmata
chromatid
chromatin
chrysalis
coenobium
coenocyte
commensal
community
convolute
corpuscle
cotyledon
cytoplasm
Darwinism
diaphragm
dichotomy
digestion
dimorphic
dominance
dura mater
ecosystem
ectoplasm
endocrine
endoplasm
endosperm
endospore
endostyle
epidermis
eukaryote
evolution
excretion
excretory
exodermis
fertilize
flagellum
folic acid

forebrain
germinate
gestation
guttation
gynaeceum
gynaecium
gynoecium
haemocoel
halophyte
herbivore
heterosis
hindbrain
histology
homospory
hypocotyl
ingestion
inhibitor
internode
intestine
isotropic
life cycle
life forms
limnology
megaspore
metaplasm
micropyle
microsome
middle ear
migration
morphosis
mutagenic
nephridia
nerve cell
notochord
nucleolus
olfactory

oogenesis
operculum
optic lobe
organelle
organogeny
ovulation
oxidation
pacemaker
perennial
pericycle
Petri dish
phagocyte
phellogen
phenology
phenotype
phycology
phylogeny
pituitary
polar body
polyploid
proboscis
protozoan
pulmonary
pyridoxal
recessive
reflex arc
reticulum
retractor
sclerotic
sebaceous
secretion
secretory
selection
sieve cell
sieve tube
sporangia

sporogony
sterility
substrate
succulent
symbiosis
synecious
synoicous
telophase
tricuspid
umbilical
unisexual
ventricle
xerophyte
zoogamous

10

achromatin
acoelomate
actomyosin
albuminoid
alimentary
androecium
antheridia
archegonia
archespore
autecology
biogenesis
biological
biometrics
biophysics
blastocoel
blastocyst
blastoderm
blastomere
blastopore
bronchiole

catabolism
centromere
centrosome
cerebellum
chemotaxis
chromomere
chromosome
coleoptile
copulation
dehiscence
dermatogen
dimorphism
embryology
entomology
enzymology
epididymis
epiglottis
epithelium
etiolation
fibrinogen
generation
geotropism
glomerulus
grey matter
guard cells
hemocyanin
hemoglobin
herbaceous
hereditary
heterodont
homocercal
homozygote
homozygous
hygrophyte
hypophysis
incubation

inhibition
integument
interferon
involution
Krebs cycle
Lamarckism
leaf sheath
leucoplast
locomotion
lymphocyte
mesenteron
metabolism
monoecious
morphology
mother cell
mycorrhiza
nephridium
nerve fibre
neural tube
nitrifying
nucleotide
oesophagus
omnivorous
osteoblast
osteoclast
parasitism
parenchyma
pathogenic
periosteum
phelloderm
photonasty
phototaxis
physiology
pineal body
polyploidy
population

prokaryote
prothallus
protoplasm
pyridoxine
saprophyte
sarcolemma
schizogony
sieve plate
splanchnic
sporangium
sporophyte
stone cells
strophiole
subspecies
succession
synecology
vegetation
vegetative
vertebrate
viviparity
viviparous

11

aestivation
allelomorph
anisotropic
antheridium
antibiotics
archegonium
archenteron
astrobotany
autotrophic
autotropism
biodynamics
blastocoele
carbon cycle

carboxylase
carnivorous
chlorophyll
chloroplast
chromoplast
collenchyma
competition
conjugation
deamination
desiccation
eccrinology
endothelium
environment
erythrocyte
exoskeleton
facultative
gall bladder
gametophyte
genetic code
germination
Golgi bodies
haemocyanin
haemoglobin
halophilous
heterospory
hibernation
homeostatic
homeostatis
infundibulum
inheritance
lipoprotein
loop of Henle
monoculture
monomorphic
muscle fibre
nematoblast

nucleic acid
orientation
parturition
pericardium
pinocytosis
plasmodesma
plasmolysis
polar bodies
pollination
polypeptide
pseudopodia
pyramidines
respiration
somatic cell
spermatozoa
sub-cellular
tapetal cell
thermotaxis
unicellular
white matter
X-chromosome
Y-chromosome
zooplankton

12

all-or-nothing
archesporium
astrobiology
back-crossing
bacteriology
basal granule
biochemistry
biosynthesis
buccal cavity
cell division
chondroblast

denitrifying
diploblastic
distribution
ectoparasite
endoparasite
endoskeleton
fermentation
flexor muscle
gastrulation
heliotropism
heterocercal
heterogamete
heterogamous
heterozygous
homoeostasis
homoeostatic
hypothalamus
invagination
invertebrate
keratogenous
mammary gland
medullary ray
microbiology
mitochondria
myelin sheath
nerve impulse
palaeobotany
phospholipid
phototropism
pyridoxamine
radiobiology
red blood cell
reductionism
reproduction
sclerenchyma
smooth muscle

spermatozoid
telolecithal
trace element
zoochemistry

13

accommodation
acotyledonous
bacteriophage
bicuspid valve
binary fission
biodegradable
bioenergetics
blastogenesis
cephalization
chemoreceptor
decomposition
dental formula
erector muscle
extracellular
Fallopian tube
fertilization
hermaphrodite
homoiothermic
insectivorous
intracellular
marine biology
micro-organism
mitochondrion
morphogenesis
multinucleate
organogenesis
ovoviviparity
ovoviviparous
palisade cells
parthenocarpy

photoreceptor
phytoplankton
plasmodesmata
proprioceptor
striped muscle
thermotropism
thigmotropism
translocation
transpiration
triploblastic

chemosynthesis (14)
extensor muscle (14)
Haversian canal (14)
multiple fission (15)
osmoregulation (14)
oxyhaemoglobin (14)
parthenogenesis (15)
photoperiodism (14)
photosynthesis (14)
poikilothermic (14)
polysaccharide (14)
vascular bundle (14)
voluntary muscle (15)

14 AND 15

bioengineering (14)
Brunner's glands (14)

Chemistry and metallurgy

2 AND 3	TNT	gold	5	boron
	4	iron		brass
azo		keto	agene	braze
DDT	acid	lead	agent	ester
DNA	acyl	lime	aldol	ether
dye	alum	meta	alkyl	ethyl
gas	aryl	mica	alloy	Freon
ion	atom	mole	amide	group
lab	base	mond	amine	imine
mu	bond	neon	amino	inert
oil	Buna	rust	anion	Invar
ore	calx	salt	arene	ionic
pH	cell	slag	argon	leach
PVA	clay	soda	assay	Lysol
PVC	coal	spin	azote	metal
RNA	coke	zinc	basic	model
sol	dyad		beryl	molal
tin	enol		borax	molar

monad
niton
nitre
nylon
oxide
ozone
phase
poise
radon
redox
resin
roast
salol
salts
smelt
solid
steel
sugar
vinyl
wootz
xenon

6

acetal
acetic
acetyl
acidic
adduct
aerate
alkali
alkane
alkene
alkyne
amatol
ammine
anneal

atomic
barite
barium
baryta
biuret
bleach
borane
borate
bronze
buffer
butane
carbon
cation
cerium
chrome
cobalt
copper
cresol
curium
decane
dilute
dipole
dry ice
energy
erbium
ethane
ferric
galena
halide
helium
indium
iodate
iodide
iodine
iodite
iodize

ionium
isomer
kation
ketone
labile
ligand
liquid
litmus
lysine
methyl
natron
nickel
octane
olefin
osmium
oxygen
period
pewter
phenol
phenyl
potash
proton
quartz
radium
reduce
refine
reflux
retort
ribose
rutile
silica
silver
sinter
sodium
solder
solute

starch
sterol
sulfur
tannin
Teflon
thoria
thoron
thymol
xylose

7

acetate
acetone
acidity
aerosol
alchemy
alcohol
alembic
alumina
amalgam
ammonal
ammonia
amylose
analyse
aniline
anodize
antacid
arsenic
aspirin
barytes
bauxite
bell jar
benzene
bismuth
bitumen
bonding

bromate	gallium	pig iron	wolfram
bromide	gelatin	plastic	yttrium
bromine	glucose	polymer	
burette	hafnium	propane	**8**
cadmium	halogen	pyrites	
caesium	holmium	quinine	actinide
calcium	hydrate	rare gas	actinism
calomel	hydride	reagent	actinium
camphor	iridium	red lead	aldehyde
carbide	isotope	rhenium	alkaline
chemist	krypton	rhodium	aluminum
chloric	leucine	silicon	ammonium
coal tar	leucite	soda-ash	analysis
cocaine	lithium	soluble	antimony
codeine	menthol	solvent	aromatic
colloid	mercury	sorbite	arsenate
corrode	methane	spectra	arsenide
crystal	micelle	spelter	asbestos
cuprite	mineral	sucrose	astatine
cyanate	monomer	sulfate	atropine
cyanide	naphtha	sulfide	Bakelite
dextran	neutral	sulfite	benzoate
dextrin	niobium	sulphur	Bessemer
dialyse	nitrate	terbium	bivalent
dibasic	nitride	terpene	caffeine
dioxide	nitrite	thorium	carbolic
ebonite	orbital	thulium	carbonic
element	organic	titrate	carbonyl
entropy	osmosis	toluene	cast iron
ferment	osmotic	tritium	catalyse
fermium	oxidant	uranide	catalyst
ferrate	oxidize	uranium	charcoal
ferrite	oxyacid	valence	chemical
ferrous	pentane	valency	chlorate
formate	pentose	Veronal	chloride
formula	Perspex	vitriol	chlorine
			chromate

chromite
chromium
cinnabar
corundum
covalent
cryolite
cyanogen
dextrose
dialysis
diatomic
didymium
dissolve
divalent
electron
emission
emulsion
enthalpy
ethylene
europium
firedamp
fluoride
fluorine
francium
fructose
glucinum
glycerin
glycerol
graphite
gunmetal
half-life
haloform
hematite
hydrated
hydrogen
hydroxyl
inert gas

iodoform
isomeric
kerosene
keto form
levulose
litharge
lone pair
lutecium
lutetium
magnesia
Manganin
marsh gas
masurium
melamine
methanal
methanol
molecule
monoxide
Nichrome
nicotine
nitrogen
nobelium
noble gas
non-metal
oxidizer
paraffin
periodic
peroxide
phosgene
platinum
plumbago
polonium
pot metal
reactant
reaction
refining

rock salt
rubidium
samarium
saturate
scandium
selenium
silicane
silicate
silicone
solution
suboxide
sulphate
sulphide
sulphite
tantalum
tartrate
test tube
thallium
titanium
tribasic
trioxide
tungsten
unit cell
unstable
vanadium
water gas

9

acetylene
acylation
alchemist
alcoholic
aliphatic
allotrope
allotropy
aluminate

aluminium
americium
amino acid
anhydride
anhydrous
apparatus
aqua regia
atmolysis
bell metal
berkelium
beryllium
bivalence
black lead
boric acid
brimstone
carbonate
catalysis
catalytic
cellulose
chemistry
chokedamp
cobaltite
copolymer
corrosion
covalence
deuterium
diazonium
digitalin
duralumin
elastomer
erythrite
flotation
fulminate
galactose
galvanize
germanium

glucoside
glyceride
guncotton
gunpowder
haematite
histamine
homolysis
homolytic
hydration
hydrazine
hydroxide
indicator
inorganic
insoluble
ionic bond
isomerism
laevulose
lanthanum
limestone
limewater
magnesium
magnetite
malic acid
manganese
metalloid
millerite
molecular
monatomic
neodymium
neptunium
nitration
oxidation
palladium
permalloy
petroleum
phosphate

phosphide
plutonium
polar bond
polyamide
polybasic
polyester
polythene
polyvinyl
potassium
pyrolysis
quicklime
raffinose
rare earth
rare gases
reductant
reduction
resonance
ruthenium
saltpetre
semimetal
solvation
stability
strontium
sulphuric
synthesis
synthetic
tellurite
tellurium
titration
univalent
verdigris
vulcanite
white lead
ytterbium
zirconium

10

acetic acid
alkalinity
alkyl group
allotropes
amphoteric
analytical
bimetallic
bisulphate
bond energy
bond length
carnallite
catenation
chalybeate
chemically
chloroform
cinchonine
citric acid
constantan
dative bond
dichromate
double bond
dysprosium
electronic
enantiomer
eudiometer
exothermic
formic acid
free energy
gadolinium
heavy water
homocyclic
hydrolysis
ionization
isocyanide
laboratory

lactic acid
lanthanide
lawrencium
metallurgy
metamerism
mischmetal
molybdenum
monovalent
Muntz metal
natural gas
neutralize
nitric acid
oxalic acid
phosphorus
picric acid
polyatomic
polymerize
promethium
rare earths
saccharate
saccharide
solubility
sphalerite
technetium
trivalence
viscometer
white metal
zinc blende
zwitterion

11

accelerator
acetylation
acrylic acid
benzene ring
benzoic acid

bicarbonate
californium
carborundum
cassiterite
chloric acid
cobalt bloom
crystallize
cyclohexane
dehydration
einsteinium
electrolyte
elimination
endothermic
equilibrium
free radical
German steel
Glauber salt
haloid acids
heterolytic
hydrocarbon
hydrocyanic
laughing gas
litmus paper
mendelevium
Mond process
naphthalene
non-metallic
oxidization
paraldehyde
phosphonate
phosphorous
pitchblende
polystyrene
polyvalence
precipitate
prussic acid

quicksilver
radioactive
radiocarbon
ribonucleic
sal ammoniac
Schiff's base
sebacic acid
sublimation
substituent
tautomerism
tetravalent
transuranic
wrought iron
zone melting

12

acetaldehyde
alkali metals
alkyl halides
atomic number
atomic theory
atomic weight
benzaldehyde
blast furnace
Bunsen burner
butanoic acid
carbocations
carbohydrate
carbonic acid
chlorination
condensation
covalent bond
deliquescent
diamagnetism
disaccharide
dissociation

distillation
electrolysis
fermentation
formaldehyde
German silver
Haber process
halogenation
hydrochloric
hydrogen bond
muriatic acid
permanganate
praseodymium
prince's metal
protactinium
radioisotope
rate constant
Rochelle salt
sulphonamide
tartaric acid
zone refining

13

Bessemer steel
carbon dioxide
chain reaction
chromium steel
hydrochloride
hydrosulphate
lattice energy
molecular mass
paramagnetism
periodic table
petrochemical
precipitation
protoactinium
recrystallize

reducing agent
sulphuric acid
trisaccharide

14 AND OVER

aufbau principle (15)
Born–Haber cycle (14)
Britannia metal (14)
carbon monoxide (14)
carboxylic acid (14)
Chile saltpetre (14)
decarbonization (15)
deoxyribonucleic (16)
diazonium salts (14)
electrochemical (15)
esterification (14)
ferro-manganese (14)
ferrous sulphate (15)
giant structures (15)
Grignard reagent (15)
microchemistry (14)
molecular weight (15)
monosaccharide (14)
nitrogen dioxide (15)
nitroglycerine (14)
organo-metallic (14)
oxidizing agent (14)
oxonium compound (15)
phosphor bronze (14)
photosynthesis (14)
polysaccharide (14)
reaction kinetics (16)
saponification (14)
trinitrotoluene (15)

Engineering

2 AND 3

ace
amp
bhp
bit
cam
cog
dam
emf
erg
fan
fit
gab
hob
hp
hub
ion
jib
key
lag
nut
ohm
oil
rpm
ram
rig
sag
tap
taw
tew
tie
uhf
vhf

4

arch
axle
beam
belt
bolt
burr
byte
cast
coak
cone
cowl
flaw
flux
fuel
fuse
gear
glue
hasp
hook
hose
jack
kiln
lens
lift
link
lock
loom
main
mill
mine
nail
nave

oily
pawl
pile
pipe
plan
plug
pump
rack
rail
reel
road
rope
rung
rust
skid
slag
stay
stop
stud
sump
tamp
tank
test
tilt
tire
tool
tram
tube
turn
tyre
unit
vane
vent
void

volt
weir
weld
wire
work
worm

5

alloy
anode
binac
blast
braze
cable
chair
chase
civil
clamp
cleat
compo
crane
crank
crate
deuce
dowel
drill
drive
elbow
emery
felly
flume
flush
force
gauge

girder
H-beam
helix
hinge
hoist
ingot
input
jenny
jewel
joint
joist
keyed
laser
level
lever
lewis
miner
model
motor
mould
oakum
oiler
pedal
pivot
plant
power
press
pylon
quern
radar
radio
ratch
relay
resin

rigid	wiper	gutter	sheave	welded
rivet	works	hinged	siding	welder
rough	**6**	hooter	sleeve	willow
rusty		ingate	sluice	
screw	aerial	intake	smiddy	**7**
shaft	analog	jigger	smithy	adapter
short	anneal	kibble	socket	adaptor
shunt	barrel	lacing	solder	air duct
slack	bit-end	ladder	spigot	airfoil
slide	blower	lamina	static	airlock
sling	bobbin	latten	stoker	air pipe
smelt	boiler	magnet	strain	air pump
spoke	bridge	milled	stress	air trap
spool	buffer	mining	strike	air tube
spout	burner	moment	sucker	autovac
stamp	camber	monkey	switch	battery
steam	clutch	nipple	swivel	bearing
still	column	nozzle	system	belting
strap	coppin	oilcan	tackle	booster
strut	cotter	oil-gas	tappet	bracket
stulm	couple	output	temper	caisson
swage	cradle	petrol	tender	casting
swape	cut-out	pinion	thrust	cathode
taper	damask	piston	tie-bar	chamfer
tewel	damper	pulley	tie-rod	chimney
tommy	derail	rarefy	tinned	cistern
tools	duplex	repair	toggle	clacker
tooth	dynamo	retard	torque	conduit
T-rail	energy	rigger	tripod	cutting
train	engine	rocket	trolly	derrick
valve	felloe	roller	tubing	digital
video	fitter	rotary	tunnel	drawbar
waste	flange	rundle	tuyere	drawing
wedge	flashe	saggar	uncoil	dry dock
wharf	funnel	sagger	vacuum	dry pile
wheel	geyser	saw pit	washer	dynamic

exciter
exhaust
eye-bolt
factory
ferrule
firebox
fitting
forging
founder
foundry
fulcrum
furnace
fuse box
gas trap
gearing
gimbals
gudgeon
hydrant
inertia
jointer
journal
lagging
lockage
locknut
machine
magneto
male die
manhole
mill-cog
mill dam
milling
monitor
moulded
moulder
mud hole
nuclear

Ohm's law
oil lamp
oil pump
pattern
pig iron
pontoon
program
pug mill
rag bolt
railway
ratchet
reactor
riveter
road bed
roadway
sawmill
sea-bank
sea-wall
shackle
shuttle
sleeper
smelter
spindle
stamper
statics
suction
sump-pit
support
syringe
tamping
templet
tension
test bay
testing
thimble
tie-beam

tilting
tin mine
tinfoil
tinning
torsion
tracing
treadle
trolley
turbine
turning
unrivet
unscrew
ventage
viaduct
voltage
voltaic
welding
wet dock
wringer
wrought

8

air brake
air valve
annealed
aqueduct
axletree
ball cock
bevelled
bridging
cam wheel
camshaft
cassette
cast iron
castings
catenary

chauffer
cog wheel
compound
computer
concrete
contrate
corn mill
coupling
cradling
cylinder
Davy lamp
dead lift
draw gear
edge rail
electric
elevator
engineer
eolipyle
fan blast
feed pipe
feed pump
fireclay
fireplug
flywheel
fracture
friction
fuse clip
galvanic
gas gauge
gas mains
gasworks
governor
gradient
hardware
hot blast
hot press

ignition
injecter
injector
ink stone
insulate
ironwork
irrigate
Jacquard
joint box
junk ring
laminate
land roll
leverage
limekiln
linch pin
Linotype
lock gate
lock sill
loop line
magnetic
mechanic
mill pond
mill race
momentum
monorail
Monotype
moulding
movement
mud valve
oil stove
oilstone
operator
overshot
ozonizer
pendulum
penstock

pile shoe
platform
pressure
puddling
pump gear
pump head
purchase
radiator
rag-wheel
railroad
recharge
refinery
register
rheostat
rigidity
ring bolt
rotatory
shearing
silk mill
skew arch
smeltery
smelting
soft iron
split pin
stamping
standard
starling
stone pit
stopcock
tailrace
telotype
tempered
template
terminal
throttle
tide-gate

tide mill
tilekiln
tinplate
tractile
traction
tractive
tram rail
tramroad
velocity
water gas
windmill
wind pump
wiredraw
wireless
wood mill
workable
workshop
wormgear

9

acoustics
aeolipyle
air engine
air filter
air vessel
amplifier
artificer
baseplate
bevel gear
blueprint
brakedrum
brakepipe
brick kiln
cast steel
chain belt
chainpump

clockwork
condenser
conductor
cotter pin
crosshead
cyclotron
datum line
dead level
diaphragm
disc brake
disk brake
dynamical
earthwork
eccentric
electrify
electrode
escalator
female die
fire brick
fish joint
fishplate
floodgate
fog signal
foot valve
force pump
framework
funicular
galvanize
gas engine
gas fitter
gas geyser
gas holder
gasometer
gas retort
gearwheel
horse mill

hydraulic
hydrostat
idle wheel
induction
inductive
inertness
injection
insertion
insulated
insulator
ironsmith
ironworks
jet engine
knife edge
laminated
lewis bolt
Leyden jar
limelight
lubricant
lubricate
machinery
machinist
magnetize
male screw
man engine
master key
mechanics
mechanism
mechanize
mild steel
millstone
mine shaft
mud sluice
nodal line
nose piece
oil-engine

oil geyser
perforate
petrol can
piston rod
pneumatic
polarizer
porous pot
power loom
programme
propeller
prototype
pump brake
pump spear
pump stock
radiation
rectifier
reflector
regulator
reservoir
resultant
rheomotor
rheophore
road metal
roughcast
sandpaper
shunt coil
sleeve nut
slide rule
smack mill
soapworks
soldering
spring box
spur wheel
stanchion
steam pipe
stock lock

stoke hole
structure
superheat
telephone
tempering
tin mining
transform
trunk line
turntable
twin cable
vibration
vulcanite
vulcanize
watermark
water tank
wheelrace
white heat
winepress
wire gauze
wire wheel
worm wheel

10

alternator
automation
automobile
bevel wheel
broad gauge
brush wheel
cantilever
case-harden
centigrade
chain-drive
clack valve
coach screw
combustion

crankshaft
crown wheel
dead weight
dielectric
discharger
diving bell
donkey pump
drawbridge
earthplate
efficiency
electrical
electronic
embankment
emery cloth
emery paper
emery wheel
engine room
escapement
fire escape
flange rail
fluid drive
footbridge
galvanized
gas turbine
glass paper
goods train
goods truck
grid system
gudgeon pin
guillotine
hair spring
heart wheel
hogger pipe
hogger pump
horsepower
hydrophore

idle pulley
Indian fire
instrument
insulating
insulation
iron heater
irrigation
isodynamic
laboratory
lamination
leaf bridge
lewis joint
lock paddle
locomotive
lubricator
macadamize
magnetizer
male thread
manila rope
mechanical
nodal point
paper cable
pentaspast
percolator
petrol tank
piledriver
pneumatics
powder mill
powerhouse
powerplant
programmer
pulverizer
pump handle
recondense
refraction
rejointing

resistance
revolution
safety-lamp
scoop-wheel
self-acting
skew bridge
smokestack
soap boiler
socket pipe
socket pole
solid state
spokeshave
steam gauge
streamline
structural
swing wheel
swivel hook
telegraphy
telescopic
television
telpherage
temper heat
thermopile
thermostat
torque tube
transients
transistor
tunnelling
unsoldered
voltaic arc
voltaplast
water crane
water power
watertight
water tower
waterwheel

waterworks
wave motion
well-boring
wind tunnel
wiped joint

11

accelerator
accumulator
air fountain
anelectrode
atomic clock
bell founder
bell foundry
block system
Bramah press
brush wheels
cable laying
candlepower
compression
computation
coupling box
coupling pin
damask steel
diamagnetic
dished wheel
driving band
driving belt
dynamometer
electrician
electricity
electrolyte
electrolyse
electronics
endless belt
engineering

exhaust pipe
female screw
frame bridge
graving dock
helical gear
incinerator
inking table
iron filings
iron founder
iron foundry
latten-brass
lock chamber
low pressure
lubrication
machine tool
maintenance
manila paper
manufactory
mechanician
narrow gauge
oil purifier
oil strainer
perforation
pile-driving
pillow block
pilot engine
power factor
rack-railway
rarefaction
retardation
revolutions
rolling mill
rubber cable
safety valve
searchlight
series-wound

service pipe
skeleton key
sleeve valve
socket joint
steam boiler
steam engine
steam hammer
stuffing box
stuffing nut
suction pipe
suction pump
summit level
superheater
swing bridge
switchboard
synchronism
synchronize
synchrotron
tappet valve
toggle joint
transformer
transmitter
trundle head
tube railway
underground
uninsulated
voltaic pile
vulcanizing
warping bank
water cement
water engine
water furrow
water hammer
water supply
welding heat
wind furnace

wire drawing
wire grading
workmanship
wrought iron

12

acceleration
aerodynamics
anti-friction
arterial road
artesian well
assembly line
balance wheel
belt fastener
blast furnace
block machine
block signals
buffing wheel
canalization
chain reactor
coaxial cable
counterpoise
danger signal
diamagnetism
diesel engine
differential
disc coupling
donkey engine
double acting
driving shaft
driving wheel
dry-core cable
eccentric rod
eduction pipe
electric fire
electric iron

electrolysis
electromotor
endless screw
exhaust valve
female thread
floating dock
flying bridge
flying pinion
founder's dust
founder's sand
friction gear
gas condenser
gas container
gas regulator
hanging valve
high pressure
hydraulic ram
hydrodynamic
inking roller
installation
jewel bearing
lubrifaction
machine tools
magnetomotor
marine boiler
marine engine
master spring
negative pole
non-conductor
nuclear power
oxyacetylene
petrol engine
petrol filter
plummer block
polarization
pressure pump

ratchet wheel
Réaumur scale
rolling press
rolling stock
service cable
short circuit
shunt winding
single-acting
sleeve button
solar battery
specific heat
spinning mill
stamping mill
steam heating
steam turbine
steam whistle
suction valve
synchronized
terminal post
thermocouple
toothed wheel
transmission
unmechanical
unmechanized
vibratiuncle
water turbine
wheel cutting
wheel-and-axle
working model

13

civil engineer
compound-wound
contrate wheel
control theory
Cornish engine

counterweight
direct current
draught engine
Drummond light
eccentric gear
electric cable
electric clock
electric light
electric motor
electric stove
electrifiable
electromagnet
engine-turning
expansion gear
floodlighting
fluid flywheel
friction balls
friction cones
friction wheel
injection cock
injection pipe
insulated wire
kinetic energy
lifting bridge
lubrification
magnetic fluid
magnetization
non-conducting
overshot wheel
pneumatic tyre
pontoon bridge
pressure gauge
printing press
rack-and-pinion
roller bearing
series winding

shock absorber
sniffing valve
standard gauge
telegraph line
telegraph pole
telegraph wire
telephone line
telephone wire
throttle valve
thrust bearing
water drainage
wave mechanics
whirling table

14

analog computer
blowing machine
diesel-electric
discharge valve
discharging rod
disintegration
eccentric strap
eccentric wheel
electric cooker
electric kettle
electrodynamic
electrostatics
electrothermic
explosive rivet
floating bridge
friction clutch
galvanized iron
hydraulic press
insulated cable
lubricating oil
magnetic needle

multi-core cable
nuclear reactor
pneumatic drill
portable engine
resino-electric
resultant force
shunt regulator
thermo-electric
three-core cable
traction engine
universal joint
voltaic battery
washing machine

15 AND 16

brake horsepower
concentric cable
digital computer
electric battery
electric circuit
electric current
electrification
electrochemical
electrodynamics

electrokinetics
electromagnetic
electronegative
electronic brain
electropositive
expansion engine
friction rollers
galvanic battery
hydraulic cement
insulating paper
irrigation canal
linotype machine
machine language
magnetic battery
magneto-electric
ohmic resistance
perpetual motion
pressure machine
railway engineer
smelting furnace
specific gravity
synchrocyclotron (16)
tensile strength
water-tube boiler

Instruments

2	dial	grid	meter
PC	dynamo	lancet	nozzle
	filter	laptop	octant
4–6	flange	laser	octile
	fleam	lens	orrery
abacus	funnel	lever	pole
camera	gasket	maser	probe
clock	gauge	Megger	relay

rule
ruler
scale
square
style
stylus
tester
toner
tool
trocar
tube
valve

7

aerator
ammeter
aneroid
balance
bellows
binocle
compass
counter
divider
monitor
pH meter
scriber
sextant
sundial
T-square
vernier
wetbulb

8

biograph
bioscope
bootjack

boot tree
calipers
computer
detector
diagraph
gasmeter
horologe
odometer
ohmmeter
otoscope
quadrant
receiver
recorder
rheostat
shoetree
solenoid
spy glass
udometer

9

aeolipyle
aerometer
altimeter
apparatus
arcograph
areometer
astrolabe
atmometer
auxometer
barograph
barometer
baroscope
callipers
clepsydra
compasses
condenser

dip circle
dynameter
dynometer
eidograph
eriometer
gasometer
generator
gyroscope
heliostat
hodometer
holometer
hour glass
litholabe
lithotome
logometer
magnifier
manometer
marigraph
megaphone
megascope
metronome
microtome
microtron
Nilometer
oleometer
optigraph
optometer
pedometer
periscope
polygraph
polyscope
pyrometer
pyroscope
rain gauge
rectifier
retractor

rheometer
rheoscope
rheotrope
rotameter
saccarium
scarifier
set-square
shot gauge
slide rule
steelyard
tasimeter
taximeter
telegraph
telephone
telescope
televisor
tellurion
tide gauge
voltmeter
wind gauge
zoeotrope
zymometer

10

acetimeter
acidimeter
altazimuth
anemograph
anemometer
anemoscope
angioscope
anglemeter
araeometer
astrometer
astroscope
audiometer

audiophone
binoculars
bow compass
calculator
calorifier
chiroplast
clinometer
collimator
cometarium
cryophorus
cyanometer
cyclograph
declinator
diagometer
drosometer
duplicator
ear-trumpet
elaeometer
elaiometer
endiometer
field glass
goniometer
gravimeter
heliograph
heliometer
helioscope
hydrometer
hydrophore
hydroscope
hyetograph
hyetometer
hygrometer
hygroscope
lactometer
lactoscope
macrometer

metrograph
micrometer
microphone
microscope
multimeter
multiplier
night glass
nitrometer
noctograph
ombrometer
pantagraph
pantograph
pantometer
pentagraph
phonograph
phonoscope
photometer
photophone
piezometer
plane-table
planimeter
pleximeter
protractor
pulsimeter
radiometer
respirator
rev counter
spirometer
steam-gauge
tachometer
teinoscope
theodolite
thermostat
transistor
tribometer
tuning-fork

typewriter
viscometer
voltameter
water-clock
water-gauge
water-meter

11

actinograph
actinometer
alkalimeter
auxanometer
beam compass
calorimeter
cardiograph
chlorometer
chronograph
chronometer
chronoscope
comptometer
cosmosphere
craniometer
dendrometer
depth-finder
dynamometer
graphometer
magnetophon
odontograph
optical lens
pluviometer
polarimeter
polariscope
polemoscope
pseudoscope
range-finder
salinometer

seismograph
seismometer
seismoscope
sideroscope
speedometer
spherograph
spherometer
stereometer
stereoscope
stethometer
stethoscope
teleprinter
thaumatrope
thermometer
thermoscope
transformer
transmitter
zymosimeter

12

aethrioscope
arithmometer
assay balance
averruncator
burning glass
camera lucida
chondrometer
control valve
declinometer
ductilimeter
electrometer
electrophone
electroscope
evaporometer
field glasses
galactometer

galvanometer
galvanoscope
harmonometer
inclinometer
kaleidoscope
laryngoscope
machine ruler
magnetograph
magnetometer
night glasses
opera glasses
oscillograph
parallel rule
psychrometer
reading glass
scarificator
sliding scale
spectrometer
spectroscope
sphygmometer
thermocouple
tuning hammer
weatherglass

13

alcoholometer
bubble chamber
burning mirror
camera obscura
chromatometer
diaphanometer
dipleidoscope
dipping needle
electric meter
electrophorus
esthesiometer

Geiger counter
pneumatometer
potentiometer
pressure gauge
probe scissors
pyrheliometer
refractometer
saccharometer
sidereal clock
spring balance
sympiesometer
watt-hour meter
word processor

14

aesthesiometer
air thermometer
desk calculator
geothermometer
hydrobarometer
interferometer
manifold writer
ophthalmoscope
radio telescope
sonic altimeter
torsion balance
wire micrometer

15

chemical balance
digital computer
magnifying glass
mariner's compass
solar microscope

Mathematics

2 AND 3

add
arc
cos
cot
lcd
lcm
log
map
pi
sec
set
sin
sum
tan

4

apex
area
axes
axis
base
cone
cosh
cube
cusp
edge
face
line
loci
lune
math
mean

node
null
plus
ring
root
sine
sinh
surd
term
trig
unit
zero

5

acute
angle
bevel
chord
conic
cosec
cotan
cubed
cubic
curve
digit
equal
field
focal
focus
graph
group
helix
index
lemma

limit
locus
maths
minus
plane
point
power
prime
prism
proof
radii
radix
range
ratio
rhomb
rider
solid
table
unity
value

6

abacus
binary
bisect
centre
choice
circle
conics
conoid
convex
cosine
cuboid
cyclic

degree
denary
divide
domain
equals
factor
figure
finite
height
heptad
isogon
matrix
maxima
median
minima
minute
modulo
moment
normal
number
oblate
oblong
obtuse
octant
origin
pentad
radian
radius
random
result
scalar
secant
sector
senary

series	mapping	**8**	helicoid
sphere	maximum		heptagon
square	minimum	abscissa	identity
subset	modulus	addition	infinite
tables	nothing	algorism	infinity
tensor	numeral	aliquant	integers
tetrad	numeric	analysis	integral
vector	oblique	argument	involute
vertex	octagon	binomial	isogonal
volume	octuple	bisector	mantissa
	ordinal	brackets	matrices
7	per cent	calculus	monomial
	polygon	centrode	multiple
algebra	problem	centuple	multiply
aliquot	product	circular	negative
average	prolate	codomain	new maths
bracket	pyramid	conoidal	numerary
cissoid	quinary	constant	numerate
commute	rhombic	cosecant	octonary
complex	rhombus	cube root	operator
concave	scalene	cubiform	ordinate
conical	segment	cuboidal	osculate
cubical	squared	cylinder	parabola
cycloid	subtend	diagonal	parallel
decagon	surface	diameter	pentagon
decimal	tangent	dihedral	positive
divisor	ternary	division	prismoid
ellipse	ternion	elliptic	quadrant
evolute	theorem	equation	quadrate
fluxion	totient	exponent	quadric
formula	trapeze	formulae	quantity
fractal	unitary	fraction	quartile
hexagon	unknown	frustrum	quotient
indices	vernier	function	rational
integer		geometer	repetend
inverse		geometry	rhomboid
lattice		gradient	rotation

septimal
sequence
sextuple
spheroid
subgroup
subtract
symmetry
tetragon
totitive
triangle
trigonal
trochoid
variable
vicenary
vinculum

9

algebraic
algorithm
asymptote
Cartesian
chi-square
chiliagon
compasses
corollary
cotangent
curvature
decagonal
dimension
directrix
dodecagon
duodenary
eccentric
ellipsoid
Euclidean
expansion

factorize
fluxional
frequency
geometric
hemicycle
hexagonal
hyperbola
imaginary
increment
inflexion
intersect
isosceles
logarithm
Napierian
Newtonian
numerator
numerical
octagonal
parabolic
parameter
perimeter
polygonal
polyhedra
pyramidal
quadratic
quadruple
quintuple
re-entrant
rectangle
remainder
set square
set theory
slide rule
spherical
tetragram
trapezium

trapezoid
trinomial

10

arithmetic
biquadrate
centesimal
co-ordinate
complement
concentric
continuity
conversion
decahedron
derivative
dimensions
duodecimal
eigenvalue
epicycloid
equivalent
expression
fractional
game theory
golden rule
hemisphere
heptagonal
hexahedral
hexahedron
hyperbolic
hypotenuse
hypothesis
inflection
irrational
multiplier
octahedral
octahedron
orthogonal

osculation
paraboloid
pentagonal
percentage
percentile
polyhedral
polyhedron
polynomial
proportion
protractor
quadrangle
quadratics
quadrature
quaternary
real number
reciprocal
right angle
semicircle
square root
statistics
stochastic
subtrahend
tangential
tetragonal
triangular
trilateral
versed sine

11

aliquot part
approximate
binary digit
binary scale
biquadratic
coefficient
combination

commutative
computation
coordinates
denominator
determinant
directrices
dodecagonal
eigenvector
equiangular
equidistant
equilateral
equilibrium
exponential
geometrical
Gödel's proof
heptahedron
hyperboloid
icosahedron
integration
logarithmic
mathematics
mensuration
mixed number
Möbius strip
obtuse angle
orthocentre
pentahedral
pentahedron
permutation
prime number
probability
progression
proposition
real numbers
rectangular
rectilinear

reflex angle
right-angled
round number
rule of three
sesqualter
submultiple
subtraction
symmetrical
tetrahedron
trapezoidal
Venn diagram
whole number

12

alphanumeric
common factor
conic section
decimal point
differential
dodecahedron
eccentricity
harmonic mean
intersection
least squares
long division
metric system
multilateral
multiplicand
Napier's bones
number theory
oblique angle
quadrangular
quadrinomial
semicircular
straight line
substitution

tetrahedroid
trigonometry
vernier scale

13

antilogarithm
approximation
circumference
common divisor
complementary
complex number
concentricity
differentiate
dihedral angle
exterior angle
geometric mean
golden section
interior angle
linear algebra
parallelogram
perfect number
perpendicular
plane geometry
quadrilateral

solid geometry

14 AND 15

alphanumerical (14)
arithmetic mean (14)
axis of symmetry (14)
binomial theorem (15)
cardinal number (14)
common fraction (14)
common multiple (14)
complex numbers (14)
decimal notation (15)
differentiation (15)
harmonic series (14)
imaginary number (15)
linear equation (14)
multiplication (14)
natural numbers (14)
proper fraction (14)
pure mathematics (15)
rational numbers (15)
unknown quantity (15)
vulgar fraction (14)

Minerals (including alloys, metals, ores, precious stones, rocks, etc.)

3 AND 4	coal	lead	rock	wad
	gold	Lias	ruby	wadd
alum	grit	marl	sard	zinc
bort	iron	mica	spar	
caix	jade	onyx	talc	**5**
cauk	jet	opal	trap	
clay	lava	rag	tufa	agate
				albin

alloy	barium	nosean	aphrite
argil	basalt	ophite	arsenic
baric	blende	ormolu	asphalt
beryl	bronze	osmium	axiline
borax	cannel	pelite	azurite
boron	cerite	pewter	barytes
brass	cerium	pinite	bauxite
chalk	cherty	plasma	biotite
chert	cobalt	potash	bismuth
emery	copper	pumice	bitumen
erbia	davyne	pyrite	bornite
flint	dipyre	pyrope	breccia
fluor	dogger	quartz	cadmium
Invar	egeran	radium	caesium
macle	erbium	rutile	calcite
magma	gabbro	schist	calcium
nitre	galena	schorl	caliche
ochre	gangue	silica	calomel
pitch	garnet	silver	cat's-eye
prase	glance	sinter	citrine
shale	gneiss	sodium	cuprite
silex	gypsum	speiss	cyanite
slate	halite	sphene	desmine
steel	humite	spinel	diamond
topaz	indium	thoria	diorite
trona	iolite	tombac	edenite
tutty	jargon	xylite	emerald
	jasper	yenite	epidote
6	kaolin	zircon	epigene
	kunkur		erinite
acmite	marble	**7**	euclase
albite	mesole		fahlerz
aplite	minium	adamant	fahlore
aplome	mundic	alumina	felsite
arkose	nappal	alunite	felspar
augite	nickel	anatase	fuscite
barite		apatite	

gahnite
gallium
granite
greisen
gummite
hafnium
helvite
hessite
holmium
hyalite
ice spar
iridium
jacinth
jadeite
jargoon
kainite
kernite
kyanite
lead ore
leucite
lignite
lithium
mellite
mercury
mullite
nacrite
niobium
olivine
orthite
peridot
petzite
pycnite
pyrites
realgar
red lead
rhenium

rhodium
romeine
sahlite
silicon
sinoper
sinople
sulphur
syenite
sylvite
talcite
thorite
thorium
thulite
thulium
tripoli
uranium
wolfram
wurgite
yttrium
zeolite
zeuxite
zincite
zoisite
zorgite
zurlite

8

achirite
adularia
aegirite
aerolite
allanite
alquifou
aluminum
amethyst
amiantus

analcime
analcite
andesine
andesite
ankerite
antimony
aphanite
asbestos
basanite
blue john
boracite
braunite
bronzite
brookite
calamine
calcspar
cast iron
cerusite
chabasie
chlorite
chromite
chromium
cinnabar
corundum
crocoite
cryolite
dendrite
diallage
diaspore
diopside
dioptase
dolerite
dolomite
eclogite
embolite
enargite

epsomite
essonite
euxenite
fayalite
feldspar
felstone
fireclay
fluorite
gibbsite
glucinum
goethite
graphite
hematite
hyacinth
idocrase
ilmenite
jarosite
jasponyx
konilite
laterite
lazulite
lazurite
ligurite
limonite
litharge
lomonite
lutecium
lutetium
magnesia
massicot
meionite
melanite
melilite
mesolite
micanite
mimetene

mimetite	siderite	aluminium	chondrite
monazite	smaltine	amianthus	cobaltine
mudstone	sodalite	amphibole	cobaltite
mylonite	stannite	anamesite	columbite
nemalite	steatite	andradite	cornelian
nephrite	stellite	anglesite	cornstone
noumeite	stibnite	anhydrite	dialogite
obsidian	stilbite	anorthite	diatomite
orpiment	tantalum	aphrisite	dripstone
pagodite	thallium	aragonite	dyprosium
pea stone	tin stone	argentite	earth flax
peridote	titanite	argillite	elaeolite
petalite	titanium	arquifoux	elaterite
pisolite	trachyte	asphaltum	enstatite
platinum	traprock	baikalite	erythrite
plumbago	triphane	basaltine	eucairite
porphyry	tungsten	beryllium	eudialite
prehnite	vanadium	boltonite	ferberite
psammite	vesuvian	brick-clay	fibrolite
pyroxene	voltzite	brimstone	firestone
ragstone	weissite	brown coal	fluorspar
rhyolite	wood opal	brown-spar	galactite
rock cork	wood rock	byssolite	gehlenite
rock salt	wurtzite	cairngorm	germanium
rock soap	xanthite	carbonado	glucinium
rock wood	xenotime	carbuncle	gmelinite
rubidium	yanolite	carnelian	granitite
sagenite	zirconia	carnotite	granulite
samarium		cat-silver	graywacke
sanidine	**9**	celestite	greensand
sapphire		cerussite	grenatite
sardonyx	alabaster	ceylanite	greystone
scandium	allophane	ceylonite	greywacke
selenite	almandine	chabazite	haematite
selenium	alum shale	chalybite	harmotome
siberite	alum slate	china clay	heavy spar
	aluminate		

hessonite
hornstone
indianite
ironstone
johannite
kaolinite
killinite
laccolith
lanthanum
latrobite
laumonite
lenzinite
limbilite
limestone
lodestone
magnesite
magnesium
magnetite
malachite
manganese
manganite
marcasite
margarite
marmolite
melaphyre
meteorite
mica slate
microdine
microlite
millerite
mispickel
monzonite
moonstone
moorstone
muscovite
nagyagite

natrolite
necronite
needletin
neodymium
nepheline
niccolite
noumeaite
omphacite
ozocerite
ozokerite
palladium
pargasite
pearl spar
pectolite
pegmatite
penninite
periclase
petroleum
phenacite
phenakite
phonolite
physalite
pleonaste
plinthite
potassium
proustite
pyrophane
quartzite
raphilite
rhodonite
rhombspar
rubellite
ruthenium
sandstone
satin spar
scapolite

scheelite
scolecite
scorodite
soapstone
spodumene
streamtin
strontium
sylvanite
sylvinite
tachylite
tantalite
tapiolite
tellurium
theralite
torbanite
torrelite
tremolite
tridymite
turmaline
turnerite
turquoise
uraninite
uvarovite
variscite
veinstone
vivianite
vulcanite
wavellite
wernerite
willemite
withamite
witherite
woodstone
wulfenite
ytterbium
zinc bloom

zirconium

10

actinolite
amianthoid
amygdaloid
andalusite
anthracite
apopyllite
aquamarine
aventurine
azure stone
batrachite
beudantite
bismuthite
bloodstone
bourmonite
calaverite
cannel coal
carnallite
cervantite
chalcedony
chalcocite
chalybeate
chrysolite
clinkstone
colemanite
constantan
cordierite
coupholite
cross-stone
dyscrasite
eagle stone
false topaz
floatstone
forsterite

gabbronite
gadolinium
garnierite
glauberite
glauconite
glottalite
greenstone
heterosite
heulandite
hornblende
hornsilver
hydrophane
indicolite
iridosmine
iron glance
karpholite
Kentish rag
kieselguhr
kimberlite
koupholite
laumontite
lead glance
lepidolite
liriconite
malacolite
melaconite
mica schist
mocha stone
molybdenum
Monel metal
nussierite
nuttallite
orthoclase
osmiridium
peridotite
phosgenite

phosphorus
picrosmine
polyhalite
pyrochlore
pyrolusite
pyrrhotite
redruthite
retinalite
rock butter
rose quartz
rothottite
safflorite
sapphirine
sardachate
saussurite
schalstein
serpentine
smaragdite
sparry iron
sperrylite
sphalerite
stalactite
stalagmite
staurolite
stephanite
talc schist
themardite
thomsonite
thorianite
tiavertine
topazolite
torbernite
tourmaline
triphylite
vanadinite
villarsite

vitrophyre
websterite
wolframite
zinc blende

11

alexandrite
amorthosite
amphibolite
amphiboloid
Babbit metal
black silver
brewsterite
cassiterite
cerargyrite
chondrodite
chromic iron
chrysoberyl
chrysocolla
cobalt bloom
crichtonite
crocidolite
dendrachite
diving stone
epistilbite
feldspathic
figure stone
hypersthene
Iceland spar
iron pyrites
labradorite
lapis lazuli
libethenite
molybdenite
Muschelkalk
napoleonite

needlestone
nephelinite
octahedrite
pentlandite
phillipsite
piedmontite
pitchblende
plagioclase
polymignite
pryallolite
psilomelane
pyrargyrite
pyrochroite
pyrosmalite
rock crystal
sillimanite
smithsonite
smoky quartz
sordavalite
sphaerulite
tetradymite
titanic iron
valentinite
vermiculite
vesuvianite
yttrocerite
zinnwaldite

12

aerosiderite
agalmatolite
arsenopyrite
artvedsonite
bismuthinite
chalcopyrite
cobalt glance

copper glance
feldspathoid
forest marble
fuller's earth
greyweathers
grossularite
hemimorphite
jeffersonite
kupfernickel
mineral black
mineral green
montmartrite
mountain cork
mountain flax
mountain milk
mountain soap
murchisonite
praseodymium
protactinium
puddingstone
pyromorphite
pyrophyllite
quartz schist
red sandstone
senarmontite
silver glance
skutterudite
somervillite
Spanish chalk
specular iron
speisscobalt
sprig crystal
strontianite
tetrahedrite
wollastonite
xanthoconite

13

agaric mineral
anthophyllite
chlorophaeite
cinnamon stone
cleavelandite
copper pyrites
emerald copper
kerosene shale
needle zeolite
rhodochrosite

14 AND 15

antimony glance (14)
arkose sandstone (15)
bituminous coal (14)
Britannia metal (14)
brown haematite (14)
Cairngorm stone (14)
chlorite schist (14)
elastic bitumen (14)
graphic granite (14)
hydromica schist (15)
quartz porphyry (14)

Physics

2 AND 3	cell	tube	gauss	relay
	coil	unit	henry	shell
aa	core	volt	hertz	solid
ac	dyne	watt	image	sonic
amp	flux	wave	joule	sound
bar	foci	work	laser	speed
bel	fuse	X-ray	lever	valve
emf	heat		light	weber
erg	kaon	**5**	lumen	
gas	lens		maser	**6**
lux	mach	anion	meson	
ohm	mass	anode	motor	albedo
ray	muon	curie	phase	ampere
rpm	node	cycle	pitch	atomic
uhf	phon	diode	polar	baryon
vhf	pile	earth	power	cation
	pion	farad	prism	charge
4	pole	field	quark	corona
	rays	fluid	radar	dipole
atom	spin	focus	radio	energy
beam		force		fusion

hadron
impact
isobar
kelvin
lepton
liquid
magnet
micron
moment
motion
newton
nuclei
optics
period
photon
plasma
proton
quanta
radome
sensor
torque
triode
vacuum
vector
weight

7

ammeter
aneroid
battery
beta ray
bipolar
breeder
calorie
candela
cathode

Celsius
circuit
coulomb
crystal
current
damping
decibel
density
dry cell
elastic
element
entropy
fallout
fissile
fission
gaseous
gravity
heating
hyperon
impulse
inertia
isochor
isotone
lattice
machine
maxwell
neutron
nuclear
nucleon
nucleus
nuclide
optical
orbital
physics
pi-meson
quantum

radiant
reactor
röntgen
spectra
statics
thermal
torsion
voltage
voltaic

8

adhesion
aerofoil
aerology
alpha ray
angstrom
antinode
armature
betatron
bevatron
Brownian
cohesion
constant
delta ray
detector
deuteron
dynamics
electric
electron
emission
enthalpy
filament
free fall
friction
fuel cell
gamma ray

graviton
half-life
harmonic
hologram
ideal gas
inductor
infrared
isogonic
kilowatt
kinetics
klystron
long wave
magnetic
magneton
molecule
momentum
negative
negatron
neutrino
overtone
particle
pendulum
polarity
Polaroid
positive
positron
pressure
rest mass
rheostat
roentgen
solenoid
spectrum
subshell
velocity
watt-hour
wave-form

9

acoustics
adiabatic
amplifier
amplitude
antimeson
barometer
black body
bolometer
Boyle's law
capacitor
coherence
condenser
conductor
cyclotron
electrode
frequency
gamma rays
generator
impedance
induction
insulator
isoclinic
kilohertz
Leyden jar
magnetism
magnetron
mechanics
plutonium
polarizer
potential
radiation
radio wave
real image
rectifier
resonance

resultant
short wave
spark coil
subatomic
threshold
vibration
viscosity

10

aberration
absorption
achromatic
antilepton
antimatter
antiproton
atomic mass
atomic pile
biophysics
cathode ray
centigrade
conduction
convection
cosmic rays
cryogenics
Dewar flask
dielectric
dispersion
distortion
electrical
electronic
Fahrenheit
geophysics
heavy water
horsepower
inductance
ionization

isodynamic
isothermal
kinematics
latent heat
mass number
nanosecond
nucleonics
omega meson
omega minus
oscillator
precession
reflection
refraction
relativity
resistance
ripple tank
Röntgen ray
scattering
short waves
shunt-wound
solid-state
supersonic
synchroton
thermionic
thermopile
transistor
transition
vacuum tube
wavelength
xerography
zwitterion

11

accelerator
accumulator
actinic rays

atomic clock
capacitance
capillarity
cathode rays
centrifugal
centripetal
coefficient
compression
conductance
declination
diffraction
electricity
electrolyte
electronics
falling body
fast neutron
fibre optics
focal length
gravitation
ground state
hypercharge
interaction
irradiation
nucleophile
oscillation
positronium
radioactive
resistivity
restitution
series-wound
solar energy
spectrogram
synchrotron
temperature
transformer
transuranic

ultraviolet
vacuum flask

12

acceleration
Angstrom unit
antineutrino
antiparticle
atomic energy
atomic number
atomic weight
band spectrum
beta particle
centre of mass
cloud chamber
conductivity
critical mass
deceleration
diamagnetism
disintegrate
displacement
eccentricity
electrolysis
electrophile
electroscope
geomagnetism
interference
kilowatt-hour
oscilloscope
permittivity
polarization
scintillator
selenium cell
specific heat
spectrograph
standing wave

wave equation
wave function

13

alpha particle
bubble chamber
chain reaction
critical angle
direct current
discharge tube
Doppler effect
electric field
electric motor
electric power
electromagnet
electromotive
electrostatic
ferromagnetic
gravitational
induction coil
kinetic energy
magnetic field
magnetic north
magnetic poles
paramagnetism
photoelectric
quantum number
quantum theory
radioactivity
rectification
scintillation
semiconductor
transmutation

14 AND OVER

breeder reactor (14)

Brownian
  movement (16)
cathode ray tube (14)
centre of gravity (15)
disintegration (14)
electric current (15)
electric energy (14)
electrification (15)
electromagnetic (15)
electrostatics (14)
ferromagnetism (14)
ionizing radiation (17)
nuclear physics (14)
nuclear reactor (14)
nuclear-powered (14)
Planck's constant (15)
potential energy (15)
specific gravity (15)
synchrocyclotron (16)
terminal velocity (16)
thermal capacity (15)
thermodynamics (14)
thermoelectric (14)
transformation (14)
Wheatstone bridge (16)

Poisons

4 AND 5

acid(s)
agene
bane
coca
drug
dwale
ergot
fungi
lead
lysol
nitre .
opium
toxin
upas
venom

6

alkali
antiar
cicuta
curare
heroin
iodine
ourari
phenol

7

aconite
alcohol
amanita
ammonia
aniline
arsenic

atropia
atropin
bromine
brucina
brucine
cadmium
calomel
caustic
chloral
cocaine
gamboge
henbane
mercury
ptomain
Veronal
vitriol
wourali

8

antimony
atropine
botulism
chlorine
chromium
ergotine
hyoscine
morphine
nicotine
oenanthe
Paraquat
pearl ash
phosgene
ptomaine
ratsbane

selenium

9

baneberry
barbitone
beryllium
chromates
colchicum
colocynth
croton oil
grapewort
hellebore
herbicide
mercurial
monkshood
nux vomica
potassium
rat poison
strychnia
sulphonal
toadstool
veratrine
white lead
wolf's-bane

10

antiseptic
aqua fortis
belladonna
chloroform
cyanic acid
mustard gas
nightshade
nitric acid

oxalic acid
phosphorus
picric acid
salmonella
snake venom
strychnine
thorn apple
weed-killer

11

blue vitriol
boracic acid
caustic soda
dog's mercury
hyoscyamine
insecticide
lead acetate
prussic acid
snake poison
sugar of lead

12

barbiturates
bitter almond
carbolic acid
fool's parsley
lead arsenate
lunar caustic
pharmacolite
water hemlock
white arsenic

13 AND OVER

allantotoxicum (14)
carbon monoxide (14)
carbonic oxide (13)
caustic potash (13)
deadly nightshade (16)
hydrocyanic acid (15)
meadow saffron (13)
sulphuric acid (13)
yellow arsenic (13)

Tools and simple machines
See also **Engineering** *(page 449)* and
Instruments *(page 458)*

3	gad	**4**	file	mule
	gin		fork	nail
adz	hod	adze	gage	peel
awl	hoe	bill	hook	pick
axe	jig	bore	hose	plow
bit	saw	burr	jack	pump
die	zax	celt	last	rake
dog		clam	loom	rasp
fan		crab	maul	rule

spud	level	chaser	planer
tool	lever	chisel	pliers
trug	mower	colter	plough
vice	parer	dibber	rammer
whim	peavy	dibble	ramrod
	plane	digger	rasper
5	plumb	doffer	reaper
	prong	dredge	riddle
anvil	punch	driver	rip-saw
auger	quern	fanner	roller
bench	quoin	faucet	rubber
besom	ratch	flange	sander
bevel	razor	folder	saw-set
blade	sarse	gadget	screen
borer	scoop	gimlet	scribe
brace	screw	grater	scythe
burin	sieve	graver	shaver
chuck	spade	hackle	shears
churn	spike	hammer	shovel
clamp	spile	harrow	sickle
clasp	spill	jagger	sifter
cleat	swage	jigger	skewer
cramp	tommy	jig-saw	sledge
crane	tongs	ladder	slicer
croze	wedge	laptop	spigot
cupel	winch	lister	square
dolly		mallet	strike
drill	**6**	mortar	stylus
flail		muller	tackle
forge	barrow	oil-can	tedder
gauge	beetle	oliver	tenter
gavel	blower	pallet	trepan
gouge	bodkin	peavey	trowel
hoist	bowsaw	pencil	wrench
jemmy	brayer	pestle	
knife	broach	pitsaw	
lathe	burton		

7

andiron
arc lamp
bandsaw
boaster
bradawl
buzz-saw
capstan
cautery
chopper
cleaver
cold saw
coulter
crampon
crisper
crowbar
cuvette
derrick
diamond
dog-belt
dredger
drudger
flippers
forceps
fretsaw
gradine
grainer
grapnel
grub hoe
hacksaw
handsaw
hatchet
hayfork
jointer
mandrel
mattock

nut hook
pickaxe
piercer
pincers
plummet
poleaxe
pounder
pricker
salt-pan
scalpel
scauper
scraper
scriber
scuffle
shuttle
spanner
spatula
sprayer
stapler
swingle
tenoner
thimble
toolbox
trestle
triblet
T-square
twibill
whip-saw
whittle
woolder

8

billhook
bistoury
blowlamp
boathook

butteris
calender
calipers
cant-hook
chainsaw
clippers
crow mill
crucible
die stock
dividers
dowel bit
drill bow
Dutch hoe
edge tool
filatory
flashgun
flatiron
flax comb
glass-pot
hand tool
hand-loom
hand-mill
handloom
hayknife
horsehoe
lapstone
mitre-box
molegrip
oilstone
panel saw
penknife
picklock
pinchers
plumb bob
polisher
power saw

prong-hoe
puncheon
reap hook
saw wrest
scissors
shoehorn
spray-gun
stiletto
strickle
Strimmer
tenon saw
throstle
tommy bar
tooth key
tweezers
twist bit
water-ram
weed-hook
windlass
windmill

9

baseplate
belt punch
bench hook
blow torch
can opener
cement gun
centre-bit
compasses
corkscrew
cotton gin
cramp iron
curry comb
die sinker
draw knife

draw-plate
drift bolt
drop forge
drop-drill
excavator
eyeleteer
fining pot
fly-cutter
fork-chuck
grease gun
hair-drier
hair-dryer
handbrace
handscrew
handspike
implement
jackknife
jackplane
jackscrew
lace frame
lawnmower
nail punch
nut wrench
pitchfork
plane iron
planisher
plumb-line
plumb-rule
rotary hoe
screw-jack
secateurs
shear-legs
sheep-hook
steam iron
steelyard
sugar mill

telescope
tin opener
tire lever
try-square
turn-bench
turnscrew
tyre lever
watermill
woodscrew

10

box spanner
bush-harrow
churn staff
claspknife
claw-hammer
coal shovel
cold chisel
compass saw
crane's bill
cultivator
drill-press
drop-hammer
edging tool
emery wheel
fire escape
grindstone
instrument
masonry bit
masticator
mitre block
motor mower
mouldboard
nail drawer
paintbrush
paper knife

perforator
pipe wrench
rotary pump
safety lamp
screw press
spokeshave
steam press
stepladder
tenterhook
thumbscrew
tilt hammer
trip hammer
turf cutter
turn-buckle
twist drill
watercrane
watergauge
water-level
wheel brace

11

brace-and-bit
breast-drill
cheese press
cigar cutter
circular saw
countersink
crazing-mill
crosscut saw
drill barrow
drill harrow
drill-plough
electric saw
fanning mill
glass cutter
grubbing axe

grubbing hoe
helve-hammer
machine tool
monkey block
paint roller
ploughshare
pocket knife
pruning hook
rabbet-plane
reaping-hook
sanding disc
screwdriver
scribing awl
snatchblock
spirit level
steam hammer
steam shovel
sward cutter
swing-plough
tape-measure
touch needle
turfing iron
two-foot rule
warping hook
warping post
watering can
weeding fork
weeding hook
wheelbarrow

12

branding iron
breast-plough
caulking iron
countergauge
cradle-scythe

crimping-iron
curling tongs
driving wheel
flour dresser
garden shears
glass furnace
hedge-trimmer
hydraulic ram
mandrel lathe
marlinespike
masonry drill
monkey wrench
palette knife
pruning knife
pulley blocks
rotary plough
sledgehammer
straightedge
trench plough
trying square
turfing spade
water-bellows
weeding-tongs

13

chopping block
chopping knife
cylinder press
electric drill
grappling-iron
hydraulic jack
mowing machine
packing needle
precision tool
sewing machine
soldering iron

spinning jenny
spinning wheel
stocking frame
subsoil plough
three-foot rule
weeding chisel

14

blowing machine
carding machine
draining engine
draining plough
fillister plane
pneumatic drill
reaping machine
shepherd's crook
smoothing plane
three-metre rule

15

carpenter's bench
crimping machine
dredging machine
drilling machine
entrenching tool
pestle and mortar
pump screwdriver
weighing machine

SPORTS, GAMES AND PASTIMES

2 AND 3

ace	out	bout	hold	putt
aim	pam	bowl	hole	quiz
bat	par	brag	hoop	race
bet	peg	card	hunt	reel
bid	pt	chip	I-spy	ride
bob	put	club	iron	ring
bow	rod	crew	jack	rink
box	run	crib	judo	rook
by	set	dart	king	ruff
bye	ski	deal	knur	sail
cap	tag	deck	lido	seed
cat	taw	dice	love	shot
cox	tie	dive	ludo	sice
cue	tig	draw	luge	side
cup	tir	duck	lure	skip
dan	top	duel	main	skis
die	toy	epée	mate	slam
fan	try	fall	meet	slip
go	win	faro	mime	snap
gym	won	foil	miss	solo
hit		fore	mora	spar
hop	**4**	form	Oaks	spin
jeu		foul	oars	suit
kit	ante	gaff	odds	sumo
ko	away	gala	over	swim
lap	bail	game	pace	tack
lbw	bait	gate	pack	team
let	ball	gear	pass	toss
lie	beat	goal	pawn	tote
lob	bias	golf	play	trap
loo	bike	grab	polo	trey
nap	bite	grip	pool	trip
oar	blow	hand	puck	trot
	blue	hike	punt	turf
	boat			

				6
vole	chess	kayak	scull	
volt	chips	kendo	serve	abseil
walk	clubs	knave	shoot	aikido
whip	coach	links	skate	angler
wide	court	lists	skier	archer
wing	craps	loser	skiff	ascent
wood	cycle	lotto	slice	ballet
yoga	dance	lunge	slide	banker
yo-yo	darts	match	slips	basset
	Derby	medal	smash	battue
5	deuce	miler	spade	bidder
	dicer	monte	spoon	birdie
alley	diver	no bid	sport	bishop
arena	dormy	ombre	spurt	bookie
bails	drama	Ouija	stake	bowled
bandy	drawn	pacer	stalk	bowler
basto	drive	pairs	start	bowman
baths	dummy	parry	steer	boxing
baton	evens	party	stump	brassy
bingo	event	piste	stunt	bridge
blade	extra	pitch	swing	bunker
bluff	fault	point	tarot	caddie
board	feint	poker	throw	cannon
bogey	field	prize	title	casino
bogie	fight	queen	touch	castle
bowls	final	quits	track	centre
boxer	fives	racer	train	chukka
break	fluke	rally	trial	circus
caddy	going	reins	trick	conker
canoe	grass	relay	trump	corner
capot	green	rodeo	vault	course
cards	gully	rugby	venue	crambo
carom	halma	rummy	wager	crease
catch	hobby	scent	whist	cruise
chase	joker	score	yacht	cup tie
cheat	joust	scrum		curler
check				

dealer	jigsaw	rattle	ten-pin
discus	jockey	record	tierce
diving	jumper	replay	tip-cat
domino	karate	revoke	torero
dormie	knight	riding	toss-up
driver	kung-fu	rowing	trophy
dry-fly	leg-bye	rubber	umpire
écarté	loader	rugger	venery
eleven	lobber	runner	versus
euchre	mallet	safari	victor
falcon	manege	savate	volley
fencer	marble	scorer	wicket
finish	marina	sculls	willow
gallop	marker	second	winger
gambit	mascot	see-saw	winner
gamble	mashie	shinny	xystus
gaming	mid-off	shinty	yorker
gammon	no-ball	skater	
gillie	not-out	skiing	**7**
glider	opener	ski-run	
gobang	paddle	slalom	acrobat
go-kart	peg-top	sledge	also ran
golfer	pelota	soccer	amateur
googly	piquet	soirée	ambs-ace
ground	player	sports	ames-ace
hammer	punter	sprint	angling
hazard	putter	squash	archery
header	puzzle	stakes	arm hold
hearts	quarry	stroke	athlete
hiking	quoits	stumps	average
hockey	rabbit	stymie	balloon
hooker	racing	tackle	barbell
hoopla	racket	tai chi	bathing
hunter	raffle	target	batsman
hurdle	ramble	tenace	batting
jigger	rapier	tennis	beagles
			bezique

bicycle	dribble	ju-jitsu	pinball
bidding	driving	jumping	pinocle
boating	end game	keep fit	pitcher
bowling	etching	kick off	pit stop
brassie	fairway	knock up	play off
bruiser	fan club	last lap	playing
camping	fencing	leg side	pontoon
canasta	fielder	line-out	press-up
captain	fifteen	lottery	primero
cassino	fine leg	love all	putting
century	fishing	mah-jong	rackets
charade	fixture	marbles	rebound
checker	fly half	matador	referee
chicane	forward	maypole	regatta
chukker	fowling	misdeal	reserve
circuit	fox hunt	net cord	reversi
classic	funfair	netball	rubicon
contest	gallery	niblick	running
cooncan	gambler	nine pin	sailing
counter	gliding	oarsman	St Leger
crampon	golf bag	oarsmen	scratch
cricket	golfing	offside	sculler
croquet	grounds	old maid	service
cue ball	gymnast	on guard	shot put
curling	hairpin	outdoor	shuffle
cycling	harrier	overarm	singles
cyclist	hawking	over par	skating
dancing	hunting	pachisi	ski jump
day trip	hurdler	pallone	skid lid
decider	hurling	partner	snooker
declare	ice rink	pastime	snorkel
defence	innings	pat ball	stadium
diabolo	jackpot	penalty	starter
dice-box	javelin	pharaoh	striker
discard	jogging	picador	stumped
doubles	joy-ride	picquet	sub-aqua

surfing
tilting
tinchel
tombola
top spin
tourney
trainer
trapeze
tumbler
vantage
vaulter
walking
wargame
weights
whip top
workout
wrestle

8

aerobics
aqualung
aquatics
away game
baccarat
backhand
backspin
ballgame
baseball
baseline
biathlon
boat race
body blow
boundary
bull's eye
bullring
bully off

canoeing
carnival
castling
catapult
ceramics
champion
charades
chequers
chess set
chessmen
climbing
commerce
contract
counters
coursing
crap game
cribbage
crossbar
cup final
dead heat
deck golf
delivery
dominoes
doublets
drag-hunt
draughts
dressage
dropkick
duelling
dumb-bell
eurythmy
eventing
exercise
face card
fair play
falconer

falconry
field day
fielding
finalist
firework
five pins
flat race
flippers
foot race
football
forehand
forfeits
foul play
fox hound
full back
full toss
gambling
game laws
gin rummy
goal kick
goal post
golf ball
golf club
gymkhana
gym shoes
halfback
handball
handicap
harriers
hat trick
heelkick
high jump
home game
Hula-Hoop
huntsman
hurdling

jiu-jitsu
jousting
juggling
knockout
korfball
lacrosse
leapfrog
left back
left half
left hook
left-wing
leg break
linesman
long jump
long stop
love game
lucky dip
mah-jongg
marathon
marksman
monopoly
motoring
napoleon
natation
ninepins
no trumps
off break
Olympiad
Olympics
opponent
outfield
outsider
palestra
pall-mall
patience
pétanque

ping-pong	sporting	ball games	dribbling
pinochle	stalking	beach ball	dumbbells
pintable	stock car	bicycling	equalizer
pole jump	swimming	big dipper	extra time
pony race	team game	billiards	favourite
pool room	teetotum	black belt	five-a-side
pope Joan	The Ashes	blackjack	flyweight
pugilism	third man	bob cherry	foot fault
pugilist	tie break	bobsleigh	forty–love
pyramids	toboggan	body punch	free-style
quatorze	trap ball	bull board	full house
quiz game	trial run	bull feast	game point
racegoer	tric trac	bullfight	gardening
racquets	tricycle	card trick	gate money
rambling	trotting	chair lift	go-karting
roulette	tug of war	challenge	goal posts
rounders	tumbling	checkmate	gold medal
runner-up	turf club	chess game	golf clubs
sack race	umpiring	clock golf	golf links
scrabble	underarm	clubhouse	golf shoes
sculling	uppercut	cockfight	grand prix
set point	vaulting	cockmatch	grand slam
shooting	walkover	conjuring	gumshield
short leg	wall-game	contender	gymnasium
sideline	wrestler	court card	gymnastic
skipping	yachting	cricketer	handstand
ski slope		crossword	hard court
ski stick	**9**	cupwinner	hatha yoga
skittles		cycle race	hopscotch
sledding	advantage	dartboard	horserace
sledging	agonistic	decathlon	ice hockey
snowball	anchorman	deck games	ice-skates
softball	archeress	decoy duck	joyriding
southpaw	athletics	dirt track	loose ball
sparring	Aunt Sally	dog racing	low volley
speedway	badminton	drawn game	motocross
	bagatelle		

Newmarket
nine holes
orienteer
pacemaker
palaestra
panel game
Parcheesi
pelmanism
philately
pogo stick
pole vault
pot hunter
potholing
prize-ring
punchball
quadrille
racehorse
racetrack
racing car
relay race
right half
right hook
right wing
safety net
sand yacht
schnorkel
scorecard
scrum half
semi-final
shinguard
shrimping
singleton
skin-diver
skydiving
sleighing
solitaire

solo whist
speedboat
sportsman
square-leg
stalemate
stool ball
stopwatch
stroke oar
surfboard
test match
tip and run
torch race
touchdown
touchline
trial game
trial race
trump card
turnstile
twenty-one
vingt-et-un
water jump
water polo
whipper-in
whirligig
wrestling
yacht club
yacht-race
yachtsman

10

acrobatics
aerobatics
backgammon
backstroke
ballooning
basket-ball

battledore
blood sport
booby prize
boxing ring
challenger
chessboard
clay pigeon
coconut shy
competitor
cover point
cricket bat
cup-and-ball
deck quoits
deck tennis
discobolus
doll's house
drag racing
drop volley
dumb crambo
equitation
fairground
fast bowler
feathering
field event
field sport
fishing net
fishing rod
fisticuffs
fives court
flat racing
fly-fishing
footballer
fox-hunting
goalkeeper
golf course
grandstand

greasy pole
groundbait
gymnastics
half-nelson
half volley
handspring
handy-dandy
high diving
hippodrome
hobby horse
hockey ball
hockey club
hockey team
hot cockles
humming-top
hunting box
ice dancing
ice skating
Indian club
indoor golf
injury time
inside left
isometrics
jockey club
karate chop
landing net
lansquenet
lawn tennis
masquerade
midget golf
Monte Carlo
outfielder
pancratist
pancratium
paper chase
pari mutuel

pentathlon
philopoena
playground
pot hunting
prize fight
punch drunk
queen's pawn
queen's rook
racecourse
raceground
real tennis
recreation
relaxation
riding whip
rifle range
roundabout
rowing club
rugby union
saturnalia
scoreboard
sea bathing
second half
seven-a-side
showjumper
shuffle cap
sidesaddle
silly mid-on
skateboard
ski running
skin diving
sky jumping
slow bowler
snapdragon
somersault
speed trial
spillikins

stamp album
stroke play
submission
substitute
surf riding
sweepstake
switchback
tauromachy
team spirit
tennis ball
thimblerig
thirty–love
timekeeper
title fight
tournament
trial match
twelfth man
volley ball
weighing-in
whist drive

11

accumulator
agonistical
barley-brake
baseball bat
bear baiting
bird nesting
bloodsports
bobsledding
boxing match
bronze medal
bull baiting
bumblepuppy
chariot race
chess player

close season
competition
competitive
county match
coup de grâce
crash helmet
cricket ball
cricket pads
croquet ball
croquet hoop
cup of honour
cycle racing
Derby winner
diving board
double fault
egg and spoon
eurythmics
fast bowling
field events
field sports
fifteen love
first eleven
fishing line
folk dancers
football fan
forward pass
gaming house
garden party
general post
goal-kick line
gymnasiarch
hang gliding
heavyweight
hide-and-seek
hockey match
hockey stick

home and away
horse racing
horse riding
hunt counter
hunting horn
ice yachting
inside right
inter-county
king's bishop
king's knight
league table
lightweight
love–fifteen
martial arts
motor racing
mountaineer
neck and neck
oarsmanship
outside left
penalty area
photo finish
picnic party
pillow fight
playing card
pole vaulter
pony trekking
prizewinner
quarterback
rabbit punch
race meeting
river sports
rouge-et-noir
royal tennis
rugby league
service line
show jumping

shuttlecock
sightseeing
silly mid-off
silver medal
single stick
skating rink
slot machine
slow bowling
spelling bee
spinning top
sportswoman
springboard
squash court
stag hunting
stonewaller
straight bat
sweepstakes
table tennis
tennis court
tennis match
theatre-goer
tiddlywinks
tobogganing
totalizator
touring club
toxophilite
track record
triple crown
uncontested
water skiing
water sports
whipping-top
wild-fowling
wing forward
winning post
winning side

winning team
world record
yacht racing

12

approach shot
bantamweight
batting order
billiard ball
billiard room
birdwatching
bobsleighing
body-building
bowling alley
bowling green
boxing gloves
brass rubbing
breast stroke
bullfighting
butterfly net
caber tossing
championship
changing room
climbing rope
cockfighting
consequences
crapshooting
cricket boots
cricket match
cricket pitch
cross-country
curling stone
deer stalking
double sculls
doubles match
draughtboard

drinking bout
Eton wall-game
field glasses
figure skater
first service
flying tackle
fruit machine
game of chance
gamesmanship
horsemanship
housey-housey
huntsmanship
jigsaw puzzle
level pegging
long distance
magic lantern
marathon race
medicine ball
merry-go-round
mixed bathing
mixed doubles
nursery slope
obstacle race
Olympic games
opera glasses
orienteering
paddling pool
parallel bars
parlour games
pigeon racing
pitch-and-toss
playing cards
playing field
pleasure trip
point-to-point
pole position

pole vaulting
prize fighter
prize winning
professional
putting green
pyrotechnics
Pythian games
quarter-final
queen's bishop
record holder
riding school
rock climbing
roller skates
sand yachting
scotch-hopper
second eleven
shadow boxing
shrimping net
shuffle board
singles match
skipping rope
skittle alley
starting post
state lottery
steeplechase
sticky wicket
stilt walking
swimming gala
swimming pool
table rapping
table turning
tennis player
tennis racket
theatre-going
thoroughbred
tiddleywinks

treasure hunt
trick cyclist
weightlifter
welterweight
wicket keeper
winter sports

13

aquatic sports
auction bridge
billiard table
blind man's buff
bubble blowing
callisthenics
centre-forward
chuck farthing
coarse fishing
county cricket
cribbage board
cricket ground
cricket stumps
croquet mallet
cruiserweight
double or quits
entertainment
equestrianism
featherweight
figure skating
finishing post
fishing tackle
football match
Grand National
ground-angling
half-time score
hare-and-hounds
horizontal bar

Isthmian games
kiss-in-the-ring
morris dancing
musical chairs
nursery slopes
Olympian games
parlour tricks
pillion riding
prisoner's base
prize fighting
record breaker
roller skating
roulette table
rugby football
skateboarding
spirit rapping
sports stadium
sportsmanship
squash rackets
stalking horse
starting price
steeplechaser
straight flush
ten-pin bowling
three-day event
track and field
vantage ground
vaulting horse
victor ludorum
weight lifting
wicket keeping

14

all-in wrestling
billiard marker
billiard player

children's party
coin collecting
conjuring trick
contract bridge
discus-throwing
divertissement
ducks-and-drakes
football ground
golf tournament
greyhound Derby
grouse shooting
hunt-the-slipper
hunt-the-thimble
marathon runner
master of hounds
mountaineering
opening batsman
putting the shot
record breaking
shove-halfpenny
speedway racing
squash racquets
steeplechasing
stock-car racing
thimblerigging
three-card trick
weight training
winter Olympics
wrestling match

15

ballroom dancing
bodyline bowling
cross-country run
crossword puzzle
Derby sweepstake

dirt-track racing
egg-and-spoon
  race
greyhound racing
javelin throwing

king-of-the-castle
leg before wicket
shooting gallery
sparring partner
stamp collecting

swimming
  costume
three-legged race
youth hostelling

THEATRE, OPERA, CINEMA, TELEVISION AND RADIO

2 AND 3

act
arc
ASM
BBC
bit
bow
box
cue
DVD
dub
fan
gag
ham
hit
ITV
mug
No
pan
pit
rag
rep
run
set
tag

TV
UHF
VCR
wig

4

bill
book
boom
busk
cast
clap
clip
crew
dais
diva
duet
Emmy
epic
exit
film
flop
foil
gaff
gala
gods

grid
hero
idol
joke
lead
line
live
mask
menu
mike
mime
mute
part
play
prop
rake
role
rush
shot
show
skit
sock
solo
spot
star
take

team
turn
tutu
unit
wing

5

actor
ad lib
agent
angel
apron
arena
aside
Bafta
baton
break
cable
cloth
clown
comic
debut
decor
drama
dry up
enact

exode
extra
farce
flies
focus
foyer
frame
halls
heavy
hoist
hokum
house
inset
lines
manet
mimer
mimic
movie
odeum
on cue
opera
Oscar
piece
props
radio
revue

scene
scrim
slips
sound
stage
stall
stunt
telly
usher
video
wings

6

acting
action
aerial
appear
backer
ballet
barker
big top
boards
busker
buskin
camera
Ceefax
chorus
cinema
circle
circus
claque
comedy
corpse
critic
dancer
dimmer

direct
dubbed
effect
encore
finale
floats
flyman
kabuki
lights
lyrics
make-up
masque
method
motley
movies
mummer
nautch
number
one act
on tour
parody
patron
patter
player
podium
poster
prompt
puppet
recite
repeat
return
ring up
rushes
satire
screen
script

season
serial
series
singer
sitcom
sketch
Sky One
speech
stalls
stooge
studio
talent
talkie
ticket
tights
timing
tinsel
troupe
TV show
UK Gold
viewer
walk-on
warm-up
writer

7

acrobat
actress
all-star
amateur
balcony
benefit
bit part
booking
box seat
buffoon

cabaret
callboy
cartoon
casting
catcall
catwalk
channel
charade
chorine
circuit
clapper
close-up
commère
company
compère
concert
console
costume
curtain
dancing
deadpan
diorama
dress up
drive in
dubbing
fan club
fantasy
farceur
feature
film set
gallery
heroine
ingenue
juggler
leg show
leotard

long run	sponsor	clapping	juvenile
maillot	stadium	clowning	libretto
manager	stagery	coliseum	lighting
matinée	staging	comeback	live show
mimicry	stand-in	comedian	location
mummery	stardom	conjurer	magician
musical	starlet	costumer	male lead
mystery	support	coulisse	morality
network	tableau	crush bar	newsreel
new wave	talkies	designer	offstage
on stage	theatre	dialogue	operatic
overact	tragedy	director	operetta
pageant	trailer	disguise	overture
perform	trilogy	dramadoc	parterre
phone-in	Trouper	dramatic	pastoral
Pierrot	tumbler	dumb show	peep show
players	upstage	duologue	pictures
playing	variety	entr'acte	pit stall
playlet	vehicle	entrance	platform
pop star	viewing	epilogue	playbill
portray	western	exit Line	playgoer
prelude		farceuse	première
present	**8**	fauteuil	producer
preview		festival	prologue
produce	applause	figurant	prompter
program	arthouse	film crew	protasis
re-enact	artistry	film star	quiz show
recital	audience	film unit	rehearse
reciter	audition	Film Four	ring down
resting	backdrop	filmgoer	scenario
revival	bioscope	first act	set piece
rostrum	blackout	funny man	showbill
royalty	Broadway	ham actor	side show
scenery	burletta	interval	smash hit
show biz	carnival	jongleur	stagebox
showman	chat show	juggling	star turn
	Cinerama		

straight
stripper
subtitle
tapedeck
telecast
teletext
thespian
third act
tragical
travesty
typecast
wardrobe
wigmaker

9

acoustics
animation
announcer
Artsworld
backcloth
backstage
bandstand
barnstorm
bit player
blue movie
box office
broadcast
burlesque
cameraman
character
chorus boy
cinematic
Classic FM
clip joint
cloakroom
Columbine

conjuring
costumier
coulisses
criticism
cyclorama
discovery
docudrama
double act
downstage
dramatics
dramatist
dramatize
drop scene
entertain
exhibitor
figurante
film actor
film extra
filmstrip
first lead
flashback
floorshow
folk dance
footlight
full house
gala night
gogglebox
green room
guest star
Harlequin
home movie
impromptu
interlude
limelight
love scene
low comedy

major role
melodrama
minor role
monodrama
monologue
movie-goer
movie star
music hall
night club
noises off
orchestra
panel game
pantaloon
pantomime
performer
photoplay
Pierrette
pit-stalls
play-actor
playhouse
portrayal
programme
projector
promenade
prompt-box
publicity
punch-line
quartette
recording
rehearsal
repertory
represent
second act
sight line
Sky Sports
slapstick

soap opera
soliloquy
soubrette
spectacle
spectator
spotlight
stage door
stage left
stage play
stagehand
stage-name
take a part
tap dancer
teledrama
title role
tormentor
tragedian
usherette
voiceover
wisecrack

10

afterpiece
appearance
auditorium
chorus girl
clapper-boy
comedienne
comedietta
comic opera
commercial
continuity
coryphaeus
crowd scene
denouement
disc jockey

THEATRE, OPERA, ETC. 499

drag artist
drama group
dramaturge
dramaturgy
fantoccini
film house
film script
first house
first night
floodlight
footlights
get the bird
high comedy
hippodrome
histrionic
horror film
horse opera
impresario
in the round
in the wings
intermezzo
junior lead
lap dancing
leading man
legitimate
librettist
marionette
masquerade
microphone
minstrelsy
movie actor
music drama
newscaster
newsreader
on location
opera buffa

opera house
performing
play-acting
playwright
prima donna
production
prompt-book
properties
proscenium
Pulcinella
puppet-show
rave notice
rave review
recitation
repertoire
repetiteur
ringmaster
screenplay
silent film
soundtrack
stage fever
stage right
stagecraft
star player
striptease
substitute
sword-dance
tap dancing
tear-jerker
television
theatre box
theatrical
torch dance
travelogue
understudy
variety act

vaudeville
walk-on part
widescreen

11

accompanist
all-star cast
art director
balletomane
barnstormer
black comedy
broadcaster
cap and bells
charity show
Cinemascope
circus-rider
cliff-hanger
comedy drama
comic relief
commentator
concert hall
credit title
curtain call
cutting room
dance troupe
documentary
drama critic
drama school
dramatic art
dress circle
electrician
entertainer
equilibrist
exeunt omnes
feature film
film theatre

fire curtain
folk dancing
funambulist
greasepaint
Greek chorus
histrionics
house lights
illusionist
impersonate
kitchen-sink
leading lady
legerdemain
light comedy
matinée idol
method actor
miracle play
off-Broadway
opera bouffe
opera singer
pantomimist
Passion play
performance
picture show
problem play
protagonist
psychodrama
Punchinello
scene change
set designer
set the scene
showmanship
show-stopper
sound effect
spectacular
stage design
stage effect

stage fright
stage player
stage school
stage-struck
star billing
star quality
star vehicle
star-studded
straight man
stripteaser
strobe light
talent scout
Technicolor
terpsichore
thaumaturgy
theatregoer
theatreland
theatricals
thespian art
tragedienne
tragicomedy
trick riding
unrehearsed
upper circle
variety show
ventriloquy
wind-machine
word-perfect

12

academy award
actor-manager
amphitheatre
cinema studio
clapperboard
concert party

costume drama
credit titles
digital radio
dramaturgist
dressing-room
exotic dancer
extravaganza
film director
film festival
film producer
first-nighter
grand guignol
harlequinade
impersonator
introduction
juvenile lead
make-up artist
melodramatic
method acting
minstrel show
modern ballet
morality play
name in lights
natural break
opera glasses
orchestra pit
picture house
principal boy
Punch and Judy
puppet-player
scene-painter
scene-shifter
scene-stealer
screenwriter
scriptwriter
show business

silver screen
song and dance
sound effects
stage manager
stage whisper
standing room
starring role
steal the show
stock company
straight part
top of the bill
World Service

13

burlesque show
cine projector
cinematograph
contortionist
curtain-raiser
dance festival
emergency exit
entertainment
musical comedy
Nouvelle Vague
pantomime dame
projectionist
remote control
safety curtain
sleight-of-hand
sound engineer
stage lighting
studio manager
thaumaturgics
theatre school
ventriloquist
video cassette

video recorder
volume control

14 AND 15

acrobatic troupe (15)
cable television (15)
character actor (14)
classical ballet (15)
continuity girl (14)
dancing academy (14)
domestic comedy (14)
dramatic society (15)
dress rehearsal (14)
features editor (14)
gala performance (15)
incidental music (15)
orchestra stalls (15)
property master (14)
proscenium arch (14)
revolving stage (14)
school of acting (14)
school of dancing (15)
shooting script (14)
situation comedy (15)
slide projector (14)
smoking concert (14)
sound-projector (14)
stage carpenter (14)
stage direction (14)
stage properties (15)
strolling player (15)
supporting cast (14)

TIME (INCLUDING SPECIFIC DATES, PERIODS, SEASONS, ANNUAL FESTIVALS, ETC.)

(H.)=Hindu; (I)=Islam; (J.)=Jewish months (variously spelled); (R.)=Roman

2–4

AD
Ab (J.)
Adar (J.)
aeon
age
ages
ago
AM
BC
BST
date
dawn
day
dusk
Elul (J.)
eon
Eos
era
ere
eve
ever
fall
fast
GMT
Holi (H.)
hour
Ides (R.)

Iyar (J.)
July
June
last
late
Lent
May
morn
Noel
noon
now
NS
oft
old
once
OS
past
PM
slow
soon
span
term
then
tick
tide
time
week
when
Xmas

year
yore
Yuga (H.)
Yule

5

after
again
alway
April
bells
brief
clock
cycle
daily
dated
delay
diary
early
epact
epoch
Fasti (R.)
flash
horal
jiffy
Kalpa (H.)
later
March
matin

month
never
night
Nisan (J.)
nonce
nones
of old
often
passé
pause
prime
prior
Purim (J.)
quick
reign
short
Sivan (J.)
so far
spell
sunup
teens
Tevet (J.)
times
today
trice
until
watch
while
years

young	latest	Sunday	diurnal
youth	latish	sunset	dog days
6	Lenaea	Tammuz (J.)	earlier
	May Day	Tebeth (J.)	elapsed
actual	memory	termly	endless
always	mensal	timely	epochal
annual	midday	Tishri (J.)	equinox
August	minute	to date	estival
autumn	modern	ultimo	eternal
before	moment	update	etesian
betime	Monday	vernal	evening
brumal	morrow	vesper	extinct
coeval	New Age	weekly	fast day
curfew	o'clock	whilom	fête day
decade	off-day	whilst	for ever
Diwali (H.)	old age	winter	half-day
dotage	pay-day	yearly	harvest
Easter	period		Heshvan (J.)
elapse	prewar	**7**	high day
extant	pro tem		holiday
faster	prompt	ageless	holy day
feriae	pronto	almanac	instant
ferial	rarely	already	interim
Friday	recent	ancient	Iron Age
future	record	antique	January
gnomon	rhythm	archaic	journal
heyday	season	bedtime	jubilee
hiemal	second	belated	Kalends
hourly	seldom	betimes	lady day
Ice Age	Shebat (J.)	by and by	long ago
Jet Age	slower	Calends (R.)	long run
Julian	slowly	century	lustrum
Kislev (J.)	sooner	chiliad	midweek
Lammas	spring	Chisleu (J.)	monthly
lapsed	sudden	current	morning
lately	summer	dawning	new moon
		daytime	

New Year
nightly
noonday
October
overdue
postwar
proximo
quartan
quarter
quicker
quickly
quintan
quondam
Ramadan (I.)
regency
rent day
sabbath
shortly
sine die
slowest
some day
sundial
sundown
sunrise
tea time
teenage
tertian
Thammuz (J.)
time gun
time lag
timeous
time was
tonight
Tuesday
undated
wartime

weekday
weekend
Whitsun
workday
Xmas day

8

aestival
annually
antecede
antedate
anterior
biannual
biennial
bimensal
birthday
biweekly
blue moon
calendar
carnival
chiliasm
chiliast
date line
daybreak
day by day
deadline
December
Dionysia
dogwatch
domesday
doomsday
duration
earliest
eggtimer
enduring
Epiphany

estivate
eternity
eventide
evermore
every day
feast day
February
festival
fleeting
forenoon
formerly
frequent
futurist
futurity
Georgian
gloaming
half-hour
half-past
half-term
half-time
half-year
Hannukah
  (J.)
hibernal
high noon
high time
hitherto
Hogmanay
holidays
Holy Week
infinity
in future
in no time
in season
interval
keep time

kill time
last time
last week
lateness
latterly
leap year
lifelong
lifespan
lifetime
long time
Lord's Day
lose time
make time
mark time
mealtime
meantime
medieval
menology
midnight
minutely
natal day
New Style
next week
noon-time
noontide
November
nowadays
oft-times
Old Style
old times
Olympics
our times
overtime
Passover (J.)
past time
periodic

postdate	aforetime	hard times	Pentecost
postpone	afternoon	hereafter	perennial
previous	afterward	hodiernal	permanent
punctual	all at once	honeymoon	postponed
quickest	anciently	hourglass	premature
right now	antedated	immediacy	presently
Saturday	antiquity	immediate	quarterly
se'nnight	bimonthly	in the past	quick time
seasonal	Boxing Day	indiction	quotidian
seed time	Bronze Age	instantly	recurrent
semester	Candlemas	interlude	regularly
sidereal	centenary	latterday	right away
sometime	childhood	lean years	Saint's day
Space Age	Christmas	light year	salad days
speedily	chronicle	local time	September
Stone Age	clepsydra	long since	sexennial
suddenly	continual	long-lived	short-term
temporal	decennary	longevity	sometimes
Thursday	decennial	lunar year	spare time
timeless	decennium	lunchtime	speech day
tomorrow	diurnally	market day	spend time
twilight	Easter Day	Martinmas	time flies
until now	Edwardian	matutinal	timepiece
untimely	Ember days	menstrual	times past
up to date	ephemeral	metronome	timetable
vacation	ephemeris	middle age	transient
weeklong	erstwhile	midsummer	triennial
whenever	eternally	midwinter	trimester
yearbook	feast days	night-time	Victorian
yearlong	flexitime	nightfall	waste time
Yuletide	forthwith	nightlong	Wednesday
zero hour	fortnight	octennial	whole time
	fruit time	out of date	yesterday
9	Golden Age	overnight	Yom Kippur
	Gregorian	past times	(J.)
Adar Shani	Halloween	peace time	
(J.)			

10

afterwards
All Hallows
Anno Domini
antecedent
anticipate
at all times
before long
before time
beforehand
behind time
biennially
bimestrial
break of day
bygone days
centennial
chiliastic
chronogram
chronology
close of day
continuous
days of yore
dinner time
Easter term
Easter time
estivation
evanescent
Father Time
frequently
Good Friday
half-yearly
hebdomadal
henceforth
Hilary term
historical
immemorial

in good time
isochronal
Lammastide
lunar cycle
lunar month
Lupercalia
Michaelmas
Middle Ages
millennium
nick of time
occasional
oftentimes
olden times
Palm Sunday
posthumous
prehistory
present day
quarter day
Quirinalia
record time
ripe old age
Saturnalia
seasonable
septennial
sexagesima
sextennial
Shrovetide
solar month
springtime
summer term
summertime
synchronal
Theban year
thereafter
time enough
timekeeper

time server
time signal
transitory
triple time
ultimately
unpunctual
vespertine
watch night
wedding day
Whit Monday
Whit Sunday
wintertime
working day
yesteryear

11

adolescence
All Fools' Day
All Souls' Day
anachronism
anniversary
antecedence
antemundane
anteriority
Bacchanalia
Bank Holiday
behindtimes
bicentenary
bygone times
chronograph
chronometer
closing time
continually
cosmic clock
crack of dawn
cuckoo clock

day and night
day in day out
Elizabethan
everlasting
fashionable
fin de siècle
fortnightly
good old days
half holiday
harvest home
harvest time
hebdomadary
immediately
interregnum
isochronism
isochronous
Judgment Day
lapse of time
leisure time
little while
long-lasting
march of time
millenarian
modern times
never-ending
New Year's Day
New Year's Eve
night and day
Passion Week
perennially
perpetually
point of time
prehistoric
prematurely
present time
prime of life

pudding time
punctuality
quadrennial
quartz clock
sands of time
seeding time
settling day
synchronism
synchronize
synchronous
tempus fugit
thenceforth
time and tide
time bargain
time to spare
Tudor period
twelvemonth
ultramodern
waiting time
Whitsuntide

12

afterthought
All Saints' Day
antediluvial
antediluvian
antemeridian
anticipation
Armistice Day
Ascension Day
Ash Wednesday
auld lang syne
betrothal day
bicentennial
carbon dating
Christmas Day

Christmas Eve
contemporary
continuously
course of time
duodecennial
early closing
Easter Sunday
eleventh hour
following day
Midsummer Day
Midsummer Eve
occasionally
old-fashioned
once in a while
post-diluvian
postmeridian
postponement
postprandial
Quadragesima
quinquennial
red-letter day
Rogation days
Rosh Hashanah (J.)
sidereal year
simultaneous
standard time
synchronized
tercentenary
time and again
time-honoured
time will tell
tricentenary
tropical year
Twelfth Night
unseasonable

13

All Hallowmass
All Hallowtide
April Fools' Day
breakfast time
calendar month
Christmastide
Christmastime
chronological
everlastingly
every other day
golden jubilee
golden wedding
holiday season
lunisolar year
Michaelmas Day
once upon a time
Passion Sunday
retrospective
St Swithin's Day
Shrove Tuesday
silver jubilee
silver wedding
summer holiday
thenceforward
Trinity Sunday
vernal equinox

14 AND 15

behind the times (14)
biological clock (15)
early closing day (15)
early Victorian (14)
Holy Innocents'
    Day (16)
in the nick of time (15)

Julian calendar (15)
lunisolar cycle (14)
Maundy Thursday (14)
Michaelmas term (14)
Mothering Sunday (15)
once in a blue moon (15)
once in a lifetime (15)
quatercentenary (15)
Remembrance Day (14)

Rogation Sunday (14)
sabbatical year (14)
St Valentine's Day (15)
synchronization (15)
synodical month (14)
Thanksgiving Day (15)
tomorrow morning (15)
Walpurgis night (14)
world without end (15)

TRANSPORT
Aviation and space travel

3 AND 4	knot	wash	drift	Airbus
	land	wind	filer	airman
ace	lane	wing	flaps	airway
air	leg	yaw	float	basket
bank	lift	york	glide	beacon
bay	loop	zoom	jumbo	bomber
bump	mach		pitch	camber
buzz	nose	**5**	plane	canard
car	prop		prang	cruise
crew	rev	aloft	pylon	cut out
dive	rib	apron	radar	drogue
dope	roll	bends	range	fabric
drag	slip	blimp	rev up	flight
fin	slot	cabin	rigid	floats
flap	span	cargo	slots	flying
fly	spar	chock	stall	gas-bag
fuel	spin	chord	strut	glider
gap	tail	cleat	stunt	hangar
gas	taxi	climb	valve	intake
hull	trim	craft		jet set
jet	UFO	crash	**6**	jet-lag
kite	veer	crate		launch
		ditch	aerial	

module
nose-up
octane
piston
ram jet
refuel
rocket
rudder
runway
Skylab
yawing

7

aerobus
aileron
air base
aircrew
airdrop
airflow
air foil
air jump
air lane
airlift
airline
airport
air rage
air taxi
air-raid
airsick
airsock
aviator
bale out
ballast
balloon
banking
biplane

birdman
bomb bay
capsule
ceiling
charter
chassis
chopper
clipper
cockpit
compass
contact
co-pilot
cowling
descent
ejector
emplane
fairing
fighter
flyover
flypast
gliding
gondola
helibus
hostess
inflate
jump-jet
landing
lift-off
Mae West
milk run
nacelle
nose-cap
on board
pancake
payload
Pioneer

re-entry
ripcord
shuttle
sponson
Sputnik
steward
tailfin
take-off
taxiing
Trident
Tristar
twin jet
Voyager
wingtip

8

aerodyne
aerofoil
aeronaut
aerostat
air brake
air force
air route
airborne
aircraft
airfield
airframe
airliner
airplane
airscrew
airspace
airspeed
airstrip
airwoman
altitude
anhedral

approach
autogiro
aviation
aviatrix
ballonet
black box
bomb-rack
buoyancy
carousel
Concorde
corridor
cruising
dihedral
elevator
envelope
flat spin
fuel pipe
fuselage
grounded
gyrostat
heliport
in flight
intercom
jet pilot
jet plane
joystick
jumbo jet
kamikaze
long-haul
moonshot
near miss
non-rigid
nose-cone
nosedive
nose down
pitching

pulse-jet
radiator
seaplane
sideslip
spaceman
squadron
stopover
subsonic
tail-skid
tailspin
tail unit
terminal
throttle
triplane
turbofan
turbojet
twin-tail
volplane
warplane
wind cone
windsock
wing-flap
Zeppelin

9

aerodrome
aeroplane
air bridge
air intake
air pocket
airworthy
altimeter
amphibian
astrodome
astronaut
autopilot

cabin crew
cosmonaut
countdown
crash-land
delta-wing
dirigible
doodlebug
empennage
fuel gauge
gyroplane
jet bomber
launching
launch pad
longerons
low-flying
monocoque
monoplane
navigator
nosewheel
overshoot
parachute
power dive
propeller
rudder bar
sailplane
satellite
semi-rigid
short-haul
sonic boom
spacecrew
spaceship
spacesuit
spacewalk
stability
stratojet
sweepback

swing-wing
tailplane
taxiplane
test pilot
touch down
turboprop
twin-screw
wind gauge

10

aerobatics
aero-engine
aeronautic
aerostatic
air balloon
air control
air defence
air hostess
air service
air steward
air support
air traffic
airfreight
anemometer
ballooning
balloonist
cantilever
cargo plane
Challenger
dive bomber
flight deck
flight path
flight plan
flying boat
fuel intake
ground crew

helicopter
hydroplane
jet fatigue
jet fighter
landing run
Mach number
microlight
outer space
oxygen mask
pathfinder
pilot error
pilot plane
robot plane
rudder-post
slipstream
solo flight
spacecraft
space probe
splashdown
stabilizer
stewardess
supersonic
test flight
turbulence
V-formation

11

aeronautics
aerostatics
afterburner
air corridor
air terminal
air umbrella
blind flying
combat plane
ejector seat

flying speed
free balloon
ground speed
hand luggage
heat barrier
heavy bomber
kite-balloon
laminar flow
landing deck
landing gear
leading edge
loop the loop
moon landing
mooring-mast
ornithopter
parachutist
radio beacon
retractable
retro-rocket
sesquiplane
slotted wing
soft landing
space centre
space flight
space rocket
space travel
stabilizers
stunt flying
vapour trail
weather-vane

12

aerodynamics
air ambulance
airfreighter
air–sea rescue

arrester gear
beacon lights
belly landing
control stick
control tower
crash landing
ejection seat
fighter pilot
flying circus
flying saucer
gliding-angle
hedge-hopping
jet-propelled
landing field
landing light
landing speed
landing strip
launching pad
Lunar Orbiter
maiden flight
manned rocket
night fighter
pilot balloon
pressure suit
pursuit plane
radar scanner
radial engine
reverse thrust
sound barrier
space capsule
space shuttle
space station
space vehicle
trailing edge

13 AND OVER

air stewardess (13)
aircraft-carrier (15)
airworthiness (13)
control-column (13)
cruising speed (13)
decompression (13)
dihedral angle (13)
engine-mounting (14)
escape velocity (14)
excess luggage (13)
fighter-bomber (13)
flight recorder (14)
forced landing (13)
ground control (13)

heavier-than-air (14)
in-line engines (13)
jet propulsion (13)
lighter-than-air (14)
looping the loop (14)
radio-location (13)
semi-retractable (13)
shock-absorber (13)
space traveller (14)
stalling-speed (13)
Stratocruiser (13)
troop-transport (14)
undercarriage (13)
vertical take-off (15)
weightlessness (14)

Boats and ships
See also **Nautical terms** (*pages 522–532*)

3 AND 4		5		6
ark	koff	aviso	ketch	argosy
bark	MTB	balsa	liner	banker
boat	pair	barge	praam	barque
brig	pram	canoe	Q-ship	bateau
buss	proa	coble	razee	bawley
cog	punt	cogge	scull	bireme
dhow	raft	craft	shell	caique
dory	saic	dandy	skiff	carvel
duck	scow	E-boat	sloop	coggle
four	ship	eight	smack	cutter
gig	snow	ferry	tramp	decker
hoy	sub	fleet	U-boat	dinghy
hulk	TBD	float	umiak	dogger
junk	tub	funny	whiff	dugout
keel	tug	kayak	xebec	galeas
	yawl		yacht	

galley
gallot
hooker
hopper
launch
lorcha
lugger
mistic
oomiak
packet
pedalo
pirate
PT boat
puffer
randan
sampan
sealer
settee
slaver
tanker
tartan
tender
trader
vessel
whaler
wherry

7

bumboat
caravel
carrack
carrier
catboat
clinker
clipper
coaster

cockler
collier
coracle
corsair
cruiser
currach
curragh
dredger
drifter
drogher
dromond
felucca
flivver
four-oar
frigate
galleon
galliot
gondola
gunboat
gunship
ice-boat
lighter
man-o'-war
minisub
mistico
monitor
mud-scow
pair-oar
pinnace
piragua
pirogue
polacca
polacre
pontoon
rowboat
sculler

shallop
steamer
tartane
towboat
trawler
trireme
tugboat
warship

8

bilander
car ferry
coalship
cockboat
corvette
dahabeah
dahabiya
derelict
eight-oar
fireboat
fire-ship
flagship
flat-boat
galleass
galliass
gallivat
hoveller
ice yacht
Indiaman
ironclad
keelboat
lifeboat
longboat
mailboat
man-of-war
sailboat

schooner
showboat
steam-tug
surf-boat
trimaran
waterbus
well-boat

9

bomb-ketch
bucentaur
cable ship
canal boat
cargo boat
catamaran
depot ship
destroyer
ferryboat
freighter
frigatoon
guard boat
guard ship
horse boat
houseboat
hydrofoil
jollyboat
lightship
minelayer
motorboat
oil tanker
outrigger
pilot boat
powerboat
privateer
prize ship
river boat

sand yacht
sheer-hulk
ship's boat
slave ship
speedboat
steamboat
steamship
storeship
submarine
transport
troopship
two-decker
whale-boat

10

banana boat
barkentine
battleship
bomb vessel
brigantine
cattleboat
cockleboat
four-master
hovercraft
hydroplane
icebreaker
monkey-boat
motor yacht
narrow-boat
nuclear sub
ocean liner
ore-carrier
packet-boat
paddleboat
patrol boat
picket boat

pirate ship
prison ship
quadrireme
repair-ship
rivercraft
rowing boat
royal barge
small craft
supply ship
survey ship
tea-clipper
train ferry
turret ship
victualler
Viking ship
watercraft
windjammer

11

barquentine
bulk carrier
capital ship
chasse-marée
cockleshell
dreadnought
factory ship
fishing boat
luxury liner
merchantman
minesweeper
motor launch
motor vessel
naval vessel
pilot cutter
prize vessel
quinquereme

racing shell
sailing boat
sailing ship
sardine boat
slave-trader
steam launch
submersible
supertanker
three-decker
three-master
torpedo boat

12

cabin cruiser
despatch boat
East Indiaman
escort vessel
fishing smack
heavy cruiser
hospital ship
landing barge
landing craft
light cruiser
merchant ship
pleasure boat
police launch
sailing barge
sailing craft
square-rigger
stern-wheeler
supply vessel
survey vessel
training ship
tramp steamer
troop carrier

13

battlecruiser
container ship
double-sculler
four-oared boat
paddle-steamer
passenger-boat
passenger-ship
sailing vessel
ship-of-the-line
trading vessel
transport

14 AND 15

aircraft-carrier (15)
cable-laying ship (15)
cable-repair ship (15)
channel steamer (14)
coasting vessel (14)
eight-oared boat (14)
flotilla leader (14)
seaplane tender (14)
submarine chaser (15)
torpedo-gunboat (14)
victualling ship (15)

Motoring

2 AND 3

AA
air
bhp
cc
cam
can
cap
car
cog
fan
fit
GT
gas
hp
hub
jam
jet
key
lap
lug
map
MOT
nut
oil
pin
pit
RAC
rev
rim
rod
run
ton
top

4

axle
belt
body
bolt
boot
boss
bulb
bush
clip
coil
cowl
dash
disc
door
drum
flat
fuse
gate
gear
hood
hoot
horn
idle

jack
lane
lock
nail
park
pink
plug
pump
road
roll
rope
seat
skid
sump
tail
tank
test
tire
tour
tube

tyre
veer
wing

5

apron
brake
cable
chain
chart
choke
clamp
coupé
cover
crank
cut in
drive
float
frame
gauge

	6	lock-up	bus stop
joint		louvre	carpark
knock	adjust	mascot	carport
lay-by	air bag	milage	cat's eye
level	big end	mirror	chassis
lever	bonnet	octane	contact
model	bumper	oilcan	control
motor	bypass	one-way	cooling
on tow	camber	petrol	dipping
pedal	car tax	pile-up	drive-in
rally	charge	pinion	driving
rev up	clutch	piston	exhaust
rivet	cut out	rebore	fan belt
rotor	dazzle	saloon	flyover
route	de luxe	signal	gearbox
scale	decoke	spokes	give way
screw	de-icer	spring	goggles
sedan	detour	swerve	gudgeon
servo	dickey	switch	hardtop
shaft	divert	tappet	highway
shift	driver	timing	joyride
spark	dynamo	torque	L-driver
speed	engine	tow bar	licence
spoke	fender	tuning	linkage
squab	fitter	winker	locknut
stall	flange		log book
start	funnel	**7**	L-plates
stick	garage		luggage
ton up	gasket	air hose	magneto
tools	grease	airlock	map-case
tread	grille	axle-box	mileage
U-turn	handle	battery	misfire
valve	hooter	bearing	missing
wheel	hot rod	blowout	mixture
wiper	hub cap	bollard	MOT test
works	idling	build-up	muffler
	klaxon	bus lane	

no entry
non-skid
off-road
offside
oil seal
oil-feed
parking
pillion
pinking
pull out
reverse
road tax
roadhog
roadmap
rolling
run into
seizing
service
skidpan
spindle
springs
starter
test run
toolkit
top gear
touring
towrope
traffic
trailer
viaduct
warning
wingnut

8

air brake
air inlet

airtight
armature
arterial
Autobahn
back seat
backfire
bodywork
brake pad
brake rod
camshaft
cat's eyes
clearway
coasting
converge
coupling
crankpin
cruising
cul-de-sac
cylinder
declutch
delivery
dipstick
driveway
fast lane
fastback
feed pipe
feed pump
flat tyre
flywheel
foglight
footpump
freezing
friction
fuel pipe
fuel tank
garaging

gasoline
gradient
guide-rod
handpump
ignition
inlet cam
knocking
lead-free
manifold
missfire
motoring
motorist
motorway
mudguard
nearside
oil gauge
oncoming
open road
overhaul
overpass
overtake
overturn
pavement
prowl car
puncture
radiator
rattling
rear axle
rear lamp
ring road
road rage
road sign
road test
roadside
roofrack
rotor arm

rush hour
seat belt
side road
sideslip
silencer
skid mark
skidding
slip road
slow down
slow lane
speeding
squad car
steering
stock car
tail skid
tailgate
taxi rank
throttle
tire pump
track rod
turnpike
two-speed
tyre pump

9

air filter
alignment
anti-glare
autoroute
back wheel
ball-valve
batteries
bench seat
brake drum
brake shoe
breakdown

bus driver
cab driver
car driver
car polish
chain-link
chauffeur
clearance
coachwork
concourse
condenser
cotter pin
crank axle
crankcase
crossroad
cutting in
dashboard
dashlight
defroster
dipswitch
direction
dirt track
disc brake
diversion
drum brake
estate car
filler cap
footbrake
framework
free-wheel
front axle
front seat
fuel gauge
gear lever
generator
Grand Prix
grease-box

grease-gun
guarantee
handbrake
hatchback
headlight
hit-and-run
indicator
inner tube
insurance
limousine
lubricate
monocoque
motorbike
motorcade
motor show
nipple key
oil engine
oil filter
overdrive
oversteer
passenger
patrol car
petrol can
piston rod
point duty
police car
prop shaft
racing car
radial-ply
rear light
reflector
revving up
road block
road sense
road works
saloon car

sidelight
side-valve
spare tire
spare tyre
spark plug
speed bump
sports car
spotlight
stoplight
switch off
T-junction
tail-light
taximeter
third gear
tire lever
tramlines
trunk road
two-seater
two-stroke
tyre lever
underpass
underseal
wheel spin
wheelbase
white line

10

access road
adjustment
alternator
amber light
anti-dazzle
antifreeze
bevel-wheel
bottom gear
box-spanner

brakeblock
brake fluid
brakelight
brake pedal
broken down
bucket seat
car licence
coachbuilt
combustion
commutator
crankshaft
crossroads
detonation
dickey seat
drive shaft
dry battery
fluid drive
four-seater
four-stroke
front wheel
gear casing
gear change
green light
gudgeon pin
headlights
horsepower
inlet valve
insulation
lighting up
low-tension
lubricator
mileometer
motorcycle
overtaking
petrol pump
petrol tank

piston ring
private car
radial tire
radial tyre
rear mirror
rev-counter
right of way
roadworthy
roundabout
safety belt
signalling
spare wheel
speed limit
streamline
suspension
tachograph
tachometer
third-party
three-speed
toll bridge
touring car
traffic cop
traffic jam
two-wheeler
upholstery
ventilator
wheelbrace
windscreen
wing mirror

11

accelerator
accessories
accumulator
anti-roll bar
blind corner

brake lining
built-up area
carburetter
carburettor
carriageway
clutch pedal
compression
convertible
crash helmet
de-luxe model
decarbonize
distributor
driving seat
driving test
exhaust pipe
exhaust port
feeler-gauge
front lights
Highway Code
ignition key
interrupter
lorry driver
lubrication
luggage rack
motor spirit
needle-valve
number plate
oil pressure
overhauling
overheating
over-revving
owner-driver
petrol gauge
pre-ignition
racing model
radiator cap

request stop
reverse gear
reverse turn
rotary valve
screen-wiper
self-starter
sliding roof
speed camera
speed limits
speedometer
splashboard
sports model
streamlined
synchromesh
tappet valve
thermometer
through road
ticking over
trafficator
traffic sign
vacuum brake
valve-timing
wheel wobble

12

acceleration
approach road
arterial road
ball-bearings
breakdown van
car insurance
clutch-spring
coachbuilder
contact-screw
countershaft
cylinder head

diesel engine
differential
driving wheel
driving-chain
driving-shaft
exhaust valve
float-chamber
freewheeling
gear changing
hazard lights
lock-up garage
miles per hour
motorcyclist
motor scooter
motor vehicle
parking light
parking meter
parking place
petrol filter
pillion rider
racing driver
ratchet-wheel
registration
repair outfit
road junction
running-board
sparking plug
starter motor
steering gear
sunshine roof
supercharger
traffic light
transmission
turbocharger
two-speed gear
warning light

13

breakdown gang
connecting rod
cooling system
driving mirror
fluid flywheel
fuel injection
hydraulic jack
induction pipe
inspection pit
licence-holder
overhead valve
petrol station
pillion-riding
power steering
pressure-gauge
rack-and-pinion
roller-bearing
servo-assisted
shock absorber
shooting brake
speed merchant
steering wheel
traffic island
traffic signal
traffic warden

14

adjusting-screw
circuit-breaker
compression tap
contact-breaker
double-declutch
driving licence
exhaust-cam axle
filling station

four-wheel drive
friction-clutch
hydraulic brake
grease-injector
lighting-up time
lubricating oil
luggage-carrier
miles per gallon
off-road vehicle
propeller shaft

reclining seats
service station
starting handle
steering column
third-party risk
three-speed gear
traffic calming
universal joint

15

carriage-builder
front-wheel drive
dual carriageway
instrument panel
insurance policy
reversing lights
road-fund licence
seating capacity
windscreen wiper

Nautical terms

2 AND 3	jib	yaw	crew	grog
	lay		deck	hank
AB	lee	**4**	dive	hard
A1	log		dock	haul
aft	man	ahoy	down	haze
bay	nut	alee	dune	hazy
bow	oar	back	east	head
box	ply	bale	eddy	helm
cat	ram	beam	fake	hold
cay	rig	beat	flag	hove
CIF	RM	bend	floe	hulk
con	RN	bitt	flow	jack
cox	rum	boom	foam	junk
ebb	run	bows	fore	keel
fid	sag	brig	foul	knot
FOB	sea	bunk	frap	land
fog	set	bunt	furl	last
gam	SOS	buoy	gaff	lead
guy	tar	calk	gale	leak
HMS	top	calm	gang	line
hog	tow	coak	gear	list
jaw	way	comb	girt	load
		cott		

loof	sink	after	cleat	ligan
luff	skid	ahead	craft	lurch
mast	slip	ahull	crank	metal
mess	spar	aloft	cuddy	misty
mine	stay	apeak	davit	naval
mist	stem	aport	depth	north
mole	step	atrip	diver	oakum
moor	surf	avast	douse	ocean
navy	swab	awash	downs	order
neap	tack	beach	dowse	orlop
oars	taut	belay	draft	pitch
peak	tend	below	embay	prick
pier	tide	berth	entry	prize
poop	tilt	bight	flake	radar
port	toss	bilge	fleet	radio
prow	trim	block	float	range
punt	trip	board	fluke	refit
quay	veer	bosun	foggy	rhumb
raft	waft	bouse	gauge	roads
rail	wake	bower	grave	ropes
rake	warp	bowse	gusty	route
rank	wave	brace	hands	rower
rate	wear	brail	hatch	royal
rear	west	bream	haven	sally
reef	whip	briny	hawse	salve
ride	winch	cabin	hitch	salvo
road	wind	cable	hoist	screw
roll	wing	cadet	horse	sheer
rope	yard	canal	hound	sheet
rove	yarn	cargo	jetty	shelf
rung		caulk	kedge	shoal
sail	**5**	chain	kevel	shore
sand		chart	lay to	siren
scud	aback	check	lay up	skeet
seam	abaft	chock	leaky	sling
ship	abeam	clamp	leech	sound
	afoul			

spirit	bridge	kedger	piston
steer	bumkin	lading	pooped
stern	bunker	lateen	poppet
storm	burton	launch	purser
surge	cablet	lay-off	rating
swell	canvas	league	ratlin
thole	careen	leeway	reefed
tidal	comber	Lloyd's	reefer
trice	convoy	locker	rigged
truck	course	manned	rigger
truss	crotch	marina	rocket
waist	cruise	marine	rudder
watch	crutch	marker	sailor
weigh	debark	maroon	saloon
wharf	diving	marque	salute
wheel	double	masted	salvor
windy	earing	mayday	sculls
woold	embark	mizzen	sealer
wreck	engine	moored	seaman
	ensign	mutiny	seaway
6	escort	needle	sennit
	fathom	offing	sheets
aboard	fender	on deck	shroud
adrift	fo'c'sle	outfit	signal
afloat	for'ard	paddle	sinker
anchor	fother	parcel	sinnet
armada	funnel	patrol	splice
ashore	furled	paunch	squall
astern	galley	pay off	square
aweigh	gasket	pay out	stocks
awning	gunnel	pennon	stormy
bargee	halser	Pharos	strake
batten	hawser	pillow	strand
beacon	hove-to	pintle	stream
becket	jetsam	piracy	tackle
billow	jigger	pirate	tender
bonnet			

thwart
tiller
timber
toggle
towage
unbend
unbitt
uncoil
undock
unfurl
unlade
unload
unmoor
unship
vessel
voyage
yawing

7

aground
athwart
backing
bale out
ballast
beached
bearing
beating
boarder
bobstay
bollard
boomkin
bowline
bow wave
boxhaul
bracing
breaker

bulwark
bunting
buoyage
caboose
calking
can-buoy
capsize
capstan
captain
cast off
catfall
cathead
cat's-paw
channel
charter
claw off
coaling
cockpit
compass
conning
cordage
corsair
counter
cresset
cringle
cyclone
dead-eye
deep-sea
degauss
dismast
dockage
dog-vane
dolphin
draught
dry dock
dunnage

ease off
ebb tide
embargo
eye-bolt
fairway
fishery
flotsam
fogbank
foghorn
foretop
forward
founder
freight
freshen
freshet
frogman
futtock
gangway
gimbals
go about
go below
grapnel
grating
graving
grommet
grummet
gudgeon
gun-deck
gun-port
gun-room
gunnage
gunwale
guy-rope
half pay
halyard
harbour

harpoon
haul off
head off
head sea
headway
heave to
horizon
iceberg
icefloe
inboard
inshore
Jack Tar
jib boom
jibstay
keelage
keelson
landing
laniard
lanyard
lashing
lastage
latches
leaking
lee-gage
lee side
lee tide
leeward
listing
loading
logbook
log-line
log-reel
lookout
low tide
lugsail
maintop

mariner
marines
marline
marling
matelot
mistral
monsoon
moorage
mooring
mudhook
oarsman
oceanic
old salt
on board
outport
oversea
painter
pennant
pooping
port-bar
quayage
rafting
rations
ratline
reefing
ride out
rigging
rip tide
rollers
rolling
rope-end
rostrum
rowlock
run down
sailing
salvage

scupper
scuttle
sea-card
seafolk
sea-lane
sealegs
sea-mark
sea mile
sea room
seasick
seaward
set sail
sextant
shallow
shelves
shipper
shipway
shrouds
sick-bay
sinking
skipper
skysail
slipway
spanker
spencer
squally
stand-by
steward
stopper
stowage
tacking
tactics
tempest
thimble
tonnage
top deck

top mast
topsail
topside
tornado
torpedo
towline
towpath
towrope
transom
trysail
tsunami
typhoon
unladen
unsling
unslung
veering
waftage
ward off
warping
wavelet
wet dock
whistle
wrecked
wrecker
yardarm

8

anchored
aplustre
approach
armament
at anchor
aweather
backstay
backwash
barbette

bargeman
barnacle
beam-ends
bearings
becalmed
berthage
berthing
binnacle
boat-deck
boathook
bolt-rope
bowsprit
broach to
bulkhead
bulwarks
buntline
castaway
caulking
claw away
clubhaul
coamings
coasting
coxswain
crossing
cruising
cutwater
dead slow
dead-wood
deckhand
derelict
ditty-bag
ditty-box
dockyard
dog watch
dog-shore
doldrums

doubling	jackstay	midships	sandbank
downhaul	jettison	moorings	scudding
drifting	jury mast	moulinet	seaborne
easterly	keel over	mutineer	sea-chest
eastward	keelhaul	mutinous	seafarer
even keel	land ahoy!	nautical	seagoing
fife-rail	land wind	navigate	sea-rover
flag-rank	landfall	neap tide	shallows
floating	landmark	ordnance	shark-net
flotilla	landsman	outboard	sheer off
fogbound	landward	overrake	ship ahoy
foot-rope	larboard	overseas	ship oars
forefoot	lead-line	paravane	shipmate
foremast	leeboard	periplus	shipment
forepeak	lee gauge	picaroon	shipping
foresail	lee shore	pierhead	shipworm
foreship	lifebelt	pilotage	shipyard
forestay	lifebuoy	plimsoll	sounding
forewind	lifeline	poop deck	spy-glass
free-port	load-line	porthole	squadron
gaffsail	loblolly	portside	stand off
go aboard	long haul	pratique	standard
go ashore	low water	pumproom	staysail
hard alee	magazine	put about	steerage
hatchway	main boom	put to sea	sternway
head into	main deck	quarters	stowaway
head wind	mainmast	reef-knot	stranded
headfast	mainsail	re-embark	streamer
helmless	mainstay	ride easy	stunsail
helmsman	mainyard	ride hard	submerge
high seas	make sail	roadster	tackling
high tide	maritime	sail-loft	tafferel
hornpipe	martinet	sail-room	taffrail
hull-down	masthead	sail-yard	thole-pin
icebound	mastless	salvable	tranship
icefield	messmate	salvager	traverse

unbuoyed	beaconage	flying jib	north wind
uncoiled	below deck	foreshore	northerly
under way	bilge-keel	foundered	northward
underset	bilge-pump	free-board	northwind
unfurled	blue peter	gangboard	ocean lane
vanguard	boardable	gangplank	orlop deck
wall-knot	boat drill	gather way	outrigger
wardroom	broadside	groundage	overboard
waterman	bunkering	half-hitch	parbuckle
water-rot	captaincy	hard aport	periscope
waterway	careenage	high water	pilot boat
waveworm	chartered	hoist sail	pilot flag
welldeck	chartroom	holystone	press-gang
west wind	close haul	house-flag	privateer
westerly	coastwise	houseline	prize-crew
westward	companion	hurricane	promenade
windlass	corposant	jack-block	quicksand
windrode	cross-jack	jack-staff	recharter
windsail	crosswind	kentledge	reckoning
windward	crow's nest	land ahead	Red Ensign
woolding	Davy Jones	lobscouse	reef-point
wreckage	dead-water	lower deck	refitment
yachting	deck cargo	loxodrome	revictual
	demurrage	maelstrom	rhumb-line
9	departure	mainbrace	roadstead
	disanchor	mainsheet	rockbound
about-ship	discharge	manoeuvre	royal mast
admiralty	disembark	midstream	Royal Navy
affreight	doggerman	minefield	rum-runner
afterdeck	dress ship	minute-gun	sailcloth
air-funnel	drift-sail	mizzentop	seafaring
all aboard	driftwood	naumachia	sea-letter
alongside	false keel	navicular	sea-robber
amidships	firedrill	navigable	seaworthy
anchorage	flood-tide	navigator	semaphore
anchoring	floodmark	neptunian	sheathing
bargepole			shipboard

shipowner	unlighted	cross-piece	liberty-man
ship's crew	upper deck	crosstrees	life-jacket
shipshape	water-line	deadlights	lighterage
shipwreck	water-sail	degaussing	lighthouse
shoreward	whirlwind	diving-bell	lookout-man
sick-berth	wind-bound	dockmaster	loxodromic
sidelight	wring-bolt	downstream	manoeuvres
sight land	yachtsman	drop anchor	marker buoy
sou'wester		drop astern	martingale
south wind	**10**	embarkment	middle deck
southerly		engine room	midshipman
southward	A1 at Lloyd's	escutcheon	mizzenmast
spindrift	aboard ship	fathomless	mizzensail
spinnaker	after-guard	fiddle-head	mizzenstay
spritsail	after-hatch	figurehead	navigating
stanchion	after-sails	fore-and-aft	navigation
starboard	alongshore	forecastle	night watch
stateroom	anchor buoy	forge ahead	ocean-going
steersman	anchor hold	freightage	orthodromy
stemfast	anchorable	freshwater	parcelling
sternmost	astarboard	frostbound	pilot house
sternpost	ballasting	full-rigged	pipe aboard
stokehold	batten down	gaff-rigged	port of call
storm-beat	Bermuda rig	harbourage	powder-room
stormsail	bilgewater	harness tub	prize-court
stormstay	Blue Ensign	heavy-laden	prize-money
stretcher	bluejacket	high-and-dry	quarantine
tarpaulin	bootlegger	jigger-mast	raking fire
telescope	breakwater	Jolly Roger	reduce sail
tide-table	cargo space	jury-rigged	rendezvous
tophamper	cast anchor	jury rudder	reshipment
trade wind	casting-net	landlocked	rope-ladder
twin-screw	catch a crab	landlubber	round-house
two-decker	chainplate	lateen sail	rudder post
unballast	charthouse	lateen yard	rudderless
uncharted	coal-bunker	lay a course	seamanlike
	cork jacket		

seamanship
ship-broker
shipmaster
ship-rigged
shipwright
signalling
skyscraper
slack-water
spring tide
square-sail
stanchions
stay-tackle
stern-board
stern-frame
sternsheet
submariner
supercargo
take in sail
tally-clerk
thwartship
tidal basin
tidal river
tiller-rope
topgallant
unfathomed
unfordable
upper works
water-borne
waterspout
watertight
wheel-house

11

abandon ship
anchor light
beachcomber

belaying pin
captainship
centre-board
chafing-gear
close-hauled
compass card
compass rose
contact mine
debarkation
depth-charge
dismastment
diving bell
diving suit
dock charges
echo-sounder
embarcation
embarkation
escape hatch
foam-crested
fore-topmast
foul weather
gallows-tops
get under way
go alongside
graving-dock
groundswell
harbour dues
harness-cask
hug the shore
keelhauling
landing deck
lifeboatman
loblolly boy
main-topmast
main-topsail
make headway

marine store
mess steward
middle watch
monkey-block
naval rating
orthodromic
paddle wheel
port charges
port of entry
press of sail
quarterdeck
range-finder
reconnoitre
riding-light
sailing date
St Elmo's fire
Samson's post
searchlight
seasickness
sheet anchor
shipbreaker
ship's doctor
ship's papers
sliding keel
snatchblock
sounding-rod
south-wester
spring a leak
standing off
steerage-way
stern-chaser
sternsheets
storm signal
three-masted
thwartships
tidal waters

torpedo tube
unballasted
unchartered
under canvas
under-masted
unnavigable
unnavigated
unsheltered
unsoundable
waterlogged
weathermost
weatherside
weigh anchor
white ensign

12

air-sea rescue
between-decks
bill of lading
breeches-buoy
cable's-length
canvas length
caulking iron
change course
collision-mat
companionway
conning tower
counterbrace
displacement
double-banked
double-manned
equinoctials
fishing fleet
floating dock
futtock-plate
ground-tackle

hard-aweather
jack-o'-lantern
Jacob's ladder
lateen-rigged
line of battle
longshoreman
magnetic mine
maiden voyage
man overboard
marine boiler
marine engine
marlinespike
measured mile
minesweeping
mizzen course
nautical mile
naval command
navigability
orthodromics
outmanoeuvre
outward-bound
Plimsoll line
Plimsoll mark
privateering
recommission
ride at anchor
ship-chandler
shipping line
ship's husband
slack in stays
sounding lead
sounding line
spanking boom
spilling line
square-rigged
starboard bow

studding sail
tourist class
training ship
transhipment
Trinity House
undercurrent
unfathomable
weatherboard
weatherbound
weather-gauge
weatherglass
westerly wind
will-o'-the-wisp

13

affreightment
cat-o'-nine-tails
close quarters
compass signal
dead reckoning
deck passenger
fishing-tackle
floating light
grappling-iron
high-water mark
hurricane deck
life-preserver
mizzen rigging
naval dockyard
naval ordnance
navigableness
northeast wind
northerly wind
northwest wind
order of battle
press of canvas

re-embarkation
royal dockyard
ship's articles
ship-of-the-line
southeast wind
southerly wind
southwest wind
spilling lines
starboard beam
starboard side
steering-wheel
weather report

14

circumnavigate
compass bearing
disembarkation

dolphin striker
futtock shrouds
hard astarboard
horse latitudes
letter-of-marque
Lloyd's Register
naval architect
powder magazine
prevailing wind
running rigging
schooner rigged
screw-propeller
ship's-carpenter
superstructure
swivel-rowlocks
topgallant mast

15

Admiralty Office
circumnavigable
command of
  the sea
companion ladder
Davy Jones' locker
loxodromic curve
marine insurance
mariner's compass
operation orders
victualling yard

Vehicles

2–4	drag	luge	tram	coach
	dray	MG	trap	coupé
Audi	duck	mini	tube	crate
auto	Fiat	Opel	van	cycle
bier	fly	pram	wain	float
biga	Ford	PSV	Yugo	Honda
bike	gig	RV	**5**	Lexus
BMW	heap	Saab		lorry
BMX	HGV	Seat	araba	Lotus
bogy	JCB	shay	artic	Mazda
bus	Jeep	skis	bogey	moped
cab	jet	sled	bogie	motor
car	Lada	SUV	brake	pulka
cart	limo	tank	buggy	Rover
DAF	loco	taxi	chair	sedan

Skoda
sulky
tonga
train
truck
Volvo
wagon

6

Austin
banger
barrow
Berlin
bowser
boxcar
calash
camper
chaise
Daiwoo
diesel
digger
dodgem
doolie
drosky
engine
fiacre
go-cart
hansom
hearse
hot rod
hurdle
Jaguar
jalopy
jingle
jitney
Lancia

landau
limber
litter
Model-T
Morgan
Morris
Nissan
oxcart
Proton
saloon
sledge
sleigh
Sno-Cat
spider
Subaru
surrey
Suzuki
tandem
tanker
tender
tipper
tourer
Toyota
troika
waggon
whisky

7

Amtrack
autobus
autocar
balloon
Bentley
bicycle
bob-sled
britzka

Bugatti
caboose
cacolet
caravan
caravel
cariole
caroche
chariot
chopper
Citroën
Daimler
dogcart
droshky
flivver
fourgon
growler
gyrocar
hackery
hackney
hardtop
haywain
Hyundai
kibitka
mail car
mail-van
minibus
minicab
off-road
omnibus
pedrail
Peugeot
phaeton
Porsche
Pullman
railcar
Reliant

Renault
scooter
sidecar
taxicab
tilbury
tipcart
tractor
trailer
tramcar
trishaw
Triumph
trolley
trundle
tumbrel
turnout
vis-à-vis
voiture

8

aircraft
barouche
brake van
brancard
britzska
brougham
buck cart
cable car
Cadillac
carriage
carriole
carry-all
carrycot
Chrysler
clarence
curricle
dustcart

equipage
fleet car
golf cart
goods van
handcart
horse car
ice-yacht
jetliner
mail-cart
monorail
motorbus
motorcar
old crock
pushbike
pushcart
quadriga
rally car
rickshaw
roadster
rockaway
runabout
sociable
staff car
stanhope
stock car
toboggan
tricycle
unicycle
Vauxhall
victoria
Zeppelin

9

aeroplane
Alfa Romeo
ambulance

amphibian
applecart
bandwagon
bath-chair
boat-train
bobsleigh
box-wagon
bubblecar
bulldozer
cabriolet
charabanc
Chevrolet
diligence
dining car
dodgem car
Dormobile
estate car
funicular
guard's van
half-track
hansom cab
hatchback
ice skates
intercity
Land Rover
landaulet
limousine
low loader
mail-coach
mail-train
milkfloat
motorbike
motorcade
muletrain
palanquin
prison van

racing car
rail coach
saloon car
sand yacht
sports car
streetcar
stretcher
tarantass
tin lizzie
two-seater
wagonette
water-cart

10

automobile
beach buggy
Black Maria
boneshaker
conveyance
donkey-cart
fire-engine
four-in-hand
freight van
goods train
goods truck
goods wagon
hackney cab
handbarrow
hovercraft
invalid cab
jinricksha
juggernaut
knockabout
locomotive
luggage van
motor lorry

motorcoach
motorcycle
pedal cycle
pony engine
post-chaise
Pullman car
Range Rover
removal van
Rolls-Royce
sedan chair
smoking car
snowmobile
snowplough
spacecraft
spring-cart
stagecoach
state coach
tip-up lorry
touring car
tramway-car
trolley-bus
trolley-car
troop train
velocipede
Volkswagen
waggonette
wagon train
war chariot
wheelchair

11

armoured car
brewer's dray
bullock cart
Caterpillar
convertible

delivery van
fire balloon
four-wheeler
goods waggon
gun-carriage
horse-lifter
jaunting-car
jinrickshaw
landaulette
magic carpet
mail phaeton
sleeping car
steam engine
steamroller
three-in-hand
transporter
waggon train
wheelbarrow

12

baby carriage
coach-and-four
coach-and-pair
covered wagon
double decker
freight train
furniture van
hackney coach
horse and cart
invalid chair
Mercedes-Benz
motor scooter
mountain bike
pantechnicon
perambulator
railway train

single decker
station wagon
three-wheeler
troop carrier
watering-cart

people carrier
shooting brake

14 AND 15

ambulance wagon (14)
bathing-machine (14)
hackney carriage (15)
invalid carriage (15)
luggage trailer (14)
passenger train
prairie-schooner (15)
railway carriage (15)
refrigerated van (15)
traction engine (14)

13

ambulance cart
covered waggon
electric train
fork-lift truck
governess cart
mourning-coach
penny-farthing

WARFARE
Air force ranks and appellations: British and US

2–4

FO
LAC
WAAF
WRAF

5

major (US)
pilot

6

airman
fitter
rigger

7

aviator
captain (US)
colonel (US)
general (US)
private (US)

8

armourer
corporal
mechanic
observer
sergeant

9

air gunner
bomb aimer
drum-major
navigator

10

air marshal
apprentice
balloonist
bombardier (US)
nose gunner
rear gunner
tail gunner

11

aircraftman
air mechanic
belly gunner
second pilot

12

air commodore
group captain
major general (US)
pilot officer

13

flying officer
master aircrew
sergeant major (US)
staff sergeant (US)
wing commander

14

air vice marshal
flight engineer
flight mechanic
flight sergeant
master sergeant (US)
squadron leader
warrant officer

15

air chief marshal
chief technician
first lieutenant (US)

16 AND OVER

brigadier general (US) (16)
flight lieutenant (16)
junior technician (16)
leading aircraftman (18)
second lieutenant (US) (16)
senior aircraftman (17)

Battles and sieges

3 AND 4			
Acre	Ivry	Taku	Anzio
Aden	Jena	Tet	Arcot
Agra	Kiev	Trak	Arras
Alma	Kut	Uhm	Basra
Amoy	Laon	Yser	Boyne
Caen	Loos	Zama	Bulge
Gaza	Lys		Cadiz
Guam	Maas	**5**	Cairo
Hué	Metz	Aduwa	Crécy
	Mons	Aisne	Crete
	Nile	Alamo	Delhi

			7
Douai	Amiens	Mantua	
Douro	Arbela	Midway	Aboukir
El Teb	Argaon	Mileto	Abu Klea
Eylau	Armada	Minden	Alamein
Genoa	Arnhem	Moscow	Albuera
Herat	Assaye	Mukden	Algiers
Ipsus	Atbara	Nagpur	Alkmaar
Issus	Bagdad	Narvik	Almansa
Kabul	Barnet	Naseby	Almeida
Kandy	Bataan	Nicaea	Antioch
Kursk	Berlin	Oporto	Antwerp
Liège	Burgos	Orthez	Badajoz
Ligny	Busaco	Ostend	Baghdad
Luzon	Calais	Peking	Bapaume
Maida	Camden	Plevna	Bautzen
Malta	Campen	Quebec	Bousaco
Marne	Cannae	Rabaul	Brienne
Meuse	Chusan	Rhodes	Britain
Miami	Coruña	Rivoli	Bull Run
Paris	Dargai	Rocroi	Cambrai
Patay	Delium	Sadowa	Cape Bon
Pusan	Dunbar	Saigon	Cassino
Rhine	Ferrol	Saints	Chalons
Sedan	Ghazni	Shiloh	Coimbra
Selle	Guarda	Tarifa	Colenso
Sluys	Havana	Tobago	Cordova
Somme	Isonzo	Tobruk	Coronel
Tagus	Jattoo	Toulon	Corunna
Texel	Jhansi	Towton	Dresden
Tours	Lützen	Tudela	Dunkirk
Valmy	Madras	Tugela	Edghill
Ypres	Madrid	Ushant	El Obeid
	Majuba	Verdun	Erzurum
6	Málaga	Vienna	Falkirk
	Maldon	Wagram	Flodden
Actium	Manila	Warsaw	Granada
Aleppo			

Gujerat
Gwalior
Iwo Jima
Java Sea
Jutland
Kharkov
Khe Sanh
La Hogue
Leipzig
Lemberg
Lepanto
Leuthen
Lucknow
Magdala
Magenta
Marengo
Matapan
Megiddo
Minorca
Moselle
Moskowa
Nam Dong
Nations
Newbury
Nivelle
Okinawa
Orleans
Plassey
Poltava
Preston
St Kitts
St Lucia
Salamis
Salerno
Sobraon
Solebay

Taranto
Vimeiro
Vitoria
Wimpfen

8

Antietam
Ardennes
Atlantic
Ayacucho
Bastille
Beresina
Bhurtpur
Blenheim
Borodino
Bosworth
Calcutta
Carthage
Cawnpore
Coral Sea
Culloden
Drogheda
Ebro Riva
Edgehill
Flanders
Flushing
Fontenoy
Fort Erie
Freiburg
Granicus
Hastings
Hydaspes
Inkerman
Jemappes
Kandahar
Khartoum

Lake Erie
Le Cateau
Lobositz
Mafeking
Malakoff
Marathon
Maubeuge
Medellin
Messines
Metaurus
Montreal
Navarino
Nieuport
Normandy
Omdurman
Overlord
Philippi
Poitiers
Potidaea
Pretoria
Przemysl
Rossbach
St Albans
St Mihiel
St Pierre
Salsette
Saratoga
Smolensk
Spion Kop
Stirling
Suvla Bay
Syracuse
Talavera
Tiberias
Toulouse
Tsushima

Valencia
Waterloo
Yorktown
Zaragoza

9

Abukir Bay
Algeciras
Arginusai
Balaclava
Barcelona
Belle Isle
Bergendal
Bluff Cove
Caporetto
Caxamarco
Chaeronea
Champagne
Charleroi
Ctesiphon
Dettingen
El Alamein
El Mansura
Falklands
Festubert
Friedland
Gallipoli
Gaugamela
Gibraltar
Hyderabad
Jerusalem
Kasserine
Kimberley
Ladysmith
Laing's Nek
Leningrad

540 BATTLES AND SIEGES

Leyte Gulf
Louisburg
Magdeburg
Mauritius
Melagnano
Mobile Bay
Nashville
Oudenarde
Pharsalus
Port Mahon
Princeton
Ramillies
Rodriguez
St Quentin
St Vincent
Salamanca
Saragossa
Sedgemoor
Singapore
Solferino
Stormberg
Stromboli
Tarragona
Tourcoing
Trafalgar
Vicksburg
Vimy Ridge
Wakefield
Walcheren
Waterberg
Waterloo
Worcester
Zeebrugge

10

Adrianople
Ahmednagar

Alexandria
Appomattox
Austerlitz
Brandywine
Brownstown
Bunker Hill
Camperdown
Cerro Gordo
Chevy Chase
Copenhagen
Corregidor
Dogger Bank
Fort George
Gettysburg
Gravelotte
Guadeloupe
Heligoland
Imjin River
Isandlwana
Kut-el-Amara
La Rochelle
Les Saintes
Malplaquet
Martinique
Montevideo
Montfaucon
New Orleans
Nördlingen
Paardeburg
Petersburg
Port Arthur
Porto Praya
Quatre Bras
River Plate
Sevastopol
Shrewsbury

Stalingrad
Tannenberg
Tel-el-Kebir
Tewkesbury
Tinchebray

11

Bannockburn
Bismarck Sea
Breitenfeld
Bunker's Hill
Cape Matapan
Chattanooga
Chilianwala
Dardanelles
Dien Bien Phu
Fort Niagara
Guadalcanal
Hohenlinden
Isandhlwana
Jameson Raid
Londonderry
Marston Moor
Masulipatam
Modder River
Pearl Harbor
Philiphaugh
Philippines
Pieter's Hill
Pondicherry
Port Stanley
Prestonpans
Quiberon Bay
Rorke's Drift
Schoneveldt
Thermopylae

Ticonderoga
Vinegar Hill

12 AND OVER

Antietam Creek (13)
Battle of Britain (15)
Bloemfontein (12)
Cape St. Vincent (13)
Cedar Mountain (13)
Chalgrove Field (14)
Chancellorsville (16)
Ciudad Rodrigo (13)
Constantinople (14)
Delville Wood (12)
Falkland Islands (15)
Flodden Field (12)
Fredericksburg (14)
Fuentes de Oñoro (14)
Harper's Ferry (12)
Killiecrankie (13)

Lake Champlain (13)
Little Bighorn (13)
Magersfontein (13)
Mariana Islands (14)
Messines Ridge (13)
Neuve Chapelle (13)
Neville's Cross (13)
Passchendaele (13)
Philippine Sea (13)
Plains of Abraham (15)
San Sebastian (12)
Seringapatam (12)
Solomon Islands (14)
Spanish Armada (13)
Stamford Bridge (14)
Trichinopoly (12)
Tsushima Strait (14)
Vittorio Veneto (14)
White Mountain (13)

Military ranks and appellations

2 AND 3

ADC
ATS
CO
CSM
GI
MP
NCO
OC
RA
RE

RSM
RTO
SAS

4

naik
para
peon
RAOC
REME
WAAC
WRAC

Zulu

5

cadet
fifer
Jäger
Jerry
major
piper
poilu
scout
sepoy

sowar
spahi
Tommy
Uhlan

6

archer
askari
batman
bomber
bowman
bugler

cornet
driver
ensign
gunner
Gurkha
hetman
hussar
lancer
marine
ranger
ranker
sapper
sutler
yeoman
Zouave

7

captain
colonel
Cossack
dragoon
drummer
farrier
flanker
general
hoplite
jemadar
lancers
marines
marshal
militia
officer
orderly
pikeman
pioneer
private

recruit
redcoat
regular
reserve
saddler
samurai
sappers
soldier
subadar
trooper
vedette
veteran
warrior

8

adjutant
armourer
bandsman
cavalier
chasseur
commando
corporal
decurion
deserter
doughboy
dragoons
fencible
fugelman
fusilier
havildar
infantry
janizary
Landwehr
marksman
messmate
muleteer

mutineer
partisan
rifleman
sentinel
sergeant
spearman

9

beefeater
berserker
brigadier
cannoneer
cannonier
centurion
combatant
commander
conscript
drum-major
estafette
field rank
fife-major
grenadier
guardsman
guerrilla
Home Guard
irregular
Janissary
junior NCO
lance-naik
lifeguard
man-at-arms
musketeer
paymaster
pensioner
pipe-major
Roundhead

senior NCO
signaller
subaltern
tactician
town major
tradesman
trumpeter
vexillary
voltigeur
volunteer

10

aide-de-camp
bandmaster
bombardier
carabineer
cavalryman
commandant
cuirassier
drummer-boy
file-leader
footguards
halberdier
instructor
Lansquenet
lieutenant
Life Guards
militiaman
other ranks
paratroops
roughrider
serviceman
skirmisher
strategist

11

arquebusier
artillerist
auxiliaries
bashi-bazouk
bersaglieri
condottiere
crack troops
crossbowman
enlisted man
gendarmerie
horse guards
infantryman
Landsknecht
moss-trooper
parachutist
paratrooper
Tommy Atkins
top sergeant

12

armour-bearer
artilleryman
brigade-major
camp follower
ensign-bearer
field marshal
field officer
horse soldier
major-general
master gunner
officer cadet
PT instructor
Royal Marines
Royal Signals
sharpshooter

staff officer
storm-trooper
territorials

13

army commander
barrack-master
color sergeant
corporal-major
dispatch-rider
drill sergeant
first sergeant
foreign legion
generalissimo
gunner officer
lance-corporal
lance-sergeant
Life Guardsman
light infantry
machine-gunner
mounted rifles
prisoner of war
quartermaster
sapper officer
sergeant major
staff-sergeant

14

colonel-in-chief
colour-sergeant
liaison officer
master sergeant
medical officer
military police
orderly officer
provost-marshal

Royal Artillery
Royal Engineers
Royal Tank
  Corps
signals officer
standard bearer
warrant officer

honorary colonel
household troops
mounted infantry
national service
orderly corporal
orderly sergeant
ordnance officer
provost sergeant

15

adjutant-general
corporal-of-horse
first lieutenant
gentleman-at-arms

17 AND OVER

lieutenant-colonel (17)
lieutenant-general (17)
quartermaster-sergeant (21

Military terms (including fortifications)

2–4	file	lay	raze	ward
	fire	levy	rear	wing
aim	flag	line	rout	zero
ally	flak	loot	ruse	
ammo	foe	man	sack	**5**
arm	foot	map	sap	
arms	form	mess	shot	abort
army	fort	mine	slay	agent
awol	gas	moat	slug	alarm
band	gun	NATO	spur	alert
base	ha-ha	OCTU	take	annex
belt	halt	park	tank	ANZAC
blip	host	plan	tent	armed
camp	hut	post	tilt	armor
defy	impi	pow	trap	array
draw	jam	push	turn	baton
duck	jeep	raid	unit	beret
duel	kern	ramp	van	beset
fife	kit	rank	war	booty
				busby

butts	order	storm	charge
cadre	party	strap	cohort
corps	peace	talus	colour
decoy	pivot	track	column
depot	pouch	troop	combat
ditch	prime	truce	convoy
draft	radar	unarm	cordon
dress	rally	waste	corral
drill	range	wheel	curfew
enemy	ranks	wound	debris
enrol	redan	yield	decamp
equip	relay		defeat
feint	repel	**6**	defend
field	rifle		defile
fight	round	abatis	deploy
flank	route	ack-ack	desert
flare	royal	action	detach
foray	sally	affray	detail
fosse	salvo	allies	disarm
front	scale	ambush	donjon
gazon	scarp	archer	double
gorge	SEATO	armour	dugout
guard	seize	assail	embark
guide	SHAEF	attack	encamp
herse	shako	bailey	engage
horse	shell	banner	enlist
khaki	shock	barbed	ensign
lager	shoot	battle	epaule
lance	siege	beaten	escape
lines	snipe	billet	escarp
march	sonar	blow up	escort
medal	sonic	brevet	Fabian
mêlée	spoil	bunker	firing
mount	squad	cartel	fleche
mufti	staff	casern	foeman
onset	stand	castle	fraise
		centre	

gabion	primer	target	canteen
glacis	pursue	tattoo	carbine
guards	raider	tenail	caserne
helmet	ransom	thrust	cavalry
hot war	rapine	trench	chamade
hurter	rappel	trophy	charger
impact	ration	vallum	chevron
inroad	recall	valour	citadel
invade	recoil	victor	cold war
invest	reduce	volley	colours
kitbag	relais	walled	command
laager	relief	war-cry	company
legion	report	zareba	conquer
limber	resist	zigzag	counter
maquis	retake		coupure
merlon	retire	**7**	crusade
mining	review		curtain
mobile	riddle	abattis	debouch
muster	rideau	advance	defence
mutiny	roster	airlift	degrade
number	saddle	air-raid	destroy
occupy	salute	archery	détente
oppose	sconce	armoury	detrain
orders	second	arsenal	disband
outfit	signal	assault	dismiss
outgun	sniper	baggage	dispart
parade	sortie	barrack	drawn up
parley	square	barrage	draw off
parole	stores	basenet	dungeon
patrol	strife	bastion	echelon
pennon	strike	battery	enguard
permit	stripe	besiege	entrain
picket	stroke	bivouac	envelop
plonge	subdue	bombard	epaulet
pompom	submit	brigade	fallout
pompon	supply	bulwark	fanfare
		caltrop	

fascine
fatigue
fortify
fortlet
forward
fourgon
foxhole
gallery
guérite
gunfire
gunnery
gunshot
half-pay
harness
holster
hostage
hostile
hutment
jamming
Kremlin
liaison
looting
lunette
maniple
martial
megaton
moineau
mounted
neutral
nuclear
on guard
outpost
outwing
outwork
overrun
parados

parapet
pennant
phalanx
pillage
pillbox
platoon
plongée
postern
priming
provost
quarter
rampart
rations
ravelin
Red Army
redoubt
refugee
regular
remblai
remount
repulse
reserve
retaken
retreat
reverse
salient
sandbag
section
service
sniping
spurred
standby
subvert
support
tactics
take out

tambour
tenable
tilting
trailer
triumph
unarmed
uncased
uniform
victory
ward off
warfare
wargame
warlike
warpath
warsong
wartime
warworn
wheeler
wounded

8

accoutre
admiralty
advanced
air force
airborne
alarm gun
alliance
armament
armature
armorial
arms race
Army List
baldrick
barbette
barbican

barracks
bartizan
bearskin
billeted
blockade
bull's eye
camisade
camisado
campaign
casemate
casualty
chivalry
civil war
collapse
conquest
cornetcy
crusader
decimate
decisive
defended
defender
defilade
demi-lune
demolish
despatch
detonate
disarray
dismount
dispatch
division
doubling
drumhead
duelling
embattle
enceinte
enfilade

ensigncy
entrench
equipage
escalade
eyes left
fastness
fatigues
field day
fighting
flanking
fortress
furlough
garrison
gauntlet
gendarme
guerilla
half-moon
hedgehog
herisson
hill fort
horn-work
invasion
knapsack
last post
lay siege
lay waste
limber up
lodgment
loophole
magazine
Mameluke
mantelet
marching
mark time
matériel
mess bill

militant
military
mobilize
movement
muniment
musketry
mutinous
on parade
on parole
opponent
ordnance
outflank
outguard
overkill
palisade
partisan
password
pay corps
petronel
pipe-clay
prisoner
punitive
quarters
railhead
ramparts
rear line
rear rank
rearward
recharge
re-embark
regiment
remounts
reprisal
retrench
reveille
ricochet

rifle-pit
roll-call
sabotage
saboteur
saluting
scout-car
seconded
security
sentry-go
services
shabrack
shelling
shooting
shot-belt
siege-war
skirmish
soldiery
spotting
squadron
stampede
standard
stockade
storming
straddle
strategy
strength
struggle
supplies
surprise
surround
sword arm
tactical
tenaille
time-fuse
tortoise
total war

training
transfer
traverse
trooping, the
  colour
unbeaten
unlimber
uprising
vanguard
vanquish
vexillar
victuals
warhorse
warpaint
war-whoop
watch-box
wheeling
yeomanry
zero hour

9

aggressor
alarm post
ambuscade
armistice
armouries
army corps
artillery
assailant
atomic war
attrition
ballistic
bandolier
banquette
barricade
barricado

battalion	elevation	Landsturm	re-entrant
batteries	embattled	legionary	refortify
battle-cry	embrasure	lifeguard	reinforce
beachhead	encompass	logistics	reprimand
beleaguer	encounter	Luftwaffe	revetment
bellicose	enfiladed	manoeuvre	revictual
billeting	enrolment	march-past	safeguard
bodyguard	epaulette	mercenary	sally-port
bombproof	equipment	musketoon	scrimmage
bombsight	espionage	Mutiny Act	semaphore
bugle call	esplanade	objective	sentry-box
bulldozer	eyes front	offensive	slaughter
cannonade	eyes right	onslaught	slope arms
caponiere	fencibles	operation	slow-march
captaincy	field rank	overpower	stack arms
cashiered	fire power	overshoot	stand fast
cavalcade	fire-drill	overthrow	stratagem
ceasefire	firefight	overwhelm	strategic
challenge	flagstaff	pack train	subjugate
chevalier	forage cap	packdrill	surrender
colonelcy	form fours	palladium	sword-knot
combatant	fortalice	parachute	taskforce
conqueror	fusillade	predictor	terrorist
covert-way	gabionade	pregnable	unguarded
crossfire	gas attack	presidial	uniformed
crown-work	gladiator	pressgang	unopposed
crow's foot	guardroom	projector	unscathed
defection	guerrilla	promotion	unsheathe
defensive	haversack	protector	unwarlike
demi-gorge	homograph	provender	war office
desertion	housewife	provision	watchword
devastate	incursion	rearguard	Wehrmacht
discharge	interdict	rebellion	white flag
disengage	invalided	reconquer	withstand
dismantle	irregular	red ensign	zigzagged
earthwork	land force	re-enforce	

10

action left
aggressive
air defence
ammunition
annexation
annihilate
arbalister
armipotent
battlement
blitzkrieg
blockhouse
breastwork
brevet rank
bridgehead
camel corps
camouflage
cantonment
capitulate
ceremonial
challenger
color guard
commandeer
commissary
commission
covered-way
crenulated
dead ground
decampment
defensible
demobilize
demolition
deployment
despatches
detachment
detonation

direct fire
dismounted
dispatches
divisional
dragonnade
drawbridge
encampment
enfilading
engagement
enlistment
ensignship
epaulement
epauletted
escalation
escarpment
expedition
fieldworks
first strike
garrisoned
glasshouse
ground fire
guardhouse
hand-to-hand
heliograph
indecisive
Indian file
inspection
investment
invincible
leadership
light horse
light-armed
limited war
line of fire
manoeuvres
map-reading

martial law
militarism
musketeers
muster book
muster roll
night-watch
no man's land
nuclear war
occupation
odd numbers
operations
opposition
outgeneral
over the top
patrolling
point blank
portcullis
presidiary
prison camp
projectile
protection
quartering
quick-march
raking fire
raw recruit
reconquest
recruiting
re-entering
regimental
rencounter
rendezvous
reorganize
reparation
resistance
respirator
retirement

revolution
rifle range
route march
rules of war
sabretache
sentry beat
sentry duty
sentry post
shell-proof
short-range
sick parade
siegecraft
siege-train
signalling
slit trench
soldiering
squad drill
state of war
stronghold
subjection
submission
submissive
subsection
subversion
surrounded
sword-fight
table money
terreplein
tirailleur
trajectory
trench foot
undefended
unlimbered
unmolested
unsheathed
vanquisher

victorious
volunteers
vulnerable
war-council
watchtower

11

action front
action right
barking iron
barrack room
battle-array
battledress
battlefield
belligerent
besiegement
bombardment
bulletproof
button-stick
castellated
colour party
countermand
countermine
defenceless
demi-bastion
disarmament
disbandment
double-march
drawn swords
dress parade
embarkation
emplacement
envelopment
even numbers
fatigue duty
firing party

firing squad
flag of truce
flying party
foot-soldier
forced march
forlorn hope
form two deep
fortifiable
generalship
germ warfare
guerilla war
hostilities
impregnable
machicoulis
mobile force
orderly room
penetration
postern gate
present arms
range-finder
rank-and-file
reconnoitre
recruitment
review order
running-fire
safe conduct
searchlight
shock troops
skirmishing
smokescreen
stand-to-arms
supply depot
trained band
trench fever
trous-de-loup
trumpet call

unfortified
unprotected
unsoldierly
unsupported
war memorial

12

advance guard
advanced base
annihilation
anti-aircraft
Bailey bridge
battlemented
break-through
bush-fighting
capitulation
casualty list
civil defence
commissariat
commissioned
conscription
counterforce
countermarch
court-martial
covering fire
disaffection
dropping fire
encirclement
entrenchment
fatigue party
field colours
field-kitchen
field officer
flying column
foot barracks
friendly fire

garrison town
guard forces
guerrilla war
headquarters
heavy brigade
hollow square
horse-and-foot
indefensible
intelligence
invulnerable
irresistible
landing party
light brigade
light cavalry
line-of-battle
machicolated
Maltese cross
mobile column
mobilization
outmanoeuvre
platoon drill
plunging fire
protectorate
quarter-guard
remount depot
retrenchment
rocket attack
running fight
ruse-de-guerre
saluting base
shock tactics
shoulder-belt
shoulder-knot
siege tactics
siege warfare
staff college

surveillance
truce-breaker
ungarrisoned
unobstructed
white feather
working party

13

accoutrements
active service
advanced guard
armored column
articles of war
assault course
carrier pigeon
cheval-de-frise
circumvallate
co-belligerent
column-of-route
counterattack
fatigue parade
field equipage
field hospital
field of battle
fighting force
flying colours
fortification
guards' brigade
interior lines
machicolation
martello tower
mass formation
Military Cross
Military Medal
mounted police
mushroom cloud

order of battle
order of the day
ordnance depot
pontoon-bridge
radiolocation
rallying point
re-embarkation
re-enforcement
regular troops
reinforcement
running battle
shoulder-strap
splinter-proof
storming-party
strategically
striking force
swordsmanship
trench warfare
unarmed combat
urban guerilla
Victoria Cross
war department

14

action stations
airborne forces
ammunition dump
armored brigade
armoured column
auxiliary force
blockade-runner
castrametation
chevaux-de-frise
demobilization
field allowance
field ambulance

freedom fighter
general reserve
liaison officer
marching orders
mechanized army
medical officer
military school
miniature-range
musketry course
musketry school
nuclear warfare
pincer movement
Pyrrhic victory
reconnaissance
reinforcements
reorganization
standing orders
supreme command
urban guerrilla
volunteer force
winter quarters

15

armoured brigade
auxiliary forces
casualty station
circumvallation
clearing station
contravallation
counter approach
creeping barrage
discharge papers
dressing-station
entrenching tool
guerilla warfare
married quarters

military academy
military college
military funeral
non-commissioned
observation post
operation orders
rearguard action
regimental march
substantive rank

turning movement

16 AND OVER

collateral damage (16)
counter-insurgency (17)
counter-offensive (16)
flanking movement (16)
guerrilla warfare (16)

Naval (British and US) and Merchant Navy (Merchant Marine) ranks and appellations

3 AND 4

cook
CPO
mate
Wren
WRNS

5

bosun
cadet
diver
middy
pilot

6

cooper
ensign
gunner
lascar

marine
master
purser
rating
reefer
seaman
snotty
stoker
topman
writer
yeoman

7

admiral
armorer
artisan
captain
deck boy
fireman
greaser

jack-tar
lookout
messman
recruit
shipman
skipper
steward
surgeon

8

armourer
cabin boy
chaplain
coxswain
engineer
flag rank
gun-layer
helmsman
messmate
ship's boy

9

artificer
boatswain
commander
commodore
cook's mate
navigator
paymaster
ropemaker
sailmaker
ship's cook
signalman
tugmaster

10

able seaman
apprentice
coastguard
lieutenant

midshipman
shipmaster
ship's baker
shipwright

11

chief stoker
electrician
flag captain
flag officer
foremastman
gunner's mate
port admiral
port officer
post captain
rear-admiral
vice-admiral
watchkeeper

12

cabin steward
chief officer
chief steward
first officer
fleet admiral
junior seaman
master gunner
master-at-arms
petty officer
powder monkey
second master
senior purser
telegraphist
third officer

13

armourer's mate
chief armourer
chief engineer
fourth officer
harbourmaster
leading seaman
leading stoker
marine officer
privateersman
quartermaster
radio operator
sailing master
second officer
ship's corporal
signal officer
sub-lieutenant
third engineer

14 AND OVER

admiral of the fleet (17)
boarding officer (15)
boatswain's mate (14)
chief petty officer (17)
first lieutenant (15)
flag-lieutenant (14)
fourth engineer (14)
leading steward (14)
lieut.-commander (14)
ordinary seaman (14)
second engineer (14)
ship's carpenter (14)
warrant officer (14)

Weapons and armour

3 AND 4

ABM
ammo
arm
arms
axe
ball
bill
bolt
bomb
bow
butt
cane
club
Colt
cosh
dag
dart
dirk
epée
foil
goad
gun
helm
ICBM
kris
mace
mall
mere
meri
mine
MIRV
pike
ram
Scud
shot
tank
taws
TNT
tuck
Uzi
whip

5

A-bomb
aegis
armet
armor
arrow
bilbo
birch
bolas
crest
estoc
flail
fusee
fusil
H-bomb
jerid
knife
knout
kukri
lance
lasso
lathi
Luger
Maxim
Minié
panga
pilum
rifle
sabre
salvo
shell
skean
skene
sling
spear
staff
stake
stave
stick
sword
targe
tawse
visor
vizor

6

ack-ack
airgun
armlet
armour
barrel
basnet
bodkin
bullet
cannon
casque
cudgel
dagger
dualin
dumdum
Exocet
glaive
gorget
gusset
heaume
helmet
jereed
kreese
lariat
lorica
mailed
Mauser
morion
mortar
musket
muzzle
napalm
parang
pellet
petard
pistol
pom-pom
popgun
powder
primer
rapier
rocket
sallet
scutum
scythe
Semtex
shield
sickle

stylet
swivel
target
tonite
tulwar
weapon
Webley
womera
zipgun

7

assagai
assegai
bar-shot
basinet
bayonet
bazooka
beldric
Bren gun
buckler
bundook
calibre
caliver
caltrop
car bomb
carbine
cordite
corslet
cuirass
curtana
cutlass
dudgeon
ejector
elf-bolt
firearm
firepot

fougade
gas mask
Gatling
greaves
grenade
gunport
gunshot
hackbut
halberd
halbert
handgun
harpoon
hatchet
hauberk
haubert
holster
javelin
long tom
longbow
lyddite
machete
megaton
missile
nuclear
Patriot
Polaris
poleaxe
poniard
priming
quarrel
shotgun
side-arm
sjambok
Skybolt
Spandau
Sten gun

surcoat
teargas
torpedo
trident
warhead
woomera

8

arbalist
arbelest
Armalite
arquebus
atom bomb
aventail
ballista
basilisk
blowpipe
bludgeon
broadaxe
Browning
burganet
burgonet
canister
carabine
catapult
cavalier
chamfrom
chamfron
chanfron
chausses
claymore
corselet
crossbow
culverin
dynamite
eel-spear

elf-arrow
falchion
falconet
field-gun
firearms
fireball
firebomb
firelock
fireship
fougasse
gas shell
gauntlet
gunsight
half-pike
haquebut
howitzer
jazerant
landmine
langrage
Lewis gun
linstock
magazine
mangonel
mantelet
Maxim gun
Oerlikon
ordnance
paravane
partisan
partizan
petronel
pistolet
plastron
portfire
pyroxyle
repeater

revolver
ricochet
ringmail
scabbard
scimitar
scorpion
shrapnel
siege-gun
skean-dhu
slow fuse
spontoon
stiletto
time bomb
tomahawk
tommy gun
vambrace
vamplate
whinyard
whiz-bang
yataghan

9

ack-ack gun
angel-shot
arrowhead
artillery
automatic
backpiece
balistite
ballistic
bandoleer
bandolier
battleaxe
Big Bertha
blackjack
Blue Water

boar-spear
Bofors gun
bombshell
bombshell
boomerang
Brown
  Bess
brownbill
carronade
cartouche
cartridge
chain-mail
chain-shot
chamfrain
chassepot
damascene
defoliant
derringer
deterrent
detonator
doodle-bug
equalizer
face-guard
fish-spear
fléchette
flintlock
gelignite
grapeshot
guncotton
gunpowder
habergeon
half-track
harquebus
headpiece
matchlock
Mills bomb

Minuteman
munitions
needle-gun
poison gas
quaker-gun
rerebrace
sling-shot
slow-match
small arms
small-bore
smoke-bomb
spring-gun
starshell
stinkbomb
sword-cane
trebuchet
troopship
truncheon
turret gun
whizz-bang
xyloidine

10

ammunition
Blue Streak
bowie knife
broadsword
cannon-shot
cannonball
coat of mail
demi-cannon
field-piece
flick knife
flying bomb
Gatling gun
knobkerrie

WEAPONS AND ARMOUR 559

Lee-Enfield
letter bomb
limpet mine
machine-gun
Minié rifle
mustard-gas
pea-shooter
petrol bomb
powder horn
projectile
recoilless
safety-fuse
shillelagh
Sidewinder
six-shooter
smallsword
smoothbore
sticky bomb
swordstick
touchpaper
Winchester

11

air-to-ground
antitank gun
armoured car
balistraria
basket sword
blockbuster
blunderbuss
bow and arrow
breastplate
cluster bomb
contact-mine
depth-charge
elephant gun

Garand rifle
germ warfare
gun carriage
hand-grenade
Kalashnikov
neutron bomb
powder flask
powder-chest
safety-catch
scale-armour
snickersnee
Snider rifle
stern-chaser

12

acoustic mine
armour-plated
Armstrong gun
battering ram
battery piece
breech-loader
cartridge-box
conventional
demi-culverin
double-charge
flame-thrower
fowling-piece
guided weapon
hydrogen bomb
landing craft
magnetic mine
mine detector
mitrailleuse
muzzle-loader
quarterstaff
rifle grenade

sword-bayonet
tracer bullet
trench mortar

13

aerial torpedo
armaments race
armor-piercing
ball-cartridge
cartridge-case
cruise missile
guided missile
high-explosive
knuckleduster
life preserver
percussion cap
poisoned arrow
semi-automatic
submachine-gun
thermonuclear
two-edged sword

14 AND OVER

air-to-air missile (15)
anti-aircraft gun (15)
armour-piercing (14)
ballistic missile (16)
blank cartridge (14)
chemical warfare (14)
duelling pistol (14)
field artillery (14)
heat-seeking missile (18)
heavy artillery (14)
horse artillery (14)
incendiary bomb (14)
miniature rifle (14)
Molotov cocktail (15)
nitroglycerine (14)
nuclear weapons (14)
plastic explosive (16)
powder-magazine (14)
rocket launcher (14)
sawn-off shotgun (14)
small-bore rifle (14)

WEIGHTS AND MEASURES

(A.)=Argentina	(f.)=fish
(B.)=Brazil	(G.)=Greece
(b.)=bread	(H.)=Hebrew
(C.)=Canada	(Hon.)=Honduras
(c.)=coal	(I.)=India
(Ch.)=China	(Ice.)=Iceland
(E.)=Egypt	(Indo.)=Indonesia
(elec.)=electricity	(Ire.)=Ireland
(Eth.)=Ethiopa	(It.)=Italy
(F.)=France	(J.)=Japan

(liq.)=liquids
(M.)=Malta
(Malay.)=Malaysia
(min.)=minimg
(Mor.)=Morocco
(N.)=Norway
(O.)=Oriental
(P.)=Portugal
(pap.)=paper
(print.)=printing
(R.)=Russia
(Rom.)=Roman

(S.)=Spain
(s.)=silk or cotton
(SA)=South Africa
(S.Am.)=South America
(SI)=Système International:
   metric system
(T.)=Turkey
(Thai.)=Thailand
(US)=United States
(v.)=various commodities
(w.)=wool
(w.y.)=worsted yarn

1–3

A4 (pap.)
aam
amp (elec.)
amu
are (SI)
as (Rom.)
aum (SA)
bar
bel
bit
BSI
BTU
cab (H.)
cho (J.)
cm (SI)
cor (H.)
cwt.
day
DIN
dwt.
el

ell
em (print.)
en (print.)
erg
fen (Ch.)
fou
ft
g (SI)
hin (H.)
in.
keg
ken (J.)
kg
kin (J. and
   Ch.)
km
lb
lea (s.)
li (Ch.)
log (H.)
lux (SI)
m
mho (elec.)

mil
min
mou (Ch.)
mu
nit (SI)
niu (Thai.)
ohm (elec.)
oka (F.)
oke (T.)
oz
pic (G.)
pin
piu (It.)
pot
rad
rai (Thai.)
rem
ri (J.)
rio (J.)
rod
sen (Thai.)
sho (J.)
SI

sun (J.)
tan (Ch.)
to (J.)
tod (w.)
tog
ton
tot
tun (liq.)
vat (liq.)
wah (Thai.)
wey (w.)
yd.

4

acre
atom
bale (v.)
barn
bath (H.)
boll
bolt
BThU.
butt (liq.)

byte
cade (f.)
case (v.)
cask (liq.)
ch'ih (Ch.)
comb
cord
coss (I.)
cran (f.)
darg
demy (pap.)
dose
drah (Mor.)
dram
drop
dyne
epha (H.)
feet
flint (R.)
foot
gill
gram (SI)
gray
hand (horses)
hank (w.y.)
hath (I.)
hide
hour
inch
iota
keel (c.)
kela (E.)
kilo (SI)
knot
koku (J.)
koss (I.)

kwan (J.)
last (f., w.)
line
link
load (min.)
mile
mina (G.)
moio (P.)
mole (SI)
mudd
muid (SA)
nail
natr (Eth.)
obol (G.)
oket (Eth.)
omer (H.)
onza (A.)
paal
pace
pack
palm
peck
phon
phot
pica
pint
pipe (liq.)
pole
pood (R)
post (pap.)
pott (pap.)
pund (N.)
raik (I.)
ream (pap.)
reed (H.)
reel (s.)

rood
rotl (E.)
sack (c., w.)
sawk
seah (H.)
seam
seer (I.)
slug
span
tael (Ch., J.)
tare
tola (I.)
torr
tret
tron
troy
ts'un (Ch.)
unit
vara (S. Am.)
volt (elec.)
watt (elec.)
yard

5

almud (T.)
angle
anker (SA)
ardeb (E.)
bahar (Ar.)
bekah (H.)
cable
candy (I.)
canna
carat
catty (Ch.)
cawny (I.)

ch'ien (Ch.)
chain
chang (Ch.)
cheki (T.)
clove
coomb
count (w.y.)
crown (pap.)
cubic
cubit
curie
cusec
cycle
debye
ephah (H.)
farad
fermi
gauge
gauss
gerah (H.)
grain
gross
henry
hertz (elec.)
homer (H.)
joule
kaneh
kikeh (T.)
legua
liang (Ch.)
libra (B.)
ligne
lippy
litre (SI)
livre (F. and G.)

lumen (SI)
maund (I.)
meter (SI)
metre (SI)
minim (liq.)
month
neper
obole (G.)
ocque (G.)
okieh (E.)
ounce
pearl (print.)
pecul (Ch.)
perch
picul (Ch.)
piede (M.)
point (print.)
poise (SI)
pound
proof
pugil
purse (T.)
qirat (E.)
quart
quire (pap.)
quota
royal (pap.)
sabin
sajen (R.)
shaku (J.)
sheet (pap.)
shock
skein (s.)
stade
stere (SI)
stone

stoup (liq.)
tesla
therm
tithe
toise (F.)
token (pap.)
tonne
truss
tsubo (J.)
ungul (I.)
vedro (R.)
verst (R.)
weber
yojan (I.)

6

ampère (elec.)
archin (T.)
armful
aroura (E. and G.)
arpent
arroba (S., P. and
    S.Am.)
assize
bandle (Ire.)
barrel (v.)
batman (T.)
bundle (v.)
bushel
calory
candle
cantar (E. and T.)
casing (pap.)
cental (C. and
    U.S.)
cental (B. and G.)

chopin (liq.)
dalton
decare
degree
denier
dirham (E.)
dirhem (E.)
djerib (T.)
double
drachm
endaze (T.)
fanega (S. and
    S.Am.)
fathom
feddan (E.)
firkin
firlot
fother
gallon (liq.)
gramme (SI)
kantar (Eth.)
kelvin
kilerg
league
libbra (I.)
medium (pap.)
megohm (elec.)
metric
micron (SI)
minute
moiety
morgen (SA)
newton
noggin
obolus (G.)
octant

octave
octavo (pap.)
oxgang
parsec
pascal
photon
pocket (hops)
pottle (liq.)
proton
quarto (pap.)
radian
rotolo
sajene (R)
schene (E.)
second
shekel (H.)
shtoff (R)
stokes
suttle
talent (G.)
thrave (Ice.)
tierce (liq.)
vishan (I.)
weight
yojana (I.)

7

acreage
boiling
braccio (I.)
calorie
candela (SI)
Celsius
centner
century
chalder

chiliad
chronon
coulomb (elec.)
dangall (L)
deciare (F.)
decibel
dioptre
drachma (G.)
ellwand
faraday
fresnel
furlong
geodesy
gilbert
gravity
half-aum (SA)
half-ton
hectare (SI)
kilobar
lambert
maximum
maxwell
measure
mega-erg
megaton
mileage
miller
minimum
modicum
oersted
outsize
pailful
per cent
poundal
quantar (E.)
quantum

quartan
quarter
quinary
quintal
röntgen
rottolo
scruple
sea mile
siemens (SI)
sievert (SI)
spindle (s.)
stadium (G.)
stature
stremma (G.)
ternary
ternion
tonnage
virgate

8

angstrom
centiare (F.)
centibar
chaldron (c.)
chaudron (c.)
chetvert (R.)
cubic ton
decagram
decigram
distance
division
elephant (pap.)
foolscap (pap.)
footrule
freezing
graviton

half-hour
half-inch
half-mile
hogshead (liq.)
imperial (pap.)
infinity
kassabah (E.)
kilodyne
kilogram
kilovolt
kilowatt (elec.)
magneton
megadyne
megavolt
megawatt
metrical
millibar
molecule
mutchkin (liq.)
parasang
plateful
puncheon (liq.)
quadrant
quantity
quartern (b.)
roentgen
sarplier (w.)
serplath
ship-load (c.)
short ton (C. and
   U.S.)
spoonful
tonelada (S. and S.
   Am.)
watt-hour
yardland

yardwand
zolotnik (R)

9

altimetry
amplitude
areometry
becquerel
bisegment
board foot
centigram
cuartilla (S. and
   S.Am.)
cubic foot
cubic inch
cubic yard
decalitre (SI)
decametre (SI)
decilitre (SI)
decimetre (SI)
decistere (F.)
dekalitre (SI)
dekametre (SI)
dimension
foot-pound
half-ounce
half-pound
hectogram (SI)
isometric
kilderkin
kilocycle
kilohertz (elec.)
kilolitre (SI)
kilometre (SI)
large sack (c.)
light year

long dozen
megacycle
megahertz (elec.)
metric ton
microgram
microwatt
milestone
milligram (SI)
nanometre (SI)
net weight
quadruple
quarterly
quintuple
scantling
steradian
threefold
troy ounce
yardstick

10

araeometry
barleycorn
barrel-bulk
centesimal
centigrade
centilitre (SI)
centimetre (SI)
cubic metre (SI)
deadweight
decagramme (SI)
decigramme (SI)
dessiatine (R)
double-demy
   (pap.)
double-post (pap.)
dry measure

eighth part
Fahrenheit
fifty-fifty
fluid ounce
hectolitre (SI)
hectometre (SI)
horsepower
kilogramme (SI)
lunar month
microfarad (elec.)
micrometre
millesimal
millilitre (SI)
millimetre (SI)
nanosecond
quadrantal (Rom.)
rutherford
square foot
square inch
square mile
square yard
super-royal (pap.)
tripartite
tron weight
troy weight

11

antiquarian (pap.)
avoirdupois
baker's dozen
candlepower
centigramme (SI)
day's journey
double-crown (pap.)
double-royal (pap.)
equidistant

fluid drachm
half and half
hand-breadth
heavyweight
hectogramme (SI)
imperial cap (pap.)
long hundred
  (eggs and f.)
long measure
milligramme (SI)
millimicron
millisecond
pennyweight
short weight
square metre (SI)
tape measure
teaspoonful
thermal unit
thermometer
two-foot rule
wine-measure
yard-measure

12

angstrom unit
areometrical
bantamweight
boiling point
cable's length
cubic measure
electronvolt
equidistance
hair's breadth
half-quartern
hand's-breadth
kilowatt-hour

measured mile
metric system
printer's ream (pap.)
quantitative
quartern loaf (b.)
Réaumur scale

13

calendar month
decimal system
featherweight
freezing point
hundredweight
hypermetrical
inside measure
linear measure
medicine glass

square measure
tablespoonful
three-foot rule

14

atomic mass unit
cubic decimetre (SI)
double elephant (pap.)
outside measure
zenith distance

15

centigrade scale
cubic centimetre (SI)
square decimetre (SI)
square kilometre (SI)

MISCELLANEOUS
Abbreviations

1 AND 2

A-1 first class in Lloyd's
Register
AA Automobile Association;
anti-aircraft; Alcoholics
Anonymous
AB Alberta
AB. able-bodied seaman
AC alternating current;
Companion of the Order of
Australia; Apellation
contrôlée (wine
classification)

AD Anno Domini (In the year
of our Lord)
AG Adjutant-General;
Attorney-General
AH Anno Hegirae
AI Amnesty International;
artificial insemination;
artificial intelligence
AK Knight of the Order of
Australia
AM Master of Arts
am ante meridiem
(before noon)

AO Officer of the Order of Australia

AS Anglo-Saxon

at atomic

AV Authorized Version

av avenue; average

b born, bowled

BA Bachelor of Arts; British Academy; British Airways; British Association

BC Before Christ; British Columbia

BCE Before Common Era

BD Bachelor of Divinity

BE Bachelor of Engineering; Bachelor of Education

bf bold face

bl bill of lading

BM British Museum

BO body odour

BP British Pharmacopoeia

bp blood pressure; boiling point

Bp Bishop

BR British Rail

br branch

BS Bachelor of Surgery; Bachelor of Science

BT British Telecom

Bt Baronet

C Celsius, centigrade

c caught, cent(s), chapter, circa

CA California; chartered accountant

ca circa (around, about)

CB citizens' band; Companion of the Bath

cb confined to barracks

CC cricket club; county council

cc carbon copy (copies); cubic centimetre(s)

CD Civil Defence; compact disc; Corps Diplomatique

CE Church of England; civil engineer; Common Era

cf compare

cg centigram

CH Companion of Honour; Confédération Helvétique

ch chapter; check; church

CI Channel Islands

CJ Chief Justice

cm centimetre

CO commanding officer; conscientious objector

Co company; county

c/o care of

CP Communist Party

cr councillor; creditor

CT Connecticut

ct cent; court

CU Cambridge University

cu cubic

CV curriculum vitae

d daughter; died; old penny; old pence

DA district attorney

DB Bachelor of Divinity

DC detective constable; District of Columbia (US)

dc da capo; direct current
DD Doctor of Divinity
dd direct debit
dg decigram
DJ dinner jacket; disc jockey
dl decilitre
DM Doctor of Medicine; Deutschmarks
do ditto
DP data processing; displaced person
Dr Doctor
dr dram; debtor; drive
DS Doctor of Science
DV Deo volente (God willing)
E east
ea each
EC East Central; European Community
ed edited; edition; editor
eg exempli gratia (for example)
EI East Indies
ER Elizabeth Regina (Queen)
F Fahrenheit; franc(s)
f feminine; forte
FA Football Association
FC football club
ff folios, fortissimo
fl floruit (flourished)
FM field-marshal; frequency modulation
FO Field Officer; Flying Officer; Foreign Office

fo folio
Fr Father; France; French; Friday
ft foot, feet
g gram(s)
GB Great Britain
GC George Cross
GI government issue (US)
Gk Greek
GM general manager; George Medal; Grand Master
GP General Practitioner
GR Georgius Rex (King George)
Gr Greek
gr grain(s); gram(s); gross
GT gran turismo
Gt great
HC House of Commons
HE high explosive; His Eminence; His (Her) Excellency
HF high frequency
hf half
HH His (Her) Highness
HM His (Her) Majesty
hp high pressure; hire purchase; horsepower
HQ headquarters
hr hour
HT high tension
ht height
hv high velocity; high voltage

Hz hertz
IA Iowa
ID Idaho; identification
id idem (the same)
ie id est (that is)
IL Illinois
IN Indiana
IQ intelligence quotient
Is Isaiah; island(s)
IT information technology
It Italian, Italy
J joule; judge
JC Jesus Christ
JP Justice of the Peace
Jr junior
Jt joint
K kelvin
k kilo; one thousand
KB kilobyte
KC King's Counsel
kc kilocycle
KG Knight of the Garter
kg kilogram(s)
KT Knight of the Thistle
Kt knight
kt knot
kW kilowatt
L lira; Latin; Liberal
l left; litre
lb libra (pound)
lc lower case (printing)
Ld Lord
LF low frequency
LP low pressure
LT low tension
Lt Lieutenant

M Mach; medium; member;
  Monsieur (Fr.); thousand
  (mille)
m metre(s); miles (s);
  masculine; married;
  meridian
MA Master of Arts
MB Bachelor of Medicine
MC Master of Ceremonies;
  Member of Congress (US);
  Military Cross
MD Doctor of Medicine;
  Managing Director
ME Middle English; myalgic
  encephalomyelitis
mf mezzoforte
mg milligram
mi mile
mk mark
ml millilitre
MM Messieurs (Fr.); Military
  Medal
MO medical officer
Mo month
MP Member of Parliament;
  Military Police
MR Master of the Rolls
Mr mister
MS Master of Science;
  multiple sclerosis
MS manuscript
MT mechanical
  transport
Mt mount
N newton; north
n neuter; noun

NA North America; not applicable

NB New Brunswick

nb nota bene (note well)

NE northeast

NF National Front

NI National Insurance; Northern Ireland

No. number (numero)

NP new paragraph

nr near

NS New Style; Nova Scotia

NT New Testament; Northern Territory

NW northwest

NY New York

NZ New Zealand

o octavo

ob obit (died)

OB outside broadcast

OC Officer Commanding

Oc Ocean

OD on demand; overdose; overdrawn

OE Old English

OF Old French

OM Order of Merit

op. opus (work)

op out of print

OR other ranks (mil.)

OS Old Style; Ordnance Survey

OT occupational therapy; Old Testament

OU Oxford University; Open University

P parking; pawn; peseta; peso

p page; penny; pence; piano

PA personal assistant; Press Association; Publishers Association

pa per annum

PC personal computer; police constable; politically correct; Privy Councillor

pc per cent; postcard; post cibum (after meals)

pd paid; per diem; potential difference

PE physical education

PG paying guest

Pg Portugal; Portuguese

pg page

pl plural; place

PM Prime Minister; Provost Marshal; Past Master; Postmaster

pm post meridiem; post mortem

PO Personnel Officer; Petty Officer; Pilot Officer; postal order; post office

pp pages; pianissimo; per pro

PR proportional representation; public relations

PS postscript; private secretary

Pt part; port

pt pint; point

Q quartermaster

q query; question

QB Queen's Bench
QC Queen's Counsel
QM Quartermaster
qr quarter, quarterly
qt quart
qv quod vide (which see)
R Réaumur; Royal; Rex;
 Regina; right; river; rouble;
 rupee
RA Rear Admiral; Royal
 Academician; Royal
 Academy; Royal Artillery
RC Roman Catholic
Rd road
RE religious education; Royal
 Engineers
RF radio frequency
rh right hand
RI religious instruction
RL Rugby League
RM Royal Mail; Royal
 Marines
RN Royal Navy
RR Right Reverend
RS Royal Society
Rs rupees
RU Rugby Union
ry railway
S Saint; Schilling; second;
 singular; shilling; son;
 south
SA Salvation Army; South
 Africa; South America;
 South Australia;
 Sturmabteilung (Nazi
 militia)

sc small capitals (printing)
SE southeast(ern)
SF science fiction
sf sforzando
sg specific gravity
SI Système International
SJ Society of Jesus
SM Sergeant-Major
Sp Spain, Spanish
sp special; specific; spelling
Sq squadron
sq square
Sr Señor; Sister
sr senior
SS Saints; Steamship;
 Schutzstaffel (Nazi elite
 unit)
St Saint; street; stone;
 stumped
SW southwest(ern)
Sw Sweden, Swedish
t ton(ne)
TA Territorial Army
TB torpedo-boat; tuberculosis
TD Territorial Decoration
TT teetotal; Tourist Trophy
tr transitive; translated;
 translator
TU trade union
TV television
uc uppercase (printing)
UK United Kingdom
UN United Nations
UP Uttar Pradesh
US United States
V volt; volume; victory

v verb, versus (against)
vb verb
VC Vice Chancellor; Victoria Cross
VD venereal disease
vg very good
VI Virgin Islands
VO Victorian Order
VR Victoria Regina (Queen)
W watt; west
WC water closet; West Central
WD War Department
wf wrong fount (printing)
WI West Indies
WO War Office; Warrant Officer; Wireless Operator
wt weight
yd yard
yr year, your

3

AAA Amateur Athletic Association; American Automobile Association
ABA Amateur Boxing Association; American Bar Association
ABC American Broadcasting Company; Australian Broadcasting Corporation
ABM antiballistic missile
Abp archbishop
ACA Associate of the Institute of Chartered Accountants
ACT Australian Capital Territory
ADC aide-de-camp; amateur dramatic club
adj adjective
Adm Admiral
ADP automatic data processing
adv adverb
AEA Atomic Energy Authority
AEC Atomic Energy Commission
AEU Amalgamated Engineering Union
AFC Air Force Cross
Afg Afghanistan
AFM Air Force Medal
Afr Africa
AGM Annual General Meeting
AID artificial insemination by donor
aka also known as
Alb Albania
Alg Algeria
alg algebra
ALP Australian Labour Party
AMU atomic mass unit
ANC African National Congress
AOB any other business
AOC Air Officer Commanding, Appellation d'origine contrôlée (wine classification)

AOF Ancient Order of Foresters
APM Assistant Provost Marshal
APR annual percentage rate
Apr April
APT Advanced Passenger Train
ARA Associate of the Royal Academy
ARP Air Raid Precautions
Arg Argentina
arr arranged; arrival; arrive
ASA Advertising Standards Authority
ASH Action on Smoking and Health
ATC air-traffic control; Air Training Corps
ATP adenosine triphosphate
ATV all-terrain vehicle; Associated Television
Aug August
aux auxiliary
ave avenue
BAA British Airports Authority
BBC British Broadcasting Corporation
BCG Bacillus Calmette Guérin (anti-tuberculosis vaccine)
BCL Bachelor of Civil Law
BDS Bachelor of Dental Surgery
BEd Bachelor of Education

BEF British Expeditionary Force
bhp brake horsepower
BIM British Institute of Management
BMA British Medical Association
BMC British Medical Council
BMJ British Medical Journal
BMX bicycle motocross
Bro brother
BRS British Road Services
BSc Bachelor of Science
BSE bovine spongiform encephalopathy
BSI British Standards Institution
BST British Standard Time; British Summer Time
BVM Blessed Virgin Mary
CAP common agricultural policy
cap capital
CBC Canadian Broadcasting Corporation
CBE Commander of the British Empire (Order)
CBI Confederation of British Industry
CBS Columbia Broadcasting System
CEO chief executive officer
CGT Confédération Générale du Travail (French trade union association)

CIA Central Intelligence Agency

CID Criminal Investigation Department

cif cost, insurance, freight

CIO Congress of Industrial Organizations (US)

CJD Creutzfeldt–Jacob disease

CMG Companion of St Michael and St George (Order)

CND Campaign for Nuclear Disarmament

cod cash on delivery

COI Central Office of Information

Col Colorado, Colossians

col column

coy company (mil.)

cpl corporal

CPO chief petty oficer

CPR Canadian Pacific Railway

CPS Crown Prosecution Service

CRE Commission for Racial Equality

CRT cathode ray tube

CSE Certificate of Secondary Education

CSM Company Sergeant-Major

CVO Commander of the Victorian Order

CWS Co-operative Wholesale Society

cwt hundredweight

DAG Deputy Adjutant-General

DBE Dame Commander of the British Empire (Order)

DCB Dame Commander of the Bath (Order)

DCL Doctor of Civil Law

DCM Distinguished Conduct Medal

DDR Deutsche Demokratische Republik (East Germany)

DDS Doctor of Dental Surgery

DDT dichlorodiphenyl-trichloroethane

Dec December

dec deceased; decimal; decimetre; decrescendo (music)

def definite; definition

del delegate

Den Denmark

Det Detective

DFC Distinguished Flying Cross

DFM Distinguished Flying Medal

Dip Diploma

div Dividend

DIY do-it-yourself

DNA deoxyribonucleic acid

DNB Dictionary of National Biography

DOA dead on arrival
doz dozen
DPP Director of Public Prosecutions
dpt department
DSC Distinguished Service Cross
DSc Doctor of Science
DSM Distinguished Service Medal
DSO Distinguished Service Order
DST Daylight Saving Time
DTs delirium tremens
DTI Department of Trade and Industry
DTP desktop publishing
ECT electroconvulsive therapy
ECU European Currency Unit
EDC European Defence Community
EEC European Economic Community
EEG electroencephalogram; electroencephalograph
EFL English as a Foreign Language
emf electromotive force
ENE eastnortheast
ENT ear, nose and throat
EOC Equal Opportunities Commission
ESE eastsoutheast

ESN educationally subnormal
ESP extrasensory perception
esp especially
Esq Esquire
EST Eastern Standard Time; electric shock treatment
est estimated
ETA expected time of arrival
etc. et cetera
ETD expected time of departure
FAO Food and Agriculture Organization
FBA Fellow of theBritish Academy
FBI Federal Bureau of Investigation
FCA Fellow of the Institute of Chartered Accountants
Feb February
fem feminine
FGS Fellow of the Geological Society
FIA Fellow of the Institute of Actuaries
fig figure; figuratively
Fin Finland, Finnish
fin finance; financial
FLA Fellow of the Library Association
fob free on board
FPA Family Planning Association
Fri Friday

FRS Fellow of the Royal Society

FZS Fellow of the Zoological Society

fur furlong

Gal Galatians

GBE Knight (or Dame) Grand Cross of the British Empire

GBH grievous bodily harm

GCB Knight Grand Cross of the Bath

GCE General Certificate of Education

GDP gross domestic product

GDR German Democratic Republic

gen gender; general; genitive; genus

GHQ General Headquarters

Gib Gibraltar

GLC Greater London Council

Gmc Germanic

GMT Greenwich Mean Time

GNP Gross National Product

GOC General Officer Commanding

GOM grand old man

Gov government, governor

GPO General Post Office

gtd guaranteed

HAC Honorable Artillery Company

HBM His (Her) Britannic Majesty

hcf highest common factor

HGV heavy goods vehicle

HIH His (Her) Imperial Highness

HIM His (Her) Imperial Majesty

HIV human immunodeficiency virus

HLI Highland Light Infantry

HMI His (Her) Majesty's Inspector

HMS His (Her) Majesty's Ship or Service

HNC Higher National Certificate

HND Higher National Diploma

Hon honorary; Honourable

Hos Hosea

HRH His (Her) Royal Highness

hrs hours

HRT hormone replacement therapy

IBA Independent Broadcasting Authority

ICA Institute of Chartered Accountants; Institute of Contemporary Arts

ICE Institution of Civil Engineers

ICI Imperial Chemical Industries

IEE Institution of Electrical Engineers

IHS Jesus, Saviour of men (Iesus Hominum Salvator)

ILO International Labour Organization

ILP Independent Labour Party

IMF International Monetary Fund

imp imperative; imperfect; imperial

Inc incorporated

inc including; inclusive; increase

Ind India; Indiana

ind independent; indicative; industrial; industry

inf infinitive; informal

int interest; internal; international

IOC International Olympic Committee

IOF Independent Order of Foresters

IOM Isle of Man

IOU I owe you (acknowledgment of debt)

IOW Isle of Wight

IPA International Phonetic Alphabet

IRA Irish Republican Army

ISO Imperial Service Order; International Standards Organization

ITA International Teaching Alphabet

ITU International Telecommunications Union

ITV Independent Television

IUD intra-uterine device

IVF in vitro fertilization

Jan January

Jas James

Jer Jeremiah

Jon Jonah

Jos Joseph

jun junior

juv juvenile

KBE Knight Commander of the British Empire (Order)

KCB Knight Commander of the Bath

KGB Komitet Gosudarstvennoi Bezopasnosti (Committee of State Security)

kHz kilohertz

KKK Ku Klux Klan

kWh kilowatt-hour

Lab Labour

lab laboratory

Lat Latin

lat latitude

lbw leg before wicket

LCC London County Council

lcd liquid crystal display; lowest common denominator

LCJ Lord Chief Justice

lcm lowest common multiple

LDS Licentiate in Dental Surgery

LEA Local Education Authority

LED light-emitting diode
LEM lunar excursion module
Lev Leviticus
LLB Bachelor of Laws
LLD Doctor of Laws
LLM Master of Laws
LSD lysergic acid diethylamide
lsd librae; solidi; denarii (pounds shillings pence)
LSE London School of Economics
LSO London Symphony Orchestra
Ltd Limited
Lux Luxembourg
mag magazine
Maj Major
Mar March
mar married
max maximum
MBA Master of Business Administration
MBE Member of the British Empire (Order)
MCC Marylebone Cricket Club
MCP male chauvinist pig
MEP Member of European Parliament
met meteorological; metropolitan
MFH Master of Foxhounds
Mgr Manager; Monsignor
MHz megahertz
mil. military

Min Minister, Ministry
min mineralogy
MLR minimum lending rate
Mme Madame
MOD Ministry of Defence
mod moderate; modern
MOH Medical Officer of Health
Mon Monday
mph miles per hour
MSc Master of Science
MSS manuscripts
MTB motor torpedo boat
MVO Member of the Royal Victorian Order
nat national; native
NBA Net Book Agreement
NCB National Coal Board
NCC Nature Conservancy Council
NCO non-commissioned officer
NCP National Car Parks
NEB New English Bible
neg. negative
NFU National Farmers' Union
NHS National Health Service
NNE northnortheast
NNW northnorthwest
nos numbers
Nov November
NPA Newspaper Publishers Association
NPL National Physical Laboratory

NRA National Rifle Association
NSU non-specific urethritis
NSW New South Wales
NUJ National Union of Journalists
NUM National Union of Mineworkers
Num Numbers
NUR National Union of Railwaymen
NUS National Union of Seamen; National Union of Students
NUT National Union of Teachers
NYC New York City
OAP old age pensioner
OAS Organisation de l'Armée Secrète; Organization of American States
OBE Officer of the British Empire (Order)
obs obsolete
OCR optical character reader (recognition)
Oct October
oct octavo
off offer; officer
OFT Office of Fair Trading; Orange Free State
OND Ordinary National Diploma
ono or near(est) offer
Ont Ontario

opp opposed; opposite
ord ordained; order; ordinary; ordnance
OTC Officers' Training Corps
Pac Pacific
Pal Palestine
Pan Panama
Par Paraguay
par paragraph; parallel; parish
PBS Public Broadcasting Service
PBX private branch exchange
pen peninsula
PEP personal equity plan
PhD Doctor of Philosophy
PLA Port of London Authority
PLC public limited company
PLO Palestine Liberation Organization
PLP Parliamentary Labour Party
PLR Public Lending Right
PMG Paymaster-General; Postmaster-General
PMT premenstrual tension
pop population
pow prisoner of war
PPE philosophy, politics and economics
ppr present participle
PPS parliamentary private secretary
pps post postscriptum

PRB Pre-Raphaelite Brotherhood

PRO public relations officer

PSV public service vehicle

PTA Parent–Teacher Association

PTO please turn over

PVC polyvinyl chloride

Pvt Private

PWR pressurized water reactor

qed quod erat demonstrandum (which was to be proved)

QMG Quartermaster-General

QMS Quartermaster-Sergeant

Que Quebec

RAC Royal Armoured Corps; Royal Automobile Club

RAF Royal Air Force

RAM Royal Academy of Music; random access memory

RCA Royal College of Art

RCM Royal College of Music

RCN Royal College of Nursing

RCP Royal College of Physicians

RCS Royal College of Surgeons

rec receipt; record

ref referee; reference

rel religion; religious

REM rapid eye movement

rep report; reprint

ret retired

Rev Reverend

rev revenue; revision; revolution

RFC Royal Flying Corps; Rugby Football Club

RGN Registered General Nurse

RGS Royal Geographical Society

RHA Royal Horse Artillery

RHS Royal Horticultural Society

RIP requiescat in pace (may he or she rest in peace)

RMA Royal Military Academy

RNA ribonucleic acid

RNR Royal Naval Reserve

ROC Royal Observer Corps

ROM read-only memory

Rom Roman; Romania

rom roman (typeface)

RPI retail price index

RSA Republic of South Africa; Royal Scottish Academy; Royal Society of Arts

RSC Royal Shakespeare Company

RSI repetitive strain injury

RSM Regimental Sergeant-Major; Royal Society of Medicine; Royal Society of Music

RTE Radio Telefis Eireann

RUC Royal Ulster Constabulary

SAD seasonal affective disorder

sae stamped addressed envelope

SAf South Africa

SAM surface to air missile

SAm South America

Sam Samuel

SAS Special Air Service

Sat Saturday, Saturn

ScD Doctor of Science

SCE Scottish Certificate of Education

sci science, scientific

SDI Strategic Defense Initiative

SDP Social Democratic Party

sec secant; second; secretary

Sen senate; senator; senior

Sep September, Septuagint

seq sequens (the following)

Sgt Sergeant

SIB Securities and Investment Board

Sib Siberia

Sic Sicily

SIS Secret Intelligence Service

Skt Sanskrit

SLD Social and Liberal Democrats

SLR single-lens reflex

SNP Scottish National Party

snr senior

Soc socialist; society

sop soprano

SPG Society for the Propagation of the Gospel

SRC Science Research Council; Student Representative Council

SRN State Registered Nurse

SSE southsoutheast

SSW southsouthwest

STD subscriber trunk dialling

stg sterling

SWG standard wire gauge

Tas Tasmania

ten tenor

TGV train à grande vitesse (high-speed passenger train)

Tim Timothy

TIR Transports Internationaux Routiers (International Road Transport)

TNT trinitrotoluene (explosive)

TUC Trades Union Congress

typ typographical; typography

UAE United Arab Emirates

UAR United Arab Republic

UDA Ulster Defence Association

UDC Urban District Council

UDI unilateral declaration of independence

UDR Ulster Defence Regiment

UFO unidentified flying object

uhf ultra-high frequency

ult ultimate; ultimo (last month)

UNO United Nations Organization

UPU Universal Postal Union

Uru Uruguay

USA United States of America

USN United States Navy

USS United States Senate; United States Ship

usw ultra-short wave

UVF Ulster Volunteer Force

VAD Voluntary Aid Detachment

VAT value added tax

VCR video cassette recorder

VDU visual display unit

Ven Venerable

Vet veterinary surgeon

vhf very high frequency

VIP very important person

viz videlicet (namely)

vlf very low frequency

voc vocative

vol volume, volunteer

VSO very superior old (brandy); Voluntary Services Overseas

War Warwickshire

WBA World Boxing Association

wef with effect from

WHO World Health Organization

WNW westnorthwest

wpb wastepaper basket

WPC Woman Police Constable

wpm words per minute

WSW westsouthwest

YHA Youth Hostels Association

yrs years

YTS Youth Training Scheme

4

ABTA Association of British Travel Agents

ACAS Advisory Conciliation and Arbitration Service

ACTH adrenocorticotrophic hormone

Adjt adjutant

advt advertisement

AIDS Acquired Immune Deficiency Syndrome

anon anonymous

APEX Advance Purchase Excursion; Association of Professional, Executive, Clerical and Computer Staff

ARAM Associate of the Royal Academy of Music

ARCM Associate of the Royal College of Music

asap as soon as possible

Asbo Anti-social behaviour Order

asst assistant

AWOL absent without leave

BAOR British Army of the Rhine

Bart baronet

BCom Bachelor of Commerce

Beds Bedfordshire

Belg Belgian; Belgium

BEng Bachelor of Engineering

BFPO British Forces Post Office

Bibl Biblical

biog biographical; biography

biol biological; biology

BLit Bachelor of Literature

BMus Bachelor of Music

Brig Brigadier

Brit British

Bros brothers

BThU British Thermal Unit

BUPA British United Provident Association

Cant Canterbury

caps capital letters

Capt Captain

cath cathedral; Catholic

cent centigrade; century

CERN Conseil Européen pour la Recherche Nucléaire

chem chemical, chemistry

Chron Chronicles

C in C Commander in Chief

Cllr Councillor

coll college

comp company; comparative; composer; composition; composito; comprehensive

cont contents; continued

Corp Corporal; corporation

CPRE Council for the Preservation of Rural England

dept department

dict dictionary

dist district

DLit Doctor of Literature

DMus Doctor of Music

DVLA Driver and Vehicle Licensing Authority

Ebor Eboracum (York)

eccl ecclesiastical

ECSC European Coal and Steel Community

Edin Edinburgh

EFTA European Free Trade Association

elec electrical, electricity

ENSA Entertainments National Service Association

Epis episcopal, epistle

Esth Esther

et al and elsewhere; and others

FIFA Fédération Internationale de Football Association

FIFO first in, first out

FRAM Fellow of the Royal Academy of Music

FRAS Fellow of the Royal Astronomical Society

FRCP Fellow of the Royal College of Physicians

FRCS Fellow of the Royal College of Surgeons

FRGS Fellow of the Royal Geographical Society

FRSA Fellow of the Royal Society of Arts

FRSL Fellow of the Royal Society of Literature

FRSM Fellow of the Royal Society of Medicine

GATT General Agreement on Tariffs and Trade

GCMG Knight Grand Cross of St Michael and St George (Order)

GCSE General Certificate of Secondary Education

GCVO Knight Grand Cross of the Victorian Order

geog geographical; geography

geol geological

geom geometric; geometry

Glos Gloucestershire

govt government

gram grammar; grammatical

Guat Guatemala

Guin Guinea

IATA International Air Transport Association

ibid ibidem (in the same place)

IBRD International Bank for Reconstruction and Development

ICBM Intercontinental Ballistic Missile

ILEA Inner London Education Authority

impf imperfect

incl including, inclusive

INLA Irish National Liberation Army

I of W Isle of Wight

INRI Iesus Nazarenus Rex Iudaeorum (Jesus of Nazareth King of the Jews)

inst instant (in the present month); institution, institute

intr intransitive

IRBM Intermediate Range Ballistic Missile

ISBN International Standard Book Number

Ital Italian; Italy
ital italic
Josh Joshua
Judg Judges
KANU Kenyan African National Union
KCMG Knight Commander (of the Order) of St Michael and St George
KCVO Knight Commander of the Royal Victorian Order
kilo kilogram
LIFO last in, first out
Lith Lithuania
long longitude
LRAM Licentiate of the Royal Academy of Music
LRCM Licentiate of the Royal College of Music
LRCP Licentiate of the Royal College of Physicians
mach machine; machinery
masc masculine
math mathematics
Matt Matthew
mech mechanics
memo memorandum
Meth Methodist
MICE Member of the Institution of Civil Engineers
MIEE Member of the Institution of Electrical Engineers
MIME Member of the Institution of Mechanical Engineers
MIRV multiple independently targeted re-entry vehicle
Mlle mademoiselle
MORI Market and Opinion Research Institute
MRCP Member of the Royal College of Physicians
MRCS Member of the Royal College of Surgeons
MusB Bachelor of Music
MusD Doctor of Music
myth. mythology
NASA National Aeronautics and Space Administration
NATO North Atlantic Treaty Organization
NUPE National Union of Public Employers
OECD Organization for Economic Cooperation and Development
OEEC Organization for European Economic Cooperation
OHMS On Her (His) Majesty's Service
OPEC Organization of Petroleum-Exporting Countries
OUDS Oxford University Dramatic Society
Oxon Oxford, Oxfordshire
Parl Parliament; Parliamentary

part participle

pass passive

path pathological; pathology

PAYE pay as you earn

PDSA People's Dispensary for Sick Animals

perf perfect

pers person; personal

plup pluperfect

plur plural

prec preceding

pred predicate

pref preference; prefix

prep preparation; preposition

pres present

Pres President

Prof professor

pron pronoun; pronunciation

Prot Protectorate; Protestant

Prov Proverbs; Province; Provost

prox proximo (next month)

PSBR public sector borrowing requirement

RAAF Royal Australian Air Force

RADA Royal Academy of Dramatic Art

RAMC Royal Army Medical Corps

RAOB Royal Antediluvian Order of Buffaloes

RAOC Royal Army Ordnance Corps

RASC Royal Army Service Corps

RCMP Royal Canadian Mounted Police

recd received

Regt regiment

REME Royal Electrical and Mechanical Engineers

RIBA Royal Institute of British Architects

RICS Royal Institute of Chartered Surveyors

RNIB Royal National Institute for the Blind

RNLI Royal National Lifeboat Institution

RNVR Royal Naval Volunteer Reserve

RSPB Royal Society for the Protection of Birds

RSVP répondez s'il vous plaît (please reply)

SALT Strategic Arms Limitation Talks

SATB soprano, alto, tenor, bass (choral music combination)

SAYE save as you earn

Scand Scandinavia(n)

SDLP Social Democratic and Labour Party

Sept September

SIDS Sudden Infant Death Syndrome

SNCF Société Nationale de Chemins de Fer Français (French National Railways)

SPCK Society for Promoting Christian Knowledge

sp gr specific gravity

SPQR Senatus Populusque Romanus (the Senate and the People of Rome)

STOL short take-off and landing (aircraft)

Supt superintendent

Surg surgeon; surgery; surgical

TASS Telegrafnoye Agenstvo Sovetskovo Soyuza (Soviet news agency)

TAVR Territorial Army and Volunteer Reserve

TEFL Teaching English as a Foreign Language

TESL Teaching English as a Second Language

TGWU Transport and General Workers' Union

Tues Tuesday

UCCA Universities Central Council on Admissions

UEFA Union of European Football Associations

USAF United States Air Force

USSR Union of Soviet Socialist Republics

VSOP very superior old pale (brandy)

VTOL vertical take-off and landing (aircraft)

Vulg Vulgate

WAAC Women's Army Auxiliary Corps

WAAF Women's Auxiliary Air Force

WASP White Anglo-Saxon Protestant

WCdr Wing Commander

WFTU World Federation of Trade Unions

WRAC Women's Royal Army Corps

WRAF Women's Royal Air Force

WRNS Women's Royal Naval Service

WRVS Women's Royal Voluntary Service

Xmas Christmas

YMCA Young Men's Christian Association

YWCA Young Women s Christian Association

ZANU Zimbabwe African National Union

ZAPU Zimbabwe African People's Union

zool zoology

5

ad lib ad libitum (as much as desired)

admin administration, administrative

Anzac Australian and New Zealand Army Corps

ANZUS Australia, New

Zealand and the United States (Pacific security alliance)

ARIBA Associate of the Royal Institute of British Architects

ASLEF Associated Society of Locomotive Engineers and Firemen

Assoc associate; association

ASTMS Association of Scientific, Technical and Managerial Staffs

Bafta British Academy of Film and Television Arts

BALPA British Airline Pilots' Association

b and b bed and breakfast

Berks Berkshire

BLitt Bachelor of Letters

Bucks Buckinghamshire

Cambs Cambridgeshire

CAMRA Campaign for Real Ale

CENTO Central Treaty Organization

Chron Chronicles

COHSE Confederation of Health Service Employers

Comdr Commander

Comdt Commandant

Corpn corporation

CSRIO Commonwealth Scientific and Industrial Research Organization

D and C dilation and curettage

DipEd Diploma in Education

DLitt Doctor of Letters

DPhil Doctor of Philosophy

DrIur Doctor of Laws

elect electrical; electricity

ERNIE Electronic Random Number Indicator Equipment

et seq et sequens (and what follows)

ex div without dividend

FRIBA Fellow of the Royal Institute of British Architects

FRICS Fellow of the Royal Institute of Chartered Surveyors

Hants Hampshire

Herts Hertfordshire

indef indefinite

intro introduction

Lancs Lancashire

Leics Leicestershire

Lieut Lieutenant

Lincs Lincolnshire

LittD Doctor of Letters

LRCVS Licentiate of the Royal College of Veterinary Surgeons

Lt Col Lieutenant-Colonel

Lt Com Lieutenant-Commander

Lt Gen Lieutenant-General

Lt Gov Lieutenant-Governor

Middx Middlesex

Mlles mesdemoiselles

MRCVS Member of the Royal College of Veterinary Surgeons

NAAFI Navy, Army and Air Force Institutes

Notts Nottinghamshire

NSPCC National Society for the Prevention of Cruelty to Children

op cit opere citato (in the work cited)

P and O Peninsular and Oriental

RAFVR Royal Air Force Volunteer Reserve

R and D research and development

ROSPA Royal Society for the Prevention of Accidents

RSPCA Royal Society for the Prevention of Cruelty to Animals

Rt Hon Right Honourable

Rt Rev Right Reverend

Salop Shropshire

SEATO Southeast Asia Treaty Organization

Sergt Sergeant

SHAEF Supreme Headquarters Allied Expeditionary Forces

SHAPE Supreme Headquarters Allied Powers in Europe

SOGAT Society of Graphical and Allied Trades

SWAPO South-West Africa People's Organization

suppl supplement(ary)

TESSA Tax Exempt Special Savings Account

trans transitive; translated; translator

Treas treasurer

UNRRA United Nations Relief and Rehabilitation Administration

vocab vocabulary

Wilts Wiltshire

Worcs Worcestershire

Xtian Christian

Yorks Yorkshire

6 AND OVER

approx (6) approximately

attrib (6) attribute; attributive

Cantab (6) of Cambridge

Cantuar (7) of Canterbury

Col-Sergt (8) Colour-Sergeant

COMECON (7) Council for Mutual Economic Aid

Cominform (9) Communist Information Bureau

Comintern (9) Communist International

DTheol (6) Doctor of Theology

Dunelm (6) of Durham

E and OE (6) errors and omissions excepted

Euratom (7) European Atomic Energy Community

intrans (7) intransitive

Lieut-Col (8) Lieutenant-Colonel

Lieut-Gen (8) Lieutenant-General

Lieut-Gov (8) Lieutenant-Governor

LitHum (6) Literae Humaniores (classics)

loc cit (6) in the place cited

Maj-Gen (6) Major-General

matric (6) matriculation

MIMechE (7) Member of the Institution of Mechanical Engineers

MIMinE (6) Member of the Institution of Mining Engineers

mod cons (7) modern conveniences

MusBac (6) Bachelor of Music

nem con (6) nemine contradicente (none objecting)

non-com (6) non-commissioned officer

per pro (6) per procurationem (by proxy)

pro tem (6) pro tempore (for the time being)

QARANC (6) Queen Alexandra's Royal Army Nursing Corps

quango (6) quasi-autonomous non-governmental organization

UNESCO (6) United Nations Educational, Scientific and Cultural Organization

UNICEF (6) United Nations International Children's Emergency Fund

verb sap (7) verbum sapienti (a word to the wise)

French revolutionary calendar

Brumaire (8) fog, Oct.

Floréal (7) blossom, April

Frimaire (8) sleet, Nov.

Fructidor (9) fruit, Aug.

Germinal (8) seed, March

Messidor (8) harvest, June

Nivôse (6) snow, Dec.

Pluviôse (8) rain, Jan.

Prairial (8) pasture, May

Thermidor (9) heat, July

Vendémiaire (11) vintage, Sept.

Ventôse (7) wind, Feb.

Greek alphabet

2	phi	**5**	**6**
mu	psi	alpha	lambda
nu	rho	delta	
pi	tau	gamma	**7**
xi		kappa	epsilon
	4	omega	omicron
3	beta	sigma	upsilon
	iota	theta	
chi	zeta		
eta			

Group terms

3 AND

band (of musicians)
bevy (of larks, quails, roes, or women)
box (of cigars)
brew (of beer)
case (of whisky or wine)
cast (of hawks)
cete (of badgers)
clan (people)
club (people)
crew (oarsmen or sailors)
crop (of farm produce)
down (of hares)
dule (of doves)
fall (of woodcock)
form (at schools)
four (card-players, oarsmen, or polo team)
gang (of elk, hooligans, labourers, slaves or thieves)
hand (at cards)
herd (of asses, buffalo, cattle, cranes, deer, giraffes, goats, or oxen)
host (of angels)
hunt (hounds and hunters)
husk (of hares)
knob (of pochards, teal, toads, or widgeon)
leap (of leopards)
lepe (of leopards)
lot (in auctioneering)
meet (of hounds and hunters)
mess (military and naval)
mute (of hounds)
nest (of machine-guns, mice, rabbits, or wasps)

nide (of pheasants)
nine (baseball team)
pace (of asses)
pack (of grouse, hounds,
    wolves, or cards)
pair (of oarsmen and various)
park (of guns or cars)
peal (of bells)
pile (of arms)
pod (of whiting or peas)
pony (betting; £25)
pool (various)
posy (of flowers)
rag (of colts)
rope (of onions or pearls)
rout (of wolves)
run (of poultry)
rush (of pochards)
sect (of religious people)
set (of various articles)
show (of agricultural
    products, dogs, horses, etc.)
side (of players)
six (of cub scouts,
    sportsmen)
sord (of mallards or wild-
    fowl)
stud (of horses and mares)
sute (of mallards or wild-fowl)
team (of ducks, horses, oxen,
    or players)
trio (of musicians)
tuft (of grass)
walk (of snipe)

wing (of plovers)
wisp (of snipe)
wood (trees)
yoke (of oxen)

5

batch (of bread and various)
bench (of bishops or
    magistrates)
blast (of hunters)
blush (of boys)
board (of directors)
brace (of ducks, partridges,
    etc.)
brood (of hens)
bunch (of flowers, grapes,
    teal, or widgeon)
caste (of bread)
charm (of goldfinches)
class (of children at schools)
clump (of trees)
copse (trees)
covey (of grouse, partridges,
    or other birds)
crowd (of people)
doylt (of tame swine)
draft (of police or soldiers)
drove (of cattle or kine)
eight (oarsmen)
field (hunters, race-horses, or
    runners)
fleet (of motor-cars or
    ships)flock (of birds,
    pigeons, or sheep)

flush (at cards)
flyer (money; £5)
genus (of animals or plants)
grand (money; £1000 or $1000)
group (photographic and various)
guard (soldiers)
hoard (of gold, etc.)
horde (of savages)
leash (of bucks or hounds)
party (of people)
plump (of wildfowl)
posse (of police)
pride (of lions)
scrum (at rugby football)
sedge (of bitterns or herons)
sheaf (of corn)
shoal (of fish)
siege (of herons)
skein (of geese, silk, or wool)
skulk (of foxes)
sloth (of bears)
squad (of beaters or soldiers)
staff (of officials or servants)
stalk (of foresters)
stand (of arms)
state (of princes)
swarm (of bees and other insects)
table (of bridge or whist players)
tribe (of goats or people)
trick (at cards)
troop (of boy-scouts, brownies, cavalry, kangaroos, lions, or monkeys)
truss (of hay)
twins (people)
watch (of nightingales or sailors)

6

barren (of mules)
basket (of strawberries)
budget (of papers)
bundle (of asparagus, firewood, and various)
caucus (of politicians)
cellar (of wine)
clique (of people)
clutch (of eggs)
colony (of gulls or people)
covert (of coots)
desert (of lapwings)
double (in betting)
eleven (cricket and other teams)
faggot (of sticks)
family (of people or sardines)
flight (of aeroplanes, doves, dunlins, or pigeons)
gaggle (of geese)
galaxy (of beauties)
harras (of horses)
kennel (of dogs)
kindle (of kittens)
labour (of moles)
litter (of cubs, pigs, pups, or whelps)
melody (of harpers)

monkey (in betting; £500)
museum (of antiques, works of art, etc.)
muster (of peacocks or soldiers)
nation (of people)
outfit (of clothes or sails)
packet (of cigarettes)
parade (of soldiers)
punnet (of strawberries)
quorum (minimum number of people)
rayful (of knaves)
rubber (at cards)
school (of porpoises or whales)
sextet (of musicians)
sleuth (of bears)
spring (of teal)
stable (of horses)
string (of pearls or racehorses)
tenner (money; £10)
throng (of people)
trophy (of arms, etc.)
troupe (of actors, dancers, or minstrels)
twelve (lacrosse team)
vestry (parochial assembly)

7

battery (of guns)
bouquet (of flowers)
brigade (of troops)
clamour (of rooks)

clouder (of cats)
cluster (of grapes or stars)
company (of actors, capitalists, or widgeon)
council (advisers or local authorities)
dopping (of sheldrakes)
draught (of butlers)
fifteen (rugby football team)
gallery (of pictures)
library (of books or music)
nosegay (of flowers)
orchard (of fruit trees)
quartet (of musicians)
service (of china or crockery)
sounder (of boars or swine)
spinney (of trees)
thicket (of trees)
vintage (of wine)

8

assembly (of people)
audience (of people)
building (of rooks)
division (of troops)
flotilla (of boats)
jamboree (of boy-scouts)
paddling (of ducks)
partners (in business or games)
regiment (of soldiers)
richesse (of martens)
sequence (at cards)
squadron (of cavalry or ships)
triplets (people)

9

army corps (of troops)
badelynge (of ducks)
committee (people)
community (of people or
  saints)
cowardice (of curs)
gathering (of people and the
  clans)
morbidity (of majors)
orchestra (of musicians)
sachemdom (N. American
  Indians)
shrubbery (of shrubs)
subtiltie (of sergeants)
syndicate (of capitalists)

commission (committee of
  enquiry)
detachment (of police or
  soldiers)
exaltation (of larks)
exhibition (of commercial
  products, pictures, works of
  art, etc.)
observance (of hermits)
shrewdness (of apes)
simplicity (of subalterns)

11 AND OVER

confraternity (brotherhood,
  usually religious) (13)
congregation (of birds or
  worshippers) (12)
constellation (of stars) (13)
convocation (of clergy or
  university authorities) (11)
murmuration (of starlings)
  (11)

10

assemblage (of clergy and
  various)
buttonhole (of flowers)
chattering (of choughs)
collection (of stamps, works
  of art, etc.)

Hebrew alphabet

Aleph (5)	Koph (4)	Shin (4)
Ayin (4)	Lamedh (6)	Sin (3)
Beth (4)	Mem (3)	Tav (3)
Daleth (6)	Nun (3)	Teth (4)
Gimel (5)	Pe (2)	Vav (3)
He (2)	Resh (4)	Yod (3)
Heth (4)	Sade (4)	Zayin (5)
Kaph (4)	Samekh (6)	

Heraldry

2–4		6	fleury	7
	animé		florid	
arms	armed	aiglet	fretty	adorsed
band	azure	apaumy	fylfot	adossed
bar	badge	argent	garter	alberia
bend	barry	armory	ground	annulet
boar	baton	at gaze	guttée	arrière
coué	bendy	attire	heater	arrondi
dawl	bowed	baston	herald	attired
delf	breys	bazant	jessed	barruly
enty	cable	bendil	knight	bearing
erne	chief	bevile	manche	bendlet
fess	cross	bezant	mascle	bevilly
fret	eagle	billet	maunch	bordure
garb	erect	blazon	mullet	bottony
gore	ermin	border	naiant	brisure
gray	fesse	bouche	Norroy	cadency
kite	field	buckle	pallet	chapter
lion	fusil	canton	rebate	chevron
or	garbe	charge	rustre	clarion
orle	gorge	checky	sejant	courant
pale	gules	chequy	shield	croslet
pall	gurge	cleché	square	dolphin
paly	gyron	cotise	timbre	dormant
pean	label	couché	vairée	emblaze
pile	motto	coward	vested	embowed
posé	pheon	dexter	voided	embrued
rose	rebus	dragon	voider	enarmed
semé	rompu	ermine	volant	endorse
vair	sable	escrol	vorant	engoulé
vert	scarp	etoile	wivern	engrail
5	torse	falcon	wyvern	ermelin
alant	waved	fillet		estoile
		flanch		fretted

fructed
gardant
griffin
Ich Dien
leopard
lioncel
lozenge
lozengy
martlet
miniver
nombril
passant
potence
purpure
quarter
raguled
rampant
roundel
salient
saltire
sea-lion
sexfoil
shafted
sinople
statant
swallow
torqued
torteau
trefoil
unicorn

8

affronté
allerion
armorist
aversant

barrulet
bevilled
blazonry
caboched
caboshed
chaperon
couchant
crescent
dancetty
emblazon
englante
enmanché
erminois
escallop
gonfalon
haurient
heraldic
insignia
Lyon King
mantling
naissant
opinicus
ordinary
renverse
roundlet
sea-horse
sinister
standard
tincture
tressure

9

aquilated
arraswise
banderole
blazoning

carbuncle
cartouche
combatant
diapering
displayed
embattled
enveloped
environed
erminites
estoillee
florettée
hatchment
lionceaux
lioncelle
Lyon-Court
regardant
scutcheon
spur-rowel
supporter

10

barry-bendy
barrybendi
bicorporal
blue mantle
cinquefoil
Clarenceux
coat-of-arms
cross-patée
difference
emblazoner
empalement
escalloped
escutcheon
fesse-point
fleur-de-lis

fleur-de-lys
king-at-arms
knighthood
pursuivant
quartering
quatrefoil
quintefoil
rebatement
surmounted

11 AND OVER

bend-sinister (12)
bendy-sinister (13)
bicapitated (11)
College of Arms (13)

counter-paled (12)
counter-passant (14)
countervair (11)
cross-crosslet (13)
cross-fleury (11)
cross-patencée (13)
Earl Marshal (11)
emblazonment (12)
engrailment (11)
escarbuncle (11)
escutcheoned (12)
garde-visure (11)

Garter King of Arms (16)
grant of arms (11)
heraldic emblem (14)
honour point (11)
inescutcheon (12)
Lyon King at Arms (14)
marshalling (11)
quarter arms (11)
Somerset herald (14)
transfluent (11)
unscutcheoned (13)

Palindromes

3				
aba	eke	Oxo	anna	civic
aga	ere	pap	boob	kayak
aha	eve	pep	deed	level
ala	ewe	pip	dood	madam
ama	eye	pop	ecce	minim
ana	gag	pup	keek	put-up
asa	gig	s.o.s.	ma'am	radar
ava	hah	tat	noon	refer
bab	huh	tit	otto	rotor
bib	mam	tot	peep	sagas
bob	mom	tut	poop	sexes
bub	mum	wow	sees	shahs
dad	nan	zuz	toot	sohos
did	non			solos
dud	nun	**4**	**5**	tenet
	oho	abba	alula	

6 AND OVER

Able was I ere I saw Elba (19)	marram (6)	reviver (7)
	pull-up (6)	rotator (7)
deified (7)	redder (6)	terret (6)
Hannah	reifier (7)	
	repaper (7)	

Seven Deadly Sins

anger (5)	gluttony (8)	sloth (5)
covetousness (12)	lust (4)	
envy (4)	pride (5)	

Seven Virtues

charity (7)	hope (4)	prudence (8)
faith (5)	justice (7)	temperance (10)
fortitude (9)	love (charity) (4)	

Seven Wonders of the World

The Colossus of Rhodes
The Hanging Gardens of Babylon
The Pharos of Alexandria
   or
The Palace of Cyrus (cemented with gold)

The Pyramids of Egypt
The Statue of Zeus by Phidias
The Temple of Artemis (Diana) at Ephesus
The Tomb of Mausolus

Signs of the Zodiac

Aquarius (Water-bearer) (8)	Libra (Balance) (5)
Aries (Ram) (5)	Pisces (Fishes) (6)
Cancer (Crab) (6)	Sagittarius (Archer) (11)
Capricorn (Goat) (9)	Scorpio (Scorpion) (7)
Gemini (Twins) (6)	Taurus (Bull) (6)
Leo (Lion) (3)	Virgo (Virgin) (5)